Anthony Lansdowne.

Window Essential Reference

New Riders

Other Books by New Riders Publishing

Windows® 2000 Essential Reference

Steve Tate, et al.

New Riders

201 West 103rd Street, Indianapolis, Indiana 46290

Windows 2000® Essential Reference

Copyright © 2000 by New Riders Publishing

FIRST EDITION: April, 2000

International Standard Book Number: 0-7357-0869-X

Library of Congress Catalog Card Number: 99-067440

04 03 02 01 00 7 6 5 4 3 2 1

Interpretation of the printing code: The rightmost double-digit number is the year of the book's printing; the rightmost single-digit number is the number of the book's printing. For example, the printing code 00-1 shows that the first printing of the book occurred in 2000.

Printed in the United States of America

Trademarks

Warning and Disclaimer

Publisher
David Dwyer

Associate Publisher
Brad Koch

Executive Editor
Al Valvano

Managing Editor
Gina Brown

Product Marketing Manager
Stephanie Layton

Acquisitions Editor
Leah Williams

Development Editor
Ami Frank Sullivan

Project Editor
Nancy Sixsmith

Technical Editors
Steve Crandall
Jeremy Godinger
Mike Kazmier
James F. Kelly
Kevin Kohut

Indexer
Lisa Stumpf

Manufacturing Coordinator
Chris Moos

Book Designer
Louisa Klucznik

Cover Designer
Aren Howell

Proofreader
Gina Brown

Composition
Amy Parker

Contents

About the Authors

Steve Tate, MCT and MCSE, has had seven years of experience with Windows NT and NetWare LAN administration. Most recently, Steve has focused exclusively on training and consulting on networking with Microsoft technologies. He was selected by Microsoft to be a member of the Windows NT 5.0 Rapid Deployment Team and has also developed exam items for Microsoft for use in Microsoft Certified Professional exams. His authoring experience includes two New Riders Publishing books: *MCSE Training Guide: Windows NT 4 Workstation* and *Windows NT Server 4: Security, Troubleshooting, and Optimization*.

Prior to teaching MS-certified courses, Steve was a trainer/consultant specializing in end-user applications training. He also dabbled in corporate life (a Systems Analyst programming in COBOL), and had stints as a PC analyst, computer salesman, and graduate student.

Jon Boggs is an MCSE, MCSD, and CNE. As a senior consultant for the eBusiness Networks practice of Xpedior Incorporated in Chicago, he has provided consulting services to a number of nationally known corporations. He is an expert at automating administrative tasks and system deployments, typically employing a mix of Windows NT/2000, SMS, and Visual Basic. Jon co-authored *Planning for Windows 2000* and served as a technical reviewer on several BackOffice-related books. He enjoys reading and biking in his spare time.

Scott Burgess is a Managing Consultant and Sr. eBusiness Architect for Xpedior Incorporated, the number one Microsoft solution provider of the year worldwide for both 1997 and 1999. Scott is an MCSE+I and is MCT certified to teach all the current Microsoft products, including the new Windows 2000 curriculum. Scott has 15 years of experience implementing and designing enterprise-wide LAN, WAN, and heterogeneous operating system environments, including OS390, AS400, UNIX, NT, and OS/2. In the past two years, Scott's focus has been centered on the in-depth beta testing of Windows 2000. Through his involvement with Microsoft's JDP program (Joint Deployment Program), Scott and his team have architected and implemented several rollouts of Windows 2000 to international customers.

Randy Cook is an independent contractor from Salt Lake City, Utah. His qualifications include Certified Novell Instructor, Master CNE, Microsoft Certified Trainer, MCSE, and the Cisco CCNA. He is currently working for Blue Cross/Blue Shield of Florida as a LAN Architect in their NT Enterprise and teaches in his spare time at Productivity Point International, Jacksonville Florida. He has an extensive background in distributive network integration and Directory Services.

Jeremy Deats (jeremy@pdq.net) is a Web application developer and e-commerce consultant with Penta, Inc. in Houston, Texas. Jeremy is a Microsoft Certified Professional in Visual Basic and is certified in IBM's Net.Commerce. When he's not hard at work, Jeremy is either spending time with his beautiful fiancée Amanda Clement or playing his guitar.

Art Henning's 14-year career with Intergraph Corporation includes a wide scope of experience in a support role for hardware, software, and networks with VAX VMS, various flavors of Unix, and WinNT, beginning with beta versions of 3.1. Art was staffed for three years as a Software Analyst and Consultant for Intergraph's NFS products, which were licensed to Microsoft and released as part of the WindowsNT Services for Unix bundle. This included certification work with Windows 2000. He currently is a Systems Administrator for one of Intergraph's MIS departments, and is an MCP.

Chris Jones is a Microsoft Certified System Engineer. He holds a B.S.B.A. in Management Information Systems and Finance from the University of Arizona. Chris is currently a Senior Systems Programmer for Intel Corporation. His experience at Intel has included engineering and implementation of enterprise Windows NT infrastructure architectures and extensive involvement in Microsoft's Joint Development Program for Windows 2000. Chris enjoys mountain biking, golf, and Tae Kwon Do in his spare time.

Thomas Lee is an independent computer consultant who has been working with Windows NT since 1993. After graduating with a BS in Computer Problem Solving from Carnegie Mellon University, he worked on two successful operating system projects (Comshare___s Commander II and ICL___s VME) before joining Andersen Consulting in 1981, where he was a manager in the London office. He has been an independent consultant since 1987. Most recently, he worked in Redmond developing Windows 2000 Microsoft Official Curriculum (MOC) training material and is presently engaged in several consulting projects relating to Windows 2000. Thomas is a Fellow of the British Computer Society and a Member of the Institute of IT Trainers, as well as being a Microsoft Certified Systems Engineer (MCSE), Microsoft Certified Trainer (MCT), and Microsoft Valued Professional (MVP). Thomas lives in a cottage in the English countryside with his wife, Susan, and daughter, Rebecca. You can contact Thomas at tfl@psp.co.uk.

Mary McLaughlin, MCSE+I, MCT, ASE, ACT, lives in the Boston area with her beloved daughter, Margaret. She started as a systems administrator 10 years ago, and has worked consistently on small- to medium-sized LANs and WANs for profit and non-profit organizations. In the last five years, her focus has been on training individuals in Windows 2000, Windows NT, and Compaq technologies. Currently, she is involved in security solutions such as firewall, VPN, and PKI technologies.

Jim Mulvey is a Microsoft Certified Systems Engineer (MCSE) and Microsoft Certified Trainer (MCT). He has a BS in Electrical Engineering from the University of Connecticut. His 13 years of experience in the IT industry include project management, architecture, systems engineering, and technical support under a variety of platforms. He is currently a Senior Consultant with Xpedior Incorporated, an eBusiness solutions provider awarded Microsoft's "Partner of the Year—Worldwide" award for 1997. His experience at Xpedior includes engagement in Microsoft's Joint Deployment

Program for Windows 2000, in which he was project manager and chief architect for one of the first production Windows 2000 Domain designs.

James O'Neill was born in 1965 and lives near Oxford, England. After doing a BSC in Computer Science at the University of Exeter, he joined the UK's biggest supplier of PCs for schools, where he planned and supported customers' networks before leaving in 1993 to work in the IT training industry. In 1995 he became Managing Director and major shareholder of SHX, a Microsoft Certified Technical Education Centre, before selling it in 1998, but continued to teach Windows NT and Microsoft Exchange. In 1999, he worked as part of Microsoft's team developing the MCP exams for Windows 2000. He married his wife Jackie in 1989 and their daughter Lisa was born in January 2000. He collects quotations and has the irritating habit of talking about himself in the third person.

David Shackelford holds a master's degree from California State University at Fullerton. His background includes working as a beekeeper, screening submissions for a popular poetry journal, and teaching NT operating system and networking courses at Hewlett Packard and Intel. He currently works for a firm in southern California as the supervisor of network operations.

Paul Papanek Stork is a Senior Lecturer and Director of the E-Ideas Lab for Weatherhead School of Management at Case Western Reserve University. Paul has an MBA from Weatherhead and is a Microsoft Certified Trainer, a Microsoft Certified Systems Engineer plus Internet, and a Certified Novell Engineer with more than 14 years of experience designing, implementing and supporting Microsoft and Novell Networks. Prior to his appointment as a lecturer at Weatherhead in January of 2000, Paul was an active member of Microsoft's Windows 2000 Rapid Deployment Program for DeCarlo, Paternite, and Associates, Inc. As a staff instructor at DPAI, he was one of the first MCTs in the Midwest to teach beta classes on Windows 2000 to other trainers and network engineers.

About the Reviewers

The following reviewers contributed their considerable hands-on expertise to the entire development process for *Windows 2000 Essential Reference*. As the book was being written, these dedicated professionals reviewed all the material for technical content, organization, and flow. Their feedback was critical to ensuring that *Windows 2000 Essential Reference* fits our readers' need for the highest-quality technical information.

Steve Crandall is a technology consultant in Cleveland, OH. An MCSE, he is also a doctoral student in the History of Technology at Case Western Reserve University. He has worked in technical support and management for a number of computer, consulting, and telecommunications firms. He is also a regular columnist for *Microsoft Certified Professional Magazine*.

Jeremy Godinger works for the Distributed Architecture team at a global financial services company, a 40,000-user environment. Recent projects include a 5000-user NT domain migration and a Windows 2000 evaluation. Projects are NT infrastructure-related and affect the entire enterprise. Certifications include MCSE and CNE. He graduated from MIT in 1997 with a BS in Mechanical Engineering and will complete his master's degree program at Drexel University in Computer Science in June 2000. He currently lives in Philadelphia, PA.

Mike Kazmier is the Director of Network Services for Binocs Systems, Inc., located in Kalispell, Montana. (Yes, they have computers in Montana.) Mike is certified as an MCSE+I, Compaq ASE, and Novell CNA. His background centers around Windows NT 4.0, enterprise-level architecture planning and deployment, and he is currently pursuing the Cisco CCNP in Routing and Switching. His company has been running Windows 2000 in a production environment since Beta 3, and has been testing and running Exchange 2000 Beta 3 for three months.

James F. Kelly is the systems/network administrator for Technology Partners International, Inc., which offers consulting services for IT outsourcing, business process outsourcing, contract management, relationship management, and contract renegotiation. He is currently a Microsoft Certified Systems Engineer (MCSE), a Microsoft Certified Trainer (MCT), and is Network+ certified.

Kevin Kohut has been applying technology solutions to business needs for more than 18 years. As a consultant, he has helped both small companies and large corporations keep pace with ever-changing information technology requirements. Currently, Mr. Kohut is the Director of Technical Operations for an Internet eCommerce company, where he is responsible for both the company's internal IS and external Web site. An MCSE+Internet, Kevin has taught courses in network design, project management, and a variety of software applications and server operating systems. As a Contributing Editor for *Microsoft Certified Professional Magazine*, he published several articles on a variety of technologies, including Microsoft Exchange, Windows 2000, and network infrastructure.

Acknowledgments

I'd like to thank Al Valvano, Leah Williams, and Ami Sullivan for their belief in this project and their commitment to getting it done right. Special thanks to my good friends Thomas Lee and Dave Shaw for their encouragement and technical expertise—without their generous help this book would not have been completed! I'd also like to thank the reviewers—Steve Crandall, Jeremy Godinger, Jim Kelly, Mike Kasmier, and Kevin Kohut.

—*Steven Tate*

Thanks to Ami and Leah and the rest of the staff there for the opportunity, all the help, and support. It was a great learning experience for me. Though I have produced technical documents in the past, this is the first time I have contributed to a project to be publicly published.

—*Art Henning*

Tell Us What You Think

As the reader of this book, you are the most important critic and commentator. We value your opinion and want to know what we're doing right, what we could do better, what areas you'd like to see us publish in, and any other words of wisdom you're willing to pass our way.

As the Executive Editor for the Networking team at New Riders Publishing/MTP, I welcome your comments. You can fax, email, or write me directly to let me know what you did or didn't like about this book—as well as what we can do to make our books stronger.

Please note that I cannot help you with technical problems related to the topic of this book, and that due to the high volume of mail I receive, I might not be able to reply to every message.

When you write, please be sure to include this book's title and author as well as your name and phone or fax number. I will carefully review your comments and share them with the author and editors who worked on the book.

Fax: 317-581-4663

Email: nrfeedback@newriders.com

Mail: Al Valvano
          Executive Editor
          New Riders Publishing
          201 West 103rd Street
          Indianapolis, IN 46290 USA

Introduction

Windows 2000 Essential Reference streamlines information about Windows 2000 to enable administrators to find the critical answers and processes they need to know quickly, without scanning through numerous pages or resources. Designed as a telescoping tutorial/reference, the book breaks Windows 2000 into major areas, which are then divided into major subcategories. Readers can "dip" into a chapter to obtain the fundamentals. If you require more information, the book is cross-referenced and set up to allow targeted additional reading, topic by topic. Finally, there is a third, more comprehensive layer of detail beyond that, enabling the reader to go deeper in particular topic areas. Sections are very highly indexed and cross-referenced to each other.

How This Book Is Organized

In order to help readers find the answers they need quickly and easily, the authors have utilized the following series of design elements in organizing this reference:

- **Tables**. Each section begins with a series of jump tables that let you know the primary topics discussed, what tasks the section will help you accomplish, and where you can find additional information.

- **Steps.** Whenever a particular procedure is complicated, problematic, or not thoroughly discussed in the help materials, the authors give you easy-to-follow steps to help you accomplish it.

- **Cross-References.** This book utilizes a series of arrows that direct you to information within and outside of the reference itself.

- **Sidebars.** Authors include useful tips, warnings, and histories in a sidebar format to avoid distracting you from the main body of the text.

- **FAQs.** Frequently asked questions are drawn apart from the text in sidebar format and signified by the use of a question mark on the left side.

- **Going Deeper.** For administrators who want more information on a particular procedure or process, the authors provide the "Going Deeper" section at the conclusion of a section.

I

The Windows 2000 Environment

1.1
Overview of Windows 2000 Architecture

You Need to Read This Section If You Want to:

- Select the appropriate version of Windows 2000 to meet your business needs.
- Have an understanding of the components of Windows 2000 and how they relate to each other.
- Be able to troubleshoot Windows 2000 with an understanding of its architecture.

Versions of Windows 2000

There are four versions of Windows 2000. All of these versions share a common base operating system. The differences between them are the additional features that are included with the product and the way that versions of Windows 2000 are "tuned" for performance.

* **Windows 2000 Professional.** This version of Windows 2000 is designed for corporate as their personal desktop operating system. You should use this operating system as your primary desktop mainly because it is tuned to perform as a network client and personal workstation.

* **Windows 2000 Server.** All the "server" versions of Windows 2000 provide a robust, secure environment for providing file, print, and application services to client computers. Windows 2000 Server is the "basic" server. Advanced Server and Datacenter Server provide additional features and support larger hardware platforms. This version of Windows 2000 provides the best server platform for most organizations.

* **Windows 2000 Advanced Server.** Use this version of Windows 2000 on servers needing more memory and processors than Windows 2000 Server can handle. It also adds clustering and network load balancing services.
  ▶ *For more information, see "Windows Clustering and Load Balancing" later in this chapter.*

* **Windows 2000 Datacenter Server.** If you have applications that require very large amounts of memory or processors, or that need more support for fault tolerance and higher availability than Windows 2000 Advanced Server, this is the operating system to run. Generally, this version of Windows will be installed on very high-end systems provided by Original Equipment Manufacturers (OEMs) and sold to larger companies through Value-Added Resellers (VARs).

You must have at least one Windows 2000 Server of any version on your network to have an Active Directory forest because only Windows 2000 Servers can be domain controllers.

For a comparison of the features of the various versions of Windows 2000, see Table 1.1.1.

Table 1.1.1   Features by Version of Windows 2000

Feature	Windows 2000 Professional	Windows 2000 Server	Windows 2000 Advanced Server	Windows 2000 Datacenter Server
Memory support (maximum)	4 GB	4 GB	8GB	64 GB

Feature	Windows 2000 Professional	Windows 2000 Server	Windows 2000 Advanced Server	Windows 2000 Datacenter Server
Processor Support (number of processors supported during a new installation)	2	4	8	32
Maximum concurrent	10	Limited by hardware capability	Limited by hardware capability	Limited by hardware capability
Active Directory (directory service)	Client	Domain Controller or Member Server	Domain Controller or Member Server	Domain Controller or Member Server
Web server	Peer Web Services	Internet Information Server v. 5.0	Internet Information Server v. 5.0	Internet Information Server v. 5.0
Network services	No	Yes	Yes	Yes
DHCP, DNS, WINS, Routing and Remote Access servers				
Remote Installation Service	No	Yes	Yes	Yes
Terminal Services	No	Yes	Yes	Yes
Transaction services	No	Yes	Yes	Yes
Fault-tolerant disk volumes (mirroring and RAID-5)	No	Yes	Yes	Yes
Network Load Balancing	No	No	Yes	Yes
Clustering	No	No	Yes	Yes

What's New in Windows 2000 Server?

Here are the highlights of what's new, compared to Windows NT 4.0:

* **Active Directory.** A new directory service, based on X.500 specifications, which replaces Windows NT 4.0 domains. Active Directory is integrated with DNS, uses industry-standard Kerberos authentication, provides transitive trusts throughout an enterprise, and employs multi-master directory replication.

* **Improved manageability.** A consistent user interface for system management (Microsoft Management Console), Group Policy, the Microsoft Installer, offline folder synchronization, and a Telnet server and Terminal Services for remote administration.

* **Enhanced networking.** Many enhancements have been made to networking services, including improved DNS, WINS, and DHCP services, Quality of Service (QoS), HTTP compression, IP Security (IPSec), Asynchronous Transfer Mode (ATM) support, Internet Connection Sharing, Virtual Private Networking (VPN), and Routing and Remote Access Service (RRAS).

* **Improved device support.** Device drivers for current hardware, Digital Video Disks (DVDs), Universal Serial Bus (USB) devices, new network adapters, scanners, printers, modems, and more. Much of the new driver support means that installation of devices and services on a system running Windows 2000 will generally not require a system restart. In fact, the number of system-invoked required restarts have been reduced from some 50 or more to fewer than seven.

* **Storage management.** Many enhancements have been made to the process of storing, retrieving, and managing files on disks and other media, including disk quotas, encryption, removable storage management, content indexing, and Distributed File System (DFS).

* **Improved performance.** Support has been added for much larger amounts of memory and more processors on newer equipment that supports such features. Additionally, job objects that enable process accounting and limits on the use of CPU time, and better use of system hardware have been added as well.

Deciding Between Windows 2000 Server and Windows 2000 Advanced Server

How do you know whether you must use the additional capabilities of Windows 2000 Advanced Server instead of the less-expensive Windows 2000 Server? Basically, it all boils down to three major differences between the versions:

* **Clustering.** Windows clustering provides multiple clustering technologies to ensure a high availability of data and applications on the network. There are two types of clustering technologies supported in Windows 2000: Network Load Balancing and Server clusters. These clustering technologies can be used separately or can be combined to provide scalability and high availability for network applications.

* **Processor Support.** Each version of Windows is licensed to provide support for a maximum number of CPUs. Windows 2000 Server supports up to four processors, Windows 2000 Advanced Server supports up to eight processors, and Windows 2000 Datacenter Server will support up to 32.

* **Memory Support.** Windows 2000 Professional and Windows 2000 Server support up to 4 GB of installed memory. Windows 2000 Advanced Server supports up to 8 GB of memory on Intel PAE-based computers (PAE is "Physical Address Extension"). Windows 2000 Datacenter Server can support up to 64 GB of memory on Intel Physical Address Extension (PAE)-based computers.

PAE allows up to 64 GB of physical memory to be used as 4 KB pages, providing better performance than is available through the earlier Intel® PSE36 driver. For more information on Intel PAE, see Windows 2000 Help.

So, if you don't need these additional capabilities of Windows 2000 Advanced Server, Windows 2000 Server will do just fine!

Windows 2000 System Architecture

Windows 2000 was designed to support local security, be portable to other hardware platforms, provide symmetric multiprocessing (SMP), have integrated networking capabilities, and provide a robust environment for client/server applications. In its design, it is highly modular, with each component of the operating system playing a well-defined role. It is essential, when supporting or troubleshooting Windows 2000, to have a basic understanding of what these components do and how they interact with each other.

Figure 1.1.1 provides a diagram that represents the basic structure of Windows 2000. The main system components that will be described in this section are as follows:

- User mode and Kernel mode
- The Executive
- The Microkernel
- The Hardware Abstraction Layer
- User mode services and applications
- Processes and threads
- Security Manager
- Memory management
- Networking

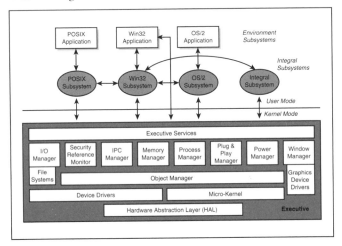

Figure 1.1.1   Windows 2000 system architecture.

Changes in the Windows 2000 Architecture

The basic architecture of Windows 2000 is relatively unchanged from Windows NT. The major changes are as follows:

- **Plug and Play Manager.** Each resource that is assigned to your device must be unique or the device will not function properly.

- **Power Manager.** When you install or uninstall a hardware device, Plug and Play works with Windows 2000 to manage the requirements of your hardware and peripherals, shutting them down or conserving them when you are not using them. And, if you are working in another program when you install or uninstall a device, Plug and Play lets you know that it is about to change your computer configuration and warns you to save your work.

- **Integral Subsystem.** Users of Windows NT will notice that the Security Subsystem has been renamed as the Integral Subsystem. This is primarily a name change (although there are some changes within Windows security that will be addressed later).

User Mode and Kernel Mode

All programs that run on the computer run in User mode, Kernel mode, or a combination of both. Technically speaking, the term "program" refers to software stored on media and ready for execution. The term "process" refers to the actual running code. In either case, the software operates in different ways, depending upon where it is used in the system.

User Mode and Kernel Mode

The terms *User mode* and *Kernel mode* are derived from the days when Windows NT was compiled to operate on multiple microprocessor architectures, such as Compaq (Digital) Alpha and other RISC-based equipment. RISC-based microprocessors generally have two "modes" of operation: User mode and Kernel mode (also known as Privileged mode). They are employed to protect the processes running on the computer. 32-bit Intel-based (x86) microprocessors use a *ring* architecture that provides four distinct layers of protection. Because Windows NT was designed to be a completely portable operating system, it was necessary to construct it in a way that would enable it to operate in a similar fashion, no matter what hardware platform it was installed and operating on. Windows NT (and hence, Windows 2000 as well) use only two of the rings of the x86 processor: Ring 0 (which corresponds to Kernel mode) and Ring 3 (which corresponds to User mode).

- **User mode.** Most applications, when started by the end user, run in User mode. To protect the core operating system from possible malfunctions in the application, these programs have limited access to the system. They run in their own protected memory space, which is allocated by the operating system. They are unable to access any memory addresses other than their own and they cannot access any hardware devices directly. When you log on and then start a program such as Notepad, you are running it in User mode and your identity is associated with the program. When the application requires the support of the system's installed hardware, such as a printer or video display device, the operating system intercepts the request and manages the operation of the device for the application.

- **Kernel mode.** Processes have a high level of privilege. All processes running in Kernel mode share the same memory and have direct access to all hardware devices, including critical devices such as the processor and video display adapters. Software written specifically to control hardware (device drivers) execute their processes in this mode. Obviously, processes that are written to be run in Kernel mode are a necessary part of the operating system and must be carefully constructed to ensure their proper operation. The core operating system programs, including Executive Services, all system managers, the Microkernel, the Hardware Abstraction Layer (HAL), and all device drivers run in Kernel mode. They are executed automatically by Windows 2000 during system boot and run under the security context of the LocalSystem account (a special built-in account) when accessing resources.

Windows 2000 services run in User mode in a specific user context. Examples of Windows 2000 services include Task Scheduler, Alerter, and Messenger. In fact, this brings up a point that may not be obvious from the diagram—although programs run in either User mode or Kernel mode, the User mode programs do not have to all run within the same user context. Windows 2000 keeps a separate user environment for each user that is running programs. An administrator can configure Windows 2000 services to use a specific user account when they run. A user can start applications in another user context by using the Run As command.

What Is a Service?

A service is a process that runs in addition to or as a companion to the base operating system. Users familiar with UNIX would know these as daemons. These services can be added, stopped, started, and paused as needed. They can also run in different security contexts to control their access to resources and provide more complete auditing within the system. In other words, a service is an application that the operating system uses to supplement its own basic functions and controls on its own. Services run in their own security context. To establish a security context, a service needs to log on to the system, just as security principals do. By default, a service logs on to the system using the System account, but you can modify this if you want.

Thus, you could have many different tasks running in different user contexts on a single computer. The capability of those tasks to access local resources will depend on the permissions that have been granted to that account. For example, if a service is configured to use the wrong user account, it will probably fail when the operating system attempts to start it.

▸ *For more information on the Run As command and Windows 2000 services, see Chapter 3.4, "Managing Services and Tasks."*

Why Should I Care About User Mode and Kernel Mode, Anyway?

There is a practical reason for knowing about the restricted (User) mode and privileged (Kernel) mode in Windows 2000. Any process that is running in User mode should not be able to crash the operating system—create a Stop error (or "blue screen of death," as it's affectionately known). Only processes running in Kernel mode can do that.

So if a Stop error occurs, one of the Kernel mode components, such as a device driver, is the likely culprit. This helps narrow the field when trying to troubleshoot Stop errors.

The Executive

The term *Executive* in Windows 2000 refers to those software components that run in Kernel mode. The Windows 2000 Executive contains the core operating system services, such as memory management, I/O management, security, interprocess communications, caching, and management of processes and objects. It also contains the device drivers for all hardware devices, such as the keyboard, mouse, sound, video, printers, network interfaces, and disk controllers. The Executive is loaded during startup as part of Ntoskrnl.exe.

▶ *For more information on device drivers and memory management, see Chapter 2.3, "Configuring Devices and System Settings."*

The Microkernel

The Microkernel, the "heart" of the operating system, schedules threads and handles the system interrupts and exceptions. It is also responsible for synchronizing activity among the various Executive services and among processors on multiprocessor computers. Unlike the rest of Windows 2000, the Microkernel always operates in physical memory and cannot be pre-empted or paged to disk.

The Microkernel is also loaded during startup as part of Ntoskernl.exe.

The Hardware Abstraction Layer

The Hardware Abstraction Layer (HAL) enables Windows 2000 to run on computers with different hardware components and numbers of processors (single or multiple processors). The HAL allows the operating system to take advantage of specific equipment features that differ from platform to platform without having to recompile the operating system to compensate. Many equipment manufacturers provide their own customized version of the HAL to take advantage of specific features of their hardware platform.

The HAL is loaded during startup as Hal.dll.

Processes and Threads

A *process* is a program that can be executed in Windows 2000. Each process has a private address space, one or more threads of execution, and a security ID (representing a security principal account) associated with it.

A *thread* is an entity within a process (kind of a process within a process) that Windows 2000 can schedule for execution. Processes can have multiple threads if the application were written as a multi-threaded application. For example, when you use Windows Explorer and open a new Explorer window, by default a new thread is created to control the new window rather than a whole new instance of the Explorer process.

When you start a new process, it runs with a specific *priority* on your computer. In general, the higher the priority, the more CPU time the process will receive. There are 32 possible thread priorities, divided into six different priority levels. The priority levels are (from highest to lowest): Realtime, High, Above Normal, Normal, Below Normal, and Low. If you do not specify otherwise, processes are started with Normal priority. You can specify the priority for a process by either changing the priority in Task Manager, or by starting the process by using the Start command with a priority parameter.

? **How Can I Tell Which Processes Are Running on My System?**

You can view a list of running process in the Windows Task Manager. To start Task Manager, right-click an empty space on the Taskbar and click Task Manager, or run taskmgr.exe. The Processes tab lists the currently running processes. To customize the display to show different information about each process, including the base priority and number of threads, choose Select Columns from the View menu.

▶ *For more information on Task Manager and starting and stopping processes, see Chapter 3.4, "Managing Services and Tasks."*

Symmetric Multiprocessing and Scalability

Windows NT and Windows 2000 were designed to take advantage of multiple processors. The method used in Windows 2000 is Symmetric Multiprocessing (SMP). In Windows 2000, this means that if there is more than one processor, threads are scheduled for the first available processor.

The Microkernel controls the scheduling of threads. By default, this allows load balancing across all available processors, although applications can change processor affinity to ensure that all threads for that application run in only one processor. The default behavior ensures that no single processor will get overloaded. By default, single-threaded applications cannot use more than one processor at a time and are, by default, scheduled for the last processor. This differs from Windows NT 4.0, which assigned all single-threaded applications to the first processor.

? **How Can I Control Processor Affinity?**

On a multi-processor system, you can use Task Manager to limit the CPUs that a given process will run in. You do this by brining up Task Manager and then selecting the Processes tab. Then, you right-click the process you wish to modify and click on Set Affinity to bring up the Processor Affinity dialog box. You can then select which processor the application will run in.

User Mode Services and Applications

There are three kinds of processes that run in User mode:

- **System processes.** These are processes that manage the User mode environment. They include Winlogon (which handles user logons), The Service Controller (which starts and stops services), and The Session Manager (which manages the user sessions). They are started by the Kernel at startup and are invoked by the LocalSystem account.

- **Windows 2000 services.** The Windows 2000 services, such as Alerter and Computer Browser, are started by The Service Controller (services.exe). Many of the standard Windows 2000 services run as threads within services.exe, so they do not appear as separate processes on the computer. They are stopped by the service controller when you either shut down the computer or use the Services console to stop the service. Most are invoked by the LocalSystem account, but many can be reconfigured to use whatever account the administrator deems necessary.

- **User applications.** Applications that are run while the user is logged on are run in User mode, and each runs in its own private memory address space. These processes are associated with an *environment subsystem* that takes the Application Programming Interface (API) calls generated by the process and translates them into the appropriate commands for the Executive. The client/server runtime subsystem (Csrss.exe) is the subsystem that supports Windows and DOS programs. It is started automatically when the system is started. Windows 2000 also includes subsystems that can be used to run fundamental OS/2 and POSIX applications; these subsystems are not started until one of these applications is started.

? **Why Should I Care About These Different Types of User Mode Processes?**

The main differences between these three types of User mode processes is how they are started and what is necessary to manage them:

- System processes are started by Windows 2000, and there's nothing that you need to do to manage them.

- Windows 2000 services can be managed only by an administrator. Use the Services console in Computer Management to start and stop services. Installing new services requires administrative authority as well. Services are not affected by users logging on and logging off at the console of the computer. In other words, services continue to run, regardless of whether a user is interacting with the system at the console or not.

- User applications can be started and stopped by whoever is logged on at the computer. When the user logs off, all the applications running in that user's interactive session are terminated as well.

Security Manager

The Security Manager is the part of the Executive that is responsible for enforcing security on all objects on the system. It runs in Kernel mode as part of the Local Security Authority process (lsass.exe).

Security is covered in more detail in "Windows 2000 Security" later in this chapter.

Memory Management

Like many other operating systems, Windows 2000 uses virtual memory to allow the operating system to use hard disk space as if it were Random Access Memory (RAM). The Virtual Memory Manager (VMM), a component of the Windows 2000 Executive, constantly evaluates the best use of memory and disk to provide a large enough file cache while also keeping as many applications as possible in memory. When the demands for cache and applications exceed the amount of available physical memory, the VMM will transfer infrequently used pages of memory to the disk. When an application needs to access one of these pages of memory that have been "paged out" to the disk, a "page fault" occurs, and the VMM retrieves the page from the disk.

The amount of space being used for the paging file is managed dynamically by Windows 2000, and it can grow and shrink as the demand for memory increases and decreases.

▶ *For more information on configuring the paging file, see "Virtual Memory Configuration" in Chapter 2.3, "Configuring Devices and System Settings."*

Processes running in Kernel mode have direct access to memory locations and other computer hardware addresses. User mode processes can only access virtual addresses provided to it by the VMM, and thus are protected from each other. In the memory map of each process, the area between 0 and 2 GB is available for program code and data; the area between 2 GB and 4 GB is reserved for referencing system code (that is, Kernel mode portions of Windows 2000).

Memory in Enterprise Class Servers

On systems that have between 2 GB and 4 GB of physical memory, Windows 2000 can be configured to limit the kernel address space to 1 GB instead of the usual 2 GB, so the remaining memory can be used for applications. This allows applications with large memory requirements, such as databases, to keep more of their data resident in memory, reduce paging to disk, and thereby improve performance. Called *four giga-byte tuning* (4GT), you enable it by modifying the contents of the boot.ini file. An application must be designed to take advantage of the larger address space to benefit from this configuration.

If your server is running Windows 2000 Advanced Server, it will be able to address up to 8 GB of memory by using a technology called Physical Address Extension (PAE) X86. On servers running Windows 2000 Datacenter Server, the amount of memory you can use jumps to 64 GB.

A key point about this extra memory, however, is that it is not used to run programs. A process can allocate and then use memory using special API calls. However, the OS will not page this memory nor will it use it to run applications. For more information about enterprise memory architecture, search Microsoft's Web site at http://www.microsoft.com.

Windows Clustering and Load Balancing

Windows Clustering consists of two features of Windows 2000 Advanced Server and Datacenter Server that enhance the availability of applications:

- Network Load Balancing enables up to 32 servers in a single cluster to be connected for TCP/IP-based services and applications. As clients connect to the cluster, their network connections are distributed among the members of the cluster. Servers can be added to or removed from the cluster while the applications remain available on the network. Clients see the network cluster as a single machine with a single IP address.

- Server clusters provide high availability by allowing applications to automatically *failover* to other servers in the cluster. Windows 2000 Advanced Server allows two computers to be connected using a supported shared SCSI disk device or up to four servers to participate in a single cluster using SCSI over Fiber Channel.

Networking

The network architecture in Windows 2000 consists of multiple layers. These layers provide device and protocol independence for network applications (see Figure 1.1.2).

The key components in the Windows 2000 network architecture are as follows:

- **Network applications.** Application programs that rely on the network to perform tasks. Examples include Web servers, browsers, messaging applications, or file and print servers. These applications typically run in User mode.

- **Network redirectors and servers.** Network programs that create and manage connections between client application programs and server applications, but may also have companion process running in the kernel. For example, the Server service is a User mode process that also relies upon the SRV.SYS component operating as an installable file system under the IO Manager.

- **Network protocols.** Protocol drivers that enable network communications to be properly coded for transmission and routing from one computer to another on the network. Examples include TCP/IP, NWLink IPX/SPX compatible protocol, and NetBEUI. These drivers run in Kernel mode.
- **Network interface drivers.** Device drivers for the network interfaces attached to the computer, such as network interface cards or dial-up networking devices. These drivers run in Kernel mode.

▶▶ *For more information on installing and configuring Windows 2000 network components, see Chapter 8.1, "Overview of Managing Network Services."*

Figure 1.1.2   Windows 2000 network architecture diagram.

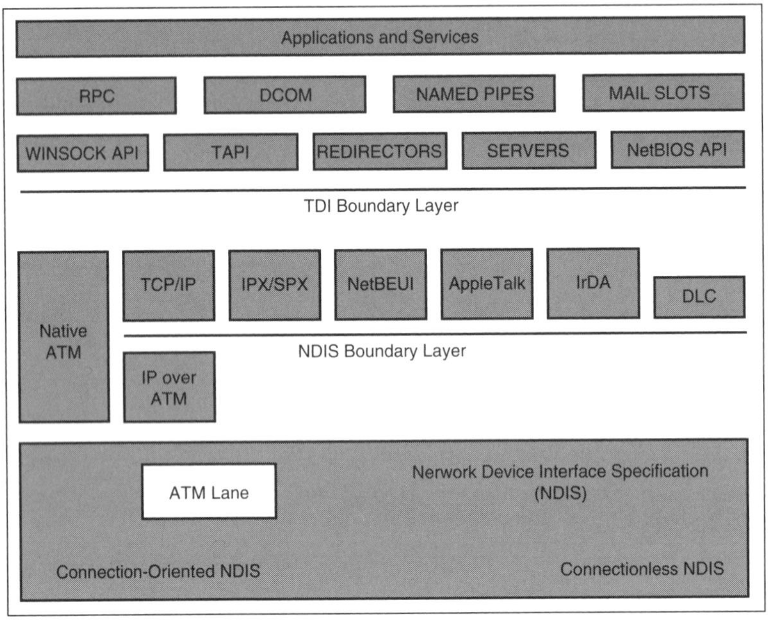

Windows 2000 Security

- Authentication
- Local security
- File system security
- Applications and security
- Network security

Authentication

Users are security principals. In other words, they have the ability to create and access resources on Windows 2000 systems. A security principal, therefore, must be positively identified before being given access to any resource. This process is known as *authentication*. After the user has been authenticated, an identity known as an access token is attached to the user's shell process. The access token contains the user's security ID (SID), a list of groups to which the user belongs, and a list of abilities or privileges that have been enabled and disabled for the user on the computer. When a user attempts to access a remote Windows 2000 computer on a network, another access token for the user is created and attached to the user's session on the remote computer. The user's access token is also attached to any other processes that the user starts on the computer.

▶ *For more information about Windows 2000 authentication, see Chapter 4.6, "Logging On and Authentication."*

Local Security

Security principals are entities that have the capability to access and use system resources. There are three types of security principals in Windows 2000: Users, Groups, and Computers. Windows 2000 resources are protected by a descriptor that identifies which security principals have access to that object and what level of access they have. This descriptor is known as an Access Control List (ACL). An ACL is constructed of one or more Access Control Entries (ACEs) that specifically describe *who* can do *what* with the object in question. All requests to use resources are passed to the Local Security Authority (LSA). The LSA enforces security on a local object such as a file or printer by comparing the user's SID (contained in the user's access token) with the permissions that have been assigned to the object (contained in the object's ACL). If the user and group SIDs in the user's access token have not been granted access to an object, the LSA will deny access.

If a system is not a domain controller, local user accounts and information about user rights and privileges are stored in the Security Accounts Manager (SAM) database on the computer. If the computer is a member of a domain, it can also refer to information about domain users from the Active Directory domain database.

If a system is a domain controller, Active Directory is trusted by the LSA on the computer. User accounts and information about user rights and privileges are stored in Active Directory instead of the local SAM database.

Figure 1.1.3 illustrates the relationship of the LSA to the SAM and Active Directory.

**Figure 1.1.3   The relationship of the LSA to the SAM
and Active Directory.**

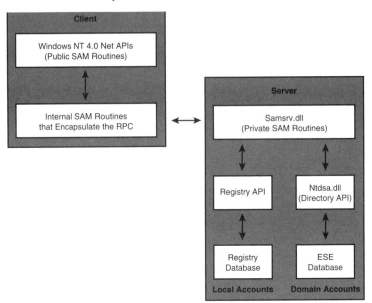

▶ *For more information on Active Directory within Windows 2000,
see Chapter 1.2, "Introduction to Active Directory."*

File System Security

File system security exists in basically two ways:

- **NTFS permissions**. On disk volumes that are using the NTFS file
  system, each file and folder has its own access control list that specifies
  the accounts that have been granted access. These permissions are
  stored as part of the security descriptor on the file or folder itself. By
  specifying security principals in the access control list on an NTFS file,
  you can control who or what has access to the file.

- **Encrypting File System (EFS)**. On NTFS volumes, users can easily
  encrypt and decrypt files, making files more secure even if the disk volume is removed from the computer or NTFS permissions are set inap-
  propriately.

  ▶ *For more information on NTFS permissions and EFS, see Chapter 5.2,
  "File Systems and Disks."*

Applications and Security

Some client/server applications need to limit access to the features of the application based on the account of the user. Applications that run on Windows 2000 have three different options for managing access to the applications:

- Use the security features of Windows 2000 to enforce security within the application by authenticating the user in a domain. This approach centralizes all user accounts so that they can be administered in one place, rather than maintaining separate account databases for each application or system. Group policies can be used to make administration of the application as granular as necessary.

  ▶ *For more information on Group Policies, see Chapter 6.3, "Group Policies."*

- Maintain a list of users and passwords that are stored with the application itself. This approach requires separate administration for each application.

- Trust a security authority outside of the domain, such as a trusted Kerberos realm. This approach allows applications to operate in heterogeneous network environments.

Network Security

Windows 2000 also provides the capability to keep data secure as it is being transmitted across the network.

- **IP Security (IPSec).** IPSec provides for secure networking over TCP/IP by providing end-to-end security for all communications on the network. To use IP Security, you modify the IP Security policy for the computers involved. For example, you could create an IPSec policy for an Active Directory domain that would require all computers in the domain to use IP Security.

- **Virtual Private Networking (VPN).** A VPN allows you to use a public network, such as the Internet, for secure data transfer between two computers. By using the Point-to-Point Tunneling Protocol (PPTP), the VPN connection acts as a "tunnel" in which all data is encrypted. You configure the VPN properties in Routing and Remote Access Service (RRAS).

- **Data encryption.** You can configure dial-up connections to use data encryption so all data sent between two computers via a dial-up connection are encrypted. Data encryption is also configured in RRAS.

1.2

Introduction to Active Directory

You Need to Read This Section If You Want to:

- Understand how Active Directory provides the platform for distributed computing in Windows 2000.
- Know how changes to Active Directory affect network clients.
- Create a new Active Directory forest and create a distributed Directory.
- Configure Domain Controllers appropriately.
- Synchronize Active Directory and other directories.

Related Topics (continued)

For More Information On ▶ *See*

Logging on to a Domain ▶ *Chapter 4.6: Logging On and*
Authentication

Administering user ▶ *Chapter 6.1: Overview of Managing*
desktops *User Desktops*

▶ *Chapter 6.3: Group Policies*

Active Directory and Windows 2000

In a network environment, information needs to be accessed by any number of computers on the network. Whether verifying a user's account and password, locating files and printers on the network, receiving important information from other users, or sending messages to users on other networks, there must be some place to store the information needed to make these things happen. In some organizations, users have to "look up" these kinds of pieces of information from a variety of sources on the network. To eliminate the need for users to search in multiple places for this kind of information, Windows 2000 provides a *Directory service* that allows Windows 2000 to store information about virtually any device or object on the network in a single database that is accessible to everyone on the network. That database is called *Active Directory*.

Active Directory provides information about users, computer, printers, network applications, and a variety of other objects of interest to network clients. Active Directory is the following:

- **Secure.** All objects and properties in Active Directory are protected by permissions that control who can access them.

- **Distributed.** In a large network environment, changes made to the Directory in one place are replicated throughout the network to other Active Directory servers (called *Domain Controllers*). This ensures that clients can access the same information from a Domain Controller near them at any time.

- **Extensible.** When Active Directory is installed, it makes available a number of predefined objects and properties that are in common use by the average organization. If these default objects need to be modified for any reason, a "template" for adding or modifying information in the Directory is included. New types of objects and new properties can easily be created to suit the needs of your organization and you can reap the benefits of Active Directory in your custom applications.

Information Stored in Active Directory

As a Directory service, Active Directory can store whatever information is useful and practical in its distributed database. Some examples of the kinds of information that can be stored in Active Directory include the following:

- **Users.** Information is stored in the Directory about network users, such as names, authentication methods, passwords, e-mail addresses, locations, phone numbers, job titles, and even Web page addresses.

- **Computers.** Information about computers on the network is stored. This data includes details about the operating system installed, its role in the network, its logical placement in the Directory, its physical location, and the persons responsible for its management.

- **Shared folders.** With Active Directory, shared folders can now be published. After information about shared folders is published in the Directory, users can search for shared folders easily by using keywords or descriptions. The folder becomes universally available, regardless of its location. This eliminates the need for users to know the server where a folder is located.

- **Printers.** In Windows 2000, the print subsystem is tightly integrated with Active Directory, making it possible to easily search across an enterprise for printers at different locations. Information about printers—such as their bin capacity, whether they print in color, and their location—can all be stored in Active Directory and searched.

- **Settings for Directory-enabled applications.** Because Active Directory is extensible, developers can use Active Directory to publish information useful to their applications. Publication is the creation, storage, and maintenance of information in Active Directory Network clients, and network administrators can use the information stored in Active Directory to find, connect to, and manage an application or service.

- **Policies.** Group Policy is a powerful feature of Windows 2000 for the central management of computers and users throughout the enterprise. Administrators may use Group Policy to specify options for desktop configurations for groups of computers and users. Group Policy is flexible and includes options for Registry-based policy settings, security settings, software installation, scripts, computer startup and shutdown, user logon and logoff, and folder redirection.

- **Active Directory configuration information.** Within Active Directory, information is stored about how Active Directory itself is organized and how the communication between servers on the network is configured.

Using Active Directory

Users can use Active Directory to do the following:

- **Log on to the network.** When users log on to a Windows 2000 Domain, credentials (username, password, or smartcard) are checked against the Directory database. If the user provided the proper information and an administrator has granted the user the ability to log on to that computer, the logon will be successful.

- **Find resources on the network.** Users can search Active Directory to locate information about other users, shared file or print resources, or any other information published in the Directory. There are a variety of methods that can be used to find information in the Directory—all of them very flexible and able to be customized as the administrator sees fit.

- **Use Directory-enabled applications.** Applications can use standard Directory access protocols to retrieve and present Active Directory data to users as part of their work. Additionally, applications can be developed that add their specific information to the Directory, extending its usefulness and simplifying its administration.

Administrators can use Active Directory to do the following:

- **Enforce security on the network.** Active Directory is the accounts database for Windows 2000 Domains.

- **Apply policies to user desktops.** Policies can be used to assign user rights on client and server computers, specify what the desktop environment should look like, decide what applications should be installed, and so on.

- **Redirect requests for resources or services to servers "near" the user's location on the network.** Active Directory stores information about the network's topology to make these decisions easier to automate. Because Active Directory "knows" the location of all objects, clients can be redirected to servers in their own location when logging on to a Domain or connecting to a Distributed File System (DFS) server.

- **Publish information in the Directory.** Good candidates for published information include frequently accessed data that needs to be highly available and localized to the clients.

- **Provide a central store that network applications can use.** Instead of having to manage application-specific configuration settings on individual desktop computers, an application can store its configuration information in Active Directory and let Active Directory make the settings available to network clients whenever they need them.

- **Configure network devices automatically through a single console.** Network devices that are configured to use Active Directory can use information placed there by the administrator to manage network traffic.

Windows 2000 Features Enabled by Active Directory

Besides the obvious task of logging on to a Windows 2000 Domain, Active Directory is integrated into many features of Windows 2000. Table 1.2.1 provides a list of these features.

Table 1.2.1   Features of Windows 2000 that Use Active Directory

Feature	Interaction with Active Directory
DNS integration with Active Directory	The DNS service can store resource records for hosts and services in Active Directory instead of on a zone file on disk. This integration enables secure dynamic updates and multi-master replication of DNS data.
DHCP with DNS integration	Allows Windows 2000 DHCP servers to update DNS information for non-Windows 2000 DHCP clients by using secure dynamic updates, eliminating the need to maintain these records manually. In addition, Windows 2000 DHCP service will start only on servers that are authorized in Active Directory to perform this role on the network.
Group Policies	Group Policies are stored in Active Directory. Client computers retrieve group policies from Domain Controllers and apply the policies to users and computers. Group Policies provide very flexible management capabilities to administrators in a Windows 2000 Domain.
IP Security	IP Security (IPSec) settings can become policy-based and are most easily implemented by using Group Policy, which requires Active Directory.
Public Key infrastructure	A Windows 2000 Domain Controller can become an enterprise root certification authority.
QoS	QoS Admission Control can be installed on a Windows 2000 Active Directory Domain Controller.
Remote Installation Services (RIS)	Remote Installation Service uses Active Directory to direct client computers to a RIS server. Like DHCP servers, Windows 2000 RIS servers must be authorized in Active Directory to perform this role on the network.
Software installation and maintenance	Using Group Policy, which requires Active Directory, most software installation and maintenance can be easily performed.

continues

Table 1.2.1   continued

Feature	Interaction with Active Directory
User data management	Using Group Policy, which requires Active Directory, users' documents can be centrally redirected to shared network locations.
User settings management	Using Group Policy, which requires Active Directory, you can most easily configure user settings management, which stores user settings for applications on a shared network location.

Perhaps the most important Windows 2000 feature that Active Directory enables is Group Policy, which is the major tool in Windows 2000 for managing the state and configuration of desktop computers.

▶ *For more information on Group Policy, see Chapter 6.3, "Group Policies."*

Industry Standards Implemented in Active Directory

Active Directory in Windows 2000 was designed to work with existing industry standards and to interoperate with other Directory services on the Internet. Active Directory supports the following standard interfaces and protocols:

- **Directory object naming.** Active Directory is derived from the X.500 model of objects and attributes. This means that information in the Directory is meant to be rich and available, as well as useful and manageable. *Objects* are distinct, named sets of attributes that represent concrete things, such as users, printers, or applications. Active Directory holds objects representing entities of various types, described by *attributes*. However, Active Directory is not an X.500 Directory; and as such, it does not support X.500 protocols. Rather, objects in the Directory are named and referenced using Lightweight Directory Access Protocol (LDAP) and other, perhaps more common and useful protocols.

- **Client access protocols.** Network clients can use LDAP and MAPI-RPC to access Active Directory.

- **Replication protocols.** Domain Controllers use either Remote Procedure Call (RPC) over IP or Simple Message Transfer Protocol (SMTP) to replicate Active Directory information throughout the enterprise.

- **Authentication protocols.** Users and computers are authenticated by using either Kerberos v.5 (the default) or Windows NT LAN Manager (NTLM) protocol (used in Windows NT 4.0 and earlier operating systems). Digital certificates, based on X.509, can be associated with user accounts in Active Directory for public-key security, for use in applications that support the Secure Sockets Layer (SSL), or Transport Layer Security (TLS).

- **Programming interfaces.** Active Directory Service Interfaces (ADSI) provides an object-oriented interface to Active Directory. ADSI can be used in Java, Visual Basic, C++, and other development environments. The LDAP C API, as defined in RFC 1823, can be used as well.

- **Interoperability with other directories.** Because Active Directory can be accessed by using LDAP, you can use LDAP-based tools to synchronize data in Active Directory with other LDAP directories. One such synchronization tool, the Active Directory Connector, is available on the Windows 2000 Server CD-ROM and is used to synchronize Active Directory with the Exchange Server 5.5 Directory.

Organization of Active Directory

Active Directory refers to both the Directory (the data about users, computers, and various other objects) and the Directory service itself (the application that runs on a Domain Controller and provides access to the Directory data). This section focuses on how the Directory is organized—that is, the hierarchical and topological models that are used to organize the information in the Directory. "Going Deeper: Domain Controllers and Active Directory," later in this chapter, will explain the distributed nature of the Directory database and its physical storage on Domain Controllers.

Building Blocks of Active Directory

In order to maintain compatibility with the LDAP standard, Active Directory uses a simplified version of the X.500 information model to represent the path to objects in Active Directory. Each Windows 2000 Domain has both a Domain Name System (DNS) name (for LDAP access) and a NetBIOS name (for backward-compatibility).

▶ *For more information on DNS names and NetBIOS names, see Chapter 4.2, "DNS and Active Directory."*

The following components are the building blocks of Active Directory:

- Objects, attributes, and permissions
- Organizational units
- Domains
- Trees and forests
- Global Catalog

Figure 1.2.1 shows an example of an object and its attributes.

Figure 1.2.1   Example object and attributes.

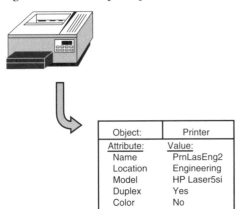

Object:	Printer
Attribute:	Value:
Name	PrnLasEng2
Location	Engineering
Model	HP Laser5si
Duplex	Yes
Color	No

Objects, Attributes, and Permissions

Active Directory consists of a collection of objects organized in containers. These objects have properties, or *attributes*, associated with them that contain descriptive information pertaining to that class of object. In order to keep these objects secure, Active Directory assigns permissions at the attribute level. Administrators or their delegates can modify these permissions as needed. For example, a user could have read access to some properties of a printer, but be denied read access to other properties. This level of granularity of permissions in Active Directory provides flexibility to administrators when delegating authority over objects in the Directory. Administration of specific attribute types, such as user passwords, can be delegated to specific groups or users in the Directory. For example, a group of Help Desk personnel could be assigned the specific permission to reset passwords on accounts within a specific Directory container that represents a business' region of collection of offices.

User and computer objects are called *security principals* because they represent agents on the network that can be authenticated. Each security principal has a security ID (SID) associated with it (one of the attributes of a security principal is its SID). Security principals can be granted access to a resource by adding their SID to the Access Control List of the resource.

▶ *For more information on assigning permissions on resources, see Chapter 5.2, "File Systems and Disks," Chapter 5.3, "Sharing Folders," and Chapter 5.5, "Sharing Printers."*

Table 1.2.2 provides a list of the object types that can be created by using Active Directory Users and Computers, along with a short list of some sample attributes for each.

Table 1.2.2   ***Some Active Directory Objects and Sample***
                 Attributes

Object	Sample Attributes
Computer	DNS name, Location, Role
Contact	First name, Last name, Full name, Display name
Group	Group name, Group scope, Group type
Organizational Unit	Description, Street, State/Province, Group Policy objects
Printer	Name, Share name, Driver name, Driver version
User	First name, Last name, Telephone number, E-mail address, Profile path
Shared folder	Name, UNC name, Description, Keywords

The definition of the object classes is contained in the Active Directory schema. Adding new attributes or properties requires a change to the schema.

Organizational Units

An organizational unit (OU) is a container in which you can create other objects, such as user objects, computer objects, or other OUs. Because an OU is an Active Directory object, it also can have permissions assigned to it. In order to create objects in an OU, you have to have the appropriate permissions on the OU.

The major benefits of using organizational units to organize objects are as follows:

- Group Policy can be assigned to OUs.

- Assigning permissions to OUs and their contents simplifies managing permissions on Directory objects and provides a simple means of delegating administration.

- Creating a hierarchy within a large Domain makes it easier to navigate and manage the objects in the OUs.

Figure 1.2.2 shows a possible OU hierarchy for the kapoho.com Domain. An OU structure can strictly follow a company's organizational chart, reflect geographic divisions, or become a combination of both. Because the hierarchy itself is transparent to the users for the most part, their best use is to use them to simplify administration.

Figure 1.2.2   The OU hierarchy for the kopoho.com Domain.

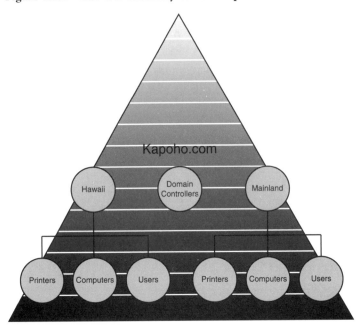

Domains

A Windows 2000 Domain is a collection of objects in the Directory. The entire Active Directory might consist of a single Domain or multiple Domains logically connected through *trusts*.

Active Directory clients use DNS to locate Active Directory Domain Controllers. Active Directory Domain names follow the standards for DNS names. For example, an organization has registered the Domain name **kapoho.com** with the appropriate Internet authorities. They could choose to name their Active Directory **Domain kapoho.com** as well (see Figure 1.2.3).

To ensure compatibility with earlier versions of Windows, Active Directory Domains also maintain NetBIOS names. Non–active Directory clients, also known as *down-level clients*, access the Windows 2000 Active Directory Domain as if it were a Windows NT Domain.

▶ *For more information on Active Directory Domain names and DNS, see Chapter 4.2, "DNS and Active Directory."*

Figure 1.2.3   Resolving a DNS name to a specific Domain Controller.

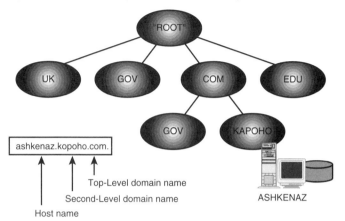

A Domain represents the following:

- **A unit of administration.** Although many administrative tasks can be delegated to specific groups of users through the use of permissions on Directory objects, there are certain special capabilities that are granted to Domain administrators, such as the ability to take ownership of any object in the Domain.

- **A unit of administrative policy.** There are policies that are Domain-wide in scope. If one of these policies is created, it will affect the entire Domain. For example, account policies (password length, password uniqueness, and so on) affect all accounts in the Domain. This occurs through inheritance of the Group Policy setting in the lower-level OUs.

- **A unit of replication.** A Domain Controller's copy of Active Directory contains all the objects in the Directory for its Domain. So, if a user logs on to the kapoho.com Domain, the Domain Controller that responds to that request will have information about all the Domain's objects in its local copy of the Directory.

A single Domain represents the simplest Active Directory design. However, an organization can choose to use more than one Domain for Active Directory. Some reasons to have more than one Domain in Active Directory include the following:

- **Partitioning administration.** When there are multiple Domains, the administrative authority of the Domain administrators is limited to their own Domain. Group Policies defined at the Domain level, such as password policies, can be implemented differently in separate Domains.

- **Partitioning replication.** A Domain's database is replicated only to other Domain Controllers in its own Domain. Having multiple Domains allows the Directory to scale to very large organizations.

- **Different Internet Domain names.** If the organization wants to continue using multiple DNS Domain names on your company's network, you will need to do some careful planning.
  ▶ *For more information, see Chapter 4.2, "DNS and Active Directory."*

Describing the path to an Active Directory object requires the following to complete:

- **Fully qualified Domain name.** This type of name appears most often in the Active Directory Administrative tools. Objects and their containers are stored in Active Directory Domains. These Domains are named using DNS-compliant names.

- **LDAP distinguished name (DN).** Because DNS describes a path only to the Domain and its Domain Controllers, a method had to be devised to store and extract information within the database. Although there are numerous protocols available to do this, a standardized method that used Internet-compliant methods was preferred. Therefore LDAP was chosen.

Trust Relationships

A *trust relationship* is a relationship between two Domains in which one Domain trusts the other (one Domain accepts the credentials from an account in the other Domain as valid). Trust relationships enable logging on to any Domain in the forest and the capability to assign permissions to a resource for any account in the Directory.

In Windows 2000, all Domains in Active Directory automatically share transitive two-way Kerberos trusts with all other Domains in the Directory.

This enables a user to log on to any computer that is part of Active Directory and be authenticated. For example, a user sitting at a computer that is a member of the usa.mcp.com Domain would be able to log on with a user account from europe.mcp.com.
▶ *For more information on trusts and the logon process, see Chapter 4.6, "Logging On and Authentication."*

Global Catalog

The Global Catalog in Windows 2000 is a collection of all the objects in Active Directory that can be searched to locate objects, no matter what Domain the object is in. For example, to locate a user in a large enterprise, you could search the Global Catalog and find the user quickly, without having to know which Domain to search.

In order to keep searches fast and to minimize the amount of replication traffic that is involved, only designated Domain Controllers play the role of Global Catalog servers, and only a subset of the attributes for objects are replicated. The Active Directory schema specifies which attributes of objects should appear in the Global Catalog. The Global Catalog servers then replicate only those attributes to each other.

By default, only the first Domain Controller in the forest is a Global Catalog server. If you want additional servers to perform as Global Catalog servers, you need to configure them as such.

Global catalog servers are an important part of your Active Directory implementation for the following reasons:

- A Global Catalog (GC) server must be available on the network for users to log on to successfully, although the administrator for a given Domain can still log on if there is no GC available.

- A Global Catalog server must be available on the network to create user accounts.

- It is much faster for users and applications to search the Global Catalog than to search multiple Domains to locate a user or a shared resource.

Because it is a Domain Controller in a Domain, each GC will have a complete replica (copy of all attributes) of all the objects in its own Domain. It will also have a partial replica (copy of selected attributes) of all the objects in the other Domains in the forest.

Figure 1.2.4 shows the relationship between the Global Catalog and the Domain-naming contexts on a Global Catalog server in a forest with three Domains.

Figure 1.2.4   How the Global Catalog is constructed.

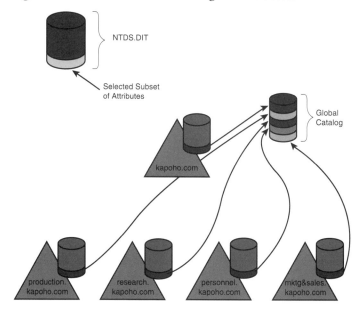

Global Catalog servers listen for queries on TCP port 3268. Any request that is received on that port will be treated as a *Global Catalog query*, and only the attributes that are published in the Global Catalog will be returned to the client. Any queries that are received on TCP port 389, however, are treated as *Domain queries*, and only objects in the Domain Controller's Domain are returned to the client (all of the attributes are available, however).

Going Deeper: Domain Controllers and Active Directory

A Domain Controller is a computer running Windows 2000 Server that has been configured as an Active Directory server. Each Domain Controller has configuration information about the entire Active Directory, along with a copy of all the Active Directory objects for its own Domain.

Active Directory uses multi-master replication, which means that all the Domain Controllers for a Domain are writable (updatable by a user) copies of the Domain database. You can connect to any Domain Controller and add users, reset passwords, or do other maintenance tasks to Directory information. After the changes have been made, they will be replicated automatically to all other Domain Controllers in the Domain.

This is a major change from Windows NT 4.0, which had only one writable copy of the Domain database (the Primary Domain Controller, or PDC) and read-only copies on other Domain Controllers (the Backup Domain Controllers, or BDCs).

In order to log on to a Domain, client computers must be able to contact a Domain Controller for the Domain. Client computers use the standard LDAP port (TCP port 389) to communicate with Domain Controllers. Queries received on that port are treated as Domain queries.

Naming Contexts

Within Active Directory, there are three *naming contexts* that define a portion of the Directory that needs to be replicated to other Domain Controllers:

- **Configuration.** This part of the Directory holds information about the configuration of the Domain Controllers: definition of sites, connection objects used to replicate information between DCs, and information about other Domains within the enterprise that are part of the same forest. The configuration-naming context is replicated to all Domain Controllers in the forest.

- **Schema.** A part of the configuration information, the schema defines to Windows 2000 the types of objects and their properties that can be created in Active Directory. It also contains the rules about what classes of objects can be created in what containers. Customizing Active

Directory to hold new object classes or new properties requires modifying the schema. The schema-naming context is replicated to all Domain Controllers in the forest.

- **Domain.** This is the information that starts at the root of the Domain and contains all organizational units and objects in the Domain. The Domain-naming context is replicated to all Domain Controllers in the same Domain.

Replication

Because all the copies of Active Directory on the various Domain Controllers are writable copies, client computers and administrators can make changes to a Domain on any Domain Controller in the Domain. The Domain Controllers then replicate the changed information to the other Domain Controllers in the Domain.

Naming Contexts and Replication

The naming context is the boundary of replication. Domain Controllers in the same namespace receive the same Domain information. It is a portion of the LDAP namespace (the portion a Domain Controller is responsible for).

The root of a Domain's naming context is the DNS name of the Domain itself. The root of an enterprise's naming context is the root of the first Domain created in Active Directory. All Domains created in the forest after that will share the same configuration data and schema. Although each Domain maintains its own Domain namespace, each Domain is dependent upon the root Domain for authority, topological information, and rules concerning how objects will be handled. They need this information to ensure database consistency.

All objects created in each Domain are children of the name of that Domain. The Domain information is stored within the namespace LDAP://ashkenaz.kopoho.com/Domain NC, with the Distinguished Name of DC=kopoho,DC=com. All other objects are referenced under that name. For example, the Organizational Unit Domain Controllers has a DN of OU=Domain Controllers,DC=kopoho,DC=com; the System container, which is usually hidden, has a DN of CN=System,DC=kopoho,DC=com.

The configuration information for the enterprise is a child of the root Domain, within the LDAP namespace LDAP://ashkenaz.kopoho.com/ Configuration Container, and an LDAP Distinguished Name of CN=Configuration,DC=kopoho,DC=com.

Likewise, the schema information for the enterprise is a child of the root Domain, and found in LDAP://ashkenaz.kopoho.com/Schema, and referenced by the DN, CN=Schema,DC=kopoho,DC=com.

The Active Directory database is physically contained on Domain Controllers within the database file NTDS.DIT. The database is controlled by the Directory service that is a process running under LSASS.EXE. NTDS.DIT contains objects from all three name contexts.

LSASS.EXE actually does not run a *service* in the purest sense of the terminology. The Directory service cannot be started and stopped in the same way services can. The Directory service is started when a Domain Controller is started, and it is stopped when the Domain Controller is shut down. Any attempt from within the Windows 2000 interface to stop the process will result in the Domain Controller shutting itself down. To run the Domain Controller without running the Directory service, restart the server in Directory Services Restore Mode.

As mentioned before, Directory replication is a full-synchronization, multi-master operation based on a ring topology. Within a Domain, almost any action taken on the database is replicated to all other Domain Controllers in the Domain. Operations that initiate replication include object creation, manipulation, moves, and deletions. For example, if a printer object is created in the OU kapoho.com/West, all other Domain Controllers also need to know that. The object is then replicated from the originating Domain Controller to all other Domain Controllers for that Domain. Again, if the object were moved from the West OU to the East OU, each Domain Controller in that Domain would need to receive an update, notifying it that the object had moved. Finally, if the object is deleted from the database (an action that all Domain Controllers need to be notified of), replication takes place again.

Object creation updates the database. To maintain an accurate record of creation, modification, movement, or deletion, objects are tracked by using a number of methods so database consistency can be maintained. The first action recorded in the database is the *originating update*, which identifies the object's place of creation. Each object is constructed of attributes, or properties, defined by the schema. Each of these attributes is tagged with a unique identifier (also known as a Globally Unique Identifier, or GUID) that initially matches the identifier assigned to the object itself.

There are two types of updates possible in the system: originating updates and replicated updates. There can be only one originating update for any event in the Directory. All other updates to Domain Controllers are replicated. When a change is initiated to the database, it is accomplished on the Domain Controller and the user is connected to at the time of creation. That object is tagged as having been created on that Domain Controller. The Domain Controllers that receive the update then update themselves and replicate the change onto other Domain Controllers. Replication by these Domain Controllers is a *replicated* update. In other words, this change didn't come from the location it originated; it was passed on from somewhere else. This activity uses a *store-and-forward* mechanism, in which the responsibility for completing replication is passed on to other servers in the system.

Keeping track of where an update originates is important because a Domain Controller can determine whether or not a proposed update was already received or not. By examining the *originating write* on the change and comparing it to what it has already received determines whether it has received that update or not. This activity is called *propagation damping*.

Propagation avoids a situation in which Domain Controllers might continue to try replicating changes to servers that already received those changes. This situation might occur because the replication topology is configured in a ring. That means an originating change will propagate bi-directionally to at least two other Domain Controllers, which in turn will propagate the change around the ring until the update has been received on all Domain Controllers. If the last server in a ring already received an update from one of its replication partners and was notified by its other replication partner that a change occurred, how could it determine whether that change was received?

When a Domain Controller is created, it is assigned a GUID. This GUID is maintained in the configuration container. This unique ID is also published in DNS, where it is used to positively identify the server—not by a friendly name, but by a unique ID that never changes. GUIDs ensure that all objects in Active Directory are *rename safe*. When the first Domain Controller is created in Active Directory, both the Domain Controller and the Directory database itself are assigned GUIDs. These GUIDs, known as the *server GUID* and the *database GUID,* are initially identical. The database GUID is used to identify the Domain Controller's database positively during replication processes.

Update Sequence Numbers (USNs)

Used by Domain Controllers to determine whether they need an update from a replication partner. The USN is a 64-bit, double-byte value that is sequentially incremented whenever a change occurs to the server maintaining it. Each time a change occurs in the Directory, it is assigned to the database as a transaction, and the number of the transaction is the USN. Through this USN, a sequential record of all transactions that have occurred on a server can be maintained. Like any reliable database transaction, the update must be properly committed to the database. If, for some reason, the transaction is aborted, the USN is not assigned.

Each object in the Directory maintains two distinct USNs: usnCreated and usnChanged. Each property on every object also maintains the same two USN values. This makes it possible to change a specific attribute without having to update the values for all other attributes, as well. When an object is created, it is stamped with the next available USN. This is the usnCreated value.

USNs are extremely important for replication. Servers determine whether or not they require updates to the Directory by examining the USNs of their replication partners. Each Domain Controller maintains a table containing the identity of a replication partner and the last USN known from that partner. Through this method, a Domain Controller can determine not only that a change has or has not occurred (the reported USN changed or didn't), it can also determine how many changes have occurred and how many changes to apply. One very important advantage of this method is its complete non-reliance upon time-based mechanisms. For the purposes of replication, server clocks don't ever have to be synchronized. All a server needs to know to receive an update is the last USN reported from a replication partner and the USN currently being reported. If they differ, an update is required.

USNs are used not only to determine what to change in the database, but also to find the changes themselves. As a result of this, USNs are indexed values in the database.

When an object is created, a database entry is made and attributes are completed with specific values. The object and its attributes are tagged with the GUID of the server's database, and the transaction is assigned two USN values: the usnCreated and the usnChanged.

Upon creation at ServerA, the usnCreated value and usnChanged value are the same. The USN was selected as the next available sequential transaction value on that server. Because both the created and changed values are identical, it shows that the object has never seen a change. Each attribute of the object has a GUID that matches all the other attributes' GUIDs. This indicates there has never been a change to this object.

The object now has to be replicated to the other Domain Controllers in the Domain. Let's say one of them is named ServerB. This server is currently at USN value 2044. The originating server announces to its near-replication partners that it has changes. This announcement includes the current (newly updated) USN from that server. The server receiving the announcement (ServerB) maintains a table containing its replication partners and the last USN received from that computer. ServerB notices that the last USN it knew about on ServerA was 1202, so there is one change on ServerA that needs to be updated on ServerB.

The usnCreated and usnChanged values now reflect the new creation on ServerB, but it still retains the originating GUID of ServerA and the attributes are still tagged with the GUID of the originating database, ServerA. What this all means is that when it was created, the object was the 1203rd transaction on ServerA, but when it was replicated to ServerB (and then created there as well), it inherited the next available transaction number on that server, 2045. The same process is used when the object is replicated to the next server in line.

Because Active Directory is a multi-master replication system, this object can be modified by an administrator while connected to a different computer.

Notice that the change affects only the attribute that was changed and the server the change was made on. All other attributes remain as they were.

This change needs to be replicated to the other Domain Controllers, one of them being ServerA. ServerB announces its change and sends its USN with the change announcement. The USN from ServerB is now 2052. ServerA compares the USN from ServerB to the previously stored USN from that computer, notes that the new USN is higher, and applies the change. However, this object already exists on this server and only the attribute needs to change.

What has changed on ServerA is the object's usnChanged value and the values of the attribute that were replicated from ServerB. Nothing else about the object (none of its other attributes) were altered.

What this demonstrates are the benefits of attribute-based replication. This replication model makes multiple-master replication possible. It also ensures a relatively low amount of replication traffic and the capability to accurately determine where changes have occurred. All this information is used for two values, maintained on every Domain Controller used to keep this all in line: the high-watermark vector and the up-to-dateness vector.

High-Watermark Vector

The *high-watermark vector* is a simple table maintained on each Domain Controller. It contains two values: the GUID of replication partner servers and the highest USN value known from that partner. Simply stated, the high-watermark vector is (from the perspective of a server needing update) the information it knows about the state of the Directory on the servers that send it Directory updates. It only regards direct replication partners.

Replication activity is always a *pull* operation, which means that when replication must take place, a server will learn of an update through an announcement from a replication partner, but will always pull it from a partner. However, before the changed information is pulled, the locally cached high-watermark vector is consulted. When a Domain Controller announces it has changes, it sends its highest USN value along with that change. When received at another Domain Controller, this value is compared to the high-watermark vector to determine whether that change must be applied. If the values match, the data does not need to change and the information is not pulled. If the high-watermark vector doesn't match the USN of the announced change, the information requires an update and the change is pulled. In other words, it is used to keep track of recent changes on replication partners. If a Domain Controller has three replication partners, the high-watermark vector has three row entries—one for each partner.

As mentioned before, replication is initiated through an announcement. This announcement contains a limited amount of information designed to allow the replication partners to determine whether they need to apply the announced change or not. In other words, it's the responsibility of each Domain Controller to determine whether or not it should apply an announced change, and it is determined by using the information sent in the announcement. It contains the following information:

- The naming context to which the change should be applied. In other words, should this change be applied to the configuration, schema, or Domain?

- The maximum number of objects to be updated (default = 100). This value ensures that the replication process doesn't consume too much link time and can be adjusted by the administrator.

- The maximum number of values to be updated (default = 100). This value also ensures control over link consumption and is also manageable by the administrator.

- The current highest USN value.

- The state vector, also known as the up-to-dateness vector.

Up-to-Dateness Vector

The *up-to-dateness vector*, another table maintained by Domain Controllers, makes it possible for them to determine whether an update has already been received. This table contains a list of all Domain databases (GUIDs) for that Domain and the highest USN received from that database. The only entries in this list are from Domain Controllers where a change has occurred. Over a period of time, this will most probably grow to include all the Domain Controllers for a given Domain.

The up-to-dateness vector makes it possible to maintain a flexible replication topology (in which replication partners might dynamically occasionally change because of changes in the network).

The up-to-dateness vector is useful because it provides information that can't be gained from direct replication partners. If a Domain has only two or three Domain Controllers, replication is relatively simple. All Domain Controllers are aware of all other Domain Controllers directly.

However, when a Domain grows beyond this size, the replication topology changes to a logical ring. This is a function of an Active Directory service called the Knowledge Consistency Checker (KCC), and it is performed automatically. Now, each of the servers receives direct replication from only two servers because it maintains a logical direct connection with only two of them. The fourth server's data changes are replicated indirectly through the other two. A fourth server (ServerD) has been added to the Domain and the KCC has configured a replication ring. Each server in the ring is directly connected to two others and indirectly connected to the fourth. ServerD receives updates from ServerA indirectly through ServerB and ServerC.

To ensure reliability and reduce latency, replication is also a bi-directional process. When a server's database is changed, it promulgates its changes to all its direct replication partners. Thus, two of the servers receive updates directly from the originating server (ServerA), but ServerD receives its update indirectly. When ServerD receives its update from one of the two previously updated servers (let's assume it's ServerB), it does so in the same way as the others, except that the change announcement contains a state vector from the originating server, although it is from a direct replication partner. This update identifies where the change actually originated.

However, the other replication partner (ServerC) doesn't know ServerD has been updated and must announce the changes it has received. It proceeds to send a change announcement to ServerD. ServerD examines the replication announcement from ServerC, and the USN value from ServerC indicates that an update should be pulled, but this announcement includes (as mentioned previously) the state vector from ServerA. Server examines the announcement, determines that the change has already been applied, and doesn't pull the change.

Let's examine in detail how this works, as follows:

1 A new user is added while an administrator is connected to ServerA. This change will eventually have to be replicated to ServerD, but Server D is not directly connected to ServerA.

2 The user account is replicated to ServerB from ServerA. ServerD still has not received the update. Recall that this replica carries the originating update USN from ServerA.

3 ServerB initiates replication with ServerD. The change announcement contains the following information:

   - Name context (Domain) of the change
   - Highest known USN on ServerB
   - Number of objects in the replication
   - Number of values in the replication
   - Up-to-dateness vector from ServerA

4 From the information supplied, ServerD determines that it needs to apply the announced update, binds to ServerB, and pulls the change.

5 ServerA replicates the new user information to ServerC by using the same method.

6 ServerC initiates replication with ServerD. The change announcement contains the following information:

   - The naming context (Domain) of the change
   - The highest known USN for this server (Server C)
   - The number of objects in this replication

- The number of values in this replication
- The up-to-dateness vector from ServerA

7 ServerC replication reply determines that ServerD already is up-to-date and sends last-object-changed USN, up-to-dateness vector, but no data!

Conflict Resolution

There are two situations in which conflicts may arise in a distributed Directory system: the attribute value conflict and the object name creation conflict. Domain Controllers must be able to determine these conditions and correct them when they arise.

Attribute Value Conflict

An *attribute value conflict* occurs when the same attribute is changed on the same object, at the same time, on different Domain Controllers. For example, an attribute this might happen to might be the user's address. If the user were to change the address at the same time as an administrator, there would be a conflict when both changes reach other Domain Controllers. When the updates replicate back to ServerD, the question is "Which attribute should be used?"

Each of the changes made are originating writes, with a state vector identifying the server the change was made on. However, although the change was originated on two different Domain Controllers, the version number of each of these changes has also been incremented equally. The servers won't be able to determine which change to apply based upon this information alone.

Recall for a moment that Directory replication in Windows 2000 does not rely upon timestamps; it relies upon the highest USN known from the server applying the change and the current version number of that attribute. When the version number is examined and determined to be higher, replication is applied.

However, when a server receives a change, but the version number is the same as a previously applied update, the timestamps are compared and the change with the latest timestamp will be applied. That's why a timestamp is applied to each change. It's a tie-breaker. In the very unlikely situation that the timestamps are identical, the change with the highest-valued state vector (up-to-dateness) GUID value will be applied. That's a final and certain tie-breaker. The GUID applied to each state vector is different because the changes originated on a different server, so one of the changes is guaranteed to be chosen. This may not be what was desired, but at least it is consistent.

A second case of conflict resolution is necessary in a loosely consistent Directory service: when an object with the same Relative Distinguished Name (RDN) is created on two different servers at the same relative time. Although unlikely, it is possible and must be addressed. For example, if a user account is created on ServerB and ServerC simultaneously, it will have to be replicated to ServerA and ServerD.

However, when the object is replicated from ServerC, there is already an object existing with that RDN. Because objects are created with a unique SID and GUID, this is a unique object, different from the one created on Server B. Because the object is different, ServerD applies the object to its database. But because the name is identical, it appends the object's GUID to the object from the server with the highest state vector (ServerC).

Orphaned Objects

Although not properly a conflict in the same sense as the previous two cases, there is one other situation the Directory service must resolve potential problems: orphaning.

All leaf objects are created in containers. However, an Organizational Unit container is an administrator-created object, so it can also be deleted. When a container object is deleted, all contents in the container are deleted as well. The Directory also keeps track of the objects that were deleted in that container and replicates their deletion. In a loosely consistent Directory, it takes some amount of time for created objects to be replicated to Domain Controllers somewhere else; deleted objects are included. During that latent period, a deleted container is still active on other Domain Controllers until replication of the deletion completes. Because of this, it's possible that an account could be created in a container that was already deleted somewhere else after the time that the container was deleted. However, that created object was not deleted by the administrator when the container was deleted. In fact, that account is not deleted at all.

If this occurs after the replication of the deleted container occurs, the created account has no container and is *orphaned*. For this reason, Microsoft created the hidden built-in container, LostAndFound. Active Directory moves all orphaned objects to this folder, where they await disposition from the administrator.

Higher-Priority Replication Issues

Under most circumstances, in a fairly well-designed network, Active Directory's default replication timings are adequate for most events in the system. There are some times, however, when certain activities deserve a little boost over the timings of normal account activity: Urgent Replication and Preferential Change.

Urgent Replication

Some activities shouldn't have to wait for the regular replication interval to occur. They may be just too important. The Urgent Replication function ensures that certain types of traffic won't be delayed by standard replication latency. These are initiated by SAM or LSA (not by LDAP writes). Urgent Replication uses RPC/IP to immediately notify replication partners of a change while bypassing the regular replication interval. Only certain events trigger urgent replication; normally, this replication is confined within the site and the site containing the PDC emulator.

The following events can trigger Urgent Replication:

- **Assignment of an Account Lockout.** Account Lockout is a feature of the security system that assigns a limit to the number of failed authentications that an account can accumulate. After the account has reached the Account Lockout threshold, it is prevented from being further authenticated for a period of time set in the system's policies.

- **Changing a Local Security Authority Secret (LSA).** These are essentially data about accounts and trusts that need to be known by all Domain Controllers concurrently.

- **Changing the Relative Identifier (RID) Master Role Owner.** This is the Domain Controller responsible for assigning unique relative identifiers to Domain Controllers in the Domain.

How Urgent Replication Lockout Is Applied

When one of the previous events occurs, that data is urgently replicated to the Primary Domain Controller (PDC) emulator for that Domain and then to the following:

- Domain Controllers in the same site and Domain as the PDC emulator.

- Domain Controllers in the same site as the originating Domain server.

- Domain Controllers in the same Domain as the originating server, or within sites that have been configured to allow change notification with the site containing the PDC emulator or the server originating the change. Enabling Change Notification Between Sites also, by definition, enables Urgent Replication.

Urgent Replication bypasses the normal replication interval. When this event is triggered, the Domain Controller immediately announces a replication update to all its replication partners. Included in this announcement are any and all accumulated changes that were not announced already. This immediate replication event travels the same replication path that normal replication does. Because the default interval within the site is five minutes, it is possible that not only would the lockout be propagated immediately, but also a number of "normal" changes as well. Because Urgent Replication is a somewhat rare event, this should not create a problem.

Managing Urgent Replication Between Sites

By default, changes applied to the Directory are replicated between sites according to a schedule determined by the administrators, and not just when changes occur. These parameters are controlled within the site connection object properties. An administrator may determine that change notifications should be replicated at the same rate as intra-site replication and may configure the system using ADSI Edit to do so. This effectively allows Urgent Replication to occur across these additional sites as well.

To determine whether or not to enable Change Notification Between Sites, consider the following:

- Is the Domain distributed across too many sites? If so, perhaps consolidating all Domain Controllers into one site might solve the problem.

- If the desired result is to maintain site affinity but urgent replication everywhere, use multiple sites and enable change notification on all the site links.

- Increase the scope of the sites to a more expansive collection of subnets—perhaps all. This might require additional bandwidth, but the expenditure here might have long-term benefits in cost and functionality.

- Is this function really an issue? If the network's sites are fairly large geographic areas, it's unlikely that a user would be able to log on to the network after the lockout, anyway. By default, all Domain Controllers in the site where the lockout occurred receive urgent replication. That being the case, a user would have to physically travel to a site location before regular scheduled replication occurred in order to defeat the lockout. That situation would be unlikely in a properly designed network.

Preferential Change

A multiple-master Directory has many advantages, not the least of which is the ability of users to change their passwords while logged on to virtually any Domain Controller in the Domain. In the previous Windows NT single-master model, if the PDC wasn't available, users couldn't change their passwords because the PDC was the only Domain Controller users could send a change request to. However, allowing password changes on any Domain Controller does have its challenges. If password changes were replicated normally on the same interval as other data, it is possible that users might, within a short while, log on to a Domain Controller that hasn't received notification of the update. This could happen if a user changed their own password, logged off, and then (due to a busy network) logged on to a different Domain Controller. This would be a rare instance, however, because users are generally always validated by the same Domain Controller, as designated by the site settings. But password changes don't always originate with end users.

Administrators and call centers will regularly reset passwords for users. Those performing this function will rarely be connected to the same Domain Controller the user is currently attached to. As a result, the password will be reset on a quite different server. The end result would be an inability of the user to be authenticated for a period of time. One way to avoid this is for the administrator to determine what server the user is logged on to, attach to that computer, and perform the password change. This process is awkward, however, and doesn't avoid the situation described previously.

What Active Directory provides is a system of Preferential Change in which any password change on any Domain Controller results in a best-effort notification by that Domain Controller to the PDC emulator. In addition, whenever a user authenticates against a Domain Controller and the logon fails because the password was incorrect, the Domain Controller will check the PDC emulator for evidence of a different password. If the PDC emulator holds a recent password change that matches the one entered by the user, it authenticates the user. Replication of the password attribute to other Domain Controllers can continue via normal replication. Although not a replication per se, this method results in a means by which other Domain Controllers can reasonably check the PDC emulator if a user's logon fails because of an incorrect password entry.

Sites

Within Active Directory, sites are defined to manage the effect Directory replication has on the physical topology of your network. The Domain Controllers store this information as part of the configuration partition.

Sites allow the administrator to identify the different locations in the enterprise that have good bandwidth and then manage the replication traffic that occurs between them. Sites also allow you to identify locations so you can localize services provided by applications. For example, Windows 2000 client computers use information about its site to determine which Domain Controller is the closest.

For a comparison of replication within a site and between sites, see Table 1.2.3.

Table 1.2.3   Comparing Intra-site Replication and Inter-site Replication of Active Directory Data

Intra-Site Replication	Inter-Site Replication
Assumes availability of high-speed connections	Makes no assumption of link speed
No compression	All data is compressed
No scheduling of replication	Replication can be scheduled
Automatic replication topology generated	Site link must be created Costs can be associated with site links Bridgehead server can be designated
Uses RPC over IP as replication protocol	Uses either RPC over IP or SMTP as replication protocol

Locating Services

One of the most important ideas behind deploying a global Directory is its capability to locate almost anything defined as an object. Virtually any network service can be represented as an object in Active Directory and therefore can be located easily through the Directory. Here are some of the more common services that can be found using Active Directory:

- **Distributed File System.** Distributed File System (DFS) shares are found by clients through site information. If there is a DFS share replica in the client's site, it will connect there.

- **Published Shares.** If you are not using DFS, you can publish shares to the Active Directory, which will make it easier to find these shares.

- **Printers.** The printing subsystem is closely integrated into Active Directory. Print servers publish their information in Active Directory. Domain Controllers in a site also manage printer maintenance. If a printer is no longer available, it will be automatically removed from the Directory by a Domain Controller in its site. Printers can be tracked and located according to site information.

How to Create Sites

The complete site-creation activity is actually a two-step process. The first task is to create the subnet object name. The second is to create the subnet objects and then associate them with the site.

Site container objects are created in the Active Directory Sites and Services snap-in. After the snap-in is open, select Sites and then select the Sites container. To create the site, right-click the container; from the popup menu, select New Site. Create a meaningful name for the site, and associate it with a site link.

When to Create New Sites

The general rule-of-thumb is to create sites whenever the network is bounded by a wide area network (WAN). Relatively slow connections between geographic locations are generally good candidates for site links. What constitutes a slow link, however?

As mentioned before, sites are bounded by connections having relatively slow or low network connectivity. However, what one person regards as slow might be deemed adequate by another. Most installations today would consider anything connected by less that a 10 MB-per-second connection to be "relatively slow." But that really depends upon the existing traffic and its relative data population. That's why the issue of net available bandwidth is such a factor. Connectivity between sites isn't so much a factor of "how much," but of "how much is left."

Domain Controllers and Sites

When a server is promoted to the Domain Controller role, its network ID is examined. Based upon that information, it's placed into a site. If no site is assigned for the server's network, the server will be assigned to the Default-First-Site-Name. If the administrator determines it should be in a different site, it can be manually moved. Active Directory will adjust itself to compensate for the server's new location. There are some rules-of-thumb that can be followed in most cases.

Certain servers and server roles should be represented in almost all sites. The most obvious is a Domain Controller. Although it's possible to create a site and never place a Domain Controller in it, there probably is no really good reason to do so. Sites should usually be large enough to require a Domain Controller. Additionally, without a Domain Controller in the site, a communications failure might make it impossible for a client to log on or locate important network services. In most cases, there are certain Domain Controller roles that should be represented in each site.

Site Coverage

In rare instances, sites may exist where there is no Domain Controller for that Domain. When that's the case, Active Directory provides a method to find a Domain Controller when one doesn't exist. During a search for a Domain Controller, the client attempts to find a Domain Controller in the site closest to the client. When the Domain being sought is a Windows 2000 Domain, the Domain Controller uses the information stored in Active Directory to determine the closest site for the client. When the Domain being sought is a Windows NT 4.0 Domain, Domain Controller discovery occurs when the client starts and uses the first Domain Controller that it finds.

Rather than just respond to a logon request with the name of any Domain Controller, the Net Logon process reads the site topology from the Directory, gets a list of all sites and subnets, and examines it. This process determines which Domains have Domain Controllers in the site. If there is no Domain Controller in that site, it queries the Knowledge Consistency Checker (KCC) to determine the replication topology for that site. If a Domain Controller determines that there is no Domain Controller for a given site, it will publish itself in DNS as an Active Directory server for that site, based upon the discovered site link cost.

What this essentially means is that DNS publishes names of Domain Controllers for each site, regardless of whether there is a Domain Controller for that Domain there. This way, every client is able to find the closest Domain Controller, regardless of location. This behavior can be disabled or controlled by modifying the Registry. An administrator can direct specific Domain Controllers to cover specific sites.

Replication Models

Recall that there are two replication schemes: intra-site and inter-site. The purpose of these models is to capitalize upon the network's inherent LAN/WAN topology and optimize traffic generated by the Directory service. The end result is a loosely consistent Directory, in which full-information convergence is constantly being accomplished. As you can see in Table 1.2.4, intra-site traffic assumes a high degree of connectivity.

Table 1.2.4   Intra-Site versus Inter-site Replication

	Intra-Site Replication	Inter-Site Replication
Transport	RPC	RPC or SMTP
Topology	Ring	Spanning Tree
Schedule	Frequency Schedule	Availability Schedule
Replication Model	Notify and Pull	Pull/Store and Forward
Compression	None	Full

Placing computers within the same site presupposes that connections between these machines will be relatively unrestricted, on-demand, and high-speed. The Directory topology created is a bi-directional ring, with no more than three hops between any other Domain Controller in the site. All Directory traffic within the site must connect using RPC connections. The default connection interval is 300 seconds, with complete end-to-end consistency being attained within 15 minutes.

Inter-site connectivity gives the administrator the ability to control Active Directory traffic through schedule and interval. This means that if the schedule is closed during a specific replication interval, no Directory information is passed. In addition, the propagation of

Directory information uses a minimum cost, spanning-tree mechanism between sites. Because of the non-connection-oriented nature of inter-site replication, SMTP can also be used to connect sites with different Domains. The KCC generates the inter-site topology automatically, but the settings on the site links are the factors the KCC considers in the process.

How the Topology Is Generated

Every Domain Controller in a site always performs topology generation in Active Directory. Each runs its own instance of a process called the Knowledge Consistency Checker (KCC). Its job is to compute the replication topology and create or delete connection objects as needed. The KCC is essentially a dynamic-link library that modifies data in the local Directory in response to system-wide changes. These are made known to the KCC by changes to the data within Active Directory.

The KCC configures replication connection objects between Domain Controllers. All connection objects define incoming replication from replication partners. Inside a site, KCCs generate their own connections. But for replication between sites, one Domain Controller per site generates all connections to all other sites. This Domain Controller is known as the Inter-Site Topology Generator (ISTG).

Each name context maintains its own replication topology. The configuration and schema share same topology because they are forest-wide operations originating in the root Domain. However, each Domain name context has its own topology because that topology is specific just to the Domain Controllers in that Domain.

Global Catalogs participate in the replication process as well. They generate their replication information by examining the Domain context of every Domain in the forest and replicate with each Domain in the forest.

The replication topology is built on sites. Each naming context results in a separate replication topology. For intra-site connections, a bi-directional ring is automatically built within sites. For inter-site replication, a spanning-tree topology is automatically created and maintained. The automatically generated topologies can also be customized or overridden by the administrator.

The KCC reviews and makes modifications to the Active Directory replication topology every 15 minutes. This ensures the propagation of data, either directly or transitively, by creating and deleting connection objects automatically as needed. An administrator can modify the KCC's behavior, and it can be triggered manually. The KCC recognizes changes that occur in the site's environment and ensures that Domain Controllers are not orphaned in the replication topology.

Intra-Site Replication Topology

The KCC generates a bi-directional ring with optimizing edges to propagate Directory information within a site. A ring avoids the problem of building too many point-to-point connection objects. If each Domain Controller were to connect to every other Domain Controller, the number of connection agreements would eventually become unmanageable. What happens is that as the number of servers in the site grows, the KCC calculates additional edges to each of the rings to ensure that Domain Controllers are connected with an average number of three hops between them. As more servers are added to the ring, the KCC optimizes the site by dynamically creating additional connection objects to reduce the latency.

These objects define a connection along one path. Although in many cases, connections seem to be created in pairs, that may not always be the case. The KCC may determine (and many times does) that a unidirectional connection object is needed to optimize the site topology. An important thing to remember here is that the connection object exists on the computer that pulls the replica. This can be demonstrated by performing a manual replication.

It's important that each Domain Controller's KCC derives the same topology as the others, so within the site, the Domain Controller's GUID is used to form the replication ring. The Domain Controller GUIDs are sorted and collected in order. Each Domain Controller will determine its replication partner by placing itself between the next-highest and next-lowest GUID in the site.

When a Domain Controller is promoted by running dcpromo, it adds itself to the site automatically. Once in, it replicates its configuration information to its partners and other Domain Controllers become aware of its presence. It really doesn't matter where in the ring a Domain Controller adds itself. Recall that the assumption accepted about sites is that they possess adequate bandwidth. If this isn't true, either the network should be upgraded or another site created.

Inter-Site Replication Topology

Inter-site topology generation is more complex than for replication within a site because Windows 2000 supports replication between sites over asynchronous transport (SMTP). With intra-site topology generation, the KCC can assume that any server can replicate to any other server. However, the same assumption cannot be made for replication between sites. All connections are represented as objects and have attributes; some are configurable. The most important of these is the designation of the source partner (the Domain Controller from which the data will be pulled) and the schedule (which determines when replication can take place).

Intra-site and inter-site connection objects are created automatically by the KCC. Under almost all situations, it is recommended to allow this behavior to continue unabated. If the network is designed well to begin with, the KCC will do a good job of optimizing itself and the Directory will work well. There are times, however, when an administrator might want to configure some manual connection objects. The KCC may be left to create the intra-site topology, but the administrator might want to massage the connections between the sites. An example of this is when an application that uses Active Directory needs to be tweaked to optimize its performance across the WAN.

It is possible to create and delete connection objects manually. This gives more control when dealing with replication over slow links. But under most conditions, the KCC will do a better job of this, and does it automatically. Manually created connection objects can be used by the KCC. In other words, if the administrator creates a connection object, the KCC will include it into its topology. The KCC will not delete manually created connection objects.

Intra-site connection objects can also be created. In fact, the administrator could go so far as to completely disable the automatic generation of the KCC's replication topology. Obviously, this isn't recommended. An administrator might attempt to compensate for a poorly performing network by doing this. However, the time to compensate for the network's weaknesses is before Active Directory is installed, and the method to compensate is to fix the problems.

When the first Domain Controller is promoted, it is the only copy of Directory information anywhere. Everything (the schema, configuration, and Domain information) is maintained on this one computer. As a site is built, it takes on a life all its own. Each additional Domain Controller adds its own connections to the mix.

When dcpromo is run on the second Domain Controller, the configuration is downloaded to it from the first Domain Controller. Recall that when dcpromo is run, the program connects and authenticates to the Domain to modify the topology. After the promotion is complete, the first Domain Controller has one connection object to the second, and the second has one connection object to the first. To fully synchronize the servers, however, all three name contexts must be replicated, which is done across the single connection. The naming contexts must replicate their information appropriately, but they don't create their own connections; they rely upon the KCC to do that. The KCC examines the contexts, determines what connections must be created to properly maintain their respective topologies, and creates the objects when appropriate. The first server's KCC is also now aware of the additional Domain Controller in the site and creates a connection object to that as well.

When a third server is promoted, the same process occurs again. The third server downloads the configuration from whatever Domain Controller it was connected to, reads the configuration, determines its placement in the ring by examining the GUIDs of the other Domain

Controllers, and creates connection objects to the others. Likewise, the other servers discover the new server, also determine its placement in the ring by the same method, and begin replication.

When a fourth server is introduced to the site, things change. When dcpromo is run, the KCC determines that it still only needs to maintain two connections to the ring. It will optimize the topology by examining its GUID, determine its placement in the topology, and begin synchronization. Because the KCC on each server uses the same method to determine the ring's topology, each server arrives at the same conclusion, and the ring is formed and optimized. This behavior continues as servers are added to the site.

Multiple Domains in a Site

Although the previous examples were interesting, most sites will probably contain a mix of Domain Controllers from different Domains. When that occurs, the site has to contend with more than one Domain naming context and more than one Domain topology. If the site must support two Domains, there will be at least three replication topologies. The schema and configuration still share the same topology. But the two Domains have their own Domain namespace and must generate separate topologies.

Although the KCC generates connection objects to optimize replication and all replication uses whatever connections the KCC creates, replication is per naming context. If Domain Controllers from different Domains are contained within a site, the KCC must generate connections to ensure that their Domain namespace is replicated as well.

Global Catalog Server

Global Catalog servers have an impact on replication and the means by which the KCC generates the site's topology.

Global Catalog servers provide a means to query any Domain for objects, regardless of whether the Domain is represented in the site or not. That's because the Global Catalog maintains a partial replica—a selected, uniform subset of attributes of every object in the forest. Only one Global Catalog is created by default in the forest—the first Domain Controller in the root Domain.

You can create a Global Catalog on any Domain Controller in the forest. Although the GC contributes somewhat to the forest's replication traffic, each site should house at least one because they are used for client logons in a multiple Domain environment. The KCC on a Global Catalog server examines the list of all the Domains from the configuration partition and pulls the Global Catalog information required from those Domains as well. It's as if the Global Catalog were a member of every Domain in the enterprise. The Global Catalog stores this information in its local Directory database: NTDS.DIT. As the number of Domains increases and the number of objects in those Domains increases, the size of the Global Catalog's Directory database increases proportionally. This isn't an alarming feature—just one that administrators should be aware of and plan for.

Standard Domain Controllers, as mentioned before, hold three partitions: the configuration, the schema, and the domain naming context for the Domains they are members of. A Global Catalog server holds more than three partitions. In addition to the standard partitions of a Domain Controller, the Global Catalog holds a mini-partition or partial replica of every Domain in the forest and maintains that in the database as well. When a server becomes a Global Catalog, that information is stored in the Configuration partition and replicated via normal Active Directory replication to all the other Domain Controllers in the forest. All Domain Controllers know the location of all Global Catalog servers because that information is kept in the Directory database on each Domain Controller. Because Global Catalog servers are Domain Controllers, they always update their information in DNS. That information is then available to the network, whether connected to the Directory or not.

When a computer starts, it queries DNS for the name of a Domain Controller in its Domain. It then sends a message to a randomly selected Domain Controller. The responding Domain Controller determines the client's site assignment, based on its IP address. It then returns the name of the site to the client. The client caches this information and uses it for subsequent Domain Controller searches. Clients find Global Catalog servers using DNS. There are entries in an Active Directory-aware DNS server that point to Global Catalog servers. These entries are similar to the information that clients gain about sites and Domains from DNS. As Active Directory grows to include other applications and services, DNS can expand to support them as well. For example, Exchange 2000 clients will be able to search the Global Catalog using MAPI, and other sockets-based clients will be able to search it using LDAP.

When a Global Catalog server is created in a site, the KCC then optimizes the topology to allow the server to participate in the ring for each naming context present in the site. Another way to think about it is to envision the Global Catalog as touching at least one Domain Controller for each Domain that exists in the site.

Inter-Site Replication Cost

Replication between sites is automatically calculated and controlled by the KCC. The KCC creates representative objects in the Directory to use when controlling its activities. Those objects are known as site links, which represent inter-site connection objects. Like intra-site replication, they represent incoming replication communication from other Domain Controllers in the Directory. However, there are a number of significant differences in the way the KCC creates inter-site replication objects. Additional parameters, such as link availability and cost factors, are also calculated to determine the appropriate connections to other sites.

The default configuration of sites in a forest is to configure a default inter-site topology using a least-cost, spanning tree algorithm. In this model, cost is administratively set to favor various routes. Additionally, replication between sites can occur synchronously by RPC over IP transport or asynchronously by SMTP over IP transport to compensate for differences in network connectivity.

Although replication within sites is optimized for LAN connectivity and requires little or no management, administrators have control over when and how replication between sites occurs. The goal is to maximize efficiency and minimize cost, and decisions must be made on the basis of your network environment, physical location, and business needs. The KCC generates the inter-site topology automatically, but the settings that administrators make on the site links are the factors that the KCC considers in the process.

Bridgehead Servers

The servers that actually house the inter-site connection objects are known as *bridgehead servers*. These servers are chosen by the KCC based on their placement in the topology and their participation in required Domain namespace. Any site with a connection to other sites has at least one bridgehead server configured. If the site has more than one Domain, the KCC will configure bridgeheads for each Domain to ensure replication of the Domain partition across the site link.

Site Links

Site links have four parameters:

- **Cost.** The cost value of a site link helps the replication system determine when to use the link when compared to other links or an accumulation of combined links. Cost values determine the paths that replication will take through the network.

- **Replication schedule.** A site link has an associated schedule that indicates at what times of day the link is available to carry replication traffic.

- **Replication interval.** The replication interval indicates how often the system polls Domain Controllers on the other side of the site link for replication changes.

- **Transport.** This parameter is the transport that is used for replication.

A site link might contain a single site on either end. This configuration would generally represent a point-to-point connection, such as a WAN link, in a geographically separated network. Site links might also contain many sites in one link. This configuration would be useful when connecting multiple LANs on a distributed metropolitan network (MAN), in which the connections are through ATM or Frame Relay, and the relative performance and cost are equal. This would allow the administrator to modify the default site-to-site replication topology into a semi- or full-mesh arrangement that mirrors the actual physical arrangement.

Each site link has an associated cost factor. These costs can range from 1 to 65,536. The default is set automatically to 100. Smaller values are considered lower cost and used in preference over higher-cost links during replication activity.

The KCC examines all site links in the topology—not just those it is connected to. Through this, it can calculate a path for efficient replication through the network, based upon cumulative costs of links. The KCC on each Domain Controller runs every 15 minutes. As the administrator modifies site links, the KCC re-evaluates all links; if the cost change was significant, then replication may be directed along a different path.

A schedule is associated with each site link. The schedule simply indicates the availability of the link. When the schedule is closed, replication doesn't occur across the link. The site link schedules can be thought of as *windows*. When the windows are open, replication can occur. Because replication is transitive, across any connection or connections, if the schedule is closed, the connection is considered not available. In other words, if replication passes through multiple site links, there must be at least one common connection open. The default schedule for site links is open always.

An interval or period also controls replication between sites. This interval determines how often replication is to occur. The default is set at 180 minutes (three hours), but can be set to as little as 15 minutes. Schedules and intervals must intersect for replication to occur. If a site link's interval activates during a time when the schedule has closed the link, then replication doesn't occur. Likewise, if the schedule is open, but an interval never activates during that time, no replication occurs.

The key factor in determining cost will be the calculated net available bandwidth between the sites. Active Directory replication traffic can be "persuaded" to use different links based upon the cost factor assigned. However, additional factors may be involved that make this impossible or impractical.

Cost can also be assigned proactively rather than reactively. If the network has a high-speed backbone that is desirable for Active Directory traffic, then a cost of 1 can be assigned.

Recall that Global Catalog servers behave as if they are members of all the Domains in the forest. Their replication is based upon every naming context in the enterprise. Therefore, a Global Catalog server's KCC creates a connection to a Domain Controller from all Domains. If a Domain Controller doesn't exist in the site where the Global Catalog is installed, the KCC will generate a connection object to a Domain Controller in that site to enable replication of that Domain's objects.

The KCC's decision to replicate with servers in another site actually originates with one server in the site. This server is authoritative for creating connections to other sites. The KCC runs on every Domain Controller, and every Domain Controller in a site shares its configuration information. However, one server in the site actually determines the inter-site topology and creates connection objects for all bridgehead servers in the site. This server is known as the Inter-Site Topology Generator (ISTG). The ISTG generates the inter-site replication topology for all naming contexts and replicates it to all the other Domain Controllers in the site. The ISTG is the Domain Controller in a site that creates the master copy of the site's Configuration.

The ISTG is, by default, first Domain Controller in the site and there is one for each site in the enterprise. All other Domain Controllers in the site, regardless of Domain, are aware of which Domain Controller holds the ISTG role and regularly examine it for changes in the site connection topology. If, for some reason, the ISTG fails, the other Domain Controllers in the site detect it and another server will be automatically chosen to fill the role. The selection criteria are by GUID.

KCC Failures

If the KCC detects a replication failure, it generates new temporary connections to ensure that replication continues. Once the connectivity is restored, the configuration will return to the previous default and continue from there. Replication failure detection is based two thresholds: the number of failures that have occurred, and the period of time that has elapsed since the last replication. Intra-site KCC evaluation is performed regularly by all Domain Controllers in the site and immediate neighbors are evaluated more often than others in the ring. Inter-site connections are dealt with by the Inter-site Topology Generator.

The ISTG is not required to be a bridgehead server. It is possible that the ISTG role could reside on a Domain Controller that doesn't have a connection to another site, and bridgeheads are being maintained on other Domain Controllers in the site.

Site Link Bridges

When sites are first configured, the assumption is that some form of routed network connects them all. When multiple sites are created, the transitive nature of the site links essentially bridges the entire network and treats the sites as if they were all physically connected. Site links provide seamless connectivity in a connected environment. This is the default behavior.

However, not all organizations possess this kind of connectivity. There are many times when the only connection between a company's locations is the Internet e-mail configured between different ISPs. In this case, there is no underlying network infrastructure to rely on. The network is not fully routed.

To deal with this situation, Active Directory allows for the creation of *site link bridges*. A site link bridge is a connectionless method of bridging site links. They aren't necessary on a single WAN because the WAN assumes routed connectivity. Site link bridges can use IP or SMTP for replication. An organization could leverage an existing Internet e-mail connection to provide a unified Directory, even if there is no actual network connection. In essence, a site link bridge operates like a bridge or router specifically for the Active Directory.

Network Ports Used by Active Directory

These settings specify the TCP and UDP port numbers on which the LDAP server listens for queries to the Global Catalog. They are not added by default; if they are not present, the default is the values shown as follows:

- **LdapSrvPort**

  HKLM\SYSTEM\CurrentControlSet\Services\Netlogon\Parameters

  Data type Range Default

  REG_DWORD 0x0 - 0xFFFF 0x0 - 0xFFFF 0x185 (389)

  Specifies the TCP port number and the UDP port number on which the LDAP server listens.

- **KdcSrvPort**

  HKLM\SYSTEM\CurrentControlSet\Services\Netlogon\Parameters

  Data type Range Default

  REG_DWORD 0x0 - 0xFFFF 0x0 - 0xFFFF 0x58 (88)

  Specifies the TCP port number for the Key Distribution Center (KDC) service on the Domain Controller.

- **LdapGcSrvPort**

  HKLM\SYSTEM\CurrentControlSet\Services\Netlogon\Parameters

  Data type Range Default

  REG_DWORD 0x0 - 0xFFFF 0x0 - 0xFFFF 0xCC4 (3268)

Table 1.2.5 contains a list of the network ports that are used by Active Directory Domain Controllers. Both the native Windows 2000 ports and the NetBIOS ports required to maintain compatibility with earlier versions of Windows are listed.

Table 1.2.5   Network Ports Used by Active Directory on DCs and Clients

Port	Used for
TCP port 53	DNS queries
UDP port 53	
TCP port 389	LDAP—Domain Controller
TCP port 3268	LDAP—Global Catalog
TCP port 636	LDAP SSL—Domain Controller
TCP port 3269	LDAP SSL—Global Catalog
TCP port 88	Kerberos v. 5

Port	Used for
UDP port 88	
User defined	Active Directory Replication (RPC over IP)
TCP port 25	Active Directory Replication (SMTP)
TCP port 137	NetBIOS name service
UDP port 137	
UDP port 138	NetBIOS datagram service
TCP port 1512	WINS
UDP port 1512	

▶ *For more information on how Windows NT 4.0 clients are authenticated and supported by Active Directory, see Chapter 4.6, "Logging On and Authentication."*

II

Installing and Configuring Windows 2000 Server

2.1

Overview of Installing and Configuring Windows 2000 Server

In This Section:

You Need to Read This Section if You Want to:

- Know how to install and configure a new computer with Windows 2000 Server.
- Be able to configure system and network settings for your server.
- Be able to identify and correct common problems that can occur when starting Windows 2000.
- Understand how Windows 2000 stores information about configuration of the operating system, device drivers, and services.

Related Topics

Installing Windows 2000 Server

Microsoft has tried to make installing Windows 2000 Server, a network operating system with a plethora of features and services, as easy as possible. Surprisingly, they've generally done a pretty good job at it, too. There are only a few choices that really have to be made during the installation process, and much of the configuration of Windows 2000 for your specific hardware is done by the Setup program.

In what follows, we'll refer to Windows 2000 Server as just Windows 2000. This should make it a bit easier for you to read.

This section provides an overview of key characteristics of the Setup process. Before you install Windows 2000, be sure to read the additional information in Chapter 2.2 *Installing Windows 2000 Server*.

There are two different kinds of Windows 2000 installations:

- **New installation.** You are installing Windows 2000 Server on a computer without trying to have it preserve any settings from a previous operating system. Typically, you start with a system containing a newly formatted disk drive or drives. For testing purposes you could set up Windows 2000 in a dual-boot configuration with other operating systems. A new installation is usually the best way to install Windows 2000 Server in a production environment.

- **Upgrade.** If the computer on which you will run Setup already has an operating system installed (for example Windows NT 4), and you want to migrate your existing applications and user accounts to Windows 2000, you should perform an upgrade. Upgrades take careful planning and testing, since the Setup program will migrate as much of the current configuration as possible, which may not be optimal for the new server.

  ▶ *For more information, see "Upgrading to Windows 2000 Server" in Chapter 2.2, "Installing Windows 2000 Server."*

Before you start Setup, you want to identify all of your hardware, and make sure that it will work with Windows 2000 by consulting the Windows 2000 Hardware Compatibility List (which can be found online at http://www.microsoft.com/hcl/default.asp). Taking the time to do this will make it more likely that you'll complete Setup successfully.

You can also automate the Setup process by creating an installation script to use with the Setup program.

▶ *For more information, see "Creating and Using Installation Scripts in Chapter 2.2, "Installing Windows 2000 Server."*

Running the Windows 2000 Setup Program

To install Windows 2000 on a computer that doesn't have an operating system already installed, you have three options:

- **From the CD-ROM.** If your computer supports booting from the CD-ROM drive, you can start the Setup program this way. This is the simplest and easiest way to start a new installation, although it may require changing your system's CMOS settings to get it started (to have it look at the CD-ROM drive to boot).

  ▶ *For more information, see "From the CD-ROM" in Chapter 2.2 "Installing Windows 2000 Server."*

- **From the Setup disks.** You can boot the computer by using four Windows 2000 Setup floppy disks. The Setup program then continues by copying files from the CD-ROM. Use this method if you want to install from the CD-ROM but your system does not support bootable CDs.

  ▶ *For more information, see "From the Setup Floppy Disks" in Chapter 2.2, "Installing Windows 2000 Server."*

- **From the network.** If you don't have a local CD-ROM drive, or you don't have the Windows 2000 CD-ROM handy, you can install from a copy of the Windows 2000 source files on the network. (Of course this assumes that they are available on a server somewhere that you can access.) This method requires that you boot from a floppy disk, create and format a disk partition on the computer, connect to a network server, and start the installation.

  ▶ *For more information, see "Installing Over the Network" in Chapter 2.2, "Installing Windows 2000 Server."*

If you want to be able to install Windows 2000 without having to use any media or other operatings sytems at all, you can use the Remote Installation Services (RIS) to download an image from a network server to the computer.

▶ *For more information, see "Remote Installation Services" in Chapter 2.2, "Installing Windows 2000 Server."*

If you have MS-DOS, Windows 95, Windows 98, or Windows NT 4.0 installed, you can start your current operating system and then run either WINNT.EXE (from DOS) or WINNT32.EXE. The first part of WINNT.EXE and WINNT32.EXE runs in your current operating system, copying some files and modifying your startup environment. Then, when the computer restarts, you boot the Setup program and then Setup continues—just as if you were installing from the Setup disks.

No matter which method you choose, the Setup program:

- Allows you to create and format a disk partition on which you can install Windows 2000, if one does not already exist.
- Copies the Setup program files to your hard disk.
- Copies the Windows 2000 files to your hard disk.
- Configures Windows 2000 with device drivers and system settings to match your hardware.
- Configures your networking components for connectivity on your network.
- Removes the temporary files used by the Setup program.
- Starts Windows 2000 for the first time.

? **How Much Do You Need to Know Before You Try to Install Windows 2000?**

The good news is that the Setup program in Windows 2000 can detect most of the information that it needs about your hardware, limiting the questions that it asks you about your preferences. You can usually accept all of the defaults suggested by the Setup program and have Windows 2000 install successfully.

The bad news? The most common problems occur from either not having hardware that meets the minimum requirements for installation, or for which you don't have the appropriate Windows 2000 device drivers. If your disk controller, video adapter, and network card are common enough, you should be OK. If not, Setup will either give you a message asking for the drivers, or you might complete Setup and have the rest of your system working fine except for that one device. For a list of tested hardware that you can use with Windows 2000 (where Microsoft has tested the device drivers for the hardware to make sure they work with Windows 2000) see the Windows 2000 Hardware Compatibility List. See http://www.microsoft.com.hcl.

The other bit of bad news is that Windows 2000 tends to assume you want to install the Operating system on to the first partition of the first drive into the directory \winnt. If you are installing from CD, or via boot disks, you cannot change these defaults, unless you use an unattend.txt file. Also, if you first load another operating system, and run WINNT.EXE or WINNT32.EXE, you are able to change these defaults.

However, there *are* a few key decisions that should not be made lightly, such as the size of the partition on which you install Windows 2000, the file system that you use (FAT or NTFS), and the network settings.

▶ *For more information on these options (and how to decide what to choose), see Chapter 2.2, "Installing Windows 2000 Server."*

Upgrading Your Existing Operating System

If your computer is currently running Windows NT 4.0 Server, you can have the Setup program upgrade Windows NT to Windows 2000 Server. If you upgrade, Setup will attempt to preserve as much as possible about your Windows NT 4.0 environment as it can in Windows 2000. You can upgrade domain controllers, member servers, and standalone servers with little trouble, although planning is required before migrating your Windows NT 4.0 domain to Active Directory. You can also upgrade Windows 95, Windows 98, and earlier versions of Windows NT.

▶ *For more information, see Appendix A, "Migrating Windows NT 4.0 Domains to Active Directory," and "Upgrading to Windows 2000 Server" in Chapter 2.2, "Installing Windows 2000 Server."*

Configuring Devices and System Settings

The Windows 2000 Setup program gets the operating system installed and configures as many of the devices on the computer that it can. However, once you finish installing Windows 2000, you have some more work to do. To make the best use of your computer's hardware, you may have to do some additional configuration of your computer. These configuration tasks fall into two main kinds of changes—system configuration settings and device drivers.

There are three types of configuration changes in Windows 2000:

- **User preferences.** These are settings that are stored on a per-user basis. They are stored in the user's profile. Examples of user preferences are such settings as the desktop colors, the location of the Taskbar, printing settings, and mapped network drive letters. Users can make changes to their own user preferences without affecting other users of the computer. See Chapter 6.2, "*Profiles.*"

- **System settings.** These are settings that affect all users of a computer. Only administrators can change system settings.

- **Device drivers.** A device driver is a software component that provides the interface between Windows 2000 and a hardware device, such as a printer or a network adapter. Only administrators can install, remove, or configure device drivers.

System Settings

Examples of system settings include

- **Date, time, and time zone.** In a distributed computing environment, the accuracy of the system time is very important.

- **Power options.** The power options affect the behavior of the system when certain components have been idle for a specified length of time. While primarily useful for laptop and desktop computers, it is important to set the power options appropriately on a network server. Unless you have a good reason, it's probably better to turn off all the power management options for servers, except for the monitor.

- **Virtual memory configuration.** The size and location of the computer's paging file can make a significant impact on server performance.
- **Startup and Recovery options.** These options affect the list of operating systems at startup and the computer's behavior when STOP errors occur.

Network Settings

The configuration of the networking components, such as the computer's name, IP address, location of name servers, etc. Windows 2000 will detect your network cards, install TCP/IP and assume the computer is DHCP client. This may be acceptable for some servers but not for others. If you wish to setup the system differently, you will need to make these changes either during installation or subsequently.

Device Drivers

Every device in your computer will need one or more device drivers to enable Windows 2000 to use the device. Since the integrity of device drivers is so important to system stability, you must be an administrator manage them.

Device drivers are installed in one of two ways:

- **Automatically.** The Windows 2000 Setup program attempts to detect hardware devices that are attached to the computer and install the appropriate drivers. You can have Windows 2000 perform this hardware enumeration at any time by using the Add/Remove Hardware wizard. Detection of new hardware is also done each time you boot up your computer—if new devices are found, Windows 2000 will install the necessary device drivers.
- **Manually.** The Device Manager tool allows you to view the status of devices, and disable or reconfigure them. You can install new device drivers by using the Add/Remove Hardware wizard and specifying the driver to be installed.

In general, it is best to let Windows 2000 detect your computer's hardware and install the necessary drivers. However, you should know how to install device drivers when needed so that you can install updated drivers or drivers for devices that were not detected by Windows 2000.

All of these settings, along with information about the device drivers that should be loaded, are stored in the Registry. See *The Registry* later in this chapter.

▶ *For more information on configuring devices, see Chapter 2.3, "Configuring Devices and System Settings."*

Configuring Network Components

The configuration of the network is something that affects every user of a computer. For this reason, Windows 2000 requires that network settings are changed only by an administrator.

There are three main network components that are necessary for one Windows 2000 computer to communicate with another:

- **Network interface.** The computer has to be connected to a network cable or other media by means of an interface on the computer—whether it's a network adapter or a modem that is used for dial-up communications. A computer attached to an Ethernet network would have an Ethernet adapter as its network interface.

- **Network protocol.** The network protocol provides a way for messages to be delivered from one computer to another by means of a common method of communicating. TCP/IP is an example of a network protocol. In Windows 2000, TCP/IP is installed as the default network protocol. TCP/IP is required if you are using Active Directory, but is optional otherwise.

- **Network services and applications.** Although the network interface and the network protocol simply provide a conduit through which messages can be delivered, the programs that have real work to do are the network services and applications. They are programs that run on the two computers that know how to send messages to each other to get useful things done, like transfer files, send and receive e-mail, submit a query to a database program, or retrieve information.

An administrator can modify the network settings for a computer by using the Network and Dial-Up Connections option in the Control Panel.

The settings for the network components are stored in the Registry. See *The Registry* later in this chapter.

▶ *For more information on Windows 2000 networking, see Chapter 2.4, "Configuring Network Components."*

The Boot Process

Installing and configuring Windows 2000 also includes managing the Windows 2000 boot process. It is important for an administrator to understand how Windows 2000 starts, what files or components are accessed, and how to recover when the system fails to boot. This will assist you in troubleshooting system boot problems.

For a description of the normal process of booting Windows 2000 and the options for modifying the boot process, see Chapter 2.5, "*The Boot Process.*" For a description of ways of recovering a system that will no longer boot, see Chapter 5.7, "*Protecting Data.*"

The Registry

The Registry is a database that stores the configuration information for Windows 2000. It consists of user settings, system settings, and information about device drivers and system services. The Registry is

- **Dynamic.** The Registry is held in the server's memory. It can be read from and written to at any time. Changes made to the Registry are available to processes on the server immediately.

- **Hierarchical.** Data in the Registry is organized in a highly structured tree of system and user information.

- **Secure.** Each entry in the Registry has an access control list and permissions associated with it. Only users who have appropriate permissions can modify information in the Registry.

You can use either Regedit.exe (which originally came from Windows 95) or Regedt32 (the Window NT registry editor) to view or modify the contents of the Registry. In general, this is not usually necessary, or desirable. The registry editors assume you know what you are doing, and mistakes can be made that can destroy your installation. So be careful.

▶ *For more information the Windows 2000 Registry, see Chapter 2.6, "The Registry."*

2.2

Installing Windows 2000 Server

In This Section:

You Need to Read This Section If You Want to:

- Run the Windows Setup program.
- Know how to automate Setup by using installation scripts.
- Understand how Remote Installation Services can automate deployments of Windows 2000 Professional computers.
- Understand how a system image can be used as a part of an automated installation.

Related Topics

Using Windows 2000 Setup

This section consists of the following topics:

- **Before you install**—decisions that need to be made before you run Setup.
- **Starting the Setup program**—ways to start Setup and the requirements for each.
- **Stages of the Setup process**—what to expect when running Setup, along with information on adding custom or updated device drivers during Setup.
- **Decisions you make during Setup**—a checklist of options you will encounter during Setup and how to configure them.
- **Reasons that Setup may fail**—the main reasons that Setup might not complete successfully.

In case you are deploying a large number of servers at once or need to be able to set up a test environment repetitively, information about automating the Setup process is included later in this chapter. Most of the time when you install a new server on the network, however, you will probably run Setup and respond to the prompts manually. Automating Setup applies equally to both Server and Professional. You will probably find automated Setup very useful when you need to deploy a group of desktop computers.)

Before You Install

Before you run the Setup program, you should answer these questions:

- Is the hardware compatible with Windows 2000?
- How will I configure the disks and partitions?
- What network settings should I use?
- What will the name and role of the computer be on the network?
- What services should I install on the server?

Hardware Compatibility

The biggest potential problems when installing Windows 2000 are all hardware-related. If Windows 2000 has trouble communicating with the main devices on your computer—the motherboard, BIOS, CD-ROM drive, or hard disk controller—Setup may fail or install drivers that make your system unstable. For this reason, you want to thoroughly check out your server's hardware first before you run Setup.

- Make sure that your hardware meets the minimum requirements. The minimum requirements for Windows 2000 Server is shown in Table 2.2.1. The minimum requirements and other details are also noted on the Microsft Web site at http://www.microsoft.com/windows2000/guide/platform/overview/default.asp.

- Make sure that your hardware is on the Hardware Compatibility List (HCL). You can obtain the latest Hardware Compatibility List from the Microsoft Web site, at www.microsoft.com/hcl/default.asp

- Check with the manufacturer of the components of your computer to see if updated versions of device drivers are available or if there are any known issues or workarounds.

- Search the technical support areas of Microsoft's Web site for articles about your hardware.

Table 2.2.1   Minimum Hardware Requirements for Windows 2000 Server

Component	Requirement
Processor	Pentium 133 MHz or higher
Memory	256 MB
Hard disk space	1 GB (actual requirement varies based on file system used [FAT or NTFS] and amount of memory)
Networking	One or more network interfaces (you can use the MS Loopback Adapter if no network adapter is physically present)
Other drives	12x or faster CD-ROM (if installing from CD-ROM)
	1.44 MB floppy disk (if starting Setup from the Setup floppy disks)
Other devices	Keyboard, mouse or other pointing device
	VGA or higher video display

Although most personal computers not listed explicitly on the HCL should install Windows 2000 Server successfully, you can run into snags. If your computer requires a custom Hardware Abstraction Layer (HAL) or if your system's BIOS is not up to date, you may not be able to install Windows 2000. If you have a disk controller that is not on the HCL, you may need to supply a driver for Setup to use during the early part of text-mode Setup.

Pay Attention to the Hardware!

The reason that you should ensure that Windows 2000 fully supports your hardware is *reliability*. If your organization will be counting on the server to do what it's supposed to do, the hardware details are critical. Taking shortcuts when qualifying the equipment can lead to endless hours of needless downtime and fruitless troubleshooting. Although building your own system from third-party supplies may be attractive in the short term, it may be false economy in the longer term.

The Disk Configuration

Normally, you install Windows 2000 Server as the only operating system on a server computer. If that is the case, you should install Windows 2000 on the first partition of the first hard disk, and format it as NTFS. After Setup is complete, you can create additional disk partitions or volumes by using the Disk Management tool in Computer Management.

▶ *For more information, see Chapter 5.2, "File Systems and Disks."*

NTFS or FAT for Your System and Boot Partitions?

In the past, I've always recommended using FAT for the System and Boot partitions. The logic was that you could always boot from the floppy to repair your installation if anything goes wrong. But Windows 2000 contains significantly more files and takes up more space than Windows NT 4.0. Using FAT on these volumes wastes a tremendous amount of space. With the recovery console, you can reboot your system and access all the files in your installation. You could use FAT 32, but I find NTFS to be just as good, and NTFS comes with the capability to set ACLs on key files, file level journaling for recovery, file and folder compression, and file and folder encryption. All in all, NTFS is probably a better bet.

It is generally best to keep the operating system on a separate partition from your applications and data. In Windows 2000 and Windows NT, use the term *system partition* to refer to the partition that you initially boot from (usually this is your C: drive) and the *boot partition* to refer to the partition that the Windows 2000 Operations system is on. By default, this is usually C: too, but it can be different.

How big should the boot partition be? Microsoft recommends that you be generous with this, especially on very large servers, to allow for adequate space for the paging file or other operating system files (such as the Active Directory on a domain controller). Although 1 GB is the recommended minimum, you should plan on at least 2 GB for the boot partition (more space will be useful, of course). You will need an even larger boot partition if the server will be a domain controller in a large domain or if your server has a large amount of memory.

▶ *For more information, see "Virtual Memory Configuration" in Chapter 2.3.*

Leave Unpartitioned Space on Your Disk!

If you plan to convert the disk to a dynamic disk later, be sure to leave at least 1 MB of unpartitioned space on the disk. Otherwise, you will be unable to convert the disk to a dynamic disk later without backing up, repartitioning the disk, and restoring.

▶ *For more information on dynamic disks, see Chapter 5.2, "File Systems and Disks."*

The disk must be dynamic if you plan to use software-based mirroring to mirror the operating system to another disk.

Other notes about your disk configuration include the following:

- If you plan to start the Setup program from DOS, Windows 95, or Windows 98, you will need to create and format a FAT partition before running Setup. If your version of Windows can create FAT32 partitions, you can create up to a 32 GB FAT32 partition for the boot partition. During Setup, you can either leave the partition as FAT or you can format it with NTFS.

- If you plan to have a dual-boot between Windows 2000 and DOS, Windows 95, or Windows 98, the first partition on the first disk should be FAT to maintain maximum compatibility with the other operating system. In this case, install Windows 2000 into its own separate partition and format it as NTFS. Windows 2000 Setup will automatically create a dual-boot between your existing operating system and Windows 2000.

Windows NT 4.0 Cannot Access NTFS5 Partitions Natively

If you plan to have a dual-boot between Windows NT 4.0 and Windows 2000, be careful. Windows NT 4.0 cannot access NTFS5 partitions natively. Windows 2000 automatically converts all of your NTFS partitions to NTFS5—either at installation time, or any time the OS is booted and detects an older version of NTFS on any disk in your system. This means that Windows NT 4.0 would then be unable to access those partitions. To enable Windows NT 4.0 to use NTFS5 partitions, you need to install Service Pack 4 (or later) for Windows NT 4.0.

What if you installed Windows 2000 before you upgraded Windows NT to Service Pack 4? It's not too late—you can copy the Ntfs.sys driver provided on the Windows 2000 Server CD-ROM to your Windows NT 4.0 System32 directory. The filename on the Windows 2000 server CD is NTFS40.SYS and is found in the \i386 folder on the CD. You should copy this to %systemroot%\system32\drivers folder for your Windows NT 4.0 installation.

Microsoft strongly discourages having a dual-boot between Windows 2000 and Windows NT because of the disk security and configuration issues involved. If you must dual-boot, make sure you install Windows 2000 on a separate partition.

▶ *For more information, see Chapter 5.2, "File Systems and Disks," and Chapter 2.5, "The Boot Process."*

The Network Configuration

Before you install Windows 2000 Server, you need to have a basic understanding of your network environment and your network hardware. Specifically, you need to know the following:

- **Network interface.** You will need to know the manufacturer and model number of the type of network interface card(s) that you will be using (for example, the brand and model number of your Ethernet card[s]).

- **Network protocols.** You will need to know which network protocols are needed by the server to communicate with other computers on the network. TCP/IP is installed by default; unless you have a good reason for installing other protocols, use only TCP/IP.

- **TCP/IP configuration information.** You will need to know the TCP/IP parameters that are required to communicate successfully on your network, such as IP address, subnet mask, default gateway, and addresses of your DNS and WINS servers, if any. The default for TCP/IP that Setup uses is to assign an address dynamically to the computer from a DHCP server. Although this may be great for testing, it is probably not a good idea for production. It is more likely that you will want to use a static IP address and configuration to avoid the possibility of the IP address not being renewed if the DHCP server were to have problems.

- **Windows 2000 Networking Service.** You will also need to know whether to install network services on your server. The services you might want to add are discussed in "Windows 2000 Components" later in this chapter.

Which Network Protocols Should You Use?

For most users, TCP/IP is probably the best default protocol. Windows 2000 installs this by default, and TCP/IP is required for use in an Active Domain environment as well as being required for access to the Internet. If you are using Novell NetWare or communicating with other non Windows operating systems, you may need to add IPX/SPX or NetBeui, which can be done while installing via unattended installation scripts or after you have loaded Windows 2000. Windows 2000 also includes Automatic Private IP Addressing (APIPA), which enables TCP/IP to be Plug and Play for small work groups.

▶ *For more information, see Chapter 2.4, "Configuring Network Components."*

Names and Roles

The next set of parameters that you will need to supply to the Setup program has to do with names and the role of your computer on the network. Specifically, you will need to provide a name for your computer and specify whether it should be a standalone or a member server. In addition, you will be asked whether to use Per Seat or Per Server Licensing (if in doubt, choose Per Server; you can change your licensing to Per Seat later if need be).

Table 2.2.2 lists the parameters that are requested from the user during this portion of Setup.

Table 2.2.2   Notes on Configuration Options During Setup

Configuration Choice	Notes
	Names and Accounts
Computer name	Name that uniquely identifies the server on the network. In order to maintain NetBIOS compatibility, limit names to no more than 15 characters. To maintain compatibility with DNS, use alphanumeric characters or a hyphen and no spaces.★
Domain name	If the computer will be joining an existing domain, you need to provide the domain name during Setup.
Workgroup name	If the computer will not be joining a domain, you can specify a work group name. The default work group name is workgroup.
Local Administrator account password	This is the password used in the local account database of the computer. Can contain up to 14 characters.
Domain controller	This option is not offered during Setup. If you want the computer to be a domain controller, configure the computer as a standalone or member server and then run Dcpromo after Setup is complete.
	Licensing
Per Seat	This option requires a license for each client computer that connects to any Windows 2000 server on the network. It is generally most economical when client computers connect to multiple servers.
Per Server	This option requires a license for each client computer that is currently connected to this server. It is generally most economical when client computers generally use only one server at a time, and not all clients are connected at the same time.
	When you specify a number of licenses for Per Server licensing, the server will prevent users from connecting to the server when all of the licenses are in use.

★*Specific requirements of NetBIOS and DNS naming are provided in Chapter 4.2, "DNS and Active Directory."*
★★*Licenses are required for all Windows 2000 services except for access to IIS, Telnet, and FTP.*

Windows 2000 Components

You will also be prompted to choose the Windows components that should be installed by the Setup program. You can add any of the services listed here after Setup finishes by using the Add/Remove Programs option in Control Panel.

The components that are available are listed as follows. Only the Indexing Service, Internet Information Service, and Microsoft Script Debugger are installed by default. The following is a list of Windows 2000 Server Components:

- **Accessories and Utilities**

Accessibility Wizard

Accessories

    Calculator

    Character Map

    Clipboard Viewer

    Desktop Wallpaper

    Document templates

    Mouse Pointers

    Object Packager

    Paint

    Wordpad

Communications

    Chat

    Hyper Terminal

    Phone Dialer

Games

    Freecell

    Minesweeper

    Pinball

    Solitaire

Multimedia

    CD Player

    Media Player

    Sample Sounds

    Sound Recorder

    Utopia Sound Scheme

    Volume Control

- **Certificate Services**

  Certificate Services CA

  Certificate Services Web Enrollment Support

- **Cluster Service (only on Advanced Server and Data Center Server)**

- **Indexing Service**

- **Internet Information Services (IIS)**

  Common Files

  Documentation

  File Transfer Protocol (FTP) Server

  FrontPage 2000 Server Extensions

  Internet Information Server Services Snap-in

  Internet Services Manager (HTML)

  NNTP Service

  SMTP Service

  Visual InterDev RAD Remote Deployment Support

  Word Wide Web Server

- **Management and Monitoring Tools**

  Connection Manager Components

  Network Monitor Tools

  Simple Network Management Protocol

- **Message Queuing Services**

- **Networking Services**

  COM Internet Services Proxy

  Domain Name System (DNS)

  Dynamic Host Configuration Protocol (DHCP)

  Internet Authentication Service

  QoS Admission Control Service

  Simple TCP/IP Services

  Site Server ILS Services

  Windows Internet Name Service (WINS)

- **Other Network File and Print Services**

  File Services for Macintosh

  Print Services for Macintosh

  Print Services for Unix

- **Remote Installation Services**

- **Remote Storage**

- **Script Debugger**

- **Terminal Services**

  Client Creator Files

  Enable Terminal Service

- **Terminal Services Licensing**

- **Windows Media Services**

  Windows Media Services

  Windows Media Services Admin

Starting the Setup Program

So now you've gathered the information that you need, you're ready to actually start the installation. Of course, in typical Microsoft style, you have options. You can install in any of the following ways:

- From the CD-ROM
- From the Setup floppy disks
- From the network
- From another operating system

These three options are discussed in the following sections.

From the CD-ROM

If your computer supports booting from the CD-ROM drive, you can start the Setup program by booting the CD-ROM. You do not need to create any disk partitions in advance for this method; you can get the Setup program to create and format the partition to hold the operating system. No network or floppy disks are required for this type of Setup. You may have to change the CMOS settings of your computer, however, to have it boot from the CD-ROM drive. For most modern servers, this is probably the best approach to loading Windows 2000.

From the Setup Floppy Disks

If your computer does not support booting from the CD-ROM, you can start the computer from Setup floppy disks. You boot the computer from the first Setup disk and follow the prompts. After the four disks are loaded into memory, the Setup program uses the CD-ROM for the rest of the installation process.

You can make a set of Setup floppy disks by using the MAKEBOOT.EXE program in the \Bootdisk folder on the Windows 2000 Server CD-ROM. If you are making the disks on a DOS or Windows computer, run Makeboot.exe. If you are making the disks on a Windows NT or Windows 2000 computer, run Makebt32.exe.

From the Network

If you don't want to use the local CD-ROM drive to install Windows 2000, you can install from another location, such as a network server.

Basically, you start the computer with DOS, Windows, or Windows NT, access a shared I386 shared folder on another computer, and then run either Winnt.exe or Winnt32.exe from the I386 directory. Use Winnt.exe if you have started your computer with a DOS boot disk; use WINNT32 if you are running from within Windows 95 or 98 or if Windows NT. WINNT32 and WINNT have a number of switches (these are described later in this chapter).

Because the Setup program needs to ensure that all the files are available on the computer throughout the installation process, Setup copies all of the source files (the entire I386 directory!) to the local hard disk. For this reason, this method requires that you have a formatted partition already available on the disk before starting Setup.

From Another Operating System

You can also start WINNT32 (or WINNT) from within another operating system. This is most often appropriate when you want to dual-boot—perhaps leaving Windows NT 4.0 or Windows 98 on your C: drive and putting Windows 2000 on the D drive. As noted previously, there are a number of options to WINNT and WINNT32, which are described in the sections that follow.

If you are installing Windows 2000 from either DOS or Windows, you must have a partition large enough to hold all the Setup files. This is the case if you are performing a network install or if you are setting up your system to dual-boot. You will need around 300–400 MB of free disk space to accommodate these files.

If you're installing Windows 2000 Professional computers, another alternative is to use Remote Installation Services (RIS).
▶ See "Remote Installation Services (RIS)" later in this chapter.

Winnt and Winnt32 Command Line Switches

The syntax for the Winnt and Winnt32 command lines is as follows:

```
winnt [/s:sourcepath] [/t:tempdrive] [/u:answer file][/udf:id [,UDF_file]]
[/r:folder][/rx:folder][/e:command][/a]
winnt32 [/s:sourcepath] [/tempdrive:drive_letter]
    [/unattend[num]:[answer_file]] [/copydir:folder_name]
[/copysource:folder_name] [/cmd:command_line] [/debug[level]:[filename]]
    [/udf:id[,UDF_file]] [/syspart:drive_letter] [/checkupgradeonly]
    [/cmdcons] [/m:folder_name] [makelocalsource] [/noreboot]
```

For a description of these switches, see Table 2.2.2 and Table 2.2.3.

Table 2.2.2 Winnt Command-Line Switches

Switch	Description
/s:sourcepath	Source location of the Windows 2000 files.
/t:tempdrive	Location for the Setup program to place temporary files. This drive also becomes the drive on which Windows 2000 will be installed.
/u:answer file	Answer file for unattended installation (requires the /s switch).
/udf:id [,UDF_file]	Uniqueness Database File and the ID for this computer within that file (requires the /u and /s switch).
/r:folder	Specifies a folder to be installed by Setup.
/rx:folder	Specifies a folder to be copied by Setup (deleted after Setup finishes).
/e:command	Command to run at the end of GUI-mode Setup.
/a	Enables accessibility options.

Table 2.2.3 Winnt32 Command-Line Switches

Switch	Description
/s:sourcepath	Specifies the source location of the Windows 2000 files. To simultaneously copy files from multiple servers, specify multiple /s sources.
/t:tempdrive:drive_letter	Location for the Setup program to place temporary files. This drive also becomes the drive on which Windows 2000 will be installed.
/unattend[num]:[answer_file]	Answer file for unattended installation.
/copydir:folder_name	Specifies a folder to be copied by Setup.
/copysource:folder_name	Specifies a folder to be copied by Setup (deleted after Setup finishes).
/cmd:command_line	Command to run at the end of GUI-mode Setup.
/debug[level]:[filename]	Creates a debug log while Setup is running.
/udf:id[,UDF_file]	Uniqueness Database File and the ID for this computer within that file (requires the /u and /s switch).
/syspart:drive_letter	Specifies that Setup should copy files to the disk and mark the disk as active (for moving the disk to another computer to complete Setup). Requires the /tempdrive switch.
/checkupgradeonly	Checks the system for compatibility with Windows 2000 and creates a log. You should run this on any system you plan to upgrade as part of the planning.

Switch	Description
/cmdcons	Adds the Recovery Console option to the boot menu. This switch must be used alone and only after Windows 2000 is installed.
/m:folder_name	Specifies an alternate location for files for Setup. Files in the folder specified with /m are used instead of the versions of those files in the source directory.
/makelocalsource	Copies the Windows 2000 source files to the local hard disk.
/noreboot	Prevents Setup from restarting the computer after the copy phase of Winnt32.

The following examples show how these options could be used:

- This example shows installing Windows 2000 from Windows 95, install while prompting for all options:

  ```
  winnt
  ```

- This example shows installing Windows 2000 from Windows 95, installing on drive D, and using x:\i386 as the source directory:

  ```
  winnt /s:x:\i386 /tempdrive:D
  ```

- This example shows installing Windows 2000 from Windows 95, installing on drive D, using x:\i386 as the source directory and an installation script named unattend.txt:

  ```
  winnt /s:x:\i386 /tempdrive:D /u:unattend.txt
  ```

- This example shows installing Windows 2000 from Windows 95, installing on drive C, using x:\i386 as the source directory, and using the computer ID Server1 from the UDF named servers.udf:

  ```
  winnt /s:x:\i386 /tempdrive:C /u:unattend.txt /udf:Server1,servers.udf
  ```

- This example shows installing Windows 2000 from Windows NT 4 installing onto drive D, and making drive D a bootable disk (for moving the disk to another computer):

  ```
  winnt32 /s:x:\i386 /tempdrive:D /u:unattend.txt
  ➡/udf:Server1,servers.udf /syspart:D
  ```

For more information on the switches that can be used with Winnt and Winnt32, see Windows 2000 Server Help.

Stages of the Setup Process

The main stages of Windows 2000 Setup are as follows:

1 The Setup program loads into memory and presents the opening screen of the Setup program—this begins the Text mode setup.

2 The Setup program prompts you for where you want to install Windows 2000—which disk and partition—and what file system (FAT or NTFS) to use.

Setup Tips

If your disk controller is not on the Hardware Compatibility List, you will need to provide the Setup program with a driver to use (otherwise, Setup will fail with an inaccessible boot device message). To provide Setup with a driver for your disk controller,
watch for the message (Press F6 if you need to install a third party SCSI driver or
RAID driver) during Text mode setup. When you see this, you should quickly press F6
and then provide a driver for a mass storage device on a floppy disk.

If your computer uses a custom Hardware Abstraction Layer (HAL), you can provide its
setup at this same prompt; however, you have to press the F5 key instead of F6 to
provide a HAL driver.

---

3   Setup copies files to the local hard disk and then prompts you to restart
    the computer (this is the end of the Text mode portion of Setup). Setup
    will automatically reboot after waiting for 15 seconds.

4   The GUI mode portion of Setup begins, prompting you for the com-
    ponents to install, networking configuration, Administrator password,
    and other information. At the end of this phase, Setup prompts you to
    restart the computer again. Depending on the speed of your system, this
    can take a considerable amount of time—possibly as long as an hour.

5   The computer starts for the first time in Windows 2000. After you log
    on for the first time, a user profile is created for the Administrator
    account. The first time you log on, you are presented with a Configure
    Your Server Wizard. This was put into Windows 2000 to assist you.
    Most skilled administrators do not need this assistance, and you can can-
    cel it if you don't need it.

What Should I Do After Setup Finishes?

At the end of Setup, your should verify the success of your installation by doing the
following:

 ■ **Check the Event Logs for Error Messages.** Error messages in the System Log
could indicate improperly functioning hardware, drivers that failed to initialize, or
configuration problems.
▶ *For more information, see "Event Viewer" in Chapter 3.3, "Using Administrative Tools."*

 ■ **Test Network Connectivity.** Verify your network configuration by using basic
network diagnostic tools (such as ping or tracert) to ensure that your server can communicate on the network.
▶ *For more information, see Chapter 2.4, "Configuring Network Components."*

 ■ **Test Your Backup Solution.** Now is the perfect time to test your tape drive or
other backup device and make a good backup of the base operating system. Don't forget to test restoring it, too!
▶ *For more information, see "Backup and Restore" in Chapter 5.7, "Protecting Data."*

 ■ **Test Your Disaster Recovery Plan.** Install and test the Recovery Console and the
Emergency Repair process on your hardware, to ensure that you can make your sys-
tem bootable in case of file corruption or disk failure.
▶ *For more information, see "Disaster Recovery" in Chapter 5.7, "Protecting Data."*

Decisions You Make During Setup

A summary of the configuration decisions that you make during Setup are listed in Table 2.2.4.

Table 2.2.4   Information you Need to Provide to the Setup Program

Setup Option	Notes
Which partition?	Create a partition that will be dedicated to the operating system, and ensure that it is at least 1 GB (larger is better). After Setup finishes, create additional partitions for applications and data.
Which file system?	FAT or NTFS? Setup uses FAT32 if you choose FAT and make it larger than 2 GB. In general, you should choose NTFS on a server unless you are setting up a dual-boot with another operating system.
Components to install	The only components that are selected by default are IIS, Indexing, and Microsoft Script Debugger. Do not add other components unless you need them because they can add unnecessary overhead to your server.
Time and Date	Make sure that the time, date, and time zone are all correct. You can have problems later in Setup if you are joining a domain and these values are not correct.
Administrator account password	Be very careful how you type the password for this account (you get to type it twice). If you forget the password or mistype it, you will not be able to log on to the computer after Setup is complete.
Computer name	Up to 15 characters; must be unique on the network; must follow NetBIOS and DNS naming rules.
Network settings	IP address, subnet mask, gateway, DNS server, etc.
Member of domain?	You can configure the server as a member of a domain later. If you want the server to be manageable immediately with domain accounts, join the domain during Setup.

Reasons That Setup May Fail

Despite your best efforts, the Setup program may fail, or result in a STOP error. Common problems include the following:

- Hardware is not on HCL—especially disk controllers.
- BIOS is out-of-date—needs to be updated
- ACPI or Plug and Play may need to be disabled in system BIOS.
- Hardware malfunction. Mismatched or erratic hardware can cause Setup to fail.
- Mismatched memory modules are a particularly pernicious problem.

?   **What Should You Do If You Get a STOP Error During Setup?**

- Check to make sure your hardware is on the HCL. You may find that the revision level on a hardware device is a generation behind or that you have a different device than you thought you had. If your hardware is not on the HCL, contact your system manufacturer or the vendor of the hardware in question. They may have produced updated drivers that will enable your instillation to succeed.

- Remove non-essential hardware devices. Physically disconnect any device that is not an essential device such as the keyboard, mouse, video adapter, and disk controller. Unplug any device that could be detected by the hardware enumeration, such as printers, scanners, tape drives, CD-ROM towers, etc. Then run Setup again, removing the partition of the failed installation and creating a new one. If this is successful, add back in hardware devices, one at a time, until the failure recurs.

- Verify the BIOS and firmware revisions of the remaining hardware if STOP errors still occur.

- Search the Microsoft Knowledge Base. Microsoft has documented a number of STOP screen (and other) errors that may occur in some systems. The knowledge base on line is at http://support.microsoft.com/search/default.asp.

Upgrading to Windows 2000 Server

If you have existing Windows NT servers on your network, a decision you will need to make is whether to leave them as Windows NT servers or upgrade them to Windows 2000. Even if your Windows NT server is chugging along contentedly, you may want to upgrade it. File and print servers should experience a healthy speed improvement in Windows 2000. You don't have to use Active Directory for Windows 2000 to provide significant benefits.

The following upgrade paths are available:

- Windows NT 3.51 or 4.0 domain controllers can be upgraded to Windows 2000 domain controllers (you must upgrade the PDC of the domain first).
- Windows NT 3.51 or 4.0 member servers can be upgraded to a Windows 2000 member server.

- Windows NT 3.51 or 4.0 standalone servers can be upgraded to Windows 2000 standalone or member servers.

- Earlier versions of Windows NT must be upgraded to Windows NT 3.51 or 4.0 before they can be upgraded to Windows 2000.

Why would you *not* want to upgrade to Windows 2000? Reasons include the following:

- If no Windows 2000 drivers exist for your computer's hardware.

- If the server is running a critical application that is incompatible with Windows 2000.

- If the server has inadequate system resources (memory and disk space) to run Windows 2000.

Before you upgrade a production server, make sure that you have a good backup of the system and that you have a viable disaster-recovery plan. You want to be able to revert to your existing configuration if for some reason the installation fails.

If your upgrade includes upgrading your Windows NT 4.0 domain to Active Directory, you need to do careful planning before starting the upgrade. If your domain has only a single domain controller, the issues are very minor. However, if you have several domain controllers or have an enterprise with multiple domains, you need to make some decisions before you start to upgrade the first domain controller.

▶ *For more information, see Appendix A, "Migrating Windows NT 4.0 Domains to Active Directory."*

Automating Setup

Manual Setup, where you sit in front of the computer and answer all the questions, may be an acceptable approach if you only have to install Windows 2000 on a few systems. But if you have a larger number, this can be very time-consuming. In such cases, you should automate the Setup.

Ways to automate the Setup process include the following:

- Using an unattended installation script
- Using Remote Installation Services (RIS)
- Using system images
- Using a bootable CD-ROM

Creating and Using Installation Scripts

With *installation scripts* (also called *unattended answer files*), you can launch the Setup program and have it use a text file to provide the additional information normally supplied by the user during the installation process—such as the computer name, the network settings, the components to install, and so on. If you provide enough information in the script, you can fully automate the Setup program so that no user input is required.

To perform an unattended installation, you perform these steps:

- Create an installation script that contains the options that you want.
- Create any installation routines that you want to run at the end of Setup.
- Run the Setup program with command line switches that specify the unattended installation script to use, or save the file to a floppy disk and use it in conjunction with installing from CD.

For more information on creating installation scripts for unattended setup, see the Windows 2000 Server Resource Kit, Deployment Planning Guide.

Sample Unattended Installation Script

As an example of an unattended installation script, following is the contents of the Unattend.txt file that comes with Windows 2000 Server. You'll find it in the \I386 folder on the Windows 2000 Server CD-ROM:

```
; Microsoft Windows 2000 Professional, Server, Advanced Server and
; Datacenter
; (c) 1994 - 1999 Microsoft Corporation. All rights reserved.
;
; Sample Unattended Setup Answer File
;
; This file contains information about how to automate the installation
; or upgrade of Windows 2000 Professional and Windows 2000 Server so the
; Setup program runs without requiring user input.
;

[Unattended]
Unattendmode = FullUnattended
OemPreinstall = NO
TargetPath = WINNT
Filesystem = LeaveAlone

[UserData]
FullName = "Your User Name"
OrgName = "Your Organization Name"
ComputerName = "COMPUTER_NAME"

[GuiUnattended]
; Sets the Timezone to the Pacific Northwest
; Sets the Admin Password to NULL
; Turn AutoLogon ON and login once
TimeZone = "004"
AdminPassword = *
AutoLogon = Yes
```

```
AutoLogonCount = 1

;For Server installs
[LicenseFilePrintData]
AutoMode = "PerServer"
AutoUsers = "5"

[GuiRunOnce]
; List the programs that you want to lauch when the machine is logged into
; for the first time

[Display]
BitsPerPel = 8
XResolution = 800
YResolution = 600
VRefresh = 70

[Networking]
; When set to YES, setup will install default networking components. The
; components to be set are
; TCP/IP, File and Print Sharing, and the Client for Microsoft Networks.
InstallDefaultComponents = YES

[Identification]
JoinWorkgroup = Workgroup
```

Creating Installation Scripts

The easiest way to create an unattended installation script is to use the Setup Manager program, which is located inside the \SUPPORT\TOOLS\DEPLOY.CAB file on the Windows 2000 Server CD-ROM. Setup Manager consists of two files—SETUPM-GR.EXE and SETUPMGX.DLL—and both are contained in the DEPLOY.CAB file.

With Setup Manager, you can select options such as the name of the computer, the network settings, which components to install, and which OEM device drivers to install. Setup Manager will save the options you select as entries in an installation script. You can even ask Setup Manager to create an answer file to duplicate the setup of another machine, as shown in Figure 2.2.1.

Figure 2.2.1   Setup Manager.

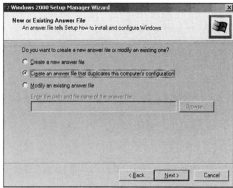

For additional help with parameters available in unattended setup, see the Unnatend.DOC file contained in Windows 2000 Server Resource Kit, Deployment Planning Guide.

Upgrade Scripts

If you are trying to script an upgrade, a small number of parameters from the installation script are used and the rest are ignored. The parameters that you can use are listed as follows:

```
[Unattended]
OemPreinstall = Yes
NoWaitAfterTextMode = 1
NoWaitAfterGUIMode = 1
NtUpgrade = Yes
OverwriteOemFilesOnUpgrade = Yes

[UserData]
ProductId = "111-1111111"

[GuiUnattended]
OemSkipWelcome = 1
```

Automating the Installation of Active Directory

At the end of Setup, you can automate the Active Directory Installation Wizard by using an answer file. You create an answer file that contains only the parameters that would appear in the [DCInstall] section of an unattended answer file. Then run the Active Directory Installation wizard by using the following syntax:

```
dcpromo /answer:<answer file name>
```

For more information about scripting Dcpromo, see SUPPORT\TOOLS\DEPLOY.CAB file on the Windows 2000 Server CD-ROM.

Adapting a Single Script for Multiple Computers

If you are installing more than one computer by using unattended answer files, you can create separate answer files for each computer. Another alternative is to create a file called a Uniqueness Database File (UDF). The UDF contains only the settings that are different for each individual computer, such as the computer name and IP address. When you run Setup, you use the UDF with a "generic" unattended answer file. The values in the UDF are substituted for the corresponding values in the unattended answer file.

The following is a sample UDF file that contains separate information for three computers:

```
[UniqueIds]
; This section lists the unique IDs (i.e., the computer names)
; of the computers this UDF applies to.  These are
; the IDs called after the /UDF:id switch when running setup.

    KAPOHO1=UserData
    KAPOHO2=UserData, GUIUnattended, Identification
    KAPOHO3=UserData
```

```
[KAPOHO1:UserData]
    FullName="Steve's Computer"
    ComputerName=KAPOHO1

[KAPOHO2:UserData]
    FullName="Thomas's Computer"
    ComputerName=KAPOHO2

[KAPOHO2:GUIUnattended]
    TimeZone=21

[KAPOHO2:Identification]
    JoinDomain=Kapoho

[KAPOHO3:UserData]
    FullName="Rebecca's Computer"
    ComputerName=Kapoho3
```

Starting a Scripted Installation

You use an installation script by providing the script file name as a
parameter to the Winnt or Winnt32 commands.

▶ *For more information, see "Winnt and Winnt32 Command-Line Switches"*
earlier in this chapter.

You can also use a script when booting from the CD-ROM, by supplying the script to Setup from a floppy disk.

▶ *For more information, see "Using System Images" later in this chapter.*

Remote Installation Services (RIS)

The methods for installing Windows 2000 described so far in this chapter
either require that you boot from Windows 2000 media (the CD-ROM or
Setup boot floppy disks) or start another Microsoft operating system (DOS,
Windows 95, Windows 98, or Windows NT 4.0) to access the source files and
run the Setup program.

What if you want to simply turn on a computer that has no operating system
installed and have Windows 2000 automatically install from the network?
That's what Remote Installation Services (RIS) does.

RIS is a service, running on Windows 2000 Server, which automates the
installation of Windows 2000 Professional for network clients. The RIS server
has a copy of the source files for the client's operating system on its hard disk.
When a client computer with no operating system starts on the network, the
client can download a fully configured operating system and desktop environment from the RIS server.

Using RIS

You cannot use RIS to install Windows 2000 Server. RIS can be used only to install
Windows 2000 Professional on client computers.

How RIS Works

The first step is to install the RIS service on a Windows 2000 Server computer. After RIS is installed, you create operating system images and place them on the RIS server.

There are two types of operating system images:

- **CD-based image.** A CD image is essentially the source files from the Windows 2000 Professional CD-ROM combined with an unattended answer file. All the files that are normally downloaded during a network installation are downloaded to the client and used by the Setup program to configure the client operating environment.

- **RIPrep image.** A RIPrep image is a fully configured client operating environment, complete with any desktop enhancements or post-installation addition of applications. The Remote Installation Preparation Wizard takes that fully configured desktop and saves it on the RIS server as a RIPrep image. When a client is installed from a RIPrep image, only the files that are required for the finished installation are downloaded to the client, with no local configuration.

The process of installing the operating system image on a desktop computer is as follows:

1 When the client computer starts up, it sends out a DHCP Discover message that includes PXE client extension tags.

2 A DHCP server on the network provides the client with an IP address. At the same time, the RIS server responds to the DHCP request with a message that provides the location of the RIS server the client should use, based on information in Active Directory.

3 The client logs on to the RIS server.

4 The RIS server provides a list of available operating system choices to the client, based on information in Active Directory.

5 The client uses TFTP to download the bootstrap program and the files from the image needed to install the operating system.

RIS Server and Client Requirements

The requirements for RIS servers and RIS clients are shown in Table 2.2.5. If the client computer does not have a compatible PXE boot ROM, you can make a floppy boot disk to use instead—as long as your network interface is on the list of supported network adapters.

Table 2.2.5   RIS Requirements

Role	Required Configuration
RIS Server	• 128 MB of RAM recommended
	• 2 GB or more available disk storage on an NTFS partition for client images
	• 10 or 100 Mbps network interface card (100 Mbps recommended)
RIS Client	• Pentium 166 Mhz or greater networked PC client computer
	• 64 MB of RAM recommended
	• One 800 MB or more primary disk drive
	• PXE DHCP-based boot ROM version .99c or greater, or a supported network adapter card and floppy disk drive (run the Rbfg.exe utility for a list of supported adapters)
Other Required Network Services	• DHCP server to assign IP addresses to client computers
	• DNS server to enable the RIS server to locate an Active Directory domain controller
	• Windows 2000 domain controller to authorize the RIS server in Active Directory and hold configuration information for pre-staged client computers

For information on installing and configuring RIS, see "Remote Installation Services" in Windows 2000 Server Help.

Using System Images

There are three additional ways of installing Windows 2000 that are based on the idea of "cloning" a completed or partially completed installation:

- **Sysprep.** For deploying Windows 2000 to multiple computers with identical hardware. You install Windows 2000 and configure the user environment with additional applications, etc. Then you run Sysprep to make a "master" copy that can be cloned on other computers. A version of Sysprep is included in \SUPPORT\TOOLS\DEPLOY.CAB on the Windows 2000 Server CD.

- **Syspart.** For deploying Windows 2000 to multiple computers that have dissimilar hardware. This method allows you to start the Setup program and then interrupt it after the file copy phase of Text mode Setup. Use the /syspart switch on the Winnt32 command line.

- **Bootable CD-ROM.** For running a CD-ROM-based installation by providing an answer file on floppy disk during Setup. To use this method, you boot from the Windows 2000 CD-ROM and then provide a winnt.sif file on floppy disk when the blue Setup screen appears. Setup uses data provided in the winnt.sif file to customize the installation and continues installing from the CD-ROM.

  ► *For more information on these deployment methods, see the Windows 2000 Deployment Guide.*

2.3

Configuring Devices and System Settings

You Need to Read This Section If You Want to:

- Add or remove devices from your computer
- Update device drivers used by your computer
- Optimize virtual memory
- Modify environment variables
- Modify startup and recovery options

Related Topics

For More Information On ▸ *See*

Overview

Windows 2000 Setup attempts to detect the hardware devices that are present on your computer, and installs device drivers for any devices that are found. It also configures basic system settings to default values. As your computer's hardware configuration changes or the operating requirements change, you can install new device drivers and modify these default configuration settings as needed.

Installing a device driver in Windows 2000 makes the following changes to your computer:

- The device driver files are copied to the *systemroot%*\System32 folder.
- Other files (such as help files, etc.) may be copied to other folders, depending on the driver's installation file.
- Entries are made in the Registry to control how the driver is started and any other configuration or run-time parameters. These Registry entries are made under HKEY_LOCAL_MACHINE\SYSTEM\CurrentControlSet\Services or HKEY_LOCAL_MACHINE\SYSTEM\CurrentControlSet\Control.

Configuring system settings in Windows 2000 consists of making changes to the Registry that affect certain core operating system functions and the Windows 2000 environment. These changes include the settings for the size and location of the paging file, the environment variables, certain options for startup and shutdown of Windows 2000, and the relative performance of foreground and background applications.

 Can I Use Windows NT 4.0 Drivers with Windows 2000?

In some cases, yes, but typically the answer is no.

▶ *For more information, see "Installing and Configuring Device Drivers" later in this chapter.*

? **I Installed New Drivers for A Piece of Hardware and the Server Will Not Restart. How Can I Get Back Into My Server to Remove the Driver?**

There are a few ways you can do this.

▶ *For more information, see "Recovering from Failed Driver Installations" later in this chapter.*

Windows 2000 can usually detect most supported hardware during a reboot, and will either automatically load the correct driver (using driver.cab) or will prompt you for the drivers. You can install device drivers and configure the system settings for a Windows 2000 computer by using Device Manager, which you can access via the System option in Control Panel (or by right-clicking My Computer and selecting Properties). A sample of the System properties dialog box on a Windows 2000 Server is shown in Figure 2.3.1.

Figure 2.3.1   System Properties dialog box, showing Device Manager.

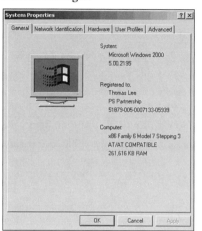

The System Properties dialog box has five tabs that allow you to view and change both system settings and device drivers:

- **General**. Displays the version of Windows 2000 that you are using, along with the processor type, the amount of installed RAM, and product registration information.

- **Network Identification**. Displays the computer name and domain or workgroup name that the computer uses on the network. If the server is not a Domain Controller, you can also change these settings.
  ▶*For more information, see Chapter 2.4, "Configuring Network Components."*

- **Hardware**. Allows you to display and modify device drivers and hardware profiles. You can also set the options for the way the system should respond when installing an unsigned device driver.
  ▶ *For more information, see "Installing and Configuring Device Drivers" later in this chapter.*

- **User Profiles**. Allows you to copy, delete, or change the type of user profiles on the local computer.
  ▶ *For more information, see Chapter 6.2, "Profiles."*

- **Advanced**. Allows you to set performance options, environment variables, and startup and recovery options.
  ▶ *For more information, see "Configuring System Settings" later in this chapter.*

Installing and Configuring Device Drivers

Before you can use a hardware device in Windows 2000 (such as a network card, disk controller, or input device), you need to install a device driver for it. A *device driver* is software that provides the necessary interface between application programs and the physical hardware itself. For example, if you install a new network interface adapter in your server, you also have to install the appropriate device driver so that Windows 2000 knows how to communicate with the adapter.

The Registry settings for devices are part of the computer's hardware profile. You can have multiple hardware profiles that load different device drivers and services. See *Hardware Profiles* later in this chapter.

▶ *For more information about the Registry, see Chapter 2.6, "The Registry."*

You can use the Add/Remove Hardware Wizard to install any device. You must be logged on as the Administrator or a member of the Administrators group to install device drivers.

Windows 2000 can use any of the following methods to install device drivers:

- **Running Setup**. During installation of Windows 2000, the hardware-detection process attempts to enumerate all of the hardware devices attached to the computer. Device drivers are automatically installed for all detected devices.

- **Starting the computer**. The Plug and Play process enumerates Plug and Play devices at system startup. If new devices are detected, their device drivers are automatically installed.

- **Scanning for new hardware**. You can use the Add/Remove Hardware Wizard to perform the same hardware-detection process and device driver installation that Windows 2000 Setup performs.

- **Manual installation**. You can use the Add/Remove Hardware Wizard to specify the device you want to install, or you can right-click the .INF file that comes with the driver and choose Install. You need to install drivers manually when you are replacing existing device drivers with newer versions or when installing drivers for devices that were not detected by the other methods.

Windows 2000 uses three types of device drivers:

- Network Device Interface Specification (NDIS) version 5.0.
- Small Computer Systems Interconnect (SCSI).
- Windows Driver Model (WDM).

WDM Drivers Work!

WDM drivers have been designed specifically to be used on both Windows 98 and Windows 2000 computers.

Think Twice Before You Install These Drivers...

If you plan to use hardware that is not on the Hardware Compatibility List, make sure to test the hardware and its device drivers before using them on a production server.

In general, you should not use Windows NT 4.0 device drivers with Windows 2000, although some may work OK. Using device drivers originally developed to run on earlier version of Windows NT can compromise the stability and reliability of your server. Be sure to test any legacy drivers before installing them on critical systems!

You need to make sure that the hardware is correctly configured before attempting to install its device drivers. For example, make sure that SCSI devices are set to the correct ID and that the SCSI bus is terminated correctly.

Automatic Installation of Devices

Drivers for all supported hardware devices should be installed automatically by Windows 2000. Installation of drivers is handled differently for Plug and Play and non-Plug and Play devices.

Plug and Play is an industry-wide, Microsoft-supported initiative to automate the installation and configuration of computer hardware. With Plug and Play, an end user should be able to dynamically add and remove devices without extensive knowledge of computer hardware and related resources.

For Plug and Play devices to be detected, your system BIOS must support the *Advanced Configuration and Power Interface (ACPI)* specification and the devices must be Plug and Play-compatible. Windows 2000 will continue to support APM and Plug and Play BIOS for backward compatibility whereas ACPI will provide support for Plug and Play and power.

The Plug and Play process automatically assigns each device whatever resources the device requires, including the following:

- IRQ level
- Direct memory access (DMA) channels
- Input/Output (I/O) ports
- Memory addresses

Plug and Play arbitrates the requests for resources from various devices, and assigns the appropriate resources to each device. If the resource requests from all devices cannot be satisfied without conflicts, the devices that did not receive resources will appear in Device Manager with a stop sign to indicate the conflict.

Plug and Play devices are detected at system startup. Depending on your hardware and the type of device, the insertion or attachment of devices after startup can also be detected automatically. For example, the insertion of a PC card into a PC card slot can be detected (and the appropriate drivers installed automatically) as long as the PC card and the computer's PC card bus support hot-swapping.

Plug and Play devices are also detected when scanning for new hardware.

▶ *For more information on Plug and Play, see the Microsoft white paper "Plug and Play for Windows 2000" at* http://www.microsoft.com/HWDEV/desinit/PnPNT5_2.htm.

Devices that are not Plug and Play will not be detected at startup or when attached to the computer. Most devices can be added by choosing Scan for new hardware in either the Add/Remove Hardware Wizard or in Device Manager, which will detect the new device.

To scan for new hardware, do either of the following:

- Reboot your system (this may be most appropriate just after adding new hardware.
- Run the Add/Remove Hardware Wizard.
- In Device Manager, right-click a device and choose Scan for hardware changes.

Device drivers will be installed automatically for any detected devices. If you have added a new device that was not detected, you will need to install the device drivers manually.

Manual Installation and Configuration of Devices

You can install devices manually by using the Add/Remove Hardware option in Control Panel.

To start the Add/Remove Hardware Wizard, do any of the following:

- In Control Panel, click Add/Remove Hardware.
- On the desktop, right-click My Computer, click Properties, click the Hardware tab, and then click Hardware Wizard.
- Run Hdwwiz.cpl (this runs the hardware wizard without needing to run Control Panel).

Why Are Some Devices Missing from the List of Available Devices In the Add/Remove Hardware Wizard?

Any devices that are enumerated by Plug and Play will not appear in the list of available devices to install   if they're present on the system, they will be installed automatically. For example, the Intel PRO 100+ network card does not appear in the Add/Remove Hardware Wizard because Windows 2000 knows that this is a Plug and Play driver. To install these types of drivers, either restart the computer or scan for new devices in the Device Manager.

If you need to install a device driver but the device is not detected, you can still install it by choosing Other and then clicking the Have Disk button. Then, supply the driver to Windows 2000 either on a floppy disk or some other path that includes the driver and its .INF file.

If you install a device that the Add/Remove Hardware Wizard was unable to detect, you will need to configure the settings for the device driver manually by using Device Manager.

Using Device Manager to Configure Devices

After a device is installed, you can display information about the device and the resources the device is using in Device Manager.

To start Device Manager, do any of the following:

- In the Administrative Tools program group, click Computer Management. Click Device Manager in the console tree.
- On the desktop, right-click My Computer and click Properties. Click the Hardware tab and click Device Manager.
- Run Devmgmt.msc (this runs the Device Manager).

Page: 1
Device Manager displays a list of devices that were either detected or for which drivers are installed. The icon for the device indicates whether the device is working properly. See Table 2.3.1 for a description of the meaning of the icons.

Table 2.3.1   Device Status Indicated by Icon in Device Manager

Icon	Status
Normal icon	The device driver has initialized successfully and there are no resource conflicts.
Stop sign on icon	Hardware conflicts prevented the device from initializing.
Exclamation point on icon	The device is incorrectly configured, or the device driver is missing or corrupt. This can also mean that the device driver is installed but the device was not connected on startup (such as a Zip drive that is not constantly needed).

If you want to override the resources or the device driver that were assigned to a device, follow these steps:

1. Bring up Device manager, right-click the device, and then click Properties. This brings up the Properties for the device.
2. Click the Resources tab.
3. Click the resource to be changed and then clear the Use automatic settings checkbox.
4. Click Change Setting and then change the value of the setting to the desired value.

Let Plug and Play Resolve Conflicts

When you manually change the resource assignment or other settings for a device, those settings will not be changed in the future by Plug and Play, even if the device is removed or a resource conflict is eliminated. In general, it is best to let Plug and Play resolve conflicts whenever possible.

Specifying the Driver Source Location

When you add a supported Plug and Play device to your system or add a driver for a device for which Windows 2000 provides a driver, the driver is installed from the Driver.cab file in the *systemroot*\DriverCache\I386 folder. The size of this file is approximately 50 MB. If the driver cannot be found in Driver.cab, Windows 2000 will prompt you for the location of the driver.

Using Driver. cab is useful, especially for traveling laptop users, but can be a waste of space for corporate users who never or very rarely update their hardware. If you want to save this space on the hard disk of client computers or if you want to centralize this file so that all clients install drivers from a consistent central source, you can change the source path in the Registry and delete the local copy of Driver.cab. To change the path, just update the data for the SourcePath value in this key in the Registry:

HKEY_LOCAL_MACHINE\SOFTWARE\Microsoft\Windows\ CurrentVersion\Setup

Updating and Removing Device Drivers

To update a device driver, display the properties of the device in Device Manager, click the Driver tab, and then click Update Driver.

To remove a device, right-click the device in Device Manager and click Uninstall. Removing the device does not actually delete the device driver itself. It removes references to the driver from the Registry so the computer does not load the driver.

Upgrading from Uniprocessor to Multiprocessor

If Windows 2000 was originally installed on a single processor computer and a second processor is added, you need to update the system software. With Windows NT 4.0, you had to perform this upgrade using the Uptomp.exe program from the Resource Kit (or reinstall the operating system). With Windows 2000, this is now much simpler and is done using the following steps:

1 From Device Manager, expand the Computer icon and make note of the computer model.

2 Right-click the computer model below the Computer icon and select Properties.

3 Begin the Upgrade Device Driver Wizard by clicking on the Update Driver button from the Driver tab.

4 Choose Display a List of Known Drivers For This Device and click the Next button.

By selecting Show All Hardware of This Device Class, you may choose from a list of supplied multiprocessor drivers or use the Have Disk button if your hardware manufacturer has provided Windows 2000-specific multiprocessor drivers.

WARNING: Do Not Select the Incorrect HAL and/or Kernel

When upgrading from uniprocessor to multiprocessor, you are replacing the Hardware Abstraction Layer (HAL) and certain other Kernel files. If you select the incorrect HAL and Kernel during the upgrade process, your server may fail to start and you will have to perform the Emergency Repair Process or run Setup to make your system bootable again. Selecting Last Known Good Configuration will not repair this because the changes are not limited to the Registry.

▶ *For more information on the boot process, see "Emergency Repair" in Chapter 2.5, "The Boot Process."*

Driver Signing

Driver signing has been implemented in Windows 2000 to improve the quality of drivers and increase the overall stability of the Windows operating system. Microsoft requires all vendor-provided drivers that ship with Windows 2000, Windows 98, and drivers published on the Windows Update Web site to be digitally signed. This ensures that the drivers have been certified by Windows Hardware Quality Labs (WHQL).

All files and drivers on the Windows 2000 installation CD are digitally signed by Microsoft. What about drivers downloaded from the Internet or provided by the hardware vendor? An Administrator can configure how Windows should handle third-party drivers. Select the System Properties icon from Control Panel, click on the Hardware tab, and select the Driver Signing button. The three options that are presented are as follows:

- **Ignore.** Install all files, regardless of the file signature
- **Warn.** Display a message before installing an unsigned file (default setting)
- **Block.** Prevent installation of unsigned files

? Code Signing: What Is It?

File signing does not actually alter the binary files themselves. After a driver is tested by Microsoft (WHQL), a catalog file is created and signed using existing Digital Signature cryptographic technology and the signed catalog file is associated with the driver package using the drivers .INF file. This association is maintained even after installation.

Recovering from Failed Driver Installations

The installation of a device driver can fail for any of the following reasons:

- Wrong driver installed (doesn't match hardware)
- Partially installed   not all files installed
- Files are corrupt
- Hardware problem

Table 2.3.2 details the solutions to these problems.

Table 2.3.2   Troubleshooting Tips for Failed Driver Installations

Problem	Solution
Wrong driver installed	If you have installed the wrong driver for a particular piece of hardware and the server will no longer start, press F8 at startup and use the Last Known Good Configuration. This will roll the HKEY_LOCAL_MACHINE\SYSTEM\CurrentControlSet Registry hive back to the previous reboot, prior to the installation of the failing driver.
Partially installed drivers	System File Checker is a command-line utility that can verify the version of protected system files and revert to a previous version by using sfc.exe */scannow*.
Files are corrupt	Uninstall or remove the device driver, restart the server, and reinstall the driver.
Hardware problem	Replace faulty hardware.

Hardware Profiles

Windows 2000 has the capability to maintain multiple hardware configurations and allows you to select which configuration you want to use at boot time. The most common use of hardware profiles is on a laptop. You may have a hardware configuration for a docking station on the network and one for undocked without the network card. By selecting the undocked hardware profile at startup, the mobile user would not have to wait for the devices and network service to fail to start.

Hardware profiles are less useful for servers, which rarely get moved or rebooted. You want to keep a server's hardware configuration as static as possible to maximize stability and availability.

A hardware profile can be used as a troubleshooting tool if you want to disable selected drivers temporarily to determine whether they are creating problems on the server. Create a new hardware profile based on the current one and then disable the devices in Device Manager for that new hardware profile.

The individual hardware configurations for each Hardware Profile are stored in the Registry under HKEY_LOCAL_MACHINE\ SYSTEM\CurrentControlSet\Hardware Profiles.

Creating a New Hardware Profile

To create a new hardware Profile, do the following:

1 From Control Panel, open the System applet and click Hardware. Click Hardware Profiles.

2 Under Available Hardware Profiles, select the (Current) profile and click Copy.

3 Provide a name for the new profile.

An administrator can also specify which profile will be the default Hardware profile and the delay, in seconds, that the server will wait for a selection before loading the default Registry settings.

Enabling/Disabling Devices and Services for a Specific Profile

Individual devices and services may be configured to load or not load as part of a Hardware Profile.

To disable devices, do the following:

1 From Device Manager, view the Properties of any device such as the Modem.

2 On the General tab, click on the down arrow in the Device Usage section and select Do not use this device in the current hardware profile (disable).

3 Click on OK.

To disable services, do the following:

1 From Administrative Tools, select Services.

2 Select the Log On tab from the Properties dialog of any Services such as Alerter.

3 Click on Enable or Disable for the selected Hardware Profile.

   ▶ *For more information on services, see Part 8, "Managing Network Services."*

Configuring Device Options Through Control Panel

Several types of devices have specific configuration options accessible through Control Panel. Table 2.3.3 lists those device types, along with notes about the issues specific to each.

Table 2.3.3   ***Hardware Devices Configurable Through Control Panel***

Device Type	Notes
Display	Configuration options for Multiple monitors: <ul><li>Must use Peripheral Component Interconnect (PCI) or Accelerated Graphics Port (AGP) card.</li><li>Windows 2000 disables the display adapter that is built-in to the system board.</li><li>You may be able to select the primary display by changing a setting in the computer's BIOS.</li><li>On the Settings tab, click Identify to arrange the order of display among monitors. Drag the icons to arrange them.</li></ul>
Mouse	The Hardware tab allows you to display the properties of the device driver being used, along with the capability to change the driver. You can also modify the resources used by the driver and run the Mouse Troubleshooter.
Phone and Modem Options	The Modems tab allows you to add and remove modems and change their configuration. Select a modem and click Properties to display the Modem Properties.
	In Modem Properties, use the Diagnostics tab to determine whether Windows 2000 is able to communicate with the modem. Use the Advanced tab to specify any modem initialization strings that you want to send to the modem before initiating a call.
	Note that some ISDN cards will not appear here and are configured directly in Device Manager.
Keyboard	Allows you to adjust Speed settings, Input Locales for languages, and Hardware device driver settings.
Sound and Multimedia	Sound schemes, audio device preferences, and hardware device configurations and resource settings.

Device Type	Notes
Wireless Link	File Transfer settings, Image Transfer preferences for Wireless Digital Cameras, and Hardware device driver settings for wireless adapters.
Scanners and Cameras	Allows you to add and configure communication properties for cameras and scanners. Click the Add button to activate the Scanner and Camera Installation Wizard.
Printers	Click Add Printer to add a new printer or right-click on a printer and choose Properties to display the properties of a specific printer. For more information on printers, see Chapter 5.5, "Sharing Printers."

Other devices may add their own options to Control Panel, which will give you more flexibility in configuring the devices.

Configuring System Settings

System settings that you can configure through Control Panel, include the following.

- Performance Options, including the size of the paging file
- Environment Variables
- Startup and Recovery Options

Performance Options

There are two general performance settings that are available through the Advanced tab of System Properties:

- **Application Response.** This setting controls the relative responsiveness of foreground and background applications.

- **Virtual memory.** This setting controls the size and location of the paging file(s) used by Windows 2000 for virtual memory.

Application Response

There are two possible settings for application response:

- **Applications.** Causes the system to give more processing time to the foreground application instead of background applications. This is the default setting on Windows 2000 Professional; it enables the foreground application to be more responsive to user input than it would otherwise be.

- **Background Services.** Causes the system to give equal amounts of processing time to the foreground application and background applications. This is the default setting for Windows 2000 Server; it allows background applications to get the same processor time as the foreground task. This is the optimal setting for a network server.

Virtual Memory Configuration

As applications make demands on memory resources, the Virtual Memory Manager (VMM) adjusts the amount of memory that is used for file caching and memory used for applications. If the demands for file caching are low, the VMM can decrease the amount of RAM used for the file cache, allowing more applications to be resident in RAM.

The VMM balances two different uses of memory on your server:

- **File caching.** VMM sets the amount of memory that is used to cache data on local and network volumes. The file cache helps improve performance reading information from disks when the information is cached in memory instead of having to access the physical disk (which is much slower).

- **Applications.** VMM sets the amount of memory that will be available for applications to use for their code and data. When the amount of memory in use by applications is larger than the available memory, the VMM stores pages of memory on the disk in the paging file.

When an application requests a new memory page and there are no more available pages of RAM, the Virtual Memory Manager must move background application data out of RAM and into the paging file to free up memory pages for the new process. The next time the background application attempts to access its data, it finds that it is no longer in RAM. The application must wait for the VMM to page other data out of RAM to make pages available for the requested data from the paging file. This is called a *hard page fault*. Page faults occur when an application looks for data in RAM and finds that it has been moved to the paging file.

Environment Variables

Environment variables are strings containing information such as a user name, path, or operating system. Environment variables provide information that Windows needs to control the behavior of applications. For example, the TMP environment variable specifies where an application places its temporary files.

- **System variables.** These variables affect all users of the system. Only administrators can change these variables. System variables are stored in the following location:

HKEY_LOCAL_MACHINE\SYSTEM\CurrentControlSet\Control\
Session Manager\Environment

- **User variables.** These variables affect only the currently logged-on user. Users can change their own environment variables. User variables are stored in

  HKEY_CURRENT_USER\Environment

Environment variables can also be used in scripting and batch files (for example, mapping a drive to the user's home directory share using the variable %USERNAME%).

If a variable is defined more than once, the last one to be processed when creating the environment is the result.

The order in which variables are processed is as follows:

1 AUTOEXEC.BAT (if the server has been configured to parse the autoexec.bat)

2 System variables (from HKEY_LOCAL_MACHINE, hardware profile)

3 User variables (from HKEY_CURRENT_USER, user profile)

Thus, any variables assigned for the user will override the same variable that was defined for the computer.

Getting Environment Variables from AUTOEXEC.BAT

Variables from AUTOEXEC.BAT are not included in the Environment Variables, by default. The AUTOEXEC.BAT is only parsed if the Registry is modified by adding the following value to HKEY_LOCAL_MACHINE\SOFTWARE\Microsoft\WindowsNT\CurrentVersion\Winlogon\ ParseAutoexec with a REG_SZ value of 1 (adds the value for all users).

Or

HKEY_CURRENT_USER\SOFTWARE\Microsoft\WindowsNT\CurrentVersion\Winlogon\ ParseAutoexec with a REG_SZ value of 1 (adds the value for the user currently logged in to Windows).

From a clean installation of Windows 2000, there would not be an AUTOEXEC.BAT without dual-boot. Some legacy applications may add this file for defining single purpose variables.

A server's current environment variables can be viewed by using the SET command at a command prompt. Consider the following example:

```
ALLUSERSPROFILE=F:\Documents and Settings\All Users
APPDATA=F:\Documents and Settings\Administrator.Kapoho2\Application Data
CommonProgramFiles=F:\Program Files\Common Files
COMPUTERNAME=kapoho2
ComSpec=F:\WINNT\system32\cmd.exe
DIRCMD=/O:GNE
HOMEDRIVE=F:
HOMEPATH=\
LOGONSERVER=\\KONA
NUMBER_OF_PROCESSORS=1
OS=Windows_NT
Os2LibPath=F:\WINNT\system32\os2\dll;
```

```
Path=F:\WINNT\system32;F:\WINNT;F:\WINNT\System32\Wbem;F:\Program
Files\Resource Kit\;C:\DOS
PATHEXT=.COM;.EXE;.BAT;.CMD;.VBS;.VBE;.JS;.JSE;.WS;.WSH
PROCESSOR_ARCHITECTURE=x86
PROCESSOR_IDENTIFIER=x86 Family 6 Model 5 Stepping 2, GenuineIntel
PROCESSOR_LEVEL=6
PROCESSOR_REVISION=0502
ProgramFiles=F:\Program Files
PROMPT=$P$G
SystemDrive=F:
SystemRoot=F:\WINNT
TEMP=F:\DOCUME~1\ADMINI~1.W2K\LOCALS~1\Temp
TMP=F:\DOCUME~1\ADMINI~1.W2K\LOCALS~1\Temp
USERDNSDOMAIN=kapoho.com
USERDOMAIN=Kapoho
USERNAME=Rebecca
USERPROFILE=F:\Documents and Settings\Administrator.Kapoho2
windir=F:\WINNT
```

Default environment variables are shown in Table 2.3.4.

Table 2.3.4   *Default Environment Variables*

Variable	Value
System Variables	
ComSpec	*Systemroot*\system32\cmd.exe
NUMBER_OF_PROCESSORS	Depends on hardware
OS	Windows_NT
Os2LibPath	*Systemroot*\System32\os2\dll
Path	
PATHEXT	
PROCESSOR_ARCHITECTURE	x86
PROCESSOR_IDENTIFIER	Depends on hardware
PROCESSOR_LEVEL	Depends on hardware
PROCESSOR_REVISION	Depends on hardware
TEMP	
TMP	
Windir	*Systemroot*
User Variables	
TEMP	*Systemdrive*\Documents and Settings*username*
TMP	*Systemdrive*\Documents and Settings*username*

Adding New Environment Variables

You can add new variables to the user's environment during the processing of a logon script by using the Putinenv utility from the Windows 2000 Resource Kit. One of the things that makes this utility useful is that it works for Windows 95 and Windows 98 clients, as well. For example, you can use Putinenv to create a %USERNAME% variable during logon script processing on Windows 95 and Windows 98 clients.

Startup and Recovery Options

The Startup and Recovery button under System Properties allows you to configure default parameters for operating system selection, and what processes should occur in the event of a system failure.

Startup Options

The System Startup options allow you to change the following:

- **Default operating system.** Selects which operating system listed in the Boot.ini should be used as the default in the system startup menu. Changing this value changes the default value in Boot.ini.

- **Display list of operating systems for xx seconds.** Allows you to set the number of seconds that the startup menu should be displayed before the default operating system is started automatically. Changing this value changes the timeout value in Boot.ini. A value of zero will prevent the boot menu from being displayed.

  ▶ *For more information on the system startup menu and the values in Boot.ini, see Chapter 2.5, "The Boot Process."*

Figure 2.3.2   Systems failure options in Windows 2000.

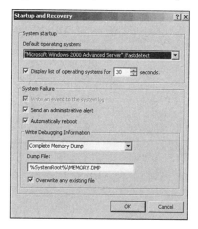

Recovery Options

The System Failure options box allows you to configure the following areas:

- **Write an event to the system log.** This box must be checked in order to write an alert when running Windows 2000 Professional. It is checked by default and cannot be unchecked in Windows 2000 Server.

- **Send an administrative alert.** When checked, an administrative alert will be sent in the event of a system failure.

- **Automatically reboot.** In the event of a system failure, the server will automatically restart itself. This will ensure the highest possible uptime for customers. Without this box checked, a system failure would leave the server unavailable until a technician restarts it.

- **Write debugging information.** This setting has four options:

  (none)   No debugging information will be written.

  Small Memory Dump. Only a summary Kernel dump will be written (64 kb). This option requires a paging file of at least 2 MB on your boot volume.

  Kernel Memory Dump. This dumps only the Kernel memory which speeds up the process of saving the dump file. Deepening on how much ram you have in your system, you need between 50MB and 800MB available for the paging rile on the boot volume.

  Complete Memory Dump. A full dump will be written to the file-name specified in the following box. This option requires that your paging file be large enough to handle the dump, system memory plus 1 megabyte.

- **Dump File.** Specify the name and location of the dump file to be created. By default, this is set to *%SystemRoot%\MEMORY.DMP* .

- **Overwrite any existing files.** You may also specify that if there is already an existing dump file to overwrite it.

If a server is configured to automatically reboot, the system log will need to be periodically monitored to determine whether STOP errors have occurred and use information in the log to determine the cause of the error. You can also determine whether a STOP error occurred recently by using the uptime.exe utility, which is a Windows 2000 Resource Kit utility that examines your computer's event log to determine system availability and current uptime.

Paging file requirements for a dump file to be generated when a STOP error occurs:

- A paging file must be located on the boot partition. (that is, where *systemroot* is located)

- Paging file size must be at least equal to physical RAM plus one megabyte.

What Good Is a "Dump File," Anyway?

A good use for the dump file is a server that experiences STOP errors at random intervals that cannot be reproduced. Because the engineer can't be there 24 hours a day to see what the server is doing when it experiences the error, a dump file can be generated when the server crashes. Later, when parsed with a Kernel Debugger, the file can show the contents of the stacks and information stored in memory when the server experienced the error helping to determine the cause of the problem.

Going Deeper: Windows 2000 Demand Paging

The paging file is a system file named PAGEFILE.SYS. By default, it's a hidden file in the root of the *systemdrive* volume. If Pagefile.sys does not exist at startup, Windows 2000 will create a new one. The default initial size is one and half times the amount of system RAM or the amount of available free space, whichever is less. For example, on a system with 256 MB of RAM, the default initial paging file size would be 384 MB.

VMM will adjust the size of the paging file as needed, up to the maximum size specified in System Properties. In general, it's best to leave the paging file settings at the default and ensure that adequate RAM is available to keep paging to a minimum and still have adequate RAM available for file caching. Optimal settings may differ, depending on the applications supported. In memory shortage situations, careful analysis is needed to determine the appropriate settings.

If the paging file is too small, Windows 2000 will dynamically allocate additional disk space up to the Maximum Size setting under System Properties. This requires additional processing time and can causes additional disk fragmentation. The combination of insufficient RAM and an inadequate paging file could cause the system to slow down greatly.

Demand paging creates a lot disk activity as pages are read from and written to the disk. The best way to observe this paging activity is to monitor the Memory:Pages/sec counter in Performance Monitor. When the Pages/sec is greater than 10–20 on a sustained basis, there is a large amount of paging activity and additional memory is probably needed.

If more in-depth information about a particular applications paging is necessary, use the Windows 2000 Resource Kit utility: Page Fault Monitor (pfmon.exe).

Optimizing Memory and Paging File Usage on Your Server

To increase performance, consider placing a paging file on multiple physical disks. Multiple physical disks can be accessed simultaneously, thus increasing throughput. If one disk is substantially slower than another, better performance may be achieved by paging only to the faster disk.

continues

Ideally, your computer should rarely need to write pages of memory to the paging file. You can't completely eliminate paging because the VMM will page parts of the operating system to disk, regardless of how much memory you have. What you want to avoid is the situation in which high levels of paging are occurring on a sustained basis.

To avoid paging, what you need to do is determine how much memory is needed to keep all of your applications resident in RAM. You can do this by adding up the working set size for all of the processes running on your server. Be sure to measure these values during periods of peak activity on the server to ensure that you have sized memory for your periods of peak demand. Next, examine the size of the file cache on the server. You can then determine the appropriate amount of memory by adding together the working sets of all the processes on the server and the memory needed for file caching.

After you have sized the RAM on the server to minimize paging, you are ready to optimize the paging file. The best starting point is the default suggested by Windows 2000   one and half times the amount of physical RAM. Then, monitor the paging activity, size of the paging file, and disk usage on the server under peak loads. If the size of the paging file grows, this indicates that the initial size of the paging file is too small. Increase the initial size to the largest size that the paging file grows to under peak demands. If the physical disk on which the paging file resides is busy more than 40%, you should consider either moving the paging file to another physical disk or creating multiple paging files. You will need to make the change and then monitor the results to ensure that you receive a performance benefit from the change.

To change the size or location of the paging file, do the following:

1 Select System Properties in Control Panel.

2 Click on the Advanced button.

3 Select Performance Options and then Change in the Virtual Memory box.

The Virtual Memory dialog box is shown in Figure 2.3.2.

Figure 2.3.3   Virtual Memory Properties in Windows 2000.

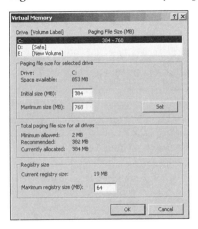

The following values can be set on the Virtual Memory Properties dialog box, as shown in Figure 2.3.3:

- **Drive details**   This shows which volumes that either can have or already have paging files created. You can choose a volume and adjust the page file details for that volume.
- **Initial size**   The size of the paging file on this volume at startup. The paging file never shrinks below this size.
- **Maximum size**   The largest size on the selected volume, to which the paging file is allowed to dynamically become.
- **Maximum Registry size**   Specifies the maximum size the Registry is allowed to dynamically become.
  ▶ *For more information on system dump files, see "Performance Options" earlier in this chapter.*

Best Practices

- Before making changes to your virtual memory configuration, monitor the demands for memory in Performance Monitor to determine the nature of the memory shortage.
- If you are not sure how much virtual memory is needed or desirable, don't change anything; let the VMM adjust the paging file size as needed.
- Consider distributing the paging file across multiple physical disks by creating multiple paging files, as long as the disk controller hardware can write concurrently to the different physical disks.
- Consider locating the paging file on a volume that is not very active in order to reduce competition for the disk resource.
- Remember to create a paging file at least equal to system RAM, plus one megabyte on the boot partition if you want to be able to get a dump of system memory.

Tuning the Paging File Size on Systems with Very Large Amounts of Physical RAM

Care must be taken when sizing the paging file on a system that is using either four gigabyte tuning (4 GT) or Very Large Memory (VLM). Because the optimal paging file size will depend on the way that applications use memory on the server, careful performance analysis under varying memory loads is needed.

▶ *For more information on 4GT or VLM, see ""Memory Management in Chapter 1.1, "Overview of Windows 2000 Architecture."*

2.4
Configuring Network Components

You Need to Read This Section if You Want to:

- Allow clients to connect to your Windows 2000 Server.
- Allow your Windows 2000 Server to communicate with other servers.
- Administer and maintain network connectivity for Windows 2000.
- Optimize your Windows 2000 Server's network performance.

Related Topics

Network Components Overview

The following components are the three key pieces involved in building any network. It's critical to understand not only what each of them do, but how they interact (see Figure 2.4.1).

Figure 2.4.1   Network connectivity requires a common protocol be bound to a network interface and a network service.

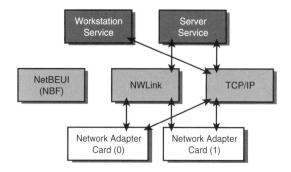

- **Network Interface cards (NICs)** are physical devices that must be installed into the server and must match the network which you will be connecting. A network interface can be Ethernet, Token Ring, Fibre, ATM, or a serial device such as a modem or ISDN device.
  ▶ *For more information, see "Adding and Removing WAN Adapters" later in this chapter.*

- **Network protocols**, also refered to as *transport protocols*, are used to transport requests or data through a network interface and across the network media. The two most commonly used transport protocol suites are TCP/IP and NWLink (IPX/SPX-compatible transport). The protocols that you install and configure must match the protocols being used by the computers you want to communicate with on the network.

- **Network services** can be defined as Client services or Server services. *Client services* allow a computer to request resources from another computer's Server service. The role of Client and Server can be difficult to define in a distributed network. When a client requests a file from a server, the roles are clearly defined. When a client requests a file from a NetWare server that is being accessed through a Windows 2000 Server via Gateway Services for NetWare, things become a bit fuzzy. Windows 2000 acts as a server to fulfill the client request while acting as a client to request the actual file from the NetWare server.

Most Windows computers play a dual role by running two services: Server service and Workstation service. When a workstation requests a file from a server, it uses its *Workstation service* to connect to the Server service of the host computer.

Configuring Network Interfaces

There are several things you need to be able to do as a Windows 2000 Network Adminstrator in relation to network interfaces. The following sections highlight some of the key activities for configuring network interfaces.

Adding and Removing LAN Adapters

Because Windows 2000 now supports Plug and Play, network adapters should be recognized automatically. If the adapter is not present, run the Add/Remove Hardware Wizard from Control Panel and add the network adapter just as you would any other piece of hardware.

? **Where Are Network Interface Settings Stored in the Registry?**
HKEY_LOCAL_MACHINE\SYSTEM\CurrentControlSet\Enum\
{ *PClorPCMCIAorISAPNPorUSB*}

Configuring Network Adapters

Device Manager can be used to configure adapters and update drivers like any other hardware. An alternate method of accessing this dialog box is as follows:

1 From the Start button, select Settings.

2 Network and Dial-up Connections.

3 Local Area Connection.

4 From the Local Area Connection Status dialog box, select the Properties botton.

5 Select the Configure button beneath the network adapter displayed at the top of the dialog box.

Adding and Removing WAN Adapters

Like other hardware, WAN adapters should be recognized automatically by Plug and Play. If the adapter is not present, run the Add/Remove Hardware Wizard from Control Panel and add the network adapter just as you would any other piece of hardware.

Configuring Dial-up Networking is easy. From the Start button, Settings, select Network and Dial-up Connections and Make New Connection. This will launch the Network Connection Wizard and allow you to select the type of connection desired.

The Network Connection Wizard will guide you through the process of configuring the following dial-up connections:

- **Dial-up to Private Network.** Guides you through creating a connection using your phone line via modem or ISDN device.

- **Dial-up to the Internet.**   This wizard guides you through connecting to the Internet by using your phone line via a modem or ISDN device.

- **Connect to a Private Network through the Internet.** Creates a Virtual Private Network (VPN) connection or "tunnel" through the Internet

- **Accept Incoming Connections.** Configures your computer to allow others to connect via phone line, the Internet, or direct cable.

- **Connect Directly to Another Computer.** Connects your computer to another by using serial, parallel, or infrared port.

For Network Interface Statistics and Quick Access To Network Settings

You can add your Network LAN adapter to the system tray. This will allow you to easily monitor the device statistics of the adapter, both Sent and Received bytes.

From the Start button, Settings, select Network and Dial-up Connections and Local Area Connection. From the Local Area Connection Status dialog box, select the Properties botton.

You will see an option at the bottom: Show Icon in Taskbar when Connected.This will place an icon in the System Tray when the adapter connects to the network.

By hovering your mouse over the tray icon, you can quickly view the status of your Network Adapter. Double-clicking the tray icon will launch a window to display this information. You select the Properties button from here to modify the network setting for this adapter.

Configuring Network Protocols

Adding and removing network protocols is a fairly simple process:

1   From the Start button, select Settings, Network and Dial-up Connections, and then Local Area Connections.

2   From the Local Area Connection Status dialog box, select the Properties botton.

3   Click on the Install button, highlight Protocol from the selection box, and click the Add button.

4   The Select Network Protocol dialog box displays a list of available protocols, or you can load custom protocols from the Have Disk button.

5   To remove a protocol, simply highlight the protocol to be removed from the Local Area Connection Properties dialog box and click on Uninstall.

Uninstalling and Removing Protocols

Although installing a protocol does not require a server restart, uninstalling a protocol does. It may be more effective to simply unbind the protocol from the adapter, which does not require a restart. You can remove it later when the server can be restarted without impacting client connections.

As a safety precaution, if all protocols are about to be removed, Windows will display a warning box and allow you to respecify protocol selections. Removing all protocols would render the system unable to communicate on the network.

Configuring TCP/IP—Client-Side Configuration (General TCP/IP Settings)

After a protocol is added to the system, it must be configured for addressing and bound to a network interface and a network service such as the Server or Workstation service. TCP/IP configuration is divided into two sections in Windows 2000: General and Advanced.

To configure a server for basic network connectivity using TCP/IP, the following tasks must be accomplished:

- **IP Address.** From the Local Area Connection Properties dialog box (see previous section on how to get there), highlight Internet Protocol (TCP/IP) and click on the Properties button. If this server will get its IP configuration information from DHCP either dynamically or by reservation, select the Obtain an IP address Automatically radio button at the top of the dialog box.

  ▶ *For more information about DHCP, see Chapter 8.2, "Dynamic Host Configuration Protocol (DHCP)."*

  If this server will have a manually entered static IP address, select Use the Following IP Address button and supply the IP address for this interface.

- **Subnet mask.** The subnet mask allows Windows to determine the network and host addresses from the IP address. If the subnet mask is incorrect, the IP address will not work for your network.

  If you have selected Obtain an IP Address Automatically, this option will be unavailable. The DHCP server will assign a subnet mask along with the IP address. If the IP address is manually entered, the subnet mask will need to be manually entered as well.

- **Default Gateway.** The Default Gateway option may also be delivered to the server via DHCP if you have selected Obtain an IP Address Automatically. If you have manually entered an IP address for this interface, you may need to configure ther IP address of the default gateway.

If configuring manually, enter the IP address of the router interface that connects the local network to external networks such as the internet. This entry may be left blank if the server is on a small non-routed network (there are no routers on the LAN).

▸ *For more information about IP Routing, see Chapter 8.6, "IP Routing."*

- **DNS.** If the server uses DHCP for IP addressing, the Obtain DNS Server Addess Automatically radio button will be available. In DHCP mode there is still the option to use static DNS server entries.

  If the server uses a statically entered IP address, DNS server addresses must also be manually entered by typing in the appropriate addresse for at least one Domain Name Service server. Windows 2000 uses DNS for host name resolution and services.

  ▸ *For more information about DNS, see Chapter 8.3, "Domain Name System (DNS)."*

Configuring TCP/IP—Client-Side Configuration (Advanced TCP/IP Settings)

For advanced TCP/IP settings, such as adding additional IP addresses or configuring IP security, select the Advanced button from the Internet Protocol (TCP/IP) Properties General tab. Then you will need to change certain fields as follows:

- **IP Settings.** The IP Addresses section is used to configure multiple IP addresses for the network interface in a static IP environment. (If the server is DHCP-enabled, the IP Address section will indicate DHCP Enabled). If the server is not using DHCP, the current IP address will be listed in the box and additional IP addresses may be added, edited, or removed. This will allow the server to exist on multiple logical networks simultaneously.

- **Default Gateway.** Additional default gateways may be assigned, edited, or removed and an administrative cost (Metric) may be assigned to each. If there are multiple paths to a destination, a packet will be sent to the interface with the lowest cost or Metric.

- **DNS.** Additional DNS servers beyond the two from the General tab may be entered, edited, or removed from the DNS Server Addresses section. DNS servers will be used based on their order on the list—highest first.

  The remainder of the DNS tab establishes the DNS suffix settings for this connection. The server may be configured with primary and connection-specific DNS suffixes such as the Servers Domain and Parent Domains. Alternately, the server may be configured with custom DNS suffixes and the order of application can be set.

Windows 2000 has the capability to maintain Dynamic DNS entries. By checking the Register This Connection's Addresses in DNS check box, the server will register its DNS name and IP address at startup. The server's suffixes may also be registered in DNS by checking the Use this Connection's DNS Suffix in the DNS Registration box.

- **WINS/LMHOSTS Netbios Name Resolution.** Windows Internet Name Service (WINS) is used for netbios name resolution. WINS server addresses may be added, edited, or removed from the WINS tab. WINS servers will be used based on their order on the list (up to 12), highest first.

  LanManager Hosts (LMHOSTS) files may be used to resolve netbios names, based on a text file mapping of names to IP addresses. Check the Enable LMHOSTS lookup box to enable the use of LMHOSTS. By clicking the Import LMHOSTS button, you may browse for files outside of the default LMHOSTS location of <systemroot>\system32\drivers\etc\.

  The Enable\Disable NetBIOS over TCP/IP (NetBT) radio buttons determine whether this connection will communicate with older legacy versions of Windows or legacy applications that require WINS or NetBT. If this connection will only communicate with other Windows 2000 computers; TCP/IP-based, non-Windows computers; or Internet hosts using DNS-aware applications, NetBT may be disabled.

  This option may also be set via DHCP automatic configuration.

  ▶ *For more information about WINS, see Chapter 8.4, "Windows Internet Name Service (WINS)."*

- **Options—IP Security.** The Optional IP Security settings allow for granular security concerning IP packets transmitted between two IP hosts on a network and apply to all connections on the server bound to TCP/IP.

  Display the IP Security dialog box by highlighting IP Security from the Options tab and clicking the Properties button. By default, IP security (IPSec) is disabled for the server. When you enable IPSec, you must choose from the three levels of security, as follows:

- **Client (Response Only).** This setting leaves the Server Service settings unsecured, but allows the Client (Workstation) Service to negotiate with secure servers that require IPSEC for communication.

- **Secure Server (Require Security).** This setting will require Kerberos trust for all IP traffic. Unsecured communication with clients is not allowed.

- **Server (Request Security).** This setting will allow unsecured communication with clients, but will always request security using Kerberos trust for all IP traffic.

- **Options—TCP/IP Filtering.** By default, all TCP/IP traffic is permitted. Using the TCP/IP Filtering dialog box, an administrator has the ability to filter traffic on a granular level, based on protocol and port address. When Permit Only is selected for a particular protocol such as TCP, only the port numbers added to the TCP Ports list are allowed to enter the interface. For example, if port number 80 were added and no others, the server would not accept any packet except default HTTP packets.

  Display the TCP/IP Filtering dialog box by highlighting TCP/IP Filtering from the Options tab and clicking on the Properties button.

  Check the Enable TCP/IP Filtering (All Adapters) box to enable filtering.

  It can be a time-consuming chore to find every port that a server needs for communication. Incorrectly entered information can cripple network communications with the server.

? **Where Are Network Protocol Settings Stored in the Registry?**
HKEY_LOCAL_MACHINE\SYSTEM\CurrentControlSet\Services\{Tcpip \Apple Talk \Nwlnklpx \Nbf }\Parameters\Interfaces (or Adapters)

The Windows 2000 TCP/IP implementation is largely self-tuning. Microsoft has added the following enhancements to increase performance and flexibility:

- Protocol Stack tuning, including increased default window sizes
- TCP scalable window sizes
- Selective Acknowledgments
- TCP Fast Retransmit
  ▶ *For detailed information on TCP/IP registry settings and modifications, see "TCP/IP Implementation Details for Windows 2000" at* http://www.microsoft.com.

Adjusting registry parameters may adversely affect system performance.

Configuring NWLink

NetWare Link Protocol (NWLink) is an IPX/SPX-compatible transport protocol used to communicate with legacy NetWare networks (prior to NetWare 5.0) or legacy Windows computers that also use NWLink.

NWLink can be added by clicking on the Install button in the Local Area Connection Properties dialog box (see previous section for help getting there). NWLink requires no configuration except for the following situations:

- Running File and Print Services for Netware (FPNW).
- Operating as an NWLink router.
- Running an application that requires the server to generate SAP (Service Advertising Protocol) packets.

If one or more of these situations occurs, the properties of NWLink IPX/SPX will have to be configured. The Internal Network Number is an eight-character hexadecimal value that uniquely identifies a server on an IPX network. No two servers may have the same Internal Network Number.

Frame types are methods of data encapsulation for transport across a network or internetwork. The most common frame types used are Ethernet 802.2 and Ethernet 802.3.

Novell Standards

Novell standardized on 802.3 as its default frame type through NetWare version 3.11. NetWare 3.12 through 4.11 changed to 802.2 and NetWare 5.0 uses TCP/IP by default.

All computers that need to communicate with one another using IPX/SPX or NWLink must be configured with matching frame types. Although multiple frame types can exist on the same physical segment, computers using differing frame types cannot communicate. Frame types are identified on a physical segment using (External) Network Numbers that consist of eight-digit hexadecimal values. so a single segment of cable may have multiple logical IPX networks:

Frame type 802.2—a network of 10002000.

Frame type 802.3—a network of 10003000.

Host addresses are represented by the network interface's MAC address and do not need to be configured.

Microsoft's implementation of IPX/SPX NWLink helps to alleviate some of the administrative overhead of configuring network addresses by implementing Auto Frame Typing. When the NWLink protocol stack initializes, Windows attempts to determine the frame type and network address currently in use on the segment. From the NWLink Properties dialog box, frame type and external network numbers can be statically specified. Click the Add button and select the Frame Type, and then supply the hexidecimal value in the Network Number box. Multiple frame types may be defined for each interface.

Adding NetBEUI to Your Configuration

NetBIOS Extended User Interface (NetBEUI) is a broadcast-based, non-routable protocol that requires no configuration. NetBEUI can be added by executing the following steps:

1 Select the Install button from the Local Area Connection Properties dialog box.

2 Select Protocol from the list and click the Add button.

3 Select NetBEUI and click OK.

Configuring AppleTalk and AppleTalk Routing

If your Windows 2000 server will be connected to an AppleTalk network to support Macintosh computers, you will need to add and configure the AppleTalk Protocol by executing the following steps:

1 Select the Install button from Local Area Connection Properties dialog box.

2 Select Protocol from the list and click the Add button.

3 Select AppleTalk and click OK.

4 From the Local Area Connection Properties dialog box, select the Properties of AppleTalk Protocol and select the Zone your server will reside in from the pull-down list.

Windows 2000 can also function as an AppleTalk Router. Use the following steps to enable and configure AppleTalk routing:

1 Start the Routing and Remote Access application from Administrative Tools after installing the AppleTalk protocol.

2 Right-click AppleTalk Routing from the list of protocols beneath the target server and select Enable AppleTalk Routing.

3 In the right pane, double-click on the connection you want to configure routing on.

4 If this server will be a seed router, check the box labeled Enable seed routing on this network. (An AppleTalk seed router propogates the AppleTalk routing table to the rest of the network. A seed router must be running on the network prior to starting a non-seed router.)

5 Fill in the appropriate Network Address or Network Range and specify the Default Zone. You may click on the Get Zones button to obtain a list of Zones from other AppleTalk routers on your segment.

6 Click OK to save your changes and exit.

Configuring Network Services

There are different flavors of Client and Server services available for Windows. If your computer wants to talk to a Microsoft server, you need a Microsoft Client (Workstation service). If your Windows 2000 Server wants to print to a NetWare server's printer, it will have to have a NetWare Workstation service (Gateway and Client services for NetWare).

Microsoft servers speak a different language from NetWare servers. Although they both have TCP/IP installed, they use different core protocols. When a client needs a file from a server, the client has to formulate a core protocol request that the server will understand. Windows 2000 uses SMBs (Server Message Blocks) as its core protocol. So in this example, the client forms an SMB request for a file, packages the SMB request inside of a transport protocol such as IP for delivery across the network, and sends the request out of the appropriate network interface. When the server receives the IP packet, it opens it up, extracts the SMB request and passes it to the server service for fulfillment.

NetWare's NCP

NetWare's equivelent to SMB is called NetWare Core Protocol, or NCP. If you wish to connect to a NetWare server for file and print services, you will have to load an NCP-based Workstation service such as Gateway and Client services for NetWare.

Table 2.4.1 lists the services:

Table 2.4.1   Windows 2000 Client and Network Services

Service	Description
Client for Microsoft Networks	Workstation service used to access Microsoft Server services using SMB core protocol.
Gateway and Client Services for NetWare (GSNW)	Workstation service used to access Novell NetWare Servers services using NetWare Core Protocol (NCP).
File and Printer Sharing for Microsoft Networks	Server service for Microsoft operating systems. Responds to clients requesting services using SMB core protocol.
File and Print Services for NetWare (FPNW)	Server service for Windows Servers. Responds to clients requesting services using NCP core protocol. (Microsoft Server allows NetWare clients to access file and print services).
Telnet Service	Server service for hosting Telnet connections.
SAP Agent	Server service that allows Windows to broadcast service availability to NetWare clients (installed by default with FPNW).

Adding/Removing Services

Adding and removing Client and Server services is accomplished with the same sequence of events as adding protocols. From the Local Area Connection Properties dialog box, click the Install button, select either Client or Service, and select the option you wish to install.

Clients, Services, and Protocols can be enabled or disabled for an interface by checking or unchecking the box next to the options in the Local Area Connection Properties dialog box.

Starting/Stopping Services

If you're a mouse person, services can be stopped or started from Administrative Tools, Services. Select the service you wish to stop or start, and click the approptiate button on the toolbar.

From the command line (or batch file/script), services can be stopped or started with the NET command. For example, NET STOP "WORKSTATION" would stop the Workstation Service and render the computer incapable of making a network connection to a server.

?   **How Do I Know the Name of a Specific Service?**

If you do not know the name of a specific service, currently running services can be listed by typing **NET START**. Quotation marks are necessary only when starting or stopping a service with a space in its name. For example, **NET STOP** "World Wide Web Publishing Services."

▶ *For more information on the NET command, see "Configuring Network Bindings" later in this chapter.*

Change Computer Name

If you need to change a computer name, execute the following steps:

1 For a Stand Alone or Member Server, select the System icon from Control Panel.

2 Click on the Network Identification tab and select the Properties button.

3 Type in the new computer name and click OK. You will be prompted to reboot before the changes will take effect.

If the server is a Domain Controller, you will be unable to change its name. You will have to run DCPromo and demote it to a Member or Stand Alone Server before you can rename the system.

▶ *For more information on Domain Controllers, see Chapter 4.3, "Configuring a Domain Controller."*

Change the Domain or Workgroup Name

The process for changing the Workgroup name is the same as changing the computer name. If you wish to change the Domain of a Member Server, the Server will have to have an account in the Domain you wish to join.

Telnet

The Windows 2000 Telnet Server allows a Telnet client to log on and run character-mode applications. By default, when a Telnet client connects to a Windows 2000 server, the client is left at a command shell at on the root of the Server's boot partition.

You can monitor and terminate Telnet sessions and configure default Telnet services settings with Tlntadmn.exe. The Telnet Administration program is a menu-driver command shell program.

The Telnet client that ships with Windows 2000 is slightly different from previous Windows Telnet applications. The Windows 2000 version is command-line, not GUI. The new client does however, have NTLM authentication capability. Both the Telnet Server service and Client service have command-line configuration settings for NTLM authentication.

There are several ways to configure NTLM Authentication for Telnet. You can use NTLM by using the set command from Telnet client by executing the following steps:

1 From a command shell, run telnet.exe.
2 Type **set ntlm**.
3 Type **open** to open a new session.

You can use the Telnet Administation program to set the NTLM authentication by executing the following steps:

1 From a command shell, run tlntadmn.exe.
2 Select option 3 to change the registry settings.
3 Select option 7 to configure the number of NTLM connections.
4 Type **Y** to confirm that you want to change this setting.
5 Enter the value that you want to change NTLM for (see value descriptions following).
6 Type **Y** to confirm your selection.
7 Exit, stop, and restart the Telnet service.

Possible values for Telnet NTLM Authentication are listed in Table 2.4.2:

Table 2.4.2   Telnet NTLM Authentication

0	NTLM not available. The Telnet server does only clear text authentication.
1	NTLM or logon prompt where NTLM is tried before the logon prompt. If the client supports NTLM but authentication fails, the server will then send the logon prompt. If the client does not support NTLM, the server sends the logon prompt.
2	NTLM Authentication only. Legacy Windows Telnet client will fail to connect.

Configuring Network Bindings

The three core components of network communication (network interfaces, network protocols, and network services) all work together to provide communication and resource delivery. The interaction between the three components can be configured and optimized for performance, availability, and even security.

By default, when you install a new network device, Windows establishes all bindings for all installed services and protocols. In Figure 2.4.1, the default bindings have been modified to prevent the Workstation service from using the NWLink protocol. Establishing all bindings by default allows the highest level of connectivity, but may not be the most efficient use of resources.

In Figure 2.4.1, NetBEUI has been unbound from all services and interfaces—reducing resource usage and the number of services to be advertised.

From a security standpoint, if Network Card (0) were attached to the Internet and Card (1) to the private network, you could unbind TCP/IP from Card (1), preventing any IP traffic from entering the private network.

You can be very granular with network bindings, for example, allowing only IP traffic to the Server service on Card (1) and only NWLink traffic from the Workstation service on Card (0).

Bindings are also hierarchical. You can configure multiple bindings to be redundant with preference for one service or protocol over another. If 90 percent of the servers are IP-based and 10 percent are NWLink, you would prefer that the Workstation service attempts IP communication before attempting IPX.

To configure network bindings, you need to access the Advanced Settings dialog box, as follows:

1 Open the Network and Dial-up Connections window and select Advanced Settings from the Advanced menu.

2 The Adapters and Bindings tab allows you to enable, disable, or set the priority of interface, protocols, and services for local as well as remote connections. To disable a service or protocol, simply uncheck the box. Highlight a service or protocol and select the up/down arrows to change the binding order.

3 The Provider Order tab allows you to configure priority for client services (for example, default network provider).

Windows 2000 supports a wide range of command-line utilities (far too numerous to list here). If you run out of CLUs to play with in Windows 2000, don't worry; the Windows 2000 Resource Kit also comes armed for command-line bear.

Useful "NET" commands are displayed in Table 2.4.3. Each command must be preceded by the word NET. (Please note this is not a complete list.)

Table 2.4.3   Windows 2000 NET.EXE Configuration Commands

Command	What It Does
START	Starts a service. If used alone, displays running services.
STOP	Stops a service.
PAUSE	Pauses a running service.
CONTINUE	Un-pauses a paused service.
COMPUTER	Adds or removes a computer account from a Domain database.
CONFIG	Displays configuration information about Servers or Workstations.
ACCOUNTS	Configures Account Policy settings.
FILE	Closes a shared file and removes the lock. If used alone, displays open files.
GROUP	Adds or removes Global Groups from the Domain changes user membership in Global groups. Lists Global Groups.
LOCALGROUP	Same as previous, but for Local Groups on server.
SEND	Sends a text message to users, computers, or domains.
SESSION	Lists or deletes sessions between your server and other computers.
SHARE	Command line creates and configures network shares on server.
STATISTICS	Displays the statistics log for the Workstation or Server.

continues

Table 2.4.3   continued

Command	What It Does
TIME	Synchronizes the Server's clock with another computer or Domain.
USE	Connects to a network resource (for example, mapping a drive to a network share).
USER	Creates and modifies user accounts on a computer or Domain. When used alone, displays user accounts on computer or domain.
VIEW	Lists computers with shared resources in a Domain or network. When used with a computer name, lists shared resources on that computer.
HELP	Describes of all NET commands and syntax.

Troubleshooting Network Connectivity

When troubleshooting network connectivity problems, never overlook the obvious. Sometimes the simple answer is the correct one. Many hours can be spent troubleshooting technical networking issues, only to discover a faulty patch cable to the wall. Table 2.4.4 lists common symptoms and their resolutions.

Table 2.4.4   Network Connectivity Troubleshooting

Symptoms	Explanation/Resolution
Windows 2000 cannot see any NetWare servers.	IPX frame type may be incorrectly set (802.2 is default for 3.12 and higher).
Computers nearby can be accessed, but not computers in other parts of the building or network.	The default Gateway setting may be incorrectly configured.
I can access a server by its IP address, but not by its name.	DNS and/or WINS may be incorrectly configured or DNS/WINS servers are unavailable or misconfigured.
Windows 2000 is configured for DHCP and my IP address is 169.254.245.174 (255.255.0.0 mask).	No response from the DHCP server, or DHCP scope is out of addresses (previous versions of Windows NT would have 0.0.0.0 in this situation).

Symptoms	Explanation/Resolution
I cannot connect to a remote server.	Ping the remote server by its IP address.
	If it responds:
(Listed to the right are steps to effectively troubleshoot IP connectivity using the Ping.exe command line utility.)	Check your name resolution settings (DNS/WINS/HOSTS file/LMHOSTS file). DNS/WINS servers could be down or misconfigured.
	If it does not respond:
	Ping a different host on the remote network.
	If it responds:
	The original server may be unavailable or misconfigured.
	If it does not respond:
	Check your Default Gateway settings, IP address, and subnet mask. If they are correctly configured:
	Ping your Default Gateway IP address.
	If it responds:
	The router may not be routing. Ping the remote, or far side router interface of your Default Gateway.
	If it does not respond:
	The router may not be functioning: Ping a host on your local network or subnet.
	If it responds:
	The router may be down.
	If it does not respond:
	Ping the Loopback address (127.0.0.1)
	If it responds:
	Check your network cables, connectors, and link lights on the network interface card.
	If it does not respond:
	Remove and reinstall networking (local protocol stack or files may be corrupt).

2.5

The Boot Process

You Need To Read This Section If You Want To:

- Diagnose a server that will not start.
- Change the default OS in a multiboot environment.
- Increase the amount of time the boot menu is presented.
- Load Windows with a minimal set of drivers for testing.

Related Topics

The Normal Boot Process

The Windows 2000 boot process is a complex, configurable sequence of events that can be configured and optimized like any other part of the operating system. A clear understanding of the boot process is essential for server maintenance and troubleshooting.

In the Windows 2000 startup process, you can configure the following:

- You can configure the boot menu. You can change the menu that appears at startup, from which you select the operating system to start. You can change the text that appears, set options, choose versions of Windows 2000, and configure a dual boot with another operating system.

- You can configure the partition that your hardware uses to find an operating system.

- You can choose which device drivers and services load and in what order.

- You can use special options in the boot process to enable the repair or restoration of your system in case of problems.

- You can disable nonessential drivers or services to speed boot time.

Windows initialization is commonly divided into four distinct phases, as follows:

- **Boot phase.** Begins when NTLDR initializes and presents the boot menu. It ends with the initialization of Ntoskrnl.exe or the selection of an alternate OS from the boot menu. Ntdetect.com scans the system hardware and returns the results to NTLDR.

- **Kernel phase.** Begins when Ntoskrnl.exe takes control. Lower-level drivers are loaded and NTLDR populates the HARDWARE key of HKEY_LOCAL_MACHINE with the results of the hardware scan completed by Ntdetect.com in the Boot phase.

- **Services phase.** Loads higher-order services and subsystems, including the memory manager. The paging file is created and all drives are autochecked.

- **Logon phase.** Includes starting Winlogon.exe, the Local Security Authority subsystem (Lsass.exe), and Microsoft Graphical Identification and Authentication modules (Msgina.dll). The Last Known Good Configuration is written to disk when the user authenticates, acknowledging that this was a good system start.

Boot Phase

Following the hardware vendor's Power On Self Test (POST) of the server, the Master Boot Record is loaded into memory. The MBR scans the Partition Boot Record table to locate the active or *boot partition*.

After the boot sector of the active partition is loaded (the partition marked as active is the one that Windows starts from), NTLDR is initialized.

NTLDR is the first step in the Windows 2000 boot sequence. NTLDR switches the microprocessor from Real mode into 32-bit mode and starts the appropriate minifile system drivers. These drivers, built into NTLDR, allow Windows to access FAT, FAT32, and NTFS file systems.

NTLDR locates the boot.ini file on the active partition and creates the Boot Loader Operating System Selection menu from the contents of the boot.ini file.

NTLDR's final responsibility is to initialize and hand over control to whichever operating system is selected from the boot menu. If no selection is made, the default operating system is loaded after the timer has elapsed (30 seconds by default).

Windows 2000 May Still Start If the boot.ini Is Missing

If NTLDR is unable to locate a boot.ini file on the boot partition, it will attempt to load Windows from the default installation location: WINNT directory on the first partition of the first physical disk of the first controller "multi(0)disk(0)rdisk(0)partition(1)\WINNT". If Ntoskrnl.exe cannot be located at this location, the boot will fail.

As long as your BIOS can handle it, Windows 2000 doesn't have a size limit on the boot drive.

If an operating system other than Windows 2000 is selected, the bootsect.dos is loaded and control is handed over to the operating system—Windows 98, for instance. This ends the Windows 2000 boot sequence.

Bootsect.dos is the boot sector of an operating system wrapped in a file and stored on the *system partition*. Unless your server is dual-boot with another OS, this file will not be present.

If Windows 2000 is selected at the boot menu, NTLDR runs Ntdetect.com, which scans the hardware and returns the list of detected hardware to NTLDR for inclusion in the Registry under HKEY_LOCAL_MACHINE\HARDWARE.

NTLDR then loads Ntoskrnl.exe, HAL, and the SYSTEM hive of the Registry for drivers that are scheduled to load at boot time. Finally, NTLDR starts Ntoskrnl.exe and the Kernel phase begins.

Kernel Phase

The Kernel phase consists of two separate tasks: one responsible for driver loading and one for driver initialization. Typically, a boot failure will occur during the initialization phase.

- **Kernel load.** The Kernel phase begins when ntoskrnl.exe takes control. The hardware abstraction layer (HAL), which masks platform-specific hardware differences from Windows 2000, is loaded immediately after the Kernel. The Registry SYSTEM hive is loaded and scanned for drivers and services that are marked to be loaded at this stage. Drivers and services are processed in groups that are enumerated in the ServiceGroupOrder subkey of HKEY_LOCAL_MACHINE\ SYSTEM\CurrentControlSet\Control. This portion of the boot process is displayed for users as a progress bar across the bottom of the screen. The actual drivers and services can be displayed by adding **/SOS** to the appropriate OS line of boot.ini.

▶ *For more information, see "Troubleshooting the Boot Process" later in this chapter.*

- **Kernel initialization.** Drivers loaded during the load phase are initialized and the SYSTEM hive is once again scanned for high-level drivers that should be loaded. The CurrentControlSet and the Clone hives are created and initialized, but not saved. In the final stage of Kernel initialization, the hardware list compiled by Ntdetect.com is stored in the Registry under HKEY_LOCAL_MACHINE\HARDWARE.

Services Phase

Session Manager (Smss.exe) begins to load the higher-order services and subsystems, including memory management and subsystems. Session Manager executes the instructions listed in BootExecute under HKEY_LOCAL_MACHINE\SYSTEM\CurrentControlSet\Control\ Session Manager. The default entries include instructions to autocheck all drives and to initialize the DFS file system under Windows 2000 Server.

▶ *For more information on the Distributed File System, see "Hierarchical Storage Management" in Chapter 5.2, "File Systems and Disks."*

After the volumes have been checked, Session Manager scans the Registry for paging file information, creates the paging file(s), and writes the CurrentControlSet and Clone control set.

The final task of the Session Manager is to load the subsystems specified in HKEY_LOCAL_MACHINE\SYSTEM\CurrentControlSet\ Control\SubSystems\Session Manager\Required.

Windows 2000 Subsystem Initialization

By default, the only subsystem started by Session Manager is the Win32 subsystem (Csrss.exe). Other subsystems such as OS2 and POSIX do not load until a corresponding application is launched.

Logon Phase

When the Win32 subsystem initializes, Winlogon.exe is started, which in turn starts the Local Security Authority subsystem (Lsass.exe) and the Welcome to Windows dialog box (Press Ctrl+Alt+Del to begin). By providing a valid set of credentials, (user account and password), the individual logging onto the server is verifying that this was a good boot of the operating system. After the user's credentials are validated, the Clone control set is copied to the LastKnownGood control set and the boot is considered complete.

Understanding boot.ini

The purpose of the boot.ini file is to provide a list of operating systems and OS modifiers installed on the system, the location of the load files for those operating systems, and information about the default OS and how to start it.

Reasons to modify the boot.ini file include the following:

- To change the path to the operating system
- To change the boot menu descriptions
- To change the boot menu delay
- To add switches that modify the way Windows loads

The following is an example of a typical boot.ini file (not a dual boot system):

```
[boot loader]
timeout=30
default=multi(0)disk(0)rdisk(0)partition(1)\WINNT
[operating systems]
multi(0)disk(0)rdisk(0)partition(1)\WINNT="Windows 2000 Server"
multi(0)disk(0)rdisk(0)partition(1)\WINNT="Windows 2000 Server VGA Mode"
/BASEVIDEO
```

Information about boot.ini is organized as follows:

- **Boot loader.** Specifies which operating system to load after the boot delay has expired and how long the boot menu will be displayed before the default OS is loaded.

- **Operating systems.** Enumerates the available operating systems and load options that will be displayed on the boot menu and where the operating system resides. An example of multiple entries in this section could be a Windows 2000 and Windows 98 dual-boot computer. The information contained in quotation marks (*"Windows 2000 Server"*) is what will be displayed in the boot menu.

- **ARC paths.** Advanced RISC Computing paths are used to locate an operating system.

- **Switches for modifying the operating system line.** boot.ini supports multiple entries in the operating system section, which allow several configurations to be maintained (for example, the capability to start Windows with standard VGA (/BASEVIDEO) support instead of the currently configured video driver).

Default Section

The "default" line boot.ini represents one of the lines under *operating systems* preceded by *default=*. This is the operating system that will load if a selection is not made prior to the timeout value expiring (the default is 30 seconds).

ARC Paths

Each line in the boot.ini file represents a Windows installation or modified load of a Windows installation. If Windows is installed in the default location of \WINNT on the first partition of the first physical disk of the first controller (IDE or SCSI with BIOS-enabled controller), the line would appear as follows:

```
multi(0)disk(0)rdisk(0)partition(1)\WINNT
```

multi(x)

The *multi( )* designator indicates that Windows should rely on the system's INT13 BIOS calls to find and load Ntoskrnl.exe. The *multi( )* designator is used when the controller is either IDE or SCSI with the BIOS enabled for INT 13 calls.

signature(xxxxxxxx)

The signature keyword identifies the target drive by its Master Boot Record. Because of the Plug and Play capabilities of Windows 2000, the SCSI controller ordinal number may vary between boots or when adding hardware. The *signature( )* syntax is used if one of the following conditions exists:

- The partition where Windows 2000 is being installed is larger than 7.8 gigabytes (GB) or the ending cylinder is greater than 1024, and the system BIOS does not support INT13 extensions.

- The disk that Windows 2000 is being installed on is attached to a SCSI controller with the BIOS disabled and INT13 BIOS calls cannot be used during the boot process.

An example BOOT.INI line using signature() would appear as follows:

```
signature(35fd6da8)disk(0)rdisk(0)partition(1)\WINNT
```

Windows 2000 Kernel Located by Master Boot Record

When *signature( )* is used, NTLDR locates the target disk by the signature stored in its Master Boot Record (independent of the controller number). If the MBR is overwritten or corrupted by a virus, Windows will fail to start and indicate a disk hardware configuration error.

▶ *For more information on recovery, see "Troubleshooting the Boot Process" later in this chapter.*

disk(x)

If the ARC path starts with *signature( )*, the disk keyword designates the SCSI ID of the target disk. If the ARC path begins with *multi( )*, the disk is always 0 (zero) because *multi* invokes INT 13 BIOS calls, which do not require disk information.

rdisk(x)

If the ARC path starts with *signature( )*, the rdisk keyword designates the logical unit number (LUN) of the target disk, normally 0 (zero). If the ARC path begins with *multi( )*, rdisk is the ordinal number for the physical disk on the controller starting with 0 (zero).

partition(x)

Represents the ordinal partition number on the physical disk, starting with 1 instead of 0. All partitions on a disk receive partition numbers except for DOS extended partitions and unused partitions.

Be Careful When Adding Drives or Using Extended Partitions

If your server won't start after creating or deleting partitions, it is because primary partitions take precedence in the numbering scheme over logical partitions. Therefore, be careful when adding drives or using extended partitions.

Using a drive letter instead of an ARC path is not recommended, except for C: for multiboot environments where C: is the system partition. Drive letters can change based on the addition or removal of disks or disk controllers.

Plug and Play Support in Windows 2000 Requires a New Controller Designator for boot.ini

The use of the *signature( )* designator in the ARC naming path is new to Windows 2000. Previous versions of Windows NT used the *scsi( )* keyword to identify SCSI controllers with BIOS disabled, by their ordinal numbers. The first controller found during system startup is designated as 0 (zero). Because of the dynamic nature of Plug and Play, the ordinal numbering of SCSI controllers could change from one system boot to the next.

Non-x86-based computers such as the Alpha required the *scsi( )* keyword in the ARC path; however, there will be no future releases of Microsoft products for the 32-bit or 64-bit Alpha platform. For more information on Alpha platform development, see http://www.microsoft.com/NTServer/nts/news/msnw/compaq.asp.

Operating System Section

The Operating System section lists the available operating systems and load options that will be displayed on the boot menu. You can use multiple entries in this section to load the same operating system in several different configurations. The maximum number of lines the boot menu will display is ten (10).

Switches on Operating System Line

Table 2.5.1 defines the available switches used on the OS Line to modify the way Windows 2000 will load and gives an example of each.

Table 2.5.1   OS Switches

Optional Switch	Explanation	Example
MAXMEM	Limits Windows to the amount of memory specified.	/MAXMEM=16
BURNMEMORY	Forces Windows to discard the amount of memory you specify as unusable.	/BURNMEMORY =64
ONECPU	Forces Windows to enable only one CPU in a multiprocessor system.	/ONECPU
NUMPROC	Forces Windows to enable only the number of processors specified in a multiprocessor system.	/NUMPROC=2
SOS	Redirects drivers being loaded during boot to the video display.	/SOS
BASEVIDEO	Forces Windows to use standard VGA for GUI mode.	/BASEVIDEO
NODEBUG	Prevents the initialization of Kernel mode debugging.	/NODEBUG
CRASHDEBUG	Same as /NODEBUG.	/CRASHDEBUG

Optional Switch	Explanation	Example
DEBUG	Enables Kernel mode debugging.	/DEBUG
DEBUGPORT	Enables Kernel mode debugging and specifies the port to connect to. Defaults to COM1 if not specified. Is overridden by /NODEBUG.	/DEBUG /DEBUGPORT= COM2
BAUDRATE	Enables Kernel mode debugging and specifies the baud rate for COM port. Defaults to 19200 if not specified. Is overridden by /NODEBUG.	/DEBUG /BAUDRATE=115200
KERNEL	Forces NTLDR to override the default selection of NTOSKRNL. EXE for an alternate Kernel.	/KERNEL= ALTKRNL.EXE
HAL	Forces NTLDR to use the specified Hardware Abstraction Layer image (HAL).	/HAL=ALTHAL.DLL
3GB	Allows Enterprise, 3 GB-aware applications to take advantage of 3 GB of user address space, leaving 1 GB for system.	/3GB
PCILOCK	Prevents Windows from dynamically allocating I/O and IRQ resources to PCI devices —System BIOS settings will be used.	/PCILOCK

continues

Table 2.5.1   continued

Optional Switch	Explanation	Example
NOSERIALMICE	Prevents Windows from scanning specified COM ports for a serial mouse.	/NOSERIALMICE= COM1,2
SAFEBOOT	Specifies a limited set of drivers to load for troubleshooting a Windows failure.	/SAFEBOOT: MINIMAL /SAFEBOOT: NETWORK /SAFEBOOT: DSREPAIR
BOOTLOG	Enables text file logging of drivers loaded during boot: <systemroot>\ntbtlog. txt.	/BOOTLOG
FASTDETECT	Turns off Serial and Bus mouse detection in NTDETECT for the specified COM port. If no port is specified, all COM ports are skipped (this switch is used by default in Windows 2000).	/FASTDETECT =COMx
NOGUIBOOT	A command shell inside of Windows 2000 is loaded instead of Explorer.exe (can be accessed by selecting F8 at startup).	/SAFEBOOT: MINIMAL /NOGUIBOOT

Using Advanced Boot Options

There are several advance boot options, listed here:

- Last Known Good Configuration
- Safe Mode (Safe Mode with Networking, Safe Mode with Command Prompt)
- Recovery Console
- Emergency Repair

Last Known Good Configuration

Windows 2000 maintains the previous configuration Registry settings in the event that you are unable to boot the system after changing service or device settings. To do so, execute the following steps:

1 At the boot menu, press F8 for Troubleshooting and Advanced Startup Options for Windows 2000.

2 Select Last Known Good Configuration from the Advanced Options Menu.

3 Last Known Good Configuration will appear in blue at the bottom of the screen, indicating that the Last Known Good Configuration has been selected and you are prompted to select the OS from the boot menu.

4 If the system has multiple Hardware Profiles, you are prompted for which Profile to boot with.

5 Windows loads, using the Last Known Good Configuration.

? **How Does Windows Know What the Last Known Good Configuration Is?**

The Last Known Good Configuration is written to disk when you acknowledge the good system start by logging into Windows. If you are unsure about the current configuration, wait until the hard disk stops accessing and system activity has stopped after the Windows logon screen appears. It is possible to log in before all the higher-level services have started. If the system fails after you log in, you no longer have a Last Known Good Configuration.

Safe Mode

At the boot menu, press F8 for Troubleshooting and Advanced Startup Options for Windows 2000. Those options are explained in table 2.5.2.

Table 2.5.2   Summary of Advanced Boot Options

Advanced Boot Option	How You Can Use It
Safe Mode	A third-party driver halts the system after GUI mode and you need to get into Windows to remove it. /SAFEBOOT:MINIMAL/SOS /BOOTLOG /NOGUIBOOT
Safe Mode with Networking	Loads the minimal set of drivers needed to access the network. /SAFEBOOT:NETWORK /SOS /BOOTLOG /NOGUIBOOT
Safe Mode with Command Prompt	Loads a minimal set of drivers and starts up in a CMD shell. /SAFEBOOT:MINIMAL(ALTERNATESHELL) /SOS /BOOTLOG /NOGUIBOOT

continues

Table 2.5.2   continued

Advanced Boot Option	How You Can Use It
Enable Boot Logging	Used to create a text log of drivers and services loaded during startup. /BOOTLOG
Enable VGA Mode	Used when you have added a new video card and need to get into Windows to update the display drivers. /BASEVIDEO
Last Known Good Configuration	Used if you have updated hardware drivers and the system will not start.
Directory Services Restore Mode	Used if Directory Services have become corrupt and you need to repair them in order to be authenticated. **ONLY FOR SERVERS WITH DIRECTORY SERVICES INSTALLED** /SAFEBOOT:DSREPAIR /SOS
Debugging Mode	Used if you need to enable debugging mode. /DEBUG
Boot Normally	Will boot using the default selection as specified in the boot.ini.
Return to OS Choices Menu	Will return you to the previous boot menu.
Recovery Console	Used if Windows will not start and you need access to the NTFS C: drive. (Recovery option is displayed on the boot menu, not the advanced menu.)

Recovery Console

Consider this possible situation. You are an administrator of a network, and you get a phone call that goes something like this:

"I managed to make my system unbootable by renaming ntdll.dll (trying to replace it to do some help checking). Unfortunately for me, my system partition was NTFS and I can't edit it from DOS. Or can I?"

The answer is yes—you can with Recovery Console. Recovery Console is a new feature for Windows 2000. Under previous versions of Windows NT, system or boot partitions formatted with NTFS were inaccessible if Windows failed to start and mount the NTFS volumes.

Recovery Console allows you to access a limited number of files and commands from a command prompt console without starting Windows.

A corrupt file that was preventing Windows from starting can be replaced without entering GUI mode.

To install the Windows 2000 Emergency Recovery Console, use one of the methods described in the following sections.

Text Mode Setup

You should use this option when Windows 2000 is not running. Execute the following steps:

1   Start your computer by using the Windows 2000 Setup boot disks or the Windows 2000 bootable CD-ROM.

2   When you receive the Welcome to Setup screen, press F10. You may or may not be prompted to insert Setup boot disk 2.

3   The next screen will allow you to log on to the Recovery Console or, if multiple Windows 2000 installations exist, a choice of installation folders is displayed.

Graphical Mode Setup

Use this option when Windows 2000 is running. Execute the following steps:

1   Click Start, click Run, and then type **<CD-ROM drive letter>:\i386\winnt32.exe /cmdcons** in the Open box, where <CD-ROM drive letter> is the drive letter assigned to your CD-ROM drive.

2   Click OK, follow the instructions on the screen to finish Setup, and then restart your computer.

You will now have an additional Boot Menu Option: Windows 2000 Recovery Console.

? **What Files Can Be Accessed by Recovery Console?**

Recovery Console allows access only to a very limited amount of your files: specifically, your *systemroot* directory and the root of all drives. Recovery Console does work with all supported file systems. Physical server security is always important because a server is most vulnerable to local access. The Recovery Console can be accessed only locally (not across the network), reinforcing the need for physical server security.

Changing the Password for Recovery Console on Domain Controllers

When you install the Recovery Console on a DC, you are prompted to supply an Administrative password for Recovery Console. If you lose the password and need to access the Recovery Console, follow these steps.

1   Press F8 while displaying the boot menu.

2   Select Directory Service Restore Mode.

3 After you log on, go to a command prompt and type **net user administrator** *.This will prompt you for a new password.

4 If you are in a multiple DC environment, you could run dcpromo, demote it to a standalone server, and then re-promote it to be a DC again. This process will prompt you for a new Directory Service Restore Mode administrator password.

Emergency Repair

If the system partition has become corrupted or system files have been deleted from the boot or system partitions of Windows 2000, the Emergency Repair process can be used to repair the system. The Emergency Repair Disk is needed when the installation directory cannot be located by the repair process or the files in the repair directory have been corrupted.

To make an Emergency Repair Disk (ERD), follow these steps:

1 Click Start, Programs, Accessories, System Tools, Backup.

2 Click the Emergency Repair Disk button.

3 The Emergency Repair process is initiated by running Setup (the ERD is not a bootable diskette). Run Setup either from the Setup disks or by booting from the Windows 2000 CD-ROM.

Setup will prompt you to press Enter to continue with the Windows 2000 setup or press **R** to begin the Emergency Repair Process.

4 Press **R**.

Setup will prompt you to press **C** to repair the system using the Recovery Console or press **R** to repair using the Emergency Repair process.

5 Press **R** to begin the Emergency Repair process.

The repair process can be accomplished by selecting either Fast or Manual Repair. Fast Repair automates the process and does not require user intervention.

The Manual Repair Process displays a list of repair options, including the following:

- Inspect Startup Environment
- Verify Windows 2000 System Files
- Inspect Boot Sector

If you do not have your ERD disk, Setup can search the drive for any Windows 2000 installations.

Creating a Windows 2000 Boot Disk

Windows 2000 cannot boot from a diskette. The files required to start Windows will not fit on a single diskette. However, if the Windows installation directory is intact (C:\Winnt, for example), the Boot Phase can be initiated from diskette and pass control of the Kernel load to *systemroot*\system32\ntoskrnl.exe. The following situations are examples of when to use a Windows 2000 boot disk:

- When files on the system partition are damaged or missing
- When a mirrored system partition member has failed (boot.ini is incorrect)
- When the MBR or PBR is damaged from a virus or disk utility, for example
- When the boot.ini file contains incorrect information (adding or removing primary partitions has reordered the partition numbering scheme)

To create a Windows 2000 boot disk, complete the following steps:

1 Format a diskette on any Windows 2000 computer by typing **format a:/u** at the command prompt.

2 Copy the following files to the diskette from the system partition of the server:

- NTLDR (this file has no extension)
- Ntdetect.com
- Boot.ini (make sure the ARC path is correct for the OS you wish to boot)
- Ntbootdd.sys (this file is necessary only on systems where Windows 2000 is installed on a drive connected to a SCSI controller without INT13 BIOS support enabled or on computers with the *signature(xxxxxxx)* keyword beginning the ARC path in the boot.ini)
- Bootsect.dos (this file is necessary only on dual-boot systems (Win98 and Windows 2000)

Troubleshooting the Boot Process

Ways to repair a system that won't boot depend, of course, on why the system won't boot. This requires knowing the order in which files and settings are accessed during the boot process so you can discover what is working and what isn't.

Basically, you need to know at what point in the boot process the system fails.

Table 2.5.3 provides common boot process problems and how to resolve them.

Table 2.5.3   Troubleshooting Common Boot Process Problems

Problem	Possible Solutions
System fails before boot menu appears	Use Emergency Repair Process to repair the startup environment.
	Create Windows 2000 boot floppy disk (with the correct ARC path in the boot.ini).
	Run Windows 2000 Setup and perform an upgrade of the existing installation (be sure to reapply any Service Packs).
System fails after selecting OS with following error message: Bad or missing ntoskrnl.exe	ARC path in boot.ini is incorrect—edit boot.ini.
	Disk configuration has changed—edit boot.ini to point to correct partition.
	Repair system files—run Recovery Console and run sfc.
	Use Emergency Repair Process.
	Run Windows 2000 Setup.
System fails with STOP error after Kernel initialization but before GUI mode	Problem with Kernel mode driver: Use Last Known Good.
	Perform a safe boot, and remove or disable recently added drivers or services.
	Perform an Emergency Repair.
	Use Recovery Console to run sfc and/or disable faulty driver or service.
System fails with STOP error after GUI mode but before logging on	Problem with Kernel mode driver or service—use Last Known Good.
	Perform a safe boot, and remove or disable recently added drivers or services.
	Perform an Emergency Repair.
	Use Recovery Console to run sfc and/or disable faulty driver or service.
System starts but keyboard or mouse is inaccessible	Repair from remote system using regedt32.exe.
	Use Recovery Console.
	Use Emergency Repair.
	Start with /PCILOCK switch to prevent a possible resource conflict in Windows 2000.
	Use Last Known Good if you were editing the Registry prior to the last reboot.

2.6
The Registry

You Need to Read This Section If You Want to:

- Have a general overview of the Registry—its purpose and power.
- Be familiar with the tools to manage Registry changes and reference information.
- Troubleshoot and/or repair Registry-related problems.

Related Topics

Introduction to the Registry

Basically, the Registry is the heart of the Windows 2000 operating system. The concept is a central repository and source for the operating system's authority. It is a set of files initially installed and configured on installation of Windows 2000. The methods and by whom the files are changed are protected and strictly controlled through the Registry editors. The Registry provides for stability of the operating system and predictability in the way it behaves and who uses it.

The Registry can be described in the following ways:

- **Dynamic.** The Registry is designed for a great deal of real-time flexibility to accommodate the needs and concerns of users and administrators. For instance, the Windows Desktop is the interface where and how most of the work gets done. Changed settings may be written (saved) to the Registry as a user logs out so the users know right where everything is on subsequent logins. They can then get right to work and not lose time and effort getting reacquainted with their desktop. From a user's point of view, the appearance of the desktop—organization, resolution, colors, sound, and behavior—can greatly impact their productivity at their workstation. All of these may be adjusted for optimal effectiveness during a user's login or be configured to change at login as one user logs out and another logs in. They can be tied to a user's SID and the nature of the Access Token given a user at login.

  HKEY_CURRENT_USER\Control Panel\Desktop\WindowMetrics dictates the appearance of the desktop on login and is unique to that user.

- **Hierarchical.** The Registry is hierarchical in two ways. Its hierarchy affects the way some tasks may have priority over or dependency on other services or devices. Specific portions of the Registry control the sequence of machine activity after the hardware BIOS and ROM boot allows Windows 2000 to initialize, start, and configure drivers; provide security; start services and devices; fully boot; and allow a user to login and access their home directory and applications.

  The Registry's actual structure is hierarchical as well. The major portion of the Registry is divided into structures called *subtrees*, and they are subsequently organized into *keys>subkeys>key values*. A specific description is provided in this chapter in a discussion of the organization.

- **Secure.** The Registry has its own security built into it, so it is protected from destructive, unwanted, innocent, and malicious intrusions.

Organization of the Registry

It's difficult to discuss the various portions of the Registry without first referencing the Registry editors. These tools allow the contents of the Registry to be viewed and administered. There are two that are provided by the operating system: *systemroot*\system32\regedt32.exe and *systemroot*\regedit.exe. Although they still access the same data, they provide different tools and methods to administer the Registry. Regedt32.exe is reminiscent of the winfile.exe (File Manager) GUI in appearance, whereas regedit.exe provides a more browser (Windows Explorer) feel.

Similarities End with Subtree Titles

Note that the titles of the various subtree windows in the regedt32.exe GUI have corresponding subtree folders in regedit.exe. The similarity of the Registry editors to various degrees end there, as evidenced by the verb-menus found in the menu bar.

Subtrees

There are five main subtrees, sometimes referred to as hives. Subtrees are the way the Registry is structured. Hives are more specifically the actual files that serve to store the information found in the subtrees. (The names and locations of the files are discussed later in this chapter in the discussion of the Registry physical storage.) The subtrees and their descriptions are as follows:

- **HKEY_CLASSES_ROOT.** Here, file extensions are registered and associated with various functions and applications. When changes (File Associations) are made in the FolderOptions>FileType applet or RightMouseClick>OpenWith, they are written here. OLE and COM functionality also find support under this key. The data is also represented in HKEY_LOCAL_MACHINE\SOFTWARE\Classes, and are linked.

Greater Customization and Security Available

Unlike NT, Windows 2000 allows for user-specific file associations as well as global associations. This provides for a greater degree of customization for the user and security for the administrator.

- **HKEY_CURRENT_USER.** This information is specific for the user currently logged in. It is associated with the user's SID and linked to HKEY_USERS\(SID). An example is the subkey HKEY_CURRENT_USER\ControlPanel\Desktop\WindowMetrics. This subkey gives the customized look and behavior of the user's desktop during their login. This data is linked to HKEY_USERS\(SID)\ControlPanel\Desktop\WindowMetrics\.

- **HKEY_LOCAL_MACHINE.** This subtree provides the authority for several functions: hardware configurations and how the various services' and devices' startup and shutdown states are maintained. NTDETECT.COM plays a significant role in how the hardware configurations are set here. As reviewed under HKEY_CLASSES_ROOT, file extensions are registered here. The Security Accounts Manager (SAM) and security policies are maintained here. Applications installed will often use this subtree to control their behavior and interaction with the OS and file system structures.

- **HKEY_USERS.** As reviewed under HKEY_CURRENT_USER, this is where the environment for various users may be directly manipulated. Each user will have an entry according to the user's SID. For Domain Controllers, Domain Accounts, and Servers, some user-specific information is stored on the local machine that the Domain User logs onto rather than on the Domain Controller.

- **HKEY_CURRENT_CONFIG.** This subtree is directly linked to subkeys in HKEY_LOCAL_MACHINE\ HKEY_LOCAL_MACHINE\ SYSTEM\CurrentControlSet\Hardware Profiles\Current. Displayed here is hardware-specific information used on startup to support the operating system's hardware dependencies.

Data Types of Values

Please note the association of key and subkey values. The value selected and the Registry editor used will dictate how the value may be viewed and edited. Each value type has its own specific editor and viewer. The value may be displayed in ASCII, binary, decimal, hex, or a combination of them, depending on the value type. A double-click on the value will open an editor or viewer for that value. The following is a description of the value types and their properties:

- **REG_BINARY.** This is usually hardware-specific data that is stored in hexadecimal format, as viewed from the regedt32.exe. By default, it will be displayed in hex, but the editor may use a binary or hex display. With regedit.exe, only the hex display is available with any relevant ASCII data.

- **REG_DWORD.** This is usually service- or device-related data. A numerical value, 4 four bytes long, which is viewed as hex data but may be edited as binary, decimal, or hex. Again, regedit.exe does not provide a binary format editor.

- **REG_DWORD_BIG_ENDIAN.** This data is stored as a 32-bit value. The data is represented weighted with the highest ordered byte first.

- **REG_SZ.** This is a terminated fixed-length text (Unicode) string. These and other SZ data types are given String editors with both Registry editors to administer the values.

- **REG_MULTI_SZ.** Multiple listings of data represented by text, whose values may be separated by spaces, commas, or other delimiters.
- **REG_EXPAND_SZ.** This is a data string whose data length may change. An example is the folder path to a file or directory for application and environmental variable support.
- **REG_LINK.** This is linked data stored in Unicode format.
- **REG_FULL_RESOURCE_DESCRIPTOR.** When viewed, this gives information such as hardware DMA, IRQ, and Memory Address Length. Data is displayed in hex and may be edited using byte, word, or dword format.
- **REG_RESOURCE_LIST.** regedt32.exe displays basic type hardware resources—interface type and bus number. May be expanded to display REG_FULL_RESOURCE_DESCRIPTOR. Regedit.exe gives only a binary editor with hex representation of the data, without regard to specific application of the data.
- **REG_NONE.** When values are not given as to data type by an application, or the data is encrypted so that Windows 2000 is unable to determine the value type.

Registry Security

The regedt32.exe editor is the only one of the two Registry editors that allows direct manipulation of security settings to specific subtrees, keys, sub-keys, and subsequent values. However, these security settings are honored by regedit.exe. These security settings are much like the security that may be imposed on an NTFS resource. By selecting the Security | Permissions tool in the menu bar, you may grant or deny access to a tree or value by user, group, or computer.

Registry Physical Storage

There are two main topics discussed here: the physical storage of the Registry hives and repair information.

Hives Storage

There are a total of 12 files that make up the Registry hives. Table 2.6.1 lists the default locations, names, and respective hives.

Table 2.6.1　Registry Hive Locations

Registry Hive	Filename	Location
HKEY_LOCAL_ MACHINE\SAM	Sam and Sam.log	*systemroot*\System32\Config
HKEY_LOCAL_ MACHINE\SECURITY	Security and Security.log	*systemroot*\System32\Config
HKEY_LOCAL_ MACHINE\SOFTWARE	Software and Software.log	*systemroot*\System32\Config
HKEY_LOCAL_ MACHINE\SYSTEM	System and System.log	*systemroot*\System32\Config
HKEY_CURRENT_ CONFIG	System and System.log	*systemroot*\System32\Config
HKEY_USERS\ DEFAULT	Default and Default.log	*systemroot*\System32\Config
HKEY_CURRENT_ USER	Ntuser.dat Ntuser.log	If install is fresh: *SystemDrive*:\Documents and Settings*Username*\ If install is upgrade from Windows 95 or 98: *SystemDrive*:\Documents and Settings*Username*\ If install is upgrade from Windows NT: *systemroot* \Profiles*Username*\

Repair Information Storage

When you create an Emergency Repair Disk (ERD) and the Option to Backup Registry is selected, a copy of the Registry files are copied to the %system%\Repair\ folder.

? **What Are the Files Ending in .sav In the \winnt\system32\config Directory?**

These are copies of the Registry keys that are created when you upgrade or restore the Registry using regrest.exe. regrest.exe is a tool provided by the Resource Kit.

Using the Registry Editor

As stated earlier, the Registry editors must be used with respect and full knowledge of what can happen if the Registry is changed. The Registry editors *do not* check for syntax or other typographical errors. The Registry is not self-healing if a problem results. To a degree, there are ways of overcoming and repairing incorrectly configured Registry entries, but the best prevention is simply—don't.

That is easier said than done, and it is sometimes unavoidable. Basically, there is no guarantee for a healthy system on reboot. It seems redundant to keep harping on this, but it is so very critical to document the changes as well as possible. Above all else, keep a good, current backup!

▶ *For more information, see Chapter 5.7, "Protecting Data."*

Overview

There are two tools that directly edit the Registry. The following is a description of the characteristics of each and the tools (commands) provided with each.

regedt32.exe Menu Commands

regedt32.exe provides the following menus: Registry, Edit, Tree, View, Security, Options, Window, and Help. They are discussed in the following sections.

Registry Menu

- **OpenLocal.** Opens local Registry. If the subtrees are already open, a second instance of them will open.
- **Close.** Will close the active subtree. If a remote computer's Registry is open, both subtrees will be closed (see Registry>Select Computer).
- **Load/Unload Hive.** Only applicable to HKEY_LOCAL_MACHINE and HKEY_USERS. Load will add a key entry if the subtree is active. It will install it directly under the subtree. Unload Hive will *remove* the active key. Be careful!
- **Restore.** Will restore a key created using the Save Key tool to an arbitrary key name.
- **Save Key.** Saves the data of a key in its binary format to an arbitrary filename.
- **Select Computer.** Allows you to open the Registry of a remote computer. You will be given the HKEY_LOCAL_MACHINE and HKEY_USERS subtrees of that computer, provided you have permissions to do so. This is a big security risk. Please be sure your Security>Permissions for untrusted accounts from another computer cannot intrude and sabotage your system across the net.
- **Print Subtree.** Prints an ASCII representation of the Registry.
- **Printer Setup.** Allows the adjustment of the selected printer properties.
- **Save Subtree As.** Saves data in ASCII format. For the sake of convenience, provide a .txt extension when naming the output file so that it will be associated with Notepad by default. Here is a truncated example of an output:

```
Key Name:        SOFTWARE\INTEL\ActiveMovie Filters\{14099BC3-787B-
                 ➥11d0-9CD3-00A0C9081C19}\Intel G711 MuLaw
Class Name:      <NO CLASS>
Last Write Time: 11/7/1999 - 10:26 AM
```

```
Value 0
  Name:            FixedSizeSamples
  Type:            REG_DWORD
  Data:            0x1
```

Please note that the name of the subtree it came from is not part of the output. This actually came from HKLM (HKEY_LOCAL_MACHINE).

- **Exit.** Closes the Registry Editor and all changes will be saved *without* confirmation.

Regardless of how your Registry editing session is ended, all changes will be written.

Edit Menu

The Edit menu provides more detailed tools for manipulating Registry data:

- **Add Key/Add Value.** Allows a user to create a key and key value. It assumes that you know how to format the key name, class, type, and value assigned. Case-sensitive issues must be observed. Key and Value names are directly related to objects and functions called by code in the operating system and applications. Note that the Data Types allowed are already provided.

If a value of a key is selected, you are provided with the following editors to change that value. If you double-click the value, the value type dictates which editor is opened, by default.

  - **Tree.** The Tree menu shows how the subtrees, keys, and values appear in the various windows as far as the default for a subtree and/or key displays as expanded or not. Collapse closes the active branch if it is expanded.

  - **View.** The View menu commands manipulate how the "split" is placed in the window. It will be moved all the way to one side or the other, or placed in the center. The Split tool allows you to move the split manually. You can also do the same thing by simply placing the cursor over the split and moving it as needed.

  - **Refresh.** Updates the view of any data that have changed due to a value changed elsewhere that is written to the Registry. For example, changes in Display Properties>Appearance will make changes in HKEY_USERS\<SID>\Control Panel\Desktop\WindowsMetrics.

  - **Find Key.** A very useful tool to find a key if you are not sure where it is or if it exists.

  - **Security.** As previously discussed, you may grant or deny access by user, group, or remote computer to the window that has focus in the editor. You do this through the Security menu.

  - **Options.** The Options menu allows a font to be selected, as well as determining how the editor responds to the user's activities during the session.

- **Window.** The Window menu affects how the various windows are arranged as well as changing the focus.
- **Help.** The Help menu is the standard menu available with all Windows products. Can be very beneficial when used.

regedit.exe Menu Commands

This is significantly less developed than the regedt32.exe counterpart, but still very effective. regedit.exe provides the following menus: Registry, Edit, View, Favorites, and Help.

Registry

Import Registry File: This task is listed first, but you have to have an Exported Registry File to use it. The data is imported by providing a GUI for browsing to the data you need to import. If the file has been saved with a .reg extension, the data may also be imported by double-clicking the file.

Exporting Registry data will by default append a .reg extension to the file. A sample output follows. Even though it is saved as text, it is formatted to work with the Registry. Use extreme caution when opening with a text editor. *Keeping the format is critical in protecting the integrity of the data.* Adding carriage returns and spaces, and otherwise changing the format can corrupt the data. By default, Notepad is the associated application for editing the file. A right-click of the mouse allows the file to be opened to an edit session. A double-click of the .reg file will place the data in the file in the respective paths of the Registry. Note that the full path of the values is provided in the data. The following is a sample output of the Export command:

```
[HKEY_LOCAL_MACHINE\SECURITY\Policy]
@=""
[HKEY_LOCAL_MACHINE\SECURITY\Policy\Accounts]
@=hex(0):
[HKEY_LOCAL_MACHINE\SECURITY\Policy\Accounts\S-1-1-0]
@=hex:
[HKEY_LOCAL_MACHINE\SECURITY\Policy\Accounts\S-1-1-0\ActSysAc]
@=hex(0):02,00,00,00
[HKEY_LOCAL_MACHINE\SECURITY\Policy\Accounts\S-1-1-0\Privilgs]
@=hex(0):01,00,00,00,00,00,00,00,17,00,00,00,00,00,00,00,03,00,00,00
```

Connect and Disconnect Network Registry allows the Registry of a remote computer to be opened and then closed.

Print and Exit commands are pretty much the same as with regedt32.exe.

Edit

These commands are different from those found in regedt32.exe, but perform similar functions. The Find and Find Next commands are more robust in that you can search value and data strings as well as keys.

View

This menu does the same as for regedt32.exe, except it does provide a status bar to indicate the current working path in the Registry.

Favorites

Can add/remove a key or subkey to a list of entries that are frequently visited.

Help

Please make full use of this! These Help tools are specific to the particular editor.

Most of these tools will respond to the default hotkeys as with other windowed GUIs.

Troubleshooting Registry-Related Tasks

Warning!

Editing the Registry may render the operating system of Windows 2000 unusable, and you may even have to reinstall it! Be certain that a current backup is available. Any of the procedures described here are unsupported and are used at your own risk.

The following is a list of basic troubleshooting tasks in relation to the Registry.

- Compare the Registry of working and non-working systems to find differences. Dump to file; use text compare tool (windiff in ResKit). By using the regedt32.exe Registry>Save Subtree As and regedit.exe Registry>Export Registry File, a text representation of the data is created. Using text-editing tools such as windiff.exe, one can compare a desired and undesired Registry key. If you modify the output of the regedit.exe Export Registry File, cut and paste from a good one, and then import that file to the anemic machine, you could repair the problem. Depending on the problem, not accounting for variations in directory structures, user accounts, hardware and configuration, IP addresses, etc. could create more problems than are solved. Also keep in mind that several subtrees and keys are linked to others. Again, go into troubleshooting/repair sessions with a planned purpose and knowledge.

- Save the key to a file and make changes; if not fixed, restore the key from the file again. If a change makes no difference, it is a good practice to return the changed entry back to its original. Not doing so could come back and haunt you later.

▪ Restore a previously working Registry by using Backup and Emergency Repair. This is a good technique with one drawback. If there have been any system changes not accounted for in the backup, you stand to lose those changes on reboot. That may result in having to reinstall software, re-create user accounts and profiles, reupdate drivers, etc.

A very good and reliable source for help and information may be found through Microsoft's TechNet database, where Table 2.6.2 was found. It is included here as a reference for you.

Table 2.6.2   Registry Troubleshooting Tips

Problem	Solution
Services and devices startup configuration	HK_L_M\System\CurrentControlSet\Services\ *service-device*\Start 0 = Boot Start (Used with core drivers) 1 = System Start 2 = Automatic Start 3 = Manual Start 4 = Disabled
Recovering from a lost or forgotten Administrator password	This procedure is rather involved and may be found in detail on several Web sites. This example was performed on an NT4.0 Domain Controller, but should be similar for Windows 2000. Access to the Resource Kit is needed. `http://netguru.net/tiptoc.htm`
Enabling DOS interrupt requests in Windows 2000 for printing	HK_CUR_USER\Software\Microsoft\ Windows NT\CurrentVersion \Windows\ DosPrint. Set from no to yes.
Change the Default Print Spool Dir	HKEY_LOCAL_MACHINE\SYSTEM\ CurrentControlSet\Control\Print\Printers Change the value of Default SpoolDirectory to the desired path.

III

Installing and Configuring Windows 2000 Server

3.1

Getting Started as a Windows 2000 Administrator

You Need to Read This Section If You Want To:

- Understand the tasks involved in administering a Windows 2000 network.
- Know where to find the tools used to administer Windows 2000.
- Create an administrative plan that takes advantage of time-saving features of Windows 2000.

Related Topics

A Day in the Life of a Windows 2000 Administrator

Being the administrator in a large oganization can be a stressful job. It can be especially stressful if you go about it the wrong way. With careful planning and design, however, you can develop a set of tools and an infrastructure for network management that can make administering Windows 2000 more fun and less stressful.

A typical administrator spends his day running from one crisis to another, trying to keep clients and servers running. He patches and fixes and troubleshoots. There is no time to take a long view of the organization's needs and the long-term strategies that will most benefit the business.

In a large Windows 2000 network, there are a number of daily tasks that need to be done. These tasks include

- Creating and modifying user accounts and resetting passwords (users forget 'em!)
- Managing printer queues and resolving printer problems
- Maintaining routers, bridges, hubs, and gateways to other networks
- Troubleshooting network connectivity issues between clients and servers
- Supporting remote users and troubleshooting connectivity problems
- Resolving desktop-configuration issues for clients
- Managing access to files and services on servers
- Configuring and troubleshooting network infrastructure devices and services
- Monitoring the availability and reliability of critical services
- Analyzing and clearing system event logs
- And so on…

In a large network, these tasks are usually done by various groups of support professionals. In a smaller network, however, there may be a single person that has to perform all these diverse tasks.

The need for an administrator to do a lot of these tasks can be drastically reduced if Windows 2000 is deployed in the right way. Specific tasks can be safely delegated to other users, and the change and configuration management features of Windows 2000 can automate much of the mundane work of maintaining desktop applications and system settings, and repairing problems. A little work put into planning a change and configuration management strategy in the beginning can save enormous amounts of time and aggravation later.

This chapter introduces you to the practices and tools that can make a dramatic difference in the daily routine of the administrator.

Knowing Your Tools

Having the right tool for the job is a critical part of efficient adminstration.

For basic maintenance of the operating system, a toolkit should include the following:

- The CD-ROMs for each operating system in your environment (Windows 2000 Professional, Windows 2000 Server, and Windows 2000 Advanced Server).
- Any released Service Packs for Windows 2000.
- A set of Windows 2000 startup diskettes.
- A Windows 2000 boot disk and Emergency Repair disk.
- Third-party tools that go beyond the tools provided by Microsoft, such as disk managers, network analyzers, and anti-virus software.
- Software and devices for troubleshooting hardware problems, such as diagnostic software, manufacturer utilities, and connectivity testers.
- The Windows 2000 Resource Kit. This contains both a wealth of technical information to assist with the less-frequent troubleshooting tasks and additional tools.

Microsoft provides a number of tools for managing resources and services on a Windows 2000 network. These tools are implemented as *snap-ins* to the Microsoft Management Console (MMC). You can start any of the pre-defined tools by running them from the Administrative Tools program group from the Start menu.

You will want to create your own custom consoles with the tools that you use most often, such as Active Directory Users and Computers, Computer Management, and Event Viewer.

▶ *For more information on creating and using consoles, see Chapter 3.2, "Using MMC Consoles."*

▶ *For more information on administrative tools, see Chapter 3.3, "Using Administrative Tools."*

Planning Ahead: Creating the Environment for Success

Most administrators get into trouble by reacting to problems rather than anticipating them.

It is critical to take the time up front to set all of the pieces in place, so they are there when you need them. Here's a short list of the key components of a well-managed network:

- A strategic plan that details how technology supports business objectives and how the use of technology will change to accommodate changes in the business.

- A disaster recovery plan. Most organizations have a plan for recovering data on servers, but no plan for recovering data on client computers. Your plan should address all of the data, wherever it is stored.

- A hardware and software inventory. It's hard to be successful supporting something you don't know much about! A good inventory is essential to identifying hardware and software issues in advance.

- A definition of standard desktop environments. The more that you can standardize a few basic configurations, the more you can automate tasks such as installing new computers, repairing systems with failing software, and replacing storage devices such as hard disks.

- A plan for auditing security. *After* a major incident has occurred is a bad time to think about this. Most security breaches within organizations are the result of unauthorized access by *employees*, not intruders. Plan accordingly. Your plan should address both network security and physical security of computers and data.

- A training plan for additional administrators. How are you going to be promoted if no one else can do your job?

- A definition of acceptable levels of performance for critical services on the network (for example, response times when performing frequent or important user tasks).

- A regular plan for monitoring server performance and baseline performance data. Having baseline data helps you to identify trends and anticipate capacity shortages before they occur.

Tips and Tricks to Automate Administrative Tasks

What you do not want to do is spend all your nights and weekends in the server room, installing software and troubleshooting problems. Here are ways to "work smart" and automate mundane management tasks:

- Use Group Policy to define logon and logoff scripts, manage the security configuration of remote computers, configure a multitude of settings for the users' desktop environments, and limit the users' ability to modify those settings.

- Use offline folders for mobile users.

- Redirect My Documents and other key folders to shared locations on the network where they can be backed up centrally.

- Create Microsoft Installer packages for applications and distribute them through Group Policy or through software distribution tools such as Microsoft Systems Management Server.

- Learn scripting. The Windows Scripting Host, when combined with Active Directory Services Interface (ADSI), is a very flexible environment for executing simple scripts that can save many hours of administrative effort. To assist you in learning scripting, Microsoft created Course 1080, "Essentials of Microsoft Visual Basic Scripting Edition 3.0 for Web Site Development," which is freely available from
  `http://www.microsoft.com/train_cert/Courses/1080Afinal.htm`.

- Create your own MMC consoles. By observing which tasks you do most often, you should be able to create one or more MMC consoles with taskpads that will save lots of time and effort. Place your console files (.msc files) on a share on the network so they are always available for you to use.

- Install Terminal Services on your servers so that you can perform remote administrative tasks in a secure way that does not require a power-user desktop environment.
  ▶ *For more information on managing desktop settings, see Part 6, "Managing User Desktops," and Part 7 "Managing Applications."*
  ▶ *For more information on consoles, see Chapter 3.2, "Using MMC Consoles."*
  ▶ *For more information on using Terminal Services for remote administration, see Chapter 8.10, "Terminal Services."*

Avoiding Crisis: Monitoring Your Network

Finally, you want to have a plan for the ongoing monitoring of your network. What are the critical services and devices that would cause disruption in the business if they were not available? Ongoing monitoring is the key to avoiding expensive and unpleasant surprises.

Decide on the key measures of availability and performance that are important to the organization and then measure them regularly. You should relate these statistics to the business goals of the company. For example, "Helped to fulfill our mission for quality customer service by ensuring that customer data was available online 99.99% of the time in the last quarter." Obviously, these key measures will vary, depending on the type of business and the risks associated with the unavailability of specific network services.

Here are some things to watch on your servers:

- The amount of free space available on the volumes
- The amount of paging activity (swapping of memory to the hard disk)
- The amount of system "up-time"
- The events in the Applications, Security, and System logs
- Key performance statistics, depending on the server type, including network traffic, CPU utilization, disk activity, and memory usage

In addition, you may find it helpful to purchase a third-party product that will monitor the availability of critical services on devices you identify, and then page or e-mail you if the services or devices are not responding.

Windows 2000 Administration Best Practices

Here is a list of best practices that you should adopt where possible:

- Never give users more authority on the network than they need to perform their work tasks.
- Use separate accounts for acting as a user and acting as an administrator on the network.
- Limit the number of administrators and guard passwords carefully. Do not make users the local administrator of their own computers unless absolutely necessary.
- To simplify administration, grant permissions to user groups, not directly to user accounts.
  ▶ *For more information, see Chapter 4.5, "Creating and Managing Groups."*
- When you need to have a log of attempts to log on to the network or of attempts to access files or printers, use Windows 2000 auditing.
  ▶ *For more information, see Chapter 5.6, "Auditing Resource Access."*
- Do not neglect the physical security of servers and other critical resources.
- Pay careful attention to the availability and reliability of critical infrastructure components such as Domain Controllers and DHCP, DNS, and WINS servers.
- Whenever you have the option of using logical names and locations for resources instead of physical locations, do so. For example, instead of using shared folders on individual servers that must be connected to by the server name, use the Distributed File System (DFS) to make the location of the file server transparent to clients.

3.2

Using MMC Consoles

You Need to Read This Section If You Want To:

- Configure the Windows 2000 Administration tools to suit your preferences.
- Place frequently used tools in a single console.
- Create custom MMC Consoles with limited capabilities and distribute them to other users.

Overview of the Microsoft Management Console

In earlier versions of Windows, Microsoft provided a number of separate tools for managing resources and services on a computer. The Microsoft Management Console (MMC) in Windows 2000 provides a single environment in which these tools can be combined in a single console with a consistent interface. Because of this approach in Windows 2000, you have the ability to create your own custom consoles that have the tools that you use most often, all in one place.

You have a lot of flexibility in how you configure your consoles. Into a single console, you can combine multiple tools, ActiveX controls, and even add Web pages. Figure 3.2.1 displays an example of a custom console that combines several network administration tools in a single console.

Figure 3.2.1　Custom Console showing various network tools in a single MMC console.

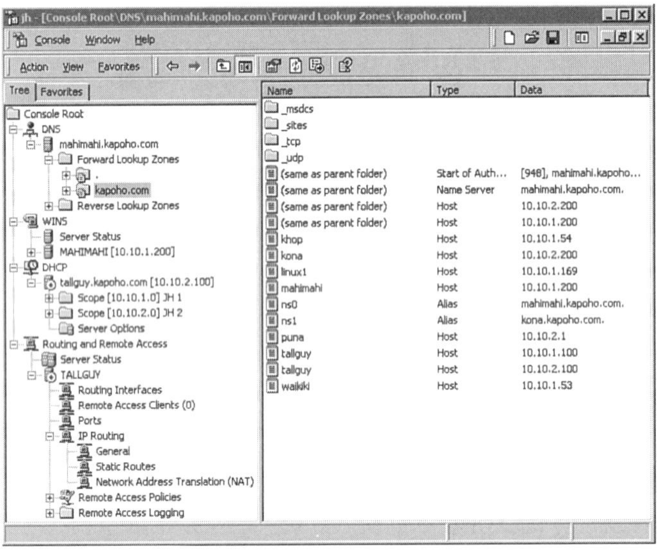

The ability to customize the management console also makes it easy for you to create custom tools to delegate specific administrative tasks. Simply create a new console, add some snap-ins, configure any other options that you want, and then save the console. Then, when another user runs the console, he will have all of the settings for the console predefined and will be able to perform only the tasks for which his account has permissions.

Key facts about the MMC:

- A console is stored as a file with an .msc extension. For example, the Computer Management Administrative tool is stored as a console file with the filename compmgmt.msc.

- You can run the MMC by running mmc.exe. This lauches MMC and starts a new console. You can also launch a specific console file from the command prompt.

  ▶ *For more information, see "Opening an Existing Console File" later in this chapter.*

- A single console can contain many separate tools called *snap-ins*. There are default snap-ins that come with Windows 2000; other snap-ins can be added to your system by installing them.

  ▶ *For more information, see "MMC Snap-ins" later in this chapter.*

- Additional tools that can be invoked by a snap-in are called *extensions*. For example, the Disk Defragmenter is an extension of the Computer Management console; it appears in the console tree under Computer Management, even though it is itself a snap-in. Not all extensions are snap-ins.

- Some snap-ins include *wizards* for performing tasks. For example, when using the Internet Information Services (IIS) snap-in, you can run the Permissions Wizard by right-clicking a server (such as Web server) and then choosing Permission Wizard from the All Tasks menu.

- You can create a window in MMC that has icons that have tasks or actions associated with them. These special windows are called *taskpads*.

  ▶ *For more information, see "Creating Custom Taskpads" later in this chapter.*

- In many tools in the MMC, you can right-click an object and choose Export list or Save As to save the information in a text file.

  ▶ *For more information, see "Exporting Console Data to a File" later in this chapter.*

  ▶ *For more information about the Administrative Tools that come with Windows 2000 Server, see Chapter 3.3, "Using Administrative Tools."*

Administering Windows NT 4.0 Systems from Windows 2000

If you have Windows NT 4.0 systems on your network and you want to use a Windows 2000 computer to manage them, you have the following options:

- Run the versions of User Manager for Domains (Usrmgr.exe) and Server Manager (Srvmgr.exe) that are on the Windows 2000 Server CD-ROM. You cannot use User Manager for Domains to administer Windows 2000 domains, but you can administer Windows 2000 computers by using Server Manager.

- Run Terminal Server on the Windows NT 4.0 computer. Then, use the Terminal Server client from the Windows 2000 computer to run User Manager and Server Manager on the Windows NT 4.0 computer. This does, however, require you to load a different version of Windows NT (Terminal Server Edition).

- Run Web-based administration on the NT 4.0 computer (from the Windows NT Server 4.0 Resource Kit). Add the URL for Web-based administration as a Web object in the Windows 2000 MMC console.

Using and Creating Consoles

Using and customizing consoles consists of these basic tasks:

- Opening a console file
- Adding and removing MMC snap-ins
- Using console menus and setting console options
- Creating custom taskpads

Standard Console Files

Table 3.2.1 shows a list of standard console files provided with Windows 2000 Server.

Table 3.2.1   Console Files Provided with Windows 2000

Console Name	Filename
Component Services	system32\com\comexp.msc
Internet Information Services	system32\inetsrv\iis.msc
System Information	<drive>:\program files\common files\Microsoft Shared\MSInfo\msinfo32.msc
FrontPage Server Extensions	<drive>:\program files\common files\Microsoft Shared\Web Server Extensions\40\bin\fpmmc.msc
QoS Admission Control	acssnap.msc
Certificates—File	certmgr.msc
Certification Authority	certsrv.msc
Indexing Service	ciadv.msc
Computer Management	compmgmt.msc
Device Manager	devmgmt.msc
Disk Defragmenter	dfrg.msc
Distributed	File System dfsgui.msc
DHCP	dhcpmgmt.msc
Disk Management	diskmgmt.msc
DNS	dnsmgmt.msc
Active Directory Domains and Trusts	domain.msc
Active Directory Users and Computers	dsa.msc
Active Directory Sites and Services	dssite.msc
Event Viewer	eventvwr.msc
Fax Service Management	faxserv.msc
Shared Folders	fsmgmt.msc

Console Name	Filename
Group Policy	gpedit.msc
Internet Authentication Service	ias.msc
Local Users Manager	lusrmgr.msc
Removable Storage	ntmsmgr.msc
Removable Storage Operator Requests	ntmsoprq.msc
Performance	perfmon.msc
Routing and Remote Access	rrasmgmt.msc
Remote Storage	rsadmin.msc
Telephony	tapimgmt.msc
Terminal Services Configuration	tscc.msc
WINS	winsmgmt.msc

All console files are located in %systemroot%\system32 unless otherwise specified.

Opening an Existing Console File

To open an existing console, either open the console file in Windows Explorer, or run MMC and then choose Open from the Console menu.

The command-line syntax for MMC is as follows:

mmc path\filename.msc [**/a /s**]

Table 3.2.2 gives a description of the different switches.

Table 3.2.2   Switch Options and Their Descriptions

Switch	Description
path\filename.msc	This is the path and filename of the console file to open. This path must include the complete path, including the .msc extension. If no filename is specified or the path is not complete, MMC will start a new console.
/a	Opens the console in Author mode, which allows the user to make changes to the console settings.
/s	Prevents display of the MMC splash screen. This option is unnecessary when you open a console file on a Windows 2000 system.

You can use system variables such as %systemroot% or %username% as part of the path on the MMC command line. For example, you could create a shortcut to Computer Management that would run, no matter on which volume Windows 2000 is installed, by using the following command line:

mmc %systemroot%system32\compmgmt.msc

MMC Snap-ins

MMC snap-ins are tools that can be "snapped-in" to place in an MMC console. They consist of .dll files, wizards, and other files that provide a specific functionality within the MMC. A number of snap-ins are installed by default as part of Windows 2000 Setup. Additional snap-ins may be installed as you add new Windows 2000 components or install third-party software applications.

Table 3.2.3 shows a list of MMC snap-ins and their functions. Some of these snap-ins have their own consoles predefined in the Administrative Tools program group. You will need to create a custom MMC console to use the others or to combine snap-ins in a single console.

Table 3.2.3   MMC Snap-ins

Snap-in	Description
Active Directory Domains and Trusts	Creates and manages trust relationships between domains. Configures native mode for the directory.
Active Directory Schema	Adds or modifies object classes or attributes in the Active Directory schema.
Active Directory Sites and Services	Defines Active Directory sites and configure, replication.
Active Directory Users and Computers	Creates, publishes, and modifies objects in Active Directory such as users, groups, computers, and shared folders.
ActiveX Control	Adds an ActiveX control to the console.
ADSI Edit	Displays and manages objects in a directory service by using ADSI.
Certificates	Browses certificate stores.
Certification Authority	Configures certificate services, and views and revokes certificates.
Component Services	Configures and manages COM+ applications.
Computer Management	Manages settings on the local computer, including the local user and group accounts, system information, Disks, Services, Shared Folders, Event Viewer, System Info, and Device Manager.
Device Manager	Lists and manages hardware devices. (Also a node in the Computer Management Administrative tool.)
DHCP	Configures a DHCP server to automatically assign TCP/IP configuration settings to network clients.
Directory Service Migration	Migrates data from Novell NDS to Active Directory.
Disk Defragmenter	Reorganizes data on disk volumes for faster access.
Disk Management	Dynamically manages disks and storage. (Also a node in the Computer Management Administrative tool.)
Distributed File System	Creates and manages DFS trees and shares.

Snap-in	Description
DNS	Configures a DNS server to resolve host names to IP addresses. (Also a node in the Computer Management Administrative tool.)
Event Viewer	Views the Event Log on the computer to observe messages. (Also a node in the Computer Management Administrative tool.)
Fax Service Management	Manages Microsoft Fax Service devices and logs.
Folder	Creates folders in the MMC console tree in which to place other snap-ins.
FrontPage Server Extensions	Adds and configures server extensions for Web servers.
Group Policy	Creates and modifies group policy objects for the local computer or Active Directory.
Indexing Service	Manages indexing and queries the index of files on a computer. (Also a node in the Computer Management Administrative tool.)
Internet Authentication Services (IAS)	Manages the Internet Authentication Service.
Internet Information Services	Manages Internet Information Services (IIS) such as the Web server and FTP server.
IP Security Policy Management	Manages IPSec policies.
Link to Web Address	Displays a Web page in MMC.
Local Users and Groups	Manages local user and group accounts. (Also a node in the Computer Management Administrative tool.)
Performance Logs and Alerts	Configures performance logs and alerts. (Also a node in the Computer Management Administrative tool.)
QoS Admission Control	Configures the QoS Admission Control Service to manage the use of network bandwidth.
Remote Storage	Manages local disks and remote storage media by using the Remote Storage service.
Removable Storage Management	Manages removable storage media such as CD-ROMs, tape drives, and optical disks.
Routing and Remote Access	Manages routing, remote access, and connection sharing. (Also a node in the Computer Management Administrative tool.)
Security Configuration and Analysis	Manages the security configuration based on a security template.
Security Templates	Creates and modifies security templates.
Services	Starts, stops, and configures Windows 2000 services. (Also a node in the Computer Management Administrative tool.)

continues

Table 3.2.3   continued

Snap-in	Description
Shared Folders	Lists and manages shared folders, sessions, and open files. (Also a node in the Computer Management Administrative tool.)
SIDWalker Security	Replaces SIDs (Security Identifiers) on Manager computers moved to a different domain.
System Information	Displays information about the hardware and software configuration of the computer. (Also a node in the Computer Management Administrative tool.)
Telephony	Manages the Telephony Service. (Also a node in the Computer Management Administrative tool.)
WINS	Manages Windows Internet Name Service (WINS) servers.

Adding and Removing MMC Snap-ins

To add a snap-in:

- From the Console menu, choose Add/Remove Snap-In.
- Click Add. A list of snap-ins appears.
- Select the snap-in to be added and click Add. If a wizard appears, answer the questions from the wizard.
- Click Close.
- If desired, modify the list of extensions by clicking on the Extensions tab. Select the snap-in whose extensions you want to modify and deselect the Add all extensions checkbox. Then, clear the checkbox for any extension that you want to remove.
- Click OK to return to the MMC.

To remove a snap-in:

- From the Console menu, choose Add/Remove Snap-In.
- Select the snap-in to be removed and click Remove.
- Click OK to return to the MMC.

Using Console Menus and Setting Console Options

The MMC.EXE shell provides a consistent way to manage consoles, independently of the particular snap-ins being used.

Using the Console Menus and Toolbars

The Console menu allows you to create a new console, open an existing console, or save a console to a file. You also use the Console menu to add or remove snap-ins, or to set the options for the console. You can also use the buttons on the console toolbar to perform these same tasks.

Creating and Arranging Console Windows

The Windows menu allows you to create new windows in the console, or to arrange the windows by cascading or tiling them. When you choose New Window from the Window menu, you get a new window, rooted at the console root.

If you want to create a new window, but have the root start at a different node in the console tree, right-click the node that you want to use and then choose New Window from Here.

Exporting Console Data to a File

In many of the standard snap-ins, you can export the information that appears in the list-view pane (the right-hand pane) to a text file.

Tools that allow you to export information from the list-view pane include the following:

- Internet Services Manager
- Computer Management
- Event Viewer
- Active Directory Users and Computers

For example, to export information from the Event Viewer to a file, follow these steps:

1 Click the desired log under the Event Viewer node in the console tree. For example, if you want to export the System Log, click System Log.

2 Right-click System Log and then select Choose Columns from the View menu.

3 Add or remove columns as desired until they are arranged the way you want them. Use the Move Up or Move Down buttons to reorder the list. Click OK.

4 Right-click System Log and then choose Export List.

5 Type a filename, select the type of text file, and click OK.

After the information has been saved in a text file, you can then print the information or import it into another application such as Microsoft Word or Microsoft Excel to perform further analysis.

Setting Console Options

You can choose Options from the Console menu to configure the console's default view, icon, and other settings. The available options are shown in Table 3.2.4, along with a brief description.

Table 3.2.4   Console Options

Option	Description
Console mode	Specifies what kind of changes that users can make to the console:
	Author mode. User has full ability to modify the console.
	User mode—full access. User is able to modify the console, except for adding or removing snap-ins or changing console options.
	User mode—limited access, multiple window. User is able to use multiple windows, but is otherwise unable to make changes to the console.
	User mode—limited access, single window. User is unable to make any changes to the console and can use only a single window.
Enable context menus on taskpads in this console	Specifies whether users can right-click and view commands that are available for objects on taskpads. If you clear this checkbox, right-clicking an object on a taskpad does not display a shortcut menu.
Do not save changes to this console	Specifies whether users can save changes to a console.
Allow the user to customize views	Specifies whether users can add windows that are rooted on items in the console.

▶ *For more information on limiting the ability of a user to change a console file, see "Distributing Custom Consoles to Other Users" later in this chapter.*

Creating Custom Taskpads

Some snap-ins have many different tasks associated with them. To find all the tasks you could perform, you would need to click on the various objects and then view the contents of the Action menu.

An alternative that simplifies this interface and makes frequently performed tasks more accessible is a feature of the MMC called *taskpads*. A sample taskpad is shown in Figure 3.2.2.

To create a taskpad, you right-click the node in the console tree for which you want to create a taskpad, choose New Taskpad View, and then complete the New Taskpad View Wizard. To modify an existing taskpad, right-click the node in the console tree and choose Edit Taskpad View.

Figure 3.2.2   Taskpad View of Services MMC Snap-in.

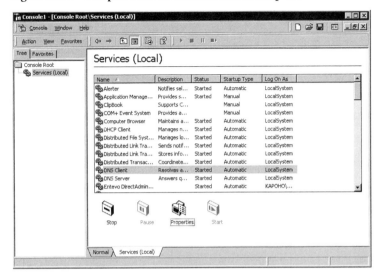

For example, to create the taskpad, follow these steps:

1 Create a new MMC and add the Services snap-in.

2 Double-click Services in the console tree.

3 Right-click Services in the console tree and then choose New Taskpad View.

4 Accept the defaults for the New Taskpad View Wizard by clicking Next until the New Task Wizard appears.

5 Accept the defaults by clicking Next until the Shortcut Menu Command window appears.

6 Choose a command (for example, Start) from the list of Available commands and click Next.

7 Click Next, select an icon for the task in the Task Icon window, and then click Next.

8 In the Completing the New Task Wizard window, click the Run this wizard again checkbox to add commands until you have added the Start, Stop, Pause, and Properties commands to your taskpad.

For more information on creating taskpads, see Windows 2000 Help.

Figure 3.2.3   MMC with System Monitor Control, Web Page Link, and Taskpad.

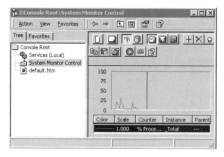

Distributing Custom Consoles to Users

For another user to run an MMC console file that you have created, the user must do the following:

- Be logged on with an account that has enough authority to perform tasks by using the console
- Have access to the console file
- Have the appropriate .dlls and other files installed that are required by the snap-ins in the console

Possible ways to distribute the console file to the user include the following:

- **Policies.** You can use the software distribution functionality in a group policy to assign or offer the console file to a user or group of users.
  ▶ *For more information, see Chapter 6.3, "Group Policies."*
- **E-mail attachments.** You can place the .msc file in an e-mail message as an attachment.
- **Shared network location.** You can place the .msc file in a shared directory on a network server. Then, you can provide the appropriate users with a shortcut to the tools in that folder. Possible ways to distribute the shortcut include via Group Policy, as part of a logon script, or via some other software distribution tool.

Limiting the Ability of Users to Modify Consoles

If you want to distribute a console to other users, but you do not want them to be able to modify it, you should choose the appropriate console mode and then turn on the Do not save changes to this console checkbox. (This checkbox is available only when you choose a mode other than Author mode.)

You can also place the console in a read-only directory on the network to prevent any changes to the console from being saved permanently.

3.3

Using Administrative Tools

You Need to Read this Section If You Want to:

- Know how to find tools for managing and administering Windows 2000 computers.
- Be aware of command-line tools that can be used in place of GUI-based tools.

Related Topics

Overview of Administrative Tools

There are three main categories of Administrative Tools:

- Standard MMC-based tools located in the Administrative Tools Program Group. These are the tools used most often in day-to-day administration of Windows 2000.
- Other standard utilities installed by default with Windows 2000.
- Additional utilities in the Resource Kit. These utilities extend the standard MMC-based and command-line utilities with other essential utilities.

Many of these tools and utilities can be used for managing remote computers on the network. For example, in the MMC-based tools, you can usually manage another computer by right-clicking the root of the console tree and then choosing the appropriate menu choice (such as Connect to another computer or Add Server). Depending on the tool, you may need administrative authority on the target system to connect successfully.

▶ *For information on the Microsoft Management Console (MMC), see Chapter 3.2, "Using MMC Consoles."*

? **Can I Manage Windows 2000 from NT 4.0?**

You cannot run the Windows 2000 Administrative Tools on Windows NT 4.0 systems. However, you can manage Windows NT 4.0 systems from Windows 2000. (See *"Managing Earlier Versions of Windows NT"* later in this chapter.) And you can also manage Windows 2000 servers from Windows NT 4.0 by using terminal services on the Windows 2000 server and the terminal server client on the Windows NT 4.0 system.

The Administrative Tools Program Group

The Administrative Tools program group can be accessed in two ways:

- **Start Menu.** From the Start Menu, click Programs, and then click Administrative Tools.
- **Control Panel.** From the Start Menu, click Settings, click Control Panel, and then double-click Administrative Tools.

Only a subset of these tools is installed by default, depending on the services that you have installed on your computer. As you install additional services, the related Administrative Tools are installed with them.

Table 3.3.1 provides a list of these Administrative Tools.

Table 3.3.1   The Administrative Tools Program Group

Tool	Description
Active Directory Domains and Trusts	Create and manage trust relationships between Domains. Configure Native mode for the directory.
Active Directory Sites and Services	Define Active Directory sites and configure replication.
Active Directory Users and Computers	Create, publish, and modify objects in Active Directory such as users, groups, computers, and Shared Folders.
Component Services	Configures and manages COM+ applications.
Computer Management	Manages settings on the local computer, including the local user and group accounts, System information, Disks, Services, Shared Folders, Event Viewer, System Info, and Device Manager.
Configure Your Server	Wizard for adding and configuring services such as DNS, DHCP, and Active Directory.
Connection Manager Administration Kit	Creates Connection Manager service profiles and provides automation of VPN connections.
Data Sources (ODBC)	Configures Open Database Connectivity (ODBC) data sources and drivers.
DHCP	Configures a DHCP server to automatically assign TCP/IP configuration settings to network clients.
Distributed File System	Creates and manages DFS trees and shares.
DNS	Configures a DNS server to resolve host names to IP addresses.
Event Viewer	Views the Event Log on the computer to observe messages.
Internet Authentication Service	Manages IAS (RADIUS) services.
Internet Services Manager	Manages Internet Information Services.
Licensing	Adds and deletes server licenses or changes licensing mode.
Network Monitor	Captures and analyzes network traffic.

continues

Table 3.3.1   continued

Tool	Description
Performance	Displays and logs information about system performance, such as the processor and disk activity.
Phone Book Administrator	Tool for administering phone books for Connection Point Services.
QoS Admission Control	Configures the QoS Admission Control Service to manage the use of network bandwidth.
Remote Storage	Manages local disks and remote storage media by using the Remote Storage service.
Routing and Remote Access	Manages routing, remote access, and connection sharing.
Server Extensions Administrator	Tool for administering FrontPage Server Extensions and FrontPage-extended Webs.
Terminal Services Client Creator	Creates disks for installing Terminal Services clients.
Terminal Services Configuration	Configures the connection used by Terminal Services clients.
Terminal Services Licensing	Tracks usage of Terminal servers to ensure appropriate licensing.
Terminal Services Manager	Manages and monitors Terminal Services sessions.
WINS	Manages Windows Internet Name Service (WINS) servers.

If you are familiar with Windows NT 4.0, you may be wondering where some things went. Table 3.3.2 lists Windows NT 4.0 Administrative Tools and their Windows 2000 replacements.

Table 3.3.2   Windows NT 4.0 and Windows 2000 Administrative Tools

If You Used this Tool In Windows NT 4.0...	...Use this Tool in Windows 2000
Backup	Start\Programs\Accessories\System Tools\Backup
DHCP Manager	DHCP
Disk Administrator	Computer Management\Storage\ Disk Management
DNS Manager	DNS
Event Viewer	Computer Management\ SystemTools\Event Viewer

If You Used this Tool In Windows NT 4.0...	...Use this Tool in Windows 2000
File Manager	File Manager (winfile.exe)
Internet Service Manager	Internet Services Manager
Network Monitor	Network Monitor
Performance Monitor	Performance Monitor
Remote Access Admin	Routing and Remote Access
Server Manager	Computer Management
System Policy Editor	Active Directory Users and Computers
User Manager for Domains	Active Directory Users and Computers
Windows NT Diagnostics	Computer management
WINS Manager	WINS

Installing the Administrative Tools

You can add the entire list of Administrative Tools to your computer by installing the Administrative Tools package from the Windows 2000 Server CD-ROM. In the \I386 folder on the Windows 2000 Server CD-ROM, double-click adminpak.msi and then follow the prompts provided by the setup program. After setup is complete, all the Administrative Tools will be available in the Administrative Tools program group.

You can also use Software Installation to deploy the Administrative Tools automatically to other computers on your network.

▶ *For more information on Software Installation, see Chapter 7.2, "Publishing and Assigning Applications."*

Other Standard Utilities

The standard utilities are installed in %systemroot%\System32. Because they are located in the system path, you can run them from a command prompt or the Run option on the Start menu.

The most useful utilities are listed in Table 3.3.3. You can get information about these utilities in Windows 2000 Help or by executing them at a command prompt with a /? parameter.

Table 3.3.3   Standard Command-Line Utilities

Utility	Description
Accessibility	Accwiz, magnify, narrator, osk
Active Directory	Csvde, dcpromo, dssetdc, esentutl, ldifde, ntdsutil, repadmin

continues

Table 3.3.3 continued

Utility	Description
Debugging/diagnostics	Drwatson, drwtsn32, eventvwr, query, runas, savedump, taskmgr, winver
Disks	Cleanmgr, convert
DNS	Dnscmd, nslookup
Files	Cacls, xcacls, cipher, clspack, compact, dfscmd, fc, sfc, ntbackup, recover, shrpubw
Networking—General	Msg, nscadmin, net, wlbs
NT 4.0 Utilities	Usrmgr, srvmgr, winfile, wizmgr
Registry	Reg, regini
Remote Installation Service	Rbfg, riprep, risetup
Routing and Remote Access Server	Mrinfo, mtrace, netsh, rasadmin, rasdial, rasphone, routemon
Scheduler	At
Scripting	Cscript, wscript
Security	Secedit
TCP/IP	Arp, evntcmd, evntwin, finger, ftp, tftp, irftp, hostname, ipconfig. Ipkern, ipsecmon, lpq, lpr, nbtstat, netstat, pathping, ping, rcp, rexec, route, rsh, tracert
Telnet	telnet, telnetc, tlntadmn, tlntsess, tlntsvr
Terminal Services	Change, chglogon, chgport, chguser, logoff, shadow, termsrv, tsadmin, tscon, tsdiscon, tskill, tsprof, tsshutdn
Windows Time Service	W32tm

Resource Kit Utilities

The Windows 2000 Resource Kit contains numerous utilities that make an administrator's life easier. There are two versions of the Resource Kit. The one that comes with Windows 2000 on the Windows 2000 Server CD-ROM is only a subset of the full version of the Resource Kit.

Table 3.3.4 has a listing of some of the most useful utilities.

Table 3.3.4   Useful Windows 2000 Server Resource Kit Utilities on the Windows 2000 Server CD-ROM

Utility	Type	Description
Computer Administration		
Kill	Command line	Terminates a process based on its name or process ID. Useful when troubleshooting via a remote command line.
Sdcheck	Command line	Enumerates permissions by examining Access Control Lists and displaying the results.
Shutdown	Command line	Shuts down a computer, either local or remote.
Registry		
Reg	Command line	Versatile command-line tool for modifying, searching, and backing up the Registry.
Service Administration		
Service Controller Query Tool (Sc.exe)	Command line	Creates, deletes, pauses, stops, and starts services from the command line.
Deployment Tools		
Setupmgr	GUI	Setup Manager creates installation scripts for unattended installations of Windows 2000.
Sysprep	Command line	Prepares a system for cloning.
Diagnostic Tools		
Depends	GUI	Dependency Walker lists all the dependent modules for a given program.
Tlist	Command line	Task List Viewer is a command-line tool that displays a list of processes currently running on the computer. Can also show the services running in each process.
Event Log Tools		
Dumpel	Command line	Dump Event Log is a command-line tool that exports an event log to a text file.

continues

Table 3.3.4   continued

Utility	Type	Description
Logevent	Command line	Command-line tool that adds custom entries to an event log.

Network diagnostic Tools

Utility	Type	Description
Browstat	Command line	Browser Status is a command-line tool that provides information about the Browser service.
Netdiag	Command line	Network Connectivity Tester runs a series of tests to identify network connectivity problems.
Pptpclnt, pptpsrv	GUI	PPTP Ping is a diagnostic tool that verifies PPTP connectivity between a PPTP client and a PPTP server.
Rpings, Rpingc32	Command line	RPC Ping is a diagnostic tool that verifies RPC connectivity between a Microsoft Exchange server and a Microsoft Exchange client.
Snmputilg	GUI	SNMP Troubleshooting tool can be used to perform GET, GET-NEXT, and SET operations for SNMP agents.

Directory Services Tools

Utility	Type	Description
Adsiedit	GUI	The ADSI Edit MMC snap-in can be used to view and modify Active Directory objects and attributes.
Dsacls	Command line	This command-line tool can be used to view and modify permissions on Active Directory objects and attributes.
Dsastat	Command line	Compares the naming contexts on two Domain controllers for consistency and retrieves other information about the status of Active Directory.
Ldp	GUI	This tool can be used to view and modify LDAP directories, such as Active Directory.
Netdom	Command line	Joins computers to a Domain and manages trust relationships.

Utility	Type	Description
Nltest	Command line	Used to list Domain Controllers, test trust relationships, and report the state of Domain synchronization for Windows 2000 and Windows NT Domains.
Ntdsutil	Command line	This command-line tool can be used to move Flexible Single Master Operations (FSMO) between Domain controllers and to remove orphaned Domain controllers from Active Directory.
Repadmin	GUI	This graphical tool can be used to display and modify the Active Directory replication topology.
Replmon	GUI	The Active Directory Replication Monitor can be used to view detailed information about naming contexts and replication on Domain controllers.
Scmmgmt.msc	GUI	The Schema Manager MMC snap-in can be used to view and modify the Active Directory schema.
Trustdom	Command line	Displays and manages trust links between Domains.

Network Administration Tools

Utility	Type	Description
Dhcploc	Command line	The DHCP Locator Utility detects and identifies unauthorized DHCP servers.
Dnscmd	Command line	Command-line tool for administering DNS servers.
Winscl	Command line	Command-line tool for administering WINS servers.

Remote Execution

Utility	Type	Description
Remote	Command line	Utility that allows remote command-line clients to run console applications on a remote command-line server. Supports only named pipes connections.

continues

Table 3.3.4   continued

Utility	Type	Description
Wsremote	Command line	The Winsock Remote Console allows remote clients to runconsole applications on a WSRemote server. Supports both sockets and named pipes connections.

Disk and File Tools

Utility	Type	Description
Diskprobe	GUI	A sector editor that allows an administrator to write information directly to physical locations on a disk.
List	Command line	A command line text display and search tool that is sparing on system performance.
Windiff	GUI	Compares two text files and displays the differences between them.

Managing Earlier Versions of Windows NT

If your network has a mixture of Windows 2000 and Windows NT computers, you will want to be able to manage both operating systems from a single desktop. Here are your options:

- Keep one of each kind of computer on hand to manage both types of clients. (This works, but takes a lot of desk space!)

- Install Terminal Services on your Windows NT servers. Then, you can use a terminal session on a Windows 2000 computer to run local copies of the Administrative Tools on the NT 4.0 server.

- Install Terminal Services on your Windows 2000 servers. Then, you can use a terminal session on a Windows NT 4.0 computer to run local copies of the Administrative Tools on the Windows 2000 server.

- Use the Windows 2000 Administrative Tools to manage the Windows NT 4.0 systems. Most tools that manage remote computers will work. Because you cannot manage accounts in a Windows NT 4.0 Domain by using Active Directory Users and Computers, the Windows NT 4.0 User Manager for Domains (usrmgr.exe) and Server Manager (srvmgr.exe) are included with Windows 2000.

? **Can I Use Any of the NT 4.0 Tools in 2000?**

Some Windows NT 4.0 tools do allow you to manage limited aspects of Windows 2000 computers, such as starting and stopping services or viewing event logs.

▶ *For more information about Terminal Services, see Chapter 8.8, "Terminal Services."*

Active Directory Administration Tools

There are three main MMC tools you will use to administer an Active Directory installation, as shown in Table 3.3.5.

Table 3.3.5   Active Directory Administration Tools

Tool	What You Can Use It For
Active Directory Users and Computers	Manage users, groups, OUs; manage GPOs for Domain or an OU and for the Domain; and seize RID, Infrastructure, or PDC Operations Master role
Active Directory Domains and Trusts	Manage manual Domain trusts and seize Domain Naming Operations Master role
Active Directory Sites and Services	Manage subnets and sites, and manage AD replication

Use ADSI Scripts

Most of the changes that can be made through these tools can be accomplished by using ADSI scripts.

If you want to start any of the Active Directory tools focused on a specific Domain or Domain controller, you can use a switch on the command line.

> **dsa.msc /Domain=example.com** would start Active Directory Users and Computers focused on the example.com Domain.

> **dsa.msc /server=dc1** would start Active Directory Users and Computers focused on the server named DC1.

> ▶ *For more information about managing Active Directory by using these tools, see Part 4, "Managing the Directory."*

Other Administrative Tools

There are a few additional tools that will help you manage your systems.

Computer Management

> Computer Management is an MMC console snap-in that allows you to view and manage important system resources such as disks, event logs, and device settings.

To start Computer Management, you can do one of the following:

- Double-click Computer Management in the Administrative Tools program group.
- Right-click My Computer on the desktop and click Manage.
- Run Compmgmt.msc.

With the Computer Management console, you can do the following:

- Manage local user and group accounts on servers that are not Domain controllers.
- Display information about the configuration of devices and operating system components.
- Start and stop services.
- Manage shared folders.
- View and manage the event logs.
- Use Device Manager to configure devices.
- Configure disks, create disk partitions, and defragment volumes.
- Manage services such as the Indexing Service or DNS.

To manage a remote computer, right-click Computer Management in the console tree and then click Connect to another computer.

▶ *For information on using Computer Management, see Windows 2000 Help.*

▶ *For information about managing devices and system settings through Computer Management, see Part 2, "Installing and Configuring Windows 2000 Server."*

Configure Your Server

Configure Your Server is a wizard that can be used to install and configure typical network services on a Windows 2000 server, such as Active Directory, DNS, DHCP, WINS, and Internet Information Server. The Configure Your Server Wizard appears when you first log on after installing Windows 2000. You can launch it at any time by double-clicking Configure Your Server in the Administrative Tools program group.

If you want to keep the wizard from starting each time you log on, execute the following steps:

1 Choose There are already one or more servers operating in my network.

2 Click Next.

3 Clear Show this screen at startup, and close the window.

Licensing

The Licensing tool in the Administrative Tools program group can be used for managing the number of licenses that your server can use. As you purchase server and client licenses for Windows 2000 and other BackOffice products, you can add them to a database of licenses. The License Logging Service in Windows 2000 then monitors license usage on your server and either denies access to clients or writes events to the System log when the number of licenses exceeds the number you purchased.

▸ *For more information on licensing, see "Licensing" in Windows 2000 Help.*

Troubleshooting and Diagnostic Tools

When troubleshooting problems in Windows 2000, the following tools and utilities will be the ones you turn to first:

- Event Viewer
- Performance Monitor
- Network Monitor
- Diagnostic network utilities such as ipconfig, nslookup, ping, and tracert
- Diagnostic Active Directory utilities such as replmon, netdom, and dsastat

---

Use Windows 2000 Help

The Windows 2000 Server Help includes articles for troubleshooting various kinds of common problems. Additional information, tools, and updates are available online from Microsoft at

http://www.microsoft.com/support

Event Viewer

As significant events occur on your computer, Windows 2000 or applications can log information to an event log for an administrator to review. The tool that you use to view these logs is the Event Viewer.

The Event Viewer is extremely useful for troubleshooting because it will often direct you to the source of a problem.

To start the Event Viewer, you can do one of the following:

- Double-click Event Viewer in the Administrative Tools program group.
- Start Manage Computer and then navigate to System Tools\Event Viewer.
- Run Eventvwr.

There are three standard logs in the Event Viewer:

- **Application Log.** This log contains events that were logged by applications. Any program can write events to this log.
- **Security Log.** This log contains events that were logged as a result of auditing, such as unsuccessful logon attempts or accesses to audited files.
  ▶ *For more information on audit events, see Chapter 5.6, "Auditing Resource Access."*
- **System Log.** This log contains events that were logged by Windows 2000 system components, such as device drivers, network protocols, and services.

If you add services to the server, you may have additional logs that are created when those services are installed. For example, when you make a server a Domain controller, the Directory Service and File Replication Service logs are added. When you add the DNS service, a DNS Server log is added, and so on.

The EventLog service starts automatically and writes an event to the system log with an event ID of 6005 at startup.

Event Types

There are five types of events that can be recorded in an event log:

- **Information.** An event that is logged for information only and does not require action by the administrator. For example, certain services log information events as they start successfully.
- **Warning.** An event that indicates some significant condition that might require action by the administrator. For example, if a dial-up interface is unavailable and will be retried, a warning message could be logged.
- **Critical.** An event that indicates a failure or significant problem, such as when a device driver fails to load successfully.
- **Success Audit.** An event that records information about a successful access attempt to a resource for which success audits are enabled.
- **Failure Audit.** An event that records information about an unsuccessful access attempt to a resource for which failure audits are enabled.

Detecting the Crucial Critical Event

If you look in the System Log and find a lot of critical events, look for the first one since the system was last restarted. Often, critical events will be related to each other. For example, if a network interface has failed or is unavailable, all the network components and services that depend on that interface will fail, too. By finding the first critical error, you can fix the lowest-level problems first.

Figure 3.3.1   Event Viewer running on a Domain Controller.

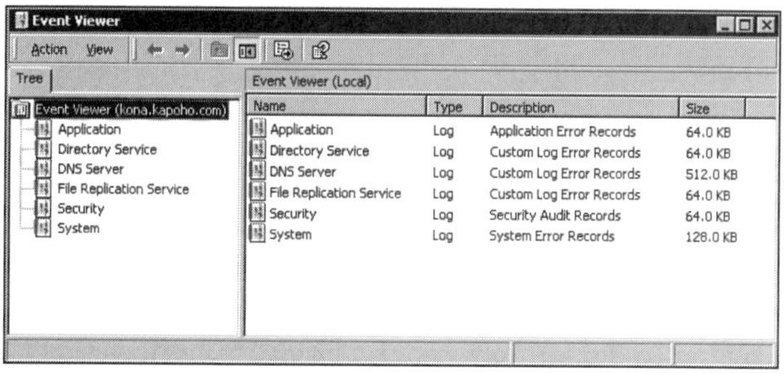

Event Log Options

Table 3.3.6 describes the options you can set for logs in Event Viewer. To modify these options, right-click the log and choose Properties. You will find additional information about Event Viewer in *Windows 2000 Help*.

Table 3.3.6   Event Log Configuration Options

Option	Description
Maximum Log Size	Determines the maximum size to which the log can grow as events are added. It should be large enough to hold any useful history. Must be in increments of 64K. Modify this setting carefully and in combination with Event Log Wrapping.
Event Log Wrapping	**Overwrite events as needed.** Allows the log to grow to its maximum size, after which the oldest events are discarded as new ones are added.
	Overwrite events older than *n* days. Works just like Overwrite events as needed, except events older than the specified number of days are discarded, regardless of the size of the log.
	Do not overwrite events (clear log manually). Allows the log to grow to its maximum size, after which no more events can be logged. This option ensures that no events are lost, but it requires the administrator to clear the log before new events can be added. If you choose this option for the Security Log, your system will stop when the Security Log is full, so use this option with care.
Default	Sets the size and Event Log Wrapping to the default values (512K log size and overwrite events older than seven days).
Clear All Events	Removes all events from the log. This is useful when the log is full or when you have reviewed the events and do not want to keep the history. There is no way to undo this action, so save the log first if you want to keep a record of the events.

Event Viewer Tips

- To view events on a remote computer, run Event Viewer, right-click on Event Viewer in the console tree, and then click Connect to another computer.

- To export events to a text or CSV file, right-click the log and then click Export List. You can also use Dumpel (a Resource Kit utility) from a command line.

- To search for specific events, right-click the log, click View, and then click Find.

- To create a filter to display only events that match specific criteria, right-click the log, click View, and then click Filter. To turn off the filter, choose All Records.

- To view the contents of a log file, right-click the Event Viewer in the console tree and then click Log View.

- You can use Logevent (a Resource Kit utility) to add your own custom events to a log, which can be very useful in troubleshooting. For example, you could have a batch file that writes events to a log as different portions of the batch file complete.

Performance Monitor

Performance Monitor is an MMC snap-in that allows you to display and log information about the demands for various kinds of resources (disk, network, memory, and so on) on your computer. It is the primary tool used for identifying performance bottlenecks. You can monitor performance of your own computer or another computer on the network.

To start Performance Monitor, you can do one of the following:

- Double-click Performance in the Administrative Tools program group.

- Run perfmon.

The performance information on a Windows 2000 computer is organized into three categories:

- **Objects.** The major types of resources or services provided by the system, such as Processor, Memory, Physical Disk, and Network Interface.

- **Counters.** The information about an object that is being measured, such as the percentage of time it is busy, the number of bytes being read or written, and the number of requests in the queue for the object.

- **Instances.** Where there is more than one of a given type of object, the specific one to be measured. For example, if there are two physical disks, there are two instances (0 and 1) of the Physical Disk object.

Useful Performance Monitor Counters

Most of what you need to know about Performance Monitor can be found in Windows 2000 Help. The hard part of using Performance Monitor is knowing what counters to monitor. Table 3.3.7 lists general counters that can be used to identify major performance issues.

Table 3.3.7   Performance Counters Useful In Identifying Performance Problems

Object\Counter	Suggested Normal Range
Memory\Available Bytes	>4MB
Memory\Pages/sec	<10 on a sustained basis
Processor\% Processor Time	<85%
System\Processor Queue Length	<2
Server Work Queues\Queue Length	<4
Network Segment\% Net Utilization	Depends on the type of network in use
LogicalDisk\% Free Space	>15%
PhysicalDisk\Current Disk Queue Length	<Number of spindles plus 2

You must install the Network Monitor Driver in order to collect data for the Network Segment object.

▶ *For more information, see "Performance Monitor" in Windows 2000 Help and "Optimizing Windows 2000" in the Workstation Resource Kit.*

Troubleshooting with Performance Monitor

When you suspect performance problems on a server, follow the strategy shown in Table 3.3.8.

Table 3.3.8   Steps for Identifying Performance Problems Using Performance Monitor

Step	What You Should Do	Example
1	Log activity for basic counters to characterize the workload of the server.	Create a log on the server that logs the objects listed in Table 3.3.7.
2	Identify resources of highest demand.	Notice that the disk-related counters are outside of normal ranges.
3	Look at additional counters that relate to that type of resource to determine the source of the demand.	Look at memory paging activity to see whether a shortage of memory is causing the demand for the disk (*Memory\Pages/sec*); look at whether the activity is primarily reads or writes (*Logical Disk\Disk Reads/sec* and *Logical Disk\Disk*

continues

Table 3.3.8 **continued**

Step	What You Should Do	Example
		Writes/sec); look at which logical disks are most busy (*Logical Disk\% Disk Time*) and whether load is balanced across multiple physical disks (*Physical Disk\% Disk Time*). Determine that a large percentage of disk activity is being generated by a specific application.
4	Change system configuration or load characteristics by either reducing demand for the resource or relocating the demand to another server.	Move a disk-intensive application to a different server or move the application's data to a different physical disk, possibly on a different controller.
5	Monitor to see whether desired results were obtained, comparing performance with earlier logs.	After moving the application, log the same counters as in step 1 and compare the results to see whether the disk resources are still in demand.

Using Performance Monitor to Create Charts and Reports

To create a chart:

1 In the Administrative Tools program group, click Performance.

2 Right-click on the chart and choose Properties.

3 Change options for the chart as desired. Pay particular attention to the Update Time interval. The shorter the interval, the more often you are collecting data and the more overhead you are creating. Click OK when done changing options.

4 Right-click on the chart and choose Add Counters.

5 Select a counter by choosing the computer to monitor, object, counter, and instance, and then click Add. Repeat this step until all desired counters are added and then click Close.

To create a report, follow the same steps as creating a chart, and then click the Report button on the toolbar to change your view to chart view. A sample chart is shown in Figure 3.3.2.

Figure 3.3.2   Performance Monitor running on a Domain controller.

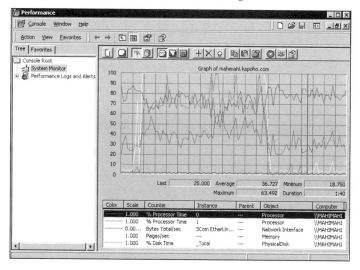

Performance Monitor is easy to use and to configure. Table 3.3.9 lists key tasks you may want to carry out and how you do them.

Table 3.3.9   Tips for Charts and Reports

If You Want To:	Follow These Steps:
Highlight a counter.	Click the highlight button or press Ctrl+H. The counter that is selected in the legend at the bottom of the chart will be highlighted.
Save your chart settings so you can use them again in the future.	Choose Save As from the Console menu and specify a filename. To use the settings, either open the file by double-clicking it, or open it from the Console menu in Performance Monitor.
Save your chart as an HTML file.	Right-click the chart and choose Save As.
Copy your chart into a document created by another program.	Copy the chart to the Clipboard by pressing Alt+Print Screen, switch to the other program, and paste it into the document.

Using Performance Monitor to Save Data in a Log

To create a log of current activity:

1 In the Administrative Tools program group, double-click Performance.

2 In the console tree, click Performance Logs and Alerts.

3 Double-click Counter Logs.

4 Right-click in the details pane, click New, and then click Create New Log Settings.

5 Type a name for the new log settings.

6 Add counters to the log settings and specify a Sampling interval.

7 On the Files tab, specify a log file name and log file folder.

8 On the Schedule tab, specify a schedule for when to start and stop the log. When done, click OK.

Performance Logs and Alerts is also available under System Tools in Computer Management.

Logging data is relatively straightforward. Here are some tips for logging that may help you:

- If you do not create a schedule for a log, the system begins logging as soon as you click OK. Be sure to specify how to start and stop logging, and set a maximum size for the log.

- If you want the system to log its performance continuously, you can configure the log file type on the Files tab to Binary Circular File. The log will grow to its maximum size, and then the oldest information will be discarded to make room for new data being added.

- Be careful about the Sampling interval that you specify on the General tab. The frequency of sampling and the amount of data being sampled directly affects the size of the log and the overhead placed on the system.

- Avoid logging counters across the network from other computers because this creates network activity that can skew your performance results. Because logging runs as a service, it is generally better to allow Performance Monitor to log data locally.

To create a chart by using data from a log file:

1 In the Administrative Tools program group, double-click Performance.

2 Right-click on the chart and choose Properties.

3 On the Source tab, click Log File and specify the filename of the log file that contains the data you want to chart. Click OK when done changing options.

4 Right-click on the chart and choose Add Counters.

5 Select a counter by choosing the computer to monitor, object, counter, and instance, and then click Add. Notice that only the counters that were logged are available to be added. Repeat this step until all desired counters are added and then click Close.

Network Monitor

Network Monitor is a tool for capturing and analyzing network traffic. It consists of a Kernel mode driver named Network Monitor Driver and a User mode application that appears in the Administrative Tools program group named Network Monitor.

You can use Network Monitor to do the following:

- Troubleshoot communications problems.
- Determine which devices are sending or receiving the most network traffic.
- Monitor for specific events.
- Observe conversations between applications on the network.

For example, a common use of Network Monitor is to troubleshoot problems with IP addressing. When a client is unable to obtain an address from DHCP, how do you know what is causing the problem? Capturing the traffic in Network Monitor eliminates guesswork because you can see the actual messages that were sent by the client and the DHCP servers.

Network Monitor Lite Versus SMS Version

Windows 2000 Server ships with Network Monitor Lite, which is limited in comparison with the version of Network Monitor that ships with Microsoft Systems Management Server (SMS). The full version has a number of enhanced capabilities beyond the Lite version. The SMS version can capture traffic on remote networks, retransmit frames, and comes with a variety of Experts that can be used to monitor and analyze network traffic.

Before you can use Network Monitor, you have to have the Network Monitor Driver installed, your network adapter must support Promiscuous mode, and you must be logged on with an account with administrative privileges.

You can start and stop capturing by choosing Start and Stop from the Capture menu. Network Monitor displays a limited amount of summary information while it is capturing network frames. After you stop the capture, you can view detailed information about each frame by choosing Display Captured Data from the Capture menu.

Configuring Network Monitor Captures

Table 3.3.10 describes the options and features you should be aware of when using Network Monitor. You will find additional information about Network Monitor in Windows 2000 Help.

Monitoring the Network Segment Object

While you are monitoring the Network Segment object in Performance Monitor, your network interface is put into Promiscuous mode, which allows you to capture all network traffic (not just traffic to or from your computer) in Network Monitor. (The SMS version of Network Monitor can place the network interface in Promiscuous mode without any help from Performance Monitor.)

In a switched network, the network card, even in Promiscuous mode, will not see all traffic on the subnet, only that traffic sent to the card by the switch. This makes Network Monitor less useful in a switched environment.

Table 3.3.10   Network Monitor Configuration Options

Option	Description
Capture Filter	Allows you to specify which traffic should be captured into the buffer. This reduces the number of frames in the capture and makes it less likely that you will overflow the buffer. Choose Filter from the Capture menu.
Buffer Settings	Allows you to specify the maximum amount of traffic to capture (default is 1 MB) and how much of each frame to capture. Choose Buffer Settings from the Capture menu.
Addresses	A database that resolves physical addresses to names for display in Network Monitor. After capturing traffic, choose Find All Names from the Display menu. All the computer names that Network Monitor can find in the captured frames will be added automatically to your address database.
Capture Trigger	Allows you to tell Network Monitor what to look for in captured frames and an action to perform if a frame with matching characteristics is captured. Choose Trigger from the Capture menu.
Display Filters	Allows you to select the frames from the capture that you want displayed. Choose Filter from the Display menu when viewing captured frames.

Diagnostic Network Utilities

A basic troubleshooting technique for resolving network communications problems is to test the various layers of the network architecture to see which components and services are working.

For a short list of network diagnostic tools and utilities, see Table 3.3.11.

Table 3.3.11   Network Diagnostic Tools and Utilities

Utility	What You Can Use It For
ipconfig	Verify the current TCP/IP configuration. Release and renew IP configuration information from a DHCP server. Register hostname and IP address with a DNS server. Display or flush the DNS resolver cache. Set DHCP Client Scope ID.
ping	Test connectivity between two IP hosts.
tracert	Display the path taken by packets from your computer to another host. Identify routing problems. Identify slow connections.
nslookup	Verify whether DNS is running on a particular DNS server. Verify the IP addresses provided by DNS for a hostname lookup. Verify the registration of service records by Domain controllers. Verify whether DNS used WINS to resolve the IP address of a specific host.

3.4
Managing Services and Tasks

You Need to Read This Section If You Want to:

- Manage and configure Windows 2000 services.
- Start and terminate tasks manually or automatically.
- Identify and resolve problems caused by errant programs (tasks).

Related Topics

Managing Services

A key administrative task in larger organizations is managing the services running on the organization's Windows 2000 servers. This chapter shows how to manage your services and automate administrative tasks.

Overview of Windows 2000 Services

Services have a unique role on a Windows 2000 system. They are different from other programs in a number of significant ways.

- Services can be started and stopped by using the Services console in Computer Management or by using the net start and net stop commands.

- Services can be configured to run automatically at startup, as part of the boot process. Settings in the Registry control at what point in the boot process the services start.

- Dependencies can be established between services, so a service will fail to start if a service that it depends on has not already started.

- Services must be able to run without any user interaction (for example, popup messages or dialog boxes). They run whether or not a user is logged on at the console, and they continue to run after users log off.

- Services are configured to run with a specific user account and password, which limits their access on the system to the access of the user account.

Services can be installed only by a user with administrative authority. Table 3.4.1 shows a list of standard services that are installed by default on Windows 2000 Server, taken from the Windows 2000 Services console.

Table 3.4.1   *Services Installed by Default in Windows 2000 Server, with Default Startup Parameters (from the Services Console)*

Name	Description	Status Type	Startup	Log On As
Alerter	Notifies selected users and computers of administrative alerts.	Started	Automatic	LocalSystem
Application Management	Provides software installation services such as Assign, Publish, and Remove.	N/A	Manual	LocalSystem
ClipBook	Supports ClipBook Viewer, which allows pages to be seen by remote ClipBooks.	N/A	Manual	LocalSystem

Name	Description	Status Type	Startup	Log On As
COM+ Event System	Provides automatic distribution of events to subscribing COM components.	Started	Manual	LocalSystem
Computer Browser	Maintains an up-to-date list of computers on your network and supplies the list to programs that request it.	Started	Automatic	LocalSystem
DHCP Client	Manages network configuration by registering and updating IP addresses and DNS names.	Started	Automatic	LocalSystem
Distributed File System	Manages logical volumes distributed across a local or wide area network.	Started	Automatic	LocalSystem
Distributed Link Tracking Client	Sends notifications of files moving between NTFS volumes in a network domain.	Started	Automatic	LocalSystem
Distributed Link Tracking Server	Stores information so files moved between volumes can be tracked for each volume in the domain.	N/A	Manual	LocalSystem
Distributed Transaction Coordinator	Coordinates transactions that are distributed across two or more databases, message queues, file systems, or other transaction-protected resource managers.	Started	Automatic	LocalSystem
DNS Client	Resolves and caches Domain Name System (DNS) names.	Started	Automatic	LocalSystem
Event Log	Logs event messages issued by programs and Windows. Event Log reports contain information that can be useful in diagnosing problems. Reports are viewed in Event Viewer.	Started	Automatic	LocalSystem
Fax Service	Helps you send and receive faxes.	N/A	Manual	LocalSystem
File Replication	Maintains file synchronization by copying files from a DFS export server to DFS import servers.	N/A	Manual	LocalSystem

continues

Table 3.4.1   continued

Name	Description	Status Type	Startup	Log On As
FTP Publishing Service	Provides FTP connectivity and administration through the Internet Information Services snap-in.	Started	Automatic	LocalSystem
IIS Admin Service	Allows administration of Web and FTP services through the Internet Information Services snap-in.	Started	Automatic	LocalSystem
Indexing Service	Indexes contents and properties of files on local and remote computers; provides rapid access to files through flexible querying language.	N/A	Manual	LocalSystem
Infrared Monitor	Supports infrared devices installed on the computer and detects other devices that are in range.	Started	Automatic	LocalSystem
Internet Connection Sharing	Provides network address translation, addressing, and name-resolution services for all computers on your home network through a dial-up connection.	N/A	Manual	LocalSystem
Intersite Messaging	Allows sending and receiving messages between Windows Advanced Server sites.	N/A	Disabled	LocalSystem
IPSEC Policy Agent	Manages IP security policy and starts the ISAKMP/ Oakley (IKE) and the IP security driver.	Started	Automatic	LocalSystem
Kerberos Key Distribution Center	Generates session keys and grants service tickets for mutual client/server authentication.	N/A	Disabled	LocalSystem
License Logging Service	Monitors license usage on the server.	Started	Automatic	LocalSystem
Logical Disk Manager	Logical Disk Manager Watchdog Service.	Started	Automatic	LocalSystem
Logical Disk Manager Administrative Service	Administrative service for disk management requests.	N/A	Manual	LocalSystem

Name	Description	Status Type	Startup	Log On As
Messenger	Sends and receives messages transmitted by administrators or by the Alerter service.	Started	Automatic	LocalSystem
Net Logon	Supports pass-through authentication of account logon events for computers in a domain.	Started	Automatic	LocalSystem
NetMeeting Remote Desktop Sharing	Supports desktop sharing with NetMeeting.	N/A	Manual	LocalSystem
Network Connections	Manages objects in the Network and Dial-Up Connections folder, in which you can view both local area network and remote connections.	Started	Manual	LocalSystem
Network DDE	Provides network transport and security for Dynamic Data Exchange (DDE).	N/A	Manual	LocalSystem
Network DDE DSDM	Manages shared Dynamic Data Exchange; used by Network DDE.	N/A	Manual	LocalSystem
NT LM Security Support Provider	Provides security to remote procedure call (RPC) programs that use transports other than named pipes.	N/A	Manual	LocalSystem
Performance Logs and Alerts	Configures performance logs and alerts.	N/A	Manual	LocalSystem
Plug and Play	Manages device installation and configuration, and notifies programs of device changes.	Started	Automatic	LocalSystem
Print Spooler	Loads files to memory for later printing.	Started	Automatic	LocalSystem
Protected Storage	Provides protected storage for sensitive data, such as private keys, to prevent access by unauthorized services, processes, or users.	Started	Automatic	LocalSystem
QoS RSVP	Provides network signaling and local traffic control setup functionality for QoS-aware programs and control applets.	N/A	Manual	LocalSystem

continues

Table 3.4.1   continued

Name	Description	Status Type	Startup	Log On As
Remote Access Auto Connection Manager	Creates a connection to a remote network whenever a program references a remote DNS or NetBIOS name or address.	N/A	Manual	LocalSystem
Remote Access Connection Manager	Creates a network connection.	Started	Manual	LocalSystem
Remote Procedure Call (RPC)	Provides the endpoint mapper and other miscellaneous RPC services.	Started	Automatic	LocalSystem
Remote Procedure Call (RPC) Locator	Manages the RPC name service database.	N/A	Manual	LocalSystem
Remote Registry Service	Allows remote Registry manipulation.	Started	Automatic	LocalSystem
Removable Storage	Manages removable media, drives, and libraries.	Started	Automatic	LocalSystem
Routing and Remote Access	Offers routing services to businesses in local area and wide area network environments.	N/A	Disabled	LocalSystem
Secondary Logon Service	Enables starting processes under alternate credentials.	Started	Automatic	LocalSystem
Security Accounts Manager	Stores security information for local user accounts.	Started	Automatic	LocalSystem
Server	Provides RPC support and file, print, and named pipe sharing.	Started	Automatic	LocalSystem
Simple Mail Transport Protocol (SMTP)	Transports email across the network.	Started	Automatic	LocalSystem
Smart Card	Manages and controls access to a smart card inserted into a smart card reader attached to the computer.	N/A	Manual	LocalSystem
Smart Card Helper	Provides support for legacy smart card readers attached to the computer.	N/A	Manual	LocalSystem

Name	Description	Status Type	Startup	Log On As
System Event Notification	Tracks system events such as Windows logon, network, and power events. Notifies COM+ Event and System subscribers of these events.	Started	Automatic	LocalSystem
Task Scheduler	Enables a program to run at a designated time.	Started	Automatic	LocalSystem
TCP/IP NetBIOS Helper Service	Enables support for NetBIOS over TCP/IP (NetBT) service and NetBIOS name resolution.	Started	Automatic	LocalSystem
Telephony	Provides Telephony API (TAPI) support for programs that control telephony devices and IP-based voice connections on the local computer and, through the LAN, on servers that are also running the service.	Started	Manual	LocalSystem
Telnet	Allows a remote user to log on to the system and run console programs using the command line.	N/A	Manual	LocalSystem
Terminal Services	Provides a multi-session environment that allows client devices to access a virtual Windows 2000 Professional desktop session and Windows-based programs running on the server.	N/A	Disabled	LocalSystem
Uninterruptable Power Supply	Manages an uninterruptable power supply (UPS) connected to the computer.	N/A	Manual	LocalSystem
Utility Manager	Starts and configures accessibility tools from one window.	N/A	Manual	LocalSystem
Windows Installer	Installs, repairs and removes software according to instructions contained in .msi files.	N/A	Manual	LocalSystem
Windows Management Instrumentation	Provides systems management information.	N/A	Manual	LocalSystem

continues

Table 3.4.1   continued

Name	Description	Status Type	Startup	Log On As
Windows Management Instrumentation Driver Extensions	Provides systems management information to and from drivers.	Started	Manual	LocalSystem
Windows Time	Sets the computer clock.	N/A	Manual	LocalSystem
Workstation	Provides network connections and communications.	Started	Automatic	LocalSystem
World Wide Web Publishing Service	Provides Web connectivity and administration through the Internet Information Services snap-in.	Started	Automatic	LocalSystem

To display the list of installed services, run Computer Management and then click the Services node in the console tree. To display a list of running services at a command prompt, type **net start**.

? **Why Don't All the Services Show Up as Separate Tasks (Separate .exe Files) in Windows Task Manager?**

Many of the standard services that are included with Windows 2000 run as threads in other tasks. For example, the Alerter, Computer Browser, and Event Log service all run as part of the Services.exe task. You can identify which task a service is part of by looking at the ImagePath value for the service in HKEY_LOCAL_MACHINE\SYSTEM\CurrentControlSet\Services*servicename*.

You can also use the tlist utility from the Resource Kit to determine which services are running within each process.

You can display the properties of a service by right-clicking the service in the Services console and then clicking Properties. The Properties dialog box has four tabs, as follows:

- **General tab.** Allows you to start and stop the service and configure whether it should start on command (Manual), automatically at every system startup (Automatic), or never (Disabled).

- **Log On tab.** This is where you configure the user account and password that the service will use. You can also enable or disable services for different hardware profiles. (The capability to disable services by hardware profile is much more useful on a Windows 2000 Professional computer than on a Windows 2000 Server computer—unless you have Server installed on your laptop!)

  ▶ *For more information on service accounts, see "Setting Service Accounts Log On Properties" later in this chapter.*

- **Recovery tab.** This tab allows you to specify how the computer should react if the service fails. You set a threshold for action if the service fails once, fails twice, or fails more than twice. You can associate a file to run (for example, a command line to execute, such as a batch file) and whether a message should be sent to users before restarting the computer (through the Restart options).

- **Dependencies tab.** When this tab is displayed, the Registry is queried to show the relationships between this service and other services. You can view a list of services that this service is dependent on (for example, the other services must be running or else this service will fail) and which services are dependent on this service (for example, which other services will fail if this service fails). These dependencies are also useful to know when starting or stopping services because they can help you start or stop the services in the fastest and best way.

Figure 3.4.1 shows the properties of Windows 2000's Telnet service.

Figure 3.4.1   Properties of the Telnet service.

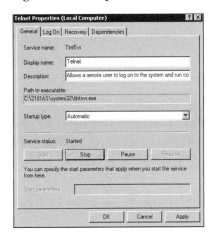

Starting, Stopping, and Pausing Services

You can use the Services console in Computer Management to manage services. With the Services console, you can select a service and then choose an action on the General tab of the service properties.

- **Start.** Start running the service. If the service has its own task (for example, its own .exe file), the task is loaded into memory and started. If the service shares a task with other services (for example, it is a part of a .exe file that contains more than one service), the thread for the service is started.

- **Pause.** The effect of pausing a service varies from one service to another. It may cause a service to stop responding (similar to stopping the service) or it may stop only certain operations performed by the service. Some services do not respond to pause or resume actions.
  ▶*For more information,* see *"Important Notes on Pausing Services" later in this chapter.*

- **Resume.** Instructs a service that has been paused to continue.
- **Stop.** Initiates a normal shutdown of the service. The service may need to close files, close network connections, or finish servicing client requests before finally terminating.

Try Not to Start and Stop Services

The general rule is to be very conservative on a server about stopping and starting services because you will disrupt the service's communications between the server and its clients. Before starting and stopping the service in a production environment, test the procedure first with a test server and client, or else wait until a time of day when users are no longer connected to the server.

To start and stop services at a command prompt, use the net start and net stop commands. For example, to start the Telnet service, type **net start telnet**. To stop the Telnet service, type **net stop telnet**. If the name of the service includes spaces, enclose the service name in quotes (for example, **net start "task scheduler"**).

Other notes on the net start command include the following:

- Before you can start and stop services at the command prompt, you need to know the name that is being used by the service. Type **net start** at a command prompt to get a list of running services.
- If the service is not currently running, you can determine the name of the service by starting the service by using the Services console in Computer Management and then running net start to get its name.
- The net help start command will give a list of standard Windows 2000 services that can be started from the command prompt. (This list will not include any third-party services that you have installed.)
- If all else fails, you can look for the service in the Registry under HKEY_LOCAL_MACHINE\SYSTEM\CurrentControlSet\Services.

The DisplayName value of the service is the name used by the net start and net stop commands.

Important Notes On Pausing Services

- When a service is paused, it will not restart again until you either resume the service or restart the computer (if the service is configured to start automatically). Use the Services console in Computer Management or the net continue command to resume the service.
- When the Net Logon service is paused, a Domain Controller will not respond to domain logon attempts, but it will continue to replicate its Active Directory information with other Domain Controllers.
- When the Server service is paused, only members of the Administrators and Server Operators groups can connect to the server.

Important Notes on Stopping Services

- When you stop a service, all dependent services are stopped. For example, when you stop the Server service, the Computer Browser and other services are also stopped. For a list of dependent services, see the Dependencies tab in the service's Properties dialog box.

- When the Server service is stopped, all inbound user connections are disconnected from the server computer. Because this can cause data loss or file corruption at the client computers, it is best to warn users to log off before you stop the Server service. A simple way to do this is to run Computer Management and connect to the server on which the service will be stopped. Right-click Computer Management, click All Tasks, and click Send Console Message.

- The order in which you attempt to stop services can make a big difference in the amount of time required to stop them all because of dependencies between them.

- Unless you are very familiar with the inner workings of a service, it is best to allow it to stop gracefully, rather than using Windows Task Manager or some other tool to terminate the service's task prematurely. Terminating a service may cause disruption and data loss at client computers or on the server itself.

Setting Service Accounts Log On Properties

All services run with a user account. Services "log on" to the system so they can be authenticated, even if no user is logged on at the console of the computer. The service can perform only actions that the account it is using has permissions to perform.

You need to be careful how you configure the properties of the user account that a service will use. Follow these guidelines:

- Grant the account the Log on as a service user right. The service must log on before it can start, and service logons require this user right.
  ▶ *For more information about user rights, see "Security Policies" in Chapter 6.3, "Group Policies."*

- Do not require the account to change its password at the next logon. Services will not change their own passwords, so there is no way for the service to log on if you require this option to be checked.

- Do not allow the account to expire. When the account expires, the service may be unable to access local or network resources.

- Place the service account in an appropriate user group and then assign permissions to the group rather than the individual accounts.

Choosing Service Accounts

In general, it is best not to use the LocalSystem account for services. Instead, create accounts specifically for services to use and then configure the services to use those accounts. The account name and password of the service accounts must be kept secure.

Some applications will require you to use an account other than LocalSystem for the service. This may be because the service needs to use this account to communicate with other computers on the network. (The LocalSystem account cannot be used on the network, only on the local computer.)

Choose service accounts carefully. Do not give services administrative authority anywhere on the network or on the local computer unless it is absolutely necessary and you have assessed the risks of configuring the service in this way.

Using SVRANY.EXE to Configure an Application as a Service

You can use Srvany to configure any Windows application so it runs as a service. This allows the application to handle requests without anyone being logged on and allows the service to run with a logon account separate from a logged-on user. When you run an application as a service, the service is not closed during logoff, so you do not need to restart the application each time you log on.

Although Srvany works best with 32-bit applications written for Windows 2000 (or Windows NT), you can use this tool to start 16-bit Windows applications as services. However, some 16-bit applications are not able to keep running after a user logs off from the computer. So test this carefully before deploying the application as a service.

Srvany does have the limitation that it is not able to respond to pause and stop requests gracefully. If Srvany is stopped, your application is simply killed with no warning. And you cannot pause Srvany. In general, it's better to try to get the service written as a proper Windows 2000 service—but Srvany is a useful tool in a pinch.

Managing Tasks

In Windows 2000, a *task* is a program started by a user (it is also known as a *process*). You can use a variety of methods to start, stop, and manage tasks.

Starting Tasks

You can start a task (process) in any of the following ways:

- At a command prompt, type the name of the program or a data file associated with it (that is, either mspaint.exe or MyDrawing.bmp).
- At a command prompt, use the Start command.
- From the Start menu, choose Run and then type the name of the program or a data file associated with it (or click Browse and select it).
- Create a shortcut to the program or a data file associated with it, and then open the shortcut.

- Run Windows Task Manager and then choose New Task (Run) from the File menu.

- Run the task with a specific user account by holding down Shift, right-clicking the program file, and then choosing Run As; or use the Run As command at a command prompt.

When you start a task, Windows 2000 allocates memory to the task and provides it with access to the processor. The amount of time on the processor that the task gets depends on the demand created by the task and the priority of the task on the computer.

Many tasks do not have a user interface or create any visible sign on the desktop that they are running. You can identify these tasks by running the Windows Task Manager. All tasks will appear in the list on the Processes tab, whether or not they have a window or taskbar button.

?   **How Do I Set Up Software Installations to Start Automatically?**

Software installation can be started automatically by using Group Policy to assign applications to users or groups.

▶ *For more information, see Chapter 7.2, "Publishing and Assigning Applications."*

The Start Command

Although you can start a task by typing the name of the program file (for example, **mspaint.exe**), this starts the task with the default behavior and priority. If you want to set the priority at which the task will run, determine the title and size of the window that it will run in, and specify a working directory for the task, you can use the parameters of the Start command to do this.

For example, if you want to start the Paint program in a maximized window with My Drawing Program in the title bar, type the following:

start "My Drawing Program" mspaint.exe /max

If you want to start the Win16 program mywin.exe in a separate memory space at a low priority, type the following:

start mywin.exe /separate /belownormal

For more information about the start command, type **start /?** at a command prompt.

Run As Command

The Run As command allows you to run a program in a different user context from your current user account. This feature is especially useful if you are troubleshooting a problem at a user's computer and you need to run a tool with administrative authority while still using the user's profile and desktop environment.

There are two ways to use Run As:

- Hold the Shift key and right-click on a program file. Then, click Run As. The dialog box that is displayed is shown in Figure 3.4.2. This option defaults to using the current user's profile and environment when running the task.

- From the command prompt, use the Run As command. Run As allows you more flexibility in specifying the environment in which the task will run. For a detailed description of the command prompt switches available, type **runas /?**.

Figure 3.4.2   The Run As dialog box.

Starting Tasks Automatically

You can have tasks start automatically in any of the following ways:

- Place a shortcut to the task in the Startup folder. To have the task start whenever anyone logs on, place the shortcut in the All Users Startup folder (\Documents and Settings\All Users\Start Menu\Programs\ Startup) or the Startup folder for the individual user (for example, in \Documents and Settings\Administrator\Start Menu\Programs\Startup for the user Administrator).

- Add the command line to a value in the Run key in the Registry (HKEY_LOCAL_MACHINE\SOFTWARE\Microsoft\Windows\ CurrentVersion\Run).

- Add the command line to a value in the RunOnce key in the Registry (HKEY_LOCAL_MACHINE\SOFTWARE\Microsoft\Windows\ CurrentVersion\RunOnce). The command will run once at next startup and then be removed from the Registry.

- Use Local Policy or Group Policy to configure logon and logoff scripts.
- Schedule tasks using the Task Scheduler.
  ▸ *For more information, see "Scheduling tasks" later in this chapter.*

Terminating Tasks

Some tasks (processes) continue to run, even after you close the window that the program was using. To stop these tasks on your system, use one of the following methods:

- Use the Processes tab in Windows Task Manager. Select the task and then click End Task.
- Use the kill utility in the Windows 2000 Resource Kit.
- Use the rkill utility in the Windows 2000 Resource Kit if the task is running on another computer.

Shutting Down the Computer

Of course, another way to terminate tasks is to shut down the computer (except that you are stopping *all* the tasks, not just one). You have to have the Shut down this computer user right before you can perform a shut down.

▸*For more information on user rights, see "Security Policies" in Chapter 6.3, "Group Policies."*

To shut down a Windows 2000 computer by using Computer Management:

1 In Computer Management, connect to the computer to be shut down.
2 Right-click Computer Management and click Properties. The Properties dialog box appears.
3 Click the Advanced tab, and then click Startup and Recovery.
4 Click Shut Down, choose the appropriate options in the Shut Down window, and then click OK.

Shutdown Utilities

The Windows 2000 Server Resource Kit includes two additional utilities for shutting down Windows 2000 computers. Shutdown is a command-line utility (for syntax help, type **shutdown /?**). Shutgui is a GUI-based tool that you can use to select the computer to shut down and send the user a warning message as a timer ticks away...

Identifying Tasks that Are Running On the Computer

When trying to identify tasks that are currently running on the computer or trying to troubleshoot task-related problems, the following tools are helpful:

- Windows Task Manager
- Performance Monitor
- Command prompt diagnostic utilities

Windows Task Manager

Windows Task Manager, often known as simply "Task Manager," is the tool you will use most often when trying to uncover hidden tasks running on your computer or diagnosing what program is using your computer's memory and processor. Figure 3.4.3 shows an example of Task Manager in action.

Figure 3.4.3   Windows Task Manager can be used to identify the processes that are creating the most activity on a Windows 2000 system.

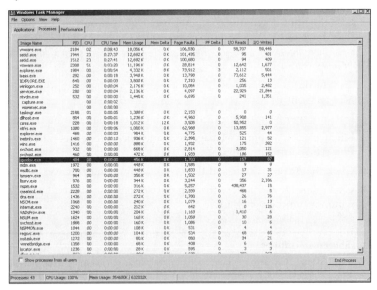

There are several ways to launch Windows Task Manager:

- Right-click on Taskbar and choose Task Manager.
- Run taskmgr.exe (or create a shortcut that does).
- Press Ctrl+Shift+Esc.
- Press Ctrl+Alt+Del and then click the Task Manager button.

Performance Monitor

You can use the Process object in Performance Monitor to monitor all the tasks and various counters, such as number of threads, amount of memory used by the task, amount of processor time used by the task, and so forth. Performance Monitor is the tool to use when you have identified the task that is creating a problem and want to know more detail about what the task is doing.

▶ *For more information on Performance Monitor, see Chapter 3.3, "Using Administrative Tools."*

Command Prompt and Resource Kit Utilities

Additional useful command prompt and Resource Kit utilities include the following:

- **Tlist.** Displays a list of tasks and their process IDs (PIDs). Use the –s switch with tlist to display the services running inside each process.
- **Pmon.** Displays detailed information about the resource usage of tasks.
- **Pviewer.** A GUI-based tool for displaying detailed information about the resource usage of tasks.
- **Kill.** Terminates tasks from the command prompt by PID or by task name.

▶ *For more information on these utilities, see Windows 2000 Help and the Tools Online Help in the Resource Kit.*

Scheduling Tasks

There are often a number of tasks that an administrator will want to run at set times, such as a virus scan or a backup. You can use the Windows 2000 Task Scheduler to create a set of tasks that can be run at some specific time in the future and have these tasks automatically start at the appropriate time.

If you want to schedule a task to run at a specific time, you can use the Task Scheduler to do that. Task Scheduler is a Windows 2000 service that starts automatically. You schedule tasks to run by using the Scheduled Tasks option in Control Panel.

? **Where Did the Windows NT 4.0 Schedule Service Go In Windows 2000?**

The Task Scheduler service in Windows 2000 is an enhanced version of the old Schedule service. It now has an enhanced user interface (although the at command still works!), and you can specify the user account that a task should use when it runs. For backward-compatibility, the Task Scheduler service is also called Schedule, so batch files that use the old name will continue to work.

When you schedule a task, it is stored in the %systemroot%\tasks folder as a .job file.

IV

Managing the Directory

4.1

Overview of Managing the Directory

You Need to Read This Section If You Want to:

- Gain an overview understanding of DNS and DNS naming.
- Gain an overview understanding of configuring a Domain Controller.
- Gain an overview understanding of managing User Accounts.
- Gain an overview understanding of managing groups.
- Gain an overview understanding of logging on and logging off.

Related Topics

Related Topics (continued)

For More Information On ▶ *See*

How clients find a   ▶ *Chapter 4.6: Logging On and*
domain controller; how   *Authentication*
users are authenticated

Tools for managing   ▶ *Chapter 3.3: Using Administrative Tools*
the Active Directory

Publishing file and   ▶ *Chapter 5.1: Overview of Managing Files*
print resources in the   *and Printers*
Active Directory

DNS and Active Directory

The designers of Windows 2000 chose the Internet Engineering Task Force (IETF) standard Domain Name System as the name resolution service to support the Active Directory. The IETF documents its standards in Requests for Comments (RFC). The fundamental specifications describing the fundamentals of DNS and DNS naming are described in the following RFCs:

- 1034 Domain Names—Concepts and Facilities
- 1035 Domain Names—Implementation and Specification
- 1123 Requirements for Internet Hosts—Application and Support
- 2181 Clarifications to the DNS Specification

In addition, Active Directory requires that the DNS service support RFC 2052, a DNS RR for specifying the location of services (DNS SRV). And the DNS server should support RFC 2136, Dynamic Updates in the Domain Name System (DNS UPDATE).

The full text of these RFCs plus others that describe different aspects of DNS, including dynamic updates and replication, can be found at the IETF Web site (http://www.ietf.org/). See the Windows 2000 Server Help for the specific DNS RFCs and Internet Draft RFCs that are supported.

Both the Active Directory namespace and the DNS namespace are very similar in design. They both follow the basic rules that each child can have only one parent and each parent can have only one child with any given name. It is important to note that every Windows 2000 domain must have a corresponding DNS domain.

Due to the Active Directory's heavy reliance on DNS, Windows 2000 Domain Controllers register several records in the DNS database. Specifically, Windows 2000 registers SRV records for Domain Controllers, Global Catalog servers, Kerberos Key Distribution Centers, Kerberos Password Change servers, and others. In addition to these records, Windows 2000 also registers SRV records, based on Windows 2000 sites, to simplify clients finding services within a site.

The DNS service that is included with Windows 2000 is the best choice for supporting the Active Directory, although third-party DNS servers can function acceptably (for example, later versions of BIND). Windows 2000 DNS has several features that are attractive to DNS administrators, such as the capability to store DNS information in the Active Directory, support for multi-master updates of DNS zones, methods for aging and scavenging records, and a process to secure DNS records using Access Control Lists (ACLs). However, you can still use third-party DNS services to support the Active Directory as long as they support the Service Locator (SRV) record as described in RFC 2052.

Configuring a Domain Controller

Domains and Domain Controllers in Windows 2000 are very different from what they were in Windows NT 4.0. In Windows NT, Domain Controllers knew only about the objects in their Domain. However, Windows 2000 Domain Controllers have three naming contexts: the Domain, the Schema, and the Configuration. The Domain context is the set of all objects and attributes in the Domain. For example, this includes users, groups, and computers. The Schema context is the knowledge of the objects (or classes) and attributes that exist for the entire forest. Finally, the Configuration context includes information on such objects as replication, the Active Directory namespace, and sites.

Domains in Windows 2000 are part of a hierarchical namespace. These Domains are connected to their parent and children Domains with two-way Kerberos transitive trusts. It is no longer necessary to maintain manually a complex web of one-way trust relationships.

However, setting up a Domain requires a lot more planning than in previous versions of Windows NT. You must plan in advance how all of the domains fit together in the hierarchical namespace and then build your forest starting with the root. You cannot build a Domain until its immediate parent exists, for example.

When setting up a Domain Controller, you need to know how that DC fits into your Domain plan. You need to decide if that DC will be a new Windows 2000 forest, a new tree within an existing forest, or a replica DC in a Domain that already exists.

Installing a Domain Controller is no longer an activity that occurs during the operating system's installation. In order to configure a server as a Domain Controller, you must run the Active Directory Wizard (DCPROMO) after the server is up and running. Also a very nice feature is the capability to remove the Active Directory (server would no longer be a Domain Controller) without reinstalling the Operating System.

Finally, if classes of objects or attributes do not exist, it is possible to extend the Active Directory schema. By using the Active Directory Schema MMC snap-in, a privileged user can add attributes to existing classes or even add new classes. This can allow an administrator to create new object types, either from scratch or derived from some other class. Active Directory-based applications or administrator written scripts can then make use of these new classes or attributes.

Extreme caution should be used in extending the Schema because classes and attributes cannot be removed; they can only be disabled. For the most part, this is not a major risk. But because the Schema is forest-wide, choosing names badly could, in extreme circumstances, affect applications from being installed in the future. Careful planning can reduce the risks.

Creating and Managing User Accounts

User creation and management in Windows 2000 is accomplished through the use of the Active Directory Users and Computers MMC snap-in. It is also possible to automate the creation and management of user accounts through the use of Active Directory Services Interface (ADSI) and Windows Scripting Host. ADSI can be used in scripting languages such as VB script or Java Script, or in full programming languages such as Visual Basic or Visual C++. The Resource Kit has a number of ADSI script samples that you can both use and adapt.

Creating a user account is usually done through the MMC snap-in. This populates only a very basic subset of attributes with data. However, after creating the account, you can edit its properties to add data to other attributes. You can also create a user account using an ADSI script.

Because Windows 2000 is a directory of data, not just an account database, there is a lot more useful information available that applications and users can take advantage of. User accounts in Windows 2000 have many more properties than in Windows NT. These properties allow you to store information about the user in the Active Directory. Some of these properties include telephone number, employee number, address, and department number. Through the Managed by property, you have the ability to link managers to employees. This allows you to build a representation of your company's organizational chart in the Active Directory.

Creating and Managing Groups

Group creation and management in Windows 2000 is also usually accomplished through the use of the Active Directory Users and Computers MMC snap-in. As in Windows NT 4.0, with the MMC tool it is possible to both select the group and add members, or to select the user and add group membership. Through the use of ADSI, it is also possible to automate group management as for user accounts.

Windows 2000 expands the types of groups available to manage your environment, providing you with several more options than just simply Global and Local groups. Windows 2000 introduces a new type of group called

Universal groups. Universal groups can contain users, Global groups, or other Universal groups from anywhere in your forest. Although Universal groups are very powerful, they exist only if the domain is in Native mode. Universal groups and their memberships are stored in the Global Catalog. Also, the behavior of Domain Local groups has been modified. In Windows 2000, Domain Local groups can contain users and Global groups from anywhere in the forest. However, they can also contain other Domain Local groups within their Domain. Once created, these Domain Local groups can be tied to ACLs or privileges on member servers and workstations within the domain.

Going Native

Windows 2000 Domains operate in one of two modes: Mixed mode or Native mode. In Mixed mode, both Windows NT 4.0 and Windows 2000 Domain Controllers can be used. With Mixed mode, you can always migrate back to a Windows NT 4.0 Domain. Once you go Native, there is no way back, but you do gain a number of cool features, including group nesting, Universal groups, and the ability to use the Domain restructuring tools in the Resource Kit, such as ClonePrincipal.

Windows 2000 also allows two classifications of groups: Security groups and Distribution groups. Security groups are used to control access to resources. These are the same types of groups that exist in Windows NT. Distribution groups are a new classification of group in Windows 2000. Distribution groups will be used by Exchange 2000, which will integrate with the Active Directory. Distribution groups are used to send e-mail.

Logging On and Authentication

Almost everything is different in Windows 2000, and the logon and authentication process is no exception. The Windows 2000 default authentication package is Kerberos, although Windows 2000 Domain Controllers also implement NT 4.0-style authentication for support of down-level clients. Kerberos is an industry standard that was developed at Massachusetts Institute of Technology (MIT).

Under Kerberos, when a user is authenticated, they are given a Ticket Granting Ticket (TGT). The TGT allows the user to get another type of ticket that is required to connect to a resource. These other tickets are called Session Tickets. When a user that has been granted a TGT needs to connect to a resource, that user contacts the Key Distribution Center (KDC) in order to get a Session Ticket for that resource. The user then presents that Session Ticket to the resource. The resource mutually authenticates the Session Ticket and allows the user access. By default, tickets in Windows 2000 are good for 10 hours. After that, they are invalid and need to be reissued. Windows 2000 handles this transparently for the user.

You can use Group Policies to change the defaults for the maximum ticket life for both user and service tickets. When you create a Domain, dcpromo also creates a default Domain policy that defines these and other Kerberos settings.

Your user token in Windows 2000 is slightly expanded from Windows NT 4.0. The Windows 2000 token contains your primary SID, the SIDs in your SIDHistory, the SIDs of any Universal groups that you belong to, and the SIDs of all Domain Global and Local groups. Because SIDHistory and Universal groups depend on the Global Catalog, they are available only in Native mode.

Of course, Windows 2000 also supports LAN Manager authentication as a fallback. This allows Windows 2000 to interoperate with Windows 95, Windows 98, and Windows NT.

4.2

DNS and Active Directory

You Need to Read this Section if You Want to:

- Understand the DNS namespace and its importance in Windows 2000.
- Be able to identify the resource records used by the Active Directory.
- Know how DNS information is stored if you are using Active Directory Integrated DNS.
- Understand how to maintain your dynamic zones through the use of aging and scavenging to prevent stale records.
- Be aware of how to use third-party DNS servers with the Active Directory.

The DNS Namespace

Previous versions of Windows NT were built on NetBIOS. To provide name resolution services for NetBIOS over the Transmission Control Prococol/Internet Protocol (TCP/IP), the Windows Internet Name Service (WINS) was created. This allows you to resolve 16-character NetBIOS names to Internet Protocol (IP) addresses.

▸ *For more information on the Windows Internet Name Service, see Chapter 8.4, "Windows Internet Name Service (WINS)."*

One of the chief designs of Windows 2000 is the removal of the dependency on NetBIOS. The designers of Windows 2000 made the decision to move to a pure IP implementation. To provide name resolution services in Windows 2000, the Internet Engineering Task Force (IETF) standard Domain Name System (DNS) is used.

DNS is a hierarchical naming system. Names in DNS are composed of host names and Domain names. The Domain names consist of a series of names separated by periods (for example, na.mycompany.com). There are two fundamental principles to the DNS namespace. First, each child can have only one parent. Second, each parent can have only one child with any given name. This works the same way as the file system on your PC. Every file can exist only in one directory and the filename must be unique in that directory.

▸ *For more information on DNS and name resolution, see Chapter 8.3, "Domain Name System (DNS)."*

In Windows 2000, all Domains and the computers in those Domains must have DNS names. Additionally, several key services register names. Chapter 1.2, "Introduction to Active Directory," provides an introduction to these concepts, including Domain Controllers and Global Catalog Servers. These service records are extremely important for the proper functioning of the Active Directory. In Windows 2000, these records are generally used for one of these three things:

- Creating the replication topology for the Active Directory. The Knowledge Consistency Checker (KCC) uses specific DNS records to create the replication topology.

  ▸ *For more information on Active Directory Replication, see Chapter 4.3, "Configuring a Domain Controller."*

- Finding the location of Windows 2000 Domain Controllers and Global Catalog Servers. Windows 2000 clients use these records to find the appropriate Domain Controller or Global Catalog Server, based on that servers proximity to the client.

- Finding the location of standard Kerberos services. Because Windows 2000 can provide standard Kerberos services to non-Windows 2000 clients, these records are important to ensure that those clients can find the correct servers. Examples of these records include the Kerberos Password Change servers and the Key Distribution Centers.

With two exceptions, Windows 2000 Domain names must follow all of the rules of DNS discussed previously. First, Microsoft's implementation of Windows 2000 DNS allows DNS names to contain UTF-8 characters. The UTF-8 character set is a superset of ASCII, as described in IETF RFC 2044. This was done to maintain compatibility with NetBIOS names used in Windows NT. Additionally, the UTF-8 character set includes support for most languages. Second, the DNS name of a Windows 2000 Domain cannot exceed 64 characters. This maximum was implemented due to a underlying limitation on DNS and UNC name lengths.

Beware of UTF-8 Names and Non-Windows 2000 DNS Server

If you are using the full UTF-8 character set and you are not using Windows 2000 DNS, you must ensure that your third-party DNS servers support these names. Otherwise, you will not be able to resolve these names, and these names could prevent your entire zone from loading.

In order to understand and design the DNS namespace to support your Active Directory implementation, you should follow these three steps:

1 Understand your current DNS namespace.

2 Plan your Active Directory based on your organizations needs.

3 Create the additional DNS zones required to support the Active Directory.

Step 1: Understand Your Current DNS Namespace

Before designing your Active Directory implementation, you need to understand your existing DNS namespace. First, you need to know whether your organization even has an existing DNS namespace. Most companies will have some sort of DNS implementation in their current environment. Second, you need to know the names and hierarchy of the current environment. Finally, you need to know if this is a public (published on the Internet) or private namespace.

Figure 4.2.1 shows an example of a simple DNS namespace. Mycompany has an external namespace of mycompany.com with subdomains of phx (Phoenix) and bos (Boston). Some of the machines in Phoenix and Boston need to be available on the Internet (public namespace).

Figure 4.2.1   Example of current DNS namespace.

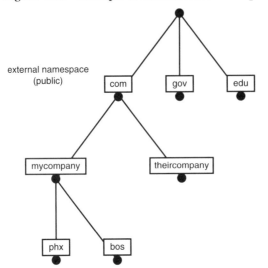

Step 2: Plan your Active Directory Based On Your Organization's Needs

Now that you understand your organization's existing DNS namespace, it is important to begin planning for your Active Directory. Some of the most basic questions that you need to answer include "How many Domains will I need?" and "What will their names be?" It is recommended that you do not overlap with your existing DNS structure. Some of the most common implementations either create a completely separate namespace from your existing DNS implementation or simply delegate a sub-domain that will become the Active Directory's forest root.

Separate Your Internal and External DNS Namespaces

One practice that is common among large companies with public DNS namespaces is to create a DNS sub-domain named CORP under their public namespace. CORP then becomes the root of their Active Directory forest. This allows separation of public and private namespaces. Also, this allows implementation of the Active Directory without requiring any changes to the existing DNS namespace.

For more information on analyzing your current environment and planning your Active Directory, see the Deployment Planning Guide that comes with the Microsoft Windows 2000 Resource Kit.

Figure 4.2.2 shows an example of Mycompany's planned Active Directory. They will implement two Domains:

- corp.mycompany.com: The root of the Windows 2000 forest.
- na.corp.mycompany.com: A single Domain for all users and computers in North America.

Figure 4.2.2   Example of Active Directory implementation

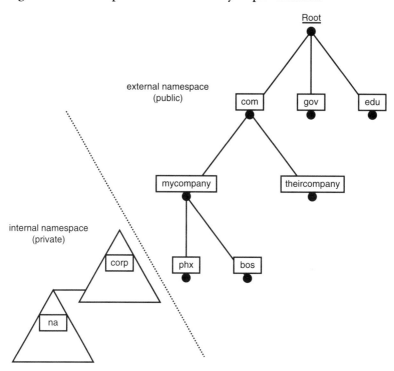

Step 3: Create the Additional DNS Zones Required to Support the Active Directory

The final step is also the easiest. After you understand your current DNS namespace and have planned your Active Directory, you should simply create the appropriate DNS zones.

Figure 4.2.3 shows an example of the DNS zones required to support Mycompany's Active Directory shown in Figure 4.2.2. DNS zones need to be created for corp.mycompany.com and na.corp.mycompany.com. By creating these zones separate from the existing PHX and BOS zones, you are able to keep your existing machines in the public namespace without needing to publish your Active Directory zones on the Internet.

Figure 4.2.3   Example of DNS zones supporting the Active Directory.

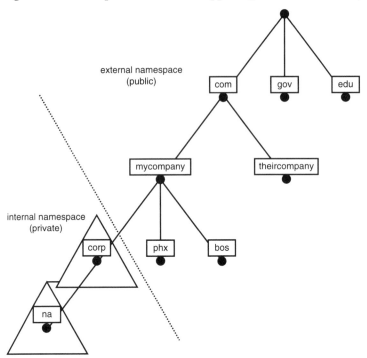

The DNS Resource Records

A *resource record* is simply an entry in the DNS database. Resource records map the names of servers or services to their location, much the way that the Windows Internet Name Service (WINS) did in previous versions of Windows NT. This referenced location can be either the physical Internet Protocol (IP) address or the name of the server.

Table 4.2.1 lists some of the common resource record types that you will encounter in Windows 2000.

Table 4.2.1   Common DNS Resource Record Types

Record	Abbreviation (DNS Type)	Description
Start of Authority	SOA	Identifies the primary server that is responsible for the zone. In dynamic DNS, only the server pointed to by the SOA can accept updates.

Record	Abbreviation (DNS Type)	Description
Host	A	Identifies the IP address of a server in the zone.
Name Server	NS	Identifies a server that can respond to DNS queries for the zone (the DNS server that is authoritative for the zone).
Canonical Name (also known as an Alias Record)	CNAME	Identifies another name as an alias for a server.
Service Locator★	SRV	Identifies the priority, weight, port, and server for a service.

★*The Service Locator (SRV) record is described in the draft RFC, draft-ietf-dnsind-rfc2052bis-02.txt. At the time of this writing, it is not currently a standard.*

Default Records Registered by a Windows 2000 Domain Controller

Because the Windows 2000 Active Directory is built on TCP/IP, Domain Controllers register several records in the DNS database. Mainly, these are Service Locator (SRV) records. These records allow clients to find the location of services, such as Domain Controllers, Global Catalog servers, Light-weight Directory Access Protocol (LDAP) Servers, and Kerberos Key Distribution Centers.

Table 4.2.2 lists the DNS records that are registered by the Netlogon service on Windows 2000 Domain Controllers.

Table 4.2.2   DNS Records Registered by Windows 2000 Domain Controllers

Record	Description
<ServerName>.<DNSDomainName>	Identifies the Internet Protocol (IP) address of <ServerName>.
_ldap._tcp.<DNSDomainName>	Identifies a LDAP server for the Domain. This record does not necessarily point to a DC.
_ldap._tcp.<SiteName>._sites. <DNSDomainName>	Identifies a LDAP server in the site and for the Domain. This record does not necessarily point to a DC.

continues

Table 4.2.2   continued

Record	Description
_ldap._tcp.dc._msdcs.<DNSDomainName>	Identifies a LDAP server for the Domain. This record will always point to a DC.
_ldap._tcp.<SiteName>._sites.dc._msdcs.<DNSDomainName>	Identifies a LDAP server in the site and for the Domain. This record will always point to a DC.
_ldap._tcp.pdc._msdcs.<DNSDomainName>	Identifies the server that owns the PDC FSMO for the Domain.
_ldap._tcp.gc._msdcs.<DNSForestName>	Identifies a Global Catalog

Only DCs that have the GC this record. |
| _ldap._tcp.<SiteName>._sites. | Identifies a Global Catalog gc._msdcs.<DNSForestName>server in the site and for the forest. This record will always point to a DC.

Only DCs that have the GC installed will register this record. |
| _gc._tcp.<DNSForestName> | Identifies a Global Catalog (GC) server for the Domain. This record does not necessarily point to a DC.

Only servers that have the GC installed will register this record. |
| _gc._tcp.<siteName>._sites.<DNSForestName> | Identifies a Global Catalog server in the site and for the Domain. This record does not necessarily point to a DC.

Only servers that have the GC installed will register this record. |
| _ldap._tcp.<DomainGUID>.Domains._msdcs.<DNSForestName> | Identifies a LDAP server for the Domain, as identified by its GUID. This record will always point to a DC. |
| _kerberos._tcp.<DNSDomainName> | Identifies a server acting as a Kerberos Key Distribution Center (KDC) for the Domain. This record does not necessarily point to a DC. |

Record	Description
_kerberos._udp.<DNSDomainName>	Same as previous, except specifies UDP.
_kerberos._tcp.<SiteName>._sites.<DNSDomainName>	Identifies a server acting as a Kerberos Key Distribution Center (KDC) in the site and for the Domain. This record does not necessarily point to a DC.
_kerberos._tcp.dc._msdcs.<DNSDomainName>	Identifies a DC acting as a Kerberos Key Distribution Center (KDC) for the Domain.
_kerberos._tcp.<SiteName>._sites.dc._msdcs.<DNSDomainName>	Identifies a DC acting as a Kerberos Key Distribution Center (KDC) in the site and for the Domain.
_kpasswd._tcp.<DNSDomainName>	Identifies a Kerberos PasswordChange server for the Domain. This record does not necessarily point to a DC.
_kpasswd._udp.<DNSDomainName>	Same as above, except specifies UDP.
<DNSDomainName>.	Identifies a DC for the Domain through a standard host lookup on the Domain name.
gc._msdcs.<DNSForestName>	Identifies a GC for the forest through a standard host lookup.
<DSAGuid>._msdcs.<DNSForestName>	Identifies a DC in the forest through a standard host lookup on the DC's GUID.

The Netlogon service registers several records that may seem redundant. However, the Windows 2000 Active Directory was designed around industry standards (Kerberos, X.500, and so on). This allows the Active Directory to interoperate with many operating systems and applications. These records are required to maintain this level of interoperability.

Storing DNS Information in the Active Directory

One of the most powerful features of Windows 2000 DNS is the capability to store DNS information in the Active Directory. If a zone is stored in the Active Directory, it is said to be "Active Directory-integrated."

In order for a zone to be Active Directory-integrated, the DNS service must be installed on a Windows 2000 Domain Controller. You can set the zone type to be an Active Directory-integrated primary zone by right-clicking on the zone, selecting properties, and setting the appropriate value in the DNS MMC snap-in. Once done, this zone will be created as a container in the Active Directory. For example, location in the Active directory of the zone mycompany.com (to support the Domain mycompany.com) would be mycompany.com\system\MicrosoftDNS\mycompany.com.

All of the resource records for that zone would then be stored as objects in that container.

DNS Objects Cannot Be Updated via ADSI Scripts

Even though the DNS records are stored as objects in the Active Directory, those objects cannot be updated through ADSI scripts. The DNS objects can be updated only through standard DNS practices (client registrations, the DNS MMC snap-in, or DNSCMD.EXE).

After this data is stored in the Active Directory, there is no longer the need to set up zone transfers, as in standard DNS. These DNS objects are now replicated just like every other object in that Domain. Should you desire to replicate that zone to a member server or a server outside of the current zone, you can still set up a standard zone transfer. However, the server that the zone is being replicated to will treat that zone as a standard secondary zone. Clients cannot update records on a standard secondary zone. The clients need to send their update requests to the SOA for the zone. The SOA for that zone on the target server will point to the Domain Controller that the data was replicated from.

Why You Should Install DNS on All Your DCs

All DCs in the Domain will contain all zone containers and record objects, even if they do not have the DNS service installed. If you plan on using Active Directory-integrated DNS, it is a good idea to install DNS on all of your DCs. This will allow all your DCs to resolve DNS queries within the Domain without going to a remote system.

In addition to the simplification in replicating DNS data, there are other benefits of Active Directory-integrated DNS:

- Multi-Master Updates
- Secure Dynamic DNS

Multi-Master Updates

Standard Dynamic DNS allows only a single Start of Authority (SOA) record for each zone. All updates must occur on the SOA and are then replicated to the other DNS servers that house that zone.

This behavior, if not modified, would create a scalability issue for the Active Directory. As Domains get large in Windows 2000, it would not be optimal if all DCs, clients, servers, and services were required to update their DNS records through only one server. The DNS server that is the SOA would be a single point of failure for record updates.

However, if the DNS zone is stored in the Active Directory, this problem is solved. The Active Directory supports updates to objects on any DC. Because the DNS records are objects in the Active Directory, they support the multi-master behavior, as well. To allow this behavior within the confines of RFC 2136, which described Dynamic DNS, Windows 2000 allows each server to own the SOA for Active Directory-integrated zones that are installed on itself.

Secure Dynamic DNS

Another issue with standard dynamic DNS is that resource records are not protected. Only the last update to the resource record is reflected in the zone. This allows other servers or services to "steal" those records inadvertently, or, even worse, you could be susceptible to a denial-of-service attack.

To prevent these issues, an Active Directory-integrated zone can be configured to allow only secure updates. However, once enabled, only Windows 2000 systems can update that zone. Each record in the Active Directory is then ACLed with the SID of the system registering that record. Then, only that server, the system account, or an Administrator can modify that record.

Put DHCP and DNS On Separate Servers

DHCP can be configured to register the host records in DNS for clients that receive leases. If this option is turned on, you should not install DHCP and DNS on the same server. Because the DHCP service runs under the context of the System account, it has the authority to overwrite secure DNS records. This allows any DHCP client to "steal" a record from another system.

▶ *For more information on installing and configuring DHCP, see Chapter 8.2, "Dynamic Host Configuration Protocol (DHCP)."*

Maintaining Zones in Windows 2000 DNS

With dynamic DNS, it is possible for records to be added to zones, but never deleted. Additionally, with the introduction of Secure Dynamic DNS, those records would be ACLed to the original owning server. If that server becomes unavailable, other servers are prevented from updating (or reusing) those records.

To solve these issues with dynamic DNS zones continuously expanding due to these stale records, Microsoft introduced the concept of aging and scavenging DNS records.

Aging and Scavenging is configured by setting parameters on both a per-zone and per-server basis. This allows you to specify which servers can scavenge which zones. Through careful planning, you can keep your zones clean and prevent having a server scavenge records that have been refreshed on, but not replicated from another server.

Table 4.2.3   Configurable Parameters for Aging and Scavenging DNS Records

Zone Parameters	Server Parameters
No Refresh interval.	Default No Refresh interval.
Specifies the time, starting at the last refresh timestamp, during which time the server will not allow the record to be refreshed.	Sets the No Refresh interval on new zones. The default value is 7 days.
Refresh interval.	Default Refresh interval.
Specifies the time, starting at the end of the No Refresh interval during which time the server will allow the record to be refreshed.	Sets the Refresh interval on new zones. The default value is 7 days.
Enable Scavenging.	Default Enable Scavenging.
Specifies whether the zone can be scavenged.	Sets the Enable Scavenging parameter on new zones. The default value is Disabled.
	Enable Scavenging.
	Specifies whether any zones on the server can be scavenged. The default value is Disabled.
	Scavenging Period.
	Specifies how often the server will perform scavenging. The default value is 7 days.

If Aging and Scavenging are enabled, a record in that zone has a period of time during which refreshes cannot occur. This is the No Refresh interval. This interval prevents excessive replication due to a short duration between refresh attempts on the client.

Updates (changing the data in the record) can occur at any time, including during the No Refresh interval.

After the No Refresh interval has expired, the record has a period of time during which it will allow refreshes. This is the Refresh interval. After the record is refreshed by the client, the No Refresh interval starts over again. If, for some reason, the Refresh interval expires, the record will be deleted at the next scavenging.

If both the server and the zone are set to allow scavenging, scavenging will occur as dictated by the scavenging period on the server.

Use Caution When Changing the No Refresh Interval

Setting the No Refresh Interval too low could cause a dramatic increase in replication traffic. As this value is lowered, the record will be refreshed more often and then replicated to the other DNS servers. However, if you increase the value too much, you could cause the size of your DNS zones to increase. Before changing these values, you should ensure that you completely understand the rate of change for your IP address-es, as well as the size of your DNS zones. This will allow you to find the proper balance for your organization.

Using Third-Party DNS Servers with the Active Directory

Although it is physically possible, choosing to use a third-party DNS server can be quite an undertaking. Microsoft has added some key features to its DNS service that makes it better prepared to support the Active Directory. For example, support for the UTF-8 character set ensures that Windows 2000 will fully interoperate with your down-level NetBIOS names. Also, the addition of Secure Dynamic DNS provides you with a level of security against denial-of-service attacks, with which a malicious user could attempt to "steal" critical service records from your Active Directory.

However, anticipating the need for some companies to run third-party DNS servers, Windows 2000 will run with non-Microsoft DNS servers as long as those servers support Service Locator (SRV) records. If your server does not support SRV records, you need to either upgrade that server or delegate the Active Directory zones to a server that does.

Assuming that your server supports SRV records, the type of DNS server that you have will determine the level of effort required to support the Active Directory. There are two general types of DNS servers:

- Servers that support dynamic updates
- Servers that do not support dynamic updates

Servers that Support Dynamic Updates.

Dynamic DNS is described in the Request For Comments (RFC) 2136, "Dynamic Updates in the Domain Name System." BIND 8.1.2 is an example of a DNS service that supports dynamic updates. As long as all of your servers that will support the Active Directory are RFC 2136-compliant, you do not need to do anything special for Windows 2000 to work. However, you do lose the benefits of Active Directory-integrated zones and Aging and Scavenging, discussed earlier in this chapter.

Servers that Do Not Support Dynamic Updates

If your server does not support dynamic updates, as described in RFC 2136, it is highly recommended that you upgrade your server to a version of DNS that does. BIND 4.9.x and earlier versions are examples of DNS services that do not support dynamic updates. Using a server that does not support dynamic updates is strongly discouraged. However, if the upgrade is not an option, you must manually update the correct DNS zones to ensure that the Active Directory will function correctly. You will need to do the following:

- Implement a manual process for updating host records for all clients and servers.
- Implement a manual process for registering Domain controller records.

Implement a Manual Process for Updating Host Records for All Clients and Servers

It should be safe to assume that if you are using non-dynamic DNS servers in your environment today, you have an adequate manual process for adding and removing host records. Having such a process in place is extremely important, especially for the host records for your Windows 2000 Domain Controllers. The Active Directory Service Locator (SRV) records will point to those host records.

Implement a Manual Process for Registering Domain Controller Records

For every Domain Controller in your forest, you will need to manually update all of the records listed in Table 4.2.2, earlier in this chapter. To assist you, the Netlogon service creates a file on each Domain Controller that contains these records. This file is %systemroot%\config\NETLOGON.DNS.

You must be very careful to enter each of the records in the correct zones. Some of the DNS records need to be in the zone for the local Domain, whereas some of the records need to be in the zone for the forest root. Maintaining the accuracy of these zones over time is also very important. If you delete and reinstall a Domain Controller, it will be necessary to update the DNS zones (because the DSAGuid will change). Also, if you remove a Domain Controller, you must remove the appropriate records from the DNS.

Due to the features that Microsoft's DNS provides, it is the ideal choice for supporting Windows 2000. As a general rule, it is not recommended that you run a third-party DNS server to support the needs of the Active Directory. However, with a solid plan and careful implementation, it is possible to set up a reliable infrastructure without using Microsoft's DNS service.

4.3

Configuring a Domain Controller

You Need to Read This Section if You Want to:

- Learn how to install the first Domain Controller in your enterprise, Domain replicas, and children Domains.

- Know how to configure subnets, sites, and site links to optimize Active Directory replication.

- Understand how to extend the Active Directory schema, mark attributes for inclusion in the Active Directory, and index items for faster searching.

- Be aware of the process to restructure the Active Directory after it has been installed.

Related Topics

Installing Active Directory

Before installing the Active Directory on your Windows 2000 server, you must have a plan. Unlike using Windows NT 4.0, you need a lot more information than just knowing if the server you are installing will be a Primary Domain Controller or a Backup Domain Controller. With Windows 2000, you must know exactly how this Domain Controller fits into your enterprise. Principally, you need to know the following about this Domain Controller:

- Will it be in a new Domain or a replica of an existing Domain?
- Will it be in a new tree or in an existing tree within your enterprise?
- Will it be in a new forest or an existing forest?

A New Domain Versus a Replica of an Existing Domain

In Windows NT 4.0, this would be the same as asking whether this server will be a Primary Domain Controller or a Backup Domain Controller. Choosing to create a replica of an existing Domain is the same as creating a BDC in a Windows NT 4.0 environment. However, because Windows 2000 allows multi-master updates of the accounts database, there are no Primary Domain Controllers and Backup Domain Controllers, just Domain Controllers. The term *replica* simply means that the Domain name context will be duplicated from another Domain Controller in the same Domain.

A New Tree Versus an Existing Tree Within Your Enterprise

A tree simply defines a hierarchical naming context. For each child in the tree, there exists exactly one parent. There are three rules that determine how trees function in Windows 2000:

- A tree has a single unique name within the forest. This name specifies the tree's root. Be aware that tree names cannot overlap. If mycompany.com is a tree, Europe.mycompany.com cannot exist as a separate tree in the forest. It can exist only as a child Domain within mycompany.com.
- The tree has a contiguous namespace. This means that children Domains are directly related to the Domains above and below themselves.
- Children Domains inherit the naming from their parent. For example, if mycompany.com is a tree, europe.mycompany.com and asia.mycompany.com would be children within that tree.

A New Forest Versus an Existing Forest

A *forest* in Windows 2000 is the group of one or more Active Directory trees. All Domains in the forest share a common schema and configuration-naming context. However, it is important to note that separate trees in a forest do not form a contiguous namespace, even if peer trees are connected through two-way transitive trust relationships.

Table 4.3.1 provides a list of other critical information needed before installing the Active Directory on a Windows 2000 server.

Table 4.3.1   Information Needed Before Installing the Active Directory

Item	Description
DNS server(s) IP address(es)	If you plan on installing DNS services on this DC, you will use this server's IP address. Otherwise, you need the IP addresses of your existing DNS servers.
	This should be configured in the Network Properties prior to installing the Active Directory.
Domain's DNS name	Based on the role of this DC in the enterprise, you may inherit part of this name from the Domain's parent.
	Example: mycompany.com
	Example: europe.mycompany.com
Domain's NetBIOS name	A NetBIOS name for the Domain is required to maintain down-level compatibility.
	Example: MYCOMPANY
Enterprise Administrator name and password	This is necessary for all scenarios, except for creating a new forest to ensure that you have the appropriate rights to join the forest.
Level of security compatability	Some Windows NT 4.0 services (for example, Remote Access Services) are not compatible with native Windows 2000 security. If you need to run these Windows NT 4.0 services against Windows 2000 accounts, make sure you specify that in the Active Directory Wizard (DCPROMO.EXE).

After you have gathered all the necessary information, you are ready to install the Active Directory. There are three main ways to install the Active Directory on a Windows 2000 server:

- The Active Directory Installation Wizard will be automatically launched upon upgrading a Windows NT 4.0 Domain Controller.

- From Configure Your Server Wizard, select the Active Directory Tab. Follow the instructions to launch the Active Directory Installation Wizard.

- From the Start menu, click Run and execute DCPROMO.EXE.

If you have gathered the necessary information prior to running the Active Directory Wizard, you should be able to follow the prompts provided. Upon completion, the Active Directory will be installed on your server.

?   **Can I Move the Domain?**

If you decide that you need to move this Domain to another location within your forest, Microsoft has provided a tool.

▶ *For more information, see "Going Deeper: Restructuring Domains" later in this chapter.*

Configuring Active Directory Replication

The first Domain Controller that you install in your enterprise will automatically be placed in the Windows 2000 site Default-First-Site-Name. If you do not configure sites and subnets in Windows 2000, all subsequent Domain Controllers will also be added to that site. If you are installing Windows 2000 on a single Local Area Network (LAN) or on a group of LANs connected with high-speed links, no further configuration is necessary.

However, if your implementation includes multiple locations that are connected with less than a T1, you will want to configure Windows 2000 sites. Windows 2000 sites not only allow you to control how the Active Directory replicates and where clients seek authentication services, but you can effectively utilize site-aware client server applications—for example, the Windows 2000 Distributed File System (DFS).

There are two types of Active Directory replication in Windows 2000. Each one has its own set of rules and behaves very differently from the other. In order to configure Active Directory Replication, you need to understand the following:

- Replication within a site
- Replication between sites
- How to use the Active Directory Sites and Services MMC snap-in

Replication Within a Site

Replication within a site is optimized to reduce the time it takes changes to reach other Domain Controllers. To do this, the Knowledge Consistency Checker (KCC) creates a bi-directional ring of connections between all other Domain Controllers in that site. However, as the number of DCs in a site grows, the replication latency continues to be increased. To solve this problem, Microsoft implemented an algorithm, ensuring that all updates are fewer than three hops from the source of the change to the destination. During the initial creation of this replication topology, it is possible for duplicate or unnecessary replication paths to exist. However, the KCC is smart enough to detect these redundant connections and remove them. Finally, it is important to note that replication within a site cannot be configured nor have a schedule applied to it.

Replication Between Sites

Replication between sites is configured to optimize the amount of data sent over the network, given your implementation's tolerance for latency. Each group of sites is connected with a site link. Each of these site links has a relative cost (that you assign). The KCC then generates a least-cost spanning tree, as calculated by the relative cost of the site links. To further optimize the data sent, replication between sites is compressed. Although this causes slightly higher utilization on the target and destination servers, it allows you to more efficiently use your physical connections. Inter-site replication can also be configured to store changes and replicate from a minimum of every 15 minutes to a maximum of every 10,080 minutes. Finally, this type of replication has a configurable schedule of one-hour blocks. For example, you can configure replication to only occur between 5:00 p.m. and 8:00 a.m., if necessary.

▶*For more information on the algorithms used by Active Directory Replication, see the Microsoft White Paper, "Active Directory Architecture."*

Using Active Directory Sites and Services

Active Directory Sites and Services is the MMC snap-in that allows you to configure Active Directory replication. Specifically, you can do the following:

- Create sites
- Create subnets
- Create IP site links

See Figure 4.3.1 for an example of using the Active Directory Sites and Services MMC snap-in.

Figure 4.3.1   Configuring sites, subnets, and site links using the MMC snap-in.

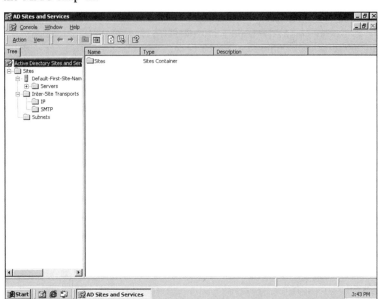

You can launch the Active Directory Sites and Services MMC snap-in from the Administrative Tools program group on the Start menu.

▶ *For more information on configuring and installing Administrative tools, see Chapter 3.3, "Using Administrative Tools."*

Leave the Default Site and Site Link in Place

Do not rename or delete Default-First-Site-Name and DEFAULTIPSITELINK in the Active Directory. A Catch-22 situation exists between sites and site links. When you create a site, you must select a site link that it uses. Also, when you create a site link, you must select at least two sites that it connects. Leaving the defaults in place provides you with a staging area when adding sites and site links.

Creating Sites

Creating a site within the Active Directory Sites and Services MMC snap-in is quite easy. You simply right-click your mouse on the Sites container and select New. Type in the name of your new site and select a site link that it will use to connect it with other sites in your enterprise.

Knowing when to create a site is more difficult. There are only two requirements for creating sites:

- All subnets within the site should be "well-connected." The physical links connecting these subnets should always be available. You do not want a site to contain subnets that are linked with a dial-up connection or a connection that is available only a few hours each day.

- All subnets within the site should be connected via LANs. If you have multiple LANs connected with high-speed links, they are also good candidates for inclusion in a single site. Microsoft recommends that all subnets within the site be connected with links greater that 64 Kbps.

Based on your infrastructure and the needs of your organization, you should attept to find the correct balance between one site and many sites. Table 4.3.2 goes over some of the basic pros and cons of small versus large sites.

Table 4.3.2   Small Number of Sites Versus Large Number of Sites

Scenario	Pros	Cons
Small number of sites	Less site and site link administration. Replication latency and complexity is minimized.	Large number of DCs in each site will impact DC performance.
		Less control over which DCs a client will select.
Large number of sites	Greater optimization of the usage of physical links is possible.	Greater replication complexity.
	Greater control over which DCs a client will select.	Higher level of administration and maintenance of sites and site links.

Create site names from general to specific. For example, USA-AZ-Phoenix. Because sites are sorted alphabetically, this allows you to find them more easily in the Active Directory Sites and Services MMC snap-in.

Creating Subnets

In Windows 2000, a *site* is a collection of subnets. Also, subnets allow clients and servers to know what site they are in. For example, if you install a new Domain Controller, and the DC's subnet is already identified, that DC will be installed in the site that the subnet belongs to.

To create subnets in Windows 2000, do the following:

1 Run the Active Directory Sites and Services MMC snap-in.

2 Right-click the Subnet container and select New Subnet.

3 Enter the address of the subnet and the subnet mask.

4 Select the site that this subnet belongs to.

If your company groups subnets together at a physical location, you do not need to create subnet objects for every physical subnet. This can greatly simplify the subnet object maintenance in Windows 2000. For example, if the Boston office exclusively uses subnets beginning with 10.1.0.0, you can define a single subnet for that location. You do this by entering **10.1.0.0** as the subnet address and **255.255.0.0** as the subnet mask. This way, you can define one subnet for the entire location, rather than manually entering each physical subnet (**10.1.1.0**, **10.1.2.0**, and so on).

Creating IP Site Links

After you decide that you need to implement multiple Windows 2000 sites, you need to plan how those sites will be connected. Inter-site transports, or site links, connect your sites and control replication and site coverage (if a Domain controller does not exist at a site).

Table 4.3.3 shows the items used to configure site links and their acceptable items.

Table 4.3.3   Configurable Items in IP Site Links

Item	Description	Range
Cost	The relative priority that is given to one link over another Given the choice, the lowest-cost link will be chosen. Used to calculate the replication topology and identify "closest" sites. By default, the cost of a site link is 100.	Min: 1 Max: 32,767
Schedule	The times that the link is available for replication. By default, the link is always available. Example: Use this to force replication to occur only during off-peak hours.	Configurable in one-hour blocks
Replication Interval	The period between the start of replication cycles. By default, sites replicate with each other every 180 minutes.	Min: 15 minutes Max: 10,080 minutes (7 days)

To create site links in Windows 2000, do the following:

1 Run the Active Directory Sites and Services MMC snap-in.

2 Select the Inter-Site Transports container to expand it.

3 Right-click the IP container and select New Site Link.

4 Enter the name of the site link and select at least two sites that will use this link.

Site links do not need to simply be point-to-point connections. It is possible for a site link to contain more than two sites. This is useful for reducing the number of site links that need to be created and managed. For example, if your company has three sites, each connected to one other with a T1, you can set up a single site link in which all three sites are members. This greatly simplifies the number of links that need to be created for large implementations.

Site Coverage

Not all sites in the Active Directory need to contain a Domain Controller. This is because of an important feature known as *site coverage*. By default, all Windows 2000 Domain Controllers will examine the sites and site links in the enterprise. The DC will then register itself in any site that does not already have a DC for that Domain.

This means that every site wil have a DC defined, by default, for every Domain in the enterprise, even if that site does not physically contain a DC for that Domain. The DCs that are published will be those from the "closest site" defined by the replication topology.

It is also possible to manually configure a DC to register in another site, regardless of the replication topology. This can be done by manually updating a Registry value on the Domain Controller that you want to register in another site. This is implemented with the SiteCoverage:REG_MULTI_SZ value in HKEY_LOCAL_MACHINE\ System\ CurrentControlSet\ Services\ Netlogon\ Parameters\.

Set this value to the name of the site or sites that you want this DC to register in. The site names exactly match the site names created in the Active Directory Sites and Services MMC snap-in. Within the SiteCoverage value, there must be only one site on each line.

Best Practices for Designing Your Active Directory Replication

- Create sites based on collections of high-speed networks. You need to decide what determines a "high-speed" network, based on your needs.
- Put DCs into those sites based on authentication and authorization needs. In some sites, it may be acceptable to use Domain Controllers in remote locations. However, be sure to assess the impact of a WAN outage.
- Configure links based on the logical WAN to optimize replication between DCs.

Modifying the Active Directory Schema

The *schema* is the set of class and attribute definitions that exist in the Active Directory. All Domains in the enterprise share the schema. You should make schema modifications only when absolutely necessary.

In most implementations of Windows 2000, it is very likely that manual schema extensions will never be required. Consequently, three deliberate safety features protect the schema.

To allow updates to be made to the schema, you must do the following:

- Configure your client to run the Active Directory Schema Manager MMC.

- Use the Active Directory Schema MMC snap-in to change the Schema Operation Master to allow schema updates.

- Be designated as a member of the Schema Administrators Global Security Group, which is located in the forest root.

Schema Modifications Are Permanent!

Schema modifications cannot be reversed and have serious implications throughout the Active Directory. After a class or attribute is added to the schema, it cannot be deleted, although it can be disabled.

Configure Your Client to Run the Active Directory Schema MMC Snap-in

The Active Directory Schema MMC is not installed by default on either Windows 2000 Professional Edition or Windows 2000 Server. To install the snap-in on Windows 2000 Professional, simply install the Administrative tools.

▸*For instructions on installing the Administrative tools, see Chapter 3.3, "Using Administrative Tools."*

On the Windows 2000 server family, you must enable the snap-in by registering the Schema Management Dynamic Linked Library (DLL). To do this, you need to run regsvr32.exe schmmgmt.dll from a command prompt.

After the Administrative tools are installed and enabled on your computer, you can then run MMC.exe and add the Active Directory Schema Console. Figure 4.3.2 shows an example of the Active Directory Schema MMC snap-in.

▸ *For more information on configuring the MMC console, see Chapter 3.2, "Using MMC Consoles."*

Figure 4.3.2   Modifying the Windows 2000 schema using the MMC snap-in.

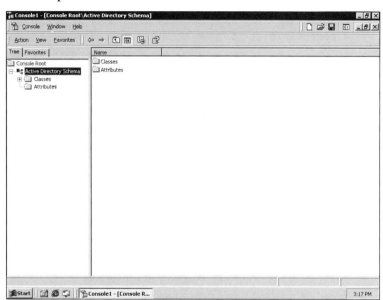

Use the Active Directory Schema MMC Snap-in to Change the Schema Operation Master to Allow Schema Updates

By default, all Domain Controllers prevent modifications on the schema. To modify the schema, you must configure the Schema Operations Master to allow updates. You accomplish this by executing the following steps:

1 Run the Active Directory Schema MMC snap-in.

2 Right-click the Active Directory Schema container.

3 Select Operations Master.

4 At the bottom of the Change Schema Master dialog box, select the checkbox to enable the option The Schema may be modified on this Domain Controller.

You will be able to do this only if you are a member of the Schema Admins Global Security group in the forest root.

The schema is also protected by a Windows 2000 Access Control List. By default, only members of the Schema Admins Global Security Group can make changes to the schema.

? **Where Should the Schema Admins Group Exist?**

Because the Schema Admins group is a Global group, your account must exist in the forest root Domain. If your forest root Domain is in Windows 2000 Native mode, you can change this group to a Universal group, which can contain users from outside the local Domain.

▶ *For more information on Windows 2000 Groups,
see Chapter 4.5, "Creating and Managing Groups."*

Common Examples of Changes You Might Need to Make to the Schema

Although it is not recommended that you extend the schema (for example, add classes or attributes), it is sometimes necessary to change the properties of existing attributes. Even though these types of changes can be reversed, you should still plan carefully prior to making these changes.

There are two main types of schema changes that might be desirable to make:

- Mark attributes for inclusion in the Global Catalog
- Index attributes in the Active Directory

Mark Attributes for Inclusion in the Global Catalog

Sometimes, it might be necessary to include certain user attributes in the Global Catalog (GC) that are not included in the GC by default. For example, one common practice among large companies is to mark the user attribute, employeeID, for GC replication. Now, an Active Directory Enabled application could query the GC for an employeeID and get the resulting user object.

To mark an attribute for inclusion in the Global Catalog:

1 Run the Active Directory Schema MMC snap-in.

2 Select the Attributes container.

3 Right-click the attribute you want to modify and select Properties.

4 Enable the Replicate this attribute to the Global Catalog checkbox.

Index Attributes in the Active Directory

The second type of change that may be desirable is to index attributes in the Active Directory. Doing so should increase the speed with with your Active Directory-enabled application can search that attribute.

To index an attribute in the Active Directory, do the following:

1 Run the Active Directory Schema MMC snap-in.

2 Select the Attributes container.

3 Right-click the attribute you want to modify and select Properties.

4 Enable the Index this attribute in the Active Directory checkbox.

Going Deeper: Restructing Domains

No matter how much planning and effort you put into your implementation of the Active directory, it will be necessary to modify parts of the design at some point in time. To be able to restructure Domains in your Active Directory, Microsoft has provided some tools in Windows 2000. Specifically, there are tools that will help you do the following:

- Move objects within a Domain
- Move objects between Domains in the forest
- Restructure entire Domains

Move Objects Within a Domain

Moving objects within a Domain is the simplest of all restructuring activities. This functionality is built into the the Active Directory Users and Computers MMC snap-in. To move an object, right-click the object and select All Tasks; then choose Move. You will be presented with a list of containers within the Domain. Simply select the appropriate destination. Other MMC snap-ins also have this functionality for the objects they manage. For example, you can move Domain Controllers between sites in the Active Directory Sites and Services MMC snap-in.

Move Objects Between Domains in the Forest

To make it possible to move objects or collections of objects from one Domain in the forest to another, Microsoft provides the MOVETREE.EXE utility in the Windows 2000 Resource Kit.

MOVETREE.EXE commands can be quite complex. A complete list of parameters can be found by running MOVETREE.EXE /? or checking the Windows 2000 Resource Kit online documentation.

Before attempting to use MOVETREE.EXE, there are a couple of things that you need to do in advance. First, the destination Domain must be in Native mode. Second, the immediate parent of the object you are moving must exist. In the following example, the OU Executives must exist in the Domain mycompany.com.

Example of a Movetree Command

Situation: You need to move a single user object John Q. Public in the OU Finance from the Domain eur.mycompany.com to the OU Executives in the Domain mycompany.com:

Movetree /start /s server1.eur.mycompany.com /d server2.mycompany.com /sdn CN="John Q. Public",OU=finance,DC=eur,DC=mycompany,DC=com /ddn CN="John Q. Public",OU=executives,DC=mycompany,DC=com /u mycompany\administrator /p mypassword

Restructure Entire Domains

In Windows 2000, it is not possible to prune and graft Domains, either within a forest or between forests. However, it is possible to achieve the same end result with a little effort.

To make it possible to restructure Domains and to aid in the migration to Windows 2000, Microsoft has jointly developed the Active Directory Migration Tool (ADMT). This tool makes it possible to move all or part of a Domain to another location. For example, you can split Domains, consolidate Domains, or effectively move Domains by executing the following steps:

1 Create the target Domain in your forest.

2 Use the ADMT to migrate the objects from the source to the target.

3 Decommission the source Domain.

Create the Target Domain In Your Forest

One drawback of the ADMT is that you cannot perform an intact Domain move. The target Domain must exist in the Windows 2000 forest as a Native mode Domain. Follow the steps described earlier in this chapter to create the new Domain. This Domain will now be the destination for the objects that you are moving.

Note: This step is not necessary if you are consolidating Domains and at least one of them is in the Windows 2000 forest. Simply pick one of the Windows 2000 Domains in your forest as the target and migrate the other Domains' objects to that Domain.

Use the ADMT to Migrate the Objects from the Source to the Target

The ADMT provides major benefits over utilities such as MOVETREE when doing major Domain restructuring or migrations. These benefits include the following:

- **Task based MMC snap-in.** The tool looks and behaves like other Windows 2000 tools.

- **Provides reporting and modeling tools.** You have the ability to simulate migrations and view reports. Reports are saved as HTML files to allow them to be posted to your intranet.

- **Provides group synchronization.** Without this tool, you would be required to migrate an entire closed set. *Closed sets* are collections of users and groups that can be moved without cloning. It is possible that the smallest closed set is the entire Domain. For example, due to the rules of group membership, you cannot move a Global group until all members of that group are in the destination Domain. Also, you cannot move users without moving their Global groups.

- **ADMT continues the operation, even if there are individual failures.** This prevents a single failure from causing the entire operation to fail.

  ▶ *For more information on the ADMT,*
  see the Microsoft Web site at http://www.microsoft.com/.

Decommission the Source Domain

If desired, you can decommission the source Domain. If this Domain is part of your Windows 2000 forest, you need to run the Active Directory Wizard on each of the Domain Controllers to uninstall the Active Directory. On the last Domain Controller (preferably the one that owns the PDC FSMO), you will specify that this is the last DC in this Domain. This will remove all references of that Domain from the Active Directory.

This step is not necessary if you are splitting Domains and the source Domain is in the Windows 2000 forest. For example, if you want to split a Domain in half, you could migrate half of the objects to the new Domain and leave half in the current Domain.

4.4

Creating and Managing User Accounts

You Need to Read This Section If You Want to:

- Add new user(s) to your Windows 2000 computer or network.
- Remove user(s) from your Windows 2000 computer or network.
- Change attributes (such as the password) of an account.
- Automate the addition, removal, or modification of user account(s).

Related Topics

Overview of User Accounts

The management of user accounts is one of the primary responsibilities of system administrators. User accounts are important because they are a fundamental unit of security and audit policies. In past versions of Windows, it was uncommon for anyone but administrators to require the ability to list user accounts. Accordingly, there was little identifying information to maintain other than Login Name, Full Name, and Description.

In Windows 2000, the strategic importance of user account maintenance has increased. Active Directory now represents not just a list of accounts, but also a database and referral point for many services that require the data to be up-to-date. The Active Directory is exposed to users often—especially in collaborative activities such as video conferencing and electronic mail. As a result, more fields have been created to help associate directory objects with real people and resources.

Although this has resulted in an increased burden on administrators, powerful new tools have come to their rescue. The traditional GUI-based management applications still exist, but additional command-line applications and API (Application Program Interface) techniques are now included. Although these new tools are sophisticated, they do not require extensive application programming experience to use.

Virtually all these new fields, functionality, and tools focus on the Active Directory. Although Windows 2000 still supports the "workgroup" networking model (utilizing local accounts), Active Directory is where the exciting improvements are.
▶ *For more information on Active Directory,*
see Chapter 1.2, "Introduction to Active Directory," and Chapter 4.2, "DNS and Active Directory."

Local (SAM) Accounts

The concept of local accounts has been carried over from the Windows NT security model. Although every Windows 2000 computer maintains a list of accounts, only non-Domain Controllers can contain local accounts.

Local accounts are sometimes referred to as *SAM accounts* because the Security Accounts Manager (SAM) service is responsible for their maintenance. The SAM service stores local accounts in an encrypted file on the local computer (%systemroot%\system32\config\sam). Local accounts are known only to the local computer, so they can be used only to authenticate to and use resources on that one computer.

Local accounts are useful in the following scenarios:

- To allow users in untrusted Domains or workgroups to access resources that exist on the local computer.

- To ensure access to a computer when Domain authentication services may be unavailable. For example, a local administration account would be needed to reconfigure a computer that cannot communicate on the network.

Local accounts may also present you with security problems. By definition, local accounts are not centrally managed, so maintaining standards throughout your enterprise may prove difficult. In addition to the security issues, the automation tools discussed later in this chapter (Command Prompt tools and ADSI) do not apply to local accounts.

To create a local account, do the following:

1 Ensure that you are logged on to the computer with appropriate credentials. You must be a member of the local Administrator's group to create local accounts.

2 Launch the Computer Management MMC snap-in. The easiest way to do this is to right-click the My Computer desktop icon and choose Manage.

3 Navigate to the Local Users and Groups section under System Tools. When you select the Users folder, a list of local accounts will appear in the right pane. If there is a red X on the icon, you are probably managing a Domain Controller, which does not support local accounts.

4 Right-click and choose New User. The New User dialog box appears.

5 In the User Name field, enter the new account's logon name. End users typically recognize the User Name as their logon name or the identification they provide to gain access to the computer or network.

6 In the Full Name field, enter the full name of the user, preferably in last, first format.

7 Enter the initial password into the Password and Confirm Password fields.

Best Practices for Local Accounts

- Use them sparingly.

- If you have implemented a Windows NT or Windows 2000 Domain model, do not permit end users to create local accounts on their computers. Instead, encourage them to engage the IT support process to have a Domain account created. Although this might seem like more work for you (and the user) in the beginning, you will have fewer problems in the long run.

- Design a predictable, secure architecture for how and where you will use local accounts. Standardize their use throughout your enterprise, whenever possible. If each system has different local accounts and different passwords, you will (or should) spend a lot of time tracking this information. Consult with your organization's security group to get input.

- Make sure that at least one local Administrator account is enabled on all workstations. This will ensure that you can gain administrative control of the workstation if it is not able to contact a Domain Controller. If you standardize the password for this account, carefully guard this password!

Domain User Accounts

For the most part, Domain user accounts are the preferred way to implement network security. Although there is additional complexity involved in maintaining a Domain architecture, Domain accounts have the following compelling advantages over local accounts:

- Domain accounts exist as objects in the Active Directory, and thus may be centrally (and securely) managed.

- Access to resources on any computer in the Domain may be granted to Domain accounts. This allows a single Domain account to have access to resources on multiple computers. To accomplish this with local accounts, each computer accessed would require an identical account and password.

- Domain accounts can be granted access to resources in other Domains when trust relationships have been established. With new support in Windows 2000 for transitive trusts, access to other Domain resources may not even require an explicit trust.

When Active Directory is first installed, a set of default accounts is automatically included in the new directory. These accounts are created for one of two reasons:

- They help you get started in effectively managing the Active Directory.

- They ensure the secure, reliable operation of an option or service that is running on computer(s) in your network. Usually, these services need to run under a specific security context other than Administrative rights.

Table 4.4.1 contains a list of default Domain accounts included in a typical installation of Windows 2000.

Table 4.4.1   Default Domain Accounts

Name	Description
Administrator	Default account for administering the automatically given full permissions to manage the Domain.
Guest	Default account for guest access to the computer/Domain. A user with no defined Domain account may be able to access limited resources with the Guest account.
IUSR_<Domain-name>	This account is created when Internet Information Services is installed. It provides permissions for anonymous users to access Web pages. ▶ *For more information, see Chapter 5.8, "Internet Information Server."*
IWAM_<Domain-name>	This account is also created when Internet Information Services is installed. It is used to start out-of-process applications spawned by IIS. ▶ *For more information, see Chapter 5.8, "Internet Information Server."*
Krbtgt	This is the Key Distribution Center Service Account, which is used by the Kerberos security subsystem to grant Ticket Granting Tickets to network clients. Kerberos is a highly secure, yet somewhat complex security architecture. More information about this account is available in RFC 1510, available at `http://www.ietf.org`.
TsInternetUser	This user account is created if Terminal Services is installed on the computer. When Terminal Services Internet Connector licensing is enabled, all Terminal Server sessions are logged in with this account. ▶*For more information,* *see Chapter 8.8, "Terminal Services."*

Administering User Accounts

As objects in the Active Directory, user accounts are available for administration by any of the various channels provided to manipulate data in the directory. These channels include GUI (Graphical User Interface), command-line scripting, and API methods. A brief overview of each method to administer user accounts is shown in the sections that follow.

GUI Interface

The Active Directory Users and Computer MMC snap-in is the most common and convenient way to administer user accounts. The snap-in is available by default on Windows 2000 servers and is installable as an optional software package (ADMINPAK.MSI) from the Windows 2000 CD.

AD Users and Computers presents a hierarchical view of the containers within the Active Directory and the contents within those containers. Users within the containers are identified in the right pane with an icon representing a person's face. If an account is disabled (not currently permitted to log in), a red X appears in front of the icon. It is generally good practice to use the Description field to make administrative notes for special cases. In Figure 4.4.1, you can see that the account for Robert Johnson has been disabled because he is on sabbatical.

Figure 4.4.1   AD Users is showing the status of different users.

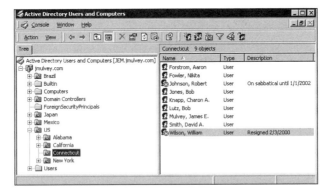

Creating and Deleting User Accounts

After you have launched Active Directory Users and Computers, and you have determined which OU should contain a new user, creating a Domain user account is very similar to the process of creating a local user:

1 Right-click the container name and choose New, User.

The New User dialog box appears. Note that the Domain name fields will be automatically included in the form.

2 Enter the information shown in Table 4.4.2 into the appropriate fields.

Table 4.4.2   New User Account Fields, Part 1

Field	Purpose
First Name, Initials, Last Name	These fields help identify the person who uses the account.
Full Name	This field populates a number of fields in the Active Directory. The most important of these is the Canonical Name. Because the Canonical Name is difficult to change, ensure that you standardize it among all users you create. Full names must be unique within the OU.
User Logon Name	Also known as the User Principal Name (UPN), the user logon name is what most users associate as their ID or account. It is the logon name they provide when first starting a session with a Windows computer. User logon names must be unique within the Domain.
User Logon Name (pre-Windows 2000)	This field provides compatibility with earlier versions of Windows. This field also must be unique within the Domain.

3 When complete, click the Next button.

A new property dialog box appears.

4 Define the password and select the appropriate settings, shown in Table 4.4.3.

Table 4.4.3   New User Account Fields, Part 2

Field	Purpose
Password, Confirm Password	If you want to set an initial password on the account, enter that password in these fields. These fields are not required, but it is strongly recommended that you set a password on all accounts in your network.
User Must Change Password At Next Logon	Check this checkbox if you want to force the next user to log in with this account to change the password.
User Cannot Change Password	Check this checkbox if you want to prevent the user from changing the password. This is useful if you have an account that is shared by many people or a computer service that runs in a user context.
Password Never Expires	This checkbox overrides any password-expiration rules and prevents the password from ever expiring.
Account Is Disabled	When checked, this option disables the account and prevents anyone from logging onto the network with it.

5 Click Next. The final screen will summarize the options chosen. Verify these settings and click Finish. The user account is then created in the directory.

Command-Prompt Utilities

The command-line utilities are well-suited for those with good Microsoft Office skills.

Two command-prompt utilities are provided with Windows 2000 that provide this functionality: CSVDE and LDIFDE.

Although generally similar, LDIFDE is more functional because it supports creation, deletion, and modification of existing objects, whereas CSVDE supports only the creation and deletion of objects.

The following sections give a brief overview of each utility and include some samples that show how to use them.

CSVDE

CSVDE is a command-line application that provides for the import or export of the attributes of many user objects at once. By transferring data between Active Directory and text files formatted in comma-separated-value (CSV) format, new objects (such as user accounts) can be created. CSV formatting allows many applications (notably Microsoft Office) to be used to manage data from Active Directory without programming.

The first line (or header) of a CSV file contains a sequential list of attribute names, separated by commas. Subsequent lines reflect the values of those attributes for the exported objects, also separated by commas. If an attribute supports multiple values (for example, a user may belong to multiple groups), the individual values are separated by a colon (:). Typically, each line after the header represents a discrete object, although it's legal to use the ampersand character (&) to continue an object's
definition to the next line.

Raw CSV files are difficult for a human to read, but applications such as Microsoft Access and Excel make them a breeze to view and manipulate!

CSVDE is run from the command prompt and requires a number of command-line parameters. In addition to the parameters defined in Table 4.4.4, additional parameters may apply, depending on whether you are exporting objects (see Table 4.4.5) or importing objects (see Table 4.4.6).

Table 4.4.4   General Options for CSVDE

Option	Description
-I	If this option is not defined, CSVDE assumes it will export data from Active Directory into a CSV file (over-writing the CSV, if it exists). The -I command-line option indicates that the CSV file (specified by the -f option) is to be read, not written to, and the utility will be importing changes into the Active Directory.

.

Option	Description
-f filename	Regardless of whether you plan to import or export information with CSVDE, you must specify a CSV file. The -f command-line option allows you to do so. After specifying -f, you designate the file with which CSVDE should work. (Don't forget to add a space between -f and the filename). This option is required to run CSVDE in any mode.
-s servername	When looking for an instance of Active Directory, CSVDE normally connects to the most convenient Domain Controller for your Domain. If you want to apply CSVDE to another Domain or perhaps a specific Domain Controller in the Domain, you can specify that server or Domain name here.
-v	This option turns on Verbose mode. In this mode, the screen will output much more information on what exactly CSVDE is doing. This option does not change the behavior or file output of the command, but simply displays more information on the console when the command is executed.
-c FromDN ToDN	This powerful option allows you to replace instances of text from the source directory name with alternative text. This could be especially useful if you are moving objects from one directory to another or want to dupli- cate objects into a test lab that doesn't have the same namespace as the production environment.
-j path	Whether you need it or not, a detailed log of activity will be generated by CSVDE. This activity log contains the same information you would receive on the console if you requested Verbose mode (the -v option). The log is always named CSV.LOG, but with the -j option, you can specify the path where the file should be stored.
-t port#	If, by some chance, you are using CSVDE to query an LDAP server that is not operating on TCP/IP port 389 (the default), the -t option will allow you to specify a different port number.
-u	Interprets CSV file using Unicode character formatting. Unicode was developed as an alternative to ASCII so that many other languages could be supported. Although Unicode-ready systems such as Windows 2000 will rec- ognize these files as text files, other systems may not. Unicode files are twice as big as straight ASCII text files, but may be necessary if your network spans non- Western countries and you expect directory information to contain non-Western character sets.
-a UserDN [Password¦ *]	Authenticates to the LDAP server using basic authentication. You must specify a login name and password.

continued

Table 4.4.4   *continued*

Option	Description
-b UserName Domain [Password ¦ *]	Authenticates to the LDAP server using the Security Support Provider Interface (SSPI) API. You must specify a login name, Domain name, and password.
-?	This option displays online help for the CSVDE command.

When using CSVDE to perform a directory Export, certain additional options are available, as shown in Table 4.4.5.

Table 4.4.5   *Export Options for CSVDE*

Option	Description
-d RootDN	By default, CSVDE will export objects at the root of the Domain container of the Active Directory. The -d option allows you to specify subcontainers within the directory or even other root-level containers in the Active Directory (schema and configuration).
-r Filter	This is a powerful option that allows you to limit exported objects to only those objects that meet specified filter criteria. When used in combination with the -d option, you can create very specialized exports that export only certain kinds of objects in certain parts of the directory.
	RFC 2254, available at www.ietf.org, contains more information about syntax and construction of LDAP search filters.
-p [Base ¦ OneLevel ¦ Subtree]	Allows you to define how far into the directory tree the command should look for objects that meet your criteria. This option can have one of three arguments:
	Base Examines only objects at the base of the directory hierarchy where CSVDE is operating. Does not search branches.
	OneLevel Examines objects at the base and one level down into any child branches of the directory hierarchy.
	Subtree Examines all objects in all child branches of the directory specified.
-l list	By default, if even one object has an entry defined for an obscure attribute, that attribute will be included in the header. CSVDE includes only object attributes that have a defined value in at least one object. If you want to ensure that an attribute is included in the export file, even if it is blank for all objects, use the -l option.
-o list	By default, CSVDE includes only object attributes that have defined values. If you want to ensure that an attribute is *not* included in the export file, even if it has a defined value, use the -o option.

Option	Description
-g	Normally, LDAP searches are performed in a paged manner, which breaks down large results into many separate pages. By delivering the result in smaller chunks, results can be processed piece-by-piece. This option disables paged searches and instead forces the entire result to be delivered at once. Although this may be more efficient, a large LDAP query result may trigger a Size Limit Exceeded message.
-m	When enabled, this option prevents the export of attributes that are specific to Active Directory objects.
-n	When enabled, this option prevents the export of attributes that contain binary values.

When using CSVDE to perform a directory Import, another option is available, as shown in Table 4.4.6.

Table 4.4.6   Import Option for CSVDE

Option	Description
-k	Normally, if CSVDE encounters an error while performing an import operation, it will halt. When this option is specified, the command will continue processing.

CSVDE Import Examples

To add a user with CSVDE, create a comma-separated file with the following minimum fields, shown in Table 4.4.7.

Table 4.4.7   Minimum Object Attributes Required to Create a User Object

Field	Description
DN	DN is short for Distinguished Name. An object's DN describes its entire path through the hierarchy of Active Directory. LDAP syntax is used to describe the hierarchy.
ObjectClass	ObjectClass defines the type of object to be created. When creating users, this is always set to user. Other values such as group and organizationalUnit are also valid, however.
sAMAccountName	This field contains the SAM account name (pre-Windows 2000 User logon name).

A sample comma-separated file containing these fields might contain the following text:

```
DN,objectClass,sAMAccountName
"CN=test user,CN=Users,DC=jmulvey,DC=com",user,testuser
```

The first line is the header, which contains the attribute names that will be specified for each object. In this case, only the three minimum object attributes are included. You can include additional attributes when creating the object, but Windows 2000 will accept only field names that are valid. If you are looking to set additional attributes, the ADSIEDIT application, available in the Windows 2000 Resource Kit, can be used to identify additional valid object field names available for import/export with CSVDE.

The second line contains values for each of the three minimum object attributes specified in the header line. Note that because the DN attribute contains commas within its value, DN is surrounded by two quote marks. This ensures that the commas do not indicate subsequent attribute values of the header.

After the import file has been created, you are ready to execute the CSVDE command.

In the following example, we run CSVDE and indicate that it should import users from the IMPORT.CSV file. In our example, the file exists on the root of drive C:. You can name the file as you like and place it anywhere that's convenient, however.

When executed, you should see output similar to the following:

```
C:\>csvde -i -f import.csv
Connecting to "(null)"
Logging in as current user using SSPI
Importing directory from file "import.csv"
Loading entries..
1 entry modified successfully.
The command has completed successfully
```

CSVDE Export Examples

The following example uses LDAP filtering to export all directory objects that have a fax number beginning with 203-555:

```
csvde -r "(facsimileTelephoneNumber=203-555*)" -f export.csv
```

The following example also uses LDAP filtering to export all organizational units in the Domain, regardless of location:

```
csvde -r "(objectClass=organizationalUnit)" -f export.csv
```

The following example is similar to the previous one, except that it exports only top-level organizational units:

```
csvde -p "Onelevel" -r "(objectClass=organizationalUnit)" -f export.csv
```

The following example exports only organizational units that exist immediately under the US organizational unit in your sample Domain (jmulvey.com):

```
csvde -d "ou=US,DC=JMULVEY,DC=COM" -p "Onelevel" -r
"(objectClass=organizationalUnit)" -f test.csv
```

The following example builds further on the previous sample to export organizational units that exist immediately under the US organizational unit in your sample Domain (jmulvey.com) and have the location field set to Boston.

```
csvde -d "ou=US,DC=JMULVEY,DC=COM" -p "Onelevel" -r
"(&(objectClass=organizationalUnit)(l=Boston))" -f test.csv
```

LDIFDE

Although very similar in operation, LDIFDE has some major functionality advantages over CSVDE. Although both utilities support the export and creation of objects, LDIFDE has the added capability to modify existing objects in Active Directory. LDIFDE also uses LDAP Data Interchange Format (LDIF) files instead of the comma-separated format used by CSVDE.

The LDIF file format describes objects by placing the contents of each attribute on a separate line in the text file. A blank line in the file indicates the start of a new object. LDIF files are more human-readable than CSV files, but more difficult to import or export from applications such as Microsoft Access or Excel. LDIF is an open standard, defined by the Internet Engineering Task Force. More detailed information on the LDIF file format standard can be found at http://www.ietf.org.

When using LDIFDE to import data, an entry is required for each object in the text file. The entry changetype indicates whether the object is to be added as a new object, or instead represents changes to an existing object. The changetype entry can be set to create, modify, or delete.

Like CSVDE, LDIFDE is run from the command prompt and requires several command-line parameters. These parameters are identical in form and function to the options available in CSVDE. (Refer to Tables 4.4.4, 4.4.5 and 4.4.6).

Adding a User with LDIFDE

To create a new Windows 2000 user using the LDIFDE command, first create an LDIF file (in this case, name it **IMPORT.LDF**). This file must contain the following minimum attributes to successfully create a new user (of course, the values for these attributes may be different):

```
dn: CN=test user,CN=Users,DC=jmulvey,DC=com
changetype: add
objectClass: user
sAMAccountName: testuser
```

Of course, additional object attributes can be defined within the LDIF file if you have more information you want to include with the user. The ADSIEDIT application, available in the Windows 2000 Resource Kit, can be used to identify additional valid object field names available for import/export with LDIFDE.

Next, execute the LDIFDE command as follows:

```
C:\>ldifde -i -f import.ldf
Connecting to "JEM.jmulvey.com"
Logging in as current user using SSPI
Importing directory from file "import.ldf"
Loading entries..
1 entry modified successfully.

The command has completed successfully
```

The new user should now exist in the Users container (as defined in the IMPORT.LDF file).

Deleting a User with LDIFDE

When deleting a user, only the Distinguished Name (DN) of the object needs to be specified. For example, to delete the test user you created previously, create a file called **DELETE.LDF** with the following contents:

```
dn: CN=test user,CN=Users,DC=jmulvey,DC=com
changetype: delete
```

Next, execute the LDIFDE command as follows:

```
C:\>ldifde -i -f delete.ldf
Connecting to "JEM.jmulvey.com"
Logging in as current user using SSPI
Importing directory from file "delete.ldf"
Loading entries..
1 entry modified successfully.
The command has completed successfully
```

The user should now be removed from the directory.

Modifying a User with LDIFDE

Creation of LDIF files when modifying users is a bit more involved than in other scenarios. After specifying the Distinguished Name (DN) and indicating a changetype of modify, a change operation identifier is used to indicate which attributes are to be modified. Finally, each attribute change is concluded with a dash on a blank line.

In the examples used here, you will use a Change Operation Identifier of replace.

For example, to change the location of your test user, create an LDIF file with the following contents:

```
dn: CN=test user,CN=Users,DC=jmulvey,DC=com
changetype: modify
replace: l
l: Boston
-
```

Next, execute the LDIFDE command as follows:

```
C:\>ldifde -i -f modify.ldf
Connecting to "JEM.jmulvey.com"
Logging in as current user using SSPI
Importing directory from file "modify.ldf"
Loading entries..
1 entry modified successfully.

The command has completed successfully
```

If you want to modify several attributes of an object at once, you do not need to respecify the object each time. Simply separate each attribute with a dash on one line and include the additional attribute function and content.

```
dn: CN=test user,CN=Users,DC=jmulvey,DC=com
changetype: modify
replace: l
l: Boston
-

replace: telephoneNumber
telephoneNumber: 617-555-5555
-
```

When this file is imported with LDIFDE, both the location and telephone number will be replaced with Boston and 617-555-5555, respectively.

Using ADSI Scripts to Manage User Accounts

API interfaces can be easily scripted with only a little knowledge of Microsoft Visual Basic.

Scripting though ADSI represents the most complex, yet most powerful way to manage user accounts in Active Directory.

Creating a user with ADSI looks like this:

```
Set ou = GetObject("LDAP://CN=Users,DC=jmulvey,DC=com")
FirstName = InputBox("User's First Name?","ADSI Create User Demo")
LastName = InputBox("User's Last Name?","ADSI Create User Demo")
Set usr = ou.Create("user", "cn=" & FirstName & " " & LastName)
usr.Put "samAccountName", Left(FirstName,1) & LastName
usr.Put "givenName", FirstName
usr.Put "sn", LastName
usr.Put "displayName", LastName & ", " & FirstName
usr.SetInfo
```

Deleting a user with ADSI looks like this:

```
Set x = GetObject("LDAP://CN=Users,DC=jmulvey,DC=com")
DeleteName = InputBox("User to be Deleted?","ADSI Delete User Demo")
x.Delete "user", "cn=" & DeleteName
```

Best Practices When Administering Accounts

- Use the Description field to make administrative notes and reminders relative to the management of directory objects.
- Use Last, First format for the Display Name field. By conforming to this standard, you will be able to more easily locate users who may prefer nicknames as their first name (for example, Robert versus Bob).
- Consider automating data feeds from other systems to keep data in the Active Directory up-to-date. For example, many corporate telephony departments maintain accurate electronic lists of employee telephone numbers, which can be integrated into appropriate Active Directory

fields. Another idea: Find out if your Human Resource department can supply updates to the organizational reporting structure. This information could be used to update the Manager and Direct Reports fields in Active Directory. There are endless possibilities here. In any event, make sure the data provided is relevant and kept up-to-date.

4.5

Creating and Managing Groups

You Need to Read This Section If You Want to:

- Understand features of traditional as well as new Windows 2000 group types.
- Add or remove groups from your domain.
- Change attributes (such as membership) of a group.
- Automate the addition, removal, or modification of groups.

Overview of Groups

In Windows 2000, *groups* allow collections of objects in the Active Directory to be referred to as a single object. Essentially, they are "one-to-many" pointers that can be used to refer to a collection of objects as a single entity. Although groups are actually references and not containers, it is common to say a group "contains" objects.

Groups are a primary tool used by system administrators to reduce the burden of managing large numbers of users. This section details the various types of groups available in Windows 2000 and focuses on the many ways administrators can manage groups themselves—both manually and programmatically—to further reduce administrative burden.

Local (SAM) Groups

Like local (SAM) accounts, Local groups are maintained by computers that are not Domain Controllers. These computers support a Security Accounts Manager (SAM) service that maintains Local groups. Local groups are known only to the local computer (they are not published in the Active Directory) and can only be assigned permissions to local resources.

▶ *For more information on the SAM service, see Chapter 4.4, "Creating and Managing User Accounts."*

In the absence of a domain architecture, Local groups still give an administrator the ability to simplify the assignment of rights. Local groups can contain local users, thereby allowing the administrator to apply user rights to a broad number of users at once.

But the real power of the Local group is realized when the computer becomes a member of a Domain. Local groups become much more powerful in a Domain configuration because only then may they contain Global groups from the Domain or trusted Domains. You will learn more about Global groups in a moment, but right now all you need to know is that some of these Global groups may originate from (and thus can be administered in) other domains. By allowing "nested group" memberships such as these, the administrator of the local computer can delegate some administrative functions to administrators in other domains. He can assign resource permissions to groups under the control of another (trusted) Domain administrator, giving that administrator the ability to control who has access to specific resources, but not the ability to change the specific permissions assigned to the resource.

This methodology is the preferred way to assign permissions to large groups of users in a trusted multi-domain environment: Users are added to Global groups, Global groups are added to Local groups, and Local groups are assigned permissions to resources.

Domain Groups

When a domain architecture is implemented, a number of additional group types become available. Each of these groups has specific characteristics and uses that make them useful in certain scenarios.

Security Groups and Distribution Groups

Although there are many different kinds of groups available in a Domain, they all fall into two broad categories:

- **Security groups**. Security groups use the power of object grouping to simplify the security process for administrators. In general, when a Security group is assigned permissions to a resource, all the members of the group receive those permissions.

- **Distribution groups**. In electronic mail systems, distribution lists allow users to send messages to groups of users. Microsoft's Active Directory strategy has a big place set at the table for electronic mail. In the near future, what were known as distribution lists will be represented as *Distribution groups*. Distribution groups may not be used to control security.

Within each of these two categories, a number of specialized groups can exist: Universal groups, Global groups, and Domain Local groups. Let's take a brief look at each one of these.

Universal Groups

Universal groups are a powerful new kind of group, available only on domains that operate in Native mode. Universal groups allow an administrator to group together objects from anywhere within the forest. If created as a Security group, administrators in any domain in the forest may assign the group permissions. Powerful Universal groups should be used carefully because their membership is replicated throughout the forest in the Global Catalog (GC). It is important to note that the GC contains a *full* membership list of the Universal group. Any changes to Universal group membership, therefore, will initiate a forest-wide change that must be replicated. For this reason, it is recommended that changes to Universal group membership be limited. One strategy to accomplish this is to have only Global groups contained within the Universal group. In this manner, individual user membership changes happen at the Global group level, but do not alter the explicit membership of the Universal group and therefore do not initiate a forest-wide replication of the group.

Universal groups can contain Domain user accounts, Global groups and other Universal groups.

Global Groups

Windows 2000 Global groups have many similar characteristics to Global groups in Windows NT 4.0. One new characteristic in Windows 2000 is that Global groups are published in the Global Catalog (GC) so that other domains in the forest can become aware of the group. However, the membership details of Global groups are not contained in the GC, so it is acceptable to make frequent changes to Global group membership because this will not impact GC replication.

Global groups may contain Domain user accounts and, if the Windows 2000 Domain is operating in Native mode, other Global groups are in the domain in which they were created.

Domain Local Groups

Domain Local groups can be created and used only on Domain Controller computers. They are analogous to Local groups on Windows 2000 Professional Workstations: They are known only to computers holding the account database (Domain Controllers), and can therefore be applied only to resources on those computers.

Domain Local groups can contain practically all other security objects: Domain User accounts, Domain Local groups (from the same domain), Domain Global groups, and Universal groups.

Nesting Groups

The group types most used in mature Windows 2000 Domain environments are Universal and Global groups. These groups differ primarily in their scope of membership: Universal groups can contain objects from any Domain, whereas Global groups can contain users from the local Domain only. It is often useful to nest groups within each other to leverage these differences in group scope to provide good cross-domain security models.

Table 4.5.1 shows the nesting relationships between the various group types in Windows 2000.

Table 4.5.1 Types of Groups in Windows 2000

	Local Groups	THESE GROUPS — Domain Groups — Security			THESE GROUPS — Domain Groups — Distribution		
		Global	Local	Universal*	Global	Local	Universal*
May Contain							
Local accounts	YES	NO	NO	NO	NO	NO	NO
Domain accounts	YES***	YES****	YES	YES	YES****	YES	YES
May Contain							
Local group	NO	NO	NO	NO	NO	NO	NO
Domain Security Global	YES	YES*	YES	YES	YES*	YES	YES
Domain Security Local	NO	NO	YES**	NO	NO	YES**	NO
Domain Security Universal	YES	NO	YES	YES	NO	YES	YES
Domain Distribution Global	NO	YES*	YES	YES	YES*	YES	YES
Domain Distribution Local	NO	NO	YES**	NO	NO	YES**	NO
Domain Distribution Universal	NO	NO	YES	NO	NO	YES	YES
Can be Referenced in ACLs	YES	YES	YES	YES	NO	YES	YES
On local computer	YES	YES	YES	YES	NO	NO	NO
Any Domain Controller in Domain	NO	YES	YES	YES	NO	NO	NO
Any domain member	NO	YES	NO	YES	NO	NO	NO
Throughout the forest	NO	YES	NO	YES	NO	NO	NO
Appear in global catalog	NO	YES	NO	YES	YES	NO	YES
Membership contained in global catalog	NO	NO	NO	YES	NO	NO	YES

* Allowed only in domains operating in Native mode.
** May contain Domain Local groups from the same domain only.
*** May contain Domain Accounts from joined or trusted domains only.
**** May contain Domain Accounts from local domain only.

Default Domain Groups

When Active Directory is installed on a computer, the directory is automatically populated with a set of default groups to help you administer the Domain (see Table 4.5.2). These groups are created in the Builtin container, and always exist in every Domain.

Table 4.5.2   Contents of the Builtin Container After Installing AD

Name	Description
Account Operators	Members can administer Domain user and Group accounts.
Administrators	Administrators have full access to the computer/Domain.
Backup Operators	Backup Operators can only use a backup program to back up files and folders on to the computer.
Guests	Guests can operate the computer and save documents, but cannot install programs or make potentially damaging changes to the system files and settings.
Print Operators	Members can administer Domain printers.
Replicator	Supports file replication in a Domain.
Server Operators	Members can administer Domain servers.
Users	Users can operate the computer and save documents, but cannot install programs or make potentially damaging changes to the system files and settings.

Creating, Deleting, and Modifying Group Accounts

Some of the most basic tasks you'll be doing as a Windows 2000 administrator include creating and deleting group accounts. There are several ways to accomplish those tasks, including using a GUI, ADSI Scripts, or a command prompt.

GUI

The Active Directory Users and Computers application supplies a Graphical User Interface (GUI) that allows an administrator to create groups. The application is very easy to use and will probably be the most common way you will create groups.

Creating a New Group Using AD Users and Computers

To create a new group, follow these steps:

1 Right-click on the container name and choose New, Group. The New User dialog box appears.

2 Enter the following information into the appropriate fields:

Field	Purpose
Group name	Defines the name of the group as it will appear in Active Directory.
Group name (pre-Windows 2000)	This field is automatically populated with data entered in the Group name field by default. However, if you want this group to appear differently in downlevel domains, you may specify a different name here.
Group scope	Group scope defines whether the group will be a Domain Local group, Global group, or Universal group. Universal groups are available only if the domain is operating in Native mode. See previous discussion for more information.
Group type	Group type determines whether the group will be a Security group or Distribution group. See previous discussion for more information on group types.

3 When complete, click the OK button. The group will then be created in the directory.

Deleting a Group Using AD Users and Computers

Deleting a group object removes the pointer from the directory, but does not delete the member objects. Any rights or permissions assigned to a group are removed when the group is deleted. To delete a group, follow these steps:

1 Start the Active Directory Users and Computers application.

2 In the left-hand window, navigate to the container that holds the group you wish to delete.

3 In the right-hand window, right-click on the group name. Select Delete.

4 You will be asked, "Are you sure you wish to delete this group?"

5 Click Yes. The group will be deleted.

Modifying Group Membership Using AD Users and Computers

If you wish to change the group membership using the GUI interface, follow this process:

1 Start the Active Directory Users and Computers application.

2 In the left-hand window, navigate to the container that holds the group you wish to modify

3 In the right-hand window, double-click on the group name. The group properties dialog box will appear.

4 Select the Members tab. This will display the current membership of the group.

5 To add a user to the group, click the Add button. A dialog box will pop up, allowing you to select additional user(s) to add to the group.

6 To remove a user from the group, select the user you want to remove and click remove.

7 When finished, click on OK.

Command Prompt

As in Chapter 4.4, the command prompt utilities CSVDE and LDIFDE are the primary tools we have to make changes from the command line.

▶ *For more information on file formats and general usage of the utilities, see Chapter 4.4, "Creating and Managing User Accounts."*

Creating Groups with CSVDE

To create a group with CSVDE, create a CSV input file with the following header contents:

```
DN,objectClass,sAMAccountName,member,grouptype
```

On the next line, define the characteristics of the group. For example, the entry below creates a local security group named "LS". The following line should be entered as one entire line with no line breaks:

```
"CN=LS,CN=Users,DC=jmulvey,DC=com",group,LS,"CN=test
↩user,CN=Users,DC=jmulvey,DC=com",2147483652
```

The first three header properties defined above are similar to the creation of user accounts in Chapter 4.4; however, the *member* and *grouptype* properties are new. As you might expect, these properties define the group membership (what objects are members of the group) and type of group (security, distribution, global, universal, etc.) you are creating.

Defining Group Membership

Group membership is specified by including the Distinguished Name (DN) of all objects you want to be members. Remember, because you are using CSVDE, you will not be able to modify membership later using this utility (you could use LDIFDE, though, among other methods). To define membership in the group, place the DN for each object in the "member" field. Separate multiple DNs with a semicolon. Don't forget to wrap the entire "member" field definition with quotation marks; otherwise, the commas in the DN will be confused as part of the CSV formatting.

Building on the prior example, if both testuser1 and testuser2 were to be added to the group, the following entry could be used:

```
"CN=LS,CN=Users,DC=jmulvey,DC=com",group,LS,"CN=test
➥user1,CN=Users,DC=jmulvey,DC
➥=com;CN=test user2,CN=Users,DC=jmulvey,DC=com",2147483652
```

Defining Group Type

As you know by now, there are several different kinds of groups. Specifying exactly which kind of group CSVDE should create can get a little tricky. The "grouptype" property is used to convey this information to CSVDE. This property expects a decimal number to be used to convey this information. As shown in the following table, the decimal values can be a little odd. To help clear up the confusion, look at the hex value column. You'll notice that the hex numbers aren't all that different. In fact, there's a pattern. This pattern will come in handy later when we show how to create groups using ADSI (Active Directory Service Interfaces). But for now, use the decimal values shown in Table 4.5.3.

Table 4.5.3   Hex and Decimal Values by Group Type

Group Type	Hex Value	Decimal value
Global Distribution	&H00000002	2
Global Security	&H80000002	2147483650
Local Distribution	&H00000004	4
Local Security	&H80000004	2147483652
Universal Distribution	&H00000008	8
Universal Security	&H80000008	2147483656

Using LDIFDE to Manage Groups

Creating, modifying, and deleting groups can all be easily accomplished with LDIFDE. The following sections contain some brief examples of how to manage groups using this versatile command prompt utility.

Creating Groups

Creating groups with LDIFDE is similar to creating users, except for
the additional *member* and *grouptype* properties. These properties were
described previously in the CSVDE sections.

▶ *For more information on user creation, see Chapter 4.4, "Creating and
Managing User Accounts."*

```
dn: CN=test group,CN=Users,DC=jmulvey,DC=com
changetype: add
objectClass: group
sAMAccountName: testgroup
member: CN=test user,CN=Users,DC=jmulvey,DC=com
grouptype: 2147483652
```

After the LDIF file has been created, execute the LDIFDE command as
follows:

```
C:\>ldifde -i -f import.ldf
Connecting to "JEM"
Logging in as current user using SSPI
Importing directory from file "import.ldf"
Loading entries..
1 entry modified successfully.

The command has completed successfully
```

The new group should now exist in the Users container (as defined in
the IMPORT.LDF file).

Modifying Group Membership

In the following example, the membership list of a group is completely
replaced with new membership information. To start, the following
LDIF import file is created:

```
dn: CN=test group,CN=Users,DC=jmulvey,DC=com
changetype: modify
replace: member
member: CN=test user1,CN=Users,DC=jmulvey,DC=com
-
```

When this file is imported with LDIFDE, the membership of the group
"test group" will be replaced with just one member: "test user1." Often,
it is more desirable to simply add users to a group rather than replace
the entire membership. For such cases, use the "add" change operation
identifier instead of "replace." In the following example, we use "add" to
preserve the current group membership and add an additional member.
"Add" works only for multi-valued properties.

```
dn: CN=test group,CN=Users,DC=jmulvey,DC=com
changetype: modify
add: member
member: CN=test user2,CN=Users,DC=jmulvey,DC=com
-
```

Deleting Groups

Deleting groups (or almost any object) is very easy with LDIFDE—only the Distinguished Name (dn) of the object needs to be specified. For example, to delete the group we created previously, create a file called DELETE.LDF with the following contents:

```
dn: CN=test group,CN=Users,DC=jmulvey,DC=com
changetype: delete
```

Next, execute the LDIFDE command as follows:

```
C:\>ldifde -i -f delete.ldf
Connecting to "JEM"
Logging in as current user using SSPI
Importing directory from file "delete.ldf"
Loading entries..
1 entry modified successfully.

The command has completed successfully
```

The group should now be removed from the directory.

ADSI Scripts

Built into Windows 2000, the Windows Script Host is an extremely useful tool for administration. Windows Script Host interprets a number of languages, including VBScript. The following examples contain some relatively simple ADSI procedure calls using VBScript code that can be run via the Scripting Host. With a rudimentary understanding of VBScript, the code can be easily customized for special needs.

If these code segments interest you, you should know that there is also a comprehensive set of ADSI-related scripts contained in the Windows 2000 Resource Kit. The Resource Kit scripts are more feature-rich than these skeleton examples that follow, but these scripts demonstrate well the basic functionality available through the Scripting Host. Each of the scripts may be executed by placing the code in a .VBS file, and using the Script Host to process the file.

Many of the scripts also contain specific directory references (jmulvey.com), which need to be changed slightly for your environment.

Creating an Empty Group with ADSI

The following code creates a new (empty) group using ADSI. After prompting the user for the name of the group, it creates the group in the Users container.

```
'First we'll set the Hex values for the groupType variable.
ADS_GROUP_TYPE_GLOBAL_GROUP         = &H00000002
ADS_GROUP_TYPE_DOMAIN_LOCAL_GROUP   = &H00000004
ADS_GROUP_TYPE_LOCAL_GROUP          = &H00000004
ADS_GROUP_TYPE_UNIVERSAL_GROUP      = &H00000008

'The Security_Enabled field is bitwise OR'd with the above types
'If the group is to be a security group. Otherwise, it's a distribution
➥group
ADS_GROUP_TYPE_SECURITY_ENABLED     = &H80000000
```

```
Set ou = GetObject("LDAP://CN=Users,DC=jmulvey,DC=COM")

'Ask the user what the name of the Group should be
GroupName = InputBox("GroupName?","ADSI Create Group Demo")

Set usr = ou.Create("group", "cn=" & GroupName)
usr.Put "samAccountName", GroupName

'Here we create a Universal Security group. Other permutations from the
➥table
'above would yield different group types. Remove the "Or
➥ADS_GROUP_TYPE_SECURITY_ENABLED"
'if you wish to create a Distribution group.
usr.Put "groupType", (ADS_GROUP_TYPE_UNIVERSAL_GROUP Or
➥ADS_GROUP_TYPE_SECURITY_ENABLED)
usr.SetInfo
```

Adding Users to a Group with ADSI

The following script code prompts for a group name and then the user
name to add to the group. Note that this code builds the DN of the
user to add to the group programmatically, rather than asking the user
for the full DN.

```
'Ask the user what the name of the Group to be modified is
GroupName = InputBox("GroupName?","ADSI add user to Group Demo")
Set group = GetObject("LDAP://CN=" & GroupName &
➥",CN=Users,DC=jmulvey,DC=com")

'Ask the user who should be added to the group
UserName = InputBox("User Name to add?","ADSI add user to Group Demo")
group.Add "LDAP://CN=" & UserName & ",CN=Users,DC=jmulvey,DC=com"
```

Removing Users from a Group with ADSI

The following script prompts for a group name and then a user name.
The script then removes the specified user from the group. Again, this
script builds the DN programmatically, instead of expecting the user to
accurately specify the full value.

```
'Ask the user what the name of the Group to be modified is
GroupName = InputBox("GroupName?","ADSI remove user from Group Demo")
Set group = GetObject("LDAP://CN=" & GroupName &
➥",CN=Users,DC=jmulvey,DC=com")

'Ask the user who should be removed from the group
UserName = InputBox("User Name to remove?","ADSI remove user from Group
➥Demo")
group.Remove "LDAP://CN=" & UserName & ",CN=Users,DC=jmulvey,DC=com"
```

Deleting a Group with ADSI

This code demonstrates how to delete a group using ADSI. It prompts
for the name of the group, and assumes the group is in the Users container.

```
Set x = GetObject("LDAP://CN=Users,DC=jmulvey,DC=com")
'Ask the user what the name of the Group to be deleted is
GroupName = InputBox("GroupName?","ADSI Delete Group Demo")
x.Delete "group", "cn=" & GroupName
```

Best Practices for Managing Group Membership

- To simplify administration, grant permissions to user groups, not directly to user accounts.
- If membership in a Universal group changes frequently, place Global groups into the Universal group and make user changes in the Global group.

4.6

Logging On and Authentication

**You Need to Read This Section if
You Want to:**

- Configure Windows 2000 computers to log
on to a Domain.
- Manage user desktop environments.
- Troubleshoot problems with logging on.
- Plan for availability of user logon and authen-
tication for your network.

Related Topics

Logging On

One of the fundamental concepts of the Windows 2000 security model is the idea that a user must log on to a Windows 2000 computer before accessing any of its resources. By enforcing a mandatory logon, Windows 2000 prevents unauthorized users from accessing the system and can prevent authorized users from having more access than the computer's administrator wants them to.

Once logged on, the computer knows who the user is and can then provide or deny access as appropriate. In a Domain environment, access to resources can be allowed or denied to any security principal in the Domain—where a security principal is a either a user or a machine.

A Windows 2000 computer that is a member of a Domain logs on to the Domain at startup. It specifies its computer account and a password, which was set by the Domain Controller when the computer joined the Domain. The most familiar way users identify themselves to Windows 2000 is by typing in their username, entering their password, and specifying their Domain in the Log On to Windows dialog box. There are other ways, though. The usual prompt for username and password can be replaced by the use of smart cards or even biometric devices such as retinal scanners. You also log on to a computer when you access it from across the network; before it lets you do that, the computer has to identify who you are and check to see what access it should allow you to have.

UPNs for Logon

In Windows 2000, users can log on just as they can with Windows NT 4.0—by typing in their user name, entering their password, and selecting their Domain name. But users can also log on specifying their User Principal Name (UPN) and password. The UPN name is the concatenation of their username (the UPN prefix), the @ symbol, and the DNS name of their Domain (the UPN suffix). If a user, Rebecca, were in a Domain called Kapoho.com, her UPN name would be Rebecca@kapoho.com. Because this is also an email alias, using UPNs is easier than having to remember separate e-mail aliases and login IDs.

In a large enterprise with a deep Domain structure, the UPN name can be tiresome to type as well as error-prone. However, by using the Active Directory Domains and Trust tool, you can create additional UPN suffixes for your Domain. After these are created, you can use the Active Directory Users and Computers tool to modify the user's properties to allow them to use a different UPN suffix when logging in. If, in the example, Rebecca's account were in the Domain jasminehouse.uk.europe.kapoho.com, her default UPN would be Rebecca@jasminehouse.uk.europe.kapoho.com. If an administrator were to add the UPN suffix kapoho.com and adjust her account properties, she could log in as Rebecca@kapoho.com.

This section will primarily focus on how to configure and troubleshoot logging on to systems that are part of a Windows 2000 Domain.

Logging on basically consists of two main activities:

- **Authentication.** Establishing the identity of the security principal (user or computer) that is requesting access to the computer.

- **Creation of the user desktop.** Performing other routine tasks such as the processing of profiles, policies, and logon scripts to configure the user's environment.

?   **What Happens After a User Enters a Username and Password?**
▶ *For more information,*
see "Interactive User Logon" later in this chapter.

There are four ways in which security principals log on to Windows 2000 systems:

- **Computer Logon.** Every Windows 2000 computer that is a member of a Domain logs on to the Domain at startup with its computer account, even before users log on.

- **Interactive User Logon.** When you enter a username and password in the Log On to Windows box, you are performing an interactive logon.

- **Network User Logon.** When you connect to a shared resource on a network server, Windows 2000 performs a remote logon to the server computer using the user's username and password.

- **Service Logon.** Windows 2000 applications can be configured to run as *services*. Services log on to Windows 2000 computers without requiring a user desktop, but they *do* run with a specific user account.

These four types of logons are described in the following sections.

Not All Processes Log On
There are also processes that run in Windows 2000 that do not need to log on. They use the System built-in account.
▶ *For more information,*
see Chapter 1.1, "Overview of Windows 2000 Architecture."

Computer Logon

If a Windows 2000 system has been configured as a member of a Domain, the system contacts a Domain Controller for the Domain at startup in order to process policies that apply to the computer and to retrieve a list of trusted Domains. After this process is complete, the system can present a logon prompt for users to be able to log on interactively.

If the system is a member of a workgroup rather than a Domain, the computer does not need to perform a computer logon.

Requirements for Computer Logon

For a computer to log on to the Domain successfully, a Domain Controller for the computer's Domain must be available and the computer must have an account in the Domain.

▶ *For more information on computer accounts, see "Configuring a Windows 2000 System for Domain Member" later in this chapter.*

Steps of the Computer Logon

When a computer logs on, the following steps occur:

1 The system locates a Domain Controller for its Domain by querying a DNS server for the IP addresses of "close" Domain Controllers.

2 The computer's account in the Domain is authenticated so the computer can perform the next two steps.

3 The computer retrieves a list of trusted Domains.

This list is used to build the list of allowed Domains for users to log on to that appears in the Log On to Windows box.

4 The computer retrieves Group Policies that apply to the computer, processes them, and runs any startup scripts.

?   **What Is a "Close" Domain Controller?**

When contacting a Domain Controller, a Windows 2000 client, as noted previously, will attempt to contact a Domain Controller that is close, thus avoiding using WAN links. To do this, the client will look for Domain Controllers in the same Active Directory site as the client.

▶ *For more information on the way sites are defined in DNS, see Chapter 4.2, "DNS and Active Directory".*

Troubleshooting Logon Problems

Troubleshooting logon problems, especially in a Domain environment can be complex and will vary with the client OS. If you fail to log in, interactively from a Windows 2000 client, some things to check include the following:

- Is the client configured to access a DNS server that contains correct Active Directory SRV records for the target Domain?

- Is that DNS server accessible?

- Is there a Global Catalog server accessible from the Domain Controller that is attempting to authenticate the user?

- If this is a Domain Controller, is the user a member of an Administrative group or has the policy for the Domain Controller been adjusted to allow other users to log in interactively?

- As with Windows NT 4.0, is the user ID and password correct, and is the account active?

Interactive User Logon

An interactive user will perform an interactive logon in two ways: Pressing the Ctrl+Alt+Del key sequence and entering a username and password in the Log On to Windows box, or swiping a smart card through a smart card reader and entering a PIN. The system will authenticate the user, and if the authentication was successful, it will start a user shell with the user's personalized desktop settings.

To log on interactively to a Windows 2000 system, you must have a valid username and password, and your account must have been granted the Log on locally user right on the computer.

▶ *For more information on user rights,*
see Chapter 6.3,"Group Policies."

The steps in the logon process are shown in Figure 4.6.1 and described in the following list.

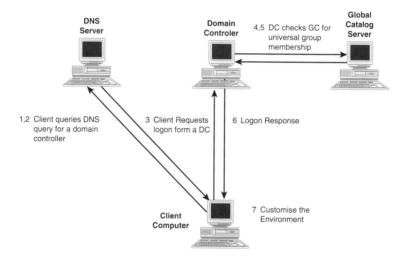

Figure 4.6.1   Logging on to a Domain.

1 If the IP address of a Domain Controller was not cached previously, the client computer locates a Domain Controller by issuing a query to the DNS to locate a Domain Controller.

2 If the DNS server has the appropriate records, they are returned to the client.

3 The client then requests authentication by sending a logon request with the user name and password to the Domain Controller, which will verify the user name and password against the Active Directory and build a list of SIDs for the user relating to any local and global groups the user is a member of.

4 The Domain Controller then sends a query to a Global Catalog server to determine universal groups to which the user belongs.

5 The GC will respond with the SIDs for these universal groups the user is a member of, which the Domain Controller can then add to the list created in step 3.

6 The Domain Controller provides a logon response to the client, which includes a list of all of the user's SIDs.

7 The client computer examines its local policies to determine which rights the user should have on the local computer. Finally, the user's profile is loaded, Group Policies related to the logged on user are processed, and any logon scripts are run.

Requirements for User Logon to a Domain

- A Domain Controller of the Domain must be available.
- A Global Catalog server must be available.
- The username and password must match the information stored in Active Directory.
- The user must have the Log on locally user right for the computer.

If no Domain Controller is available, and the user has logged on to the Domain at that computer in the past, the user will be logged on with cached credentials. If you do not want credentials to be cached, you can disable this feature by using a Group Policy.

▶ *For more information on these objects,*
see Chapter 6.3 "Group Policies."

▶ *For more information about requirements for authentication in a multiple Domain environment,*
see "Going Deeper" later in this chapter.

Logging On Automatically at System Startup

You can configure a system to log on automatically with a specific user account whenever it is restarted. This is useful for kiosk computers or other special-purpose computers.

Be careful how you use this feature, though. You probably *don't* want to have your servers log on automatically. The account that you use and its password are easily visible to anyone who can access the Registry, so it's not very secure. You should be running your applications as services rather than interactively on your servers anyway, so there's no need to log on at the console.

Limit Automatic Logons

The best practice is to limit automatic logons to Windows 2000 Professional systems that will be used for public use. You should make sure that the account that you use has very limited access to resources on the computer or on the network. You certainly don't want to make the account a member of the Administrators group unless you like reinstalling the operating system when users mess it up!

To log on automatically at system startup, execute the following steps:

1 Run regedt32 and navigate to
   HKEY_LOCAL_MACHINE\HKLM\SOFTWARE\Microsoft\Wind
   ows NT\CurrentVersion\Winlogon.

2 Double-click the DefaultDomainName and enter the Domain name.

3 Double-click the DefaultUserName and fill in the default user name.

4 Create a new string value named **DefaultPassword** and enter the user's
   password.

5 Create a new string value named **AutoAdminlogon** with a datatype of
   REG_SZ and set this to a value of 1.

6 Reboot and you should now automatically log in as the user you
   entered.

To stop the computer from logging on automatically, change the data
for the Autologon value to No and restart the computer.

The username and password that you use to log on automatically are
stored in the Registry. Anyone who can access the Registry at that
computer, whether from the console or remotely, can see the username
and password. Do not make the user account a member of the local
Administrators group, and give the account minimal access to the
computer.

Network User Logon

Whenever a user attempts to access a Windows 2000 computer's shared
resources by connecting to a named share on the computer, the computer must first establish the user's identity before granting access to the
share. This process is called a network user logon or remote logon.

For example, when you map a network drive to a shared folder on a file
server, you need to log on to the computer before you can access the
share. The network redirector performs this task for you automatically,
using your current credentials.

1 **Authenticate the user.**   The steps to authenticate the user are
   different, depending on whether Kerberos or NTLM is being used.

   - If Kerberos, the client requests a service ticket for the remote server
     from the Domain Controller and then presents the service ticket to
     the remote server.

   - If NTLM, the client requests a NetBIOS session with the remote
     server, which then has to authenticate the user by querying a
     Domain Controller for the user account.

2 **Grant or deny access to the requested resource.**   The server
   checks the user's identity against the permissions assigned to the
   resource and against the user rights that have been granted to the user.

Service Logon

Applications can be run as services in Windows 2000, which allows them to run in their own user context with their own user account and password, independently of any interactive user session.

Windows 2000 comes with many standard services that start automatically when the system starts, such as the Server service and the Net Logon service. Other services are configured to start on demand. The user account that is used by the service is configured through the Computer Management console.

▶ *For more information about services,*
see Chapter 1.1, "Overview of Windows 2000 Architecture."

1 **Start the service.**   Services can be started by the local system at system startup by configuring them to start automatically. An administrator can also start and stop services by using one of the management tools or by using the **net start** and **net stop** commands.

2 **Authenticate the user.**   The username and password that is associated with the service is authenticated. The account must have the Log on as a service user right.

3 **Create a user context for the service on the computer.**   If a user environment for the user account does not already exist, a new user environment will be created. The service will be limited by the permissions and rights assigned to the service on that computer.

Configuring Systems to Log On to a Domain

Network clients can log on interactively to Windows 2000 Domains by using several different client operating systems. The steps for configuring the Domain logon for each operating system are described as follows.

Logging On to a Domain from Windows 2000

Before a Windows 2000 system can be configured as a Domain member, an account for the computer must exist in the Domain. Domain Controllers are already members of the Domain and require no additional configuration.

Joining a computer to a Domain has the following effects:

- The DNS Domain name of the computer is automatically changed to be the same as the name of the Domain. For example, the computer called kona would have a TCP/IP hostname of kona.kapoho.com after joining the kapoho.com Domain.

- At startup, the computer will log on to the Domain in order to retrieve a list of trusted Domains and to process Group Policy for the computer.

- You can log on to the computer and be authenticated with an account from any Domain in the forest. User profiles, Group Policies, and logon scripts are retrieved from the network and processed.

- You can grant permissions for resources on the local computer to users and groups from any Domain in the forest.

Best Practices for Adding Windows 2000 Computers to Active Directory Domains

- Limit the number of people that can add computers to Domains.

- Control the capability to add computers to the Domain by managing the permissions on the default Computers container in the Active Directory Domain.

- Consider using Domain-wide OUs, filtered by group to control the specific permission to add computers to that Domain. For more granular control, you could create the GPO at OU level, thus delegating control to add computers to specific OUs to smaller groups of users.

- Create an account specifically for creating computer accounts. Use this account when adding computers to the Domain. This is a good idea if you are performing scripted installations (which show the username and password in clear text) because the account will have only the minimum abilities required.

- Use the NetDom Resource Kit utility to add computers to the Domain without having to visit individual desktops.

- For larger organizations, also develop ASDI-based scripts to add computers.
  ▶ *For more information on modifying groups with ADSI,*
  see Chapter 4.5, "Creating and Modifying Groups."

Configuring a Windows 2000 System as a Domain Member

Before you can configure a Windows 2000 system to log on to a Domain, you must meet these requirements:

- A computer account must be added to the Domain. The computer account can be created in advance or at the time of joining the Domain. The user adding the computer to the Domain must have permission to create a computer object in the container in the Domain. By default, the Computers container at the root of the Domain is used, and Domain administrators have permission to create new computer objects in it.

- The user adding the computer to the Domain must be a member of the local Administrators group on the computer.

- A Domain Controller for the Domain must be available.

- A Global Catalog server must be available.

You can move a Windows 2000 computer from one Domain to another by simply changing the settings in Network Identification in the Network option in Control Panel.

You cannot change the Domain membership of a Domain Controller. You must demote it by running dcpromo.exe before you can join the computer to a different Domain.

For step-by-step instructions, search for the "Join a Domain" topic in Windows 2000 Help.

Best Practices for Distributing Administration of Computer Accounts

The strategies for distributing administration depend on the size of your organization and whether authority for administration is centralized or delegated.

- For small Domains, simply add the user or users responsible for account creation into the Domain Administrators group. For small Domains or for users who should have extensive authority, make them a member of the Domain Admins group.

- To increase security, create a special Administrators account, which should be used only to perform account maintenance and give the password to that account to the individuals responsible for account administration. When administration activities are required, the user can either log in to the special account or use the RUNAS command to run the MMC with elevated privileges.

- For moderate-sized Domain environments with centralized security, you can create a separate group to perform account maintenance. Just create a new Domain local group and add this group to the Domain administrators group for the Domain in which they can create users.

- For a Domain environment with a decentralized administration, create a Domain local group for each OU or sub-OU who can create objects. Then, grant that group the right to create objects in the OU. Finally, add the users who will be carrying out the maintenance to the appropriate local group.

Logging On to a Windows 2000 Domain from Windows NT 4.0

Windows 2000 Domains appear like Windows NT 4.0 Domains to Windows NT 4.0 clients. When Windows NT 4.0 clients log on to a Windows 2000 Domain, they locate a Domain Controller by performing a NetBIOS name query (via WINS, lmhosts, or a broadcast). They then use the NTLM authentication protocol to authenticate the user or computer. System policies and logon scripts are retrieved from the Netlogon share of the Domain Controller.

If the Windows 2000 Domain is in Mixed mode, only the computer's Domain and the Domains that are directly trusted by that Domain will appear in the Domain list box in the Log On to Windows dialog box. If the Windows 2000 Domain is in native mode, all of the Domains in the Windows 2000 forest will appear as possible Domains to which they can log on.

Configuring a Windows NT 4.0 System as a Domain Member

Configuring a Windows NT 4.0 system as a member of a Windows 2000 Domain is no different from configuring it as a member of a Windows NT 4.0 Domain. As far as the system is concerned, the Windows 2000 Domain Controller behaves just like a Windows NT 4.0 Domain Controller.

Joining the Domain consists of two steps:

1   Create a computer account. You can do this in advance by creating a computer object in the Computers container. You can also do it at the client by specifying the username and password of an account that is a member of the Domain Admins group in the Windows 2000 Domain or has the necessary permissions to create a computer object.

2   In the Network option in Control Panel, change the name of the Windows NT 4.0 system's Domain to the Downlevel Domain name (NetBIOS name) of the Windows 2000 Domain that was assigned when the Domain was created. Usually, this is the leftmost part of the Domain's full DNS name. For example, if the Domain is called mcp.com, enter **MCP** as the Domain name.

After the required reboot, you'll be able to log on to the Windows 2000 Domain as if it were a Windows NT 4.0 Domain.

Logging On to a Domain from Windows 95/98

Windows 95/98 systems can either log on to the network as part of a workgroup or they can log on to a Domain:

- **Workgroup logon.** The user specifies a username and password to use on the network, but no Domain Controller is contacted, and no user policies or user logon scripts are retrieved from the network.

- **Domain logon.** The user specifies a username, password, and Domain name. The computer then locates a Domain Controller for the Domain and authenticates the user. If a system policy file (config.pol) is found in the Netlogon share of the Domain Controller, it is processed. If there is a user profile in the user's home directory or logon scripts associated with the user's account, they are processed, too.

Windows 95 and Windows 98 systems do not require a computer account in a Domain to log on.

Configuring a Windows 95/98 System for Domain Logon

You configure a Windows 95 or Windows 98 system to log on to a Windows 2000 Domain by changing the properties of the Client for Microsoft Networks.

Use the Network option in Control Panel to display a list of installed components. Set the Primary Network Logon to the Client for Microsoft Networks. Then, modify the properties of the Client for Microsoft Networks to include the name of the Domain and select the Log On to Windows NT Domain checkbox.

After you restart the computer, you will be prompted to supply your username, password, and Domain name whenever you log on.

Going Deeper: How a Windows 2000 System Authenticates a User

A Windows 2000 system authenticates a user by locating a Domain Controller and then using the appropriate authentication protocol to authenticate the user. The process is transparent to the user, except for the need to provide a username and password.

? **Why Go Deeper with Authentication If It Is Transparent to the User?**

If you understand how authentication works in Windows 2000, it makes troubleshooting logon and authentication problems a lot easier! It also explains how trusts work in a multi-Domain network.

The purpose of the authentication process is for the user to prove to the system that the user should be allowed access. The computer authenticates the user (verifying his identity) and then builds an access token on the computer that contains all of the Security Identifiers (SIDs) that are associated with the user's account.

The computer will locate a Domain Controller by using either the Windows 2000 Resolver and DNS, or else by using the NetBIOS Resolver and NetBIOS name resolution.

Windows 2000 supports three authentication mechanisms: Kerberos, Windows NT LAN Manager (NTLM), and Secure Socket Layer/Transport Layer Security (SSL/TLS). The authentication protocol that is used depends on the application that is requesting access to the resource.

When logging on to a Domain, Windows 2000 clients use the Kerberos authentication protocol by default. They will, however, use NTLM if Kerberos authentication is not available (for example, when logging on to a Windows NT 4.0 Domain). NTLM is also used by Windows 2000 systems that are not members of a Domain.

Locating a Domain Controller

Windows 2000 systems use two different methods of locating Domain Controllers:

- The Windows 2000 Resolver uses DNS (and the DNS cache) to locate Domain Controllers
- The NetBIOS Resolver uses queries for a NetBIOS service to locate Domain Controllers.

Windows 2000 systems try the Windows 2000 Resolver first, and will use the NetBIOS Resolver only if no Domain Controllers can be located by DNS.

The Windows 2000 Resolver

The Windows 2000 Resolver queries DNS for specific SRV resource records to locate Domain Controllers. The process is explained as follows:

1 The client queries DNS for a list of Domain Controllers in its site. These Domain Controllers are identified in DNS as LDAP SRV records in

   `_ldap.<sitename>._sites.dc_msdcs.<Domain>`.

2 The client sends an LDAP UDP query to port 389 on the Domain Controllers to identify which Domain Controllers are available.

3 The client uses the responses to the query to determine the closest Domain Controller in its site. If no Domain Controllers respond, the client queries DNS for LDAP SRV records in

   `_ldap._tcp.dc_msdcs.<Domain>`

4 The client attempts to locate one of them.

5 The client sends its logon request to the Domain Controller.

The NetBIOS Resolver

If the Windows 2000 Resolver is unable to locate a Domain Controller via DNS, the NetBIOS Resolver is tried.

The NetBIOS Resolver queries the NetBIOS interface for entries for the *Domainname* <1B> NetBIOS name that identifies Domain Controllers. If the system is a WINS client, the WINS server is queried for *Domainname* <1B>, which provides a list of Domain Controllers in the Domain. The client will then connect with one of the Domain Controllers in the list. If WINS is not available or has no name registration records for *Domainname* <1B>, the client will broadcast to attempt to locate a Domain Controller.

Kerberos Authentication

Kerberos is an authentication protocol that provides for mutual authentication of clients and servers using an industry-standard protocol. Kerberos is based on shared secrets cryptography. Windows 2000 supports Kerberos version 5.

On Windows 2000 Domain Controllers, the Kerberos Key Distribution Center (KDC) service authenticates Kerberos clients. This service provides both the Authentication Service (AS) and a Ticket Granting Service (TGS) needed in Kerberos authentication. The KDC service is part of the Local Security Authority process of Windows 2000 (lsass.exe), uses Active Directory as its account database, starts automatically, and cannot be stopped.

In a nutshell, Kerberos authentication works as follows:

1   When a user logs on, the client computer submits a request for authentication to the KDC (Domain Controller)

2   If the request is successful, the KDC sends the client a Ticket Granting Ticket (TGT). This ticket is used as a session ticket for all communications with the KDC.

3   Whenever the client needs to initiate a connection to a server (network logon), the client uses the TGT to request a session ticket for the server from the Ticket Granting Service (TGS) running on Domain Controller.

4   If the client is allowed to access the server, the TGS sends a ticket back to the client.

5   The client presents the session ticket to the server with which it wants to communicate. The server accepts the identity of the client because the ticket indicates that the user has been authenticated by a trusted authority (the Domain Controller). See Figure 4.6.2.

6   Optionally, the server can identify itself back to the client.

Figure 4.6.2   Authentication in a single Domain.

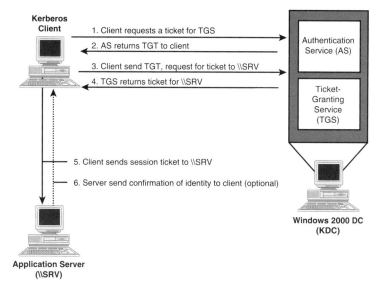

Kerberos tickets are kept in a local cache and are aged. When they have expired, they cannot be used anymore. This forces the client to get a new ticket from the KDC when it needs to connect to a remote server. (Existing connections aren't affected by expired tickets, only attempts to create new connections are.)

> **? How Do I Figure Out Which Tickets Have Been Issued to My Computer?**
>
> You can see which tickets have been issued to your computer by using the kerbtray.exe application from the Windows 2000 Resource Kit. You can also view Kerberos tickets by using the klist.exe console command.

The default length of time that Kerberos tickets are valid is eight hours, but you can modify this interval by using a Group Policy for the site, Domain, or Organizational Unit. Windows 2000 will flush the cache and destroy all existing tickets when a user logs off. Because Kerberos tickets are time-sensitive, it is very important to synchronize the system time on client computers with the Domain Controller. The Windows Time service automatically synchronizes the time among Domain Controllers in a forest.

Windows 2000 Domains are the equivalent of Kerberos realms. Cross-realm authentication occurs in Windows 2000 through the use of trust relationships. The Key Distribution Center Service account krbtgt is used to authenticate a Domain Controller when authenticating users or computers in other Domains.

> **?** **Where Did Kerberos Come From?**
>
> The name *Kerberos* comes from the name of the three-headed dog that guarded the gates at the entrance to Hades in Greek mythology—like the three roles in Kerberos authentication: client, server, and Key Distribution Center (KDC).
>
> The specification for the Kerberos protocol can be found in RFC 1510. Kerberos was originally developed at the Massachusetts Institute of Technology (MIT).
>
> ▶ *For more information, see* http://www.mit.edu.

Single Domain Kerberos Authentication

The steps of authenticating a user whose account is in the same Domain as the computer is described in the following list:

1 The user logs on with username and password. The client sends an authorization request to the KDC service on the Domain Controller.

2 The Domain Controller queries the Global Catalog in order to include all group Security IDs (SIDs) associated with the user's account.

3 The Domain Controller returns a Ticket Granting Ticket (TGT) to the client, which includes the SIDs of the user and the groups the user is in.

4 The client uses the TGT to send a request to the Domain Controller for a session ticket for the user to the local computer.

5. The Domain Controller returns a session ticket for the user to the local computer. The rest of the logon process can now continue (creating a user desktop, processing Group Policy, and so on).

As a result, you must have a Domain Controller and a Global Catalog server available to be authenticated in a Windows 2000 Domain.

Multiple Domain Kerberos Authentication

When there are multiple Domains in Active Directory, the process of authenticating a user can be more complex. When a Domain Controller receives an authorization request for an account that is not in its Domain, it generates a referral, which consists of a session ticket to a Domain Controller that has a better chance of being able to authorize the user.

Suppose you have three Domains named example.com, usa.example.com, and asia.example.com in a single Active Directory forest. A user sits down at a computer that is a member of the usa.example.com Domain and then logs on with an account in the asia.example.com Domain. What happens? The authorization request is referred from one Domain to another until a Domain Controller from the asia.example.com Domain is contacted that can authorize the user.

Note that this situation—a user logging onto a computer using an account in a Domain different from the Domain the computer is a member of—will occur less often in Windows 2000 than in Windows NT 4.0.

In Windows NT 4.0, it was good practice to have the computer in a child Domain (the resource Domain) and the user account in the partner Domain (the account Domain). With Windows 2000, it is only roaming users, using someone else's computer, that will do cross-Domain logon. Users using their own computers, even roaming users using their laptops, will tend to be authenticated by the Domain that their computer is a member of.

The steps for authenticating rebecca@asia.kapoho.com using Kerberos are shown in Figure 4.6.3, and described in the following list.

Figure 4.6.3   Authenticating an account from a trusted Domain.

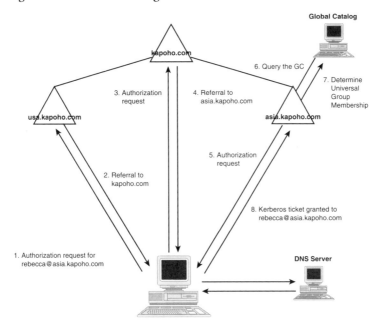

1 The user logs on as rebecca@asia.kapoho.com. The client computer sends an authorization request to a Domain Controller in its home Domain, usa.kapoho.com.

2 The Domain Controller responds with a referral, which consists of a session ticket to a Domain Controller in the parent Domain kapoho.com.

3 The client sends an authorization request to a Domain Controller in kapoho.com, using the session ticket from the previous step.

4 The kapoho.com Domain Controller responds with a session ticket to a Domain Controller in asia.kapoho.com.

5 The client sends an authorization request to a Domain Controller in asia.example.com, using the session ticket it got from the example.com Domain Controller.

6 If the DC successfully authenticates Rebecca, the asia.kapoho.com Domain Controller queries the Global Catalog to determine Universal Group membership.

7 The GC will return all Universal groups that Rebecca is a member of.

8 The asia.example.com Domain Controller returns a session ticket to the client computer for Rebecca, and the logon process can continue.

Thus, there are four Domain Controllers that are involved in authenticating JDoe: the Domain Controllers in usa.example.com, example.com, asia.example.com, and a Global Catalog server. All four Domain Controllers would have to be available on the network in order for Rebecca to log on. If any of these four servers is not available, the logon will fail. In addition, the client would also need to have access to a DNS server capable of resolving the necessary DNS records to allow the client to contact the various Domain Controllers.

Keep Domain Trees Flat

The need for these servers to be available affects the placement of Domain Controllers on your network and your site design. As a practical matter, it's a good idea to keep your Domain trees flat rather than deep because it reduces the number of points of failure for logon throughout the enterprise, as well as reducing the number of referrals. You can also mitigate some of this risk and possibly improve performance through the use of cross-link trusts.

NTLM Authentication

The Windows NT Lan Manager (NTLM) protocol was the default for network authentication in Microsoft Windows NT version 4.0. In NTLM authentication, it is the computer that is receiving the connection request (the server) that has to authenticate the user.

Although Kerberos has replaced NTLM in Windows 2000 as the default, it is still used in these situations:

- When connecting to a Windows 2000 computer that is not a member of a Domain

- When connecting to a computer that is running an earlier version of Windows

- When logging on to a Windows 2000 computer that is a member of a Windows NT 4.0 Domain

Computers that are running Windows networking clients, such as Windows NT 4.0, Windows 95, and Windows 98, are able to log on to a Windows 2000 Domain by using NTLM and can find a Domain Controller using the NetBIOS name of the Domain. To these clients, the Windows 2000 Domain behaves just like a Windows NT 4.0 Domain.

Windows 2000 computers can use NTLM when logging on to a Windows NT 4.0 BDC; however, no Group Policy objects or logon scripts will be processed.

Windows 95 and Windows 98 computers that have the Directory Services client software installed log on to the Domain by using the NTLM authentication protocol. After logging on, these clients will use Kerberos instead of NTLM when connecting to network servers. For example, the client computer will use Kerberos to obtain a session ticket when connecting to a service on a Windows 2000 computer.

Single Domain NTLM Authentication

When a client logs on to a Domain by using the NTLM protocol, the client presents a logon request to a Domain Controller. The Domain Controller authenticates the user and returns a logon response to the client that includes all of the user's SIDs.

Every time the client connects to a new server on the network (that is, a new NetBIOS session is requested), the server has to query a Domain Controller to authenticate the user. If a Domain Controller is unavailable when the client attempts to connect to a server, the user cannot be authenticated and the session will be denied—even if the user was successful logging in to the Domain only moments before.

Multiple Domain NTLM Authentication

If the Active Directory Domains are in *Mixed* mode, trusts are not transitive for clients using NTLM. A user will only be able to log on using accounts from the computer's Domain or Domains directly trusted by the computer's Domain. For example, a user at a computer in usa.example.com would be unable to log on with an account from asia.example.com unless a cross-link trust was created directly between the two Domains.

If the Active Directory Domains are in *Native* mode, the user can be authenticated by any Domain in the forest, even if NTLM is used.

Troubleshooting

When troubleshooting problems with logging on or connecting to a network resource, here are the first things to check:

- Make sure that you have network connectivity. Try pinging a known server on a remote IP subnet.

- If logging on interactively, check the username and password to ensure that they are entered correctly (passwords are case-sensitive; usernames are not). If necessary, reset the user password in Active Directory.

- Verify the configuration of TCP/IP, especially the name server addresses (DNS and WINS). Verify that the name servers are online and responding.
- Verify that all Domain Controllers required for authentication are available. Verify that a Global Catalog server is available.

Table 4.6.1 shows troubleshooting tips dealing with interactive logon.

Table 4.6.1   Troubleshooting Interactive Logon

Symptom	Explanation/Resolution
Bad username or password	If the username or password is typed incorrectly, the message The System could not log you on displays. Make sure your user name and Domain are correct and then type your password again. Letters in the password must be typed using the correct case. Make sure that Caps Lock is not accidentally on.
No Domain Controller found	If the system cannot locate a Domain Controller, the message The system cannot log you on now because the Domain <Domain name> is not available will appear. If the user has not logged on at that computer before, he will not be able to log on. Verify the availability of appropriate records in DNS for the Domain Controllers and Global Catalog server in the Domain name shown.
	If the user is logged on using cached credentials, he will be unable to change his password until a Domain Controller is available.
	Verify that the Domain Controllers are configured as WINS clients and that a WINS server is available. Also verify that the computer is a WINS client. Verify the spelling of the Domain name.
	Check DNS for appropriate SRV records for Domain Controllers. Use Nslookup to verify how DNS responds to queries for Domain Controllers.
	Check WINS for appropriate entries for Domain Controllers. Use Nbtstat to verify that the Domain Controllers are registering the correct NetBIOS names.
Wrong desktop settings	The desktop configuration at the end of the logon process is the result of the

Symptom	Explanation/Resolution
	profile, policies, and logon script for the user. Verify the settings in Active Directory for the user account and the contents of the policies for the organizational units that the user belongs to.
No logon prompt appears at startup	The system may be configured to log on automatically.
Policy problem	Use the Group Policy tools from the Resource Kit, including Gpresult.exe, to resolve policy issues.
Other problems	Verify that the NetLogon service is running on the computer. Look at the System Log in Event Viewer for possible error messages.
Some Domains in the forest do not appear in the drop-down list	If the Windows 2000 Domain is in Mixed mode, trust relationships for Windows NT 4.0 clients are not transitive. Only Domains that have the computer's Domain will appear in relationships or change the Domain to Native mode.

See Table 4.6.2 for troubleshooting tips regarding network logon.

Table 4.6.2   Troubleshooting Network Logon

Symptom	Explanation/Resolution
Access denied	The user's account cannot be authenticated, the user has inadequate permissions to the requested share, or the user has inadequate rights on the server. If no trust exists between the user's Domain and the Domain of the server, specify the Domain name and user-name of an account with adequate access to the server when connecting.
Network path not found	The server is unavailable on the network, there is a network connectivity problem, or the path was entered incorrectly.

Table 4.6.3 shows troubleshooting tips involving service logon.

Table 4.6.3   Troubleshooting Service Logon

Symptom	Explanation/Resolution
Service failed to start	Look for error messages in the System Log in Event Viewer.
	▶ *For more information, see "Event Viewer" in Chapter 3.3, "Using Administrative Tools."*
	Make sure that the service account has adequate permissions to files or other objects accessed by the service.
	Make sure that the service account has the Log On as a Service user right and that the username and password are correct.

V
Managing Files and Printers

5.1

Overview of Managing Files and Printers

You Need to Read This Section if You Want to:

- Gain an overview of what is covered in the rest of this section.
- Understand some of the changes introduced by Windows 2000.

Related Topics

File Systems and Disks

Within any PC-based operating system, the physical hard disks that are connected to the computer are divided into one or more partitions. To make use of each partition, it is formatted to contain a file system. Different operating systems can understand different file systems. The formatted partition is sometimes called a *logical drive* to contrast it with the physical hard disk. Microsoft operating systems have traditionally used a letter to represent each logical drive, whether that drive is local or on a network server.

Within Windows 2000, the partitioning of disks is controlled through the Disk Management snap-in for the Microsoft Management Console. This snap in is included in the pre-configured Computer Management MMC console (see Figure 5.1.1).

Figure 5.1.1   Disk management within the MMC, showing a single Basic drive.

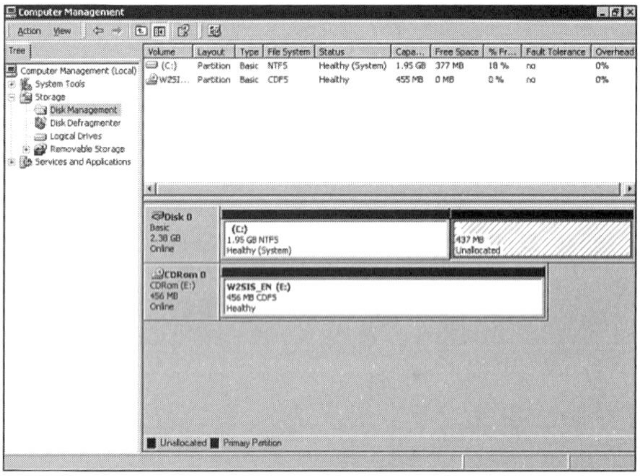

From within the Disk Management section of the console, you can see the physical disks connected to the system, how they have been divided into partitions, and the resulting volumes. Partitions can be created and deleted and volumes can be formatted, although formatting can also be done from Explorer and from a command prompt with the FORMAT program that has been familiar since MS-DOS.

One useful feature of this console is the capability to manage computers remotely, and that includes managing the disks. There are two wholly new features of Windows 2000 that are managed within this console. The first is that a volume is not required to have a drive letter. A volume can be mounted into a folder within an NTFS volume; this may be as well as or instead of having a letter assigned to it.

The second major new feature is that Window 2000 considers a disk to be either a *Basic* disk, or a *Dynamic* disk. Basic disks use the same partitioning system as all previous Microsoft operating systems with two classes of partitions: Primary and Extended. Primary partitions can contain only one volume, but extended partitions can contain more than one. Versions of MS-DOS up to version 5.0 could support only a single Primary and single Extended partition, and using multiple Extended partitions can cause problems.

Dynamic disks support some of Windows 2000's more complex functionality, such as extending volumes, spanning them over multiple physical disks, and support for mirroring, striping and RAID 5 implemented within the operating system (although technologies such as RAID 5 may be better implemented in hardware). However, dynamic disks are not compatible with prior operating systems.

The disk management snap-in for the MMC provides access to the property pages for a volume; and these are also available from within the Windows explorer. These provide control over sharing of the root folder and, in the case of NTFS volumes, its security, compression and quota management. As in Windows 95 and 98, the tools property page gives access to backup, error checking and defragmentation tools, but a new Windows 2000 is the clean-up facility, which looks for files that can be removed or compressed to save space (see Figure 5.1.2).

Figure 5.1.2   The disk clean-up utilities for Windows 2000 makes it easier to release disk space.

Sharing Folders

There are many ways that you can make the contents of a file accessible to multiple users. One of the oldest ways is the file transfer protocol that is found with just about all implementations of TCP/IP; this allows you to download files, work on them, and return them to the server. Similar processes are possible with some of the extensions that have been grafted onto HTTP, so files can be accessed through a Web browser. Normally, sharing folders means that you make part of a local disk available to other users on the network who can connect to it and use it much as they would on their own machine. So, in a typical Microsoft operating system, a computer connected to a shared folder sees an additional drive letter or perhaps a desktop shortcut.

There is more than one way for client computers to gain access to shared folders. Microsoft clients use a protocol called Server Message Blocks (SMBs), Apple computers use the Apple File Protocol (AFP), Unix machines use the Network File System (NFS), and Novell clients communicate with servers using the Netware Core Protocol (NCP). Like Windows NT 4.0 before it, Windows 2000 supports Microsoft Networking as both a Client and a Server; it can share files and printers with Macintosh clients and use Macintosh printers. Client support for Novell networks (both NDS-based and older bindery-based NetWare V2 and V3.systems) is built-in. In the case of the server products, it can act as gateway between Microsoft clients using SMB and NetWare servers. Additional software can be purchased to allow Windows 2000 to also act as a NetWare Server, or NFS Client or server.

Distributed File System

In a Microsoft network, the shared folders can be found within the servers that host them. Normally, the combination of shared folder and server is written using what is known as a universal naming convention (or UNC) name in the form \\server\folder. On a large network, finding things can be difficult because the users don't know which server hosts the resource they are seeking. Active Directory in Windows 2000 helps with this because information about shared folders can be published and searched by users. However, a user may still need a bewildering array of drive letters and shortcuts to connect to shared folders they need.

With the World Wide Web, we have become used to the idea of links in one place that take us to somewhere else. And it is links that drive the Distributed File System. The idea of DFS is simple: shared folders can contain links that store the UNC name of another shared folder. Although these links look like subfolders, when a user tries to access the subfolder, the network client software on their computer recognizes a link and connects to a shared folder that it points to. This might be on the same server or a completely different server that might not even be running Windows 2000.

Sharing Printers

As with sharing files, Windows 2000 has more than one way of sharing printers. Printers can be shared with other computers running Microsoft operating systems using Server Message Blocks. Windows 2000 computers can connect to printers on Unix computers using the LPR protocol (this protocol is also supported by some laser printers that connect directly to the network). By installing the optional Print services for Unix service, Windows 2000 computers can offer their own printers to clients that support this protocol. Windows 2000 servers can also share their printers with Apple Macintoshes, although Windows 2000 Professional machines cannot. Both can use the AppleTalk protocol to send jobs to printers.

One notable new feature in Windows 2000 is the integration of Internet Information Server with Printing. This allows information about a printer to be checked from a browser, but it goes further than that. Users of Windows 2000 client computers can click a link on a Web page to connect to a printer. The biggest change is that the Hypertext Transfer Protocol, which is normally used for reading Web pages and (less frequently) used to upload pages to a server, can now be used to submit print jobs. Combinations of firewalls and proxy servers may mean that HTTP is the only protocol that can get out of a site from a user's desktop, or it may be that HHTP is the only protocol that can come in to a server from the outside world. HTTP printing provides a useful way of accessing printers in spite of such limitations.

Printing is also one of the places where users gain a benefit from Windows 2000's Active Directory. Instead of needing to know the name of the server where a printer is located in order to connect to it, the printer now appears in the directory, which is searchable. This means that a user in large organization can search for a printer, based on its location and capabilities, without needing to know which server is in which building, which printer types can print double-sided, and so on.

Protecting Data

Protecting the data on a system takes a number of forms. The first is protection against hardware failures of various types. Because hard disks contain moving parts and magnetic media, they can be expected to fail eventually. To provide fault tolerance against disk failures, the server versions of Windows 2000 implement disk mirroring and RAID 5 within the operating system. In addition, Windows 2000 provides a backup program that Microsoft has licensed from Veritas to cope with human errors as well as hardware failures.

Protecting data means protecting it from unauthorized access, whether that means modifying it, deleting it, or simply reading it. One of the cornerstones of the security design in Windows 2000 is aiming to meet the C2 security standard defined by the US Department of Defense. Two of the basic principles of C2 security are mandatory logon (that is, before using the system you must identify yourself) and discretionary access control (every resource on the computer is owned by someone and that owner has the power to determine). The NTFS file system in Windows 2000 controls access to resources based on each file and each folder having an owner who controls who may have access to the file or folder using a Discretionary Access Control List. This list contains the details of users and what they may do to the resource.

Auditing Resource Access

Just as permissions may be set on resources by using an access control list, so a user's successes or failures in accessing the resource can be audited. This is controlled through what is sometimes called a System Access Control List, but can be thought of as an audit control list. A Discretionary Access Control List says "Allow this user read access" or "Forbid this user write access." Auditing allows the owner to say "Record in the security log if this user succeeds in deleting files in this folder," "Record in the security log if any user fails in an attempt to write to files in this folder," and so on.

Internet Information Server

Windows 2000, like Windows NT 4.0 before it, has a Web server built in. This provides a little more than the capability to build Web sites—it can manage and troubleshoot Windows 2000. Windows 2000's network places allow shortcuts to Web servers to be created, and from these files can be copied to and from Web servers that support the necessary extensions. In addition, printer information can be found through a Web interface (see Figure 5.1.3. By pointing a browser at `http://server/printers`, it is possible to find which printers are connected to the server and what is in their queues, to make a standard connection (the same connection that would be made through the Control Panel Printers folder) without leaving the browser. It is also possible to deliver print jobs to the printer using the HTTP protocol.

Figure 5.1.3   Windows 2000 provides a web interface to printing.

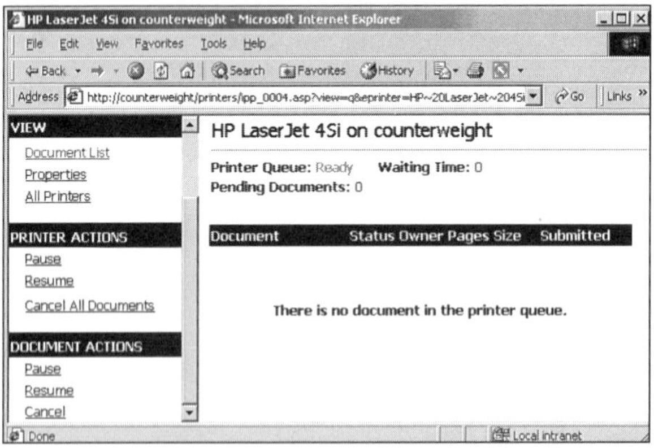

The rest of Part 5: "Managing Files and Printers," will cover each of these components of management in more detail.

5.2

File Systems and Disks

You Need to Read This Section If You Want to:

- Understand the arrangement, partitioning, and formatting of disks.
- Set NTFS permissions.
- Limit users' disk space using quotas.

Related Topics

File Systems

There are three basic choices for file systems in Windows 2000. They are FAT, FAT32, and NTFS. The following sections describe each in detail.

File Allocation Table (FAT)

The FAT file system divides the sectors of the physical disk into allocation units known as *clusters*. Directories contain the name of each file and a pointer to its first cluster. The File Allocation Table itself has an entry for each cluster; each of these entries contains either the pointer to the next cluster or an end-of-file marker. The creation date of the file and its size are stored in the directory, together with a single byte of file attributes. These attributes identify whether the file is read-only, hidden, reserved for the operating system, or needs archiving. These attributes are normally visible to the user. Further attributes also identify entries for subdirectories and volume labels.

FAT16 has existed in its present form in MS-DOS since version 4.0. *16* means that the File Allocation Table uses 16-bit numbers to represent each entry. This gives a maximum of 65536 entries in the File Allocation Table, which leads to a problem for modern systems. Although typical disks on DOS 4.0 systems were 40–60 MB (meaning that the cluster size could be as small as 1 K), modern systems have disks more than 100 times that size, and bigger disk partitions mean bigger clusters. After the disk is bigger than 64 MB, the cluster size must increase to 2 K. Beyond 128 MB, the size must increase to 4 K bytes, and so on. This becomes very wasteful of space because even if there is only one byte in the file, a whole cluster must be allocated. MS-DOS has an absolute maximum of 32 K in a cluster, so the absolute maximum size that a FAT16 partition can be (without losing compatibility) is 2 GB. This is not adequate for modern systems. Dividing the disk into multiple partitions reduces the problem, but only slightly.

FAT directories were designed to support filenames of eight characters with a three-character file extension (often called *8.3 naming*). This naming system has never been popular. Starting with Windows 95, a workaround has been used to create long filenames. This involves creating a short name and then storing the long name as additional entries in the directory (11 characters at a time). It also involves turning on both the directory and volume label attributes to prevent access by operating systems such as DOS or Windows NT 3.1, which don't understand long names on FAT. This solves the 8.3 filename problem, but introduces another. The FAT directory is a simple list; putting multiple entries in the list for the same file means that more entries must be checked when searching through the directory to find a file. Thus, searching large directories in which the files have long names is slowed down. There is a finite number of entries possible in a root directory and using long names uses them up.

FAT's attributes are relatively simple—one byte and eight possible attributes. This does not allow for compression to be turned on or off on a file-by-file or folder-by-folder basis, nor does it provide for storing security information or extended attributes such as those needed by Macintosh client computers. Finally, the file system does not perform read-after-write verification. This is expected in server file systems because it allows the operating system to detect bad disk sectors and work around them. It is possible to add this to FAT, but Microsoft has implemented it only in its higher-level file systems.

Despite these shortcomings, FAT16 works well if it is dealing with small partitions that have relatively few files on them. If you create a partition to hold a paging file and nothing else, formatting it with FAT is a good choice. In most systems, however, NTFS is preferred as a general-purpose file system.

Prior to the release of Windows 2000, some Windows NT system administrators liked to keep their operating system files on FAT file systems. Because FAT works with MS-DOS, if there was a problem with the operating system, it was possible to boot from a floppy disk and replace files to repair the system. Under Windows 2000, the Recovery Console makes this unnecessary.

FAT32

FAT32, as the name implies, is FAT—but with 32-bit numbers internally. It is not designed to operate with fewer than 64 K clusters, but it can go up to 2^{32} clusters (about 4 billion). That means that the cluster size can be as small as the size of a disk sector (which is almost always 512 bytes). FAT32 needs a larger cluster size only when partitions reach 2 TB.

In most other respects, it is the same as FAT. However, although FAT16 can be read by just about all operating systems, FAT32 can be used only by Windows 2000, Windows 98, and Windows 95 OEM Service Release 2. (OSR-2 is sometimes called the B revision because the about dialog box launched from the Help Menu has a B on the version number.) DOS, OS/2, and the original release of Windows 95 cannot read FAT32. Perhaps more significantly, Windows NT 4.0 and earlier are also unable to read this file system. Prior to the release of Windows 2000, upgrading from Windows 98 or Windows 95 OSR2 meant reformatting the disk and starting again.

NTFS: The New Technology File System

NTFS was developed from HPFS, the High Performance Filing System, which was introduced in OS/2. Early versions of Windows NT provided HPFS as well as NTFS to aid OS/2 users migrating their servers to Windows NT, but this was dropped with the release of Windows NT 4.0.

NTFS has a more complicated filing system than FAT. The major difference is that the information about file allocation is not stored at the start of the partition; instead, it is stored in bands throughout. This means that a file system can be expanded later because the new space just has bands of allocation information in it. With FAT, the allocation table would have to be enlarged and cluster sizes might have to change (especially in the case of FAT16).

The directory structure of NTFS is different as well. It copes better with searching large directories by using a binary tree structure instead of a list. This means that fewer files need to be examined when searching. Internally, there is native support for long filenames and extensible attributes. This allows NTFS to store security information, such as Access Control Lists, auditing information, and ownership information. It also provides the extra attribute needed to support file-by-file compression. In Windows 2000's implementation, it supports encryption—storing the information needed to decode the file as part of the extended attributes. Macintosh files also require additional information; it is stored as extended attributes. NTFS' allocation units are normally single disk sectors, but NTFS has the capability to store small files without using a sector and to store the data for a very small files in their extended attributes.

NTFS also provides support for links within the file system; the same file can be referenced by entries in two different folders, which is required for Posix support. Posix also demands that the file system should be able to discriminate between upper- and lowercase letters. Before the arrival of long filename support, Microsoft operating systems treated all filenames as uppercase. NTFS has something of a split personality on what is normally called *case sensitivity*. Although it preserves case, it doesn't discriminate on case *except* when running Posix applications.

With these extra features, especially security, some software insists that it use an NTFS partition. Posix applications are one case, but a more common one is the system information used by Active Directory.

NTFS has the capability to support very large file systems, indeed. It uses 64-bit numbers, so the biggest size that it supports for both file and partition size is 2^{64} bytes. This is a huge number.

2^{64} is about the same as 16 x 10^{18}, or 16 exabytes. We rarely get to use SI unit prefixes above mega and giga, terra sometimes sees the light of day, but the next two (peta -10^{16} and exa -10^{18}) are rare. If you like to follow the progression millions, billions, trillions, quadrillions, an exabyte is a quintillion. One thing is for sure: Disk technology will have moved on a little before we need to use this size. If your hard disk can write 1 MB per second, it would take 1000 billion seconds to write an exabyte. There are only 3 million seconds in a year. So it would take something like 300,000 years to write it.

The only visible change in NTFS between the release of Windows NT 3.1 and NT 4.0 was the addition of file-by-file compression in NT 3.5. However, there have been significant additions in Windows 2000. This change comes with a warning for anyone who is running Windows NT 4.0 (or prior) while testing Windows 2000 on the same computer. The NTFS file system has changed and is no longer readable using the NTFS driver provided with the release version of Windows NT 4.0. Windows NT Service Pack 4 and above includes an updated driver to address this. NT systems that have not been updated to this level will not be able to read an NTFS file system that has been accessed in any way under Windows 2000.

NTFS security comes in the following four sections:

- **Logon.** Every user—a person or service running on a computer—must uniquely identify themselves.
- **Ownership.** Every resource on the system is owned by a user (which may be the computer itself).
- **Permission.** Access to any resource is at the discretion of its owner, who determines which users have access and what that access can be.
- **Auditing.** Any time a user exercises a permission that has been granted to them, the exercise of that permission can be recorded.

When a folder is accessed remotely across a network, the shared folder has a set of permissions associated with it, even if the underlying file system is the CD file system or FAT, neither of which have the capability to support permission settings. It is useful to think of these permissions as a filter that blocks inappropriate access to the file system.

By contrast, NTFS is the only file system that supports local security. With a FAT or CDFS file system, any user at the computer where the files are stored has full access to them, but NTFS controls what a user can see, regardless of whether they are local or remote, and the owner of the file or folder can control the type of access granted to each Windows account. If the user is working remotely, the permissions on the shared folder may block certain types of access. If access is allowed through the share, NTFS may or may not allow access to the files. This is sometimes described as giving the most restrictive set of permissions.

As a follow-on from local security, Windows 2000 now has disk quotas. Quotas work using the ownership extended attribute on files. The quota system totals the size of the files for each user and checks to see if the user has exceeded a pre-set quota. Obviously, FAT volumes have no way of identifying the owner of a file, so quotas are available only on NTFS volumes.

The differences between NTFS in Windows NT 4.0 and Windows 2000 are as follows:

- **Changes to permissions.** Windows 2000 has the capability to deny specific types of access; NT 4.0 only has the capability to deny all access. Some permissions that were combined in NT 4.0 have been separated in Windows 2000 (Create Files in a folder and Create Sub-folders are now separate permissions). Permissions inherit differently. Windows NT 4.0 used to set the Access Control Lists of files and folders to match their parents when created, but changing parent's permissions did not always change the children's permissions as expected.

- **Encryption.** Windows 2000 has the capability to encrypt files on NTFS file systems. The encryption process is transparent to the user.

- Quotas were not present in NTFS before Windows 2000.

- **Defragmentation.** In common with all the file systems under Windows 2000, NTFS now supports defragmentation.

Comparison of File Systems

Table 5.2.1 summarizes the differences between the three file systems.

Table 5.2.1   Windows 2000 File Systems Features Comparison

Feature	FAT	FAT32	NTFS
Supported by	DOS, OS/2, Windows 95, Windows 98, Windows NT, Windows 2000	Windows 95, OS/2, Windows 98, Windows 2000	Windows NT Windows 2000
Minimum size of volume	None	32 MB	5 MB
Maximum size of volume	2 GB	32 GB(if formatted under Windows 2000)	16 MB
Default cluster size	Varies with partition size		512 bytes
Long filenames support	Windows 95, Windows 98, Windows NT 3.5, Windows NT 4.0, Windows 2000	Yes	Yes
Defragmentation utility in operating system	Yes (DOS 6, Windows 9X, and Windows 2000 only)	Yes	Yes (Windows 2000 only)

Feature	FAT	FAT32	NTFS
Compression	Whole Drive only under DOS 6 and Windows 9X (Not readable under NT or Windows 2000)	Whole Drive only under Windows 9X (Not readable under NT or Windows 2000)	Enabled for files or folders (NT 3.5 and later, Windows 2000)
Encryption	No	No	No/Yes (Windows 2000 only; not available for compressed files files)
Quotas	No	No	Yes (Windows 2000 Only)
Ownership/ Permissions/ Auditing	No	No	Yes (Windows 2000 only)
Supports mounting of file systems	Child only (Windows 2000 only)	Child only (Windows 2000 only)	Parent or Child (Windows 2000 only)
Use on complex partitions	Yes	Yes	Yes
Can extend	No	No	Yes (but not system or boot volumes)
Support of Macintosh and Posix	No	No	Yes
Read-after-write	No	No	Yes (Servers only)

File System Format

Hard disks, floppy disks, and CDs all contain file systems. CD-ROMs use their own file system (CDFS), floppy disks are formatted with FAT16, and hard disk partitions have a choice of FAT16, FAT32, and NTFS. Only when a partition has been created and formatted with a file system do we have a usable volume. Reformatting an existing volume erases all the data stored on it.

There are multiple ways of formatting a disk.

Formatting Through the GUI

Using Explorer, you can simply right-click on the disk and choose Format.

The resulting dialog box tells you the size of the partition, allows you to choose the file system, and allows you to override the default cluster size. The volume label helps to identify the disk. If the NTFS file system is selected, you have the option to turn on compression in the root folder of the drive, and this will inherit down into subfolders.

Quick format skips the step of checking for bad sectors. On a FAT file system, it creates a new FAT; on NTFS, it removes the pointer to the root directory, effectively making the whole disk appear to be free space.

There is a second GUI-based way of formatting the partition; that is through Disk Manager, which is discussed later in this chapter.

Formatting from the Command Prompt

Format can also be run from the command prompt for formatting hard disks. The syntax is as follows:

format *volume* [**/fs:***file-system*] [**/v:***label*] [**/q**] [**/a:***unitsize*] [**/c**] [**/x**]

The parameters are as follows:

volume   This is usually the drive letter for the volume; however, because volumes can be mounted within an NTFS volume, it can also specify the mount point or internal name for the volume (you can find this out by using the MOUNTVOL command).

/fs:*file-system*   Specifies the file system to use: FAT, FAT32, or NTFS. Remember that FAT32 and NTFS have minimum sizes bigger than the capacity of a floppy disk, so don't use this switch when formatting floppies. This switch must be specified when formatting a new partition, when reformatting a volume format will use the existing file system.

/v:*label*   Specifies the volume label. If you omit this switch, Windows 2000 prompts you for the volume label at the end of the format process. If you want no volume label, you can use **/v:** to avoid the prompt, which can be useful in batch files.

/a:*unitsize*   Allows the allocation size to be forced, although normally the default size will work well. Possible values are 512, 1024, 2048, 4096, 8192, 16K, 32K, 64K.

/q   Quick format, does not scan for bad sectors, so it is best avoided on new partitions and used only when reformatting.

/x   If the volume is in use, this switch forces it to dismount, if necessary, before it is formatted. Doing this can be dangerous—first, any open handles to the volume will no longer be valid, so programs may crash; second, the data on the disk is probably still live and will be lost.

The Convert Command-Line Utility

Convert allows a volume to be converted from one file system to another without the loss of data that would result from reformatting. Windows 2000 does not have a process for converting a partition from FAT16 to FAT32. The only conversion process Windows 2000 supports is converting from FAT16 or FAT32 to the NT file system (NTFS). The process is one way; if it proves necessary to convert from NTFS to FAT, all data must be backed up, the volume can then be reformatted, and the data is restored.

Convert is a command-line utility. It was provided with the first versions of Windows NT, where it was possible to convert FAT to HPFS and both FAT and HPFS could be converted to NTFS. In Windows NT 4.0 and Windows 2000, HPFS has been withdrawn. However, Convert still needs to be run with the /FS:NTFS to specify the end file system. The syntax is as follows:

Convert *Drive* **/fs:**NTFS [**/v**]

The parameters are as follows:

Drive   The drive letter for the volume to be converted.

/v   Verbose mode, which provides extra information as it runs.

If files are open, the conversion will be scheduled for next reboot. Convert does this by writing the command-line into the registry to be run at startup.

NTFS Permissions

As mentioned earlier in this chapter, NTFS is the only one of Windows 2000's file systems to support local security. Within Windows 2000, user accounts, groups, and even computers (collectively referred to as *security principals*), all have a Security IDs, or SIDs. A SID is a unique number; part of it identifies a security principal, and part of it identifies the Domain or individual computer where the SID was issued.

When permissions are set on an object, such as a file or folder, the SID of the user or group and the permissions assigned to them are recorded in an Access Control Entry, or ACE. An ACE identifies a single user or group and their permissions. However, many objects will have ACEs for multiple users and groups: The list of entries for an object is known strictly as a Discretionary Access Control List (usually, the Discretionary is omitted and it is just called Access Control List, or ACL).

Whenever a user logs on to Windows 2000, the SIDs that represent the user and all the groups they belong to are looked up and stored in a data structure known as an *Access Token*. When the user attempts to access a file or folder, the SIDs on the Access Token are compared against the SIDs on each ACE in the ACL. When they match, it means the permission part of that ACE applies to that user.

If a user belongs to multiple groups (and so has many applicable ACEs) or if permissions are granted to the user and to a group they belong to, the rule for combining the ACEs to get the users effective permissions is simple. If the permission is granted anywhere, the user receives that permission. (As you will see shortly, there is a codicil to this: unless the permission is explicitly revoked.)

Example of the Way Permissions Combine

Table 5.2.2. shows how permissions combine. In this table, no permission has been set for the user as an individual: JDoe is neither granted nor denied access. Two groups that user belongs to have been granted access. One has Read Access, and one has Read and Write access. The total set of permissions granted is Read and Write; nothing has been denied so the user has Read and Write access.

Table 5.2.2   Combining Permissions

User JDdoe	<No Access Control Entry Ace>	Access Control List does not refer to this individual user
Group Everyone	Grant Read	Read access has been granted; Write access is neither granted nor forbidden
Group Sales	Grant Read /Write	Both Read and Write access granted
Total Granted	**Read/Write**	
Total Denied		
Total Effective	**Read/Write**	

Table 5.2.3 develops these permissions further. A further group is added to the ACL and this group is denied access. The import rule is that if a subset of permissions is granted without explicitly denying the others, they remain. If a permission is denied anywhere, then the permission is revoked.

Table 5.2.3   Combining Permissions with a Mixture of Grant and Deny Access Control Entries

User	Jdoe	<No Ace>	Access Control List does not refer to this individual user
Group	Everyone	Grant Read	Read access has been granted; Write access is neither granted nor forbidden

| Group | Sales | Grant Read/Write | Both Read and Write access granted |
| Group | Technical | Deny Write | Write Access forbidden; Read access is neither granted nor forbidden |

Total Granted	**Read/Write**
Total Denied	**Write**
Total Effective	**Read**

Figure 5.2.1   File permissions look similar, but do not have List Folder Contents.

As you can see, the user interface in Windows 2000 presents six simple permissions, which seem self-explanatory. A little experiment shows that Full Control includes all the others, Modify includes everything—except for Full Control. Read and Execute include both Read and List Folder Contents. But there are some obvious things missing from the simple permissions. Where, for example, is the permission to delete things? And what is the difference between Modify and Full Control? As it turns out, each of the six simple permissions is made up from a combination of more complex permissions, and these can be viewed through the Advanced button.

There are 13 advanced permissions, and they map on to the six simple permissions, as shown in Figure 5.2.1. When you look at advanced permissions, you should not only look at the permissions being set on the Access Control List, but also on what objects those permissions apply to. Read and Execute shows the same advanced permissions as List Folder contents. List Folder Contents applies to the folder alone, but Read and Execute permissions apply to the folder and all its contents.

Figure 5.2.2   Advanced permissions.

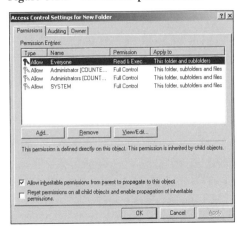

Some explanations of these permissions might be useful.

Traversing a folder means passing through it on the way to another folder. If a user is not allowed to traverse a folder to which they have no permissions, they will not be able to access a subfolder in which they do have permissions. However, this is frequently a cause of problems, so Windows 2000 has a user right called Bypass Traverse Checking. This right allows access to folders, regardless of the setting of the traverse permission in the parents. This right is granted to everyone by default, but this can be changed in the local security policy or the Active Directory group policy.

Reading a file is reading the data within it, but reading a folder is getting a list of its contents—hence, the same permission has different meanings and descriptions of Read Data and List Folder.

Note that Windows 2000 discriminates between opening to Execute a File and opening to Read Data. Note also the way that Execute File and Traverse Folder share the same check box in the user interface.

Windows 2000 also discriminates between writing data to a new file and appending data to an existing file. Writing to a folder would be adding items to it, so Write Data corresponds to Create File, and Append Data corresponds to Create Folders. It might be helpful to think of Create Files as Write to Directory because this is the permission required to rename a file, and Create Folders is needed to rename folders.

Reading and Writing attributes and extended attributes include the capability to change view and change attributes such as read-only, and extended attributes such as those used by Macintosh clients and by NTFS encryption.

Delete Sub-folders and Files replaces a Windows NT 4.0 permission known as File Delete Child, which could be granted only as part of Full Control. This permission, which now stands on its own, overrides any permission set on files that would prevent you from deleting them.

Delete is the permission to delete the file or folder itself.

The final two permissions are concerned with the setting of permissions. Change Permissions allows the owner of a file to nominate others who will be allowed to set control access. Such a person is able to take permissions away from the owner. The owner always has the right to set permissions, however. The Take Ownership permission allows a user to make themselves the owner of a file or folder. Administrators do not have automatic access to everything under Windows 2000; however, they do have the right to take ownership of any file or folder—once they own it, they can set permissions.

Ownership is a simple concept. Normally, the owner of a file or folder is the person who created it. Ownership can be offered by setting the Take Ownership permission (which is included in Full Control), but it cannot be given; instead, it must be taken by the new owner. There is one special case: Administrators can always take ownership—they do not need the Take Ownership permission to do so. However, Administrators should be aware that this causes all permissions on the object to be reset.

Permissions in Windows 2000 have only minor changes from Windows NT 4.0. Permissions that were once a single permission have been divided. In particular, Windows NT 4.0 had a permission called No Access, which blocked all other permissions. This was useful, but there were some situations where it was cumbersome. For example, if you want guest users to be able to read from a folder but not to write to it and you want all other users to have write access, you set Read access for the guests group and Read/Write access for other groups, making sure that everyone who wasn't a guest was included in these groups (but checking that no guest account was included in them).

In Windows 2000, the No Access permission disappears. Now, each permission that can be granted can be denied. The No Write Access for Guests issue is now much easier. Everyone gets Read and Write access, but Write access is denied to guests.

The other major difference between Windows 2000 and NT 4.0 permissions is inheritance. Under all the versions of Windows NT and with HPFS under OS/2, you might have a set of permissions on the root folder, a folder in the root, and a file in the folder. If you changed the permissions at the root, the folder and the file would not be affected unless you asked for permissions to be propagated to child folders and files. But this sometimes had unexpected consequences. Consider the following example.

You have a folder named users, which has a subfolder for each network user. The users' (root) folder has Read access for everyone; each subfolder has full access for a single user and nothing set for anyone else. Now, you want to give the administrator access to the users' folders. Granting the administrator account full control in the parent folder would not change the access in the subfolders unless you request that the newly set permissions be applied to subfolders and files. Doing this will delete all the permissions on the users' subfolders and replace them with the newly set permissions on the parent folder.

Windows NT 4.0 had a command-line utility named CACLS (change ACLs) to work around this problem, but it was difficult to use.

Windows 2000 solves this by allowing permissions to inherit down into a file or folder from its parent. This behavior can be disabled with a check box on the main security page. For example, the group Everyone can have access to a root folder, but that permission does not carry down into subfolders.

When inheritance is disabled, the option is given to copy the permissions that had been inherited onto the file or folder. This saves having to re-enter all the permissions that were previously inherited.

Figure 5.2.3   Removing inheritance gives the option to retain the information that was inherited.

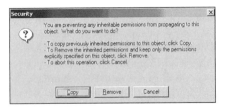

When editing permissions from the Advanced dialog box, the administrator can decide whether permissions will inherit into subfolders and into files, or not. For example, permissions granted to administrators can be set to carry down into subfolders, but those granted to ordinary users may not. Unlike some systems, it is not possible for a folder to determine the type of permissions that inherit into it from above.

Auditing is controlled in a very similar way to the setting of permissions, and this is much the same as Windows NT 4.0. The owner of a file has the ability not just to control access to a file or folder, but also to record who attempts to access it. Auditing records the exercise of the permissions, and whether they succeed or fail.

Figure 5.2.4   Inheritance and the lower-level permissions can both be controlled.

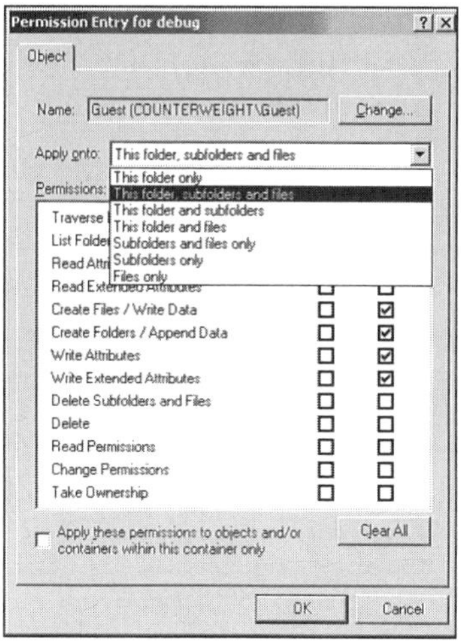

Internally, auditing and permissions are managed similarly by NTFS. Both use a form of Access Control List. The owner creates a Discretionary Access Control List to determine who is allowed what access to the files. Some Microsoft documents refer to the audit settings stored on each file or folder as a System Access Control List. The Advanced button on a security page allows access to the Auditing settings, which look very similar indeed to the settings for permissions.

Copying and Moving Files with NTFS

When a file or folder is created on NTFS, its permissions and auditing are inherited from its parent folder and the owner is initially the user who created it. One slightly unexpected behavior is that Windows 2000 sets files created by the Administrator account to be owned by the group administrators. But new administrators are often confused by the following question: "When a file is moved or copied, does it keep its existing settings or is it treated as a new file?"

The easiest way to understand this is to ask "Can the operating system do this simply by adjusting entries in the directory *or* does it have to rewrite the file?" If the file is rewritten (a copy or a move to a different volume), it is treated as a new file and gets an updated owner and permissions to suit its new location. If the move is within a volume, the permissions are preserved.

File and Disk Utilities

When managing files and disks, there are several functions that you need to be aware of. The following sections discuss the tasks of encryption, compression, defragmentation, and recovering deleted files.

Encrypted Files

A new feature of Windows 2000 is the capability to encrypt files on the disk. Although this provides some protection against unauthorized reading of the file, it needs to be understood clearly to avoid problems.

The process is very simple. From the properties of a file or a folder, the user clicks the Advanced button and selects a check box.

Figure 5.2.5   Advanced Attributes, used to turn on compression or encryption.

Windows 2000 also has an attribute to control the behavior of its free text indexing service.

When the Encrypt Contents check box is ticked for a folder, it has the effect of turning on encryption for the files in the folder. When encryption is turned on for a file, Windows 2000 creates an encryption key for the file and uses a secret key algorithm to encode the file using that key. Secret key algorithms are less CPU-intensive than public key algorithms, which makes them a good choice if large amounts of data are to be encrypted. With secret key algorithms, the same key is used for encoding and decoding and must be kept secret, which poses a problem—how to pass the key back and forth without the risk of discovery. Public key algorithms solve this problem by using one key to encode and another to decode; the encoding key can be made public, provided that the decoding key remains private.

The approached used by NTFS is to use a secret key algorithm to secure the file and to use a public key method to protect the secret key. It locks up one key by using another key—a construction sometimes called a *lockbox*. The secret key is locked by using the users' public key, and they unlock it by using their private key. This way, the (large) file is encrypted with a CPU-efficient method, and the CPU-intensive method is used only to encrypt the (small) secret key.

Windows 2000 uses X509 certificates to exchange public keys. X509 is a standard for stating "This public key belongs to this entity and can be used for this purpose." The certificate is normally issued by a certification authority, which digitally signs the certificate; someone using the certificate can say "This claims to be the private key for encrypting e-mail to John Doe, and I can trust that it really is his key because this Certification Authority says so."

You can see the certificates that have been installed for users by loading the Certificates snap-in for the Microsoft Management Console.

Passing unseen by the user, the Encrypting File System retrieves an X509 certificate, which is marked as authorized for EFS: If the user does not have a certificate, EFS creates one.

See for Yourself

You can see the X509 process in action in the Microsoft Management Console . Follow these steps:

1 Log on as a new non-administrative user.

2 Start the MMC (run mmc.exe). With the empty console, add the Certificates snap-in.

3 Go to Personal Certificates.

4 Encrypt a file, and you will see a new certificate appear.

Note that the certificate applies to one user only, and contains the public key for EFS to create a lock box containing a secret key specific to that file. To decode the file, EFS requests the private key that matches the public key. This happens in the background—if EFS is used over a network, the server and client computer must both be Windows 2000 computers in an Active Directory Domain. The computer acting as server must be trusted for delegation in order for the requests for keys to succeed, but by default only Domain controllers are trusted. This can be set or checked on the property sheet of the computer in the Active Directory Users and Computers console.

As described so far, encryption is confined to a single user. It is important to realize that if a user encrypts a file, they cannot then share it with other users; but the possible problems go a little deeper than that. Suppose a user had Full Control access to a shared folder and maliciously (or foolishly) encrypted all its contents? Suppose a user with confidential information leaves the company and their account is deleted? Then, it is found that all their files are encrypted.

There is a simple solution: Why create just one lock box? Why not make multiple copies of the secret key, and allow the user who encrypted the file to open one lock box and have another box that can be opened by a trusted individual who contains the "spare" key? That is exactly what Windows 2000 does—it nominates Encrypted Data Recovery Agents and creates an additional lock box for each one. By default, there is only one recovery agent—the administrator—but the agents can be changed by using the Security Policy Console or Active Directory group policies.

The File Recovery Certificate

If you use the Certificates console while logged on as Administrator on a standalone computer, you will see that the account has a personal certificate for file recovery. A copy of that certificate is also stored in the local security policy, and EFS uses the public key from the certificate to create a second lock box.

You can use the Certificates console to export the certificate and private key for a user to a file (for backup purposes). Having done this, the certificate and private key can be deleted. This means that if someone breaks into recovery agent's account, the key is not there for the intruder to recover any encrypted files. Nothing can be recovered unless the certificate and private key are reinstalled, so if you undertake this process for safety (which is especially worthwhile on a Domain Controller), you must make sure the exported certificate and key are stored safely.

Compression

Since Windows NT version 3.5, it has been possible to compress NTFS files and folders. Explorer has the option to show compressed files in a different color (blue instead of black), and it can be turned on or off from the View page of the Folder Options dialog box.

In Windows 2000, compression is turned on and off from the same Advanced Attributes dialog box that is used to turn on encryption. Files cannot be both compressed and encrypted If you encrypt files that are already compressed, NTFS uncompresses them (in a sense), so they do not appear as compressed via the UI.

The compression attribute is treated in much the same way as security information. When a file is moved within the same NTFS volume, its attributes are preserved. If a new copy of the file is created (by copying within a volume or moving to a different volume), the compression attribute is inherited from the destination folder.

Defragmentation

All disks suffer from a phenomenon known as *fragmentation*. When accessing the data on the disk, the distance that the disk head needs to travel is a significant factor. If a large file is written in several parts, the head has to move back and forth, and wait for the disk to rotate to the place where the data is stored. Files are created and deleted on a file system, and after it has been in use for a little while, it becomes necessary to reuse the space that was occupied by deleted files. However, the pieces of free space may be smaller than the file size, so there is no option but to write data in multiple fragments.

This obviously has a detrimental effect on the performance of the system, so the contents of the disk need to be rearranged periodically. The goals of defragmentation are as follows:

- Every existing file should be stored in a group of contiguous disk blocks.

- To allow new files to be created as a contiguous block, the free space should be contiguous.

- Files in the same folder should lie close together on the disk.

Under Windows NT, Microsoft did not provide any disk-defragmentation software, although it was possible to boot under DOS or Windows 95 and defragment a FAT file system (DOS was a risky option because it ran the risk of destroying any long filenames). It was left to the third-party market to provide defragmentation software for NTFS, and the most successful product was DiskKeeper from Executive Software. Windows 2000 includes a licensed version of DiskKeeper.

Defragmentation can be started in several ways, one being from the tools page of the properties of a drive (in the style of Windows 9x).

Figure 5.2.6   Defragmentation in progress—this disk was heavily fragmented (one file of 231 K was in 435 pieces).

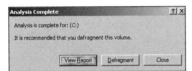

Recovering Deleted Files

When a file is deleted from a local disk by using Explorer, it is not actually deleted; instead, it is moved to the Recycle Bin. Windows 2000 preserves files in the Recycle Bin; in fact, this can make the problems of fragmentation worse because the space occupied by the file is not handed back and the operating system is forced to write new files into whatever small fragments are available.

The operation of the Recycle Bin is quite straightforward: Each volume keeps a hidden directory named Recycler. Within this directory, there is a folder for each user's deleted files. These folders are named with the Security ID (SID) of the user. When a file is deleted in Explorer, it is moved to this folder (to force a *true delete*, the file can be deleted with the Shift key held down or deleted from the command prompt). The Recycle Bin icon that appears on the desktop and in the root of each volume provides a view of all the files in the Recycle Bins on all drives.

Figure 5.2.7   Viewing the contents of the Recycle Bin.

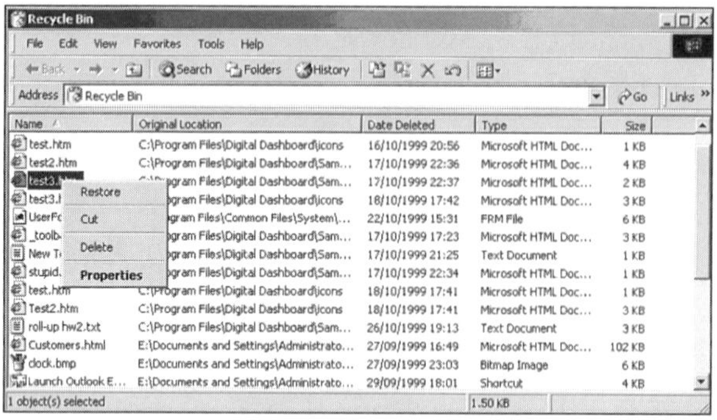

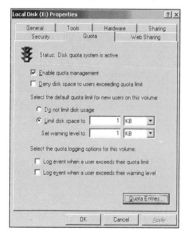

Restoring a file is as simple as choosing the file and clicking on Restore from the File menu, or right-clicking the file and choosing Restore.

The Recycle Bin can be manually emptied (by right-clicking it and choosing Empty); to prevent it from using too much disk space, its properties allow its disk usage to be capped at a fixed percentage or disabled entirely.

Disk Quotas

One of most requested additions for Windows NT was the capability to limit the amount of space used by a specific user. This has been added in Windows 2000. The system works by calculating the sum of file sizes for each user owning files on the disk. The quota system can prevent users writing to the disk if it would take them over their quota or simply log an event to the event log. Quotas work by the owner of a file, so it applies to users and not groups, and they work with the uncompressed file size; if a user exceeds their quota, compressing files will not help.

Figure 5.2.8   Quota management.

Enabling the disk quotas consists of the following steps. First, all quotas management must be turned on for the required drive. The next step is to decide whether there will be a default limit and whether a warning should be logged at a lower level. Finally, the following decisions can be made: Are users exceeding the quota denied disk space? And/or is the event logged? This sets the default. The Quota Entries button shows the amount of disk space used by each user and allows different limits to be set for different users. There are two noteworthy options of this dialog box. The first is that from the Edit menu, all the entries may be selected, copied, and pasted into a report or database to track disk usage. The second is that setting up identical quotas on multiple drives across many servers can be a slow process. The File menu allows entries to be exported and reimported.

Figure 5.2.9   Quota entries.

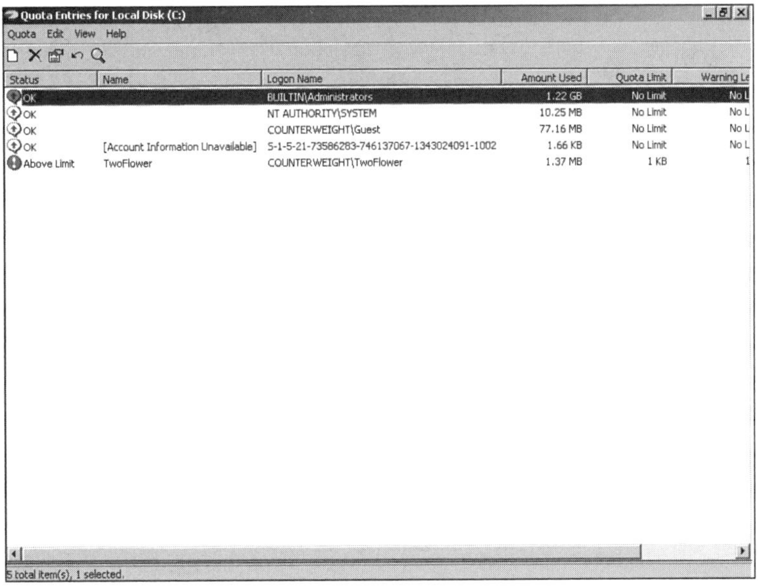

Disk Configuration

Disk partitions are created using the Microsoft Management Console, specifically within the Computer Management console. This has a branch named Storage (with a section named Disk Management under Storage), which controls the creation and deletion of partitions, controls the setting of disks as basic or dynamic, and provides a route to the volume's properties, including the ability to format it.

Basic and Dynamic Storage

Prior to the release of Windows 2000, information about the volumes on a drive was held in the partition table, which is part of the Master boot record at the start of the disk. In Windows NT, the information about what each partition was used for was stored in the Registry. This is still supported as a basic disk in Windows 2000. Dynamic disks have a database at the end of the disk to store volume information. This database is replicated among all the dynamic disks in a system. Volumes on dynamic drives can be created, removed, and extended without having to reboot the system.

When Windows 2000 is first installed, the disk is configured as a basic disk. New partitions can be created on a basic disk and can be formatted with any of the file systems. However, these partitions cannot be extended or mirrored, and no other fault-tolerance can be configured.

The disk management part of the console uses a wizard to create partitions. The wizard is started by right-clicking a piece of free disk space and has four input dialog boxes, followed by a summary before the partition is created. The wizard begins by asking whether the partition should be a primary or extended partition. Older versions of DOS could only support a disk with a single primary partition, although Windows NT, Windows 9X, and DOS 6.0 can all support multiple primary partitions. The other reason for choosing an extended partition is that a disk can contain only four partitions, but an extended partition can contain multiple volumes.

The second dialog box of the wizard asks for the amount of space the partition should use; the third confirms the drive letter to use (or where the file system should be mounted if no letter is desired); the final entry screen allows the administrator to select the formatting details for the drive.

The context menu that is called up by right-clicking the partition in disk administrator has options to open or explore the disk, to view its properties, and to format or delete it. There is one further option: to change the drive letter and path.

Each volume may have a single drive letter; in addition, it can be mounted into one or more folders of an NTFS file system. This is useful for making multiple partitions appear to be a single volume, especially because basic disks do not allow partitions to be extended. Mounting file systems in this way reduces the number of drive letters needed. Very few systems actually get to 26 drive letters, but it can be confusing to have 10 or 12 drives. It also allows the amount of space in a folder to be constrained (to the size of the mounted volume) and allows different quotas to be enforced for what appear to be different parts of the same disk.

Figure 5.2.10   Inheritance and the lower-level permissions can both be controlled.

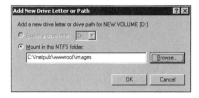

However, the only way to provide a single seamless volume is to extend it. The disk needs to be converted to a dynamic disk *before* the volume is created and the volume needs to be formatted with NTFS.

After the disk has been converted, the partitions on it are referred to as simple volumes. They're called *simple* because they are made from a single partition on a single disk. There are four complex volumes, and these include Windows 2000's fault-tolerant disk arrangements. Therefore, to provide fault-tolerance within the operating system rather than in hardware, the disks concerned must be converted to dynamic. However, after this conversion has been done, the disk will be inaccessible to other operating systems.

A *spanned volume* uses different size areas on multiple drives. (Under Windows NT, this was known as a *volume set*.) There is no fault-tolerance in a spanned volume: If one drive fails, all the data is lost, so it may be safer to use mounted file systems instead. Mounted file systems limit where in the folder hierarchy space may be used; spanned volumes do not.

A *striped volume,* sometimes called *RAID 0*, spreads information over multiple disks. It gives high performance but, like a spanned volume, it has no fault-tolerance. It contains between 2 and 32 drives that may fail, but if any fail, all the data is lost.

A *mirrored volume,* sometimes called *RAID 1*, holds all the information in the volume twice on separate disks. It offers the greatest level of fault-tolerance—it is highly unlikely that the second drive will fail before the first is replaced, but 50% of the disk space is redundant. The performance of mirroring is good, but not as fast as a striped set.

A *RAID 5 volume* uses the capacity of one of its drives to hold parity information (in Windows NT, it was known as *stripe set with parity*). This means it needs to have at least three drives and can go up to 32.

A *RAID* stands for a Redundant Array of Inexpensive Disks (some people use the term *independent disks,* but the original proponents of RAID talked about different levels of RAID, in comparison with a Single Large Expensive Disk, or SLED).

RAID 0, striping, is not redundant, RAID 1 is disk mirroring, and RAID 2–5 are all arrays that use some of their capacity to hold information that will allow the data of a failed drive to be reconstructed. RAID 5 distributes this information among all the drives in the array.

RAID 5 performs as well as a stripe set for read operations and for large writes. However, the overhead of calculating and writing the parity makes it inefficient when dealing with many small writes or situations in which the data is written and read only once (for example, paging files). It is slightly less reliable than a mirrored volume (because there is more chance of two drives from an array of five failing than both drives in a mirror pair). It is generally considered better to use RAID hardware than to provide it in software. If this is done, Windows 2000 sees the RAID array as a single disk.

Creating a dynamic volume is reasonably simple. Again, it uses a wizard, and like the Partition Wizard, it has four dialog boxes for input and a summary. Although the Partition Wizard begins by asking about primary or extended partition, the Volume Wizard begins by asking if the user wants to create a simple volume, spanned volume, striped volume, mirrored volume, or RAID 5 volume. All but simple volume will be disabled if the computer has only a single disk.

The second dialog box in the wizard is concerned with selecting the disk or disks that the volume will use, and how much space will be used. The last two input dialog boxes deal with which drive letter or mount point to use, and how the volume should be formatted.

NTFS volumes, which are created on dynamic drives, can be extended but only if they were created on a dynamic disk. This means the system disk can be made dynamic (which allows it to be mirrored), but the system partition cannot be extended because it is always created while the disk is basic. The interface for doing this is a wizard that is almost identical to the one used to create the volume in the first place. Suitable pieces of unallocated space are chosen and the disk is extended without the need to reboot. The disk cannot be contracted again, however; and if a drive fails, the whole volume is lost.

Mounting volumes overcomes this concern, as mentioned earlier. It also allows multiple file systems to appear to be a single volume (although this may simply cause confusion), and it allows different quotas to be set on different folders. However, if one mounted file system is full and another has free space, that space may not be helpful.

Best Practices

- Choose hardware RAID over software RAID when the budget allows it.
- Avoid spanned volumes if possible. Multiple drives mean more chance of failure, and a failure of one will mean the loss of data on all. Use Mounted volumes.
- Mounted drives give the appearance of a single folder tree, but the space in each folder will be restricted.

- Format all hard disks with NTFS unless the system will run different operating systems at different times *or* if an application planned for a server gains significant performance improvement on FAT.

- Use the Recovery Console if you need to repair a damaged system based on NTFS.

Removing a Volume

You have two methods of performing this:

- **Method 1.** If the partition is more than 2 GB, Windows 2000 Setup allows you to delete, re-create, and reformat the partition as FAT32 during Text mode setup. If it is less than 2 GB, your choices for formatting are only FAT or NTFS, and you can try Method 2.

- **Method 2.** Boot from the four setup disks or the Windows 2000 CD, press **R** to repair, and press **C** for Recovery Console. Use the commands DISKPART and FORMAT to perform the operations.

5.3

Sharing Folders

**You Need to Read This Section If
You Want to:**

- Share folders.
- Publish folders in Active Directory.
- Administer shared folders.
- Monitor shared folders

Overview of Shared Folders

Since the first MS Net products of the mid 1980s (through LAN Manager, Windows for Workgroups, Windows NT, Windows 9X, and Windows 2000), Microsoft networks have all worked using *shared folders*. The user does not refer to an absolute path to the file, but uses an alias for the folder. A workstation user or server administrator creates the aliases; for example, the alias INSTALL might be D:\PUBLIC FILES\SOFTWARE\INSTALL. If necessary, the path associated with one of these aliases can be changed, so if a disk becomes full, the administrator can move a shared folder to another disk on the server and make the alias point to the new shared folder. Printers are shared in the same way, with an alias representing the printer (for example, BIGLASER might be the alias for a printer).

The terminology used by Microsoft when talking about these aliases has varied a little over the years; they have been called *shares* (which covers shared folders and shared printers), *share points*, or *shared directories*. With *Directory* being used to mean Active Directory and *folders* being used to mean the places where files are stored, the name has now evolved into *shared folders*.

The NET SHARE command can be issued at the command prompt or from a batch file to share folders and printers in Windows 2000 in the same way that it was used back as far as MS Net, but sharing is usually configured through the GUI. Microsoft Network servers provide client computers with a list of shared folders and printers, which can be seen when browsing the server from the GUI or by using the command **NET VIEW\\SERVERNAME** at the command prompt. Shared folders whose share name ends with a $ sign are not shown in this way, and can be accessed only by typing their names. The network server software automatically creates some of these *administrative shares* when it starts. Exactly what is created varies slightly from product to product. In Windows 2000, there is one for each hard disk volume: C$, D$, and so on; and one named ADMIN$ for the operating system directory. If the computer shares printers with the network, a PRINT$ share will be created to provide access to printer drivers.

Default Admin Folders

The administrative shares will normally be re-created on bootup unless the following Registry keys are set (manually or via policy):

HKEY_LOCAL_MACHINE\System\CurrentControlSet\Services\LanmanServer\Parameters\ AutoShareWks to 0 (Dword)

(Professional and Server use the same key.)

Creating a Shared Folder

Shared folders can be created though the GUI or with the NET SHARE command, which can be used in batch files as well as at a command prompt.

There are two main ways to set up sharing through the GUI (even within the GUI, there is more than one way). The most common way, however, is to call up the property pages for the folder to be shared and then use the sharing page. It is possible to go directly to this page by choosing Sharing from the Folders context menu or the File menu in Explorer. Only Administrators and members of the Server Operators group are allowed to create shares on Windows 2000 Server systems. Windows 2000 Professional does not have a Server Operators group; on Windows 2000, Professional, Administrators and Power Users have the ability to add and remove shares.

Troubleshooting Tip

When logged-in with a user with the power to create shares, you will see shared folders represented by a different icon form: non-shared folders (a hand offering the folder). If no folders appear to be shared and the sharing item is missing from the Folders context menu, the current user does not belong to the correct groups. You can use the RUNAS feature to create a shared folder without logging off and on again. For example, you can start the Computer Management console with a different user account and use the Shared Folders option.

The first option in the folder is to determine whether or not the folder is shared. If it is, the alias for the share can be specified, together with a comment, to describe what is in the folder to make it easier to select the correct one.

Next, there is a box to specify how many users may connect to the share. Depending on the license settings used in Windows 2000, the operating system may limit the number of simultaneous connections—in Windows 2000 Professional, this is fixed at 10. In Windows 2000 Server, if the computer is configured for per-server licensing, no more connections will be allowed when the number of licenses is reached. It is generally considered that per-seat licensing is more flexible; if this is chosen, connections will be allowed beyond the server's configured limit (although an error will be logged). The connection limit can be used as an aid to license enforcement, not just for the file sharing, but also for applications run from the server.

Another Use for the Connections Limit

One other use of the connections limit is to provide a workaround for Microsoft's lack of a method to limit the number of simultaneous connections by a user. If a share is created with only one connection allowed and a user's logon script connects to this share, the script can log the user off if the connection fails (which implies that the account is in use on another station).

A new feature of Windows 2000 is the capability to take folders offline, which is sometimes called *client-side caching*. The server can tell client computers whether they can or cannot cache certain shared folders. If caching is enabled, there are three possible behaviors. Manual Caching for Documents does not cache any files on the user's computer *unless* the user requests it. Automatic Caching For Documents will cache files that the user opens, but will not cache other files unless the user requests it. Automatic Caching for Programs will cache files that are not to be changed; the files will be downloaded to the user's computer and run from there. It is useful for read-only data as well as programs, but will not push changes back to the server.

Another GUI method is the Microsoft Management Console. In the Computer Management MMC console, under the System Tools, Shared Folders branch, it is possible to see the Shares, Connected Users, and Files that are being used. The Shares branch shows each of the shared folders, and from the MMC's Action menu (or by right-clicking Shares), select the option to create a new file share. This provides a dialog wizard to set up the new share. The first dialog box takes the name of the folder to be shared, the alias to use, and the description to show when the client is given a list of shares. The second dialog box sets the security options for the share. After the share is set up, it is possible to set the other settings, such as caching and maximum users.

The command-line method uses the NET SHARE command. In its simplest form, it is issued in the form NET SHARE ALIAS=PATH (that is, NET SHARE INSTALL="D:\PUBLIC FILES\SOFTWARE\INSTALL).

Optional command-line switches that can be used with Net share are the following:

- **/Remark.** Comment text that sets the remark to appear when the list of shares is browsed.
- **/Users:xx** or **/Unlimited.** Sets the number of users allowed to use the share.
- **/Cache:Automatic /Cache:Manual** or **/Cache:No.** Controls the use of caching.
- **/Delete**. Deletes a share when it is no longer needed.

Setting permissions, however, needs to be carried out through the GUI.

Setting Permissions On Shared Folders

Different Microsoft networking products have different ways of providing security. Simple systems such as MS Net and Windows for Workgroups use password-level security, in which each shared folder has a password associated with it. The password must be supplied to connect to the folder. This does not work well on large networks. Windows NT and Windows 2000 use user-level security, in which the user supplies a name and password. Based on that, access to resources is either granted or refused. Under normal circumstances, the user will log in to the network and the network client software will supply their credentials to every server they connect to, without bothering the user again. Only if the user connects to a server that requires different logon credentials do they have to re-enter any information. The concept of Domains, which Microsoft networks have used since LAN Manager V2, was created to ensure that the same credentials are valid on all servers. Although users will not notice, in Windows 2000 the way the credentials are validated has changed with the arrival of Kerberos authentication.

Windows 2000 shared folder permissions are set for groups and/or individual users. The permissions act as filters to allow the administrator to say "Pass this kind of access from this user (or group) through to the file system."

If the file system is FAT or CDFS, which do not support local security, permissions can be applied only through filtering things out at the shared folder level. In effect, FAT has full access for everyone and CDFS has read access for everyone. However, when we look at NTFS, we can set permissions on the file system, on the shared folder, or both. If permissions are set on the file system, the share can be set to everyone having full control. Conversely, if permissions are set on the share, everyone can be given full control at the file-system level. However, shared folder permissions have two major limitations. First, they allow the granting (or denial) of access at only three levels: Read Only, Change, and Full Control. Second, these permissions apply to all files and subfolders accessed through the shared folder. NTFS gives a greater degree of finesse in controlling access. Like NTFS permissions, shared folder permissions are cumulative; if a user receives permission as an individual or as a member of a group at least once, they are granted the permission. If the permission is denied at least once, it is denied. If it is both granted and denied, it is denied.

If users have no access at the share level, their requests will not reach the underlying file system, even if they have full control. If they have Full Control permissions at the share level, but some folders beneath the shared one have Read Only or No Access, requests will reach the file system and will be denied.

Another way of talking about the way NTFS and share permissions combine is to think of the most restrictive access being granted. If you calculate the effective share permissions and then calculate the effective NTFS permissions, whichever is more restrictive will win (you must be granted access in both places or you don't have it).

A Little Background on Microsoft's Security Model

The main benefit that comes from working with Domains is that a user can connect to many servers by using the same logon credentials. As far as the user is concerned, they enter their password to log on in the morning and never have to re-enter it, even if they connect to additional servers during the day. In the background, the network client software passes the user's logon credentials to any server that needs them. If the network is properly structured, all servers will work from the same set of accounts. So, if a Domain Controller validated the account name and password when the user logged on, all servers in the Domain (and connected Domains) will accept the account as valid. If a server should fail and need to be rebooted, the client software reconnects just as transparently as it connected in the first place. The client software attempts to continue with a session; the server will have forgotten that the session existed. On receiving an error from the server, the client logs in again and the whole process is transparent to the user.

This poses a problem for the administrator because if users are disconnected from the system to allow maintenance to be carried out, as soon as any action on the client computer requires use of the server, the connection will be re-established.

How Clients Search for (and Find) Shared Folders in the Browser

Browsing gives users the ability to choose the server and shared folder required from a list instead of typing it. One server provides the client with a list of all the available servers, and the user's chosen server provides a list of available resources. So, the act of browsing is divided into browsing servers and browsing one server's resources. Resource browsing is as old as Microsoft networking. In MS Net, as in Windows 2000, the command line NET VIEW\\SERVERNAME will return a list of shared folders and printers. With Windows-based networks, this process usually happens from within the GUI rather then the command line. Choosing Run from the Start menu and entering **SERVERNAME** will produce a list of shared resources at the server.

Since LAN Manager, Microsoft networks have supported some form of server browsing. In LAN Manager, servers sent broadcasts to the network and clients maintained a list of servers whose broadcasts they had received. Windows NT and Windows 2000 Server have the option to make these broadcasts to support networks that continue to have LAN Manager clients.

When Windows for Workgroups arrived in 1992, there had to be a change in the way browsing was managed. Instead of the few servers and many clients model of LAN Manager, every computer on the network could be a server—if only in the peer-to-peer sense. It would have been inefficient to retain the broadcast model. Windows for Workgroups introduced the browsing model, which has been used in all subsequent Microsoft operating systems.

First of all, if the network is very large, it should be divided into manageable pieces. If the computers belong to Domains, this accomplishes the task, but if the network is not Domain-based, the browsing model provides *workgroups*. Workgroups are loose affiliations of computers—computers can move between workgroups and start their own workgroup if no suitable one exists. Workgroups have no role in security—that is the major difference with Domains. Not only do Domains share accounts, but Windows NT and Windows 2000 machines cannot join a Domain unless the administrator allows it. Windows 9x and Windows for Workgroups computers don't *belong* to a Domain in the same way. They can choose a Domain to log users on to the network, and they can decide where they wish to appear in the browsing hierarchy. For browsing purposes, workgroups and Domains are equivalent, but workgroups exist solely for browsing and Domains exist primarily for sharing accounts.

In every workgroup or Domain, one computer acts as the master browser. When the server service starts on a computer, it attempts to contact the master browser for its workgroup or Domain. If the master browser cannot be found, the machine calls a browser election. Some machines can be configured to want to be master browsers, and they will call a browser election without even seeing if there is a browser on the network. Normally, the machine calling the election will propose itself for the role of browse master. There are two exceptions, however. The first is when an existing browse master shuts down and calls an election to ensure that another machine takes on the job. The other is that as browse masters they can also be configured to not want the job.

Using the Maintain Server List Registry Setting

Whether a machine sets out to be browse master, accepts the job if it is the most suitable, or doesn't keep the list at all is governed by the Registry setting Maintain Server List under

HKEY_LOCAL_MACHINE\SYSTEM\CurrentControlSet\Services\Browser\Parameters

It can be set to Yes, No, or Auto.

When a machine proposes itself, the election packet sent out on the network contains the server's name, uptime, operating system, role (Domain Controller, Server, Workstation), and whether it seeks the job or is just willing to serve (which is the default state). Other computers in the Domain or workgroup receive the election packet. Based on these details, if they think that they should be a browser instead, they will send a election packet putting themselves forward. When machines see a superior machine propose itself, they withdraw from the election.

Superiority is defined by role (Domain Controllers outrank servers, which outrank workstations), operating system (Windows 2000 outranks NT, which outranks Windows 9x, which outranks Windows for Workgroups 3.11). If two machines have the same role and operating system, but one has been keeping a backup copy of the browse list, it will be superior. Otherwise, the one that has been running longest wins. In the unlikely event that both machines were booted simultaneously, the contest goes to the machine whose name is alphabetically first.

At the end of the election process, one machine will have proposed itself and seen no proposals from other machines that beat it. It takes on the role of master browser and sends out another packet asking any members of the workgroup or Domain to register. Periodically, the master browser announces itself to the network, primarily for the benefit of other workgroups and Domains. When a browse master sees an announcement for another workgroup or Domain, it is added to a list that can be sent to clients.

After the master browser is established, all server computers in the workgroup or Domain register with it when their server service starts, and they renew this registration every 12 minutes. When client computers want to browse the network, they contact the master browser. However, to reduce the load on the master browser, the clients do not query it directly. Instead, it gets a list of backup browsers and queries them instead. The master appoints backup browsers based on the number of machines on the network. When machines register, they will offer to act as backup browsers (unless this has been disabled through the Registry), and the master accepts or declines the offers as needed. These backup browsers get a list of servers from the master every 15 minutes. When clients want to browse a workgroup or Domain, they first connect to its master browser and obtain a list of backup browsers. After that, all queries are directed to the backup browsers. These browsers can give a list of other workgroups and Domains, and a list of servers. When the user chooses a server, the browser service has done its job and the communication is then directly with the server.

Monitoring and Testing Shared Folders

The Computer Management console has a Shared Folders section under System Tools. It provides information about shared folders, connected users, and open files (in a similar way to the Server icon in Control Panel under Windows NT). It is possible to set up and remove shared folders and to change their properties within this console, and to see which files are open and which users are connected.

It is possible to disconnect users through the MMC. However, as was explained earlier, if the connection is broken, the client will simply re-establish it. This can be a problem if the administrator disconnects a user or chooses Disconnect All users from the context menu for Sessions) because the connections will be re-established. Before disconnecting, some steps need to be followed to ensure that the connection won't be re-established. This might be a question of removing a share or setting its permissions to prevent access. Alternatively, the administrator may prevent new users from logging on by pausing the Net Logon service. This works for Domain Controllers and users logging on to member servers with Domain accounts, but it is not available if the machine sharing the folders is a Windows 2000 Professional computer or a standalone server. Users can be logged off and new connections refused by stopping the server service (in the same console under Services and Applications, Services)

Connecting to Shared Folders

There are two ways to use a shared folder. The established way is to connect a drive letter on the client to a shared folder at the server. It is often referred to as *mapping a drive to a shared folder*. This can be done from the command prompt or in a batch file (such as one used in a logon script) by using the following NET USE command:

```
NET USE <drive>   \\ <computername>\<sharename>
```

For example, you might see the following:

```
NET USE H: \\HERCULES\INSTALL
```

These names, in the form \\<*computername*>\<*sharename*>, are called universal naming convention names (UNC names). They are universal because they can be used to connect to any kind of file- and print-sharing resource. On a Windows 2000 workstation with Netware support, UNCs are used to represent the path to the Netware resource. The UNC forms part of the file path, and it is subject to similar considerations (for example characters that are illegal in a filename are illegal in a share name). On machines that do not run Windows 2000 or Windows NT, problems may result from using long share names or names that contain spaces. For example, a Windows 95 computer may not be able to obtain a list of shares when browsing a computer that has a single long shared folder name, even if the other folder names are valid to Windows 95.

To disconnect a shared folder from the command line, the command is as follows:

```
NET USE <DRIVE> /DELETE  (/delete can be abbreviated to /d).
```

The drive letter can be replaced with *. When connecting, this connects to the next free letter; when disconnecting, it terminates all connections.

The following is a list of other useful switches:

- **/USER:USERNAME.** Allows the connection to be made as a user other than the current default user. The username may simply be the account name; it may be in the form DOMAIN/USERNAME, and the Domain name can the simple (NT4 /NetBIOS Style) or the dotted (Internet FQDN style); or with Windows 2000, the name can be in the form User@Domain.

- **/PERSISTENT:YES** or **/PERSISTENT:NO.** Turns on and off the remembering of connections. If you don't want a connection to be re-established in the next session for the user, use /PERSISTENT:NO.

- **/HOME.** Connects a user to their home directory, specified as part of the settings for their Domain account.

NET USE is normally used for logon scripts. Ad hoc connections are usually made through the GUI. The user can find the resource in the Active Directory by using the browser and selecting Map Network Drive, or by choosing it from the File menu. Alternatively, the user can right-click the My Computer or My Network places desktop icons or choose Map Network drive from the Tools menu in Explorer.

Windows Scripting Host can also map drive letters to UNC names by using the function WSHNetwork.MAPNetworkDrive and remove connections by using WshNetwork.RemoveNetworkDrive. There is a pair of demonstration scripts (one VB script and one Java script) to demonstrate these in the WSH Samples collection on the Microsoft Web site. A link to this page is contained in the Online help for WSH.

There is a letter-free way of connecting to the shared folder: Use the UNC directly. This works at the command line; for example, XCOPY \\HERCULES\INSTALL\DRIVERS C:\DRIVERS /S will copy the Drivers folder and all its subfolders from a server to the local hard disk.

It is also possible to make shortcuts through the GUI. The resource can be dragged and dropped to create a shortcut, or a new shortcut can be made in a folder (or on the desktop) by right-clicking and choosing New, Shortcut. The UNC name can be entered as the path for the shortcut, and the job is done.

Windows 2000 takes shortcuts a stage further with the My Network Places folder, which has replaced the Network Neighborhood found in Windows 95 and Windows NT 4.0.

Network Neighborhood showed the user the machines in their workgroup or Domain (the list obtained from a Browser server) with a shortcut to the entire network, which gave a list of Workgroups and Domains known to the browser. The user could then navigate to the resource they needed. The Network Neighborhood also had a folder associated with it—Nethood. Shortcuts could be made to servers or shared folders and (manually) placed in this folder to make navigation easier.

My Network Places introduces three differences from the Network Neighborhood. First of all, it supports shortcuts to more than just UNC names—it allows shortcuts to FTP sites and publishing-enabled Web sites.

Second, the first icon displayed in My Network Places is Add Network Places, which produces the Add Network Place Wizard (the same way that the first icon in the Printers folder is Add Printer, which produces the Add Printer wizard).

The third change is that properties for My Network Places gives a dialog box, Network and Dial up Connections, which can also be launched from Control Panel. It is from here that protocols and Network Interface Cards are managed (as was the case with the properties of Network Neighborhood in Windows NT 4.0). Network and Dial up Connections, however, has an icon (Make New Connection) that has taken over from the Remote Access Service (RAS) phone book in Windows NT 4.0. Infrared and direct cable connections, and Inbound RAS are also configured from here.

Easy Access to Dial-up Connections

You can make shortcuts to any of your dial-up connections on the desktop or Start menu. If you use multiple dial-up connections, it is worth making them accessible from the Start menu. You can do this by calling up the properties for the taskbar and selecting Expand Network and Dial-up Connections on the Advanced page.

My Network Places contains a wider range of shortcuts and makes them easier to create than was the case before, but there is one subtle difference that might be missed if you are moving from Windows 9x or NT 4.0. The shortcuts don't have the traditional shortcut arrow on them. If you right-click them and call up their properties, they have only a single General property page, and the only thing that can be changed on this page is the label for the shortcut.

Shortcuts in My Network Places are proxy-server aware. If Internet Explorer has been configured to use a proxy server for HTTP and/or FTP protocols, the network place will use the proxy. There is only one difference between proxied places and those on the local network: If you look in Explorer, local network places are expandable in the Folders pane, just like logical drivers, but proxied connections are not. However, as parts of these sites are visited, they appear under Internet Explorer in the browser.

Publishing Folders in the Directory

Shared folders can be published in Active Directory. Unlike shared printers (see Chapter 5.5, "Sharing Printers"), publication cannot be set to happen automatically and the administrator must add the share through the Active Directory Users and Computers Console. To do this, simply open the console; select the container where the shared folder is to appear; and choose New, Shared folder from the Action menu. The resulting object stores a UNC name for the resource, a description, and some keywords to facilitate searching.

However, there are a number of pitfalls with published folders:

- Users' home folders, folder redirects in group policies, and entries in My Network Places must be UNCs; they can't be shared folder objects in Active Directory.

- The NET USE command cannot connect to an Active Directory path. Thus, if a drive is to be connected from a logon script, it must be a UNC name, or Windows Scripting Host must be used to look up the UNC name from Active Directory.

- Users cannot search the directory for shared folders from the Start menu. They have to navigate to My Network Places/Entire Network/Directory and choose Find from the context menu.

- Mapping a drive to a folder published in AD maps to the UNC name. If the UNC name in the Active Directory changes, the UNC is not updated.

Two best practices come out of these restrictions:

- If published folders are to be searched, it is useful to create a shortcut to the directory object. From there, the search should be started.

- If Active Directory is to be used to allow folders to be accessed correctly after being moved, shortcuts should be made to the Active Directory folder object instead of mapping drive letters. Then, opening the object will requery the directory each time. Windows Scripting Host can be used to automate the creation of these shortcuts.

Creating a Shared Folder Object in the Directory

Windows 2000 allows shared folders to be found through Active Directory. This is best thought of as an alternative to network browsing, which was described earlier. When a user connects to a shared folder by going through Active Directory, the client computer retrieves the UNC path for the shared folder and makes the connection using the UNC name. In the current state of Windows 2000, the Active Directory name (NTDS://style name) cannot be used to connect a network drive letter or make a network place in My Network Places.

Although shared printers can be published in the directory automatically, shared folders must be added manually. This is done by selecting an Organizational Unit in the Active Directory Users and Computers MMC console, and choosing New, Shared Folder from the context menu. After the folder has been added as an Active Directory object, it can be given a description and keywords to aid users locating the desired folder.

There is no reason why shared folders must be confined to Windows 2000 servers; the shared folder object is simply a mechanism for storing the UNC path to a resource.

Clients can search Active Directory by going to the Entire Network icon in My Network Places. With Entire Network, they will find each type of network listed. Microsoft Network allows the network to be searched by using traditional browsing methods. Directory takes users to Active Directory, and they can navigate into different containers to find other users and groups, send mail, and find shared folders. When a folder is found, the user can choose Create Shortcut, which puts a shortcut on their desktop. This shortcut remembers the path through Active Directory to reach the shared folder. If the user maps a drive to the folder, the connection is made using the folder's UNC name.

It is possible to search Active Directory for shared folders, although the method is not immediately obvious because it does not appear on the search part of the Start menu. Instead, it appears on the context menu for the directory or any of the containers within it. From here, it is possible to search for shared folders in the Directory by using keywords or their name.

5.4

Distributed File System (DFS)

You Need to Read This Section If You Want to:

- Set up and use a Distributed File System.

Related Topics

DFS Overview

The Distributed File System, DFS, provides an additional way of navigating through shared resources. Normally, shared folders are self-contained. A shared folder on one server has no connection with shared folders on other servers or even on the same server.

DFS was first introduced as an add-on for Windows NT 4.0 Server. The idea was simple: Shared folders could contain links to other shared folders. These links look just like subfolders, so the client computers would interpret them transparently and hop from one server to another without the user being aware of what was happening.

With DFS, a user might see the following three Universal Naming Convention (UNC) names:

\\SERVERX\INSTALL\DRIVERS

\\SERVERX\INSTALL\WIN2K

\\SERVERX\INSTALL\APPLICATIONS

Those names would make you think that all three were subfolders of a folder shared as INSTALL. In practice, DRIVERS might be a subfolder, but WIN2K might be a link to SERVERY and APPLICATIONS might be a link to SERVERZ (see Figure 5.4.1).

Figure 5.4.1   The client sees a shared folder with subfolders, but DFS routes some virtual folders to other servers.

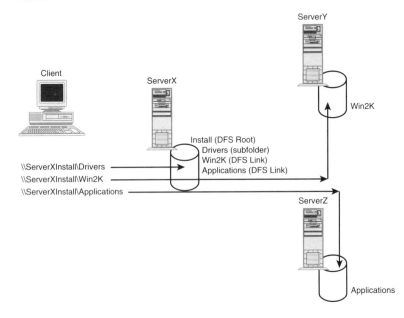

Windows 2000 provides some significant extensions to the original DFS ideas (some Microsoft documents refer to DFS 4.0 for the Windows NT 4.0 version and DFS 5.0 for the Windows 2000 version). In a Domain environment, Windows 2000's DFS can use Active Directory to store and replicate information about the DFS roots and DFS links. When the root is stored in Active Directory, it becomes possible to refer to the shared folder by using the Domain name instead of the server name. The directory provides the client with a referral to the server that hosts the root folder; there may be more than one server hosting the same root, which allows for fault-tolerant roots. If the clients needed to connect to a named server and if that server failed, they would not be able to follow their links to folders on servers that were still running.

DFS is built around roots and links. Each server can host a single DFS root, which is just a shared folder. It might be a standalone DFS root or Domain DFS root, integrated with Active Directory. Domain DFS roots can be accessed as either \\Domain\share (fault-tolerant) or as \\Server\share (not fault-tolerant). Standalone root shares are simply accessed as \\server\share. Computers running the older (4.0) version of the DFS client software always use the \\server\share format, which allows them to use Domain DFS roots, but without the fault-tolerance benefits.

Active Directory replicates information about Domain DFS roots. When a user connects to a Domain DFS root using the Domain name, Active Directory is queried to obtain the necessary information to take the user to the correct share on the correct server. The client computer does not know that the name in the UNC path is a Domain name, and relies on DNS to route it to a suitable server. If the client computer is not configured to use a suitable DNS, it has to connect to the server by name. This is because the client can find a server using a NetBIOS name, unique to that server—but with Domain DFS roots, no single server "owns" the Domain name. Attempting to connect using the Domain name will simply cause a Server Not Found error. Usually, the problem is caused by the client computer using a DNS that is not authoritative for the Domain concerned. Each Domain Controller should be registered as a host for the Domain name. In other words, if the Domain name is abc.com, a server might be called dc1.abc.com. Additionally, Domain Controllers in this Domain register themselves as the host abc.com. DNS resolves attempts to contact abc.com to any of its Domain Controllers that have registered with it.

▶ *For more information, see Chapter 4.2, "DNS and Active Directory."*

The DFS roots contain DFS links that connect to UNC names somewhere on the network. A link can point to multiple replicas of the same information to provide fault-tolerance. When DFS is integrated with Active Directory, the option exists to automatically replicate information between the different replicas.

DFS imposes a limit of one root per server and only one level of links under the DFS root. So it is impractical to link every shared folder on the network through DFS.

DFS links are simply a way of storing UNC names, which allows the servers to run a mixture of operating systems. No check made by DFS to ensure that a user who is able to access the DFS root can access all the linked shares. The UNC names for the links may be hosted on standalone servers or servers in unconnected Domains, which do not recognize the users credentials. Unlike when connecting to a conventional shared directory, the user is not prompted for logon credentials if they do not have access to the shared folder at the end of the link. They simply receive an Access Denied message.

All permissions in DFS are enforced at the file system level or at the share level in exactly the same way as with conventional shared folders. The management interface for DFS does present permissions but this is to control the management of the roots and links rather than access to the files and folders.

DFS is managed using a snap-in for the Microsoft Management Console. Wizards are used to create roots and links.

Setting Up a DFS Root

As discussed previously, there are two types of DFS roots that integrate with Active Directory: Standalone roots and Domain roots. The wizard begins by asking which type of root is required, and although there are additional steps for the Domain root, the process is similar in both cases. Whichever type of root is chosen, the first step in the setup process is to select the server where the root will be hosted. If an Active Directory root is being created, the Domain is selected as a preliminary step in selecting the server. Figure 5.4.2 shows this process. Note the message in the dialog box, saying that a server can host only one root.

Figure 5.4.2   Selecting the server to host the DFS root.

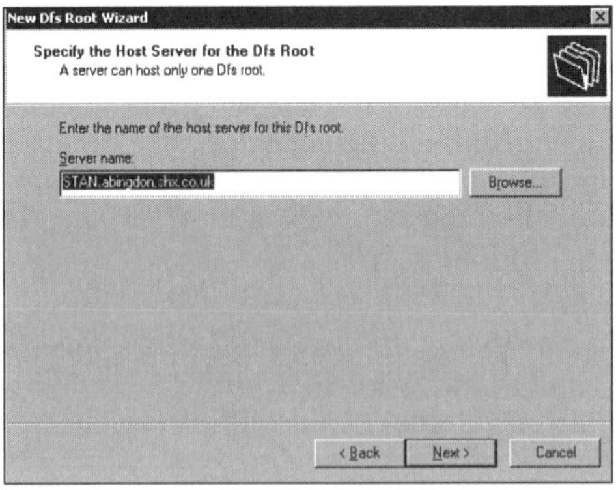

After the server has been chosen, the next step is to identify the shared folder where the links will be stored (see Figure 5.4.3). This shared folder can contain ordinary files and folders as well as DFS links. The shared folder may be an existing folder or may be created specifically for the purpose.

Figure 5.4.3   Selecting the shared folder for the DFS root.

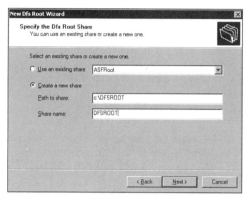

At this point, the user can connect to the root share at the server using its UNC name. However, one of the main advantages of Active Directory-based DFS is that the root share can have multiple replicas. There is no load-balancing or fault-tolerance if the user goes to the same server every time. So, when the wizard is being used to create a Domain DFS root, it prompts for a name to be used for the share that must be unique within the Domain (see Figure 5.4.4). Although every server might call its DFS Root DFSROOT (because that is unique within the server), they would have to be called Server1DFS, Server2DFS, and so on to be unique within the Domain. The DFS root is then accessible through at least two names: \\Domain\Server1DFS and \\Server1\DFSROOT. If the root has multiple replicas, it will also be accessible as \\server2\dfsroot (and so on).

Figure 5.4.4   Providing the unique name for a Domain DFS root.

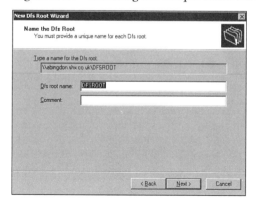

To provide fault-tolerance, the user should connect to the \\Domain\Share version of the name. This cannot be found by browsing, however, as a server-based resource can be found. Instead, the UNC name must be typed in or found through Active Directory. The UNC for Domain DFS root can be published in Active Directory in the same way as any other shared folder.

▸ *For more information, see Chapter 5.3, "Sharing Folders."*

When a user connects to any shared folder that has been found by using Active Directory, their client computer looks up the underlying UNC name and uses it to make the connection. The UNC may be stored to reconnect in the future. With a normal (non-DFS) shared folder, this can cause problems if the resource is moved to another server, even if the directory entry for the folder is updated. The client computer does not requery the directory, so the user will reconnect to the original (stored) UNC, which may no longer exist. Domain DFS roots do not suffer from this problem: If the location of a DFS root changes, its share name is preserved. And because the UNC is the combination of Domain name and share name, the UNC is unaffected. If resources are expected to move from one server to another, Active Directory shared folders can be something of a liability, but DFS provides a useful workaround.

After the DFS root has been created, DFS links can be inserted directly beneath it. There is an option to create a new link rom the context menu for the DFS root.

Although the text box for the link name allows \ characters to be entered, it produces an error message—the links must appear directly under the root. The UNC name for the destination is entered in the Send the user to this shared folder box. The comment can not be seen by the user, but it is there to aid administration.

When clients connect to a DFS link, the software on the client caches the details of shared folder they have been redirected to instead of going back to the root server each time. To allow for the possibility that the link will change, the cache doesn't last for the whole user session; instead, the information is cached for 30 minutes by default.

Configuring DFS for Fault-Tolerance

When DFS links are created, the links themselves can be made fault-tolerant by setting up multiple replicas for the same link .This is available for both Standalone DFS roots (even in DFS 4.0) and Domain DFS roots

If both replicas are on servers running Windows 2000 and both are held on NTFS file systems, it is possible to select automatic replication. Windows 2000 has a service, the *File Replication Service (FRS)*, which is normally used to replicate the SYSVOL folder used by Active Directory. DFS uses this service to perform automatic replication. When replication is configured, one replica is specified as a master. When this copy has been replicated to all the other servers, the replication works as a multiple master model—changes to any copy are replicated. A very similar mechanism controls the replication of SYSVOL for Active Directory.

Providing replicas of the links alone leaves a single point of failure: the root server. Additional replicas can be set up at root level, and this works in a very similar way to replica links. The restriction of one DFS root still applies: A server that is already hosting a root cannot be configured to host a replica from another server. The process of setting up replicas at the root level is wizard-driven and is almost identical to setting up the initial root. After roots are configured with multiple replicas, they can be replicated in the same way as the links.

Configuring DFS in a Multi-site Environment

Because Active Directory divides the network into sites based on IP subnets, it is possible for DFS to decide whether one replica is in the same site as the client. It can then route the client to that replica instead of a replica in another site (which might be on the other side of a slow Wide Area Link. If the administrator of the network is using Active Group Policies to deploy software then Active Directory DFS becomes very useful because the Group Policy refers to a single UNC name, which is directed to a server near the user. With automatic replication, the administrator has to copy the files to the server only once.

▶ *For more information, see Chapter 6.3, "Group Policies."*

DFS Clients

No DFS software is available or planned by Microsoft for 16-bit client computers (DOS and Windows 3.x).

For computers running Windows NT, DFS is not supported prior to NT 4.0 Service Pack 3. NT 4.0 Service Packs 3 and later have DFS client support, but this only supports standalone-style access (client computers must use \\Server not \\Domain names). DFS server functionality for Standalone roots can be installed as a network service on NT 4.0 servers.

Windows 95 did not include DFS support. A client for DFS 4.0 (Standalone roots) was downloadable. Windows 98 included this functionality. Both can be upgraded to full Windows 2000 DFS functionality using software provided in the clients folder of the Windows 2000 server CDs. However, Microsoft expects Windows NT 4.0 users who want this functionality to upgrade to Windows 2000 Professional, so no similar update is provided for NT 4.0.

Creating a Pseudo-DFS

If you create a network place in the My Network folders container, what is created is actually a folder that contains two files. One of these files is a hidden file named desktop.ini, which controls the "special behavior" of the folder. If you start a command prompt, move to the Documents and Settings folder, and run DIR *.ini /p /ah /s, you'll find a number of these folders. Windows 2000 also uses desktop.ini for special-purpose folders such as fonts. The other thing that is present in the Network Places folder is a shortcut file named target.lnk.

Interestingly, Network Places can be dragged out of the My Network Places folder (which creates the folder and moves the files), but it cannot be dragged back in again. At first glance, these shortcuts look like the same ones you get when you click on a shared folder and choose Create Shortcut, but closer examination reveals that a shortcut created with Create Shortcut has a little arrow on it and is just a .lnk file (those created with Add Network Place have no arrow). Explorer will also thread them together in the folders pane.

5.5

Sharing Printers

You Need to Read This Section If You Want to:

- Create and manage shared printers.
- Make printers accessible through Active Directory.

Sharing Print Resources

From the earliest days of Microsoft Networking, printers have been shared in a very similar way to files. In MS Net, the physical port (LPT1 , LPT2, or COM1, COM2) where the printer was connected was shared with an alias name, in exactly the same way that folders were shared. When the user wanted to connect to a printer, they connected a local printer name on their computer (LPTx but *not* COMx) to the universal naming convention (UNC) name for the shared printer at the server. In early versions of Windows, the logical printers that Windows understood were tied to a name such as LPT 1 or COM1—Windows did not understand the idea of a a purely network printer.

Windows NT 3.1 was the first to have logical printers that could be bound to a UNC name rather than an LPTx style printer name.

Overview of Sharing Printers

Many printers are now attached to the network cable rather than to a port on a server. However, because most normal printers do not have hard disks or adequate RAM to buffer a large number number of pages, something needs to manage the printer's queue. This is doubly the case with printers that use the DLC protocol because they tend not to drop connections once established, so only one computer can print to them in a session. Because the server can print to many more printers than it has ports attached, it is possible for dozens, even hundreds of printers to be managed from a single print server.

Sizing a server that services very large numbers of queues is difficult. The exact requirements for a print server vary widely, with the major factors being the number of print queues, the type of connection, the size and type of the jobs submitted, and the frequency with which they are submitted. If planning a large print-only server, start with 64 MB of RAM plus 2 MB per printer as a minimum. Only continuous monitoring will tell you whether the server has sufficient RAM, CPU performance, and disk throughput for the task.

The Windows 2000 system monitor—an ActiveX control that is normally used from the Microsoft Management Console—provides some counters to help. The Print Queue object allow the number of jobs, speed of printing queue length, and errors to be monitored. It also allows CPU load, rate of disk I/O opetations, and memory load/number of page operations to be monitored. By monitoring levels of CPU and disk activitiy when printing is taking place, it is possible to predict at what level of print serving the computer's disk or CPU will be saturated.

Managing Printers

Windows NT and Windows 2000 have the capability to divide the printing process into two parts. The first part is done by the application program when the user submits a print job: It creates a generic set of Windows commands. These commands are sometimes called *Graphics Device Interface (GDI)* commands and a file of these commands was called a *journal file* in early versions of NT, but is now called an *Enhanced Meta File (EMF)*. A component called a *print processor* takes this file and renders into into "Raw" printer commands. There are two queues in the this process: one queue of EMF files waiting for the print processor and one of Raw files waiting to be fed into the printer.

Whereas other operating systems might call the place where printer jobs are sent a *print queue*, this would just be confusing. Windows NT and 2000 simply talk about sending jobs to a printer, which is the logical rather than physical entity. The rendered jobs are fed out of the parallel port or over the network by a print monitor, but there is no reason why they should not be sent to multiple physical printers known as a *printer pool*. To avoid talking about physical printers, we tend to use the term *printing devices*. Monitors and print processors are plug-in components. To allow Apple Macintosh clients to print to all the printers supported by Windows 2000, the Printing Services for Macintosh adds an extra print processor that translates Postscript files. Also, to cope with different kinds of network-attached printers, extra monitors may be installed.

Setting up a printer can be as simple as choosing the printer and port, and deciding whether or not it is to be shared. When connecting to a network printer, the client computer can find out the default settings for the printer, the type of driver needed, and from where the driver may be downloaded— usually from a shared folder called PRINT$ on the print server. There are additional printer settings, which may be set from the properties of the printer, but the setup process is guided by the Add Printer Wizard found in the Printers folder (choose Settings on the Start menu or through Contol Panel).

The first question the wizard asks is whether the printer is a local or network printer. Many printers can be queried using Plug and Play techniques to find out their make and model, and the option for this exists in the wizard. If this is not chosen, the administrator will be presented with a list of printers.

The second step is to choose the port to which the printer is connected (see Figure 5.5.1).

Figure 5.5.1   Selecting the printer port.

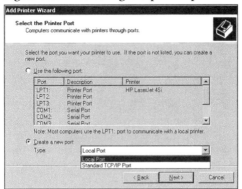

If the printer is connected to the network, a new port needs to be created. Selecting a local port allows UNC names (they are not local at all)
to be entered. This means that a printer pool exists with some of its
members on other servers. Members of a pool are not used on a round-
robin basis; all jobs will be routed to the first member of the pool unless
it is offline. Standard TCP/IP allows for Raw or LPR-based printing to
be configured. If the printer is non-Plug and Play, the next step is to
select the printer from a list

All jobs submitted to this logical printer will be rendered with this
driver, so if a printer pool is set up, all the printers should be identical—
or at least capable of using the same drivers and settings. The next step
is to give the (logical) printer a name—Windows will normally choose
one based on the driver selected. If the printer is to be used by DOS or
Windows 95 clients, the share name for the printer needs to be eight
characters or fewer.

If the printer server is a member of a Window 2000 Domain, there is
the option to publish the printer in the directory (the significance of
this is explained shortly).

When the printer has been defined, more options are available through
its property pages (see Figure 5.5.2).

The General page lists some features of the printer that may be published in the directory. Some of these are obtained from the driver (for
example, whether the printer can print in color); some, such as the
location and comment, are supplied by the admistrator. Printing preferences let the administrator set a default paper tray, page orientation, and
so on; and the test page provides a very obvious test of whether things
are working.

The Sharing tab controls the sharing of the printer and whether or not
it is to be published in the directory, which is discussed later.

The Ports tab allows the rendered print jobs to be sent to a different
port or for a printer pool to be configured so that one logical printer
feeds jobs into multiple physical devices on different ports.

Figure 5.5.2   The General printer properties page.

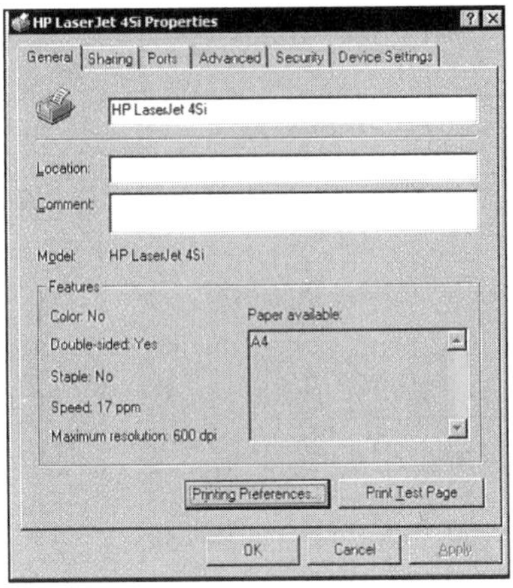

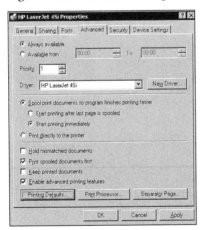

The Advanced page contains many settings, which allow the administrator to define different logical printers with different priorities (the lower the number, the higher the priority) and to make printers available only at certain times (see Figure 5.5.3). Defining two logical printers to use the same print devices allows some useful combinations. Privileged users may be allowed to use one queue that has a higher priority, allowing them to go to the front of the queue. Alternatively, users with very large jobs to print can submit them into a queue where they will only be printed at quiet times.

Figure 5.5.3   The Advanced printer properties page.

The behavior of jobs as they reach the print monitor can be defined: The monitor can be told to start printing as soon as there is something to send to the printing device, or to wait until the job has been completed or until the spooling of jobs can be disabled altogether (although this is not desirable). By default, printing starts as soon as possible. This works well unless there are print jobs that take a very long time to be sent to queue (for example, a program that prints a 10-page report at the rate of one line per minute) because nothing can print while this job in progress. It would be better to set Start printing after last page has spooled or Print spooled jobs first. If there are two jobs in the queue—one that is being spooled from an application program and a lower-priority one that has finished—the lower-priority one will be printed first.

The Advanced page provides the following options:

- **Separator pages.** Identifies which print job is which and who it belongs to. This is useful on a busy printer, but it just wastes paper on a lightly loaded printer with small print jobs. A less obvious use for separator pages is to ensure that the printer is correctly set at the start of a job. By putting control codes into a separator page file and sending it to the printer, anything left from a previous job can be reset.

- **Hold mismatched documents.** Tells the print monitor to check the printer and document settings for paper sizes that do not match (for example, printing a document set for U.S. letter-sized paper on a printer loaded with European A4 size). Many printers simply stop and ask to be loaded with the other paper size; in this case, it would be better if the job remained in the print queue.

- **Keep printed documents.** An option for either debugging or security, it means that the spool files are not removed from the print server after they have printed.

- **Printing defaults page.** Controls whether multiple pages are to be on a single booklet printing, Print last page first options, and so on. For compatibility purposes, it is possible to turn this off from the Enable advanced features checkbox.

- **Print processor button.** Allows the default data type for the printer to be changed. Normally, Windows NT and Windows 2000 clients identify the type of job they are submitting (usually an EMF file). 16-bit clients and Windows 95 machines cannot do this, so they must have a default type assigned to them. Simple DOS programs may submit plain text, which may need to be rendered for the printer. Other DOS programs and Windows 95 or Windows 3.1 will render their output into Raw printer commands: Raw is the default type, and should be changed only if you are setting up a printer for simple DOS programs.

The Print processor dialog box also allows a printer to be set to use the Mactinosh print processor (called SFMPrint, to stand for Service for Macintosh) instead of the default one (WinPrint).

The Device Settings page of the printer properties allows the admistrator to tell Windows how the printer is configured. The exact options vary from printer to printer, but they include the amount of memory fitted, the type of paper loaded, and so on.

Managing Printer Permissions

Printer permissions are managed using Access Control Lists (ACLs), which work the same way for many Windows 2000 objects, such as files and folders. Only Administrators and Power Users groups can create printers on Windows 2000 Professional and standalone servers. In Windows 2000 Domains, the Power Users group is replaced by a number of operator groups: The Printer operators and Server operators groups can manage printers, too.

There are three basic levels of permission: Print, Manage Documents, and Manage Printers. The advanced permissions actually show three more: Read Permissions, Change Permissions, and Take Ownership. Normally, Read Permissions is given with any of the others, Change Permissions is granted by administrators, if required, and Take Ownership is set in the rare event that the owner of the printer needs to be changed. As with file ACLs, these permissions can be granted or denied.

By default, the Administrators (and Power Users or Operators groups) have full control for the printer. Everyone is given print permission and the special group Creator/Owner is given Manage documents privilege. *Manage documents* can usually be read as Manage other people's documents or Manage all queued documents. The Creator/Owner group is useful for folders in which you want to say "Everyone can read, everyone can add files, but only the person who put a file into this folder can delete or change it." With print jobs, we want everyone to be able to pause or delete their own jobs, but not those of others. Creator/Owner says "Whoever submitted this job can do things to this job only."

Managing Documents

The Printers folder can be accessed from Control Panel or from the Settings entry on the Start menu. It is also accessible to a user with administrative powers by connecting to \\<SERVERNAME>. This shows shared folders and printers together with a shortcut to the Printers folder. The default view shows Large icons, but by choosing Details from the View menu it is possible to see what is currently in the queue for each printer and the printer's status.

From the File menu in the Printers folder, there is an option to configure server properties.

? How Do I Stop the Server Sending those Notification Messages and How Do I Move the Spool Directory?

Many people do not realize that the the Printers folder gives access not just to the printer properties but to a set of properties for the whole server. Server properties appears on the File menu for the Printers folder (it is also on the context menu that appears when clicking the background part of this window). Server properties allows the available forms (paper sizes) to be configured, which can be assigned to individual printers; drivers for other operating systems can be added to the download area; ports can be managed from the Advanced page. Two useful settings can be set: the location of the spool directory and Notify when remote documents are printed.

Right-clicking a printer in the Printers folder provides access to its properties, and allows the printer to be paused or all the jobs in the queue to be cancelled

Opening a single printer gives a view of the documents currently in the queue on that printer (See Figure 5.5.4).

Figure 5.5.4   Viewing the jobs on a single printer.

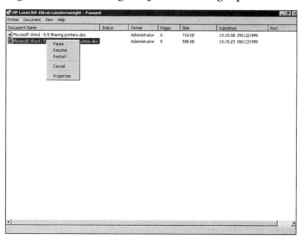

Right-clicking on a document allows its owner or an operator to pause it (allowing other jobs to overtake it) or cancel it. After a job has been paused, it can be resumed; if paper has jammed in the printer, it can be restarted from the beginning of the document.

The properties of the document allow the owner or operator to change its priority, change the time at which it will print, and view the settings it will use (see Figure 5.5.5).

Figure 5.5.5   Setting the document properties.

Publishing Printers in the Directory

Besides storing details of computers and users, Windows 2000's Active
Directory can store information about shared folders and shared printers. In
the case of printers, the information stored in the directory includes most of
the information on the general page of the printer. This information is then
accessible to Active Directory clients and is said to be *published* or the object
(the printer in this case) is said to be *listed*. When a printer is shared on a
computer that belongs to a Windows 2000 Domain, the administrator has the
option to publish the printer in the directory by checking the box labeled
List in the Directory. The printer shown in Figure 5.5.6 has recently been
published and the note under the check box says that the directory has not
completed.

Figure 5.5.6   Sharing a printer.

Active Directory clients have a Find Printer option on the search part
of the Start menu. Programs that use the standard Print dialog box in
Windows also have the option to connect to or find a new printer
when the user prints a document. The user can search for a printer
based on its location or capabilities.

Figure 5.5.7 shows that the find was started from the Print dialog box.
This user has searched using the location of the printer, but could have
used the Advanced tab to search for a color printer.

Figure 5.5.7   Finding a printer.

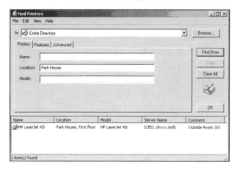

By default, printers published in Active Directory cannot be seen. This is because they are not published into a visible container, but appear beneath their computer, and computer objects are not normally treated as containers with the Active Directory Users and Computers console. To see the printer (to gain access to its properties or to move it to a browsable container), it is necessary to right-click in the Containers pane of the the console and select View, Users, groups and computers as containers. The view of the computer changes to become a container that contains the printer. (See Figure 5.5.8.)

Figure 5.5.8   Moving a printer after setting computers to be viewed as containers.

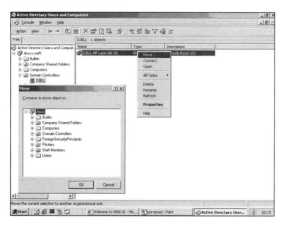

After the printer is visible in Active Directory, its entry can be modified from any computer that can manage the directory (see Figure 5.5.9).

Figure 5.5.9   Configuring the Directory entry for a printer.

5.6

Auditing Resource Access

You Need to Read This Section If You Want to:

- Audit files and printers.

Related Topics

For More Information On ▶ *See*

File and folder permissions ▶ *Chapter 5.2: File Systems and Disks*

Managing rights ▶ *Chapter 3.3: Using Administrative Tools*

Overview of Auditing

Auditing is one of the major principles of the C2 security specification that Windows 2000 (like Windows NT before it) was designed to meet. The principles of the system are the following: users should uniquely identify themselves to the system (mandatory logon), every resource should have an owner who can regulate access to it (discretionary access control), and it should be possible to record what access has taken place (auditing).

Auditing on Windows 2000 is controlled through the security policy. The policy allows the administrator to enable the recording of success and/or failure events in a number of categories. These include attempts to log on to the system, attempts to access files and printers, and attempts to manage user accounts or change to the system policy (see Figure 5.6.1.).

Figure 5.6.1   Enabling auditing—object access allows file printers to be monitored.

After auditing is enabled, events begin to appear in the Security part of the Event Log. Note that only administrators have access to this log—unlike the System and Application Logs, which are visible to all users. The size of the Log and policy for overwriting it can be set within the Event Viewer. Windows 2000 can be configured to shut down if the Security Log becomes full. To do this, a Registry entry must be created under the key HKEY_LOCAL_MACHINE\SYSTEM\CurrentControlSet\Control\Lsa The value is named CrashOnAuditFail and is a REG_DWORD with a value of 1. The computer must be rebooted before a change in this value will come into effect.

If the system halts with the message Audit failed, the procedure is to log on as an Administrator, clear the log from Event Viewer, and reset the Registry setting.

Auditing Access to Files

The NTFS file system maintains two Access Control Lists for every file or folder. One of these controls access to files or folders, and is usually just called *the* Access Control List. More accurately, it is the *Discretionary* Access Control List. A second list that is very similar in structure controls auditing. This is called the *System* Access Control List.

The Discretionary Access Control List contains Access Control Entries (ACES), which set the permissions for users and groups. Each ACE contains a Security ID (SID) for the user or group and the access to be granted or denied.

The *System* Access Control List is made up of similar ACEs. They contain SIDs, similar to their Discretionary counterparts, and contain lists of permissions. But instead of determining whether an attempt to use the resource is allowed or forbidden, the System ACE specifies if Success and/or Failure should be logged.

Auditing is controlled from the Security property page for the file or folder; selecting Advanced security reveals another dialog box that has an auditing page on it. From here, it is possible to review auditing settings, and add new users and groups whose access should be audited (see Figure 5.6.2.).

Figure 5.6.2   Configuring auditing for a folder.

Configuring auditing requires a degree of care. Even quite a simple operation such as running a program or editing a file requires more than one permission, and auditing all accesses, by all users, to all files will not only slow the system down, but so much information will be logged that it will be impossible to find anything. Therefore auditing must be used selectively.

Figure 5.6.3   Viewing audit events in the Security Log.

All 12 of these events were caused by enabling audit for word document, and then opening and closing it. Auditing was not enabled for the folder, so the creation and deletion of word's temporary file was not logged.

▶ *For more information, see Chapter 3.3, "Using Administrative Tools."*

Auditing Access to Printers

Printers have a very similar Access Control List (ACL) structure to files and folders, although with a different set of permissions that reflect printing activities rather than file access ones. Like files, there is a Discretionary Access Control List that controls access to the printer, and a System Access Control List that governs what is audited.

The auditing is controlled from the equivalent security dialog box to one for files (that is, from within the properties dialog box for the printer, the administrator chooses Security, clicks Advanced, and then goes to Auditing).

5.7

Protecting Data

You Need to Read This Section If You Want to:

- Understand Windows 2000's fault-tolerance features.
- Understand the backup facilities built into Windows 2000.
- Understand the basic steps in disaster recovery planning.

Overview of Data Protection

Threats to data include natural disasters, such as fire, and created ones such as sabotage and operator error. Protecting it covers both prevention and cure aspects—in the same way that you would lock your car and might have a alarm and/or immobilizer, yet still have insurance against theft...wouldn't you?

Virus Protection

Viruses are a fact of life for modern computer systems. Some people talk about Trojan Horse programs (trusted programs that contain something unexpected. A virus is any program that propagates itself—an infect program becomes a Trojan Horse. Many viruses—perhaps the majority—do no harm to the systems they infect, but they still need to be removed. In a lot of cases, the cost of a virus is not the damage it does, but the time and bother involved in tracing and removing it. Hoax warnings of viruses also waste considerable quantities of people's time, so several of the suppliers of anti-virus software maintain Web pages that list the hoaxes.

Viruses are programs and they have to be executed to spread. A virus can't be spread on a pure data file, such as a GIF or TXT file. Macros blur the boundary between data and programs—most of the Microsoft Office suite of applications now support Visual Basic for Applications, and therefore are prone to virus attack. This is particularly worrisome because if a virus erases your hard disk, you know where you stand and can restore from a backup, but a virus in a spreadsheet program might make slight changes to data each time a file is used. Eventually, the file will be useless; so will many generations of it. Any version backed up will either be out-of-date, corrupt, or both.

Office 2000 provides a defense against macro viruses. Macros can be digitally signed by their authors. Certificate Server, which is part of IIS, can issue certificates for the purpose of signing code. Office can be told to run only those macros that have been signed with certificates from a specified source. This can be enforced with a network policy. Signing known safe macros and preventing users from running any others provides a quick and fairly painless way of stamping out macro viruses in the same way that Internet Explorer can be configured to reduce the risk of ActiveX controls or Java applets harming the system.

There are three main sources of viruses and Trojans: files brought in on floppy disks, files downloaded from the Internet, and files received through e-mail. There are lots of choices of virus-scanning products. Many of these are memory-resident and scan files as they are opened. Although this has a performance penalty associated with it, it is quite small on fast hardware. This on its own should be enough to catch viruses, and in many organizations the measures stop there. However, some organizations like to scan files as they are downloaded from the Web or passed through e-mail. Because anything passing through these scanners will be scanned at the desktop, it seems a sensible move to use products from different vendors in each place. As new viruses are written, different vendors add rules to recognize them. Vendor A may learn about one new virus before Vendor B, but another virus might be detectable first with Vendor B's software. Running software from both vendors improves the chances of detecting new viruses, albeit at the cost of having two sets of software to maintain. Some organizations might want to use more than two products for different roles, but eventually the maintenance overhead outweighs any gain.

Viruses running on Windows 2000 or Windows NT need to have a suitable level of authorization to cause damage. This usually means they need to run in the security context of an administrator. The virus may want to reformat the hard disk (which normal users cannot do) or to attach itself to a system file to which only the administrator has write access. Windows 2000 has two useful tricks to avoid logging on as Administrator at all times. The first is the Run As feature. This is provided by a Windows 2000 service (the RUNAS Service) If you hold down the Shift key and right-click a program or a shortcut to a program in Explorer or on the Start menu, the context menu contains the Run As option (see Figure 5.7.1). Selecting it gives the option to supply alternative credentials to run that one program. This allows an administrator to log on with a normal user account and then to assume their administrator powers, as needed.

Figure 5.7.1   Using Run As from the Start menu.

There is a also a command-line Run As command (runas.exe) that can be used in a shortcut to avoid the need to shift and right-click. It is possible to modify the shortcuts on the Start menu to be the following:

> runas/user:USER NAME "COMMAND"

This will pop up a console window, prompting for the password to be typed in.

Run As provides one method of avoiding viruses at the server; a second is to avoid doing anything at the server computers. This can be achieved by connecting to the server using Terminal Services. This not only avoids the need to physically go to the server, but if the administrator has logged in with a privileged account and introduced a virus into the client computer, the Terminal Services client software cannot introduce the virus into the server. It only passes keyboard and mouse operations to the server and receives screen updates in return.

Best Practices for Virus Protection

- Consider possible infection scenarios. Ask yourself when and how a virus will be detected and removed for each one.

- It is inefficient to use the same software to scan files on arrival, on opening, and for periodic scans of a server. If you want to do all three, consider using different brands of software.

- Old viruses are more likely to be detected by other people before they reach you. New viruses are a greater risk, so develop a strategy to keep your scanning software up to date.

Fault-Tolerance

There are three forms of hardware-based fault-tolerance:

- Uninterruptible Power Supply (UPSes)
- Fault-tolerant disk system
- Clustering

UPS

Power failures under Windows 2000 are unlikely to cause major damage to the system—such as corrupting a disk volume—especially when NTFS is used. As well as eliminating this risk, protecting the system with a UPS has three main benefits. First, it may avoid the system going down at all. Power fluctuations (brownouts) and short interruptions will not take down a server or critical workstation. Second, any information that is in RAM would normally be lost in the event of a power failure. In the case of some client server systems, there may be a significant amount of information that has not yet been committed to disk. Third, if a system is not shut down cleanly, it will often go through process of checking the disk and then databases may also need to be checked for consistency. This may take hours. The system will come back online sooner if it is shut down cleanly.

Unless Windows is aware of the UPS, it will not provide the last two functions. Therefore, there is a UPS service that monitors activity on serial ports to check activity from the UPS. There are three basic signals: two allow the UPS to signal failure of the main power supply and when its batteries are low. The third signal allows the computer to tell the UPS to switch itself off after a shutdown has been completed. These settings are set through the Power Options applet in Control Panel.

The UPS service did not change from Windows NT 3.1 to 4.0, but it has been rewritten for Windows 2000 and was developed for Microsoft by UPS manufacturer APC. It supports APC's devices and generic devices. If using a UPS from another manufacturer, you should either use the software provided with the UPS or configure it as a generic device (see Figure 5.7.2). Before you do this, you need to check the signaling polarity. (Does it signal that power is working or that power has failed?)

Figure 5.7.2   Installing a generic UPS.

After the UPS has been installed, its behavior can be configured (see Figure 5.7.3). This includes the time to wait before sending a warning— to allow for minor fluctuations in power and the frequency with which warnings are sent to say that the server is running on battery power

Figure 5.7.3 Configuring the UPS.

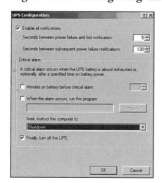

The most important part of setting up the UPS is what to do when the battery is close to running out. The UPS itself may signal this, or it can be determined based on the time the UPS has been running on battery power. Before the operating system itself shuts down, it may be necessary (or it will at least speed the process) to run a program or batch file to shut down various services. The command to run is specified similar to a scheduled task.

When choosing a UPS and when setting the critical alarm time, there is a quick calculation you should do:

(Time to run command) + (Normal Shutdown time) > (UPS Run time)– (Margin for error)

The only way to find out what these are is to test the system. If in doubt, shorten the critical alarm time.

Fault-Tolerant Disk Systems

Although many organizations choose to use disk systems that provide fault-tolerance in hardware, server versions of Windows 2000 provide mirroring and RAID 5 in software. In addition, the NTFS file system provides read-after-write verification and is transactional (if a write is not committed to the disk, it is reversed out).

Mirroring involves writing information to two disks; if one disk fails, the other takes over. The drawback of mirroring is that 50% of the disk capacity is redundant. Compared to a single disk, it provides a small improvement on read operations (because two reads can be performed simultaneously—one from each disk) and write operations (where the data has to be written to two disks) give the same overall performance as a single disk.

RAID 5, whether in hardware or software, provides a general perform-ance improvement by writing to multiple disks in parallel, with the capacity of one of the disks being used to hold parity information. Storing the parity on one disk would create a bottleneck: one of the distinguishing features of RAID 5, compared with some of the rarely used levels, is that it distributes the parity evenly among all drives. So, in an array of four drives, three-fourths of each is data and one-fourth is parity. RAID systems can give very large capacity, which has implica-tions for backup. RAID 5 improves performance for read operations. Writing large blocks of data is also fast, but the need to write parity means that small writes perform less well. When a disk fails in a RAID, the system continues to run unless a second disk fails before the first is replaced and the parity is rebuilt.

With Windows NT and Windows 2000, the system partition (which the BIOS uses to start the system—drive C) and the boot partition (the one that holds the operating system files—usually the same partition) can be mirrored in software. They cannot be stored on a software RAID 5 system. Hardware RAID systems are transparent to the operating system and so not subject to this limitation. If the primary disk in a mirror pair fails, the system will continue to run, but it will not be possible to reboot the computer. To get around this when a mirrored system is configured, it is useful to create a fault-tolerance boot disk.

Windows NT and Windows 2000 put their own boot sector on a disk when it is formatted. This boot sector attempts to load a file called NTLDR. (You can see this by trying to boot a computer from a floppy disk that has just been formatted with Windows 2000. You should see the message BOOT Can't find NTLDR.) NTLDR uses a file called boot.ini to know from where the operating system itself should be loaded. Here is a sample boot.ini file:

```
[boot loader]
timeout=30
default=multi(0)disk(0)rdisk(0)partition(2)\WINNT
[operating systems]
multi(0)disk(0)rdisk(0)partition(2)\WINNT="Microsoft Windows 2000
```

```
Professional" /fastdetect
multi(0)disk(0)rdisk(0)partition(1)\WINNT="Microsoft Windows 2000 Server"
/fastdetect
```

The boot loader section specifies how long the boot menu should be displayed and the default operating system. The operating system's section specifies the path to the operating system files, the command-line startup switches (if any), and the text to display on the boot menu.

The path to the operating system is known as an ARC path because it was defined by the Advanced RISC Consortium. The parts are described in the following list:

- **MULTI(x) or SCSI(x).** *Multi* means disk controller supported by the BIOS or a BIOS Extender. *SCSI* means load a driver named NTBOOTDD.SYS. 0 is used to mean the first such controller, 1 is the next, and so on.

- **DISK(x).** The SCSI target number. For Multi types, it is always 0.

- **RDISK(x).** The SCSI Logical Unit Number (LUN). (Most modern SCSI disks have a SCSI Target controller built into them and the disk is LUN 0.) For multi disks, this is the disk number. Again, 0 is the first disk, 1 is the next one, and so on.

- **PARTITION(X).** The logical partition number PARTITION(0) refers to the whole disk, PARTITION(1) is the first partition.

After NTLDR has built the menu and an operating system is selected, NTLDR invokes a program called NTDETECT.COM; this does the hardware detection before the operating system Kernel is loaded.

If NTLDR, BOOT.INI, NTBOOTDD.SYS (if applicable), and NTDETECT.COM are placed on a floppy disk, the system can be booted from it. If the boot.ini is modified to boot from the secondary disk in the mirror pair, this allows the system to be rebooted if the primary disk fails.

Clustering

Windows 2000 Advanced Server and Data Center Server allow servers to be arranged in clusters. The function of a cluster is to allow a service to continue to run, even if the computer running it should fail—even if that failure is in the operating system. Not all services can be clustered. Servers in a cluster use a private network connection to monitor the health of the services. If one server detects that a service has failed on another, it can start that service itself. For this to work, the computers must share a disk—a single SCSI bus is used to link a SCSI host adaptor in each machine with an external disk, usually a hardware RAID system.

There is a second form of clustering known as the network load balancing service—this allows multiple computers to use a single IP address and the computers agree among themselves which one will handle any given connection request. This can be used to provide fault-tolerance if multiple computers can hold the same data.

EFS and EFS Recovery

Abuse of the encrypting file system is another possible cause of data loss. NTFS in Windows 2000 allows files to be encrypted; when this is done, they can be decoded only by the person who encrypted them or the nominated "recovery agent," who is usually the administrator. To avoid breaches in security, some sites export and delete the certificate needed for file recovery so it must be reloaded before EFS security can be bypassed.

If the certificate used in encrypting the file should become lost, the user will no longer be able access their files and will need the administrator to recover them. This could happen if a user always works from the same client computer and so does not have a roaming profile. Their certificate is stored on the client computer, but it can be used to encrypt files on a server. If the client computer should fail, the certificate would be lost; at this point, the administrator would have to recover the files for a user. It would be good policy for the user's EFS certificate to be backed up, even if nothing else on their computer is backed up.

▶ *For more information on EFS and EFS Recovery,*
see Chapter 5.2, "File Systems and Disks."

Backup and Restore

The backup program used by Windows NT did not change from version 3.1 through version 4.0. Windows NT's scheduling service (sometimes called the AT service) was one of the few things left in the operating system from OS/2. Windows 2000 has a new backup program (although it is still called NTBACKUP.EXE and supports the old command-line switches to aid migration) and a new scheduling service (although the new schedule service can be add to Windows NT 4.0). The functionality of the RDISK program that Windows NT 3.5 and 4.0 used has been transferred to the backup program.

The backup program can store data on tape or to a file, which can be stored on a hard disk, floppy disk, or network drive. It can be started by calling up the properties for a disk volume and clicking Backup Now on the Tools page, from the Start menu (by default under Accessories, System tools), or from a batch file or command line—including running it as a scheduled task.

The program is presented in the form of a four-page tabbed dialog box. The Welcome page has links to wizards for Backup, Restore, and Create Emergency Repair Disk. These are also available from the Tools menu. The Backup and Restore pages allow files to be backed up and restored without using the wizard.

After files have been selected for backup, the administrator can save the selection to a file for later use or start the backup (see Figure 5.7.4.) If the selection is saved, the backup operation can be scheduled to run at a later date.

Figure 5.7.4   Saving the selection of files in backup.

Note that this system has no tape drive, so the destination file cannot be changed.

As well as selecting files, the backup program can back up system state. This is divided into three parts on Windows 2000 professional computers and stand-alone servers. The three parts: the boot files, COM+ class registration data-base, and the Registry. On Domain Controllers, two more sections are added: Active Directory and Sys Vol. To restore Active Directory information, it is necessary to boot the machine into a special Recovery mode. This is done by pressing the F8 key during the boot process. To log on to the machine, it is necessary to use the Windows 2000 Administrator account that existed before it was promoted to being Domain Controller. When the information is restored, it can be overwritten by other servers; a restore can be made author-itative by using the NTDSUTIL program.

After a selection of files has been made, backup can be started (see Figure 5.7.5). Some of the items set through the Tools, Options menu can be set or overridden from the Advanced backup options dialog box when the job is started.

Figure 5.7.5   Starting a backup job and setting the Advanced options.

One of the options to set is the type of backup. There are five types of back-up, which all hinge around the "archive" file attribute. All files, whether on NTFS or FAT, have four basic attributes: Read Only, Hidden, System, and Archive. Whenever a file is updated, the Archive attribute is set to indicate that it needs to be backed up. A backup program will normally reset the attribute to indicate that the file has been backed up. Table 5.7.1 describes your backup options for you.

Table 5.7.1   **Backup Options**

Type	Files Backed Up	Archive Bit Is Then
Normal	All files	Reset
Copy	All files	Unchanged
Incremental	Only files with Archive set	Reset
Differential	Only files with Archive set	Unchanged
Daily copy	Only files changed that day	Unchanged

As you can see, there are four permutations of backup, based on how the archive attribute is handled; the daily backup is really a special case of the differential. How do these work in practice? In most circumstances, Normal and Copy backups will place more data onto the backup media—whether it is a tape or a file. This may mean that Incremental or Differential backups need to be used to back up onto a single tape or to complete the backup within and an available window. However, when it comes to a restore, these methods will take longer to restore than a Normal backup.

Consider the following strategic options:

- Full backup every day
- Full backup on Monday; Incremental backups on Tuesday, Wednesday, Thursday, Friday
- Full backup on Monday; Differential backups on Tuesday, Wednesday, Thursday, Friday
- Operator error wipes all information from the disk over the weekend
- Requires only Friday's tape(s) to be restored
- Requires Monday's, Tuesday's, Wednesday's, Thursday's and Friday's tapes
- Requires Monday's and Friday's tapes (because the archive attribute is not reset; Tuesday's changes are the tapes for Tuesday, Wednesday, Thursday, and Friday)

A backup can be set as a scheduled job, either from Schedule Jobs or from the Start Backup button. In either case, it can be viewed through the Schedule page, which shows all the scheduled backup jobs, or through the Scheduled Jobs applet in Control Panel (see Figure 5.7.6). This allows you to see the exact command line that the backup program's scheduling wizard constructs. You can also get to the same information by double-clicking the scheduled backup within the backup program's Schedule tab, and clicking the Properties button. Jobs can be deleted from this dialog box or the Control Panel applet.

Figure 5.7.6   Viewing the properties of a backup job through Control Panel.

While the backup is running, a display shows what is being backed up and the overall progress (see Figure 5.7.7). One enhancement over the Windows NT backup program is that the number and sizes of files are totaled before they are backed up to given an estimate time to run. This can be turned off through the Tools, Options menu.

Figure 5.7.7   A backup in progress.

When a backup is complete, its log information can be read (see Figure 5.7.8). Clicking the report button from the end of backup dialog box loads the log file into Notepad. This is skipped if the program is run as an automated command line. The Tools Report menu then displays a list of the logs that are available to view or print (see Figure 5.7.9).

Figure 5.7.8   At the end of a backup, the status displays.

Figure 5.7.9   Printing a backup log after the event.

Restoring files is very similar to backup. The first step of the process is to read the catalog of backed-up files from the file or tape. It is then possible to choose what is to be restored, and whether it is to go to its original location or to an alternate location (see Figure 5.7.10). It is possible, when choosing the location, to flatten the folder hierarchy being restored and place everything in a single folder. The Advanced options allow files to be restored with or without their security.

Figure 5.7.10   Restoring files.

Disaster Recovery

There are many potential threats to systems. These include sabotage from people inside and outside the company, theft of equipment, fire, and flood (including floods caused by failures of the building's own plumbing or fire-suppression systems). In some parts of the world, terrorist bombs are a threat, and in others, earthquakes must be allowed for.

A disaster is anything that results in the complete destruction of the computer system, although this will almost always be part of a wider picture. If the building has been left unusable, the plan should include where people will be accommodated. It should also decide which other parts of the organization can take over the work. The function of the disaster recovery plan is to define how normal (or at least near normal) services will be restored to users. Because this restoration will be happening in a chaotic environment (after a bomb, earthquake, fire, or flood) the plan is important.

The plan should define which services will be restored and in what sequence, where specialist equipment will come from, and how data will be backed up and restored (including the storage of tapes). As the services provided on the network evolve, it is necessary to update the plan. It should also be tested. At the very least, tapes should be restored to another system using a different tape drive. There are plenty of anecdotes of system administrators who believed they had good backups until they came to try to restore them. A full-scale test of the disaster recovery plan can be expensive—it will involve most of an organization's IT team and will probably have to be done outside normal working hours. To be realistic, it must be done offsite (the site has been destroyed and your temporary site may not have the facilities that you are used to) and the telephone system will probably be undergoing a similar reconstruction to the IT systems. Keep in mind that if the site is destroyed, so is the networking infrastructure, so you need to be able to build at least a temporary network. Because many companies outsource this sort of thing to specialists, they need to be included in the plan and any testing of it.

5.8

Internet Information Server

You Need to Read This Section If You Want to:

- Configure public Web hosting.
- Set up an intranet Web server.
- Allow Internet file transfers to and from the server.
- Learn more about Windows 2000's Web services.

Related Topics

Introduction to Internet Information Server

Microsoft Internet Information Server is a richly featured commercial Web server that supports all the most recent standards of Internet protocols, including the following:

- HTTP
- FTP
- SMTP
- NNTP

With the release of Windows NT 4.0 Server, Microsoft began including Internet Information Server with the operating system. Because the Internet has evolved so quickly over the past five years, Microsoft was forced to update its Web server before it was ready to release the newest version of its operating system, so in late 1997, an Option Pack for NT was released to bring about IIS 4.0.

Internet Information Server 4.0 was a significant release in that it introduced many advanced Web server features, a completely new local management interface, the latest version of protocols, and updated versions of Microsoft's server-side scripting objects.

Internet Information Server 5.0 (also referred to as *Internet Information Services 5.0* in most of the official Microsoft documentation) is introduced with Windows 2000.

Internet Information Server 5.0 adds the following new features:

- Better performance (IIS engine now optimized for speed)
- Clustering (on Windows 2000 Advanced Server)
- Replication (on Windows 2000 Advanced Server)
- Process throttling
- Bandwidth throttling
- Integrated setup
- IIS configuration backup features
- WebDAV support
- Streamlined security administration
- New security features (integration with the new Active Directory Services)
- New version of the Active Server Pages scripting engine

IIS 5.0 supports server-side programming though CGI, ISAPI, or Microsoft's proprietary Active Server Pages. Other scripting technologies (Perl, Cold Fusion, Java Servlets, and so on) can be added with third-party applications.

Installing and Configuring Internet Information Server

Microsoft's IIS is part of a standard Windows 2000 Server install. You have the option of installing IIS 5.0 when you first install Windows 2000, or you can add it at any time. If you wish to install IIS as part of the Windows 2000 install, you will find the process to be intuitive and painless.

If you have installed Windows 2000, you probably already have Internet Information Server installed. When you are prompted with the list of Windows 2000 Server components to pick from, you'll notice that the option for "Internet Information Services" is checked by default. Microsoft has it set so that a standard IIS configuration is installed when you setup Windows 2000. To check, go to Start, Programs, Administrative Tools and look for Internet Services Manager.

If you need to install IIS after you install Windows 2000, or if you want to add or remove components from the standard IIS install, you can do so by following these steps:

1   Go to Start, Settings, Control Panel.

2   Double-click the Add/Remove Programs icon.

3   Click the Add/Remove Windows Components button and then click the Components push button near the top of the form.

   After the Windows Components Wizard starts, click Next.

4   On the form that follows, you have a list box containing optional components for Windows 2000; click on Internet Information Services. To install IIS with the default components selected, click the Next button; if you want to add or remove IIS components, click the Details button.

   Under Details, you have the option of installing select IIS components. By default, you have Common Files, Documentation, FTP Services, IIS Snap-in, Internet Services Manager (HTML version), SMTP Services, and WWW Services.

   Check the FrontPage 2000 Server Extensions option if you want to allow developers to connect to your Web server using Microsoft's FrontPage 2000 (FrontPage, a WYSIWYG HTML editor, is commonly used on the Windows platform for Web development).

   Check the NNTP option if you want the ability to host newsgroups from this Web server.

   Check Visual InterDev RAD support if you want to allow developers to connect to your server with Visual InterDev 6. Visual InterDev is part of the Microsoft Developer Studio and provides developers with a source control tool for developing Active Server Pages and HTML documents.

5   To configure IIS, open up the Internet Information Services Management Console. You'll notice a tree view in the left form with Internet Information Services as the top branch and your server name appearing directly below. The branches below your Windows 2000 server name will be for the Web (http) and FTP sites that you will create for this server.

6   To configure master properties for this server, highlight the server name branch and right-click Go into Properties. A pop-up window appears. Select WWWServices and click Edit.

Here, you can define server-level master properties. You'll want to give the server a description, do performance tweaking, set your default home directory, and so on. In most cases, you'll find that the default settings will be adequate.

Administering WWWServices

The WWWServices serves up HTML files, images, audio, and anything else supported by the latest http standard. When a user http connects to your Web server using their Web browser, your WWWService is what responds back.

You can connect to your Web server locally by opening up your Web browser and typing in **http://localhost/** or using the loop back IP address **http://127.0.0.1/**.

If your Web server is going to be inside a firewall on your Local Area Network, your users can access the Web server by using either your internal server IP number (for example, **192.168.11.10**) or by http, connecting to the WINS system server name.

http://192.168.11.10/

http://test2k/

If your Web server is going to be a public Web server hosting Internet Web sites, you'll use your static IP number assigned by your Internet service provider. Of course, you'll want to register your static IP number with a Domain name at InterNIC so that you can change http://87.1.2.50/ to **http://www.myWebsite.com/**.

▶ *For more information, see the Network Solutions Web site at* http://www. networksolutions.com/.

When you http connect to your Web server using the localhost or loop back IP address, the first thing you see is the localstart.asp page, warning you that you do not have a default document set. The following steps walk you through creating and setting a default document for the Web server.

1   First, check and see which files the server is set to accept as a default document. In the IIS Manager Console, highlight the Default Web Site branch, right-click, and open up Properties. Click the Documents tab.

2 You see a default.htm, default.asp, and iisstart.asp in a list box. These are the files that your Web server will search for when someone tries to http connect. The Web server prioritizes these in the order in which they are listed. So, if by chance you have a default.asp and a default.htm in the same directory, the default.htm will be displayed and the default.asp will not. Following this logic, if you create a default.htm or a default.asp for your default Web site, your page will display instead of the iisstart.asp page you are currently seeing.

3 You need to know where the physical location of the default Web site resides on the hard drive. To find this out, click on the Home Directory tab.

Notice that the default directory is set to point to the \InetPub\www-root\ directory on the server. It's common practice (but not required) on IIS to leave \InetPub\wwwroot\ as your home directory and create subdirectories under \wwwroot for your virtual directories and virtual servers. There are a few other things to look at while you're here. Under the Local Path, you see a group of checkboxes. By default, Read, Log visits, and Index this resource should all be checked. Check Script source access if you want to allow your Web developers to run Active Server Pages, Perl, or any other form of server-side scripting (if you want to allow for CGI executables to run, you need to set the script permissions drop-down menu). Check Directory browsing if you want to provide a user with a hyperlink-capable file list in the absence of a default document.

4 Let's create a new default.htm file and save it to \InetPub\wwwroot\. Open up Notepad and type in the following HTML script:

```
<html>

<head>

</head>

<body>

<h1>

Welcome to Internet Information Server 5.0

Web site still under construction.

</h1>

</body>

</html>
```

5 Be sure and save your file as **default.htm**. After you are done, open your Web browser and try to http connect to the Web server. You should see rather large black text on a white background, displaying the message defined in the HTML document.

Running Scripts On the Server Poses a Security Hazard

Allowing your Web developers to run scripts on your server can be a security risk. Most server-side scripting languages allow developers limited access to the file system on the Web server; CGI executables will have complete control of the file system. Most responsible Web administrators will require the source code for all CGI executables to be submitted to the Web master or an on-staff Web developer for review and approval before installation. Check Write only if you want to grant visitors the right to upload content to your server.

▶ *For more information, see "Administering IIS Security" later in this chapter.*

You have successfully configured a default Web page. To change things back to the way they were before, simply delete the default.htm file from \Inetpub\wwwroot\.

Administering FTP Services

The File Transfer Protocol is one of the oldest Internet protocols—it existed long before http. Users will connect to your FTP server using an FTP client application. Unlike the Web browser market, in which Microsoft's Internet Explorer and Netscape's Navigator fight for presentation standards, there are many popular FTP client applications. This is because FTP does not require any user interface; it simply allows you to transfer files to and from an FTP server. The Windows 2000 operating system comes with two FTP clients. You have the option of the FTP console application (which you will make use of for this section) or the FTP client that's built into Internet Explorer 5.0.

Despite its age, FTP is still the most popular way to upload files from one place to another over the Internet. Take a look at the default FTP site's properties.

To get to the Properties page, open up the Internet Information Services Management Console and expand the tree in the left form area to show the Default FTP Server. Single-click Default FTP Server, right-click, and then go to Properties.

Under the FTP Site tab, you may want to change the number of limited connections, based on your bandwidth restraints. If you have little bandwidth and are getting a high volume of connections, it will make things slow for everyone.

Under the Security Accounts tab, you can select whether or not you want to allow anonymous access (by default, anonymous access is turned on). When guests log on to your FTP site as anonymous, they are entering your system and will have certain security limitations. You can assign the user account to use for the anonymous guest (by default, this is IUSR_*). In addition to the anonymous account, you can also add user accounts to this list. All user account information for your FTP services will be handled by the Windows 2000 User Manager.

▶ *For more information on setting up and managing Windows 2000 user accounts, see Chapter 4.4, "Creating and Managing User Accounts," and Chapter 4.6, "Logging On and Authentication."*

Under the Messages tab, you can set up a welcome message that your guests will see after login. The Home Directory tab allows you to set the physical directory on the hard drive where the files will reside, and the Directory security tab allows you to restrict access by denying access to specific users based on IP number and subnet masking.

The following steps walk through setting up the default FTP site:

1 For this site, you're going to leave the default properties for the FTP Site and Security Accounts tabs. Click on the Message tab and type the following:

   ★★★
   Welcome to the Emmerison Corporate FTP Server
   ★★★

   = No file ratios
   = Please upload into incoming directory

   Any questions, please e-mail:
   Webmaster@emmerison.com
   ★★★

2 You want to set it so only Administrators can upload files to the root directory, and anonymous users can only upload to \incoming. To do this, you must change the security settings on the ftproot directory. In Windows Explorer, get the properties on the \ftproot branch. Deselect Allow Inheritable Permissions, remove the Everyone user, and add the IUSER_★ account and the Administrator user account.

3 Set the permissions so that IUSER_★ has only read and list folder contents checked. Set it so that Administrator has everything checked.

4 Create a subdirectory under ftproot named **\incoming**; set the security on this folder so that IUSER_★ has read, write, and list folder permissions.

5 Create an **\incoming** folder under \InetPut\ftproot\.

6 Open up a command prompt from Start, Programs, Accessories. At the command prompt, type **\ftp 127.0.0.1** to start the console-based Windows FTP client and attempt to connect to the local FTP server though the loop back IP number.

Now, you can use the GET and SEND commands to FTP files to and from your directory.

Creating and Managing Virtual Directories and Servers

The default Web site is usually the root Web site that is reached whenever someone http connects to the Web server. Internet Information Server allows you to create virtual directories and virtual servers to allow your Web server to distribute content around multiple physical drives and host more than one site at a time. Suppose you have a corporate intranet Web site that can be reached at http://intranet.mysite.com/. You want to add a message board to the site and you want to set up your message board in a directory outside the wwwroot. The best way to achieve this is with a virtual directory.

A *virtual directory* is simply a Registry reference that's made to a physical directory on the hard drive. Suppose you placed the files for your message board directory inside a directory under C:\server\aspcode\mboard. The virtual directory will make it possible for users to access your message board application at http://intranet.mysite.com/messages/.

To create a new virtual directory, execute the following steps:

1 Highlight the default Web site (or whatever Web site you'd like to add this virtual directory to) and right-click. On the pop-up menu, select New, Virtual Directory.

2 You'll be prompted by the Virtual Directory Creation Wizard, which will walk you though the painless process of creating a new virtual directory.

3 On the second wizard screen, enter in your Alias. This is the name as it will appear after the slash on your IP number or Domain name.

4 Next, you'll be prompted to select the Web site content directory, which is the physical hard drive directory where the file will lie. Using the previous example, you should select the following:

    c:\server\aspcode\mboard\

5 Finally, you're prompted with a list of permissions. Read and Run should be selected. Check Execute only if you must allow CGI or ISAPI applications to run, but check Write only if you want to allow users to write information to the server (you will check this only very rarely). Select Browse only if you want to give the user the ability to get a list of all the files in this directory as a list of hyperlink filenames. Remember that you can change the permissions at any time by going into the properties of this virtual directory.

Using Secondary Drives for Virtual Directories

You can point your virtual directory to a physical directory that exists on a hard drive other than the drive from which you host IIS.

This is appropriate when the server is configured with multiple smaller hard drive partitions or when you have exhausted the amount of drive space on your primary hard drive where IIS resides.

A virtual server acts as if it were an additional instance of IIS. Each virtual server can have its own properties and security. You can create a new virtual server by highlighting your server name in the management console (the branch under Internet Information Services), right-click, and go to New, Web Site.

When to Use Virtual Servers

It's best to create a new virtual server when you do the following:

- Set up a new Web site that's large enough to have virtual directories assigned under it.
- Add segregated security and administration for the new site being added.
- Add virtual Web hosting, and hosting more than one site that will be in need of a registered URL.

You are prompted with the Web Site Creation Wizard. Proceed though the wizard and enter in the description for your new site. Next, you will be prompted to enter the IP address and port settings. Here, you can assign your new site an IP number (if this is a public Web site, this IP number must be in the range of IP numbers you have been authorized to use). You can also use the default IP number of your Web server and assign the new site a unique port number.

For this example, assign a unique port number. Leave the IP address set to [All Unassigned] and change the port number to 190.

Finish up the wizard by selecting the physical directory for the new site.

Now, if you want to connect to this new site, you can reach it by opening up the Web browser and typing in the IP number of the server, followed by a colon and then the port number: **http://127.0.0.1:190/**.

By making use of virtual servers, it is possible to register multiple URLs and host multiple Web sites on the same instances of IIS.

Using Indexing Services

The Microsoft Indexing Service attempts to maintain a catalog of searchable keywords related to documents in a given directory or set of directories. Documents that can be indexed are as follows:

- HTML documents
- XML documents
- ASCII text documents
- Microsoft Active Server Pages documents
- Microsoft Word documents
- Microsoft Excel documents
- Microsoft PowerPoint documents

With Windows 2000, indexing services are now tied into Microsoft's new Active Directory technology. This allows for your indexing services to extend beyond the Web server. In fact, all your hard drives can now be indexed and searched on. You can also query the Index catalog on other servers on your network. You may have noticed when you open up a search for "Files in Folders" that you now have the option to search for specific text in files. This is achieved though the same indexing service that powers the Web site index.

Previous versions of Index Server offered their own Administrative tool in the form of a Microsoft Management Console (MMC) plug-in. Under Windows 2000 indexing, administration is done though Computer Management. To open the Computer Management Console, go into Programs, Administrative Tools, and select Computer Management. You'll see a management console plug-in with a tree view on the left and Computer Management (local) at the top of this hierarchy.

Branch down one and you will see System Tools, Storage and Services, and Applications. Expand out Services and Applications. Select Indexing Services and notice on the toolbar whether the service is stopped or started. (You can also right-click Indexing Services to obtain this information.) If the service is stopped, you can start the service by clicking the right triangle on the toolbar or by going to the pop-up menu for Index Service and selecting Start. After you are sure that the service is running, expand out Indexing Services. Under Indexing Service branch, select Web. You'll then see two subfolders—one for Directories and one for Properties. You will also see a Web page: Query the Catalog. At any time, if you want to run a search to see what's in your catalog (or the catalog of a remote computer), Query the Catalog is a useful tool to use.

To add or remove directories, click Directories. You'll notice a list of directories in the right form—these are your current directories being indexed by Index Service. If you want to remove a directory from this list, simply highlight the directory and hit the Delete key.

If you want to add a directory to this list, right-click and go to New, Directory.

With Index Service running, Web developers can easily query the Index catalog and allow Web users to perform Web-based searches for the content on the site.

Administering IIS Security

Internet Information Server has three levels of security:

- Restricting IP address and Domain name security
- NTFS permissions
- IIS permissions

Of these, the most basic level of security is the NTFS security that's built into the file system. If you open up Windows Explorer and set the permissions on a physical directory that's registered to a virtual directory or virtual server, these permissions will apply the same way to the Web users as they would to local users.

To set up security on your default Web site using NTFS, execute the following steps:

1 Open up Windows Explorer and branch down to InetPub->wwwroot.

2 Get the permissions on this directory by opening up Windows Explorer and branching down to the physical directory you're looking for.

3 Highlight that directory, and then right-click and select the Security tab, deselect Allow inheritable permissions, and remove Everyone. Add only the users you want to access this directory.

4 After the changes have taken place, open up your Web browser and try and connect to your default Web site. You will be prompted to log in before you can view any content.

On top of NTFS permissions, you have Internet Information Server permissions. You set these in the properties of your Web site. Here, you can assign site operators and set global site permissions that will apply to all users for this Web site.

Site operators have the capability to do the following:

- Enable site login
- Allow or restrict anonymous access to the site
- Create welcome and exit messages
- Configure site security
- Configure bandwidth restraints

IIS also allows you to restrict users based on their IP address or Domain name. With this security feature, you can deny or grant access to all users coming from a Domain. If you want to grant access to a Web site only to people coming from inside your company and you know all users inside your company will be assigned an IP number between 38.234.10.0 and 38.234.10.255, you can grant access to just this range of IP addresses. To do this, click the Directory security tab and click Edit for IP address and Domain name restrictions.

One last thing you should be aware of is the way IIS handles passing the username and password from the client PC to the server. Under the Directory Security tab, click Edit for Anonymous access and authentication control.

You'll notice that the Integrated Windows authentication checkbox is checked by default. This has replaced the IIS 4.0 Challenge/Response type. If anyone will connect to this Web site from outside your local area network, this is the option you'll want to go with. If you choose to go with the clear text option, IIS will attempt to pull the client's Windows username and password from the local SAM.

VI

Managing User Desktops

6.1

Overview of Managing User Desktops

You Need to Read This Section If You Want to:

- Understand profiles.
- Understand policies.
- Understand the scope of the Windows 2000 customization options.
- Differentiate between the use of profiles and policies.

Related Topics

Overview of User Desktop Management

To date, the control and maintenance of the corporate user environment, mainly the desktop, has been only partially attainable. The initial Windows NT integration of profiles and policies allowed light customization and control, but lacked the robust scope that was truly needed. Windows 2000 addresses this need, providing functions such as hierarchal processing, extensible parameters to meet unique corporate needs, secure maintenance and delegation, and a single integrated interface for modifications to Group Policy Objects. This chapter will delve into the options for architecture and application of profiles and Group Policy Objects in your Windows 2000 environment.

Customizing the Environment

Modification to the desktop environment to fit the personal and functional needs of the user and organization is one of the most understated and attractive features of the Microsoft desktop OS. Several forces drive customization, as follows:

- Software installation
- User interaction
- Administrative interaction

Regardless of the way desktop customization occurs, the end result can create a highly functional or incredibly dysfunctional working environment. The scope of desktop customization can range from a simple icon being placed on the desktop—as is common with software installation—to the complete elimination of the desktop modification feature. For instance, a KIOSK machine could be configured by an administrator to allow only the execution of the Web browser to remove the chance of misuse of a public workstation. With that said, it is important to understand the component pieces that make up the customization toolset and what they can offer.

Profiles

So what is a profile, and how do I use it to make my computing environment more consistent for my users? A *profile* is a set of preferences and default configurations for the corporate computing environment. Profiles are physically stored either locally or remotely, and can potentially exist for every user in the organization. The physical layout of this information is broken into two locations: a directory structure and a Registry hive file called Ntuser.dat. By default, at logon time, a profile specific to the user is generated and stored locally. The generation of this profile is created from base settings shipped with Windows 2000. The data contained in Windows 2000 profiles is as follows.

Ntuser.dat contains the following:

- User-definable settings relative to the Control Panel interface.
- Look and feel of NT Explorer—for instance, persistent drive mapping would be stored here.
- Taskbar location and size, as well as program groups and program items.
- Network printer connections.
- Bookmarks that were created in the Help for Windows 2000.
- Any default accessories settings such as the view for the calculator set to scientific as opposed to standard.

Directory structure contains the following:

- **Application data.** This information consists of application-specific data (for instance, Internet-explore log information).
- **Cookies.** Web-based identification files.
- **Desktop.** Files or shortcuts that live on the desktop.
- **Favorites.** Shortcuts to favorite locations.
- **Local Settings.** Subfolders within this directory are Application Data, History, and Temporary Internet files.
- **My Documents.** Maps to the My Documents folder on the user desktop (in addition, a single subfolder exists in this profile called My Pictures).
- **NetHood.** Contains shortcuts to the My Network Places items.
- **PrintHood.** Contains shortcuts to the Printers folders items.
- **Recent.** Similar to the History function in IE, this directory stores the most recently accessed documents and folders.
- **Send to.** Contents of this folder are used to build the Sends to function when you right-click a file, folder, or shortcut.
- **Start menu.** Holds the stucture for what will appear under the Start button, and programs pop up.
- **Templates.** User template items.

Now that you know the components of a profile, take a look at the implementation of a standard profile to be used as a starting point for the desktops in your environment.

User accounts in the Windows 2000 Active directory have a Profile Path property that directs the system to the proper location to retieve and store updates to the settings specific to the logged-on user. This profile can be created by the administrator and copied to the designated profile location as part of the user-creation process. The result of performing these actions will be a common starting point for all new users.

The common starting point is a great benefit to new employees who are expecting certain icon placements, colors, or sound schemes as a result of initial orientation training. However, having a common, enterprise-wide desktop that is not modifiable by the user adds even greater value. Consistent desktop and Start menu look and feel can seriously reduce help desk calls. When calls do occur, the mean turnaround time for resolution is decreased creating mandatory user profiles.

Mandatory user profiles are unique in that the Ntuser hive file has a .man file extension and the NTFS file permissions for the directory structure have the read permission set for the user or users who will use the profile. No other NTFS rights are granted. Although this will allow in-session modifications to the environment, the environment will be restored from the read-only server copy at the next logon. The manipulation of the user environment relative to the look and feel of the desktop is only part of the customization toolset addressed by Windows 2000.

▶ *For more information on the mechanics of implementing mandatory user profiles, see Chapter 6.2, "Profiles."*

Group Policy Objects

The second and significantly more formidable administration mechanism is called a Group Policy Object (GPO). By definition, a *GPO* is a collection of enforced rules that are applied to users or computers. If you worked with policies in NT 4.0, you will have a good foundation for understanding the functionality of group policies in Windows 2000. If you never had the opportunity to take advantage of this tool in previous versions of NT, you will be pleasantly surprised at the level of control the implementation of this feature will give you over the environments you are responsible for.

GPOs in Windows 2000 are made up of two components:

- **Group Policy Container (GPC).** The GPC houses version information, status information, and a list of extensions. The GPC is stored in Active Directory as an object and is part of the Domain partition of the Active Directory database. This is significant relative to what replication topology it will follow, and which DCs will have a copy of the GPO for application to the users or computers within the directory structure.

  ▶ *For more information on replication and database partitions, see Chapter 1.2, "Introduction to Active Directory.*

- **Group Policy Template (GPT).** The GPT is stored in the %systemroot%\sysvol\ \domainname \Policies\{guid}. A *guid* is a globally unique identifier that is generated for every object in Active Directory. Placement in the sysvol folder of the DC is a very deliberate one. All directories and subdirectories under sysvol are replicated Domain-wide. The replication of GPT information follows the same replication topology as the GPC; this ensures that every DC in the Domain has the required information to apply the GPO. The GPT stores machine- and user-specific data relating to security, application installations, boot, logon, logoff, and shutdown scripts, as well as look and feel.

View and configuration of group policies are performed through the Group Policy snap-in within the MMC. Representation of the types of modifications that can be set within any specific policy is broken down into computer configuration and user configuration sections (see Figure 6.1.1).

Figure 6.1   Group policies are logically divided up into two groups: computer configuration and user configuration.

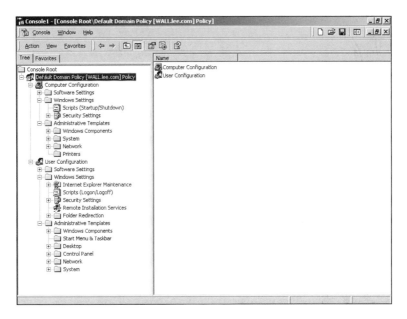

Windows NT 4.0 and 3.x processing of user policies occurred based on an individual policy named with your user ID, a policy with the name of a group you belonged in, and then the default user policy if neither of the two previous conditions were met. Machine policies were applied similarly—if a policy existed with that machine's name, the policy would take effect if the default machine policy would not be used. Application of Windows 2000 Group Policy Objects is heirarchical and occurs from the top down: Site, Domain, and then Organizational unit (see Figure 6.1.2).

Figure 6.1.2   Group Policy Object order processing.

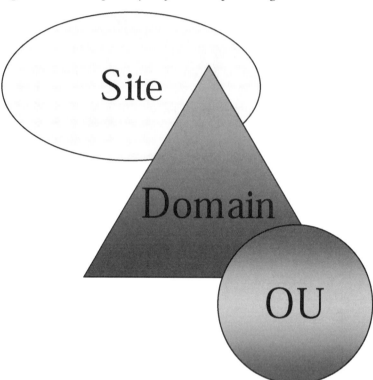

Policies apply based on the ojects (user or computer) location in the hierarchy as well as their membership in security groups.

The rest of Part 6, "Managing User Desktops," will go into further details on both profiles and Group Policies.

6.2
Profiles

You Need to Read This Section If You Want to:

- Understand the creation of local profiles and how to manipulate the default behavior.
- Create and implement roaming and or mandatory user profiles.
- Generate user profile templates.

Related Topics

Profiles

Chapter 6.1 discussed the content of the profiles in Windows 2000, as well as a general definition of what they are and how profiles might be utilized in you environment. This section will detail each type of profile and show you how to customize and implement the profile that is right for your users and desired IT goals.

Local Profiles

Three types of profiles are available to structure and standardize your desktops: local profiles, roaming profiles, and mandatory profiles. This chapter will delve into local profiles first because they are the building blocks for the other two types.

Profile generation occurs by default in Windows 2000, much as it did in previous versions of NT. However, there are some changes. One of the initial differences is the base location for the default profile. On a pristine install of Windows 2000, the structure shown in Figure 6.2.1 will exist on the installation drive.

Figure 6.2.1   The Documents and Settings folder contains the All Users and Default Users subdirectories used to generate the local profile at initial login.

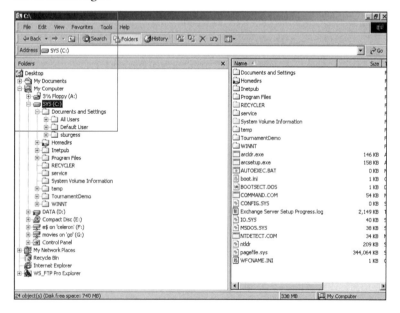

The first time a user successfully logs on to a machine, the list of existing pro-files is checked. If a profile for the user exists, it is used to build the desktop and appropriate settings for the environment. If a local profile does not exist, the Default Users profiles, stored within the Documents and Settings folder, are used to create the initial desktop and user environment.

▶ *For more information on what is stored within the ntuser.dat and default user sub-folders, see Chapter 6.1, "Overview of Managing User Desktops."*

The newly generated profile is stored under the Documents and Settings directory in a folder with the same name as the user that just authenticated. For instance, if three people have logged on to a machine since it was first installed (user1, user2, and user3), the directory structure under the Documents and Settings folder would contain the following folders: All Users, Default Users, user1, user2, and user3.

Implementing a Standard Default User Profile

The following steps walk you through the implementation of a standard default user profile:

1 Create an account either local or in AD. For the purpose of this exer-cise, call it **templateaccount**.

2 Log on to a clean build of Windows 2000.

3 Customize the desktop to fit your organization's needs (icon placement, desktop schemes, standard mapped drives, standard network printers, IE settings, start menu items, Windows application configurations such as Outlook Express, and so on).

4 Log off and log on with an account that has administrative authority.

5 Open up My Computer and double-click on the winnt installation drive letter.

6 Double-click on the Documents and Settings folder and then on the templateaccount folder.

7 At the top of the window under the Tools drop-down list, select Folder Options. Within the Folder Options dialog box, select the View tab. Ensure that the Show hidden files folders radio button is selected and that both the Hide file extensions for known types and Hide protected operating system files options are unchecked.

8 Within the templateaccount folder, select all folders and files and copy them.

9 Click the back button, right-click on the Default Users directory, and select Paste.

10 Validate your modifications by logging on with an account that has not yet been used on this machine.

The result will be a newly generated profile that will be the same every time a new user logs on.

This method would be used if the changes to the environment were significant (detailed changes to IE, mapped drives and printers, colors and font sizes, application settings that are profile-dependent). For one-off changes, you have the ability to work with the existing default user directory structure and Ntuser.dat file.

Modifications within the file structure are relatively straightforward. For instance, to create a program group on the Start menu, you would do the following:

1　Go into the Default Users directory in Documents and Settings.

2　Double-click the Start menu folder.

3　Double-click the Programs folder.

4　Create a folder with a name representative of the application you intend to create a shortcut for (for example, **Co. XYZ Applications**).

5　Double-click the newly created folder.

6　Double-click and select the new shortcut; then browse the application executable and click OK.

After you create the new shortcut, you will notice that it did not appear in your current Start menu. This is because the default user profile is used only at profile-creation time. To add a modification to the existing profiles as well as any future profiles that are created on this machine, the All Users subdirectory under Documents and Settings needs to be modified the same way.

Manually Modifying the Ntuser.dat File

Manual modification of the Ntuser.dat file is a little more involved. The Ntuser.dat file is a Registry hive file. Therefore, it can be manipulated by regedt32.exe just like the Registry. To make manual edits to the default Ntuser.dat file, perform the following steps:

1　Launch regedt32 from the Run prompt.

2　Set the focus on the HKEY_USERS pane.

3　Left-click the top of the HKEY_USERS hierarchy.

4　From the Registry drop-down list, select Load Hive.

5　Browse to the Ntuser.dat file in the Default Users directory under Documents and Settings, and click OK.

At this point, you can manually modify the settings to suit your needs.

It's important to note that these techniques would be used in deployment situations when you use disk duplication technology or Remote Installation Services (RIS). In the next section, you will learn how to deploy roaming user profiles to currently deployed Windows 2000 desktops.

Roaming User Profiles

In a user-by-user basis, you can define a profile path on the Profile tab of the User Account Properties dialog box. This function allows for a central copy of the user profile to be stored and accessed from any workstation. This implementation is called a *roaming user profile*. To implement roaming user profiles, the following steps must be executed:

1 Create an account, either local or in AD. For the purpose of this exercise, call it **roamtemplate**.

2 Log on to a clean build of Windows 2000.

3 Customize the desktop to fit your organization's needs (icon placement, desktop schemes, standard mapped drives, standard network printers, IE settings, Start menu items, Windows application configurations such as Outlook Express, and so on).

4 Log off and log on with an account that has administrative authority.

5 Double-click My Computer and left-click Properties.

6 Select the User Profiles tab, and highlight the roamtemplate profile.

7 Click Copy to and select a location on your network (\\SERVER\SHARE\ROAMING profile template).

8 In the Permitted to use portion of the dialog box, click Change and select the authenticated users group. This information is embedded into the Ntuser.dat file and limits the security groups that will be allowed to use the profile.

9 Click OK.

10 Open up Explorer and create a share under a test user's home directory. For this example, it will be called **profiledata**.

11 Locate the network share point you copied the roamtemplate profile to and copy its contents to the profiledata subdirectory for the test user account.

12 Open up the Properties dialog box for the testuser account and click on the Profile tab.

13 Enter in the UNC path to the profiledata directory and click OK.

14 Log on to the workstation with the test user account and verify proper profile application.

To deploy profiles to existing users/desktops, perform steps 11 through 13 and repeat for each user.

The implementation of roaming profiles allow administrators in existing Windows 2000 environments to customize the desktop without visiting each machine. However, neither local nor roaming profiles address the need to limit the users' ability to modify the default environment.

Mandatory User Profiles

Mandatory user profiles, unlike local and roaming profiles, remove the users' ability to permanently change their desktop environment. In the implementation of a local or roaming profile, changes to the workspace are saved upon exit. However, changes are not saved with mandatory profiles. Restated, in-session changes are permitted, However, after the logon session has ended, the original settings are restored when the user logs back on. To implement mandatory user profiles, the following steps are necessary:

1　Create an account, either local or in AD. For the purpose of this exercise, call it **mandatorytemplate**.

2　Log on to a clean build of Windows 2000.

3　Customize the desktop to fit your organization's needs (icon placement, desktop schemes, standard mapped drives, standard network printers, IE settings, Start menu items, Windows application configurations such as Outlook Express, and so on).

4　Click Change and select the authenticated users group. This information is embedded into the Ntuser.dat file and limits the security groups that will be allowed to use the profile.

5　Click OK.

6　Open up My Computer and browse the mandatory profile template directory that you just copied the profile to.

7　Double-click it and left-click Properties.

8　On the Security tab, set the Everyone permission to read. Remove all other checkmarks for the Everyone group.

9　Add the Administrators group if it is not already in the security list, and give it full control.

10　Click OK.

11　Double-click the mandatory profile template directory.

12　Rename the Ntuser.dat file to **Ntuser.man**.

13　Set up a test account to have its profile point to the \\SERVER\SHARE\MANDATORY profile template directory.

14　Log on as the test user to verify policy application. Make modifications to the desktop and log out.

15　Log back in and verify that the changes you made did not take effect.

Now that you have a good understanding of what the individual policies are and how to implement them, it's important to understand the order and conditions under which they will get applied (see Figure 6.2.2).

Figure 6.2.2   Profile processing and application flow.

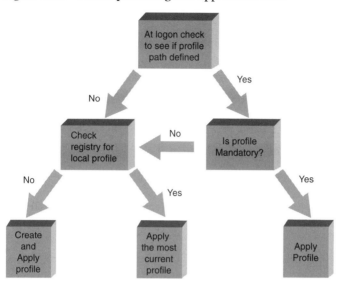

Profiles, as you understand them from the previous pages, are made up of directory structures and Registry files, but profiles are not limited to just those definitions. Profiles are also defined within the Active Directory and have several more components (see Figure 6.2.3).

Figure 6.2.3   Profile definitions within AD are made up of profile path, the logon script, and the Home folder.

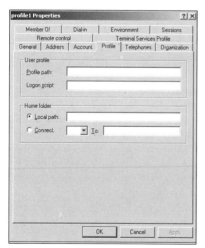

Logon Script

The logon script portion of the user profile defined within AD can take several forms. Most common is a CMD file that performs tasks such as drive mapping and printer mapping. Implementations to date have been cumbersome, especially in large environments where different physical locations or job responsibilities require different resources. For example, a 30-story building with users on every floor (each floor contains four to eight departments with unique printing and storage needs) would require somewhere on the order of 45 individual logon scripts if no third-party or add-on products were used. This is because each department would have one or two local printers that would have to be associated with each department's users. In addition, each department would have its own departmental-based share as well as corporate-wide shares. Although this is a functional method, it is a very high-maintenance feature. As movement, attrition, and hiring occur, each would cause the application of a series of scripts to assign the correct resources. Current unsupported products in the Resource Kit (kixstart) make short work of this issue, allowing enumeration of NT security group membership to determine what resources get assigned, effectively allowing two or three scripts to do the work of many. The disadvantages of using such tools are as follows:

- Login time is greatly extended as processing of these enormous scripts is slow.

- Downlevel clients require installation of particular dlls to function properly.

- The scripting languages are proprietary and at times very cryptic, requiring an extended learning curve.

- You are now tied to a non-portable solution. If the underlying technology (the OS) changes, you will be forced to re-engineer the entire set of scripts.

To address these issues, several new features have been put in place. The first of these is Windows Scripting Host (WSH). WSH is an open shell environment built into the Windows 2000 OS. WSH interprets Visual Basic script and Jscript, as well as several other common scripting languages. This allows the power of programming logic and API-level calls to be no more than a few keystrokes away in your favorite text editor. The second is the implementation of Group Policy objects as a means of specifying startup/logon and logoff/shutdown scripts based on the user or computer location within the site, Domain or organizational unit structure.

▶ *For more information, see Chapter 6.3, "Group Policies."*

Home Folder

The Home folder can be specified to automatically map a drive to a network share location, allowing a predetermined letter to represent a secure backed-up point of storage for user information. Applications may use the Home folder as the default location that the Save and Open dialog boxes access.

My Documents Folders

The control over where the My Documents folder points can be set by using profiles, as previously discussed, or it can be controlled via GPOs from within Active Directory. Although the My Documents folder is not centrally administered within the user account profile dialog box, it is an integral part of the desktop environment as the default open and save starting point for most newer applications.

Offline Folders

Much like the My Briefcase function in previous Microsoft OSs, offline folders allow you to specify a folder such as My Documents to be made available offline. This allows you to work while not connected to the network and then synchronize any changes to data at the next connection to the wire. Synchronization Manager enforces the rules you configure for when synchronizations will occur. You can access settings by double-clicking My Computer, and then by clicking on the Tools drop-down list and Synchronize.

Best Practices

- Always bear in mind that the implementation of a roaming or mandatory profile requires the profile to be copied to the local system prior to it being implemented.
- Utilize Group Policies to control the application of profiles in a Remote access environmet.
- If the driver for using profiles is forcing the storage of the My Documents folder to a network location, consider using Group Policies instead. Using this mechanism will remove the time lag and bandwidth utilization from having the My Documents folder coppied locally.
- Manage the size of your profiles using the options within Group Policies.

6.3
Group Policies

You Need to Read This Section If You Want to:

- Architect an effective manageable Group Policy object strategy.
- Effectively reduce the total cost of ownership of your environment.
- Granularly control access to the features of Windows 2000.
- Control the application of Group Policy objects in your environment.
- Troubleshoot the GPO configurations in your environments.

Introduction to Group Policies

Group Policies are the rules by which the environment is configured. They are created and replicated throughout a Domain. A Group Policy Object (GPO) is made up of two distinct physical pieces: a Group Policy container and a Group Policy template. Together, these two pieces provide all information regarding the settings of a Group Policy object. The application of the GPO on objects within the hierarchy of Active Directory is the foundation of the reasoning process for a functionally effective GPO design. We already know that the processing order is top-to-bottom within the AD hierarchy, but the options within that processing order are much more granular.

Creating Group Policies

Two group policies are created and linked to containers in your hierarchy by default. They are creatively called the Default Domain Policy and the Default Domain Controller's Policy, and are each linked to the Domain container and the Domain Controller's OU container, respectively. To generate your own GPOs, you need to be logged on with the appropriate account. The default permissions allow Enterprise Administrators and Domain Admins total control over Group Policy settings. The following steps walk you through creating a Group Policy object:

1 Ensure that your account is a member of either the Domain administrators or Enterprise administrators groups.

2 Log on to a system with the appropriate Administrative tools installed—specifically, the Active Directory Users and Computers snap-in (dsa.msc) (see the sidebar on Administrative tools).

3 Open Active Directory Users and Computers and set the focus on the OU you want to apply a GPO to.

4 Right-click on the OU, left-click on Properties, and then select the GPO tab.

5 To create a new GPO and link it to the existing container, click the New button.

6 A new entry will appear in the Group Policy Object links list with the name highlighted and in Edit mode. Change the name to be representative of the settings you will configure within the GPO.

The policy you've just created is blank and is based on a set of default administrative templates contained within the sysvol folder on the DC on which the GPO was generated. These templates are extensible and you can modify them to suit the needs of your organization. Additionally, you can create your own extensions to the existing default Group Policy object components currently defined. For instance, you may have custom software settings that you want to centrally administer relative to its behavior and configuration. Information on how to create your own extensions can be found in the Windows 2000 SDK.

After the GPO has been created, you will want to modify the settings within it to accomplish any number of tasks oriented around the configuration of the desktop and application environment. Click the Edit button on the Group Policy tab. This launches the Group Policy editor and provides a single interface to modify both Computer and User configuration settings. The list that shows up on the Group Policy tab of the container's property page shows links to GPOs that live in Active Directory. Modifications to that GPO could affect multiple objects in the directory. To ensure that the settings you configure will be applied only to the appropriate target containers, open up the Properties page for a particular GPO and click on the Links tab. Use the Find Now button to search for any containers that this policy has been linked to (see Figure 6.3.1).

Figure 6.3.1   Links provides a method of finding all containers the policy has been linked to.

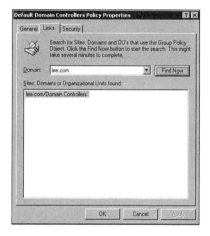

Administrative Tools

Windows 2000 Administrative tools can be found on the Server, Advanced Server, or Data Center Server CD within the I386 directory; or it can be found in the winnt\ system32\ directory on any of the previously stated platforms. The single file that is required is called adminpak.msi. This 15 MB file installs all of the administrative mscs and properly registers the associated dlls required to operate the Admin tool set properly. Currently, the installation of these tools is supported only on the Windows 2000 platform.

Group Policy Processing

Some base rules and options to be aware of regarding the use of Group Policy objects are as follows:

- GPOs get applied to containers, not leaf objects.
- Multiple GPOs can be associated with a single container.
- Multiple GPOs defined on a single container are processed in a set order.
- The Machine or User component of a GPO can be excluded from evaluation in the GPO processing sequence.
- GPO inheritance can be blocked.
- GPO inheritance can be forced.
- GPOs can be filtered through the use of ACLs.

The following example shows GPO application at several different points in the hierarchy (see Figure 6.3.2).

Figure 6.3.2   Hierarchy defining site, Domain, and OU layout for shinyapple.msft Domain.

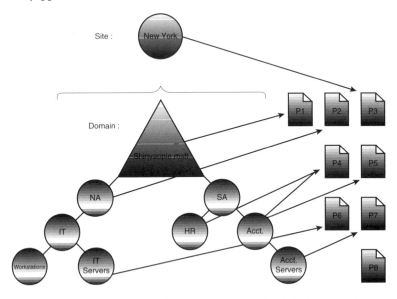

Given the structure shown in Figure 6.3.2 with the default processing options, the application of GPOs in the hierarchy occurs, as shown in Table 6.3.1.

Table 6.3.1   Default Group Policy Processing Based On
shinyapple.msft Domain

Object	Applied Policies, In Order
New York Site	P3
shinyapple.msft Domain	P3, P1
NA Organizational Unit	P3, P1, P2
SA Organizational Unit	P3, P1
IT Organizational Unit	P3, P1, P2
HR Organizational Unit	P3, P1, P4
Acct. Organizational Unit	P3, P1, P4, P5
Workstations Organizational Unit	P3, P1, P2
ITServers Organizational Unit	P3, P1, P2, P6
Acct. Servers Organizational Unit	P3, P1, P4, P5, P7

To clarify the variations of GPO processing, take a look at the following scenarios of policy application based on the hierarchy defined in Figure 6.3.2.

GPO Setting Conflict Resolution

Scenario: The P3 and P1 policies both have the logon banner setting defined. Conflict occurs and the winner is always the GPO closest to the object where the policy is getting applied. Hence, the P1 policy logon banner setting will take precedence.

GPO Inheritance

Scenario: The P3 policy has a logon banner enabled and the P1 policy does not, so the P3 policy setting will apply. Although the SA Organizational Unit has no defined policy, it will still receive the logon banner from the New York site GPO, as well as any GPO settings from the New York site P1 policy, because of the inheritance of the GPO settings from its parent container.

The previous two scenarios described GPO processing and application when a single policy is applied to an OU. Processing of multiple GPOs on a single OU adds another variable to the equation.

Multiple GPOs Linked to a Single OU

Scenario: GPO P4 and P5 have multiple settings configured and are both linked to the Acct. OU. A machine configuration policy has been set in the P4 GPO to allow members of the Accounting Global Group to have logon locally permission to any machine within or beneath the Acct. OU in the hierarchy. A machine configuration policy has been set in the P5 GPO, as well as defining logon locally rights to any machine within or beneath the Acct. OU in the hierarchy. However, the Accounting Global Group has not been defined as a security group with the permissions to log on locally. The P5 policy is displayed in the Domain Controller's Properties/Group Policy tab at the top of the list above policy P4 (see Figure 6.3.3)

Figure 6.3.3   Multiple group policies can be linked to the same object, whether that is a site, a Domain, or an Organizational Unit.

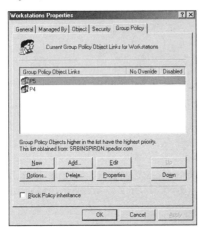

Because multiple policies linked to the same OU are applied from the bottom up, the logon locally settings defined in the P5 policy are processed last and will be applied. Therefore, members of the Accounting Global Group will not be able to directly log on to any computers within the Acct. OU or any of its sub-OUs. The processing order can be modified via the up and down buttons in the lower-right corner of the Group Policy tab.

Of interest is the capability to exclude portions of GPO from being evaluated. This positively affects overall login time for the end user. Fewer settings to evaluate means faster processing of the inherited and accumulated Group Policy settings that get applied. This can be configured on a GPO-by-GPO link basis and is done as follows:

1   From within the Active Directory Users and Computers snap-in, high-light the appropriate container and bring up the Properties dialog box GPO tab.

2   Set focus on the GPO you wish to modify.

3   Click the Properties button.

4   You can choose to exclude either the user configuration or machine configuration portion of the policy from inclusion in GPO application processing.

5 After you select the section of the GPO you want to disable, you are prompted by a dialog box, explaining that all settings previously applied to objects by this GPO will be reversed.

This eliminates the issues that NT 4.0 policies had with not properly cleaning up after themselves and effectively tattooing a box until another policy changed any settings that the removed policy made.

This setting is tied directly to the GPO itself. Simply put, any container that the policy is currently linked to will no longer receive the settings in the disabled portion of the policy

Block Policy Inheritance

Further flexibility in GPO processing is derived from the capability to block inheritance of policies from parent containers. For example, if you wanted only the settings defined at or below the IT organizational unit to be applied, you could select the Block Policy Inheritance checkbox on the IT OU Group Policy properties page. In doing so, the P1 and P3 GPO would not get applied to the IT, Workstations, or IT Servers OUs. This is a gross setting and applies to all GPOs that are assigned higher in the hierarchy.

The next setting that can affect GPO processing is the No Override option.

No Override

Unlike Block Policy Inheritance, the No Override option affects GPOs on a GPO-by-GPO basis, not on a container-by-container basis. This setting will affect the individual conflict resolution at a settings level, regardless of where the target objects are set in the hierarchy beneath it. If you bring up the Properties page for the shinyapple.msft Domain and set the No Override option on the P1 GPO, all settings within that GPO will be applied. You use this option when the settings must be applied to all objects that reside lower in the hierarchy. Security settings are a good example of when this option is useful. When the Block Policy Inheritance checkbox has been selected, No Override always takes precedence.

Group Policy Filtering

One of the last ways to modify GPO processing is to filter applications based on security group membership, user account, or machine account. This can be accomplished by using Access Control Lists much like ACLs in the NTFS file system. ACL for Group Policy objects are configured on the policy itself and will affect the object, regardless of where it is linked. For a policy to apply to an object, the object must have Read and Apply Group Policy set to Allow. If Apply Group Policy is removed, the security group or user account in question will not get the policy applied to it.

The component piece that hasn't been discussed yet is the Local policy that exists by default on all Windows 2000 systems. Much like 9.*x* and NT, the administrator has the capability to configure a Local policy on the workstation if desired. In fact, the processing order is as follows: Local policy, Site policy, Domain policy, and Organizational Unit policy (L, S, D, OU). If conflicts occur between the Site, Domain, or OU policy, the Local policy always loses.

Debugging

To log processing of user profile and system policy, follow these steps:

 1 Use Registry Editor to add the following Registry value (or modify it, if the value already exists):

   Key:
KEY_LOCAL_MACHINE\Software\Microsoft\WindowsNT\CurrentVersion\Winlogon

      Value: UserEnvDebugLevel

      Value Type: REG_DWORD

      Value Data: 0x10002 (Hex)

 2 After you make this change, restart the computer.

      The log file is written to the %SystemRoot%\Debug\Userenv.log file.

Now that you have a complete understanding of how the policies get applied in your environment, Table 6.3.2 details what mechanisms initiate that application. There are several different ways to kick off GPO application.

Table 6.3.2   Group Policy Initiation

User Policy	Machine Policy
Logon	Boot
Policy Refresh Interval	Policy Refresh Interval
Secedit /refreshpolicy user_policy	Secedit /refreshpolicy machine_policy

All settings—with the exception of logon/startup scripts, logoff/shutdown scripts, and any software installation either assigned or published—are refreshed by default every 90 minutes, with a variable plus or minus 30-minute offset. This is driven by the client-side GP engine and is based on the last time the client received a policy refresh. When the process is initiated, the version numbers of all applicable policies are compared with the local versions. If local and remote version numbers do not match, the entire GPO is reapplied; otherwise, no update takes place. The default refresh rates for Domain Controllers is five minutes.

Clients that Can Use Group Policy

As you implement Windows 2000 in your environment, there will be a period of transition in which legacy operating systems will exist until upgraded. It is important to understand the scope of GPOs in this type of environment. The following list describes which operating systems can take full advantage of Group Policy objects.

- **Windows 2000 Server.** Computers running Windows 2000 Server can either be ordinary member servers of the Active Directory or Domain Controllers (DCs). Group Policy fully supports both.

- **Windows 2000 Professional.** Group Policy fully supports client computers running Windows 2000 Professional.

- **Windows NT 4.0 Workstation and Server.** These clients continue to be fully supported by NT 4.0-style System Policy, for which the System Policy editor (poledit.exe) is provided. The administrator uses poledit.exe to write NT 4.0-style .adm files.

  Windows NT 4.0 does not use the Active Directory and Windows NT 4.0 computers do not have local Group Policy Objects, so Group Policy does not apply.

- **Windows 98 and Windows 95.** For Windows 95 and 98 clients, you need to use the System Policy Editor provided with Windows 98 or Windows 95, and copy the resultant .pol file to the SysVol folder. The System Policy editors supplied with Windows 2000 or Windows NT are not compatible with Windows 98 or Windows 95. Group Policy does not apply.

- **Windows NT 3.51, Windows 3.1 and DOS.** Group Policy does not apply.

Logon and Logoff Scripts

Windows NT allowed a script entry to be associated with each user account to accomplish any number of initial tasks required to set up the user's environment at logon time. This functionality is available on a user-by-user basis on the Windows 2000 platform as well. In addition to that base feature, you now have the ability to apply startup as well as shutdown scripts. On top of the added script types (startup and shutdown), the advent of the Windows Scripting Host shell allows you to perform true application logic in the form of Visual Basic script or Jscript. With that said, let's look at some options for assigning scripts in Windows 2000.

- **Scripts specified in the User Object.** These scriptsare handled in the same manner as NT 4.0 clients and exist mainly for compatibility reasons. Windows 2000 or NT 4.0 clients look for these scripts in the Netlogon share of the server; if not found, they look in the NT 4.0 script style location %SystemRoot%\system32\Repl\Import\Scripts. The Netlogon share is on Sysvol (sysvol\Domain.name\SCRIPTS) and is automatically replicated by FRS. Replication for the NT 4.0 location must be set up manually, as is required for NT 4.0.

- **Scripts specified by Group Policy.** This method allows for the OU-specific application of scripts. In other words, as users are added to an OU that has logon scripts defined in the GPO for that OU, those users will receive the defined logon or logoff script by means of membership within that OU. This is the most flexible of the two options.

Several other issues exist relative to scripts and migration to the 2000 platform. Because coexistence occurs in most environments, at least for a short time, you need to plan to upgrade your NETLOGON export server last. This is because of the change in the replication services used in Windows 2000. File replication service (FRS) is not backward-compatible with the NT replication service. To bridge this gap, you need to facilitate a mechanism for synchronizing netlogon and scripts directories on the different platforms because down-level clients could potentially validate on any DC.

With Windows NT, the user logon scripts ran in the security context of the user. For user-oriented scripts, this holds true for Windows 2000 as well. However, the startup and shutdown scripts run under the security context of the local system.

Delegating Administration of Group Policies

As with Organizational Units, you can delegate control of the Group Policies within your enterprise. Access Control List entries allow for link only or modify only. This is particularly useful if you wish to lock down the creation of unauthorized Group Policy objects and centralize that creation. This is a healthy tack to take; in doing so, you eliminate the chance that an unauthorized setting or action is allowed on the workstation or server desktop. Due to the one-to-many implementation of GPOs, a central architectural team can be put in charge of a common set of policies that all individuals with delegated rights to sections of the directory would have the ability to link with. They would select the GPOs that fit their particular needs and link them to containers that they have delegated authority to, but would not be able to author their own or modify those that already exist.

Using Group Policies to Manage User Documents and Offline Folders

One of the most useful options you have available within Group Policies is the ability to redirect user folders to network or specific local locations. The folders included in this feature are as follows:

- Application data
- Desktop

- My Documents
- My Pictures
- Start menu

The folder redirection is one part of the Intellimirror technology, whose goal is based on the need to allow for completed configuration and data availability, regardless of what workstation the user is sitting at. This also inherently allows for system failure without loss of user data or settings.

Redirection is configured in the User Configuration/Windows Settings/Folder Redirection section of the Group Policy object. Each of the previously stated folders is displayed. To configure redirection, right-click the folder of your choice and left-click Properties. The initial tab, labeled Target, allows for the following three choices:

- **No administrative policy specified.**

- **Basic.** Redirects everyone's folder to the same location. This allows a UNC path variable such as %username%, so that one redirection policy can accommodate multiple users. However, all accounts must be located under a single network share.

- **Advanced.** Special locations for various user groups. An implementation of this setting could use user security group definitions within the hierarchy to redirect to separate servers because of the ability to specify unique UNC paths for each group (see Figure 6.3.4).

Figure 6.3.4 Individual locations can be specified for folder redirection based on security account.

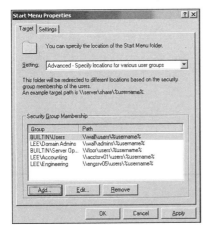

Best Practices for Group Policy Architecture and Application

- Use descriptive titles for your Group Policy objects. This helps to determine at a glance what the functions are.

- If either the user configuration or computer configuration segments of the GPO have no settings configured, disable that portion. This will decrease overall processing time and server load.

- Use caution when exercising the Block Inheritance and No Override functions. Troubleshooting becomes very convoluted in an environment that overuses these functions. The majority of the reasons to use these features can be addressed by a well-thought-out GPO design.

VII

Managing Applications

7.1

Overview of Managing Applications

You Need to Read This Section If You Want to:

- Automatically install software on a Windows 2000 desktop.
- Make programs available for installation in Control Panel/Add and Remove Programs.
- Have software available to users no matter where they login.

Related Topics

For More Information On ▶ *See*

Windows 2000 Software Distribution and Management

Installing software on user desktops is one of the most time-consuming tasks for LAN administrators. Whenever a user needs new software, someone has to go to the user's workstation and perform the install manually. Secure operating systems such as Windows NT complicate this even more because security rights are often required to install many software packages. Even if users are knowledgeable enough to install software themselves, they don't always have enough security rights to do the install. Public area workstations that seem to need every application, and roaming users who use a variety of workstations complicate the problem even more. Finally, the increasing pace of new releases guarantee that software installation is a never-ending task. LAN administrators can spend most of their time just installing, upgrading, troubleshooting, and removing software from workstations. In the past, the only solution to this dilemma was complex software distribution systems such as Microsoft System Management Server 2.0.

?   **How is Software Distribution Different in SMS?**

Systems Management Server 2.0 provides advanced features for software distribution that are not handled by software installation in Windows 2000: licensing and metering, queries of workstation status prior to installation, management of distribution points, and reporting of installation success or failure. SMS also supports software distribution to all Windows platforms.

Windows 2000 has a solution to this time-consuming problem that does not require additional software. Using Group Policy Objects (GPOs), software can be distributed to groupings of users or computers in the Active Directory. Software can be pre-installed on a computer, installed the first time a user needs it, or simply made available for installation in a categorized list. Three basic tasks make these software installations possible:

1 Obtain a Windows Installer package, repackage the application using a third-party tool, or create a .ZAP file.
   ▶ *For more information, see Chapter 7.3, "Windows Installer."*

2 Copy the software and package file to either a network share or a DFS node that is accessible by the users who will be doing the install.
   ▶ *For more information, see Chapter 5.4, "Distributed File System (DFS)."*

3 Create a package in Software Settings under either the Computer or User section of an appropriate GPO.
   ▶ *For more information, see Chapter 7.2, "Publishing and Assigning Applications."*

Distributed File System (DFS)

DFS is a virtual file system that separates the structure presented to a user from the physical storage locations where the files are stored. The DFS root represents the top of the virtual hierarchy and can be either standalone or fault-tolerant. The use of a fault-tolerant DFS root requires Active Directory, but it supports multiple synchronized DFS child nodes. When a user requests access to a fault-tolerant child node, Active Directory uses its physical site structure to determine which DFS node to use. The use of fault-tolerant DFS nodes as storage locations facilitates the efficient distribution of installation source code throughout an enterprise network.

Publishing and Advertising Applications

Software can be either published or assigned for installation. Assigning an application adds shortcuts to the Start menu on the Windows 2000 desktop. Choosing one of these shortcuts will launch Windows Installer to install the application. Assigned applications may also be invoked by accessing a file ending in an extension associated with that particular application. For example, double-clicking on a file with an .xls extension might launch the installation for Microsoft Excel.

Publishing will add the software to a list of programs available for installation in the Add and Remove Programs icon of the Control Panel. Published applications have the option of also being installed when a user accesses an associated file with the proper extension.

Publishing and assigning applications can be combined with Users and Computers in three ways:

- **Published to a User.** Applications published to a user will appear in the Add New Programs list under the Add and Remove Programs icon in the Control Panel. Users can install them by clicking on the entries.

- **Assigned to a Computer.** Applications assigned to a computer will install during computer startup.

- **Assigned to a User.** Applications assigned to a user will install Startup menu entries and Registry settings during logon. Installation will complete the first time a user chooses the menu entry or accesses a data file with an associated extension. The application can also appear in the Control Panel with Published Applications.

Applications Cannot Be Published to Computers

Published applications must be invoked from the Add and Remove Software in the Control Panel to complete installation. Because only a user can complete this type of install, applications cannot be published to computers.

▶ *For more information, see Chapter 7.2, "Publishing and Assigning Applications."*

Windows Installer

The Windows Installer service is a toolset that Microsoft created to standardize and enhance the process of installing applications. The tools are freely available to software vendors and are supported by Windows 95, 98, NT, and 2000 operating systems. But only Windows 2000 desktops support using Installer to install software packages embedded in a GPO.

Active Directory can use Windows Installer to install three different types of packages:

- **Native installer files** are obtained from the original software vendor. For example, Microsoft uses Windows Installer to install Office 2000. Native installer files can also be created in Visual Studio for applications developed in-house. Native installer files support the fullest set of features. For example: critical file repair, first-use installation, feature set-based installation, and so on.

- **Repackaged applications** are created using a third-party tool to take a before and after install snapshot of a target workstation. A sample third-party tool, WinINSTALL LE, ships on the Windows 2000 CD. Repackaged applications do not support all the advanced features that Native installer files do.

- **A Zero Administration Package (.ZAP)** file is a text file that contains the command line, install parameters, and file extensions for an application's normal setup program. ZAP files support the fewest features of any Windows Installer package.

  ▶ *For more information, see Chapter 7.3, "Windows Installer."*

Upgrading, Patching, and Removing Applications

Applications that have been installed using a GPO Installer package can also be upgraded, patched, or removed. Upgrading an existing application involves installing a new application in place of the old one, and can be either mandatory or optional. Complete removal of the old application may be required during the upgrade.

Sometimes, an upgrade simply requires replacing certain files, not installing a completely new version of the software. This is called *patching*. Patching applies only to applications that were installed using Native Installer Files. A patch is applied by obtaining an .MSP or .MSI file from the original vendor. The new files and the patch file are copied to the original shared location and a new package is created in the GPO that handled the original install.

Applications can also be removed using a GPO after their usefulness has expired. Special care needs to be taken during repackaging if an application is to be removed later. Applications installed via a .ZAP file cannot be removed automatically. They can be removed only if their Setup program provides for an uninstall parameter, which is then used to create a new .ZAP file to control the uninstallation.

▶ *For more information, see Chapter 7.2, "Publishing and Assigning Applications."*

7.2

Publishing and Assigning Applications

You Need To Read This Section If You Want To:

- Make applications available for users to choose to install.
- Preinstall applications on specific computers.
- Choose specific features to be installed
- Update applications with new releases.
- Modify existing applications by installing patches.
- Uninstall programs when they are no longer needed.
- Fine-tune software installation through Group Policy settings.

Related Topics

For More Information On	▶ See
Creating Group Policies	▶ *Chapter 6.3: Group Policies*
User and computer desktop configuration settings	▶ *Chapter 6.2: Profiles*
Sharing a subdirectory	▶ *Chapter 5.3: Sharing Folders*
Creating a DFS node	▶ *Chapter 5.4: Distributed File System (DFS)*
Deploying Windows 2000	▶ *Chapter 2.2: Installing Windows 2000 Server*
Redirecting data folders	▶ *Chapter 6.3: Group Policies*

Publishing Applications

Publishing applications makes software available for end users to install, but it leaves choice and control in the hands of the user. When planning for software distribution, it's a good idea to use published applications for programs that everyone may use, but not everyone will choose to install. For example, suppose your company allows users to work in either Microsoft Excel or Lotus 1-2-3. By publishing both applications, you can allow users to choose which one to use without installing both applications on every computer.

Published applications do not automatically install on a workstation when the GPO containing them is processed. Nor are shortcuts visibly added on the desktop or the Start menu. Instead, published applications appear in a categorized list under the Add/Remove Programs icon in Control Panel. (See "Setting Software Installation Defaults" for ways to create categories).

Users must choose to install an application that is published. Even users without administrative security permissions will be able to install applications by using the heightened security privileges of the Windows Installer Service.
▶ *For more information, see Chapter 7.3, "Windows Installer."*

Because a user is always involved in the installation of a published application, applications cannot be published through software settings on the Computer side of a GPO.

Published applications can also be invoked by accessing file extensions associated with the application (for example, a .doc file for Microsoft Word). This behavior is controlled by a checkbox (Auto-install this application by file extension activation) that may be chosen when publishing an application (see Figure 7.2.1). The checkbox is selected by default when publishing or assigning an application. Because multiple programs can use the same file extension, applications must be prioritized so that only one application will install when a file extension is invoked.
▶ *For more information on how to adjust application precedence, see "Setting Software Installation Defaults" later in this chapter.*

Figure 7.2.1   Configuring a software installation package.

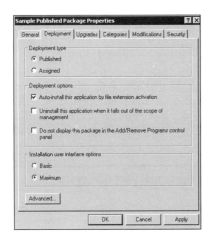

Assigning Applications

Assigning applications to computers or users is a good way to preinstall or give the appearance of preinstalling applications. Assigning applications to users is a good way to support roaming users who log in from a variety of workstations. Assigning applications to computers can be used to preinstall common software packages used by everyone. Computer assignments can even be used as part of a deployment strategy, which uses RIS to install the operating system and assigned applications to install standard software.

Applications assigned to users will only install desktop and Start menu short-cuts when a user logs on. This minimizes the time required for installation during logon. It also limits the amount of disk space required unless a user actually uses the assigned program. Applications assigned to computers will fully install during computer startup. Both types will create file associations in the Registry for the application.

Startup/Logon/Installation Delays

Installing software takes time. A user's perception of the time it takes will depend on whether you choose to publish or assign applications. Publishing allows the user to decide when to spend the time to install an application. Assigning to a computer delays the logon prompt while software is installed, but users are often more tolerant of delays during startup. Finally, assigning to a user is the most intrusive because it installs when a user tries to use an application. However, applications installed this way will break up the installation time by installing features one at a time as they are needed. Although the total time used for installation will probably increase, breaking it up into smaller bits may lessen a user's perception of that time.

Assigning applications to a user will guarantee that the user will have it available on every desktop when needed. But the application will completely install only if the user actually needs it. Until then, it will simply appear to be installed through the creation of Registry entries and shortcuts. Of course, that means there will be a delay while the application is installed the first time a user starts it on a new workstation.

Assigning an application to a computer will preinstall the application on that workstation the next time the workstation restarts. The application will be immediately available to anyone who needs it. Also, because the application is being installed before a user logs on, there is no way to limit access to the application. It will automatically be installed as part of the All Users profile.

Using Install on First Use When Applications are Assigned to Computers

Applications assigned to users install by only adding Registry entries and Start menu shortcuts. This decreases the time and disk space required during the logon process. A similar effect can be achieved with applications assigned to computers by using a transform (.mst file) to set the features of the program to Install on first use. Windows Installer will then install only Registry entries and Start menu shortcuts during the initial install. When a user invokes the application, installation will be completed just as it is when applications are assigned to users.

Applying Transforms

Transform (.mst) files are used by Windows Installer to choose which features and/or products to install from a given "Native" Installer file. Transform files may be provided by a vendor, but are more commonly created using a wizard provided by the vendor. For example, the Microsoft Office 2000 Resource Kit includes a Custom Installation Wizard that can be used to create an .mst file.
▶ *For more information on components, features, and products, see Chapter 7.3, "Windows Installer."*

Suppose you have two groups of users: administrative assistants and accountants. The only Office application the administrative assistants really need is Word, and you want to limit their installation to that product because they are working on older workstations and have limited disk space available. You would also like to eliminate the Grammar Checker feature from their installation to save space. The accountants need the full range of Office applications, especially Excel. They also need some custom add-ins and COM objects that are used by some custom spreadsheets. To accommodate these two sets of installation requirements, you need to complete the following steps.

1　Create a network-accessible distribution point (either a share or a DFS node) and complete an administrative install to this location (for some applications, this simply means copying the contents of the CD).

Hint: Not all the CDs will be needed if you are installing a subset of features. But one network location can be used by a number of GPOs, so you may want to copy everything to this one location and reuse it.

2 Run the Custom Installation Wizard twice and choose the products and features that you want included/excluded in each installation. Save the results in two different .mst files on the network share.

3 Create two GPOs that will apply to the appropriate users, either by linking them to appropriate OUs or by restricting Read and Apply Policy security to appropriate Groups.

Hint: Use security restrictions sparingly because they are much more difficult to track down when troubleshooting.

4 Create a package in each GPO and immediately add the appropriate .mst file to the Modifications tab of the package properties. Either Assigning or Publishing will work in this scenario, but Publishing will require users to complete an extra step before the application is usable.

Applying Transforms to a Package

Transforms are available only with "Native" Installer files and must be added to a Software Installation Package before the package is saved to the GPO. To use a Transform, make sure you choose the Advanced assign or publish option when creating the GPO. Choosing to either Assign or Publish a package and then opening the properties of the package will not give you access to the ADD button on the Modifications tab.

Upgrading Applications

Upgrading an application can mean a number of different things. Usually, upgrading means replacing one version of an application with a newer release of the same application for example, replacing Office 97 with Office 2000). It could also mean replacing one application with a completely different application (for example, replacing Lotus 1-2-3 with Microsoft Excel). Finally, it might simply mean applying a service pack or patch to an existing application.

Varying support is available for upgrading applications that were originally installed through GPO Software Installation. Complete replacement of an application is accomplished through an .msi file. Patching an application is accomplished through an .msp file.

Upgrades can be either optional or mandatory. An option also allows for a preceding application to be completely removed prior to installation of an upgrade.

Setting Software Installation Defaults

Software installation defaults can be controlled by accessing the properties of the software installation object in any GPO (see Figure 7.2.2). Settings on the General tab and File Extensions tab are defaults for this particular instance of software installation.

Figure 7.2.2   Setting software installation defaults.

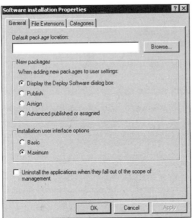

The General tab contains settings that control the defaults used when a new package is created. You can choose a default location to look for .msi files. You can also specify whether new packages will default to giving you a choice, being published, being assigned, or taking you directly to the properties page. The default user interface level and uninstall characteristics can also be set. All of these defaults can be overridden through the properties page of a package after it is created.

The File Extensions tab deals with the problem of too many applications using the same file extension. If more than one application, installed through Group Policy Objects, uses the same file extension, you can adjust which application will be installed if the user invokes a file with a particular extension. For example, suppose your company supports the use of both Microsoft Word and Corel WordPerfect for editing files with the extension .doc. Both applications are published through GPOs. Only one of these applications can be automatically installed when a user double-clicks on a .doc file in Windows Explorer.

Application precedence controls which application will be installed when a user invokes a particular file extension. To adjust the relative priority of applications, choose a particular file extension in the Select file extension drop-down box. Application priority can then be altered by using the up and down buttons. The application at the top of the list will be given priority for installation. For example, an administrator allows a group of users to install either

Word or AMI Pro by publishing them in a particular GPO. The users choose which to install through Add/Remove programs in Control Panel. But the apps can also be installed based on file extension invocation. Changing application priority allows you to specify whether Word or Ami Pro will be installed if a user double-clicks on a .doc file. If the priority is not changed, the last package added to the GPO will be installed.

?   **Why Can't I See All My File Extensions?**

The file extensions list visible in any particular GPO is limited to those extensions used by applications published or assigned by that particular GPO. Extensions used by a particular application must be preset in the .msi package file. If an application is published or assigned through another GPO or if it doesn't normally use a particular file extension, those extensions will not be visible.

The Categories tab contains a list of all the software installation categories that have been created for this domain. You can customize the list using the Add, Modify, and Remove buttons. Categories are set in an individual GPO but stored as a Domain-wide attribute. The trick is to figure out which Domain is affected. If you are editing properties on a GPO created through an OU, it affects the Domain containing the OU. Domain GPO properties are associated with the Domain where they were created. Site GPOs can be created only by a member of Enterprise Admins and are stored in the SYSVOL of the forest root Domain, so they affect the root Domain of the forest. GPOs that are linked to an additional OU, Domain, or site affect the Domain where they were originally created. Linked GPOs can be identified by looking for a Domain name in parentheses after the GPO. After categories have been created here, they can be used on the Categories tab in individual packages to categorize the way software is listed under the Add/Remove Programs icon in Control Panel.

Removing Applications

Uninstalling applications cleanly has always been a problem in the Windows environment. Some vendors have created uninstall routines that will remove most of the Registry settings, shortcuts, icons, files, and directories used by an application. But this type of support is not universal and each vendor implements it differently.

The Windows Installer service supports two levels of uninstallation support. The first is a simple clean removal of application. The second is the capability to "roll back" an installation by replacing the files and Registry entries removed or changed during an installation.

▶ *For more information, see Chapter 7.3, "Windows Installer."*

This clean removal and rollback are available only for applications installed through .msi files. Applications installed through .zap files cannot be automatically uninstalled or rolled back. If the setup program of an application supports an uninstall switch, these applications can be removed by creating a new .zap file that contains the uninstall command line. Software installation makes use of this capability to remove applications installed using .msi files through GPOs. Applications can be removed in three ways:

- An optional setting on the Deployment tab (refer to Figure 7.2.1) allows for an application to be automatically uninstalled when this GPO no longer applies to the user or computer. For example, when a user or computer is moved from one OU, site, or Domain to another, applications assigned or published through the old GPO will be removed if this checkbox is set.

- Packages can also be manually removed from a GPO by right-clicking and choosing the Remove task. When a package is removed from a GPO, a dialog box is presented that allows for forced removal of the application from any workstations where it was installed. This option is only presented once.

- An application can also be removed through the Add/Remove Programs icon in Control Panel.

   Note: Assigned applications cannot be permanently removed. They will be reinstalled during the next startup or logon, depending on whether they were assigned to computers or users.

Creating Software Policy Templates

Application packages provide varying support for customizing the user's environment. Some applications, such as Microsoft Office, provide wizards that support creation of a user profile to control items such as the shortcuts and the location of various files. But other programs will install only the basic application. One workaround for packages that lack this type of customization is to create a custom administrative template. This .adm file can be loaded into the GPO along with the software package. Customization of the user's environment can then be handled by modifying the Registry through the .adm file.
▶ *For more information, see Chapter 6.3, "Group Policies."*

Some applications support both the wizard approach and use of an .adm file. For example, Microsoft Office 2000 ships with a set of .adm files that allow for customization. The Microsoft Office 2000 Resource Kit also includes utility programs for creating profiles and using them as part of an .mst deployment (refer to "Applying Transforms").

Controlling Software Deployment through Group Policy Object Settings

There are four locations under Administrative Templates in a GPO that control the behavior of Group Policy and software installation. Two of these locations, one under User and one under Computer, control the workings of the Windows Installer Service and will be dealt with in Chapter 7.3, "Windows Installer." The third location is the Group Policy settings under Computer Configuration/Administrative Templates/System/Group Policy. Table 7.2.1 lists the major settings in this area that affect the behavior of software installation. These settings are all disabled by default except the slow link detection that defaults to a connection rate of 500 kbps. The fourth location, under User Configuration/Administrative Templates/System/Group Policy, contains no settings that have a particular effect on software installation.

Table 7.2.1 How Settings Affect the Behavior of Software

Setting	Effect
Apply Group Policy for computers asynchronously during Logon	If enabled, the Logon prompt will not wait until policy updates are complete. Depending on the time required to install applications assigned to computers, Logon may finish before software installation is complete.
Apply Group Policy for users asynchronously during Logon	If enabled, the desktop may appear before applications assigned to users finish installing. Because these applications normally install only shortcuts and Registry entries, this is unlikely.
Group Policy slow link detection	This setting determines the speed used as a threshold value for determining what is a slow link. Slow links are used most often to prevent policy processing and software installation across dial-up connections. (See "Software Installation Policy Processing" for ways to override this setting for software installation.)
Software Installation Policy Processing	This allows two settings that affect software installation to be set. The Allow processing across a slow network connection option allows for software installation, even over a slow connection. The Process even if the Group Policy objects have not changed option reapplies the software installation policy, even if it has not changed. This will enforce software settings made through software installation, even if the user has manually changed the setting after installation. It requires more time, but it will enforce standardized software installation policies.

Going Deeper: Practical Applications

Now that you understand the differences between publishing to a user, assigning to a user, and assigning to a computer, take a look at how you might use these to manage desktops in a network. We'll also discuss the licensing considerations behind each implementation.

Publishing to a User

You publish applications to users when you want to make an organized list of applications available for anyone who needs them to install. Publishing is best when you can't predict who might need to use the specific application or when the users of an application don't fit your Domain/site/OU structure. You'll need either a site license or enough licenses to cover everyone covered by the GPO. Although everyone who has access to the application may not install it, they could—so you'll have to license for that eventuality. Applications that fit into this model are the following:

- Applications developed in-house that are available to everyone, but not used by everyone
- Public utility programs such as disk defragmenters, backup utilities, etc.
- Office suites such as Office 2000 for companies with a select agreement

Assigning to a User

Assigning applications to users is the best way to support roaming users. A roaming user might be a temporary clerical person who is assigned a different desk on a regular basis. Or it might be a LAN administrator who wants specific utility programs available when they sit down to troubleshoot someone else's workstation. It could even be any user in an environment who uses a "hoteling" concept in their office without purchasing laptop computers for everyone. That way, everyone gets their own programs, no matter which specific computer they are assigned to today. Applications assigned to users follow them around the network. You should also use *folder redirection* to ensure that data follows the users as well.

▶ *For more information, see Chapter 6.3, "Group Policies."*

Applications installed this way should always be set to install in the User's profile, not in the All User's profile. If you do that, you'll only need enough licenses for users covered by the GPO. The application files may be physically installed on multiple workstations, but it will not be usable by other users. Applications that fit this model include the following:

- Office suites: Office 2000, for example, where licenses are purchased for individual users.

- Client front-ends: Small client programs for n-tiered client/server development systems.

- Licensed utility programs: Disk Imagers such as *Ghost*, troubleshooting tools such as Norton Utilities, and help desk research engines such as Technet.

Assigning to a Computer

Applications assigned to a computer automatically install on startup into the All Users profile on a computer. This makes them available to anyone who later logs on to that computer. Standardized image installation is one possible use for this type of deployment. By using the Windows 2000 Setup Manager, you can create an unattended install script for Windows 2000 professional or server

▶ *For more information, see Chapter 2.2, "Installing Windows 2000 Server."*

Then, use application assignment to preinstall a standardized set of programs on first boot. Of course, you'll need enough licenses to cover every computer installed using this method. Any application that should be installed on every workstation for every user is a candidate for this type of installation. Virus scanners are probably the best example of this type of program.

Best Practices

- Verify network share security. Use network shares to hold the installation source code and .msi files for applications being installed through GPOs. Always verify that average users have Read access to the share. Inability to read the share is the most common problem when software fails to install through a GPO.

- Use fault-tolerant DFS nodes. Fault-tolerant DFS nodes will use the IP address of a workstation to determine which physical network share to use when fulfilling a software installation request. It also provides fault-tolerance, which prevents the need to redeploy packages to recover from installation failure.

- Organize software deployment. Don't assign an application to one group of users and then publish it to another. You should also try to avoid deploying the same application through two different GPOs. Instead, create one GPO and link it to different OUs. You should also be careful not to have the same application installed twice along the same branch of an OU hierarchy. The more structured and organized your deployment planning and documentation, the easier it will be to troubleshoot later.

7.3
Windows Installer

You Need to Read This Section If You Want to:

- Repackage applications using WinINSTALL LE.
- Create .zap installation files.
- Install patches to current applications.
- Control the behavior of the Windows Installer through Group Policy Settings.

Related Topics

Windows Installer

The Windows platform has never had an integrated software-installation system. Instead, software developers have been responsible for creating their own installation routines. Most of these routines use script-based engines, which create directories, install files, and establish Registry entries. This approach coupled with a lack of standardization has led to several problems:

- Difficulty uninstalling applications because some vendors do not adequately track the use of shared files
- Configuration problems due to overwriting existing system .dlls with incorrect versions
- Inability to repair applications where files have been corrupted
- Incomplete "rollback" of failed installations
- No support for installation with security privileges higher than the end user

The Windows Installer service resolves all of these problems. The Windows Installer service consists of three parts:

- An operating system-resident installation service
- A set of standards for component management
- An API for applications and tools to access the resident service

Windows 2000 uses the installer service with Group Policy Objects (GPOs) to automate software installation. The service is also available for Windows 95, Windows 98, and Microsoft Windows NT 4.0, but these operating systems cannot read GPOs. Office 2000 is probably the most popular use of the Windows Installer service, but more applications are sure to follow.

Components, Features, and Products

Instead of working with individual files and Registry entries, the Windows Installer works with components, features, and products.

Components are the smallest building blocks used by Windows Installer. A *component* is a collection of files, Registry entries, and shortcuts that are installed or uninstalled as a single unit. For example, the Registry entries and .dlls, which make up the Spelling Checker in Microsoft Office, are a component. Files, Registry entries, and shortcuts are never part of more than one component. This prevents conflicts created when different programs install or uninstall the same component. Because there is no overlap between components, it doesn't matter whether the same component is installed twice. Different features can make use of the same component, but different components can't make use of the same file. This allows for transaction-based installation, which also facilitates rollback. It also supports installation on first use.

Components are created and handled by programmers who create the software. End users interact with Windows Installer at the Feature level and do not need to concern themselves with specific components.

Components provide an easy way to track critical files for automatic repair when they become corrupted or overwritten. Components also make it easier to patch or upgrade applications by upgrading an entire component.

Features are collections of components, which relate to a specific function of a product. Features can also be collections of other features. Features are often nested to present a more usable view of installation for the user. When a user does a custom install of an application such as Office, they are viewing a list of all the features available for installation. Features, like components, are single entities and do not overlap. Because they don't overlap, features can be used to do an Install on First Use.

At the highest level, Windows Installer uses products. *Products* are represented by a single .msi file, which contains the database of features and components that make up the product. (see Table 7.3.1) Microsoft Office 2000 is an example of a product and PowerPoint 2000 is a feature. If you purchase Microsoft PowerPoint 2000 alone, it would be the product and the graphical import filters would be individual features.

Windows Installer File Types

The Windows Installer service makes use of a number of different file extensions. Table 7.3.1 summarizes the different files and their uses.

Table 7.3.1   Capabilities of Various Package Types

File Type	File Name Extension	Description
Windows Installer packages	.msi	This is the primary file used by the Windows Installer service. Software vendors will normally provide you with these files, but they can also be created using a third-party repackaging tool. The file should be stored in the same network share as the installation source files.
Transforms	.mst	Modification files customize the installation of an .msi file. They can be used to select which features of a product to install. For example, an .mst file created by the Office Resource Kit Installation Wizard might be used to choose to install Word, Excel, and PowerPoint, but not Access.

continues

Table 7.3.1   continued

File Type	File Name Extension	Description
Patches	.msp	Bug fixes and service packs can be distributed using this file. Patches are used only to make minor changes in an existing software package and to distribute new versions of existing files. Patches cannot remove components or features, they can only modify them. They also cannot change the names of shortcuts, files, or Registry keys in this form.
.zap files	.zap	These files are similar to unattended setup scripts and are created with a normal text editor. They can only be published, not assigned. Because they use a program's normal setup routine, all the standard requirements apply to the setup. This means that the user must have administrative rights to install the program and that only programs that support unattended installation from the command line can be installed without further user intervention.
Application assignment scripts	.aas	These files are created when a package is added to Software Installation in the computer or user portion of a GPO. They are stored under the packages GUID on the SYSVOL of Domain Controllers where the package was created, and contain information that controls the assignment or publication of the package. They are binary files and cannot be directly edited.

"Native" Windows Installer Packages

"Native" Windows Installer packages provide the highest level of functionality, including support for the following:

- Installing features on first use
- Running features from CD or network

- Installation of only selected features of a product
- Automatic repair of critical files in a component
- Storing multiple versions of system .dlls for various programs
- Rollback of failed installs

Microsoft Visual Studio Installer

"Native" Installer files are normally obtained from a vendor. But what if the application is developed in-house? Microsoft has made an add-on available for Visual Studio, which will allow you to make your own .msi file. Information about this free addition to Visual Studio can be downloaded from http://msdn.microsoft.com/vstudio/downloads/vsi/default.asp.

Authority Used by Microsoft Installer

To install a new application on Windows 2000 or Windows NT requires administrative permissions. Only an administrator can create the menu entries and Registry entries required for software installation. Because the Windows Installer service operates as a service, it can install applications in a higher-security context by using the service account.

Repackaging an Application

Applications without .msi files can also be repackaged, but that has certain limitations. When a vendor does not supply an .msi file, you can use a third-party utility to repackage the application as an .msi file. Microsoft includes one such tool with Windows 2000, WinINSTALL LE (Light Edition) from Veritas Software. WinINSTALL LE can be used to create new .msi files and also to change some of the information in existing .msi files.

▸ *For more information, see "Customizing Packages" later in this chapter.*

Repackaged applications have certain limitations when compared to "native" .msi files. The limitations are as follows:

- No support for feature-driven installation. All features installed when taking a snapshot will be installed by the package.

- Critical files cannot be designated. Automatic repair of files if corrupted or overwritten will not be possible.

- Installation must be done on a similar workstation. If there are major differences between the sample workstation where the application was repackaged and the final workstation, the application may not work.

? **How do I Repackage a Simple Application?**

1 Install and configure a sample workstation without the application.

2 Using a third-party application, record the current state of the workstation, including files and Registry entries. This is the Before record.

3 Install the simple application.

4 Using the same third-party tool, record the current state of the workstation. This is the After record.

5 Calculate the files and Registry entries added by comparing the After and Before records.

6 Fine-tune the list of differences. Add needed files, shortcuts, and Registry entries such as runtime modules. Also remove unneeded files, shortcuts, and Registry entries such as temporary install directories from the package.

7 Compile the resulting list of files, Registry entries, and shortcuts as an .msi file.

8 Test the resulting package on another sample workstation.

Create .zap Installation Files

Files called .zap files can also be used to install files, which do not have a native .msi file. They provide the lowest functionality of any file type used with Windows Installer. They can be used only to publish applications; an .msi file is required to assign applications.

The .zap files are created using a standard text editor. Only two entries in one section are required. The [Application] section must contain both the FriendlyName and SetupCommand entries. The FriendlyName creates a name for the application to be listed under in Add and Remove programs. The SetupCommand entry specifies the command line, which is used to install the program. The [ext], [CLSIDs], [progIDs] sections and all other settings in the [Application] section are optional.

A Sample .zap File

```
; ZAP file for MYEDITOR.EXE

[Application]
; Only the FriendlyName and SetupCommand parameters are required
; Other parameters are optional, but will set the normal contact information
➥for
; a package if included
; FriendlyName is the name of the package that will appear in the GPO or the
➥Add and
; Remove Programs icon in Control Panel
; FriendlyName = "My Text Editor"

; SetupCommand is the full command line which will install the application.
; Parameters for unattended setup should be included here. Long file names
➥should be
; surrounded by quotation marks. The path should be either the complete path
➥or
; relative to the location of the .zap file.
```

```
; For example:
; SetupCommand = "\\MyServer\My File Share\setup.exe" /unattend:yes
; or simply
; SetupCommand = setup.exe /unattend:yes
SetupCommand = install.exe

; The following are optional parameters
DisplayVersion = 3.2
Publisher = In House Productions
URL = http://www.MyHouse.com/myeditor
LCID = 1033
Architecture = intel

[ext]
; The Extensions section is optional, but specifies file extensions that
➥will be
; associated with the program. These extensions will also be used to launch
; installation for the published app if invoked. A leading dot is ignored if
; added, but the trailing '=' is required. Anything after the '=' will be
➥treated as a
; comment and ignored.
.TXT= plain Text
PRG= Source Code for a program
PPS=

[CLSIDs]
; The CLSIDs section is optional. If included it will contain a list of
➥CLSIDs that will
; invoke installation of this application. After the '=' sign will be listed
; LocalServer32, InProcServer32, and/or InprocHandler32 to specify which
➥process
; will handle the install. The entries look like this:
{00027800-0000-0000-D000-000000000064}=LocalServer32
{00028500-0000-0000-B000-000000000064}=LocalServer32, InProcServer32

[progIDs]
; The progIDs section is optional. It specifies the Program Ids of
➥application which
; will cause this app to install. The format is 'CLSID = ProgramID'
{00027800-0000-0000-D000-000000000064}=MyApp.Editor

{00028500-0000-0000-B000-000000000064}=MyCompiler.Editor
```

Customizing Packages

Third-party apps such as WinINSTALL LE can be used to modify some of
the information in either a repackaged or original .msi file. Almost anything
in an .msi file can be edited by opening it in the WinINSTALL LE's Windows
Installer Package Editor. However, changing many of the entries in an .msi
file runs the risk of ruining the .msi files' capability to install the application.
Changes to features and components should be handled through either Patch
(.msp) files or Transform (.mst) files.

▶ *For more information, see Chapter 7.2, "Publishing and Assigning Applications."*

There are items that may be safely modified directly in the .msi file. The items
are primarily used to change default vendor contact information to internal
support information for your company. For example, you may want your users
to call an internal help desk rather than the vendor's 800 number when they

experience a problem. The items that may be safely changed include the following:

- **Contact.** A contact person for information about the application.
- **Online Support.** An email address for support information.
- **Phone.** A phone number for support calls.
- **Helpfile URL.** An Internet or intranet URL in which additional help on installing the application may be found.
- **Update Info URL.** An Internet or intranet URL in which information about updates or patches may be found.

Modifying Windows Installer Behavior

There are four locations under Administrative Templates in a GPO that control the behavior of Group Policy and Software installation. Two of the locations, one under User and one under Computer, control the application of GPOs and were dealt with in Chapter 7.2. The other two locations, one under Computer and one under User, control the actions of Windows Installer. Tables 7.3.2 and 7.3.3 list the major settings in these areas that affect the behavior of software installation. You should be careful about making changes in this area. Only the Disable Windows Installer setting will result in more restricted security. All the other settings have the potential to loosen security. Many of them leave potential entry points for virus infection of your network. Finally, some of the settings must be set under both the User and Computer sections of the GPO in order to be effective. These dual settings are noted in the table.

Table 7.3.2   Settings from Computer Configuration\ Administrative Components\Windows Components\Windows Installer

Policy	Details
Disable Windows Installer	This setting can be used to disable manual use of Windows Installer. After enabling this setting, you can choose between three options: • Never. Allows the use of Windows Installer by GPOs and manual invocation by the user. • For non-managed apps only. Windows Installer can only be used when invoked by a GPO. • Always. Windows Installer is disabled and cannot be used.

Policy	Details
	This setting will not prevent users from installing apps, which do not require use of the Windows Installer.
Always install with elevated privileges	By default, the Windows Installer service account can be used only to install with elevated security privileges when installing published or advertised applications. This setting allows Windows Installer to use the elevated privileges when installing Windows Installer-based applications manually as well.
	This setting will not be effective unless you set it both in the Computer and User sections of the GPO.
Disable patching	This setting disables the installation of .msp (patch) files by Windows Installer. Because patches replace portions of installed programs, they can be used to introduce virus-contaminated files into a healthy system. Some administrators prefer to avoid this possibility by not processing .msp files.
Disable IE security prompt for Windows Installer scripts	Software installed across the Internet is one of the prime sources of viruses on computers. In order to prevent unauthorized installation, a prompt is generated whenever Windows Installer is invoked in response to a Web link. Companies who use an intranet as a software distribution mechanism may want to use this setting to disable the prompt.
Enable user control over installs	Features chosen for installation by application of an .mst (transform) file cannot normally be overridden during installation by the user. This setting allows users to select or deselect features during an installation started by a GPO.
Logging	This setting is used to change the default options for logging activity of the Windows Installer service. Disabling this setting will not disable logging; instead it will revert logging to the default settings (iweap).

Table 7.3.3   Settings from User Configuration\ Administrative Components\Windows Components\Windows Installer

Policy	Details
Always install with elevated privileges	See the same setting in Table 7.3.2.
Disable rollback	To roll back a failed installation, any files replaced or deleted during the installation must be temporarily stored. This setting disables saving those files. This will conserve on the use of disk space, but will also prevent clean uninstallation and rollback of a failed installation.
	This setting will be effective if it is set in either the Computer and User side of the GPO.

VIII
Managing
Network Services

8.1

Overview of Managing Network Services

You Need to Read This Section If You Want to:

- Design a TCP/IP network infrastructure.
- Select an IP addressing scheme.
- Manually or automatically configure TCP/IP clients.
- Access the Internet from your internal network.
- Manage the configuration of your servers.

Physical Network Planning

Windows 2000 uses the TCP/IP protocol suite by default and Active Directory requires that you use TCP/IP. But there are other protocols. Windows 2000 also supports NWLink (IPX/SPX), NetBeui, and AppleTalk. Because TCP/IP is the most widely used protocol and the default for Windows 2000, this section will focus on implementing TCP/IP. You should keep in mind that other protocols may also be necessary to support legacy network applications on your LAN.

The first step in planning your TCP/IP network is to take stock of what you have now. Find out what you have in place—how many segments or rings, how many hosts, what protocols, and what capabilities of the routers or bridges used to connect the network together. You should also try to predict the amount of future growth to expect.

Next, you need to consider what network capabilities are needed to support your business. For example, does your company need access to the Internet? Do you need support for protocols other than TCP/IP? Are there applications that use NetBIOS or host name resolution?

Finally, if you are using Active Directory, you need to consider how your subnets will be used to divide your network into physical sites. Sites are defined as a collection of TCP/IP subnets that share a high bandwidth connection. They are created in the Sites and Services MMC. Active Directory will use sites in your network to control logon traffic, replication traffic, and access to network services such as Distributed File System (DFS) resources.

▶ *For more information, see Chapter 1.2, "Introduction to Active Directory."*

After you know what your network looks like and your business requirements, it's time to translate that information into an IP addressing scheme.

IP Addressing

After you know how many physical segments or rings, the maximum number of hosts per segment, and the location of default gateways, it's time to decide on an IP addressing scheme. To do that, you need to understand what is possible. In TCP/IP, each host is identified by a unique 32-bit IP address. When used with a subnet mask, each address is divided into a two-part address, consisting of a network ID and a host ID. The network ID identifies the particular subnet where the workstation or server can be found, just as the street name in your address identifies the particular street where you live. The host ID identifies an individual workstation or server on the subnet, just as your house number identifies your house on the street. Houses on other streets may have the same house number, but not the same street address. The subnet mask is used to mask certain portions of the IP address. The 0 bits mask out the host ID portion of the address, leaving just the Network ID. The 1 bits are used in a similar fashion to mask out the Network ID, leaving just a host ID. The following is a typical 32-bit IP address, subnet mask, and the resulting network and host IDs.

```
11011000 10100000 01100100 10010011
216.160.100.147
IP Address
11111111 11111111 11111111 11100000
255.255.255.224
Subnet Mask
11011000 10100000 01100100 10000000
216.160.100.128
Network ID
00000000 00000000 00000000 00010011
0. 0. 0. 19
Host ID
```

Working with the pure 32-bit IP addresses is easy for computers but difficult for human beings. To make it easier for humans, IP addresses are expressed in dotted decimal notation. Dotted decimal notation separates the 32-bit address into four 8-bit octets that are converted to decimal (base 10). The octets are then separated by periods.

In the same way that you use a street address to find a house, a TCP/IP network uses the combination of network and host ID to route traffic around a network. But this requires that each 32-bit address is unique throughout the entire system. Because the Internet is international in scope, each IP address must be unique worldwide. To ensure that each address is unique throughout the world, an organization was established to distribute IP addresses. The Internet Assigned Numbers Authority (IANA) distributes IP addresses by dispensing licenses for ranges of IP addresses. There are five classes of address ranges that the IANA distributes. The addresses are classed according to the starting bit patterns of the leftmost octet and the default subnet mask. Table 8.1.1 summarizes the details of each address range.

Table 8.1.1   IP Address Classes

Class	Leftmost Bits	First Octet	Default Subnet Mask	Licenses Available	Potential Hosts/License
A	0	1–126	255.0.0.0	126	16,777,214
B	10	128–191	255.255.0.0	16,384	65,534
C	110	192–223	255.255.255.0	2,097,152	254
D	1110	224–239	N/A	Used for Multicasting	
E	1111	240–254	N/A	Reserved for Experimental Use	

If your network will be connected to the Internet, you must ensure that all the IP addresses on your network are unique for the Internet. An alternative is to use either a Proxy server or Network Address Translation server to keep addresses on your internal network from being seen on the Internet.

▶ *For more information, see Chapter 8.7, "Connection Sharing."*

If your network will be connected to the Internet through a connection-sharing device or will not be connected to the Internet, you can use any IP address range that you wish. IP addresses will still need to be unique within your internal network. However, the IANA has reserved certain address classes for use in just this situation. The available "private" address classes are listed in Table 8.1.2.

Table 8.1.2   IANA "Private" Address Classes

Class	Network ID	Default Subnet Mask
A	10.0.0.0	255.0.0.0
B	172.16.0.0	255.240.0.0
C	192.168.0.0	255.255.0.0

You can use these addresses on your own network, even though other people may be using them on their own internal networks. Routers on the public Internet will ignore these addresses, but they will work effectively if kept on your own internal network.

If you have only one subnet, you can also use Automatic Private IP Addressing (APIPA) to automate TCP/IP address configuration. Windows 98 or Windows 2000 DHCP clients that support AIPA will automatically config-ure themselves with an address in the range of 169.254.0.1 to 169.254.255.254, with a subnet mask of 255.255.0.0 when they can't contact a DHCP server. Like the private address ranges, this range of addresses is not used on the Internet.

Name Resolution and Service Registration

Although dotted decimal notation is easier for humans to understand than 32-bit addresses, it's still not an easy way to remember how to access network resources. Humans prefer accessing network resources through names that are more easily remembered. We would rather access a printer called HRPrinter or a server called ACCOUNTING1 than 192.168.245.32 and 208.224.35.67. But in order to use the more easily remembered names, there must be some mechanism in place to resolve the names back to the IP addresses used by the computers when networking.

Windows 2000 supports two types of name resolution: NetBIOS and Host Name Resolution. Both translate from human naming conventions to IP addresses. Although Windows 2000 is beginning to move away from NetBIOS naming in favor of the more efficient DNS naming convention, NetBIOS naming is still supported for the sake of legacy applications.

Only One Windows 2000 Option Requires NetBIOS Naming

Many Windows 2000 services can use either NetBIOS or DNS naming conventions, but only one requires that NetBIOS naming still be in place. Restricting a user to logging on from only certain workstations requires that the workstations be identified using their NetBIOS names. You may decide to continue to support NetBIOS naming for many reasons, but this feature will require that you keep using NetBIOS naming.

NetBIOS

NetBIOS names are 16-byte addresses. The first 15 bytes are available for you to use. The 16th byte identifies the type of NetBIOS resource associated with this name. For example, a hexadecimal value of 20 identifies the server service associated with a computer. When another computer uses the net use command to connect to a network share on SERVER1, it uses NetBIOS to look for the NetBIOS name 'SERVER1   [20h]'. Because SERVER1 is not 15 characters long, the name is padded with spaces and the 16th character is added. When this name is found, the IP address associated with the name is returned. A connection can then be made using the IP address.

The process used to resolve NetBIOS names depends on the configuration of the workstation. Workstations can be configured as one of four different node types:

- **B-node (Broadcast).** Broadcasts a request for name resolution to every workstation on its subnet. B-node is inefficient and has two problems: Broadcasts are processed by every node on the subnet; and routers rarely forward broadcasts, so only NetBIOS names on the local subnet can be resolved.

- **P-node (Peer).** Uses a NetBIOS name server (NBNS) (for example, a WINS server) to resolve NetBIOS names. P-nodes never resolve names using broadcasts.

- **M-node (Mixed).** A combination of B-node and P-node. This configuration uses broadcast by default and queries a WINS server if the broadcast resolution fails.

- **H-node (Hybrid).** Similar to M-node, but now WINS is tried first and Broadcast is used only if WINS fails to resolve the name.

Windows 2000 workstations are installed as B-node or H-node by default, depending on whether a WINS server address is entered or not. In anything but the smallest and simplest networks, H-node is the preferred mode for all workstations.

▶*For more information, see Chapter 8.4, "Windows Internet Name Service (WINS)."*

Host Name Resolution

Host name resolution is the preferred method in Windows 2000 for resolving names to IP addresses. Host names can be much longer than NetBIOS names—up to 255 characters—and a single resource can have multiple different names or aliases. Host names are also made up of multiple parts. A Fully Qualified Domain Name (FQDN) includes both a simple Host name and a Domain name in the form of *host.subdomain.domain.com*. To resolve the host name, you must also resolve the Domain portion of the FQDN. When a name resolution call uses simply the host name (for example, ping servers), the Domain name is assumed to be the same as the Domain name of the caller.

Host names are resolved through a multipart process, as follows:

1 First, the name will be checked against the resolver cache on the computer requesting the name resolution. The cache contains entries for names that were resolved recently or that were preloaded through the use of a HOSTS file.

2 If the name cannot be resolved in the cache, a call is made to the first DNS server listed in the client's TCP/IP configuration.

3 If the DNS server does not have a zone file that contains the Domain portion of the FQDN being searched for, a recursive lookup is started via the root servers in that DNS server's configuration. After a DNS server is found that supports the proper Domain, a request is sent to that server for resolution of the host name portion of the request.

4 If a proper DNS server cannot be found or the host name lookup fails, an error is returned to the requesting computer. Depending on the error, other DNS servers in the client's configuration may also be queried.

5 If DNS is unable to resolve the host name and the DNS server is configured to use WINS for host name resolution, the DNS server will pass the host name portion of the FQDN to a WINS server for resolution as a NetBIOS name.

Windows 2000 DNS servers support dynamic DNS, which allows Windows 2000 computers and DHCP servers to update host records on a DNS server automatically.

▶ *For more information, see Chapter 8.3, "Domain Name System (DNS)."*

Service Registration

Just as there are two types of name resolution, there are also two ways to access services in a Windows 2000 network. The Microsoft Browser service supports automatic registration of network service providers through NetBIOS naming. Active Directory in Windows 2000 uses an alternate method of accessing network services through DNS SRV service records.

Service locator (SRV) resource records are a relatively new part of DNS. They allow the use of DNS query operations for locating network services. For example, in Windows 2000, a workstation attempting to find a Domain Controller to log on through will search for a Lightweight Directory Access Protocol (LDAP) service in DNS. The DNS will query its zone file for an SRV record that represents that service. It will then return the name of an appropriate Domain Controller running the LDAP service. Windows 2000 currently uses this functionality for LDAP, Kerberos authentication, and Distributed File System services. Other services will be added in the future.

The Microsoft Browser service is used primarily by downlevel workstations trying to access network services through NetBIOS over TCP/IP (when a Windows 98 user clicks on Network Neighborhood, for example). Similar functionality is continued in Windows 2000 for legacy compatibility. One computer on each subnet will be elected as the Master Browser. The Windows 2000 PDC emulator will be shown preference in this election, and then NT 4.0 BDCs, other Windows standalone servers, Windows 2000 Professional, NT Workstation, and other Windows-based computers (in that order). Computers designated as browsers maintain the browse lists, which contain all shared resources used on the network. The Master Browser on each network will forward resource lists to the Domain Master Browser for synchronization with other Master Browser lists. When a user clicks on Network Neighborhood or My Network Places, the local Master Browser is queried for a list of computers and Domains offering NetBIOS-based services.

Many of the tasks that users have traditionally done using the Browser service can now be accomplished in Windows 2000 using the Active Directory. Network shares and network printers can be published in the Active Directory so users can find them by using the Search features of Windows 2000. This allows even more functionality than browsing because keywords and location information can be published along with the shares and printers to enhance the functionality of a search.

Managing Client Network Configuration

There are three different ways to configure your network clients: manually, dynamically, and automatically. To use either dynamic or automatic configuration, just set the TCP/IP configuration on the client to obtain an IP address automatically. Client configuration is set in the Properties dialog box under the TCP/IP protocol in each specific connection in Network and Dial-up Connections.

Dynamic Configuration

Dynamic configuration is accomplished through the use of a Dynamic Host Configuration Protocol (DHCP) server. A properly configured DHCP server can configure all the settings that a client needs, including IP address, subnet mask, default gateway, DNS server, NetBIOS node type, and WINS server. Windows 2000 computers are configured to use DHCP by default. DHCP client configuration is also supported in Windows 95/98 and NT.

▶*For more information, see Chapter 8.2, "Dynamic Host Configuration Protocol (DHCP)."*

Automatic Configuration

If a client is configured to use a DHCP server for configuration, but fails to contact a DHCP server, Automatic Private IP Addressing (APIPA) will be used. APIPA will automatically configure the client with an address from the range 169.254.0.1 to 169.254.255.254 and a subnet mask of 255.255.0.0. No other options will be set, including DNS server, WINS server, or default gateway. APIPA is designed for use on single-segment networks that are normally not connected to the Internet. This allows for NetBIOS name resolution through broadcast and removes the need for a WINS server, DNS server, or default gateway.

Windows 98 Also Uses Automatic Private IP Addressing

Windows 98 also uses APIPA if a DHCP server is not available, and it uses it when Internet Connection Sharing is enabled. In Windows 2000, Internet Connection Sharing uses an address space of 192.168.0.0 instead. Because APIPA normally doesn't set a default gateway, the Windows 2000 implementation is easier to troubleshoot.

▶*For more information, see Chapter 8.7, "Connection Sharing."*

Manual Configuration

TCP/IP properties can be configured manually on any computer running Windows 95/98, NT, or 2000. But this is a very time-consuming task that should be avoided, if possible. Reservations can be used if you want to guarantee the use of specific addresses on specific computers. But even when using a DHCP server and reservations, some computers will need to be manually configured. For example, Active Directory Domain Controllers, WINS servers, and DNS servers should all have static addresses. You can manually configure the TCP/IP properties of specific interfaces in Network and Dial-up Connections by right-clicking on an interface and selecting Properties, selecting the TCP/IP protocol, and pressing the Properties button.

▶*For more information, see Chapter 2.4, "Configuring Network Components."*

Managing Server Network Configuration

Most of the Administrative tools in Windows 2000 have now been enhanced to allow them to function on remote machines over the network. DNS, DHCP, and even disk management can now be done from within an MMC simply by right-clicking on the snap-in and selecting Connect to another computer.

▶ *For more information, see Chapter 3.2, "Using MMC Consoles."*

For those few occasions when you need to configure something using an Administrative tool other than an MMC snap-in, there is another alternative. All versions of Windows 2000 server ship with a two-connection copy of Terminal Services for use in Remote Administration. To remotely administer a Windows 2000 server, simply do the following:

1 Enable Terminal Services in Remote Administration mode.

2 Load the Terminal Services client onto your workstation.

3 Establish a TCP/IP connection with the server across the LAN or via a dial-up Remote Access Server (RAS) connection.

4 Run the Terminal Services client and log in to the remote server.

You will now see a duplicate of whatever would be on the desktop of the remote server. You can now run third-party utility programs, such as virus checkers, just as if you were sitting at the console of the remote server.

▶ *For more information, see Chapter 8.8, "Terminal Services."*

Windows 2000 servers can also take an active role in the routing of a TCP/IP network. They support industry-standard routing protocols such as Routing Information Protocol (RIP) and Open Shortest Path First (OSPF). They are even capable of routing multicast packets in a limited multicast-enabled network. Using servers in this fashion will require advanced knowledge of how TCP/IP routes traffic and how routers update routing tables on neighboring gateways.

▶ *For more information, see Chapter 8.6, "IP Routing."*

Managing Server Network Performance

Most of the work required to manage server network performance can be summed up in two activities: planning and monitoring. The physical planning of network subnets, gateways, and the placement of servers will have the greatest impact on the performance of network servers. A balance must be maintained between the benefits of load-balancing and fault-tolerance, which have a tendency to centralize servers; and the placement of network resources close to the potential users of the services provided by those servers. The role of sites in Active Directory can also be used to fine-tune some of these performance characteristics. A well-designed network will have servers placed to facilitate load-balancing and fault-tolerance without requiring all network traffic to cross too many routers to reach network servers.

After a TCP/IP and Active Directory infrastructure is planned, you must also undertake a proactive monitoring of the network to guarantee continued performance. The use of Network Monitor, Event Logs, and Performance Monitor should be planned to facilitate an ongoing view of the network. Use of these tools will guarantee that you can identify and repair performance problems before users become aware of them. The Resource Kit also contains a number of useful activities for managing a server's network performance.
▶ *For more information, see Appendix D, "Resource Kit Utilities."*

8.2
Dynamic Host Configuration Protocol

You Need to Read This Section If You Want to:

- Plan a DHCP deployment.
- Configure DHCP scopes and options.
- Integrate DHCP with DNS or WINS.

Related Topics

Overview of DHCP

The role of DHCP (Dynamic Host Configuration Protocol) is to provide reliable and consistent TCP/IP configuration information to clients on a network. Using a centralized database and an address lease arrangement, DHCP allocates IP addresses and other TCP/IP configuration data to clients. It does this so wasted addresses are kept to a minimum and duplicate IP addresses are prevented. The alternative to DHCP, static address configuration, is labor-intensive and not practical for larger networks.

New Features

Windows 2000 Server supports DHCP and offers a version of the service that has some enhancements over the Windows NT 4.0 implementation. The new features are as follows:

- A new management interface with additional reporting and monitoring tools. DHCP is administered through an MMC snap-in, and the tool set includes the capability to check service statistics and graph DHCP activity.

- Direct integration with the Windows 2000 Dynamic DNS service (DDNS). DHCP is now able to dynamically create and remove records in the DNS database. This expands the power of DNS' name-resolution capabilities and solidifies Windows 2000's adherence to TCP/IP standards by enabling WINS to be removed from the network infrastructure of some Windows 2000 Domains.

- Support for multicast address allocation. DHCP can now dynamically provide multicast addresses to clients and servers, which are taking advantage of multicast technology implemented in services such as teleconferencing.

- Preventing unauthorized DHCP servers. Windows 2000's DHCP must be authorized in the Active Directory to come online and provide DHCP services. This requirement keeps unauthorized servers from disrupting address allocation.

- Finer granularity for IP options assignment. New class and vendor IDs have been created that allow an administrator to assign IP options based on pre-assigned criteria such as desktop versus laptop users and LAN versus RRAS users. Because of this, options in a scope are not necessarily common to every client who uses the scope.

- New built-in Local and Global groups for DHCP administration. The need to delegate responsibility for DHCP administration to personnel who aren't necessarily required to have full administrator privileges led Microsoft to create additional groups to make the delegation of partial administrative authority easier.

    ▶ *For additional configuration and implementation information covering these features, see "Installing and Configuring DHCP Server" later in this chapter.*

Defining DHCP Components

There are three main components involved in the functioning of DHCP:

- **DHCP server.** This is a system running Windows 2000 Server and configured with a static address. It has the DHCP service installed and maintains a database that it uses to manage the information it provides clients. The service is administered using the DHCP MMC, which can be accessed locally on each DHCP server or run remotely from an administrator's workstation.

- **DHCP clients.** Many flavors of network clients support DHCP, including some versions of Linux and Unix. Here is a condensed list of the Microsoft clients that support DHCP:

  - All Windows operating systems
  - Network Client 3.0 for MS-DOS
  - LAN Manager version 2.2c

- **DHCP relay agents.** Because the DHCP mechanism relies on network broadcasts for initial client configuration, a DHCP server can only service a network that is local to it. To overcome this limitation, systems and routers can both be configured to forward client DHCP requests from remote subnets to a DHCP server for servicing. Systems and routers set up to forward DHCP requests are called *relay agents*. DHCP was built on and is compatible with BOOTP technology, and routers configured to forward BOOTP broadcast packets (UDP port 67) to a DHCP server are considered relay agents.

BOOTP Defined

The protocol *BOOTP* is used primarily with diskless workstations and thin clients, in which the boot process of a system brings the system onto the network prior to loading a full operating system. This happens so the system can use operating system files located centrally on a network file server. The system booting from the network uses BOOTP to obtain an IP address or locate a network file server.

IP Address Lease Process

DHCP is a service that responds to client requests. When a DHCP client boots up on a network for the first time, it initiates a four-step process:

1. The client broadcasts a request for an IP address on UDP port 67. This request is known as a *DHCP Discovery broadcast*.

2. Any DHCP servers on the local subnet respond to the client with a direct DHCP Offer. If there are no local DHCP servers, but a relay agent has forwarded the client's broadcast to a remote DHCP server, that server responds with a DHCP Offer.

3 The client takes the first offer it gets and responds with another broad-cast (known as a *DHCP Request*). This request confirms the IP address it received. A relay agent forwards this broadcast as needed. A server whose offer was not accepted puts the IP address it offered back in its address pool.

4 The DHCP server whose offer was accepted responds with a *DHCP Acknowledgment* message that includes a lease duration and any other configuration information that the server has been set up to give. When the client receives this acknowledgment, it then binds the new address to its IP stack and proceeds to use it.

Address Selection Algorithm

A DHCP server gives addresses starting at the bottom of a scope's range and working to the top. It does not give a previously used, expired address to a new client until all unused addresses are exhausted. After all addresses are used at one point or another, the server then assigns addresses that were released or expired, based on the amount of time that the address has been available. The addresses that have been unused the longest are the server's first choice for reuse. As with all lease assignments, the server utilizes conflict-detection techniques to make sure the IP is, in reality, unused.

IP Auto-configuration

If the client is running Windows 98 or Windows 2000, cannot contact a DHCP server to obtain an IP address, and IP Auto-configuration has been enabled, the client configures itself with a temporary IP address. It uses the temporary IP address, but also continues to send out DHCP Discovery broadcasts every five minutes.

▶ *For more information on IP Auto-configuration, see "DHCP Clients" later in this chapter.*

IP Address Conflict-Detection

Both DHCP servers and DHCP clients have ways to check for IP duplication. The DHCP server can be configured to ping an IP address before it assigns that address to a client. This option is turned off by default because it slows IP address allocation.

▶ *For more information on configuring conflict-detection, see "Enabling Server-side Conflict-Detection" later in this chapter.*

The DHCP client has its own way of detecting duplicate IP addresses. Before a client replies to a DHCP Offer with a DHCP Request, it sends out an ARP broadcast on the local subnet to determine whether there is already a local host using the IP address that the DHCP server offered. If it determines that the address is already in use, it sends a DHCP Decline broadcast back to the DHCP server and makes another DHCP Discovery broadcast. The server that received the DHCP

Decline response marks that particular IP address in its pool as bad and keeps from reissuing it again by adding it to its list of active leases with the name BAD_ADDRESS. If you see entries in the Active Leases list for BAD_ADDRESS and you are able to determine (by pinging and other means) that the system that causes the error is no longer on the network, that address can be released back into the pool by deleting it from the Active Leases list.

IP Lease Renewals

The IP address that is provided to the client is good as long as the lease duration lasts. The default lease time is three days and can be modified by an administrator. Renewals take place as follows:

- At the halfway point in the lease period, the client will attempt to contact the DHCP server and renew its lease by sending a directed DHCP Request. If it is successful and is able to renew, the client gets a full new lease on the same address it was using. If the client fails to contact the server at the 50% point of the lease duration, it continues to use the leased IP address.

- When $7/8^{th}$ (87.5%) of the lease time has expired, the client again tries to contact the DHCP server to renew the lease. If it fails, it continues to attempt renewal at regular intervals until the lease expires. At that point, it drops the address it is using and initiates a DHCP Discovery broadcast every five minutes until a server responds.

- In addition to renewals timed at different intervals in the lease duration, the client also renews its lease each time it restarts, even if the lease it previously had expired while it was offline.

If any of the IP configuration options that the DHCP server provides to its clients change since the client's last renewal, they are updated on the client as needed.

Denied Renewals and Negative Acknowledgments

If the client's lease expired while it was offline and the IP address it was using was given to another client, the DHCP server responds to the client's renewal request with a Negative Acknowledgment *(NACK)*. Another time a NACK can occur is when the scope that the client got its lease from has been deactivated by an administrator. Any time a client receives a NACK in response to a renewal request, it immediately stops using its IP address and sends out DHCP Discovery broadcasts to obtain a new IP address lease.

Installing and Configuring DHCP Server

The question of where to put your DHCP server and how many of them to use is a good one. A DHCP server can service a very large user base, so the essential factor is availability. For a single non-routed LAN, there is no compelling reason to have more than one DHCP server. Because no existing clients lose their IP addresses until at least half of the normal lease period has passed, there is usually enough time for the DHCP server to be rebuilt or replaced in case of a hardware failure.

▶ *For more information on DHCP server unavailability, see "Frequently Asked Troubleshooting Questions" at the end of this chapter.*

In a network with several routers but no WAN links, one server might be able to do the job just fine, but at least two are better for providing redundant scopes. This is assuming, of course, that the server is running on reliable hardware that meets the minimum operating system specifications. If you are using more than one DHCP server for redundancy, place them on separate network segments, in case the router goes down or the connection between them is otherwise inoperable.

▶ *For information on setting up redundant scopes, see "DHCP Scopes" later in this chapter.*

Multi-homing your DHCP servers provides reliable coverage of multiple subnets, but if your routers are acting as relay agents, make sure your DHCP servers aren't sending replies to the client from multiple interfaces. This should not cause any errors, but does result in unneeded traffic.

Putting a DHCP server on either side of a slow WAN link is a good practice. As much as possible, give every site the resources it needs to function at a local level if WAN links temporarily go down. Because a valid lease is a requirement for network connectivity, a local DHCP server is insurance against DHCP lease-related downtime.

Installation Process

Because of new authentication safeguards used in Windows 2000 DHCP, the first DHCP server you install must be installed on either a Domain controller or a server that is a member of the Domain if you use Active Directory in your Windows 2000 Domain. Do not install the first DHCP server on a workgroup or standalone server.

▶ *For more information on Active Directory, see Part 4, "Managing the Directory."*

To install the DHCP service on a Windows 2000 Server, have your Windows 2000 source files handy and do the following:

1 Open the Windows Components Wizard in the Administrator Tools menu.

2 Scroll through the list of components and click Networking Services.

3 Click Details.

4 Scroll through the list and check the box next to Dynamic Host Configuration Protocol (DHCP). Click OK.

5 When and if prompted, enter the path to the Windows 2000 distribution files and click Continue.

6 After installing the service, the system restarts. After it restarts, the DHCP management console can be used.

Connecting to a Remote Server

If you are using the DHCP console at an actual DHCP server, that server will appear in the console's list of servers that can be administered. To administer a DHCP server that is not installed on the system that you are running the DHCP console on, you need to connect to that server in order to administrate it. Do this by executing the following steps:

1 Open the DHCP console and select DHCP.

2 Choose Add Server from the Action menu.

3 Select the server you want to administer from the console.

Authorizing the DHCP Server

The first time you connect to a freshly installed DHCP server, you might get the following message: The DHCP Server *servername* is not authorized in the directory…

As was mentioned earlier in this chapter, Windows 2000 Server introduced a new mechanism to prevent unauthorized DHCP servers from functioning in an Active Directory-administered Domain. Without registering in the Active Directory, a Windows 2000 DHCP server cannot activate a scope. This mechanism holds true only for DHCP running on Windows 2000 Server—it does not apply to DHCP servers running on Windows NT 4.0 or other operating systems. To authorize a DHCP server in the Active Directory, do the following:

1 Log on as a user who has membership in the Enterprise Administrators group.

2 Open the DHCP console; select DHCP.

3 Click Manage authorized servers from the Action menu.

   A dialog box appears.

4 Click Authorize server.

5 Enter the name or IP address of the DHCP server that you want to authorize and click OK.

To see whether a given DHCP server has been authorized in the Active Directory, use the Active Directory Sites and Services Console to look in the Configuration container found in the \Configuration\Services\ NetServices folder.

DHCP Scopes

A scope is used to set aside a range or pool of consecutive IP addresses to distribute to clients. The scope also has properties that determine the lease time for the addresses it gives out and the IP configuration options that will be provided to clients. A scope can span up to a single subnet. To combine scopes into a larger administrative entity, superscopes (discussed later in this chapter) need to be used.

Creating a Scope

To create a new scope, highlight a server in the Console, choose New Scope from the Action menu, and the New Scope Wizard will walk you through scope creation. Before you start, try to determine the following:

- The starting and ending addresses of the range you want to use.
- The subnet mask used on the subnet in question.
- Whether there are any clients using static addresses in the range you specified that need to be excluded from the pool.
- How long the lease duration needs to be for IP addresses leased from this scope.
- What IP configuration information you want to pass on to the clients in addition to an IP address and a subnet mask.
- Whether you need to reserve specific IP addresses for specific clients. An example is a Web server whose IP configuration you want to be updated by DHCP, but you want to ensure that it always has the same IP address.

Suppose that you have used the New Scope Wizard to create a scope. You are now ready to add all the details to the scope's configuration.

Creating Exclusion Ranges

Exclusion ranges make it easier to allocate pools of addresses for scopes. Rather than having to work around addresses that are already dedicated to specific clients with static configurations, a large range of addresses can be selected for a scope, and the addresses already in use can be excluded from use by DHCP.

If you are creating an exclusion range on a scope that is already active, be careful. You cannot exclude a range of addresses that includes an active lease. You have to delete the active lease and retry the exclusion. It is best to create all exclusions prior to activating the scope.

▶ *For more information on activation and deactivation, see "Activating and Deactivating Scopes" later in this chapter.*

To create an exclusion range, do the following:

1 Highlight Address Pool in the scope you want to configure.

2 Choose New Exclusion Range in the Action menu.

3 In the Add Exclusion dialog box, enter the starting IP address for the exclusion range.

4 If you want to exclude more than one address, enter an ending address in the appropriate field.

5 Click Add to finalize the exclusion range.

Configuring Scope Redundancy

To ensure that having more than one DHCP server for your enterprise is actually helpful, scopes should be split up between two or more servers. This is done by creating identical scopes on multiple servers and then using exclusion ranges to exclude the addresses that the other DHCP server or servers are offering to clients. Make sure that these scopes are identical as far as reservations and IP configuration options.

In the following example, ServerA and ServerB both have scopes defined for the same subnet, and the two servers have been placed in separate subnets. ServerB is on the subnet covered by the scope, and has been given the lion's share of the addresses.

ServerA:
Range   204.181.180.30 to 204.181.180.254
Exclusion   204.181.180.190 to 204.181.180.254

ServerB:
Range   204.181.180.30 to 204.181.180.254
Exclusion   204.181.180.30 to 204.181.180.189

As you can see, the ranges are the same, but the exclusion ranges serve to split the serviced addresses. ServerA is holding a pool of 65 addresses, whereas ServerB is local to the scope's subnet and has 189 addresses to distribute. If either server is unavailable, the other server can cover the clients for this subnet. Most leases will be drawn from ServerB's larger pool because ServerB is local to the hosts it is servicing. If ServerB becomes unavailable, ServerA can offer valid leases for a period of time until ServerB is brought back online, provided the routers between ServerA and the client's subnet serve as DHCP relay agents.

Another scope can be created on each server to distribute the addresses on ServerA's subnet. In this arrangement, the bulk of the addresses are given to ServerA and the remainder to ServerB for fail-over. This is how scopes are made redundant.

Viewing and Changing Scope Properties

To view and change a scope's configuration, highlight the scope whose properties you want to view and choose Properties from the Action menu. The scope name, range of the scope, and lease duration display on the General tab.

The range of the scope can be increased, but not decreased. It cannot be shifted up or down. Any address that is in the scope range must remain in the scope range. If an address is in the range that you do not want to be distributed by DHCP, use an exclusion to exclude it.

The other tabs in the Scope Properties are Dynamic DNS and Advanced. Dynamic DNS is covered later in this chapter. The Advanced tab serves to define which types of clients DHCP should allocate addresses to: DHCP clients, BOOTP clients, or both. The default setting is to service only DHCP clients.

Setting a Lease Duration

A scope's lease duration has a bearing on the amount of network traffic that DHCP clients will generate, especially when DHCP is configured to send updates to DNS. Traffic should be monitored so that an accurate picture of the actual bandwidth being used by the DHCP processes can be gauged. In reality, however, DHCP doesn't cause an undue amount of traffic when compared to several other network services such as the browser service and the different name-resolution options.

Lease duration also affects the length of time that a DHCP might be offline before any real problems will be encountered. If the lease time is set to be 10 days, for example, most clients have a remaining lease duration of between five and 10 days because of the continuous nature of the lease-renewal process. If the DHCP server disappeared for three days and the network environment was otherwise stable, the only clients that would encounter trouble would be new clients that never received an initial IP lease. All other clients would have at least five days left on their leases.

The downside of having a long lease duration is that changes to the scope IP options take longer to propagate out to clients. If, for example, a new DNS server were brought into the enterprise, it would take at least five days before the large majority of clients would receive an updated DNS entry from the DHCP server.

Setting Optional Configurations

As discussed earlier, DHCP facilitates the assignment of most client IP-configuration information. These options can be configured at the server level, the scope level, the class level, or the individual client level. The levels are listed here in order from the general to the specific:

- **Server level.** Server level options apply to all the scopes existing on a particular server. Configure options at this level with care. Several options exist that should not be configured here: options that are subnet-specific, such as Router.

- **Scope level.** This is the standard level at which to set options, and options at this level should be used as much as possible.

- **Class level.** Class level options configure information for a mixed client base with varying needs, such as Windows 2000-specific options, special DNS servers for laptops, and other unique needs.

- **Client level.** Options set here are combined with a reservation. Use this level sparingly because there are few reasons to set options here instead of the class or scope level, and client overrides can lead to administrative confusion.

Granularity is the name of the game, and options set at a higher level are overridden by options set at a lower level. Options set at the client level override all other set options.

Information manually configured at the client overrides any option DHCP offers.

To set scope-level optional configurations that DHCP will pass on to its clients, follow these steps:

1 Select Scope Options in the console tree.

2 Click Configure Options in the Action menu. A list of available options displays.

3 Check the box for the first option you want to configure. A Data Entry area is available for you to enter configuration information. For options that allow multiple entries, the order in which entries are created here specifies the order in which the clients use the entries.

To configure options at the server level, right-click the server and choose Set Pre-defined Options from the fly-out menu.

To configure options at the class level, click the Advanced tab in any of the other option-configuration areas, select either Vendor Class or User Class from the pull-down menus, and choose the options that you want to configure for that class.

To configure options at the client level, right-click a reservation and choose Configure Options from the fly-out menu.

The most commonly configured options are as follows:

- Router [code 3].   Sets the default gateway. This address must be local to the clients receiving it.
- DNS server [code 6].   Specifies one or more DNS servers.
- DNS Domain name [code 15]   Sets the Domain name for the client. This plays a role in dynamic DNS updates.
- WINS Server [code 44].   Specifies one or more WINS servers.
- NetBIOS node type [code 46].   Sets the node type that controls NetBIOS name-resolution order.

Windows 2000 clients can use the following additional options:

- Perform router discovery [code 31].   Allows clients to dynamically discover and use routers.
- Static route [code 33].   Sets one or more static routes.

DHCP clients running under other platforms, namely Unix and Linux, support many of the other IP options on the Available options list. If an option is not supported by a client, it is ignored and does not register an error.

Creating Reservations

Reservations are used when you want to allow a client to receive configuration-option updates during its renewals, but you want to guarantee it a permanent, non-changing IP address. To allow the DHCP server to recognize a unique client when it requests an IP address, the server must be preconfigured to recognize that client's unique MAC (Media Access Control) address. Any communication that a client makes includes this MAC address, so a client with a reservation can be easily identified by the server.

If more than one DHCP server is being used to supply addresses to clients in a single subnet, the reservation should be created on both DHCP servers. If the reservation were created on only one server, the client might get a different IP address from the other server that was not aware of the reservation.

To create a reservation, do the following:

1 Highlight Reservations in the console tree.

2 Choose New Reservation from the Action menu.

3 In the resulting dialog box, type the required information. Be careful when entering the MAC address and do not use hyphens.

4 Click Add to finalize a reservation and click Close when finished.

To determine the MAC address of a client, type **ipconfig /all** at any
Windows 2000 or Windows NT client. If the client is running
Windows 9x, type **winipcfg.exe** in the Run menu. The field called
Physical Address shows the MAC address that you need.

If there is an active lease using the address that you are trying to reserve,
the reservation will fail. If the address is in use, you have to go to the
client and release the address by typing **ipconfig /release** at that
client's command prompt. If the client is running Windows 95x, run
winipcfg.exe and click Release.

Activating and Deactivating Scopes

After a scope is created and configured, all that remains is to activate it.
Once activated, it will be able to service clients existing on the subnet
for which the scope is configured. To activate a scope, select it and
choose Activate from the Action menu. Deactivating a scope is done in
the same fashion.

Thought and care should be given when removing a scope. If you
delete a scope, any clients that were using IP addresses that the deleted
scope provided will continue to use them until their leases run out.
Bringing up a new scope that includes the same addresses will not force
the clients to release their addresses. To force all the clients to quickly
obtain addresses from the new scope, an administrator would have to
use the command line at each workstation to release the old address and
acquire a new one.

The solution to this dilemma is to not delete active scopes outright, but
instead use them to aid in any migrations. If you want to move client
addresses to a range defined in a new scope, create the new scope, activate it, and then deactivate the old scope. As clients try to renew their
addresses at the old scope using DCHP Request packets, the DHCP
server will return DHCP NACKs (negative acknowledgments) to the
clients. They are then forced to drop their IP addresses and start from
scratch in the lease process. Deactivating a scope causes any renewals of
addresses in that scope to be denied, and reclaims the IP from the client.

As you can see, you probably also do not want to deactivate an active
scope frivolously. If you need to stop a server from giving out any more
addresses in a scope for awhile, create temporary exclusion ranges that
keep the remaining unleased addresses out of circulation. This prevents
any new addresses from being given out, but also allows the clients who
currently have addresses from being forced to drop them.

Using Superscopes

Superscopes are groupings of distinct scopes that make it easier to manage multiple scopes in an enterprise (but not in the way you might think).

A superscope handles situations in which more than one logical IP subnet exists on a single network segment. This might happen during a migration from one addressing scheme to another, when two scopes are used during an overlap period. It is also used when it is necessary to put more clients on a single network segment than could be handled by the size of a single available logical IP subnet. Finally, it is necessary when multiple logical IP subnets and their respective scopes exist on the same network segment and more than one DHCP server is responsible for the scopes.

Here's an example of the last scenario. Two different class C networks are being used on the same non-routed LAN, and each has its own scope that is administered by a separate local DHCP server. The trouble with this is that when a DHCP server receives a renewal for an unknown IP address from a DHCP client on its LAN, it will issue a NACK, assuming that the client was recently moved to the local subnet from a remote location. On receiving a NACK, the client is forced to release the IP and start from scratch in the lease process. Nothing ensures that this client will receive an address from the same scope that it was a member of before it tried to renew.

To remedy the situation, each DHCP server configures an additional scope, using the identical range of addresses that the other server is using. Each server then excludes the entire range of addresses on the new scope and combines both old and new scopes into a superscope. The new scopes are then activated.

In the new configuration, each server knows that two logical IP subnets exist on the same segment, and does not issue NACKs nor hand out addresses to clients using the other server's scope. New clients join the scope of whichever server responds first to a DHCP Discovery broadcast unless a client reservation has been configured.

To create a superscope, right-click on the server in the console tree and select Superscope from the New menu. If there are no existing scopes or if all scopes are members of superscopes, this option is unavailable.

The Create Superscope Wizard walks you through choosing which scopes will be members of the superscope. Additional scopes that exist within a superscope are known as *child scopes*.

Using Multicast

Multicast technology allows a specific group of systems to share a special multicast IP address and to be communicated with as a group by systems broadcasting to the multicast address. Windows 2000 DHCP servers implement a standard for dynamic assignment of multicast addresses called Multicast Address Dynamic Client Allocation Protocol (MADCAP). The most common use for multicast technology is conferencing when a subgroup of hosts needs to be sent the same information in a connectionless (UDP) format.

Using multicast requires both client and server-end configuration. After the DHCP server has been set up with a multicast scope, addresses from that scope are utilized only after MADCAP applications on the client request addresses from the scope.

A multicast scope can be created via the following steps:

1 Right-click the server in the console tree and select Multicast scope from the New menu.

2 After the Create Multicast Scope Wizard comes up, name the scope and click Next.

3 Configure the range of multicast addresses that will be available. These are addresses in a special range, from 224.0.0.0 to 239.255.255.255.

4 Set the Time To Live (TTL). This option specifies the number of routers across which multicast traffic created by these clients will go. Each router the multicast traffic crosses will decrement the TTL by one until the TTL is 0 and the multicast packet expires.

5 Type a unique number for the multicast scope in the Scope ID field.

6 Click Next.

7 Set any reservations needed.

8 Click Next.

9 Set a lease duration.

10 Click Finish.

To set a multicast scope to expire after a certain period, do the following:

1 Right-click the multicast scope and choose Lifetime from the fly-out menu.

2 In the Multicast Scope Lifetime dialog box, click Multicast scope expires on.

3 Specify a date on which the scope will expire.

4 Click OK.

Dynamic DNS Integration

If you are running the Windows 2000 versions of DHCP and DNS on your network, you can allow either your DHCP server or DHCP clients to create records on your DNS server. After the DHCP server returns the final DHCP Acknowledgment to the client that includes IP configuration options, either the client or the server (depending on the configuration options) contacts the

DNS server and makes a DNS update request. This update request creates a host (A) resource record in the DNS database. The DHCP server then sends a DNS update request to the DNS server for the client's pointer (PTR) record, which allows reverse IP-to-name lookups.

Enabling Dynamic DNS Updates

As mentioned, the DHCP server can be used to update its client's address (A) and pointer (PTR) records. To set up dynamic DNS updates, follow these steps:

1 From the Action menu, choose Properties.

2 Click the DNS tab.

3 Check the Automatically update DHCP client information in DNS check box.

The other settings that were listed in the DNS tab can be configured as follows. If the Update DNS only if DHCP client requests radio button is selected, Windows 2000 DHCP clients can update their own information in DNS, and other legacy clients have their updates taken care of by DHCP. If the Always update DNS radio button is selected, DHCP always handles DNS registration, regardless of what kind of clients it provides its services to.

Normally, a DHCP server requests that the DNS delete records for hosts whose IP leases have expired. To prevent address (A) records from being deleted when an IP lease expires, clear the Discard forward (name-to-address) lookups when leases expire checkbox.

Finally, the Enable updates for DNS clients that do not support dynamic updates checkbox allows the DHCP server to update records for legacy clients such as Windows 95 and Windows NT 4.0.

Working with RRAS

When a Routing and Remote Access Server is configured with the Use DHCP to assign remote TCP/IP addresses option, it takes out a lease for each port it is configured to use for its clients. It also takes an extra for its own connection-processing purposes. Thus, if a RRAS server is configured to use 16 modems and provide addresses via DHCP, it takes up 17 addresses from the DHCP address pool and holds them for its potential clients. Each of these leases is marked with the RRAS server's name in the list of DHCP clients viewable in the Address Leases area of the console. The leases for these addresses are renewed on the standard schedule by the RRAS server.

IP options set by the DHCP scope are ignored for the addresses provided to the dial-up clients, and options are instead provided by the RRAS server.

This is true, except in cases where the special Default remote access class IP options are used. To see these options, do the following:

1 Right-click Scope Options in an appropriate scope and choose Configure Options from the fly-out menu.

2 Click the Advanced tab.

3 In the User Class drop-down menu, choose Default remote access class.

4 Scroll through the Available options list.

One useful configuration for remote access clients is a lease time that is more appropriate for dial-up users. This is option 051 Lease. The lease time for this option is set in seconds. A 60-minute (3600 seconds) lease is recommended. This allows enough time for the DHCP server to be taken offline for a reboot or brief maintenance without disrupting any existing RAS connections.

▶ *For more information, see Chapter 8.5, "Remote Access Service (RAS)."*

Enabling Server-side Conflict-Detection

Server-side conflict-detection consists of the DHCP server pinging an address in its scope before allocating it to a requesting client. The ping request must fail for the DHCP server to proceed and give the client an IP lease, so the more pings that are configured, the longer the lease process will take. Each ping takes approximately a second. If the ping is successful, the DHCP server selects another address and attempts to ping it before allocating it to a client. To set up conflict-detection, do the following:

1 Right-click the server in the DHCP console and choose Properties from the fly-out menu.

2 Click the Advanced tab.

3 Set Conflict detection attempts to a number greater than 0 (a number higher than 2 is not advised).

4 Click OK.

Server-side conflict-detection is disabled by default because its functionality is largely duplicated by the client. As mentioned previously, the client's conflict-detection is implemented through an ARP broadcast on its local subnet, rather than a ping.

Enabling Logging

When logging is enabled, the DHCP server keeps track of lease requests, renewals, expirations, and denials; and writes them to a log that is in %system-root%\System32\dhcp by default. The log is called DhcpSrvLog, and the extension depends on the day of the week on which it was created. A log file created on Sunday, October 24, 1999 would be called DhcpSrvLog.Sun. Log files are created only on days during which there was activity to log, and a given log file is overwritten after a week, assuming that activity takes place exactly seven days later.

To enable logging, do the following:

1 Right-click the server in the DHCP console and choose Properties from the fly-out menu.

2 On the General tab, select Enable DHCP audit logging and then click OK.

Maintaining the DHCP Database

The DHCP database relies on the same Jet 4.0 database engine that is used by Microsoft Exchange Server. There is no ceiling on the number of client lease records that the database can hold. The DHCP database is largely self-maintaining, and it compacts itself periodically during idle time. It needs to be compacted because the size of the database is not actually dynamic. It grows as records get added, but does not shrink when they are removed. In addition to keeping the database size in check and eliminating unused space, compaction is also the standard way to resolve Jet-corruption errors.

Compacting the Database

Although the database compacts itself periodically, it never takes itself offline when compacting, so it does not do as efficient a job as it could. Thus, it is helpful to periodically take the DHCP server offline by stopping the DHCP service and manually compacting the database. Depending on the number of clients serviced by DHCP, the database should be compacted every one to four months. Servers that maintain more than a thousand clients should be compacted monthly, whereas servers that maintain a smaller client base can have their databases compacted less frequently.

To compact the database manually, follow these steps:

1 Open a command prompt.

2 Type **cd %systemroot%\system32\dhcp** to change to the DHCP database directory.

3 Type **net stop dhcpserver** to stop the DHCP service.

4 Type **jetpack dhcp.mdb temp.mdb** to use the Jetpack.exe utility to compact the database.

5 Type **net start dhcpserver** to restart the DHCP service.

The Jetpack utility copies the database, without the excess space, to the temporary database. It then deletes the original dhcp.mdb and renames temp.mdb to dhcp.mdb. The process is not a long one.

Recovering from Corruption

It is possible for the database to become corrupted. When it does become corrupted, error events show up in the Event Log referencing the Jet database—typically errors 510, 1022, and 1850. Sometimes, compacting the database offline fails to properly repair it. When this happens, you have a few different options. You can restore the database from a tape backup, if you made one, or generate a new database file by deleting or renaming the old one.

Moving the DHCP Database to a New Server

One potentially difficult task that falls into the category of database maintenance is the migration of the DHCP database from one server to another. You might need to do this for scalability reasons (a more powerful hardware platform is needed to support DHCP activity, for example) or when the existing server becomes undependable. There is no click-and-drag way to move the database to a new server. Perform the next steps at the computer that currently has the DHCP database you want to migrate:

1   Stop the DHCP server service. You can use either the command line or the console to do this.

2   Go to Computer Management in the Administrator Tools, open the Component Services area, and disable the DHCP Server Service.

3   Copy the DHCP folder from systemroot\System32\Dhcp to a temporary location on the destination server.

   Don't put it in the %systemroot%\system32\Dhcp folder on the destination server yet.

4   Start the Registry Editor(Regedt32.exe)from the Run menu and go to the following key: HKEY_LOCAL_MACHINE\SYSTEM\ CurrentControlSet\Services\DHCPServer

5   Save the key to a file by choosing Save Key from the Delete the original DHCP folder on this server.

6   Uninstall the DHCP Server if you will continue to use this Windows 2000 Server build.

   Complete the following steps on the server that you are migrating DHCP to:

1   Install the DHCP on the server and restart the system.

2   Stop the DHCP service.

3   Go to the location where you stored the DHCP folder from the old server and rename the System.mdb file in it to **System.src**.

4   Replace the *systemroot*\system32\Dhcp directory on the new server with the DHCP directory that you copied from the old server. Overwrite files when prompted.

5   Start the Registry Editor(Regedt32.exe)from the Run menu and go to the following key: HKEY_LOCAL_MACHINE\SYSTEM\ CurrentControlSet\Services\DHCPServer

6   Highlight the DHCPServer key and use Restore from the File menu to restore the Registry key that you saved earlier. Answer Yes to the prompt that asks if you want to overwrite the key. Close the Registry editor.

7   Open the DHCP console and start the DHCP Server service by using Action, All Tasks, Start.

8   Use Action, All Tasks, Reconcile All Scopes.

This ensures that there are no inconsistencies in the database and that the Registry entries that govern DHCP are in line with settings that the database stores.

DHCP Clients

Client-side DHCP is largely a hands-free area, but there are some behaviors and configurations that every DHCP administrator should know. Windows 98 and Windows 2000 bring a new feature to the client: IP auto-configuration. There are some valuable tools for client-side DHCP administration that are worth mentioning. In addition, using class-level IP options requires some client-level configuration. These three areas are covered in the following sections.

Auto-configuration

By default, all Windows clients are configured to use DHCP. As was stated earlier, DHCP clients running Windows 2000 can automatically configure themselves with an IP address and a subnet mask if a DHCP server is unavailable. If the client did not have a previous lease, it gives itself an IP address from a class B network reserved by Microsoft: 169.254.0.0, and the subnet mask is 255.255.0.0. The client makes an ARP request for the address it intends to use before taking an address. From that point on, it will use the new address, but will continue to try and contact a DHCP server every five minutes. When a DHCP server responds, it replaces its self-configured address with the one that the DHCP server provides.

If the Windows 2000 client has a lease but cannot reach a DHCP server to renew it on boot-up, the client attempts to ping the default gateway that it had been provided with its lease. If the ping succeeds, the client keeps its lease and follows the normal rules for renewal intervals. If the client fails to ping the default gateway, it discards the lease and auto-configures itself, as described previously.

Verify, Release, Renew

To verify client DHCP information, type **ipconfig /all** from the command line on a Windows 2000 or NT client, or type **winipcfg.exe** on a Windows 9x client. The result of that command will show you, among other things, what the address of the client's DHCP server is, what IP address that client is using, and what the lease acquisition and expiration times are. You can also see what the client's class ID has been set to.

Sometimes, it is necessary to force a client to release an address, for example, if a client took an address that was meant to be reserved for another client. To do this at a Windows 2000 or NT client, type **ipconfig /release**.

To force the client to renew a lease or to get a new lease if it was just forced to release one, type **ipconfig /renew**.

Setting Class ID Information

If you created special class-level IP options, you need to configure your Windows 2000 clients to be members of the classes you set up by configuring a class ID on each client. Ipconfig is used to set class IDs. Class IDs are set on a per-adapter basis, and the adapter must be specified in the configuration. The syntax is as follows:

    ipconfig /setclassid "Adapter string" classID

To set a class ID called GatewayClassID on a Windows 2000 DHCP client using an ethernet adapter on a LAN, type the following:

    ipconfig /setclassid "Local Area Connection" GatewayClassID.

To show existing class ID information, use the following command:

    ipconfig /showclassid "Adapter string"

This configuration could be scripted for centralized administration via Systems Management Server or any of many other script-deployment solutions, but scripting is beyond the scope of this book.

Frequently Asked Troubleshooting Questions

To wrap up this coverage of DHCP and lay some common misunderstandings and "gotchas" to rest, here are a number of questions and answers regarding DHCP:

Question: I thought that Windows 2000 prevents rogue DHCP servers from being installed on my network and giving addresses to clients, but I found some clients that received addresses from an unregistered server. What's going on?

Answer: Windows 2000's version of DHCP prevents non-registered Windows 2000 servers from running the DHCP service on an Active Directory network. DHCP servers running NT 4.0 or some Unix variant will still be able to hand out addresses without authorization, however. This means that the efficacy of this security feature is quite limited. The client information will tell you which subnet the rogue server is on, and you will have to deal with the problem by finding the physical system and disabling the DHCP service on it.

Question: Assuming that leases are constantly being given out, they are also constantly expiring, and any server downtime will affect some clients. What happens then when the DHCP server becomes unavailable?

Answer: First, although leases are often given out, the most frequent activity on a stable DHCP network is actually lease renewals. On a network with a DHCP server online and with activated scopes, leases never expire because the DHCP server is always available to renew them anytime one reaches half its lease-life. If the DHCP server has not gone offline recently, every DHCP client in the network still has at least half its lease-life left. This means that if the scope's lease duration is set at three days and the DHCP server goes offline, no existing address leases will expire for at least 36 hours, or half the lease life. That is usually ample time to configure a replacement server if the original configuration was adequately documented.

Question: One of my users powered up their system on a Wednesday morning and got an IP conflict message, and now she has no network connectivity. There were no problems on Tuesday. I understood that between server-side and client-side conflict-detection, that was not supposed to be able to happen. Am I wrong?

Answer: If you think that IP conflict-detection will prevent all IP conflicts, yes, you are wrong. Conflict-detection only keeps the DHCP server from giving out an address that is already in use on the network, and both the client and the server are only able to detect a conflict through active, real-time probing. If another system has a duplicate IP address but is powered down, it is not detected. Your client will get the IP address, but when that other system is brought online, the IP conflict will rear its ugly head. What must have happened to your user is that someone manually configured a conflicting address on another system and brought the system online before your troubled user's system was brought online. Because your user's system already had a valid lease, no new conflict-detection was involved. Address renewal does not invoke the conflict-detection measures.

To take care of this problem, use **ipconfig /release** to release the client's IP address. This alone is not enough because the client does not actually have any network connectivity at this point to tell the server to remove its lease from the Active Lease list. As the administrator, you then have to delete that client system's lease from the DHCP server's Active Leases list. After those two things are done, reboot the client system. When it comes back online, it will broadcast a request for a DHCP address and the DHCP server will provide a new and different IP address.

Question: I think that the server running the DHCP service in my network is behaving erratically. What are my options for fixing it?

Answer: You might try compacting the database to fix any corruption that may be causing problems. If that does not work, you can back up the database and the Registry keys. Then, remove and reinstall the DHCP service, an easy variation on what was described in the "Moving the DHCP Database to a New Server" section. After doing this, reinstall whichever Service Pack you are currently running. This should solve any file problems if the trouble is not with the database itself.

If problems persist, it might be best to start relatively fresh; consider rebuilding DHCP on a different server. Leave the existing DHCP server online, but install the DHCP service on a new server and configure it using the console, from which you can view the configuration on both servers. Manually configure the new server with the same scope ranges and scope options that the original DHCP server had (provided they were not the source of your troubles), making sure to note any exclusions and reservations. Ensure that the scopes on the new server are deactivated until you are ready to bring clients on to it. When you are ready, activate the scopes on the new server and deactivate the scopes on the old server. Do not delete the scopes on the old server! When clients try to renew their leases on the old server, it will issue NACKs to them because of the presence of the deactivated scopes. It will force the clients to the new server for their leases. By the time half of the lease time has passed, you should see most of your clients in the Active Leases list on the new server.

Question: I made a reservation for a particular host on my network, and it keeps managing to get a different IP address than the one I reserved for it. What might be the cause?

Answer: Could be several things. First, if there is another DHCP server somewhere in your enterprise that is providing addresses for the subnet that your host is on, it had better have the same reservation configured. Otherwise, it might be supplying your host with illicit addresses. The big tipoff is the fact that the host in question will not show up in the Active Leases list on the server you expected to see it on.

Second, are you sure you did not make a typo when you specified the MAC address of the host? If you did (it is easy to do!), that reservation will never stick. It is possible to get the MAC address of a host by going to the Active Leases list and double-clicking an individual entry. You can do a Copy and Paste to get that exact number into the reserved address field. Alternately, if you are on the same subnet as the host, you can ping the host and then copy the MAC address of the host from your local ARP cache.

8.3

Domain Name System (DNS)

You Need to Read This Section If You Want to:

- Understand the DNS name-resolution process.
- Plan for DNS in your enterprise.
- Deploy and configure Windows 2000 DNS.
- Understand the changes introduced to DNS in the Microsoft Windows 2000 implementation.
- Find and resolve problems with name resolution.

Related Topics

Related Topics   (continued)

For More Information On   ▸ *See*

Subnetting and IP   ▸ *Chapter 8.1: Overview of*
addressing   *Managing Network Services*

Configuring DHCP   ▸ *Chapter 8.2: Dynamic Host*
servers   *Configuration Protocol (DHCP)*

Windows Internet   ▸ *Chapter 8.4: Windows*
Name Service   *Internet Name Service (WINS)*

Overview of DNS

In the context of the Internet age, the technological counterpart to the Postal addressing system (state, city, street, block, and building) is the Domain Name Service. Not that DNS is responsible for actually transporting packets across networks; it works as a human-friendly addressing system to allow you to use host names to refer to computers you need to communicate with, rather than having to memorize the IP addresses of the hosts. On the other hand, computer systems need IP addresses if they want to send data to remote systems, and DNS is the established way for systems to translate host names into IP addresses.

DNS is the global standard for the way names are resolved to addresses on the Internet, and it is increasingly becoming the primary way names are resolved in LANs. Windows 2000 moves Microsoft toward this goal by using DNS name resolution instead of NetBIOS name resolution as the default way of resolving computer names to IP addresses in Windows 2000 Domains. DNS is also a critical service for Windows 2000 Domains because it is required for Active Directory to function.

▸ *For more information on the interdependance of DNS and Active Directory, see Chapter 4.2, "DNS and Active Directory."*

To start off on the right foot, it should be made clear that DNS Domains and Microsoft administrative Domains are not the same thing. Microsoft Domains, such as those Windows 2000 uses, function on much more of a local level and primarily exist for the purposes of security, resource allocation, and user administration.

On an organizational level, the DNS namespace functions much like a file system. There is a root above which you cannot go, and there are sub-Domains beneath it. Each Domain functions like a folder, in that a Domain can hold individual host records or other sub-Domains, much as a folder might hold individual files and subfolders. A diagram of the hierarchy looks like an inverted tree, as shown in Figure 8.3.1.

Figure 8.3.1   Sample DNS hierarchy.

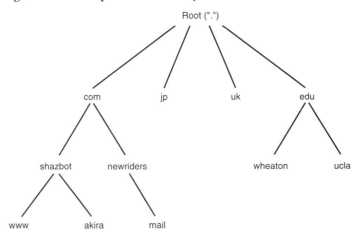

The Domains at the top of the tree, such as .com and .edu, are controlled by the Internet Assigned Numbers Authority (IANA), which delegates the task of providing second-level Domain names to those who request them. Second-level Domain names are granted to individual organizations largely on a first-come, first-served basis. After an organization has a second-level Domain name, sub-Domains can be created within the namespace of the second-level Domain. For example, if I register the name `shazbot.com`, I can then freely create the sub-Domains `support.shazbot.com` and `sales.shazbot.com`. A DNS path that includes both a host and the intervening Domains up to the root is known as a Fully Qualified Domain Name, or FQDN. If I add a Web server to the sales sub-Domain named www, the FQDN would be `www.sales.shazbot.com`.

At the root of this inverted tree are the root servers, which allow name resolutions to be made from within one top-level Domain to another (just as you must often move through a file system's root directory to change the branch of the folder hierarchy).

▶ *For more information about the root servers and their role,*
see "DNS and Name Resolution" later in this chapter.

Up until recently, the service that DNS provided was limited to static addresses. Although DHCP could give out addresses and WINS was able to integrate with DNS to resolve those addresses, DNS itself couldn't register them automatically. All entries in the DNS database had to be created manually. That has changed with the version of DNS that is implemented in Windows 2000. Microsoft included Dynamic Domain Name Service, or DDNS, a new DNS technology whose full specifications can be found in RFC 2136. DDNS allows DNS to integrate directly with DHCP to dynamically register and unregister clients from its database, expanding the number of hosts that can be resolved. When DDNS works properly, life is much easier for the network administrator.

▶ *For more information,*
see "Dynamic DNS" later in this chapter.

DNS and Name Resolution

The DNS name-resolution process can be outlined as follows:

1   A name resolution service (known as a Resolver) running on a client sends a query to its local DNS server.

   This kind of query, in which only a good resolution or a failure can be returned, is known as a *recursive query*.

2   If the local DNS server is unable to resolve the query from its own zone files and cache, it will make queries to other name servers on the behalf of the client Resolver.

   These queries are known as *iterative queries*.

Iterative queries are different from recursive queries in that they are willing to accept either a resolved IP address or a referral to another DNS server. Let's say that a user is trying to reach the corporate Web site for a company in Pakistan. If the client Resolver in the shazbot.com Domain asks its local DNS server to resolve www.fareast.co.pk, it will most likely go straight to the top of the Domain space and query one of the 13 root DNS servers. That root DNS server will respond to the local DNS server with an address for the DNS server authoritative for the pk namespace. Figure 8.3.2 shows the iterative query process.

Figure 8.3.2 The iterative query process.

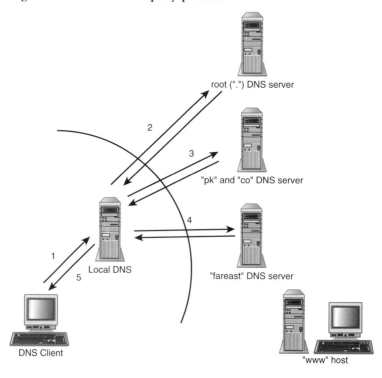

The local DNS server then sends another iterative query to the pk DNS server. Assuming that the DNS server authoritative for the pk namespace also is authoritative for co.pk, it replies with the address of the DNS server authoritive for the fareast.co.pk Domain.

Finally, the local DNS server queries the fareast.co.pk DNS server and gets a resolution for www in that namespace. The resolved IP address is passed back to the client Resolver, and the client is then able to establish a connection to that Web server.

During this process, the local DNS server cached all the information it received, and if another client on the network made a request to resolve www.paktravel.co.pk, the DNS server would communicate directly with the co.pk name server whose IP address it had cached and skip querying a root server.

As you can imagine, local DNS servers rarely go to a root server to resolve an address in the com top-level Domain, because the popular com DNS server addresses are nearly always cached.

If you were wondering how WINS is integrated into the DNS name-resolution process, it's like this: If a DNS server that is authoritative for a zone fails to locate a record in its zone file that was requested by a client Resolver, it may query one or more WINS servers, provided that it is configured to do so. If a queried WINS server has a record for that name, it provides that name-IP mapping to the DNS server, which in turn supplies it to the querying client.

DNS Zones

Administration in DNS is highly distributed. Responsibility for administrating a Domain within the namespace is assigned on the basis of zones. Actually, the essence of a zone is a file stored on a DNS server, known as a *zone file*. This file contains information about a portion of the Domain namespace. The server that has the master zone file for a Domain is considered the primary DNS server for that Domain, and any server that has either the master zone file or a copy of it is considered *authoritative* for that zone. A zone can contain a single Domain and all its sub-Domains, or it can contain one or more sub-Domains. One administrative unit could be responsible for the support.shazbot.com sub-Domain, which might be a zone by itself, whereas another unit could be the primary for the shazbot.com and sales.shazbot.com Domains. Figure 8.3.3 illustrates the relationship between zones and Domains.

Figure 8.3.3   Domains and zones.

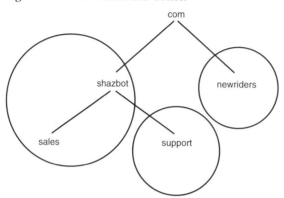

Primaries and Secondaries, Masters and Slaves

Every Domain and sub-Domain has a single name server that is considered the primary name server for the zone that the Domain is part of. Although other name servers, known as *secondaries*, may keep copies of the zone file, changes can be made only at the primary, which has the master copy. The mechanism used to transfer the zone file from one name server to another name server is known, appropriately enough, as a *zone transfer*.

Master servers are the servers that are on the giving end of a zone transfer. At first glance, it might seem like this should be the very same as a primary, but the difference is that a secondary can actually request a zone file from another secondary, making the server that provided the zone file to the other server a *secondary master* server. The secondary name server that is on the receiving end of a zone transfer is called a *slave*. This designates its position as the receiver in the zone transfer relationship.

Secondary name servers, like backup Domain Controllers in a Windows Domain, are needed for load balancing and redundancy. Unlike the Domain Controllers, however, it should be noted that a name server can play the role of both a primary for one or more zones and a secondary for one or more other zones. In the previous example, the primary name server for the zone that includes shazbot.com and sales.shazbot.com might be a secondary name server for the zone that includes support.shazbot.com, and vice versa. As far as a client is concerned, there is no difference between a primary and a secondary name server because both will resolve names in the same fashion.

As discussed in Chapter 4.2, "DNS and Active Directory," a zone can be integrated into the Active Directory. When this is done, all Domain Controllers with the DNS service installed can serve as primary name servers for that particular zone, in that they can receive and process updates to the zone. At this point, there is no longer a master zone "file" for that zone because the information in the zone has been broken down into objects and stored in the Active Directory. A zone that is Active Directory-integrated can still have secondary name servers. A good scenario for this would be secondary name servers that are maintained by an ISP for external redundancy or a stripped-down name server that is exposed to the public Internet on the outside of a firewall. These secondary name servers still maintain actual zone files, even though the master has been added to the Active Directory. It should also be noted that a Domain Controller running the DNS service can maintain both Active Directory-integrated zones and standard non-integrated zones. The latter will still exist on the server in the form of zone files.

Redundancy

Creating a redundant name server environment requires two things. First, at least one secondary name server must be created. The ISP that provides the Internet connection will often configure a DNS server within their organization to serve as a secondary, and although this will help remote hosts find your key servers, your firewall and network security arrangement may not allow your internal hosts to query an external DNS server in the event that the primary server fails. In that case, configuring a secondary name server in your internal network is necessary for redundancy.

Free DNS Server Service

Maybe you are thinking that you want to have a simple external DNS server to provide basic name resolution for your public servers to the Internet population. Or, perhaps after beginning to learn how much is involved in setting up DNS, you feel that your network is too small (fewer than 10 hosts) to be worth the overhead of using Windows 2000's DNS. If this is the case, Granite Canyon Corp., LLC offers a free public DNS service. It offers, free of charge, to maintain primary or secondary zone files for smaller companies and organizations. For more information, head to http://soa.granitecanyon.com.

Secondary servers can be invaluable in the reconstruction of a failed primary zone server. The zone file kept by a secondary can be recopied to the primary in the event that the primary's zone file is lost or badly misconfigured. If important records have very recently been deleted from the primary zone file, stop the DNS service on the secondary to prevent a zone transfer from occurring and use the unchanged zone file on the secondary to reconstruct the missing records.

▶ *For more specifics about reconstructing a failed primary,*
see "Going Deeper" later in this chapter.

The second requirement for redundancy is that the DNS clients must be configured to query at least two name servers. In the Network Control Panel on a Windows client, the IP addresses for multiple name servers can be entered and a search order can be specified. The client will always use the first server specified on its list, and will only move to the next server on the list if the first cannot be contacted. If the first is contacted and it doesn't have a record for the host name that the client wants resolved, no other name server will be queried.

A conceivable (albeit temporary) problem situation would be a client that is configured to query a secondary name server first and then the primary. If a new record had been added to the zone file on the primary, but no zone transfer had happened yet, name resolution for that particular host would fail because the secondary name server would return a No record response to the client and the client would not then query the primary.

Installing DNS

Before installing DNS, make sure that the DNS client has been properly configured on the server. The DNS client on the would-be DNS server should point at itself for DNS resolution. This is necessary to ensure that Dynamic DNS properly registers the new server.

When you are ready to install DNS, have the Windows 2000 source files handy. Here are the initial steps to take to install DNS:

1 From the Control Panel, open Add/Remove Programs.

2 Select Configure Windows from the choices in the left pane.

3 Click Components. The Windows NT Server Setup window opens.

4 Select Networking Options and click Details. This opens the Networking Options list window.

5 Select Microsoft DNS Server and click OK to close the window and continue the installation.

6 Click Next. The necessary files are loaded from the source CD.

   After the installation finishes, Setup returns to the Add/Remove Programs window, which can be closed. Happily, there is no need to restart.

7 Open DNS Management from the Administrator Tools menu.

   The DNS Management console opens and quckly passes control to the Configure New Server Wizard.

8 Click Next.

   The Setup Wizard looks for a root server. This search uses the DNS client Resolver on the local machine, so if it is not configured as a DNS client, a Root Servers Not Found window opens.

At this point, you need to decide how this server fits into your existing architecture. It could be one of the following:

- A primary DNS server in a standard (non–Active Directory) environment
- A primary DNS server in an Active Directory environment
- A secondary DNS server for an existing standard primary name server
- A caching-only DNS server

Each of these scenarios will be dealt with in turn, but the first configuration is the reference point for configuring the others.

Installing a Standard Primary DNS Server

If you are installing a new standard primary server, it is because you are creating a new zone for a Domain or sub-Domain. Because there should only be one server acting as the primary DNS server for a standard (non-Directory-integrated) zone, you should not create a new primary for an existing zone unless, for example, you need to manually maintain parallel DNS systems for distinct internal (private) and external (public) networks. If you create more than one primary DNS server for a zone, only one should be configured to accept dynamic updates.

At this point, let's continue with the installation:

1 Select This Is The First DNS Server On This Network. This assumes that this DNS server's zone is at the top of a Domain, right under a com, net, gov Domain. Choosing this means that this server will use the public DNS structure and will use the root hints file to resolve names with InterNIC's root servers.

2 When the Add Forward Lookup Zone window comes up, leave Yes selected and click Next.

3 The Select Zone Type window will appear. You have three options at this point and your choice will determine the role this server will play in your DNS infrastructure. Because we are setting up a new DNS server for a zone that will not be integrated into Active Directory, choose Standard Primary from the options and click Next.

4 At this point, you are asked for a zone name. If the DNS Domain administered by this zone is a top-level Domain, type the appropriate Domain name, including the trailing dot. If you are creating a new zone for shazbot.com, you would type **shazbot.com**. If the Domain to be created is a child Domain, type the fully qualified name: For example, the sub-Domain sales would be added by entering **sales.shazbot.com**. If the trailing dot is left off, it will automatically be added by the wizard. Click Next when finished.

5 The File Name window will appear. By default, the New File option is selected. The wizard automatically creates a possible name for the zone file by adding a .dns extension to the name of the Domain. If you are migrating from a previous installation of DNS, you may also specify an existing zone file by choosing the Existing File option and specifying a path. This mechanism allows you to convert a non-Windows 2000 implementation of BIND-compliant DNS to a Windows 2000 version. Click Next.

A completion summary window will appear, detailing all the choices you made.

6 If any mistakes were made, use the Back buttons to make changes. Click Finish to create the zone files.

Installing an Active Directory-Enabled Server

Making a DNS server Active Directory-enabled is merely a matter of choosing to make the zones on the server Directory-integrated. In the previous example, choose Active Directory-integrated. This will make the zone you create part of Active Directory. You can then go on to name the zone. Because the zone will exist in the Active Directory, you will not be asked to name a zone file.

If you are trying to move a zone from a non-Windows 2000 DNS environment into a Windows 2000 DNS Active Directory-integrated environment, you will need to migrate the zone first into a standard primary zone and then later convert that zone into an Active Directory-enabled zone.

▶ *For more information on the process for converting a zone into an Active Directory-enabled zone, see Chapter 4.2, "DNS and Active Directory."*

Installing a Secondary DNS Server

When a standard primary DNS server already exists for a zone, a secondary server can be installed for redundancy or as the first step in the process of retiring the primary. Remember that a DNS server can serve as both a primary for one or more zones and a secondary for one or more other zones.

1 Continuing from the previous instructions, choose Standard Secondary and then click Next.

You are prompted for the name of the Domain.

2 Enter the name of an existing Domain that you want this server to hold records for and then click Next.

A Master Servers window will appear.

3 Enter the IP address of a server that currently holds the zone file that the secondary will need a copy of.

Multiple addresses can be entered and will be used to contact a master server in the event that the first on the list fails.

4 Click Next when finished.

A summary of actions will be displayed.

5 Click Finish, and the zone will immediately be created.

The zone will be populated with data if the server was able to copy a zone file from a master server. If the secondary fails to contact a master, a red X appears on the zone folder.

This server can also serve as a primary zone server if a new zone is created on it.

Installing a Caching-Only DNS server

A caching-only server is not authoritative for any zone because it doesn't have a local zone file and isn't a Domain Controller in an environment with Active Directory-integrated zones. It merely accepts queries from clients and goes through the resolution process for those queries. The results of successful queries are, as usual, cached; when possible, the server will answer queries from its cached information. Administrators should be warned, however, that Windows 2000 handles caching in some new ways, adding support for negative caching. The new caching features, if not understood, could mystify an uninformed administrator.

Caching-only servers are useful for sites that need local name resolution but don't want to maintain and administrate a zone. Smaller organizations whose DNS Domain records are maintained by their ISP and who want to minimize name resolution over their WAN link can benefit from setting up a caching-only server.

To set up a caching-only DNS server, install the DNS server service as you would normally set up any DNS server, but do not create any zones. Make sure that the server has the proper root hints file configured.

Creating Zones

Zones are added whenever a new DNS namespace is created or an existing one is expanded. When a new zone is created, it is either a zone for a second-level Domain, which is the creation of a new DNS namespace such as shazbot.com, or it is a zone for a child Domain, which is an expansion of an existing namespace such as sales.shazbot.com.

Zone-creation is fairly straightforward: Just highlight Forward Lookup Zones in the console tree and choose New Zone from the Action menu. A wizard will walk you through the zone creation.

Creating Reverse Lookup Zones

As mentioned earlier in the overview, reverse lookup zones allow IP addresses to be resolved to host names in situations in which that information is desired. You may be wanting to create a new reverse lookup zone if a new network was added to your enterprise.

The process for creating a reverse lookup zone is nearly the same as that for creating a forward lookup zone. Highlight Reverse Lookup Zones in the console tree and choose New Zone from the Action menu. Spend some time reviewing what you know about how reverse lookup works before creating a new zone because it is easy to get things wrong here.

Although it complicates things to bring this up, the Windows 2000 DNS configuration console also allows an administrator to create separate reverse lookup zones for individual subnetted networks in which a non-default IP subnet mask is being used. To set up reverse lookup zones for these types of networks, use the Advanced view during the reverse lookup zone configuration and specify the subnet mask and proper subnet. Don't use use the network address field in the wizard; instead, use the name field. The name for a zone might look like the following:

64/26.180.181.204.in-addr.arpa

This name specifies a 26-bit subnet mask and a zone that governs hosts numbered from 65 to 126. For more information, see RFC 2317.

Zone Transfers

Periodically, zone information is transferred from the master server(s) to slave servers. This transfer of zone information is initiated in two situations:

- When the primary name server, having detected a change in the zone, sends out a notification to any secondary servers it has been configured to notify.

- When a secondary name server starts its DNS service or when a refresh interval defined in the zone SOA record is reached.

In response to either of these situations, a secondary name server will query the master server to compare its local zone file serial number with that of its master. If the number has changed from the last time that the secondary queried, the secondary requests a zone transfer. The type of zone transfer that then takes place depends on two things:

- Whether both the master and the slave server are Windows 2000 servers

- How out-of-date the zone file on the slave server is

Zone Transfer Types

If both servers are running Windows 2000, the option to use an incremental zone transfer (IXFR) exists. This allows the slave server to make a request for a subset of the records held on the master server. The capability to have DNS servers request partial zone files makes DNS traffic more efficient because less information needs to cross the wire when the zone file is updated. When one of the DNS servers is not running Windows 2000, a standard zone transfer (AXFR) takes place. The AXFR involves requesting the entire zone file from the master server.

Assuming that both servers are Windows 2000 and that IXFR is possible, there is another condition that has to be fulfilled for IXFR to be implemented. A Windows 2000 server maintains a zone log file that contains a fairly small changes delta of recent zone additions and deletions. It is able to use this zone log file to calculate how many serial numbers back the update being sent to the slave server needs to go. If the zone file on the slave is too old to be updated incrementally, an AXFR transfer will take place instead. The mechanism works as follows:

1 Something triggers the need for updates, either a notification from the primary server or the refresh value on a slave's zone file.

2 The slave sends an IXFR request to the master server. This request includes the serial number on copy of the SOA record that the slave server is maintaining and specifies that an incremental update would be preferred.

3 The master server compares the serial number given it by the slave server with the serial number in its own SOA record.

4 If the comparison shows that the slave's copy of the zone file is only a few revisions old, the master will collect the appropriate changes delta and send them back to the slave as an incremental update (IXFR).

5 If the master determines that the slave's copy of the zone file is too old to be updated by the changes delta, it will send the slave a copy of the entire zone file (AXFR).

Resource Records

As mentioned in Chapter 4.2, "DNS and Active Directory," resource records (RRs) are the smallest unit in the DNS database. They are what make up the zone files, and each individual record either performs some IP address/hostname mapping, sets DNS functionality parameters, or provides information about advertised services. The most common records are as follows:

SOA Record

The SOA (Start of Authority) record is the first record in a zone file.
The following is an example of an SOA record:

```
shazbot.com.   IN SOA argus.shazbot.com. alyosha.exchange.shazbot.com. (
```

```
1
; Serial/Revision number
```

```
3600
; Refresh after 1 hour
```

```
600
; Retry after 10 minutes
```

```
86400
; Expire after 1 day
```

```
3600 )
; Minimum TTL of 1 hour
```

Each segment of the SOA record is explained in the following list.

- **shazbot.com.** Tells which Domain the zone file is authoritative for.

There are Really Two Dots in "Dot Com"

Notice the trailing periods on the names in the SOA record. Those final periods represent the root of the DNS namespace, and their inclusion in certain records is crucial. The Windows 2000 interface will adjust your records as needed to include or exclude the trailing root dot. For the sake of clear punctuation, the final trailing dot will usually be omitted in this text, except in specific examples.

- **argus.shazbot.com.** Lists the name of the primary name server for the zone.
- **IN.** Stands for Internet, which is the standard class of DNS records.
- **SOA.** Designates the record type.
- **alyosha.exchange.shazbot.com.** The mail address of the person responsible for administering the zone. The first "." can be replaced with an "@" when one needs to actually write the administrative contact. In this case, alyosha@exchange.shazbot.com would be the working contact address. The DNS server will not send mail to a contact; the address exists for

the convenience of other administrators who may need to contact the administrator of a particular Domain. If, for example, you detected a hacking attempt on your network that originated in the shazbot.com Domain, retrieving the SOA record for shazbot.com might help you reach someone in that Domain who is knowledgeable about the goings-on there.

- **Serial Number.**   This is a counter that is incremented by one every time data in the zone file is updated. This value is important because it controls zone-file replication between master and slave servers.

- **Refresh.**   This entry tells secondary name servers how often they should check the master for an updated zone file.

- **Retry.**   This is the frequency, in seconds, with which a secondary will try to contact the master if it fails to reach the master after the normal refresh interval.

- **Expire.**   If the secondary is unable to reach the master after this number of seconds has passed, the secondary completely stops resolving queries for this zone.

- **Minimum TTL.**   TTL stands for Time To Live, and it sets the amount of time that servers are allowed to cache the queries it received from this zone.

- **NS Record.**   The NS (Name Server) record is used to designate each DNS server in the Domain. Here is an example NS record:

```
shazbot.com.
IN NS  argus.shazbot.com.
```

A and CNAME Records

The A (Address) and CNAME (Canonical Name) records are used to create name-to-address mappings. The A record is where the rubber meets the road in the name-resolution system; it is the information that most DNS queries are looking for.

If a host has multiple addresses, in the case of multiple network cards being installed or more than one IP address bound to a card, multiple records are created referencing the same name but varying the IP address, and then additional unique A records are usually created. If kusanagi.shazbot.com were multihomed, its entry might look like this:

```
kusanagi.shazbot.com.
IN A

204.181.180.40
kusanagi.shazbot.com.
IN A

204.181.176.14
akira.shazbot.com.
IN A

204.181.180.40
voltron.shazbot.com.
```

```
IN A

204.181.176.14
```

CNAME records (commonly called Alias records by Microsoft) are used when one wants more than one name mapped to a single IP address. A CNAME record doesn't map directly to an IP address, it maps to an A record. Here's an example of two CNAME aliases of one of the previous A records:

```
www
IN CNAME
akira.shazbot.com.
ftp
IN CNAME
akira.shazbot.com.
```

From this example, you can see that CNAME records are useful for creating aliases that allow servers to be used for multiple purposes. Although there are few real problems one would run into if one created multiple A records for the same IP address, the few that exist, mainly involving *sendmail*, suffice to encourage the use of CNAME records.

It should be noted that Windows 2000's use of Dynamic DNS can make the use of CNAME records potentially risky because CNAME records aren't checked as possible duplicates when new records are dynamically created. On the brighter side, CNAME records can be profitably put to use in a temporary fashion to ease the migration of an host from one name to another. They can also be used when implementing Round-Robin DNS, which is discussed in the "Configuring DNS Servers" section of this chapter.

PTR Records

The PTR (Pointer) record is used to allow inverse DNS queries. It allows one to map an IP address to a name, which is the opposite of what an A record does.

When DNS was first being set up, a special Domain called in-addr.arpa was set up for the purpose of making reverse lookups possible. The trick to doing an inverse query (also known as a reverse lookup) is to be able to get DNS to read IP addresses, such as names, and resolve them without having to teach the zone file parser any new tricks. The problem is that an FQDN reads from right to left, from most general to most specific: akira.shazbot.com resolves root to com to shazbot to akira. IP addresses work from left to right: First, the network portion, which is less specific; then the host, which is more specific. What happens in a PTR record is that the IP address gets reversed so that the order of specificity maps to that of an FQDN. The top of the reverse lookup tree is in-addr.arpa, which is added to the inverse IP. A PTR record for 204.181.180.40 would look like the following:

```
40.180.181.204.in-addr.arpa.
IN PTR
akira.shazbot.com.
```

This allows `40` to be mapped to an individual host, and `180.181.204` to be mapped to a particular network or Domain. The servers responsible for the `in-addr.arpa` zone keep track of several tiers of reverse Domains, and responsibility for full records such as the previous one is in the hands of DNS administrators on individual networks such as yours. Keeping PTR records is optional, but commonly done because it makes the Internet a friendlier place.

MX Records

The MX (Mail Exchanger) record allows mail arriving in a Domain to be properly routed to a mail server. The example shows two MX records:

```
mail.shazbot.com.
IN MX
10 nikita.shazbot.com.
mail.shazbot.com.
IN MX
20 olga.shazbot.com.
```

There are often multiple mail servers in a large enterprise, and part of the MX record allows an administrator to set a preference level and route to one server over another, assuming that both servers are available to receive mail. The lower the preference value, the more preferred the server is. In the previous example, `nikita.shazbot.com` has a preference value of 10. This means that it will be the preferred mail server. If it fails to respond to a host trying to send mail to the `shazbot.com` Domain, the sender will then try to send to `olga.shazbot.com`, which had a higher preference level of 20.

SRV Records

SRV records are used, among other things, to locate Domain Controllers and the various servers that participate in an AD environment. The RFC covering the functionality of SRV records is still in draft form as of this writing, but can be found at

```
ftp://ftp.is.co.za/Internet-drafts/draft-ietf-dnsind-rfc2052bis-05.txt
```

▶ *For more information, see Chapter 4.2, "DNS and Active Directory."*

Dynamic DNS

Dynamic DNS (DDNS) automates the process of A and PTR record creation and deletion and works in tandem with DHCP. Updates are always made on the primary name server in a standard zone. In a zone that has been integrated with AD, any Domain Controller running the DNS service can process a record update.

On a Windows 2000 DNS client, the dynamic update process follows this sequence:

1. The client makes a query to its configured name server to retrieve the SOA record for the zone in which it is a member. It uses this record to identify the primary server it needs to contact and the zone it needs to register a record in.

2. The client sends an assertion message, which serves to ascertain whether or not a record already exists for the client. If the client has changed its name or IP address since it last registered, a negative response will be received.

3. If the client receives a response that the record does not exist, the client will respond with an official update request to add the record. If the record already exists with all the same data, no changes are made to the zone file. If the name or IP address changed, the old record will be deleted and a new one created.

4. If the update fails, the client will try to register itself with another primary server (AD-integrated only) or will wait five minutes and then try again. If that fails, it will wait 10 minutes and retry. If that fails, the client will wait 50 minutes and then start the process again.

?   **Did You Know?**

The client-side mechanism that governs dynamic updates on a Windows 2000 client is the DHCP client service, even if that client is not configured to use DHCP.

The role Windows 2000 DHCP servers play in dynamic updates is important, but in a purely Windows 2000 environment, they can be taken completely out of the loop. By default, a DHCP server attempts to register only PTR records for any of its Windows 2000 clients. Windows 2000 clients can register their own PTR records, but reverse name resolution works best in a dynamic environment when the DHCP server is responsible for creating and deleting these records as leases are given out and expired. In a network in which older Windows clients exist, the role of the DHCP server is essential. It handles both A and PTR record registration and is responsible for removing both of these records when the leases that generated them are no longer valid.

There are both client and server sides to the dynamic update mechanism, and there are several different configurations that result in host registration. See Table 8.2.1 for a summary of the participants and their needs.

Table 8.2.1   Dynamic Update Client Configuration Chart

Windows 2000 clients configured statically	Register their own A and PTR records.
Windows 2000 clients configured dynamically with a Windows 2000 DHCP server	Can register their own A records, but by default the DHCP server registers their PTR records. DHCP server can be configured to process both A and

	PTR.
Windows 2000 clients configured dynamically with a Windows NT 4.0 DHCP server	Register their own A and PTR records.
Legacy Windows clients configured statically or dynamically with a Windows NT 4.0 DHCP server	Manual registrations, if desired. No dynamic registration available. Clients do not self-register.
Legacy Windows clients configured dynamically with a Windows 2000 DHCP server	The DHCP server registers both the A and PTR records for the clients if configured to do so. Clients do not self-register.
Windows 2000 RAS clients	Register both A and PTR records.
Legacy RAS clients	No registration.

By default, records dynamically created in the zone file via an update directly from a client are not removed when the host leaves the network. Over time, old entries can accumulate and make the zone file unwieldly and inaccurate.

▶ *For information on options for automatic scavenging and removal of old records, see Chapter 4.2, "DNS and Active Directory" and the online help.*

Configuring DNS Servers

The following section details a number of configurations that are typically implemented by DNS administrators.

Root Hints

For a name server to be able to begin resolving host names in its namespace, it must have a way of contacting the root servers for the namespace that it is interacting in. If the server is responsible for resolving hostnames in the public Internet, it must have the IP addresses of the public root servers. If the server exists within a private namespace that is not part of the public namespace, it must have the addresses of the servers in that private namespace that fulfill the roles of root servers. The IP addresses initially provided to a DNS server to allow it to traverse the namespace to which it belongs are called *root hints*. The root hints are stored in the cache.dns file located in the %systemroot%\system32\dns folder.

If you are configuring a server that will serve as a root server of a private namespace, delete the cache.dns file. If the server you are configuring is in a private namespace but is not a root server, you need to use the DNS console to change the root hints, replacing those that exist for the public namespace with the names and addresses of your root server or servers.

Round-Robin

When a DNS server is configured as load-balanced by rotating responses among a certain set of hosts when resolving a particular hostname, it is known as *round-robin* load-balancing. Round-robin is simple to configure. Merely add multiple A records for a single name, each with an IP address of one of the hosts that you want to rotate between. See the following example:

```
www

IN A

204.181.176.14
www

IN A

204.181.180.38
www

IN A

204.181.180.39
```

In this listing, you see three entries in the shazbot.com zone file. When a client requests a resolution for www.shazbot.com, the name server will return the first IP address on the list that maps to www. The next time a client requests www.shazbot.com, the name server will return the next address that maps to www. When the last instance of www is reached, the next query will rotate back to the first instance of www.

Prioritizing Local Subnets

Microsoft recently added a mechanism, both for NT 4.0 and for Windows 2000, that allows DNS to deviate from the rotation pattern established by round-robin for the sake of making resolution more efficient. Local subnet prioritization allows a server to parse existing records in which a single host name is mapped to more than one IP address, and provide an appropriate resolution based on the home subnet of the requesting client. For example, if a large corporate intranet were mirrored to six servers across the nation, clients could use the local subnet prioritization mechanism to be directed to the closest intranet server instead of relying on the semi-random distribution that round-robin provides. Like round-robin, multiple A records are created, all with the same hostname, each with an IP address for a different server offering the same service. By default, both round-robin and local subnet prioritization are turned on.

> **? Round-Robin Broken?**
>
> Local subnet prioritization is overriding round-robin and not allowing it to come into play in local, high-traffic scenarios. In this situation, you may want to disable local subnet prioritization. To do this, go to the following location in the Registry:
>
>   HKLM\SYSTEM\CurrentControlSet\Services\DNS\Parameters
>
> Add this entry if it doesn't already exist:
>
> LocalNetPriority
> Data Type : REG_DWORD
> Data : 0
>
> In the data, 0 is disabled, 1 is enabled.

Forwarders

There are situations in which a DNS server will be configured to forward recursive queries to another name server. Counterintuitively, the server that the queries are forwarded *to* is called the forwarder, not the one that actually forwards. One example of a situation wherein a forwarder would be useful is a network in which bandwidth to the Internet is at a premium, but DNS services for the network are provided at the ISP or in another remote network. Every client would normally be set up to query a name server external to the network and would use the connection to the Internet. Configuring a local, zoneless name server to forward queries to an external server and then configuring the clients to query the local name server would result in an efficient concentration of caching that would reduce traffic over the line. Note that configuring a forwarder is not something that is done on the actual forwarder. A server is known as a forwarder if another server is forwarding queries to it. A root server cannot be configured to forward queries.

Testing Tools

There are four main tools for testing and monitoring DNS that an administrator should be familiar with. They are your main weapons against any problem that may crop up with name resolution. ping needs no introduction, but the others might. They are ipconfig, nslookup, and dnscmd. All of these are run from the command-line.

ipconfig

Functionality has been added to the old ipconfig utility to make it more of a friend to DNS. In the same way that it was previously tied into DHCP, it is now integrated with DNS. Here are the newly added command-line switches:

/registerdns

> This switch will cause the Windows 2000 client to reregister all of its DNS records and renew its lease with DHCP.

/flushdns

> This switch will empty a Windows 2000 client's Resolver cache, all cached information, including wrong or outdated entries. This will not solve the problem of a misconfigured host file.

nslookup

This is an important standard tool for DNS diagnosis. The following shows an nslookup session in which a simple query was made to resolve a host name. In the first block, in which nslookup is loaded, the default name server is displayed. In the second block, a query is made to resolve www.bungie.com and is successful. Note that the query results displayed include the querying server's information again:

```
C:\nslookup
Default server: akira.shazbot.com
Address: 204.181.180.40

> www.bungie.com
Server: akira.shazbot.com
Address: 204.181.180.40

Name: www.bungie.com
Address: 209.125.9.70
```

If your server did not query the DNS namespace to resolve this name but answered it from its cache, your results would look as follows:

```
> www.bungie.com
Server: akira.shazbot.com
Address: 204.181.180.40

Non-authoritative answer:
Name: www.bungie.com
Address: 209.125.9.70
```

If you want to change to a different server, merely specify that server's name after issuing a server command.

```
> server ns.donet.com
Default server: ns.donet.com
Address: 205.133.113.129
```

Now, any queries made will use this server. The following query lists the mail servers at New Riders. The -t MX specifies that the query is only looking for mail servers. Leaving that parameter out would cause all records in that zone to be returned unless the server was configured not to do so.

```
> ls -t MX newriders.com
[ns.donet.com]
newriders.com.

MX
10
usrlms006.prenhall.com
```

Table 8.2.2   NSLOOKUP Interactive Command-Line Parameters

Help or ?	Displays a list of available options, including a short description of each.
Set all	Displays the default DNS server and any enabled options for the session.
Set domain	Changes the default Domain name to whatever name is specified. This name is used in any search if no other name is specified.
Set recurse or Set no recurse	Governs whether the queried name server is allowed to query other servers if it does not have the requested information in its zone files or cache.
Set type	Changes the type of information that a query is looking for (A, CNAME, MX, SRV, etc.).
Set debug	This option toggles the display of packet information that can be useful.
Exit	Quits nslookup.

That should be enough to get you started. There are many good resources for learning nslookup's advanced features, and this guide will leave that honor to them. Familiarity with this tool will pay off.

dnscmd

DNSCMD is a command-line interface for administrating DNS. It allows you to do most of the things that you can do in the console at the command-line. You use dnscmd to script DNS tasks such as configuring new DNS servers and other management jobs. For a complete command list for this utility, type **dnscmd /?**.

Best Practices

The following are a series of general rules to follow when working with DNS:

- Never create more than one CNAME record for an individual A record. It is best to use CNAME records as sparingly as possible, especially in the context of Dynamic DNS. There is no mechanism that will keep conflicts from arising if a machine registers a name in an A record that is already being used by another CNAME record.
- No resource record should ever point to a CNAME record. For example, I wouldn't create a CNAME record called mail and point an MX record at mail.shazbot.com. Most resource records that point at other records should only be pointing at A records. This ensures that things will only be as complex as you can handle.

- Build fault-tolerance into your DNS architecture. Make sure that every zone has at least one secondary server, even if that server is a non-Windows 2000 server in your ISP's network.

- Seriously consider name-resolution traffic flow and determine how best to use caching servers to reduce both traffic and the time a name resolution takes to complete.

- Pay attention to SOA serial numbers on your master and slave servers. The difference in the serial numbers in the zone files on each will tell you how well the slave servers are doing at keeping up. Never change the serial number in the primary zone file to a lower number. If you do so, the slaves will never update again unless you change theirs to an even lower number. Use the serial number on the primary to force full (AXFR) zone transfers if you are worried about slaves only partially updating.

- Active Directory-integrated zones can make life a lot easier. Redundancy and fault-tolerance are built into AD and should be well-leveraged by a DNS administrator. Let your Domain Controllers wear the name of server hats. The only exception to this rule would be servers that sit on the outside of your firewall. It is best to use a non-Domain Controller that is a secondary server in that role.

- Get out there and use the extensive DNS resources that exist on the Internet. Newsgroups, FAQs, RFCs, tutorials, and other documentation are abundant and a balm to the DNS administrator's weary brain. A good place to start is http://www.dns.net/dnsrd/, which is a clearinghouse for DNS-related resources.

8.4

Windows Internet Name Service (WINS)

You Need to Read This Section if You Want to:

- Understand when it is appropriate to use WINS.
- Install and configure WINS.
- Back up and restore the WINS database.
- Set up replication between WINS Servers.

Related Topics

Overview of WINS

The Windows Internet Name Service keeps a dynamic database that allows clients to register their names and to resolve the names of other systems to IP addresses. The dynamic nature of WINS allows it to have up-to-the-minute information on the systems it keeps track of. WINS is similar to DNS in that it maps names to IP addresses The names that it maps are not host names, however, they are NetBIOS names, which represent users and services located at specific IP addresses.

A NetBIOS name is special because it has a fixed, 16-character length; and it contains within itself a code that tells what kind of resource or service it refers to. If the computer name has fewer than 15 characters, the space between the name and the end of the name is filled with spaces. The 16th character is always the resource indicator.

A computer named Akira might register the following name:

```
    AKIRA        [00h]
```

▶ *For a list of the resource codes, see "NetBIOS Names Reference" at the end of this chapter.*

On boot-up, a WINS client registers its computer name in the WINS database and may register one or more services that it is running. For example, a Windows 95 client with file-sharing enabled would register an extra name for its server service, and a Domain Controller would register an extra name describing itself as a Domain Controller. A typically configured Windows 2000 Professional system will register a Server service, a Workstation service, and a Messenger service that map to the name of the logged-on user.

If another computer tries to register a unique name that is currently registered, the WINS Server will deny the name registration. In addition to registering their names on bootup and logon, WINS clients also release their names on shutdown. A record for the released name stays in the database, but WINS will generally not deny another host who attempts to register with the same name if the first name owner has released it.

Not only computers and users create entries in the WINS database, but also groups. Records for computers and users are called *unique* records, whereas those for groups are called *group* records. A group record is created when a representative or figurehead of a particular group registers itself in the database. A good example of a group record is a record created to allow clients to find a Domain Controller for authentication. Group records have multiple unique IPs but not unique names because the goal is to allow the clients to retrieve a list of multiple addresses that can fulfill a specific purpose such as domain authentication. A listing for a group record that exists for domain authentication purposes would use the Windows 2000 domain's name for the name portion of the record and include the IP addresses of up to 25 Domain Controllers.

The client who queries the WINS Server to find a Domain Controller would be given this list of names and would choose one in its local subnet, if available, for authentication. If there is no local Domain Controller, the client will select an alternate from the list.

DNS Integration

Before Windows 2000 brought us Dynamic DNS, the closest you could get to worldwide dynamic name resolution was DNS in combination with DHCP and WINS. DHCP clients would automatically become WINS clients, and DNS was configured to query WINS when it was asked to resolve a name that wasn't found in its zone file. This allowed, conceivably, a client Web browser to make a request across the Internet to a user computer configured with DHCP and running a Web server.

Even though Windows 2000 Server uses DNS technology that allows dynamic name registration, it is possible to enable what is known as WINS Lookup in the DNS configuration. This will allow the DNS server to access the WINS database for added resolution power.

▶ *For more information on how to set up this option, see Chapter 8.3, "Domain Name System (DNS)."*

Database Replication

When the enterprise is large enough, it sometimes justifies having several WINS Servers to service client queries and registrations in separate locations. To allow proper browsing and prevent duplicate names in the network, these WINS Servers must have some way to synchronize their databases. The process by which this is done is called *replication*.

▶ *For more information, see "Configuring WINS Replication" later in this chapter.*

WINS Record Properties

So far, we have talked only about different ways in which records make their way into the WINS database. Because this is a dynamic database, there is also a need for a mechanism to remove unneeded records. Each record that enters the database is given several properties that determine the length of time it will remain in the database. These are the properties:

- **Renew Interval.** This value determines how often a client will reregister its name in the database. The default is six days.

- **Extinction Interval.** This value sets the amount of time between when a record is marked Released and when it is marked Extinct in the database. The default is six days.

- **Extinction Timeout.** This determines how long a record is extinct before it is eligible for scavenging. The default is six days.
  ▶ *For more information about scavenging, see "Maintaining the WINS Database" later in this chapter.*

- **Verification Interval.** This interval determines how long a WINS Server will keep a record that was replicated to it before it queries the other WINS Servers to make sure that the record is valid and should still be kept. The default is 24 days.

These settings are optimal and should be only changed after proper consideration.

When to Use WINS

Although Windows 2000 brings a feature set that allows one to do without WINS, WINS is still usually needed for networks supporting earlier non-Windows 2000 Microsoft clients.

▶ *For more information on which clients are supported and how they are configured, see "Configuring WINS Clients" later in this chapter.*

If you are fortunate enough to be administering a network that has a pure Windows 2000 client base, your best name-resolution solution is not to use WINS at all, but to put all your eggs in the sturdy DNS basket. Windows 2000 clients do not require NetBIOS support for name resolution.

In another scenario—a network that exists within the bounds of a single unsubnetted network—WINS is not strictly necessary because clients can broadcast to resolve names. Implementing a WINS Server can serve to reduce broadcast traffic, and clients can be configured to use WINS to resolve both local and remote addresses in a larger environment, thereby cutting down on broadcast traffic over the whole enterprise.

WINS Not Specific to Domain

Note that a WINS Server's functionality is not specific to a particular Windows 2000 domain. A WINS Server could service a score of small Windows 2000 domains, and a network of properly replicating WINS Servers could take care of a couple of domains that contain ten thousand clients apiece. WINS doesn't care particularly about the domain membership of its clients; it merely accepts name registration and responds to queries.

One benefit of having a WINS Server in a network in which all the clients are WINS clients is that it is easy for an administrator to have a centralized, current list of all the systems on the network. This can help troubleshoot duplicate IP addresses and can tell you where certain users are logged on.

Windows 2000-Specific Features

Windows 2000 brings a revised version of WINS with some new and useful improvements. The most noticeable difference is the use of the MMC for WINS administration, but there are other important additions under the hood. Here are some of the most important new features:

- **Export Function.** This allows the administrator to output the entire WINS database to a comma-delimited text file. To make use of this feature, go to the Action menu in the WINS console and choose Export while the desired server is selected.

- **Persistent Connections.** A WINS Server can now be configured to keep a connection open to its replication partners; by doing so, increase replication speed and reduce the overhead of creating and tearing down connections.

- **Immediate Record Deletion.** Until NT 4.0's Service Pack 4, an administrator could not delete individual records from the database without using a command-line utility.

- **Read-Only Console Access.** There is a new, built-in, local users group called WINS USERS, whose membership allows read-only access of the WINS database. This feature allows an administrator to provide read-only access to others for delegated tasks like duplicate IP hunting.
  ▶ *For more information on local groups, see Chapter 4.5, "Creating and Managing Groups."*

Installing WINS

The system running the WINS service should be a Windows 2000 Server with adequate processor and disk resources. These steps take you through the installation process:

1 Open the Add/Remove Windows Components Wizard found in the Add/Remove Programs Control Panel.
  ▶ *For more information about the Windows Components Wizard, see Chapter 8.1, "Overview of Managing Network Services."*

2 Scroll through the list of components and click Networking Services.

3 Click Details.

4 Scroll through the list and check the box next to Windows Internet Name Service (WINS). Click OK.

5 When and if prompted, enter the path to the Windows 2000 distribution files and click Continue.

6   When the installation is finished, you will not be prompted to restart your system, but it is advisable if you can spare the downtime. At this point, WINS management can begin.

7   Make sure that the WINS Server is configured to use itself for WINS resolution and registration. Check the Advanced TCP/IP properties to make sure this is the case.

Configuring WINS Servers

If your network is only using one WINS Server, setting up WINS is one of the easier things you will have to do in your job. After the service is installed and clients are configured with the IP address of the WINS Server, your configuration is mostly finished. Your main tasks with WINS will be related to maintenance. If you have multiple WINS Servers, you will need to configure replication among them. Maintenance and replication will be covered in this section.

Adding a WINS Server to the Console

If the system that you run the WINS administration console from is not a WINS Server, the first thing that needs to be done is to add a WINS Server to the console so that it can be administered. The following steps walk you through this:

1   Open WINS from the Administrator Tools menu.

2   In the console tree, click WINS.

3   Use the Action pull-down menu and select Add Server.

4   In the WINS Server field of the Add Server dialog box, type the name of the WINS Server you want to add, or use Browse to locate the WINS Server by name on your network.

You must be logged on as a member of the Administrator's group to configure a WINS Server.

Starting and Stopping the WINS Server

Some maintenance operations, such as restoring the WINS database, call for stopping the WINS service. This can be done with the Start and Stop options in the WINS console Action menu.

As usual, the service can also be stopped or started from a command line run locally on the WINS Server with `net stop wins` or `net start wins`.

Using the Pause option stops the WINS service from processing any more queries or registrations, but doesn't reinitialize the service.

Maintaining the WINS Database

Although WINS installation and initial configuration is quite simple, there are several important tasks that need to be done to keep WINS functioning properly. These maintenance tasks involve ensuring that records are current and accurate.

Scavenging

In a multi-server WINS environment, records referencing released and removed clients that were originally registered at other WINS Servers accumulate in the database of each WINS Server. The process of removing these records is called *scavenging*. At regular intervals, every month or so, the database should be scavenged to remove information that is not current. Scavenging will happen automatically according to the interval set in the Server Properties. To scavenge the WINS database manually, choose Scavenge from the Action menu.

Deleting and Tombstoning Entries in the WINS Database

Sometimes, you want to bypass the graceful expiration approach, and delete records directly and immediately from the database. One reason you might want to do this is if a system gets its IP address changed and is subsequently powered-off without the opportunity to release its name from the database. On rebooting, the system comes up with a new IP and the same name, and tries to register itself. The WINS Server will deny the name registration because it already has an entry for that name using a different IP address. In this situation, there is little to do except delete the record or change the IP address back to what it was. Using the Action menu in the WINS console while the server whose database you want to administer is selected, click on Find by Name. This should allow you to specify the entry you want to delete.

1 After you have found the entry you want to remove, select it and click Delete in the Action menu. A Delete Record dialog box will appear.

2 At this point, you have two choices. You can merely delete the record locally, or you can delete the record locally and mark it for deletion on other replication partners.

If the record did not originate on this server, choosing to delete it only locally will probably result in the record reappearing after the next replication. To prevent this happening, you should choose to replicate the deletion.

Replicating a deletion to other WINS Servers is known as *tombstoning*. When viewing the WINS database, a cross next to a record means that the record is extinct and that there is an outstanding command to replication partners to delete the record. Tombstoned records are removed by scavenging or after the normal Extinction Interval and Timeout.

Deleting an Owner from the Database

The occasion might arise when you need to delete all the records in the database that were originally registered at a particular WINS Server. This process is similar to that of deleting an individual record, except that it will happen on a larger scale.

1 Choose `Delete Owner` in the `Action` menu and choose the WINS Server whose records you want to remove from the local database. You will then see the same options that we saw when we deleted a record.

2 You can either choose to delete the records locally or tombstone them for deletion on other WINS Servers.

Tombstoned records are removed by scavenging or after the normal Extinction Interval and Timeout.

Checking Database Consistency

Part of maintaining the database is regularly checking it for consistency. This process compares the records it received via replication in its database with the original records that are being stored at other WINS Servers. When consistency checking is configured to run automatically, it does so at 2:00 a.m. each morning by default. To turn this feature on, do the following:

1 Choose Properties from the Action menu.

2 Click the Database Verification tab.

3 After the Database Verification settings window comes up, select the Verify database consistency every 24 hours checkbox.

4 Make sure that the other default settings are what you desire and modify them if needed.

To manually initiate a consistency check, choose Check Database Consistency from the Action menu and choose Yes when prompted.

Backing Up and Restoring the WINS Database

WINS has its own built-in mechanism for backing up the WINS database. After it is configured with a backup directory path in the WINS Server Properties (in the Action menu), it performs a backup on the database every three hours. This interval can be adjusted. When the backup runs, WINS

creates a \Wins_bak\New folder in the path specified. When no path is configured, the default backup path is in the root folder of the system partition.
Do not back up the database to a network drive.

In the event that the WINS database needs to be backed up immediately, such
as to test a new backup path, the Action menu in the WINS console has a
Backup Database option that performs a backup on demand.

If your WINS database has become corrupted, you will want to restore it
from backup. This process must be performed locally at the system whose
database needs restoring, not remotely from another system. To restore the
database, follow these steps:

1 Stop the WINS service on the afflicted server. This may take several
   minutes, so make sure it stops before proceeding.
   ▶ *For more information, see Chapter 3.4, "Managing Services and Tasks."*

2 Delete all files in the WINS database folder on the system whose database you want to restore. The path for that folder can be found in the
   Advanced tab in your WINS Server's Properties in the Database Path
   text box.

3 Open the WINS console, and after selecting the ailing server in the list,
   choose Restore Database from the Action menu. If the Restore option
   is grayed-out, refresh the view and make sure that the WINS service has
   stopped.

4 In the Browse for Folder dialog box that comes up, point to the folder
   that was configured as the backup directory. WINS requires that this
   path be the same path that was configured as the backup path. This
   would be a problem if the database backup has been moved to a new
   path.

If this fails to fix the problem, another solution is to stop the WINS service,
delete all database (.mdb) files in the WINS system directory, and start the
WINS service again. This will cause a blank database to be created, and the
database will rebuild itself over time.

Configuring WINS Replication

When more than one WINS Server exists in an enterprise, replication is
required. During replication, WINS Servers pass collections of new records
back and forth, rather than copies of the entire database.

Building a replication topology requires defining the relationships between
the WINS Servers properly. Relationships between replication partners can be
defined as being Push, Pull, or Push/Pull.

- In a Push situation, thresholds are set that initiate replication when a
  certain number of new records has been reached.

- Configuring a server to Pull means setting it to query another server
  to check for changes at set time intervals. The default interval is
  30 minutes.

- In a Push/Pull relationship, both servers have a threshold at which they will push records to each other, but both also have an interval at which they will query the other for new records to be replicated. In either event, any new records or changes to existing records will be replicated.

Setting Up Replication

To set up WINS replication for a Windows 2000 Server, follow these steps and guidelines:

1 From the WINS console, select Replication Partners and then choose New Replication Partner from the Action menu.

2 In the New Replication Partner dialog box that appears, enter the name or IP address of the WINS Server that you want to replicate with. After clicking OK, the server you added should show up in the Replication Partners list.

3 By default, replication partners are set up to be in a Push/Pull relationship. If you want to change this, right-click the Replication Partner icon and select Properties from the menu. The Properties dialog box will appear.

4 Select the Advanced tab. From this tab, you can set up a relationship that either only pushes or pulls. This might come in handy, for example for sites that have an unreliable WAN link, and it isn't critical that replication happen throughout the day. A pull interval could be configured that ensures that replication only happens late at night.

5 In the Pull Parameters section, enable the Use Persistent Connection feature. This is almost always a good thing. Be careful about setting the pull interval too low because the WINS service may choke on registrations and query resolution if it is constantly processing replication.

To manually initiate replication, right-click Replication Partners and select Replicate Now from the menu. You will be asked to confirm, and will then be notified that the job has been queued.

Best Practices: Replication

If there are going to be problems with your implementation of WINS, the likelihood of them having to do with replication is high. Here are some guidelines that will help ensure that your deployment is a happy one:

- The topology of a WINS replication network can vary, but WINS has a well-deserved reputation for turning any but the most simple replication arrangement into a huge mess. The worst topology one could choose is a circle in which replication flows in a single direction. The best topology is that of a hub and spokes wherein one server has a Push/Pull relationship with each of the other servers, and none of them replicates to any other server but the central one.

- Don't *ever* have a WINS Server in a multiple WINS Server enterprise that isn't replicating with the others. If you administer a branch location and decide that you want to have a local WINS Server instead of using the corporate one, you *must* coordinate things so your local WINS Server is integrated into the wider WINS network. Enterprise-wide name resolution must be centralized and act as a single organism.

- Don't put a WINS Server in every subnet. If there are no WAN links involved in your enterprise, two WINS Servers will suffice for fault-tolerance. A single WINS Server with a Pentium II processor and at least 64 megs of RAM should be able to service the requests and registrations for up to 15,000 clients. Less is more.

- Don't deploy more than 20 WINS Servers. Even if you have a vast enterprise, other things need to change before you need to deploy this many servers.

- Don't feel obligated to put a WINS Server at every remote site. If the WAN link is fast enough, there are fewer than 300 clients, and there is enough bandwidth available, it might be far better to have your clients register and query across the link directly. The only caveat in this situation is that you configure clients with a proper node type, one that allows the clients to continue to go about their local business if the WAN link goes down.

  ▶ *For more information on node types, see the section on NetBIOS name resolution in Chapter 8.1, "Overview of Managing Network Services."*

- If your enterprise spans multiple locations, make sure that your central WINS Server is well-centralized, so that its clients and replication partners will have to cross as few networks as possible.

- Avoid creating static entries in the WINS database. A static entry in the database can easily be forgotten about and cause mysterious trouble later on when the computer's address is changed. After these static entries begin to replicate, they can be troublesome to remove.

WINS Clients

As has been discussed, the WINS service exists primarily for backward-compatability and will be used more frequently to support older clients than Windows 2000 clients. WINS supports a wide variety of clients. Here is a condensed list:

- All Windows (2000, NT, 9x, WFW) operating systems
- Microsoft LAN Manager
- MS-DOS Clients
- OS/2 Clients
- Samba-enabled Linux and Unix hosts

Each of these operating systems typically has an option in the networking configuration that allows at least two addresses to be specified for WINS Servers. In the event of the first address failing, the second address will be used.

Solving the Windows 95 WINS Problem

A known shortcoming with Windows 95 clients using WINS is that if there is only one WINS Server specified in the TCP/IP configuration on the client, NetBIOS name resolution will fail regularly if the second field is left blank. If an initial query to the WINS Server times out, the client tries to move to an alternate server instead of querying the server again, and when it finds that none is configured, it gives up. This problem can be solved by putting the same address of the single WINS Server in both fields, which allows the client to properly continue to poll in the event of a timeout.

The easiest way to deploy WINS to clients is to have them automatically configured via the scope option in DHCP. When this is done, clients automatically become WINS clients when they receive an IP address from DHCP. One smart move is to make sure that the DHCP lease interval is the same as the six-day WINS renewal interval. This will cut down on lease renewal traffic and allow the services to work more smoothly together.

▶ *For specifics on how to manually configure a Windows 2000 system to use WINS, see Chapter 2.4, "Configuring Network Components."*

Monitoring WINS

Specialized Performance Monitor counters are installed on a Windows 2000 Server when WINS is installed. Table 8.4.1 lists a few key counters and their descriptions.

Table 8.4.1   WINS Performance Monitor Counters

Counter Name	Description
Queries/sec	Number of NetBIOS name queries that are being received per second.
Releases/sec	Number of release messages received per second.
Total Number of Conflicts/sec	This is an average of group and unique name conflicts detected by WINS per second.
Unique Registrations/sec	Number of unique name registrations detected per second.

As you can imagine, having any substantial number of conflicts per second warrants investigation.

These counters should be used in combination with other counters for services running on the server so the relative impact of each service can be measured. The best way to use performance counters is to regularly benchmark the service's performance so that any real deviations from a standard can alert you to potential issues. Having a set of benchmarks whose differences you can map directly to specific changes in your network and the number of clients using the service gives you a valuable planning tool for expansion.

▶ *For more information on monitoring WINS, see Chapter 3.3, "Using Administrative Tools."*

NetBIOS Names Reference

Early in this chapter, we noted that for all Microsoft operating systems that support and use NetBIOS names, the first 15 characters of a name can be specified by a user and the 16th character of the name (00–FF hex) always indicates a resource type. Records in the WINS database use NetBIOS unique and group names, and knowledge of the various names will go a long way toward making sense of the WINS mappings database. The following tables detail the different names found in the WINS database.

Table 8.4.2   NetBIOS Unique Names

Format	Description
computer_name[00h]	Registered by the Workstation Service on the WINS client. In general, this name is called the NetBIOS computer name.
computer_name[03h]	Registered by the Messenger Service on the WINS client. This service is used by the client when sending and receiving messages.
computer_name[06h]	Registered by the Remote Access Service (RAS) on the WINS client (when the RAS Server service is started).
domain_name[1Bh]	Registered by each Windows NT Server 4.0 Domain Controller running as the domain master browser. This name record is used to allow remote browsing of domains. When a WINS Server is queried for this name, a WINS Server returns the IP addresses of the computers that registered this name.
computer_name[1Fh]	Registered by the Network Dynamic Data Exchange (NetDDE) services.
computer_name[20h]	Registered by the Server service on the WINS client.
computer_name[21h]	Registered by the RAS Client service on the WINS client (when the RAS Client is started).

continues

Table 8.4.2   continued

Format	Description
computer_name[BEh]	Registered by the Network Monitoring Agent Service and appears only if the service is started on the WINS client computer.
computer_name[BFh]	Registered by the Network Monitoring Utility.
username[03h]	User names for the currently logged-on users are registered in the WINS database. Each user name is registered by the Server service component so that the user can receive any net send commands sent to that user name. If more than one user logs on with the same user name, only the first computer logged on with that user name registers the name.

Table 8.4.2   NetBIOS Group Names

Format	Description
domain_name[00h]	Registered by the Workstation Service so that it can receive browser broadcasts from LAN Manager-based computers.
domain_name[1Ch]	Registered for use by the Domain Controllers within the domain and can contain up to 25 IP addresses.
domain_name[1Dh]	Registered for use by master browsers, of which there is only one per subnet.
group_name[1Eh]	A normal group name. Any computers configured to be network browsers can broadcast to this name and listen for broadcasts to this name to elect a master browser.
group_name[20h]	A special group name called the Internet Group is registered with WINS Servers to identify groups of computers for administrative purposes.
__MSBROWSE__[01h]	Registered by the master browser for each subnet. When a WINS Server receives a name query for this name, the WINS Server always returns the network broadcast address for the requesting client's local network.

For more detailed information on NetBIOS names, see Microsoft TechNet article Q119495. For information on creating WINS static mappings, see article Q140064.

8.5

Remote Access Service (RAS)

You Need to Read This Section If You Want to:

- Configure Windows 2000 Remote Access Service servers.
- Manage the type of Remote Access you allow to your local area networks.
- Understand Remote Access Service policies.
- Understand Microsoft's RADIUS server, IAS.

Related Topics

Overview of Windows 2000 Remote Access Server

Windows NT 3.1 Remote Access Server supported IP, IPX, NetBEUI, compression, and basic encryption. Windows NT 4.0 RAS added two more protocols, PPP and PPTP, plus new features such as autodial and demand-dial routing. Now, Windows 2000 Remote Access Server supports even more protocols, for example, L2TP, IPSec, EAP, and RADIUS. Windows 2000 operating system offers fully integrated routing, API availability for developers to accommodate custom protocols or tools, a simpler Network and Dial-up Connections interface for the RAS user, and centralized management for the RAS administrator through the Routing and Remote Access MMC snap-in.

Windows 2000 RAS allows point-to-point, point-to-LAN, LAN-to-LAN, and LAN-to-WAN connections. In previous releases, RAS on Server was limited to 256 simultaneous connections, but now RAS is limited only by the capability of the hardware installed in the server. W2K RAS supports IP, IPX, NetBEUI, and Apple Talk. Windows 2000 Professional has been enhanced to accept one incoming call per media type, for a total of three possible inbound sessions, through the NIC, a modem, or serial device.

This chapter discusses installation, configuration, and troubleshooting of a Remote Access Server. A referential overview of Virtual Private Networks and IPSec is included to very briefly acquaint you with a few security options for RAS. But first, we discuss a basic review of the underlying architecture in order to establish a baseline.

NDIS.sys, now version 5.0, is still alive and well, wrapping network protocols to the network driver interface. NDISWAN.sys provides a miniport interface to the NIC driver at the MAC layer per IEEE 802.3 specifications, and an LLC interface to WAN miniport drivers. Each physical device in the server has an associated WAN miniport driver. Moving up the OSI, inbound connections all pass through one RAS server interface, but each outbound connection gets its own interface.

A packet is compressed and encrypted by NDISWAN.sys, the PPP packet is passed up to the WAN miniport driver, and it then goes to the dial-up adapter. After the Remote Access server's Telephony API deals with the actual call connection, the RAS components can negotiate directly with the WAN miniport driver. Finally, NDIS handles any subsequent calls from IP, IPX, NetBEUI, or AppleTalk. Voilá! The client is talking to the server and/or the network as if directly connected.

Armed with this compressed understanding of what is happening behind the scenes, you can now learn how to install Window 2000 Remote Access Server.

Installing RAS Server

As always, check Microsoft's HCL before purchasing any components. Windows 2000 Remote Access Server can be installed on Windows 2000 Server or Advanced Server as a standalone server or as a Domain Controller. Installing RAS is a bit of a misnomer here, because it is fully integrated with the Windows 2000 operating system. So, simply use the Microsoft Management Console and the RRAS (Routing and Remote Access) snap-in as the API to gain administrative access to the Remote Access service. This chapter describes Remote Access Server only, so routing issues will not be discussed. The following list details how to open the RRAS MMC and enable the service.

 1 Open the Routing and Remote Access snap-in in the MMC; or choose Start, Programs, Administrative Tools, Routing and Remote Access from the menu.

    You will see the local computer selected by default. Alternatively, you can right-click Server Status and choose Add Server, which brings up a dialog box that allows you to select either the local machine, choose a specific machine by name, select all RRAS servers, or search the AD for the server.

    After adding the server, the server object appears in the console tree under Server Status.

 2 To enable Routing and Remote Access service on the server added, right-click the server object and choose Configure and Enable Routing and Remote Access.

    This launches the Routing and Remote Access Wizard.

Don't Forget to Set the Incoming Connections

An Incoming Connections dial-up network connection must exist in the Network and Dial-up Connections folder in order to enable the service. If one is not already configured, the wizard gives you an opportunity to do so.

Configuring RAS Servers

Many administrative configuration tasks completed through the MMC are done using property pages, and configuring RAS servers is no exception. After the server object is added and the service enabled, right-click the server object and choose Properties from the menu to view the RAS server's property sheet.

The RAS server property sheet shows the following:

- It shows whether the server is a router and/or a Remote Access server.
- It shows the authentication providers, methods, and accounting providers (authentication and accounting providers are Windows and RADIUS).
- It shows authentication methods, including those available with Windows NT 4.0 RAS, plus new support for Extensible Authentication Protocol (EAP).
- It shows how to assign IP and/or IPX addresses. Note that the protocol tabs appear only if the protocol is configured on the server.
- It shows default PPP options for Multilink, LCP extensions, and software compression on the server.
- It even shows logging preferences.

To assign dynamic IP addresses to the RAS client, a static pool can be created on the RAS server or addresses can be retrieved from a DHCP server on the LAN. If you choose to use DHCP, you must set up the DHCP Relay Agent using the IP address of your DHCP server; otherwise, requests from the RAS clients will not be passed. Furthermore, when the RAS client connects, DHCP can only assign the minimum parameters required for IP configuration: an IP address and subnet mask. Other parameters, such as DNS and WINS, come from the RRAS connection properties itself.

> **Configure IP Pool of Address for RAS**
>
> Configuring a pool of IP addresses on the RAS server eliminates the dependency of the RAS server contacting DHCP, thereby simplifying the process. However, this pool of IP addresses must not overlap configured address ranges that are available on any network DHCP servers, nor on any previously defined address on the network. Avoid this common error by keeping the pool of addresses available to your RAS client unique to the network.

RAS Ports

To view or configure a RAS port, right-click Ports, choose Properties, and double-click the device representing the port you want to configure. The Configure Device property sheet offers the following options:

- Allow Remote Access connections (inbound only).
- Allow demand-dial routing connections (inbound and outbound).
- Set the phone number for the device. The phone number entered is used as the Called Station ID when setting the Remote Access policy, discussed later in this chapter. If this is an L2TP or PPTP port, an IP address should be entered in this field rather than a phone number. The IP address entered must be the address configured on the VPN server's interface where the connection is received.
- Set the maximum port limit for that device.

To view the status of a specific RAS port, select Ports and then right-click the physical device you want to view, listed in the details pane on the right. The Port Status Property sheet comes up, listing the name of the device, its condition, the number of bytes passed in or out, error information, and network registration information.

Multilink

Windows NT 4.0 RAS was Microsoft's first Remote Access Service version that was compliant with the specifications of RFC 1990, enabling Multilink. In an effort to increase throughput for a given remote dial-up session, Multilink offered the capability to combine multiple physical links into a single, wider logical connection. Modems and ISDN lines connecting to the RAS server could thereby be combined to enable greater bandwidth. Of course, technology today now offers DSL or cable modem connections of greater throughput, but not all remote locations offer this capability.

To enable Multilink on a server, open the RAS server's property sheet, select the PPP tab, and select the Multilink checkbox. Once enabled, Windows 2000 will apply the associated RAS policy to this particular server's PPP connection for a given connection attempt. So, don't forget to enable Multilink on the Dial-in Profile associated with the RAS Policy used by the client that will be attempting a Multilink connection. To do this, open the Remote Access Policy that will be applied against the RAS server's configuration for the connection attempt and click Edit Profile. Multilink options are to default to server setting, disable, or allow *x* number of maximum ports. Remember, as was true with earlier RAS implementations, Multilink with callback enabled is available only for ISDN connections. Consider the Bandwidth Allocation Protocol (BAP) if you want to increase the number of ports/phone numbers available to users. Check online help for more details.

Encryption

Encryption is configured explicitly for the Remote Access Service in the same Dial-in Profile property sheet described in the previous paragraph. Remember that today's VPN capabilities are much more secure than the simple encryption capabilities offered here. However, it is a nice option if the server or client cannot or is not using more sophisticated encryption protocols. VPN capabilities are reviewed in the next section.

There are four types of encryption settings:

- **No Encryption.**   Use this option to allow unencrypted connections. Clear the checkbox to require encryption.
- **Basic.**   For dial-up and PPTP-based VPN connections, Microsoft Point-to-Point Encryption (MPPE) with a 40-bit key is used. For L2TP over IPSec-based VPN connections, 56-bit DES encryption is used.

- **Strong.**   For dial-up and PPTP-based VPN connections, MPPE with a 56-bit key is used. For L2TP over IPSec-based VPN connections, 56-bit DES encryption is used.

- **Strongest.**   For dial-up and PPTP-based VPN connections, MPPE with a 128-bit key is used. For L2TP over IPSec-based VPN connections, triple DES (3DES) encryption is used. This option is available only on North American versions of Windows 2000.

IAS Tie-in to Encryption Settings.
If you use the Windows 2000 version of RADIUS called Internet Authentication Service, the service references the settings configured previously for user VPN and dial-up connections.

Configuring RAS Users and Clients

Windows 2000 RAS scrutinizes connection attempts based on the user and the computer.

For user accounts, Remote Access Admin or User Manager for Domains was used in Windows NT 4.0 to assign Remote Access permissions to user accounts. Computer Management-Local User Manager or Active Directory Users and Computers MMC snap-ins are used in Windows 2000.

To configure individual accounts, select the user account, choose the Dial-in tab, and configure permission as allow access, deny access or control access through a Remote Access Policy. Use Remote Access Policies when you need to set up several users or have several different types of RAS connectivity that you want to configure for various groups in your organization. Policies and Profiles are discussed in the next section.

Other user properties that can be configured are verification of caller-id (hardware and telephone connection must support this), callback options, static IP addressing, and static IP routing. However, these options are not available in Mixed mode.

For computer accounts, RAS clients need a modem from the HCL, an analog line or other WAN connection, and Remote Access software. Keep in mind that Microsoft PPP clients cannot use AppleTalk.

Table 8.5.1 summarizes the various dial-up clients and Windows 2000 capabilities. (This is a condensed list from RAS help.)

Table 8.5.1   ***Windows 2000 RAS and Dial-up Clients***

Dial-up Networking Client	Supported Windows Windows 2000 RAS PPP Features	Unsupported 2000 RAS PPP Features
Windows 2000	Multilink	
	Bandwidth Allocation Protocol (BAP)	
	Microsoft Challenge Handshake Authentication Protocol— (MS-CHAP) and MS_CHAPv2 (with NT 4, SP4 and later)	
	Challenge Handshake Authentication Protocol (CHAP)	
	Shiva Password Authentication Protocol (SPAP)	
	Password Authentication Protocol (PAP)	
Windows NT v. 4.0	Multilink MS-CHAP and MS-CHAPv2 (with NT 4.0 SP 4 and later) CHAP SPAP PAP	BAP and EAP
Windows NT v. 3.5x	MS-CHAP, CHAP, SPAP, and PAP	Multilink, BAP, MS-CHAPv2, and EAP
Windows 98	Multilink	BAP and EAP
	MS-CHAP and MS-CHAPv2 (with Win98 SP 1 and later) CHAP SPAP PAP	
Windows 95	MS-CHAP CHAP and EAP SPAP PAP (with the Windows Dial-Up	MS-CHAPv2, Multilink, BAP,
	Networking 1.3 Performance and Security Upgrade for Windows95)	
	MS-CHAP v2 over VPNs only, not dial-up (with the Windows98 SP 1 and later)	
Any PPP client	RAS will negotiate authentication with any PPP client, provided LAN	

continues

Table 8.5.1   *continued*

Dial up Networking Client	Supported Windows Windows 2000 RAS PPP Features	Unsupported 2000 RAS PPP Features
	and authentication protocols are configured properly. See third-party documentation for additional details.	

Remember that with Windows 2000, the identity of the client is used to authenticate any session to a shared resource. In previous version of Windows, these sessions were null sessions that were not authenticated. Be sure that proper permissions, memberships to domains, or trusts are in place.

For automated setup of RAS clients, Rasdial is an excellent command-line utility that ships with Windows 2000 RAS. Create a batch file and call it by using Rasdial. Automatic backups to or from remote computers can be scheduled using Windows 2000 Task Scheduler, dial-up networking, and Rasdial.

RAS Policies

By default, Windows 2000 RAS ships with a default RAS policy, found in the RRAS snap-in under the Remote Access server by selecting the Remote Access Policies object and reading the details pane on the right (Allow access if dial-in permissions is enabled). This default policy allows any dial-in access controls set up on the user object to be enabled. (Please refer to the previous section on how to enable RAS on the user object.) If the default policy is deleted, RAS access will be denied. As you determine the various needs of groups of users in your organization, design a RAS policy to meet those needs, create and apply new policies, and leave the default policy alone. It is possible to bring back the default policy if it is accidentally deleted (refer to the help provided with Windows 2000 RAS). Figure 8.5.1 shows the default RAS Policy property sheet included with Windows 20000 RAS, showing the standard attributes of a RAS Policy.

▶ *For a general description of policies, see Chapter 6.3, "Group Policies."*

Note the four settings that make up a policy's settings:

- Policy name
- Conditions to match (rule)
- Access control (permissions)
- Profile

Figure 8.5.1   FC Default RAS Policy property sheet.

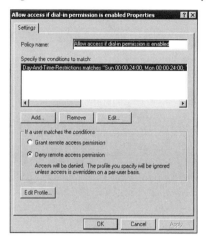

As you can see, a Remote Access policy defines the parameters that apply for a given connection attempt. An RAS policy is made up of conditions, permissions, and profiles. Note the four settings that can be made on this property sheet (refer to Figure 8.5.2). For example, you may have one policy defined to meet standard employee needs, and another policy for accounting personnel.

First, when a connection attempt is initiated, its conditions are compared with a rule (shown in the Specify the conditions to match field). All attributes of the condition must be true for the rule to invoke the policy. Once found, the policy permits or denies the attempt, enforcing all configured attributes of the policy. Table 8.5.2 describes the various attribute types that can be used in a RAS policy.

Table 8.5.2   RAS Policy Attributes

Attribute Name	Description
NAS IP Address	The IP address of the network access server (NAS). This attribute is a character string. Use this attribute for an IAS server if you have one.
Service Type	The type of service being requested: PPP, a Telnet login, or RADIUS. Use this attribute for an IAS server if you have one.
Framed Protocol	Stipulate the type of framing for incoming packets, such as PPP and X.25. Use this attribute for an IAS server if you have one.

continues

Table 8.5.2   continued

Attribute Name	Description
Called Station ID	The phone number of the RAS server. Either the software or hardware will support reading this number when the attempt is made, or you can manually type it in for each port.
Calling Station ID	The phone number used by the caller. Again, this functionality must be supported by the hardware and software.
NAS Port Type	The type of media used by the caller: analog, ISDN, or VPN.
Day and Time Restrictions	The day of the week and the time of day of the connection attempt, commonly called *TOD*. The day and time is relative to the date and time of the server providing the authorization.
Client IP Address	The IP address of the RADIUS client. Use this attribute for an IAS server if you have one.
Client Vendor	The vendor of the network access server (NAS) that is requesting authentication. For Windows 2000 RAS server, it is the NAS manufacturer.
Client Friendly Name	The name of the RADIUS client computer that is requesting authentication. This attribute is designed for the IAS server.
Windows Groups	The names of the Windows 2000 groups to which the user attempting the connection belongs. Note that built-in local groups of standalone Windows 2000 RAS servers cannot be used here.
Tunnel Type	The type of tunnel being created by the requesting client. Use this condition to specify profile settings such as authentication methods or encryption strengths for a specific type of tunneling technology to support whatever the user's connection is configured to request.

Next, Remote Access permissions are either granted or denied as con-figured in the matching policy. Remember that user accounts can be configured to deny Remote Access permissions, and this finer-grain permission overrides Remote Access policy permission. However, if the user account is configured for access through the Remote Access Policy option, the policy determines if the connection is ultimately granted or denied.

Finally, after a connection attempt is authenticated, the policy further defines the type of access allowed. This is done through the permission associated with a user account or permissions associated with the policy itself. Several properties are defined through profiles:

- Dial-in constraints. Idle timeout and maximum session length, TOD, and media limits.
- Multilink. The maximum number of ports that can be used.
- Authentication. EAP, MS-CHAP v2, MS-CHAP, CHAP, PAP, SPAP, or None.
- Encryption. None, Basic, Strong, or Strongest (for VPN connections)
- Advanced. For RADIUS connections.

In conclusion, a Remote Access Policy is the union set of a matching rule, access controls, and associated profile. When all the conditions of a policy are met, the policy is applied to the connecting user and computer.

Internet Authentication Service

Windows NT 4.0 Option Pack was Microsoft's first RADIUS implementation, compliant with the specifications of RFC 2138 and 2139. Now, Windows 2000 ships with both a Remote Authentication Dial-In User Service (RADIUS) client and a RADIUS server called Internet Authentication Service, or IAS.

RAS can behave like a RADIUS client and provide information to a RADIUS server that is used for authentication and accounting purposes. The RADIUS server can be either IAS or an external third-party server. Also, multiple servers can be configured to provide fault-tolerance. IAS as a RADIUS server validates client requests based on authentication and authorization, plus it provides accounting for users who connect using dial-up or VPN connections.

There are several advantages to using Microsoft's RADIUS solution:

- IAS as a RADIUS server offers support for RAS policies and EAP.
- It is fully integrated with the Active Directory.

If your organization supports many RAS servers, administering these servers becomes time-consuming. Set up Windows 2000 as an IAS server and set up your RAS servers as RADIUS clients. IAS centralizes the administration of your RAS servers regarding authentication, authorization, and accounting.

When a RADIUS client contacts IAS, IAS responds to the client with authentication parameters that may be ignored by RAS. Other authentication parameters sent by the RADIUS server are used by RAS for the connection, such as type of frame and type of service. If a Windows 2000 RAS server authenticates against a Windows 2000 IAS server, a shared secret must be configured that is used to encrypt messages passed between them.

If RADIUS is your authentication provider, the Extensible Authentication Protocol (EAP) can be used as an authentication method, extending the PPP packet, if desired. To configure this, select the Remote Access Policy, choose Edit Profile, and select the EAP box.

Troubleshooting Dial-up Connections

First, be sure the computer hardware is functional, cabling is connected, and WAN links are up. Slow WAN links used by connections that require strong encryption can slow transmissions and cause timeout errors or erroneous messages such as Domain Controller could not be found. Check the throughput of the connection using modem diagnostics utilities or client dial-up software.

After confirming that issues are not hardware-related, proceed up the OSI model and eliminate one layer at a time. Given the complexity of RAS and the various architectures and technologies that it uses, it is easy to spend a lot of time chasing down the wrong path because an immediate first impression clouds logical deduction. Do not underestimate the benefit of using basic scientific troubleshooting methodology. Comparison with the OSI helps to isolate the *source* of the problem, not the symptom; and it forces you to look at the whole picture, rather than focusing in on immediate first impressions. Furthermore, generic error messages can often mask the true source of a problem because assumptions about the cause of the error messages are made.

Check the TCP/IP, DNS, and phone number settings. I remember working with a user for two days because they were getting access denied messages when attempting to connect. The server wasn't logging any errors, nor were there any connection attempts for this user. The user had been able to connect successfully in the past from other remote locations. I painstakingly reviewed the settings and functionality of the ISP's service and the user account, thinking that they had inadvertently been changed when someone may have made modifications for other needs. It turned out to be user error—the area code of the RAS phone number for this newly entered remote connection was off by one digit. The user was actually calling some unknown RAS server on the Internet who responded with an access denied message!

Be aware the Multilink connections that are configured for callback are supported Windows 2000 RAS and dial-up clients on ISDN lines that have two channels for data, one channel can be calling while the other channel is free to accept the return call. Modems cannot do this.

Given the many configurable aspects of RAS, problems occur due to minor discrepancies between user, client and server, and multiple policy configurations. Try to come up with a few broad-based RAS policies to meet your constituents' needs when designing your RAS security policies. Overlapping policies can be very problematic and can largely be avoided given proper planning.

Verify that the appropriate policy or user setting is being applied by the server, the correct access control parameters are set, and that the profile is configured as desired. For example, check that the level and type of encryption for a user matches the server port and policy. Also, discern whether it is authentication or authorization that is the problem.

Testing and Monitoring RAS

Windows 2000 comes with nifty tools to test and monitor RAS. First, the command-line NetShell utility, netsh: Netsh queries interfaces, protocols, and the RAS on Windows 2000 computers. It can also query other services such as DHCP and WINS. Netsh uses the RAS context to make queries to RAS protocols. See Windows 2000 help, or type **Netsh ras ?** at the command line.

Windows NT's Performance Monitor has become a couple of MMC snap-ins. You can still type **perfmon** at the command line, which will bring up the MMC with the System Monitor and Performance Logs and Alerts Snap-ins. Use this tool to monitor RAS activity on the computer. Performance Logs and Alerts offer several performance objects to monitor. For example, the RAS port object monitors activity per media type and per tunnel. RAS totals offer additional counters for overall activity.

Don't forget to check the RAS log file. Remember that the RAS log file will provide you with additional detailed information regarding RAS server.

Overview of VPNs

Many companies are increasingly concerned about security because of Remote Access users. One way the administrator can increase the security of RAS connections is through the use of Virtual Private Networking. The following section simply introduces the concept of a VP; and PPTP, L2TP, and IPSec as protocols available to Windows 2000 RAS administrators. Keep in mind that there are volumes of books available on these subjects, and this section simply alerts you to some of the alternatives available to you.

As acronyms go these days, often their meaning is not intuitive to their functionality. However, VPN, or Virtual Private Network, is a very intuitive acronym: Virtual (the creation of an abstract concept through protocols), Private (not accessible to the general public), Network (nodes and devices that are able to communicate). VPNs are used to connect a user, computer, or network to another user, computer, or network—typically through a third segment that is untrusted or unprotected. VPNs are commonly used to allow remote mobile users to connect to the corporate LAN securely or to connect two discontiguous segments.

This part of the chapter is a high-level overview of PPTP, L2TP, and IPSec for your convenience. These protocols can be used over your RAS connections to provide increased security using encryption. Volumes of information are available on these protocols and VPN security, and changes are being made daily. Heck, I've received over 120 messages from one security list alone in a one month period, with others even more active.

Windows 2000 server offers integrated routing with RAS, VPN technology and Active Directory. IPSec is fully integrated with the Windows 2000 operating system. Routed tunnels are supported using Layer 2 protocols PPTP and L2TP, even for demand-dial and Multilink routing. IP security can be centrally managed by using the Active Directory or RADIUS. In fact, a lot had been done to enhance IP communication capabilities, such as faster stack implementation and providing a better scaling for computers with multiple processors.

In 1996, Point-to-Point Tunneling Protocol (PPTP) and Layer 2 Tunneling Protocols (L2TP) were the foremost tunneling protocols in development in the market. PPTP was spearheaded by a consortium of companies, including Microsoft, Ascend, and 3COM; L2TP was spearheaded by Cisco. In 1997, standardization and planning brought about full deployment by 1998, plus the directive to eventually merge these two similar protocols because they were intended for the same purpose. By 1999, pervasive VPN technologies abounded: smart cards, which provided the RAS user with apparent seamless, secure, integration to devices and connections. Both L2TP and PPTP encrypt and encapsulate at the Data Link layer, creating a PPP frame.

There are two ways to control secure Remote Access: through the user object and through policies. New capabilities allow policies or profiles to assign per-call attributes. Use the RRAS MMC snap-in to assign additional attributes to a call or manage RAS by groups rather than users. Please see the discussion earlier in this chapter regarding RAS user properties and RAS policies.

When Windows 2000 RRAS is installed, five objects representing PPTP and five objects representing L2TP are available by default. First, a look at PPTP, L2TP is discussed, and finally you get discussion of IPSec.

PPTP

PPTP is available for all platforms (Windows 95, Windows 98, Windows NT 4.0+, and Window 2000) for both client-to-server and server-to-server connections. PPTP cannot be used with IPSec; rather, MPPE encryption may be used. MPPE is the lower-level encryption capability that Microsoft has offered in its earlier operating systems. PPTP will encrypt IP, IPX, and NetBEUI traffic and then encapsulate it in an IP header.

L2TP

L2TP is available for client-to-server connections for Windows 95, Windows 98, Windows NT 4.0+, and Windows 2000; but server-to-server connections are supported only by Windows 2000. L2TP/PPP can be used in conjunction with IPSec encryption to establish secure transport mode connections. L2TP also encrypts IP, IPX, NetBEUI traffic.

IPSec

IPSec can only be used between computers running the Windows 2000 platform. Windows 95 can use it if it has a third-party IPSec client installed; no IPSec client for Windows 95 is available from Microsoft. IPSec works at Layer 3, and offers IPSec Transport mode and IPSec Tunnel mode. IPSec Transport mode encrypts traffic between two nodes, and IPSec Tunnel mode secures IP traffic between two networks. Windows 2000 IPSec provides multicast and multiprotocol supports, proprietary PKI User and machine authentication, and proprietary IP tunneling.

Use the Microsoft IP Security Management snap-in to centrally manage policies.

In conclusion, options available to create secure solutions include the following:

- Remote access VPNs
- Branch office VPNs
- Extranet VPNs
- Intranet VPNs

If you are looking for a client-to-server or server-to-server solution and have a limited budget, PPTP is the best pick. If you are looking for a client-to-server or server-to-server solution with the strongest security out of the box, L2TP with IPSec is the best pick (using Tunnel mode for server-to-server connections).

8.6

IP Routing

You Need to Read This Section If You Want to:

- Set up a dial-on-demand router interface.
- Use dynamic routing with hardware-based routers.
- Use IP multicasting.

Related Topics

For More Information On ▶ *See*

Establishing a dial-out connection ▶ *Chapter 8.5: Remote Access Service (RAS)*

Creating a user account ▶ *Chapter 4.4: Creating and Managing User Accounts*

Activating Internet connection sharing ▶ *Chapter 8.7: Connection Sharing*

Installing SNMP support ▶ *Chapter 2.3: Configuring Devices and System Settings*

IP Routing Overview

Even the smallest networks today rarely consist of a single TCP/IP subnet. Many small networks are connected via routed dial-up connections to the Internet. Larger networks may consist of many TCP/IP subnets interconnected by WAN links. Networks that consist of more than one subnet must have some mechanism for forwarding IP traffic to the proper destination network. This is called *IP routing*. IP routing uses default gateways, or routers, on a subnet to forward traffic to the proper destination subnet. These routers can be either hardware devices or routing software installed on a PC. The Routing and Remote Access Service provides this functionality in Windows 2000.

▶▶ *For more information on RAS, see Chapter 8.5, "Remote Access Service."*

Routers store the path followed to a destination subnet routing tables. These routing tables can be static or dynamically learned from other routers. Routers use routing protocols, such as Routing Information Protocol (RIP) and Open Shortest Path First (OSPF), to learn the routes to other networks. Windows 2000 supports both static and dynamic routing tables. Dynamic routing support in Windows 2000 is extensible. Other vendors may create support for additional routing protocols such as Interior Gateway Routing Protocol (IGRP) from Cisco.

Demand-Dial Routing

Demand-dial ports on a Windows 2000 router will automatically activate when necessary to forward IP addresses in the routing table. You create a demand-dial through the Demand-Dial Wizard or by activating Internet Connection Sharing. Right clicking on the Routing Interfaces entry in RRAS activates the wizard. The wizard will walk you through the following steps to create the demand-dial interface:

1 Assign a name to the demand-dial port, for example, RemoteLink. Note: This name is used on a later page as the username for the remote router to access this side of the connection, so abide by normal user naming rules.

2 Select whether the connection will be over a modem or VPN. This choice will affect the next several pages of the wizard.

3 Choose the modem to be used for dialing out or choose what type of VPN to create.

4 Specify the phone number to be dialed or the address of the VPN connection.

5 Select checkboxes to control routing. Checkboxes include support for IP routing, IPX routing, dial-out user settings, support for plain text password, and use of a dial-out script. Selection of these checkboxes will control additional pages presented by the wizard.

6 Choose or edit an existing script to be used for connecting to the remote router.

7 Specify a password to be used by the remote router to connect to this Windows 2000 router. The remote router will use the username we assigned in step 1 (in our example, it was *RemoteLink*).

8 Specify the userid, domain, and password for the Windows 2000 router to use to connect to the remote router.

By default, the demand-dial port will be opened whenever someone on your internal network tries to access a host not on your internal network. You can control usage by adding filters and scheduling availability. Demand-dial filters are different from IP filters because they are applied prior to opening the interface. Right-clicking on the demand-dial port and selecting the appropriate entries from the menu applies demand-dial filters and scheduling. You can filter opening of the demand-dial port by entering source or destination network addresses and then specifying whether the port will be opened only for these addresses or for all addresses but these. Using the Dial Out Hours menu, you can specify the hours of the day when the port will be available or unavailable.

Routing Protocols

Dynamic routers use routing protocols to update routing tables by exchanging information about known routes. Most dynamic routers use one of three routing protocols; Routing Information Protocol (RIP), Open Shortest Path First (OSPF), or Enhanced Interior Gateway Routing Protocol (EIGRP). RIP and OSPF are industry-standard protocols available in Windows 2000. EIGRP is a CISCO proprietary protocol that is not currently available in Windows 2000.

Routing Information Protocol (RIP)

RIP is the easiest dynamic routing protocol to set up. It is a distance vector protocol that uses hop counts plus a cost to calculate the best path to take to a destination network. Windows 2000 supports both RIP versions 1 and 2. Version 2 adds a number of advanced capabilities, including support for the following:

- Multicast routing updates. RIP version 1 sends updates to individual routers one at a time. In RIP version 2, updates are sent simultaneously via multicast protocol to multiple routers.

- Simple password authentication. A password can be set to prevent unauthorized routers from passing on updates to routing tables.

- Route filtering. Filters can be applied to keep certain routers from learning about particular subnets and routes to reach those subnets.

- Peer filtering. Filters can be applied, which will keep certain routers' updates from being applied to this routers table.

To add the RIP protocol, execute the following steps:

1 Right-click the General entry under IP Routing in RRAS.

2 Select New Routing Protocol and then choose RIP version 2 from the selection box.

3 After you have added RIP, you can add individual interfaces to the RIP protocol by right-clicking the RIP protocol entry and choosing *New Interface*.

4 Each interface can then be configured by right-clicking on the interface and selecting Properties. A summary of the configuration tabs is follows:

  - **General.** Entries on the General tab control the operation and version level of RIP on the interface. Incoming and outgoing packets can be set to either version 1 or 2 of RIP. A password used for authentication of RIP 2 updates can also be set.

  - **Security.** Use this tab to adjust which routers the Windows 2000 router will accept updates from. Options vary from Accept all to limiting updates to a specific list of routers by IP address.

  - **Neighbors.** Use this tab to adjust which routers the Windows 2000 router will send updates to. Options vary from broadcast/multicast to all to limiting updates to a specific list of routers by IP address.

  - **Advanced.** Checkboxes on this tab enable or disable advanced features of RIP such as split-horizon and poison-reverse processing. The timing of RIP updates can also be adjusted on this tab.

RIP Versus OSPF

The RIP routing protocol is the easiest of the dynamic routing protocols to enable in Windows 2000. However, because every RIP router must maintain a routing table for the whole network, it loses efficiency in a large network. The availability of areas in OSPF segments the network and decreases the overall size of the routing tables that must be maintained. OSPF's link state database system also leads to faster adaptation to changes in network topology and guarantees that routes are loop-free.

Open Shortest Path First (OSPF)

OSPF is a link state routing protocol. Instead of broadcasting or multicasting its routing table, OSPF sends other routers the status of its links. These links are then added to a link state database on each router. This database provides an efficient map of the network's topology. This makes OSPF more scalable and responsive to change than either RIP 1 or 2. Its scalability and responsiveness comes from the low overhead required to pass updates, even in very large networks. However, its scalability comes at the expense of greater complexity in planning, configuring, and administering OSPF router ports.

As the size of the link state database increases the load on system resources increases as well. To facilitate scalability, OSPF divides the network into areas. Each area is connected to other areas using a backbone. Routers maintain link states only for their own area and for the backbones. This effectively segments the database and the network into a manageable size. Routers directly connected to the backbones are known as Area Border Routers (ABRs).

To add the OSPF protocol, execute the following steps:

1 Right-click the General entry under IP Routing in RRAS.

2 Select New Routing Protocol and then choose Open Shortest Path First from the selection box.

3 After you have added OSPF, you can add individual interfaces to the OSPF protocol by right-clicking the OSPF protocol entry and choosing New Interface.

4 Each interface must be configured by right-clicking on the interface and selecting properties. A summary of the configuration tabs follows:

   ▪ **General.** Entries on this tab control whether OSPF is enabled on this interface (the default is disabled), which area the interface is part of (area 0.0.0.0 is the default), the password to be used for security (default is 12345678), and the relative priority of the interface (default is 1). A set of radio buttons controls whether updates are sent via broadcast, point-to-point transmission, or nonbroadcast multiple access (NBMA). (Note: You must check the Enable OSPF checkbox to enable OSPF on the Windows 2000 router.)

   ▪ **Neighbors.** Use this tab to adjust which routers the Windows 2000 router will send updates to. Options vary from all to limiting updates to a specific list of routers by IP address.

   ▪ **Advanced.** The timing of OSPF updates can be adjusted on this tab.

In a multi-area OSPF network, you must also adjust the properties on the OSPF protocol itself. Tabs on this property page will allow you to specify other areas in your network. The General, Areas, Virtual Interfaces, and External Routing tabs will allow you to configure the Windows 2000 router as either an Area Boundary Router (ABR) or an Autonomous System Boundary Router (ASBR).

Multicasting

Most network routers support unicasting of traffic. Unicast traffic has one source and one destination. Windows 2000 also supports routing of multicast traffic. Multicast traffic can be directed at any host that is listening for the multicast traffic. Multicast traffic is used to distribute multimedia efficiently to many workstations at the same time or synchronize data by distributing files or database updates to multiple hosts at the same time. Routing of unicast traffic is easy because only one subnet is the destination. Multicast routing requires intelligent decisions by the router about whether to forward multicast traffic onto a subnet or not because a host may or may not be listening for multicast traffic on a specific network.

Multicasting is controlled by modifying properties on interfaces in the Internet Group Messaging Protocol (IGMP) section of IP routing in RRAS. To enable multicasting, you need to check the Enable IGMP checkbox, and choose either the IGMP router or IGMP proxy mode radio button on the General tab.

IGMP Router Mode

IGMP router mode is the default setting when IGMP support is enabled on an interface. In IGMP router mode, the interface will listen for IGMP Membership Report packets. If any packets are received, multicast traffic will be forwarded through that interface.

When an interface is set to IGMP router mode, a router tab becomes available in the Properties panel. This allows access to default settings for the IGMP router environment. You will not normally need to change these settings.

Windows 2000 RRAS Is Not a True Multicast Router

Windows 2000 RRAS servers use IGMP to participate in a multicast routed network, but they are not able to exchange updates to a multicast routing table on their own. In a complex network Windows 2000 RRAS servers will only be aware of local IGMP hosts and IGMP membership requests passed to them by IGMP proxies. This has the potential to leave gaps in the network that will block multicast traffic. For example, suppose that two Windows 2000 RRAS servers are connected to each other through interfaces that are configured as IGMP routers, not IGMP proxies. If no host on that shared network requests IGMP traffic, IGMP traffic will not be forwarded through that network, even if a host on the other side of one of the routers requests multicasting support.

IGMP Proxy Mode

In IGMP proxy mode, Windows 2000 acts as a proxy multicast host and passes on IGMP Membership Reports which have been received on other interfaces running in IGMP router mode. This will inform an upstream router to forward multicast traffic to the IGMP proxy interface. The Windows 2000 RRAS server can then forward the multicast traffic through the appropriate IGMP router interfaces to downstream hosts. You can only have one interface per server set to IGMP proxy mode and the IGMP router default settings tab is not available.

IGMP proxy mode is designed to pass IGMP Membership Report packets from a small intranet to a multicast capable portion of the Internet. This will allow multicast traffic that originates on the Internet to be forwarded to the intranet.

Testing and Monitoring IP Routing

Monitoring interfaces used for IP routing is done through the RRAS MMC and log files. Individual ports can be monitored under IP Routing/General. This area will display the same statistics as the individual status page associated with each interface. You can also monitor the full IP routing table right clicking on IP Routing/Static Routes and choosing Show IP Routing Table.

Logging

Logging of activity on Windows 2000 router interfaces can be activated on the General tab on the Properties page of each IP Routing section entry. There are four levels of logging from none to maximum logging. Log entries are written to the Internet Authentication Service Log that is normally found in Winntsystemroot/system32/logfiles. Logging uses system resources such as disk space and memory and should be used sparingly.

Tracing

Windows 2000 also has an extensive tracing capability that can be used to troubleshoot problems on your network. A set of Registry keys is used to enable storage of tracing information in files. One subkey for each routing protocol, such as OSPF or RIPV2, is found under the HKEY_LOCAL_MACHINE\SOFTWARE\Microsoft\Tracing key. Under each subkey is a set of keys that control tracing. The values for each key and their usage are listed as follows:

- EnableFileTracing—Tracing is enabled by setting this key to a value of 1. The default is 0.
- FileDirectory—This is the default path to the tracing files. The tracing file will be named after the protocol being traced. By default the files are in the Winntsystemroot\Tracing folder.
- FileTracingMask—This determines the level of tracing information logged to the file. The default value is FFFF0000, which reflects the minimum, while FFFFFFFF is the maximum.
- MaxFileSize—This controls the maximum size of the tracing log file. The default value is hex 10000 or 64K.

Tracing also consumes system resources and should be used only when necessary to troubleshoot problems on the network.

SNMP Support

You can also use SNMP to manage your Windows 2000 routers. Windows 2000 routers have a fully compliant SNMP agent. The agent is installed when you install the SNMP service. SNMP is a standard Windows 2000 component, added through Add/Remove Programs in Control Panel. The Windows 2000 SNMP agent supports the following routing MIBs:

- Internet MIB II
- IP Forwarding Table MIB
- Microsoft RIP version 2 for Internet Protocol MIB
- Wellfleet-Series7-MIB for OSPF
- Microsoft BOOTP for Internet Protocol MIB
- Microsoft IPX MIB
- Microsoft RIP and SAP for IPX MIB
- Internet Group Management Protocol MIB
- IP Multicast Routing MIB

Scripting Router Configuration

NETSH is a command-line utility that can be used to script the configuration of a Windows 2000 router. To create a script of the current configuration pipe it to a text file using the netsh dump>filename command line. You can then edit the textfile as needed. The script can then be reapplied using the command netsh –f filename. For more information on writing a script file see the helpfile associated with RRAS.

Static routes can also be scripted from the command line by using the route command. For example, route add 192.168.20.0 mask 255.255.255.0 192.168.40.1 would add a route to the 192.168.20.0 network through the 192.168.40.1 interface. Adding these commands to a command file that runs at startup would rebuild a static routing table each time the computer starts up

▶ *For more information on startup scripts, see Chapter 6.3, "Group Policies."*

Going Deeper: Practical Applications

As we have seen, Windows 2000 provides a wealth of possibilities when it comes to IP routing. In this section, we'll look at scenarios in which you might use these tools to solve specific problems. Remember that using a Windows 2000 server as a complete replacement for a dedicated hardware router will probably not be cost-effective. But there are many times that an existing Windows 2000 server could take on some IP routing functions and prevent the purchase of an additional hardware router. The following scenarios are not meant to suggest that these are the only valid uses of Windows 2000 IP routing. They are meant to suggest some good potential uses. You may think of others that are just as valid.

Demand-Dial Routing

There are three scenarios in which demand-dial routing can be a potential effective solution:

1 Internet connections using Network Address Translation (NAT). Demand-dial routing works very effectively with NAT to provide automatic connection to the Internet when an internal network resource requires access to an Internet resource.

   ▶ *For more information on NAT, see Chapter 8.7, "Connection Sharing."*

2 WAN connections to small remote offices. Small offices often need connectivity to a corporate WAN. Mail delivery, file synchronization, administration, and so on are all done more easily across a WAN connection. But full-time WAN connections can be expensive, even if they are across relatively slow leased lines. Demand-dial routing provides an automated way to create intermittent connections to a corporate WAN network. Using technologies such as Integrated Services Digital Network (ISDN) can even provide relatively good bandwidth using this feature.

3 Fault-tolerant backup routes. No matter how well-designed your network is, things happen and network segments go down. By creating demand-dial routing ports on Windows 2000 servers and setting the costs appropriately, you can create backup routes that will automatically activate if a regular WAN connection is unavailable.

Multicasting

Most of the traffic on IP networks is unicast traffic. In other words, it came from a specific computer and is going to a specific computer. For most applications, that's fine, but as multimedia becomes more and more popular, there are a growing number of cases in which one computer is sending information that would be of interest to multiple users working on multiple workstations. You can use unicast IP traffic to send the information, but that means sending the same information multiple times, tying up the host server, and creating lots of additional traffic. Or you could send the information via multicast traffic.

But in a routed network, multicasting requires special routing support. If you are in a large corporate network, this is done best through sophisticated hardware routers that fully support the multicasting protocol. But in many networks, the source for almost all multicast traffic is the Internet. If that's the case for your network, a group of Windows 2000 routers can allow you to use multicasting. Simply enable the default IGMP proxy mode on all the router interfaces in your network, except the ones that lead to the Internet. These should be configured as IGMP routers. This will allow multicast traffic that originates on the Internet to be accepted by any workstation on your network.

RIP and OSPF

Larger corporate networks that need the dynamic support that these protocols provide normally use routing protocols such as RIP and OSPF. As stated earlier, in this kind of network it is usually most cost-effective to use hardware routers designed for nothing but routing. But even in these environments, there is the occasional corner of the network that needs a router, but can't really justify the expense of an additional hardware router. If a Windows 2000 server already exists in this location, it could be the perfect answer. Of course, adding a dynamic routing protocol to an already overloaded server is not a good idea, so make sure that the server has additional performance capacity before turning adding these protocols.

8.7

Connection Sharing

You Need to Read This Section If You Want to:

- Share an Internet Dial-up connection with other computers.
- Connect a home or small office network to the Internet.
- Connect a network using private TCP/IP addressing to the Internet.

Related topics

Overview of Connection Sharing

Connecting a network to the Internet has traditionally meant doing one of two things. Either you purchase an expensive firewall/proxy device or you purchase enough live Internet addresses for all of your network's computers. Windows 2000 now offers a third alternative, Network Address Translation (NAT). NAT provides a mechanism for translating internal "private" TCP/IP addresses (into TCP/IP addresses usable on the Internet. By default, NAT only processes IP packets from the Internet that are in response to internal requests. This provides a limited form of security that may be acceptable for some networks.

To enable connection sharing, you will need at least two network interfaces—one for your internal network and one for the Internet. The connection to the Internet can be either a permanent connection, such as an Ethernet NIC, or a temporary connection, such as an ISDN modem.

Connection sharing can be done in two ways: Internet Connection Sharing (ICS) or full Network Address Translation (NAT). ICS is a preconfigured form of NAT that is easier to set up but can be used only under certain specific conditions. ICS cannot be used if your internal network contains more than one subnet, has a DNS server, has a DHCP server, or uses static TCP/IP addresses. NAT is more flexible, but requires more networking knowledge during installation. Table 8.7.1 compares the use of ICS and NAT.

Table 8.7.1   NAT Versus ICS

	Internet Connection Sharing (ICS)	Network Address Translation (NAT)
Configuration	Simple Checkbox	Multi-step process
Internal Address	Automatically set to 192.168.0.1	Any valid address acceptable (Multiple interfaces also supported)
External Address	Single address supplied by ISP	Support for multiple addresses supplied by ISP (Multiple interfaces also supported)

	Internet Connection Sharing (ICS)	Network Address Translation (NAT)
Subnets Supported	Only the 192.168.0.0 subnet	Multiple routed internal networks
DHCP Support	Internal Interface hands out 192.168.0.0 addresses like a DHCP Server	Workstations can be manually addressed or use a DHCP server
DNS Support	ICS Server acts as a DNS proxy to forward requests to external DNS servers	Workstations use either an internal or external DNS server
Other limitations	No additional Domain Controllers, Gateways,or Static IP	No specific limitations

How Network Address Translation (NAT) works

NAT works by translating the TCP/IP header and TCP/UDP ports in packets, which are forwarded to and from the Internet. If more than one internal workstation is trying to reach the Internet at the same time, NAT can randomly choose a port to track the different requests, even if using the same external (Internet) address and port. Source addresses are translated in outbound packets and destination addresses are translated back on inbound packets. The NAT router maintains a table, which keeps track of the addresses translated. Figure 8.7.1 shows how NAT would handle two simultaneous requests to a Web server on the Internet.

Figure 8.7.1   A NAT server translates source and destination addresses as needed to facilitate communications.

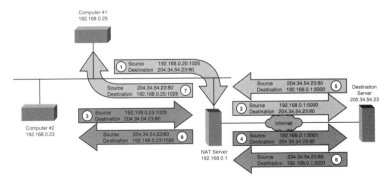

Basic NAT is only able to translate source and destination addresses in the ip header. If addresses are also included in the data portion of the frame, a more specialized process called a *NAT editor* is required. For example, FTP stores IP address information inside the data packet in the FTP header itself. A NAT editor can be loaded, which will also translate this information. Protocols such as PPTP are also a problem because they use a non-standard IP header. Windows 2000 includes NAT editors for the following: FTP, ICMP, PPTP, and NetBIOS over TCP/IP. Proxy software that can be loaded on the client is also included for the following: H.323, Direct Play, LDAP-based ILS registration, and RPC.

Heads Up!

Protocols such as L2TP, which encrypt even the header, cannot be processed by NAT.

In addition to handling translation functions, NAT in Windows 2000 also provides name resolution and address assignments. These features are normally used only when NAT is invoked through ICS. Name requests from internal computers that reach the NAT server are forwarded to Internet DNS servers and then returned to the original requestor. The NAT server can also give internal workstations addresses to use if a DHCP server is not available on the internal network.

Configuring Connection Sharing

ICS is configured through Network and Dial-Up Connections in the Control Panel. It is configured by turning on a single checkbox, either while creating a new dial-up connection, or on the Sharing tab in the Properties page of an existing connection. If the connection is a modem or ISDN card, you should also check the Dial-on-demand checkbox in the Sharing tab. Enabling ICS will make all the changes reflected in Table 8.7.3

Table 8.7.3   ICS Changes

Item	Change
Internal Address	Set to 192.168.0.1 with a subnet mask of 255.255.255.0.
External Interface	Enabled.
Routing Table	A static route for 0.0.0.0 pointing to the external interface is added to the routing table.
Internal Clients	Internal clients are given an address between 192.168.0.2—192.168.0.254, with a subnet mask of 255.255.255.0 and 192.168.0.1 as a DNS proxy server.

Windows 98 Also Supports Internet Connection Sharing

Windows 98 also supports Internet connection sharing. Because Windows 98 does not support a DHCP server, the 169.254.0.0 address range is used on the internal network. 169.254.0.0 is the default address range assigned to DHCP clients who are unable to contact a DHCP server when requesting a TCP/IP address. This is appropriate for a small home or office network, but it doesn't provide enough control for a larger, more complex corporate network.

Configuring NAT requires making changes, both to the NAT server and to the workstations on the network that will use NAT. This means that configuring NAT is more involved than simply turning on ICS. However, the NAT protocol is more versatile and less limited then ICS. NAT is configured in the Routing and Remote Access Service MMC.

If the Routing and Remote Access service has not been configured and enabled, choose Internet connection server in the RRAS Configuration Wizard. Answering the wizard's questions is all that is necessary to complete the configuration of NAT. Then, make the appropriate changes to the workstations (see step 9 that follows).

To configure NAT after RRAS is already configured and enabled, make the changes to the NAT Server and workstations listed below:

1 Configure the internal LAN adapter to use an appropriate private TCP/IP address with no default gateway.

2 Enable routing on your external LAN adapter port by entering a default gateway on the Internet. If the port is a modem or ISDN connection, create a dial-on-demand interface to enable routing.
    ▸ *For more information on creating a dial-on-demand interface, see Chapter 8.6, "IP Routing."*

3 Create a default static route that points to the external LAN adapter or dial-on-demand port. Do this by entering a route with a destination of 0.0.0.0 and a subnet mask of 0.0.0.0 which points at the external interface.
    ▸ *For more information on creating a static route, see Chapter 8.6, "IP Routing."*

4 Add NAT to the General IP Routing object in RRAS by right-clicking the entry and choosing New Routing Protocol. In the Select Routing Protocol box, choose Network Address Translation and then press OK.

5 Add your Internal and External interfaces to the NAT routing protocol by right-clicking the new NAT IP routing protocol and clicking on New Interface. In the Interfaces box, choose your Internal interface. Repeat for all additional External and Internal interfaces.

6   Select each interface that was added in step 5 and set the External interfaces to Public interface connected to the Internet on the General property tab. Set Internal interfaces to Private interface connected to private network. It is also recommended that you select the Translate TCP/UDP headers checkbox on External interfaces.

7   Configure the NAT DHCP Allocator or set up a DHCP server. NAT can be used as a DHCP Allocator by entering an IP Subnet and Subnet mask on the Address Assignments tab of the NAT protocol Properties page. Specific addresses can be excluded from the subnet using the Exclude button. The DHCP Allocator only supports DHCP for a single range of addresses.

▶ *For more information on installing a DHCP server, see Chapter 8.2, "Dynamic Host Configuration Protocol (DHCP)."*

8   Configure the NAT server as DNS Proxy or set up a DNS server with appropriate Root Hints. To enable the NAT server to forward name resolution requests for internal clients, click the Clients using Domain Name System (DNS) checkbox on the Name Resolution tab of the NAT protocol Properties page. A second checkbox, Connect to the public network when a name needs to be resolved, should also be checked if the External interface is demand dial port.

▶ *For more information on installing a DNS server, see Chapter 8.3, "Domain Name System."*

9   To configure workstations to make use of the NAT server, simply edit their TCP/IP protocol page to Obtain an IP address automatically and Obtain DNS server address automatically. The DHCP allocator or the DHCP server on your network will provide appropriate addresses.

Choosing IP Addresses for the Internal and External Networks

If you use ICS, internal network addresses are chosen for you automatically. Your internal NIC will be reset to the address of 192.168.0.1. The rest of the 192.168.0.0 subnet is automatically allocated as DHCP addresses for clients on the internal network. Your ISP will provide you with the address of your External interface.

If you chose NAT, you can use any addresses that you want on the internal network, but using one of the "private" address ranges is perhaps the best choice (see sidebar). These addresses can be distributed through either the NAT server itself or a DHCP server. Your External interface(s) will use addresses supplied by your ISP just like ICS. The only difference is that ICS is limited to one address only.

Internet "Private" Address Ranges

It is getting harder and harder to obtain valid IP address ranges from the Internet Assigned Numbers Authority (IANA). Because many companies can no longer find enough valid addresses to use on their corporate intranets, the IANA has established three ranges of IP addresses for use inside company networks. NAT allows these addresses to be used on a corporate intranet and then translated for use on the public Internet. The private network address ranges include:

Class A range 10.0.0.0 with the subnet mask 255.0.0.0

Class B range 172.16.0.0 with the subnet mask 255.240.0.0

Class C range 192.168.0.0 with the subnet mask 255.255.0.0

Another range of IP addresses is used for Automatic Private IP Addressing (APIPA). APIPA uses the Class B range 169.254.0.0 with a subnet mask of 255.255.0.0. Windows 98 or Windows 2000 DHCP clients assign these addresses automatically when they can't contact a DHCP server. This range of addresses is also not used on the Internet.

Configuring Inbound Connections

NAT is normally used only for requests that originate on your internal network for the Internet. For example, a Web browser requests a new HTML page from a Web server. The NAT server directs the returned page to a client based on the outbound request. But what if you want Internet users to have access to services on your internal network (for example, hosting a Web server on your intranet that is accessible from the Internet as well)?

Security is a Concern with Inbound Connections

NAT provides limited security by not allowing access to the internal network by any packet that is not in response to a request that originated on the internal network. When you configure inbound connections, you are allowing requests that originate on the Internet to access your internal network. Inbound connections open specific ports on the outside interface of the NAT server and map them to specific ports on an internal network server. For example, you might map port 8080 on the external interface to port 80 on a specific Web server inside your network. Security on the internal server is the only security imposed on usage of these ports. Because the packet is already inside your network at that point, this is a security concern. Remember that each external port that you map to an internal port punches another hole in your NAT server and is another way for a hacker to try to invade your network.

To support inbound connections from the Internet, you should do the following:

1 Configure the internal resource server with a static IP address, subnet mask, DNS server, and default gateway. (An Internal interface on the NAT server should be the address used for the DNS and default gateway.)

2 On the Special Ports tab of the External interface's Properties page, configure an Incoming and Outgoing IP address and port. (Note: the Incoming address can be a range of IP addresses.) Remember that you are looking at this from the Internet, so Incoming and Outgoing are reversed from your normal point of view. Incoming on this tab means the External address and port on the NAT server that a user will use to reach the resource on your Intranet. Outgoing is the static address and port number you configured in step 1.

Use this feature sparingly because it poses a potential security risk for your private network.

Configuring Applications and Services

Some applications and services will still not work using NAT because they require specific port numbers to function. Applications such as this can be configured to use special ports on the Translation tab of the NAT protocol Properties page. You can add an application definition by clicking Applications and then clicking the Add button. Provide a name for identifying the application and the specific port mappings that should be used when running this application through the NAT server.

Testing and Monitoring Connection Sharing

Because the ICS service can be configured without turning on the Routing and Remote Access service, the only way to monitor it is through Network and Dial-up Connections. Right-clicking on either the Internal or External interface and choosing Status will display information about the speed, duration, and byte flow of the connection.

Monitoring the full NAT service is done through the RRAS MMC and log files. Ports used for NAT can be monitored under the IP Routing/General. This area will display the same statistics as the individual status page associated with each interface. You can also monitor the activities of the NAT server itself under IP Routing/NAT. The Internal and External interfaces will be listed here, along with the number of Mappings, Incoming Packets Translated, Incoming Packets Rejected, Outgoing Packets Translated, and Outgoing Packets Rejected.

If you are using the NAT server as a DHCP Allocator or DNS proxy, information about the functioning of these services can be gained by right-clicking on IP Routing/NAT and choosing either Show DHCP Allocator Information or Show DNS Proxy Information.

Finally, you can look for detailed information on the functioning of NAT in the Internet Authentication Service Log. This log is normally found in Winntsystemroot/system32/logfiles. The level of logging for NAT is set on the General tab of the NAT protocol Properties page. There are four levels of logging—from disabled to logging all events, warnings, and errors.

Best Practices

- Use NAT in conjunction with a firewall. In larger environments where NAT is used simply to support connection of private IP address ranges to the public Internet, a firewall should be used to provide security. The security provided by NAT is too simplistic for larger, more complex environments.

- Use ICS for small offices or homes that have a single subnet. ICS is very easy to enable and allows a small office or home to use a single connection for Internet traffic. In a limited environment like this, the security provided by ICS is acceptable.

- Use NAT to conserve licensed IP addresses. IP addresses that can be used directly on the Internet are becoming more and more difficult to obtain. NAT facilitates reserving these scarce resources for interfaces that actually connect directly to the Internet, without limiting your use of TCP/IP within the corporate environment.

- Implement a DNS server inside your network. When using NAT, it is best to have a DNS server on your internal network that can forward requests to the Internet root servers when necessary. If your only DNS server is the one provided by your ISP, all requests for host name resolution will have to be processed by the NAT server. An internal DNS will resolve internal host names without involving the NAT server.

8.8
Terminal Services

You Need to Read this Section If You Want to:

- Upgrade an NT 4.0 Terminal Server installation.
- Remotely administer Windows 2000 Server.
- Activating a Terminal Server Licensing Server.
- Run programs after disconnecting a session.

Related Topics

For More Information On ▶ *See*

Creating a dial-in connection

▶ *Chapter 8.5: Remote Access Service (RAS)*
▶ *Chapter 3.4: Managing Services and Tasks*

Overview of Terminal Services

Remote access can be accomplished in two ways: remote access or remote control. Remote Access Service(RAS) provides connection to network data resources using dial-up links or virtual private networks, but processing still occurs on the local workstation.

▶ *For more information, see Chapter 8.5, "Remote Access Service (RAS)."*

Terminal Services provides a multi-user remote control solution. The Terminal Services Server sends screen data only to the client and receives keyboard and mouse input only from the client. Because the processing takes place on the Terminal Services server, local processing requirements are minimal and can be fulfilled by "thin client" devices or software. These devices can be solid state devices, older low-powered computers, computers running any version of Windows, or computers running operating systems such as Unix or Macintosh. Non-Windows computers require third-party software.

Terminal Services is a good solution for situations in which physical security of the data is an issue. "Thin client" devices can be solid state devices without a hard or floppy disk drive. This prohibits the use of local software or copying the data, thereby ensuring the security of the data and stability of the applications. Solid state devices can also be more cost-effective in harsh environments such as factory floors. The devices are interchangeable, leading to less downtime and lost productivity. Finally, the total cost of ownership (TCO) will be lower because of the centralization of software maintenance and installation. Upgrades, Service Packs, and new software needs to be loaded only on the Terminal Services Server, not on every workstation.

Installing and Configuring Terminal Services

Terminal Services can be installed in one of two modes: Remote Administration mode or Application Server mode. Remote Administration mode supports only two concurrent connections, but does not require the purchase of Terminal Services Client Access Licenses. It is primarily designed to allow system administrators direct access to Windows 2000 Servers. Application Server mode provides remote execution support for "thin client" devices.

To install Terminal Services in Remote Administration mode, follow these steps:

1 Access Add/Remove Windows Components under Add/Remove Programs in the Control Panel.

2 Scroll down the list of components and select Terminal Services.

3 When asked which mode to install, choose Remote Administration Mode.

No further configuration is needed. Two concurrent connections are automatically licensed for Remote Administration mode, but the second one is rarely used. This means that there is no need to modify programs for multisession access. Attaching with a thin client to a server running in Remote Administration mode will give you essentially the same view as you would get logging in to the server locally. After you have attached and logged in, you can use your view of the remote server's desktop to run all of the normal applications that you can run locally. This allows access to programs and third-party utilities that cannot be run from a remote workstation.

Upgrading from Windows NT Server 4.0 Terminal Server Edition
You cannot upgrade a Windows NT 4.0 Terminal Server to Remote Administration mode; it will automatically be installed in Application Server mode. If you want to upgrade an existing Terminal Server to a Remote Administration server you should do a clean install of Windows 2000 server instead. Then re-install all applications.

To install Terminal Services in Application Server mode, follow these steps:

1   Choose a domain member server that has an NTFS partition. NTFS will provide the security necessary when running multiple user sessions on the same file system.

2   Access Add/Remove Windows Components under Add/Remove Programs in Control Panel. Scroll down the list of components and select Terminal Services. When asked which mode to install, choose Application Server mode.

3   If a Terminal Services Licensing Server does not exist in the network, be sure to select Terminal Services Licensing as well as Terminal Services.

4   Activate the Terminal Services Licensing Server (see "Terminal Server Licensing" later in this chapter).

5   Reinstall any applications that were detected and reported during Terminal Services setup. Install any additional applications that users will need access to on the Terminal Server.

6   Configure defaults in the Terminal Services Configuration MMC. You can use this tool to specify a maximum number of allowable connections, connection encryption level, single program startup versus desktop, connection timeouts, automatic logon, and other defaults that affect the way a client connects to Terminal Server.
    ▶ *For more information, see "Application Server Mode Configuration" later in this chapter.*

7   Modify the Terminal Server Profile Settings tab on each user who will have access to the Terminal Server.

> **? Where Should I Install a Terminal Services Application Server?**
>
> Terminal Services are not a "magic bullet" when it comes to resource requirements such as CPU and memory. Although users will share system memory when running the same programs, the fact that multiple active users are using system resources will stress any server. This means that it's not a good idea to use servers running in Application Server mode to be a domain controller or run Back Office applications such as Exchange.
>
> A Terminal Server requires a minimum of 128 MB RAM and at least a Pentium processor. Additional RAM should be added for each user, ranging from 10 MB for light users to 21 MB for power users. Terminal Server also works well with multiple processors. But the only real way to tell how large to make your server is to test it in a lab. After you have gauged memory and CPU requirements for a few users, you can estimate the requirements for a larger number of users. For example, if a single processor Pentium computer with 256 MB of RAM support 25 light users in your environment then a quad processor Pentium with 1 GB of RAM will support 100 users. Of course, you also have to be careful that hard disk and network access don't become bottlenecks, but memory and CPU are usually the constraints on a Terminal Server.

Application Server Mode Configuration

Terminal Server is configured through the Terminal Services Configuration MMC on the Administrative Tools menu. The default configuration is normally acceptable for servers running in Remote Administration mode. There are two areas in the MMC where configuration settings can be made. General Server configuration settings can be made under the Server Settings folder in the MMC. Configuration of user defaults and connection settings can be made on the properties page of each connection.

The Server Settings folder contains six configuration items:

- **Terminal Server Mode.** This shows whether you are running in Remote Administration or Application Server mode. You can change this setting only by removing and reinstalling Terminal Services through Add/Remove Programs in Control Panel.

- **Delete Temporary Folders On Exit.** This specifies whether to delete temporary folders when a client disconnects or during the regular server cleanup period.

- **Use Temporary Folders Per Session.** This specifies whether to create temporary folders on the server for each client when they connect.

- **Internet Connector Licensing.** The Internet Connector license is an alternate license that can be purchased from Microsoft. See "Terminal Server Licensing," later in the chapter for more details.

- **Active Desktop.** This disables the Active Desktop of the server to preserve system resources for client connections.

- **Permission Compatibility.** Windows 2000 restricts access to certain sections of the Rregistry and system files by default. Some legacy applications will not work without this access. This setting allows a weakening of permissions to a level similar to NT 4.0 Terminal Server.

Right-clicking the connection and choosing Properties from the menu can configure individual connections. The Properties page contains the following eight tabs.

- **General.** The General tab allows the choice of Low, Medium or High encryption from traffic between the Terminal Server and Client. You can also specify whether to default to standard Windows Authentication when other authentication systems (for example, smart card authentication) are also available on the Terminal Server.

- **Logon Settings.** This tab allows you to provide default logon information for any client attaching to this connection. This will allow users to automatically log on to the Terminal Server when connecting. A checkbox allows you to require a password, even if a default user account is supplied.

- **Sessions.** The Sessions tab allows you to set default timeout and reconnection characteristics for connections. Session settings can also be made on an individual client basis on the Sessions tab of a User account's properties page.

- **Environment.** This tab can be used to substitute an initial program for a user's normal desktop. Although this limits a user's access to other programs, it also results in a significant decrease of the memory requirements for that user's session. You can also disable the use of wallpaper on client desktops in this tab. An initial program can also be set for individual users on the Environment tab of a user account's properties page.

- **Remote Control.** This tab controls default settings for shadowing of a user's session. Shadowing allows an administrator to observe and interact with another user's desktop. These are defaults and can be overridden on the Remote Control tab in a User account's properties page.

- **Client Settings.** This tab enables or disables mapping of client resources such as drives, printers, LPT ports, COM ports, Clipboard, and audio features. Drive and audio mapping is available only on Citrix Metaframe clients.

- **Network Adapter.** This tab allows you to set the maximum number of client sessions supported over a specific interface or all interfaces in the Terminal Server.

- **Permissions.** The Permissions tab is used to limit access to the Terminal Server to specific users or groups. There are three basic levels of access: Full Control, User Access, or Guest Access. Full Control will grant a user administrative rights over other sessions on the Terminal Server. User Access provides the capability to log on to a session, query for session information, send messages to other sessions, and connect to another session. Guest Access allows a user to logon only to a session on the Terminal Server. Guests will have no access or knowledge of other sessions running on the server. Access at each level can be either Granted or Denied.

Terminal Server Licensing

Running Terminal Services in Application Server mode requires activation of a Terminal Services Licensing Server. Terminal Services servers use one or more licensing servers to obtain and manager CALs for devices connecting to the Terminal Server. Retrieving an activation code from the Microsoft Clearinghouse activates Terminal Services Licensing. The activation codes can be obtained via a direct Internet connection, WWW form, FAX, or telephone call.

An activated Terminal Services License server can manage four different types of licenses:

- **Normal Terminal Services CALs.** These are normal Terminal Services CALs purchased for individual Terminal Services devices.

- **Terminal Services Internet Connector licenses.** These are bulk licenses available for placing Terminal Servers on the public Internet. Each connector license supports 200 concurrent connections.

- **Built-in licenses.** Windows 2000 clients have built-in license for Terminal Services.

- **Temporary licenses.** When the License Server runs out of valid licenses, it will distribute temporary licenses good for 90 days. This will allow you to temporarily run a Terminal Server while evaluating or waiting for new purchased licenses to arrive.

The Terminal server must be able to find the License Server. In a Windows 2000 domain, the License Server must be on a domain controller to be discovered through DNS. In an NT 4.0 domain, the License Server will be discovered through NetBIOS broadcasts. The scope of who will use a License Server is selected during activation. You can activate a License Server for use in an enterprise or domain/workgroup. The enterprise configuration uses sites to limit the visibility of License Servers.

Configuring Applications for Shared Access

Because only one session is normally used in Remote Administration mode, applications do not need to be configured for shared access. But applications must be configured for shared access if using Application Server mode. If applications are installed prior to activating Terminal Services, you will receive a list of applications that should be reinstalled to achieve proper configuration.

Applications can be configured for shared access automatically during installation. There are two ways to configure applications for shared access during installation:

- Start the application's setup program from the Add/Remove Programs icon in Control Panel.

- From a command prompt type **Change User /Install** prior to running the application's setup program. Then run Change User /Execute after the setup program completes.

It is best to install programs when no one is connected to the Terminal Server. This means either installing before activating client access or disconnecting all users manually from the server.

▶ *For more information, see "Connecting and Disconnecting Sessions" later in the chapter.*

Some programs need additional tuning to work correctly in a multi-user environment. Typically, these programs write configuration information to a proprietary .INI file or to HKEY_LOCAL_MACHINE. Either of these practices will make multiple user access to the application difficult. Application compatibility scripts are provided to patch these applications. Always check for an Application compatibility script before installing an application on terminal server. They are located under the *<systemroot>*\Application Compatibility Scripts\Install\. The scripts should be run after the application is installed normally. Some programs may still exist that are not compatible but do not have a script. These programs should not be used with Terminal Services.

Installing Terminal Services Clients

Windows 9x, Windows NT, Windows CE (CE 3.0 only), and Windows 2000 clients are included with Terminal Services. There are several methods available for installing Terminal Services clients, depending on the operating system of the client:

- **Diskette Installation.** The Terminal Service Client Creator program on the Administrative Tools menu allows you to create diskettes that you can use to install either a 16-bit client (Windows 3.1) or 32-bit client (Windows 9x. Windows NT, and Windows 2000).

- **Network Installation.** You can also install the clients from a network share by sharing *Winntsystemroot*\system32\clients\tsclient\net. This will allow network access to either the win32 or win16 directories, from which you can run SETUP.EXE.

- **Windows CE, Handheld PC Edition Version 3.0.** This client is available on the Windows 2000 CD in valueadd\msft\mgmt\mstsc_hpc. Windows CE services must be installed on your desktop PC before you can install this client. The client installation program is run on your desktop computer and transferred to the CE device through your standard synchronization method.

- **Non-Windows Operating Systems.** Clients for Macintosh, Unix, and Windows CE (prior to CE 3.0) are available from Citrix via the Metaframe product. Installing the clients is as easy as running SETUP.EXE from either the appropriate diskette or a network share. The installation wizard will ask for an organization, acceptance of the EULA, and whether the install is for all users or just for you.

Connecting and Disconnecting Sessions

You can either log off or disconnect from a Terminal Server session. Both are available on the Start menu. The command lines logoff and tsdiscon will also log off or disconnect a session, respectively.

Logging off closes the session and stops all programs that the user was running. Disconnecting leaves the session running on the Terminal Server. You can reconnect later and pick up where you left off. While you are disconnected, the session continues to run your applications, except the user interface has been disconnected. This is a good way to run time-consuming tasks such as large queries.

Administrators can also log off or disconnect users from the Terminal Services Manager. Right-clicking on a user will allow you to log off a user and terminate the attached session. Right-clicking a session will allow you to disconnect a user from a session. The session will continue running. Administrators can also set default timeouts for when a disconnected, idle, or active session will be disconnected/logged off. These timeouts can be set in the individual user properties on the Session tab or in the Terminal Services Configuration MMC.

Best Practices

- Install Terminal Services on a member server, but install Terminal Services Licensing on a domain controller. Terminal Services uses a significant amount of memory, CPU, and network traffic. A domain controller requires the same resources.

- Install Terminal Services in Remote Administration mode on every Windows 2000 server in your network. This will allow you to remotely administer your Windows 2000 servers without adding a significant performance load to your system.

- Install Terminal Services and applications on an NTFS partition. Security is essential in this type of multi-user environment in which data files may be shared.

- Use the tsshutdn command to shut down the Terminal server. Using the Shut Down option on the Start menu will not notify users before ending their sessions.

- After you have installed Terminal Services and applications, do not remove Terminal Services without reinstalling all applications. Programs that were installed while Terminal Services was in effect were changed for multi-user access and may not work properly in single user mode.

- Start users who need access to only one program without a desktop by using the Initial Program option. This will conserve system resources and improve security.

- Assign users who will be logging on to Terminal Server a specific Terminal Server profile. Many of the settings used in a normal profile are too graphics-intensive for efficient use in a Terminal Services session. Creating a specific profile allows the user to store a profile just for Terminal Services sessions.

IX
Appendices

Appendix **A**
Migrating NT 4.0 Domains to Active Directory

Designing Your Active Directory

Although this appendix will highlight the most important factors in an Active Directory (AD) migration, it is by no means a complete discussion of the subject. Many of these topics deserve their own chapter in order to be thoroughly discussed. For a much more complete discussion of this subject, please read *Planning for Windows 2000* (available from New Riders).

Before you begin a domain migration from Windows NT to AD, you have to know how your finished AD will be structured. Although people sometimes take vacations where they leave home without knowing exactly where they'll end up, an AD designed in such a manner will be anything but a vacation.

Designing a useful, stable, and flexible AD will require the careful planning of three AD components:

- Domains
- OUs
- Sites

Planning a Domain Structure

Windows 2000 domains have changed significantly from Windows NT. Due to the removal of many of the limitations inherent in NT domains, most of the design principles for NT domains are invalid when applied to Windows 2000. In most environments, only a single domain will comprise your AD structure, whereas many NT environments use two or more domains in a master-resource relationship.

In creating a Windows 2000 domain structure, you should follow these steps:

1 Evaluate the current environment.

2 Decide where Windows 2000 domains are appropriate.

3 Determine the proper placing of the domain within the tree or forest.

Evaluating the Current Environment

The primary factors influencing your AD design should be your company's physical and functional structure, and your administrative requirements. At this point in the process, you should answer questions such as the following:

Organizational Structure

- What is the size of the environment? Is it local, regional, national, or global?
- How many employees work in each location and for each division?
- What is the growth rate and expansion plan?
- Within the organization, are there subgroups with different network, language, or security needs?

Network Topology

- What is the LAN speed and structure?
- What IP subnets are used in each location?
- What is the WAN structure?
- What is the current LAN/WAN utilization?
- Are any network links currently saturated?

Administration

- Is the network managed centrally, or are administrative tasks distributed between multiple groups or locations?
- Do administrators have differing levels of priviledge?
- Are different administrators tasked with administrating different areas of the domain? (For example, areas such as user accounts, group rights, and RAS access.)

Creating Domains

You should begin your AD design process by planning on having only one domain, and then add others only when truly necessary. Although your current Windows NT domain model won't be a completely accurate guide, it may reveal situations in which multiple Windows 2000 domains are required. See Table A.1 for more information.

Table A.1   Comparison Between Windows NT and Windows 2000 Domain Designs

Windows NT Domain Structure	Likely Windows 2000 Domain Structure
Single domain	Single domain
Master-resource	Single domain, although multiple domains are possible
Multi-master	Multiple domains are likely, although a single domain might work, possibly with child domains
Complete trust	Multiple domains are likely

Four reasons why additional domains might be required are

- **Political pressure.** This is the most common reason for multiple domains. Privacy or autonomy are often reasons given for creating an additional domain. However, OUs can often meet the need just as well, without the administrative difficulty of managing multiple domains.

  ▸ *For more information on OUs, see "Planning an OU Structure" later in this appendix.*

- **Domain replication traffic.** Creating multiple domains isolates them from the replication traffic of other domains, and if done properly, can balance that traffic between multiple domains. This is typically an issue only in very large domains.

- **Domain policies.** If two or more groups require different values for a domain-level setting such as Minimum Password Length or Account Lockouts, multiple domains (or a compromise) are required.

- **International differences.** Because different countries typically use different languages, currency, and business practices, it's best to separate each country into its own domain. Additionally, this will limit replication traffic across what are traditionally slow and expensive WAN links.

Placing Domains

After the number of domains has been determined, you must arrange them into the AD. For the many organizations that have only a single domain, they will attach that domain to a single tree in the AD. Only if you have multiple domains must you consider whether a forest or tree layout is preferable.

Forests work best for companies that are a conglomeration made of several distinct entities. Navigation and administration of forests are more difficult than trees. However, users at these conglomerates typically don't need to access resources outside their own entity.

Another concern when placing each domain is in deciding the DNS name to be used. The root domain name must be chosen with extreme care; changing this name after it is implemented can be a very painful process.

Planning an OU Structure

After organizing your domain structure, it's time to fill each domain with *organization units (OUs)*. OUs are best used for segmenting administrative tasks. Another reason for separate OUs is to separate users with differing Group Policy requirements. Finally, thanks to inheritance, OUs can be used for simplifying administration of resources.

There are several important considerations when designing the OU structure of a domain:

- Shallower OU structures perform better than deep hierarchies.
- OUs should represent static structures.
- OUs should be organized by location, function, or both.

- Inheritance from parent OUs can be leveraged to simplify security administration.

The objective of these considerations is to help you avoid having to reorganize OUs at a later date. With a proper initial design, most original OUs should be effective throughout the life of the AD. Analysis of your organization's structure will help you create the best design for your environment.

Planning a Site Structure

In Windows 2000, the concept of a site is used to achieve three objectives:

- To throttle replication traffic
- To isolate workstation logon traffic
- To identify resources by proximity.

In general, each physical location should reside in its own site. Most environments have only a single link between any two locations, which makes defining inter-site links an easy task. If you have redundant links between two sites (even if the secondary link is routed through an intermediary site), you should define a cost and schedule to each link so that the primary link is favored.

Restructuring NT Domains

After you define your desired AD structure, you may note some disparity between it and your current NT domain structure. Because the domain models differ so much between NT and Windows 2000, many organizations may need to reorganize their domain structure. Typically, this will involve folding one or more domains into another domain. By nature, this process can be quite challenging and requires a great deal of planning.

Restructuring Considerations

Ideally, your NT domain structure will mirror your planned AD domain structure. If so, you can stop reading this appendix at this point. Otherwise, you should consider the following:

- **User and Machine Accounts.** These have to be migrated to the destination domain.

- **Groups.** Global groups need to be migrated, and local groups have to be re-created where necessary.

- **Permissions.** All types of permissions—such as file, share, and registry rights—need to be remapped to accounts in the destination domain.

- **User Rights.** User rights, domain security policies, and system policies have to be transferred to the destination domain. Where there are conflicts, compromises will be required.

- **Services.** Services that use user credentials for logon rather than the LocalSystem account have to be remapped to use accounts in the destination domain.

- **Applications.** A number of applications, usually those that run on the server (such as the BackOffice products) may require reconfiguration or reinstallation to move to a new domain. Wherever possible, server applications residing on DCs should be moved to member servers to facilitate migration.

- **Member Servers.** Member servers have to join the destination domain.

- **Workstations.** Client machines need to be moved to the destination domain.

- **Domain Controllers.** Non-2000 domain controllers should have any services they provide migrated to other servers, and then the DCs of the source domain should be taken offline. BDCs can be reinstalled as part of the new domain, although it is best to leave the PDC intact for a period of time, just in case there's a need to back out of the reconfiguration.

There are two approaches to consolidating domains. The first method is to migrate prior to deploying Windows 2000. The alternative is to migrate as a part of your deployment or after the deployment is complete. Each has its own advantages, and is best used in different situations.

Pre-Migration Consolidation

Consolidating domains prior to migrating to Windows 2000 is the typical approach if more than 30 percent of your domains will be consolidated. This is because the more domains that must be upgraded, the more complex the Windows 2000 migration process becomes. To assist companies in this process, Microsoft has created the SIDWalker suite of tools, available in the Windows 2000 Resource Kit (see Appendix D, "Resource Kit Utilities," for more information). As with many utilities, this tool is rather basic; third parties provide more advanced products. Such tools are available from vendors such as Mission Critical, FastLane Technologies, and Aelita. However, there are several important points that should be recognized prior to embarking on a pre-Windows 2000 migration domain consolidation:

- Don't consolidate domains if the combined SAM database will be larger than 40 MB. Although an AD domain will be able to exceed 40 MB in size, NT-type SAM databases encounter performance problems once they become this large.

- Domain replication traffic will increase on the destination domain in proportion to the size of the source domain. This will place additional burden on the LAN, WAN, and domain controllers.

- If a chief reason for multiple domains was to allow for delegation of administration, these domains should be consolidated only after migrating.

Post-Migration Consolidation

If you will be consolidating less than 30 percent of your domains, it's best to wait until after deploying Windows 2000 before performing the consolidation. Of course, if you have multiple domains due to SAM size or administration delegation needs, post-migration is the only valid timeframe for consolidating these domains. However, there is a fair amount of work you can accomplish prior to the migration or consolidation. Wherever possible (and especially for new services), utilize member servers to provide server service. This will allow you to move them to the destination domain without having to move the service to a new computer (as would be the case if the source machine were a DC).

Windows 2000 Migration

After you define your AD structure and perform any pre-migration domain consolidation, it's time to deploy Windows 2000. Prior to migrating, be sure to make one or more complete backups of all the servers. You should synchronize and then power down one of the BDCs prior to migrating any machines, so you can quickly recover if a major problem occurs. Begin by migrating the PDC, follow with the BDCs, and finally migrate the member servers and workstations. For master/resource and multiple master domain models, migrate the master domain(s) first. If you have a complete trust model you truly plan to migrate, the order isn't important. Be sure to leave each Windows 2000 domain in mixed mode until all domain controllers in a given domain have been converted to Windows 2000. After this is complete, you can make the irreversable switch to native mode, which allows you to take advantage of universal groups and group nesting.

Appendix **B**
Command Prompt
Quick Reference

Windows 2000 offers a rich variety of tools for controlling operations from the command line. Despite the name *Windows*, many functions of the OS can be controlled with a simple command prompt. There are probably two reasons for this. First, nearly everything that can be done from a command line can be automated via a batch file. This is the most important reason for an administrator. Second, it's often faster to retrieve information from a command line than a window.

This appendix describes many of the most common command-prompt utilities. They are divided into five groups, depending on their function. Although many utilities are listed, this is by no means a complete list. For example, NTBACKUP can be automated from the command line, but isn't included here because it typically uses a GUI interface. Also, the Resource Kit utilities are quite often used from the command line. For more information on these utilities, see Appendix D, "Resource Kit Utilities." Finally, commands that are specific to the MSDOS, OS/2, or POSIX subsystems have been excluded.

Networking Utilities

As the name implies, this category is occupied by programs that are network-specific. It's unlikely you will use these utilities on a machine that's not connected to a network. Note that many of the programs in other sections may be network-capable (such as AT, COPY, and DIR) but are not included here because they weren't created specifically for a networking purpose.

ATMADM

If you use an ATM network card, this utility will report information about ATM usage and configuration.

CLUSTER

Windows 2000 Clusters can be managed by using the CLUSTER command. This command has quite a few options; for full information, refer to the Windows 2000 Online Help.

EVNTCMD

You can use EVNTCMD to display SNMP events.

IPXROUTE

The IPXROUTE utility allows you to set IPX source routing options for the current logon. However, these changes are not saved when you log off.

IRFTP

IRFTP is a utility used to initialize wireless file transfers between machines.

NET

The NET utility dates back to the LAN Manager days, and is quite powerful in a number of areas. It can do things such as configure user and computer accounts, modify groups, send network messages, control file and print shares, map network drives, and synchronize the computer's time with the domains. For more information on NET, consult the Windows 2000 Online Help.

NETSH

NETSH is a powerful utility new to Windows 2000. It allows you to configure network services such as DHCP, RAS, routing, and WINS from the command line.

IP Networking Utilities

The previous section discussed general networking utilities. These utilities were protocol-independent (with the exception of IPXROUTE) and could be used whether the machine is running IP, IPX, NetBEUI, or any combination of the three. This section is dedicated to applications that require the machine to be running IP as one of its protocols.

ARP

The ARP utility is used to view or delete IP to hardware address mappings used by the ARP protocol of IP.

FINGER

FINGER is the Windows 2000 implementation of the Finger client, which is typically used on the Internet by UNIX systems to display information about users, such as whether they're logged in.

FTP

For a command prompt-based FTP client, use FTP. This is an IP-based system for transferring files between computers.

HOSTNAME

Running HOSTNAME simply returns the name of the local computer.

IPCONFIG

IPCONFIG allows you to list all the IP addressing information for the local machine. This tool also allows you to renew and release DHCP leases and DDNS names.

LPQ

LPQ is used to report the status of a remote printer using the LPD service. It is similar to the UNIX utility of the same name.

LPR

Just as with the UNIX version of the utility, LPR sends a print job to a remote printer being shared by LPD.

NBTSTAT

The NBTSTAT utility is concerned with the NetBIOS names registered by a machine. You can list all the names registered by the local or a remote computer, and reregister the local names with WINS. This utility is also useful if you know a machine's IP address, but aren't sure what the machine's name is.

NETSTAT

The NETSTAT utility is similar to the UNIX tool of the same name. It displays usage statistics for the IP protocol and shows current IP connections to and from the local machine.

NSLOOKUP

NSLOOKUP is a powerful DNS query tool with many options. It can be very useful to a DNS administrator troubleshooting a name-resolution problem.

PATHPING

PATHPING is a utility that combines the features of PING and TRACERT into one. It also computes statistics for the route between the two machines, aiding you in discovering where problems might exist in the route.

PING

The venerable PING command is used to verify that a machine on the network is online and reachable.

RCP

The RCP utility is similar to the UNIX tool of the same name. It's used to copy files between machines over the network.

REXEC

The REXEC service runs a specified command on a remote machine. It has a basic level of security.

ROUTE

ROUTE allows you to display or manipulate the routing table used by IP on the local machine.

RSH

The RSH tool serves the same purpose as REXEC. The main difference is that they connect to different server services.

TFTP

TFTP stands for Trivial File Transfer Protocol. This is the TFTP client for transferring files to or from a TFTP server. Because there is no security on these transfers, they're rarely used in practice, except for booting network devices such as routers or BOOTP clients.

TRACERT

TRACERT uses a series of ICMP packets on an IP network to discover the route packets take between two machines. It's useful for discovering routing and network problems.

Utilities

The category of utilities is used to group commands which modify data or make some other permanent change to the OS. This includes things like adjusting file security, deleting files, or changing the system time.

ASSOC

This utility can view, modify, or delete the associations Explorer makes between a file's extension and its file type.

AT

The AT command is used to schedule commands to run at a future time. Previously scheduled jobs can be cancelled. As an added benefit, AT can be used to schedule jobs on remote machines.

ATTRIB

ATTRIB is familiar to DOS users, and it has the same essentially unchanged function under Windows 2000. It is used to modify file attributes, such as making a file read-only or hidden.

CACLS

CACLS stands for Change ACLS. It can modify or display ACLs on files. Although it excels at this for files, oddly enough, it does not support directories with the same level of capability.

CHCP

The CHCP utility is used to set the active code page, which determines which language will be used for I/O at a command prompt.

CHKDSK

Disk corruption can sometimes be fixed by CHKDSK. If a volume is in use, it can be checked at the next system startup.

CHKNTFS

The CHKNTFS utility can be used to modify the way AUTOCHK functions on volumes at startup time. Among other things, the countdown time and list of excluded drives can be modified.

CIPHER

As the name implies, CIPHER is used to encrypt and decrypt files and directories that are stored on NTFS volumes. It can also report the encryption status of files.

CMD

This command starts a new command prompt. CMD supports a number of parameters; one of the more interesting is name completion, which matches what you type against file or directory names, thus saving you some keystrokes. For information on all the CMD options, run **CMD /?.**

COMP

The COMP command is used to compare two or more files for differences. This utility is not nearly as powerful as WINDIFF from the Resource Kit.

COMPACT

COMPACT can alter or display the status of compression on files and directories stored on NTFS volumes.

CONVERT

If you need to convert a FAT volume into an NTFS volume while retaining the data, this is the utility to use.

COPY

The COPY command is familiar to DOS users, and is essentially unchanged from that version. It is used to copy files from one location to another.

DATE

The DATE command is used to display or set the current system date.

DEL/ERASE

Both DEL and ERASE are the same command, used to delete files.

DISKCOMP

DISKCOMP can be used to compare two floppy disks for differences.

DEBUG

The DEBUG tool is a carryover from DOS,; and is used for advanced debugging of DOS-based programs. Most administrators will never use this utility.

DISKCOPY

DISKCOPY can be used to duplicate a floppy disk.

DISKPERF

To enable the Physical or Logical Disk counters in the Performance utility, you must run DISKPERF. This is because enabling these counters negatively impacts system performance by a few percentage points.

DOSKEY

DOSKEY is yet another DOS command that has been retained in Windows 2000. It can be used to create shortcuts for various commands. Much of its functionality is already built into CMD.

ECHO

The ECHO command is used to print information back to the console, usually from a batch file.

EDIT

EDIT is a character-based text editor. In terms of capability, it's almost on par with Notepad.

EDLIN

The predecessor of EDIT was EDLIN. EDLIN is comparatively ancient. For some reason, it's still included in Windows 2000, even though no one uses it any more.

EXE2BIN

EXE2BIN converts .exe files into .bin files, which may be useful for software developers. It's unimportant to most administrators.

EXIT

You use EXIT to quit an instance of CMD and return you to the calling program (which could be another CMD prompt or the Windows shell).

EXPAND

The EXPAND command is used to decompress files created by Microsoft's compression utility. These files typically have an underscore (_) as the last character in their extension, such as "EXPLORER.EX_".

FC

FC, which stands for File Compare, functions just like COMP. However, FC is a bit more configurable. Just as with COMP, you will find that although the WINDIFF Resource Kit utility is more powerful and offers a GUI interface, FC is more useful in batch operations.

FIND

The FIND command searches for text strings within files. This command is a common component of more complex batch files.

FINDSTR

Just as with FIND, FINDSTR searches for text within files. However, FINDSTR recognizes regular expressions for defining search criteria, making it more powerful than FIND.

FORMAT

FORMAT works just as it did in DOS, formatting disks in preparation for their use. However, the Windows 2000 version supports formatting volumes as FAT, FAT32, or NTFS.

FTYPE

Although ASSOC sets the description for a file type, FTYPE sets the program and method for opening a given file type. The two should be used together if file types are managed from the command line.

LABEL

The LABEL command is used to display or set the volume label on a partition.

MD/MKDIR

MD and MKDIR are the same utility. They create new directories. If you specify intermediate directories that don't exist, MD will create them.

MODE

The MODE utility is another carryover from DOS, and it's unlikely that you'll need to use it. It allows for configuration of LPT and COM ports, and the keyboard and console.

MOUNTVOL

MOUNTVOL, a new feature of Windows 2000, is used to display, create, or delete volume mount points.

MOVE

The MOVE command is similar to COPY; you use it to move files from one location to another.

PATH

The PATH command displays or sets the list of directories to be searched for an executable when it's not in the current directory.

PENTNT

This program was written as a workaround for a well-publicized flaw in some of the original Pentium (not Pentium II or III) CPUs. The flaw made errors in certain floating-point division operations. This program will tell you if you have a system with the problem. If you do, the utility will enable a software workaround for floating division to prevent the problem from occurring. This is not a concern for the majority of today's systems.

PRINT

PRINT is yet another command with a DOS heritage. It is used to print text files to LPT ports.

QBASIC

QBASIC is the Microsoft interpreter for the MS implementation of BASIC, which is a simple programming language.

RD/RMDIR

RD stands for Remove Directory, and it does just that. It can also be configured to delete any files and subdirectories if desired.

RECOVER

The RECOVER command is used to recover any usable information from a file that has one or more bad sectors on its disk. It's very rarely used in practice because unless the file is plaintext, the creating application is typically unable to read the recovered file.

REN/RENAME

The REN command is essentially a subset of the MOVE command, except it can't move files between directories.

REPLACE

REPLACE is similar to COPY or MOVE, with the additional logic in place to optionally overwrite only older files or only copy new files.

RUNAS

This command allows the user to run a program in a different user's context (provided that they have the user's password). This means that an administrator could have a non-administrative logon they use for day-to-day work, and use the RUNAS command to launch administrative tools in an admin user's context on an as-needed basis.

SORT

The SORT command is a powerful command for sorting files. It is used occasionally in batch files, or by the administrator as a quick way to sort a list of items.

START

START is a powerful command for launching other programs. You can control the environment, priority, and window state of the new program. You can also halt the current process until the new program finishes running.

SUBST

The SUBST command creates a virtual drive letter that maps to a directory. This is useful for routinely accessing long paths or for running programs that navigate the entire drive structure which you want to limit to certain areas.

TCMSETUP

TCMSETUP is used to set up the telephony client on a machine.

TIME

This utility allows you to display or set the local machine's time.

TREE

The TREE command displays a hierarchical view of the directories on a drive. The output is similar to the left pane of Windows Explorer.

TYPE

TYPE is used to display the contents of a file to the screen.

VERIFY

The VERIFY command allows you to specify whether Windows should confirm that files copy correctly by reading newly created files. By default, this is off.

VOL

VOL is a display-only subset of the LABEL command.

XCOPY

The XCOPY command is a much more powerful version of COPY. For example, it can optionally copy files newer than a certain date or exclude files whose names or path match a certain string.

Batch Commands

The last section was composed of programs that you can run at any time. However, the commands in this section usually make sense only in the context of a batch file. Although they all run outside of batch files, they usually aren't useful when used that way.

CALL

CALL is used to launch one batch file from another. It effectively is a GOSUB or function-like command because the source file halts until the called file completes running. Operation then resumes in the source file. By using the CALL :LABEL syntax, a different section in the same batch file can be called.

ENDLOCAL

ENDLOCAL, used in conjunction with the SETLOCAL command, specifies that all local changes should be discarded.

FOR

The FOR command allows you to perform an operation on multiple files meeting certain criteria. Common uses of FOR are with the /L switch for counting or with /F for operating within files. FOR becomes especially powerful when combined with the CALL command, such as "FOR /F %%I IN (FILE.TXT) DO @CALL :PROCESS_IT %%I".

GOTO

GOTO is used in conjunction with line labels, which start with the : character. GOTO makes the next line to be executed the one following the line label used in the GOTO. One special case exists of this is "GOTO :EOF", which specifies that processing of this file should end.

IF

The IF command allows for conditional execution of statements based on logic. IF can evaluate the current error level, compare two strings, or determine whether a certain file exists. IF statements are very common in batch files.

REM

REM, which stands for REMark, is used to instruct the command prompt to ignore a line in a batch file.

Redirection and Conditional Execution Symbols

A number of symbols are used to communicate with the command prompt. Without them, the command prompt and any batch files would be significantly limited. The symbols and their functions are listed in Table B.1.

Table B.1   Symbols Used for Redirection and Conditional Execution

Symbol	Purpose
>;batch commands>	Redirect output from one command to a text file. If the file exists, it is overwritten.
>>>;batch commands>	Same as >, except that output is appended to the previous contents of the file.
2>;batch commands>	Same as >, except that standard error is redirected instead of standard out.
2>>>;batch commands>	Same as >>, except using standard error.
<	Redirect input to the command from a text file.
[vb]	Pipe the output from one command to another.
&	Chains together multiple commands on one line and executes all of them.
&&	Same as &, but only executes the second command if the first succeeded.
[vb][vb]	Same as &, but only executes the second command if the first fails.

continues

Table B.1   continued

Symbol	Purpose
()	Used to group multiple commands as if they are on the same line even if they're not. Typically used for IF...ELSE statements.
^	Escape character. Tells the command prompt to pass the following symbol to the program being run as an argument rather than interpreting it in the shell.

PAUSE

PAUSE does just what it says. It halts execution until a key is pressed.

POPD

POPD works hand-in-hand with PUSHD, and restores the current directory saved by PUSHD.

PUSHD

This command saves the current directory for later use with POPD and then CDs to another directory.

SETLOCAL

SETLOCAL informs the command prompt to save the current environment for later restoration by the ENDLOCAL command.

SHIFT

The SHIFT command is used to adjust the numbering of any arguments.

Environment Commands

The final group of commands are those that apply to the command shell itself. They don't modify any data, and although they're used often in batch files, they're not specific to them.

CD/CHDIR

Although CD can be used to display the current directory, its chief purpose by far is to enable you to make a different directory the current directory.

CLS

CLS is used to clear the screen of all output.

COLOR

If you don't like the default gray text on black background of the command prompt, you can change it with the COLOR command. Unfortunately, this changes the entire command prompt, not just one line.

DIR

DIR is a tool for listing files and directories in a wide variety of formats.

GRAFTABL

This command allows the display of extended characters for a given code page in the command prompt. It is rarely used in practice.

HELP

HELP is a command-line reference utility for many of the commands in this appendix.

MORE

The MORE command displays text one page at a time. It's often used to slow down and break up output from another program in order to make it more readable. MORE is often on the receiving end of a pipe command, such as "TYPE FILE.TXT |MORE".

PROMPT

The PROMPT command can be used to change the command prompt from the familiar "X:\>" to many more unique styles.

SET

SET is a very powerful command that establishes or retrieves the value of an environment variable. Using the /A argument, you can cause SET to perform basic math functions. With the new /P argument, you can set a variable based on user input.

TITLE

The TITLE command sets the window title for a command prompt. This can be useful for communicating status or distinguishing between multiple command windows.

VER

VER simply displays the OS and version.

Appendix C
Sample Batch Files

This appendix presents you with two batch files. It's highly unlikely that you'll find these useful as-is in a production environment. However, the purpose of these samples is to convey the power of batch files and show you some tricks you may not have considered. This appendix goes hand-in-hand with both Appendix B, "Command Prompt Quick Reference," and Appendix D, "Utilities Resource Kit." You will likely find yourself flipping back and forth between these appendices.

RAND.BAT

One of the best functions a sample program can perform is to play a game. This makes it fun for everyone to figure out how the sample works, and modify it for different variations. For this reason, our first example (shown in Code Listing C.1) is a simple Guess-the-Number game. Note that this batch file will run only on Windows 2000 and later, although it doesn't test to see whether this is the case.

Code Listing C.1   The RAND.BAT Game

```
01 @ECHO OFF
02 REM Guess the Number Game
03
04 REM Begin by picking the random number.
05 SET /A ONES=%RANDOM:~-1%
06 SET /A TENS=%RANDOM:~-1%
07 IF %TENS%==0 SET TENS=
08 SET ANSWER=%TENS%%ONES%
09
10 REM Initialize variables.
11 SET GUESSES=0
12 SET GUESS=0
13
14 ECHO Guess the number!
15 :TOP
16 ECHO.
17 SET /P GUESS=Pick a number between 0 and 99:
18
19 REM Validate the input's length
20 IF NOT %GUESS%==%GUESS:~-2% GOTO BADANSWER
21
22 REM Validate that the input is a number
23 SET /A ONES=%GUESS% %% 10 2>NUL
24 SET /A TENS=%GUESS% / 10 2>NUL
25 IF %TENS%==0 GOTO ONESCHK
26 IF NOT %GUESS%==%TENS%%ONES% GOTO BADANSWER
27 GOTO VALID
28
```

```
29 :ONESCHK
30 IF NOT %GUESS%==%ONES% GOTO BADANSWER
31
32 :VALID
33 SET /A GUESSES=%GUESSES% + 1
34 IF %GUESS%==%ANSWER% GOTO YOUWIN
35 IF %GUESS% LSS %ANSWER% GOTO TOOLOW
36 GOTO TOOHIGH
37
38 :TOOLOW
39 ECHO Your guess of %GUESS% was too low. Try again.
40 GOTO :TOP
41
42 :TOOHIGH
43 ECHO Your guess of %GUESS% was too high. Try again.
44 GOTO :TOP
45
46 :BADANSWER
47 ECHO Invalid input.
48 ECHO Your guess must be an integer between 0 and 99.
49 ECHO.
50 GOTO TOP
51
52 :YOUWIN
53 ECHO.
54 ECHO YOU WIN!
55 ECHO %GUESS% was the right answer.
56 ECHO It took you %GUESSES% trys.
57 ECHO.
58 GOTO :EOF
```

Line 1 begins in the standard manner. 99 percent of all batch files begin with @ECHO OFF to prevent the code from being output to the screen and cluttering things up. (Note that REMing out this line by placing **REM** in front of @ECHO OFF can be quite helpful for troubleshooting.)

The first interesting thing that happens is at line 5, where the %RANDOM% environment variable(a new feature of Windows 2000) is used. Using the %RANDOM:~–1% syntax tells the OS to give us the last digit of a random number, which ensures that the digit will be somewhere between 0 and 9.

Another interesting event happens at line 7, where the script has to handle the special case of the 10s digit being a 0. The reason for this is that the command interpreter is capable of utilizing decimal, hexadecimal, or octal notation. In this case, a 0 should be avoided because this would mean the number would be interpreted as being octal. This would be a problem if the ones digit were 8 or 9, because 08 and 09 are invalid octal numbers. This line also shows a traditional use of the IF statement. Two IF statements that use more advanced forms of the statement will be examined later.

The next important line is line 15. This is the top of the loop, which is the main body of the program. It's the first use of a label within the script. Next, look at line 16. Although you should be familiar with the ECHO statement, you may not know that "ECHO." will allow you to print a blank line to the console.

The capability to have the command interpreter ask the user for input has been missing prior to Windows 2000. Line 17 shows a practical application of this new feature. Using SET /P easily allows for user input in batch files.

At line 20 is an advanced use of the IF statement. If the user's guess isn't equal to the last two characters of the guess, the guess is too long. In this case, the script needs to inform the user of the error and give them another chance. Thus, a GOTO is used to send execution to the BADANSWER label. Although you could also use the IF…(commands) syntax, this isn't as useful as a GOTO in this case because other sections of the file use the BADANSWER section.

After validating the length of the input, the script needs to verify that the input is numeric. Otherwise, it won't be able to determine later whether the guess was too high or too low. For this reason, at line 23 the number is broken into two characters through the modulus and integer division operators. One thing to note is that the script redirects error to NULL through the 2>NUL command. This relates back to the issue discussed in line 5. In this case, certain strings, such as "5b" would be interpreted as hexadecimal numbers, which produces error messages at the console unless they're redirected to NULL. Because the error is not harmful, it can be ignored and hidden from the user.

The final important line in the batch file is at line 35. Here, the script decides if the user's guess (which by this point is known to be incorrect) is too low or too high. By using the advanced LSS statement with the IF, the script will compare the guess with the answer and it can then give the user the appropriate answer. Using the IF…(commands) ELSE (commands) syntax would also work here, but an ELSE command is best used if the following conditions are met:

- Either the IF or ELSE require multiple commands
- They both resume execution at a common point after the IF
- Neither the IF commands nor the ELSE commands are duplicated elsewhere in the batch file

VIRUPDATE.BAT

A common task many administrators face is to update one or more files on all their servers. Although tools such as SMS exist to meet this need, not many environments have this kind of tool available. Therefore, you may find this tool very interesting. As an example, this batch file updates a hypothetical antivirus scanner with a new data file to enable protection against the newest viruses. It is shown in Code Listing C.2.

Code Listing C.2   The VIRUPDATE.BAT Script

```
01 @ECHO OFF
02 SET SUCCESS=0
03 SET FAIL=0
04
05 SET PROGNAME=%~n0%
06
07 CALL :LOGIT Beginning operation...
08 ECHO.
09
10 FOR /F "eol=;" %%I IN (SERVERS.TXT) DO CALL :DOIT %%I
11
12 ECHO.
13 CALL :LOGIT Operation completed.
14 CALL :LOGIT Successes: %SUCCESS%
15 CALL :LOGIT Failures:  %FAIL%
16 ECHO.
17
18 GOTO :EOF
19
20 :DOIT
21 CALL :LOGIT Updating server %1...
22 IF NOT EXIST \\%1\ADMIN$ GOTO SRVDOWN
23 CALL :LOGIT Stopping AntiVirus Service on %1...
24 SC \\%1 STOP VIRUSSVC
25 CALL :LOGIT Updating virus definitions on %1...
26 IF EXIST \\%1\VIRUSUPDATE\VIRUS.OLD DEL \\%1\VIRUSUPDATE\VIRUS.OLD
27 IF EXIST \\%1\VIRUSUPDATE\VIRUS.DAT REN \\%1\vIRUSUPdATE\VIRUS.DAT
➥VIRUS.OLD
28 COPY NEWVIRUS.DAT \\%1\VIRUSUPDATE
29 IF NOT EXIST \\%1\VIRUSUPDATE\VIRUS.DAT GOTO COPYPROB
30 SC \\%1 START VIRUSSVC
31 CALL :LOGIT Server %1 completed.
32 ECHO.
33 SET /A SUCCESS=%SUCCESS% + 1
34 GOTO :EOF
35
36 :SRVDOWN
37 CALL :LOGIT ERROR! Server %1 unreachable.
38 SET /A FAIL=%FAIL% + 1
39 GOTO :EOF
40
41 :COPYPROB
42 CALL :LOGIT ERROR! Problem during file copy to %1.
43 SET /A FAIL=%FAIL% + 1
44 GOTO :EOF
45
46 :LOGIT
47 ECHO %*
48 ECHO %* >>%PROGNAME%.LOG
49 GOTO :EOF
```

The first unusual line in this script is at line 1. Here, the script sets PROG-NAME to equal the name of the batch file (with no extension). This allows you to later write to a log file, which will automatically have the same program name as the script without any recoding. This is a standard feature of any batch file I write that does logging.

The second unique line is at line 7. Here is an elegant solution to a problem many administrators have. They want to both report information to the console and also log it to a file. Rather than include both lines anywhere this happens, you can call LOGIT, which does both and then resumes executing on the line after CALL.

Line 10 is the heart of the program. This FOR statement reads the SERVERS.TXT file line by line, ignoring any that begin with a ";". For each line, it calls the DOIT section and passes it the name of the server. This allows you to perform the same actions many times with a great deal of ease.

An important event occurs at line 24. Here, the script uses the SC utility from the Resource Kit to stop the antivirus service prior to updating the file. Although SC isn't documented in the appendix on the Resource Kit (Appendix D), it is quite useful for this type of batch file, when you need to manipulate services remotely from the command line. Also of note is the use of %1 throughout this section. This is because the CALL statement used at (C) to start the DOIT section makes the server an argument, and this is how arguments are referenced.

Another lesson about arguments exists at line 47. Here, rather than saying %1 %2 %3[el], %* is utilized, which says to use all the arguments. Note that you can't use "CALL :LOGIT" with no arguments to print a blank line. The command interpreter will reduce line 47 to just "ECHO", which will cause it to print the message "ECHO is off." Instead, if you want to print a blank line, use "CALL :LOGIT."

Notice that lines 33, 38, and 43 implement a system for reporting the total number of systems updated and errors encountered. By utilizing the mathematical capabilities of SET /A, the script can perform addition using environment variables. During development of the script, these numbers are useful for troubleshooting, especially if, when added together, they don't match the number of servers listed in SERVERS.TXT. After the script is used in production, these numbers will immediately tell you how successful the update was.

On a related note, examine the two sections beginning on lines 36 and 41. Often, batch files will perform this type of repetitive operation but not include any sort of error handling. Although this works for smaller operations, this is not the approach to use in a major enterprise. By executing these sections when one of these error conditions occurs, you are better able to discover any errors that occurred and then fix them.

Finally, it's important to discuss line 49. A GOTO :EOF is used here for two reasons. First, it's best practice to end a file with this statement, in case you add lines later. This way, you don't start running the appended lines by accident. Also, you need to end each section initiated by a CALL with GOTO :EOF or the end of the file. Both LOGIT and DOIT end with a GOTO :EOF for this reason.

Appendix D
Resource Kit Utilities

All too often, I see frustrated Windows NT/2000 administrators posting questions on the Internet, asking how to perform a given task. Many times, they can easily achieve their intended result by using a tool from the Windows 2000 Resource Kit. These tools, many of which have been carried over from the Windows NT Resource Kits, are often worth their weight in gold. Knowing the capabilities of each tool in the Resource Kit can go a long way towards making the life of an administrator easier.

Your Mileage May Vary

The content in this chapter is based on the beta Release Candidate 2 of the Windows 2000 Server Resource Kit. The utilities listed here may differ from what is included in the shipping product. Although packaging has yet to be announced by Microsoft, NT Resource Kits have typically had both a Server and a Workstation version. If this tradition continues for Windows 2000, it's likely that not all of the utilities listed here will be included in the 2000 Professional Resource Kit.

In many cases, administrators may wish to script one or more tools to automate repetitive tasks and reduce human error. Table G.1 lists all the Resource Kit utilities by their intended function (as they are discussed), and shows which can be automated via the command line. If you are familiar with the NT Resource Kits, you may want to look at only those in the table that are listed as being new to Windows 2000.

Table D.1 Resource Kit Utilities by Function

Utility	Scriptable?	New?
Disk and File Utilities		
DFSUTIL.EXE	★	★
DSKPROBE.EXE		
FILEVER.EXE	★	
RSDIAG.EXE	★	★
RSDIR.EXE	★	★
WINDIFF.EXE	★	
Migration Utilities		
CLONEPR.DLL		★
DOMMIG.DOC		★
SIDWalker Suite		★

continues

Table D.1   continued

Utility	Scriptable?	New?
Network Utilities		
ADSI Edit		★
DNSCMD.EXE	★	★
DSACLS.EXE	★	★
DSASTAT.EXE	★	★
KSETUP.EXE	★	★
KTPASS.EXE	★	★
LDP.EXE		★
MOVETREE.EXE	★	★
NETDOM.EXE	★	
NLTEST.EXE	★	
REMOTE.EXE		
REPADMIN.EXE	★	★
REPLMON.EXE	★	★
SDCHECK.EXE	★	★
SEARCH.VBS	★	★
WSREMOTE.EXE	★	★
PC Management Utilities		
DUMPCHK.EXE	★	
KILL.EXE	★	
MEMSNAP.EXE	★	★
MSICUU.EXE		★
MSIZAP.EXE	★	★
W2000MSGS.CHM		★
POOLMON.EXE		★
REG.EXE	★	
TLIST.EXE	★	
Performance Utilities		
PMON.EXE		
PVIEWER.EXE		
Troubleshooting Utilities		
ACLDIAG.EXE	★	★
APMSTAT.EXE	★	★
BROWSTAT.EXE	★	
DEPENDS.EXE		
GFLAGS.EXE	★	
NETDIAG.EXE	★	★
PPTP Ping		★
SNMPUTILG.EXE		

Microsoft Scriptlt

Although it's not a part of the Resource Kit, Scriptlt is a useful tool for automating keyboard input to any open windows. This can be an effective method for automating GUIs (such as those in the Resource Kit) and application setups. Scriptlt can be downloaded from http://technet.microsoft.com/cdonline/content/complete/windows/winnt/winntas/tools/scriptit.htm.

Disk and File Utilities

The Resource Kit wouldn't be complete without including utilities for working with files and disks. Of these, you may find DSKPROBE, FILEVER, and WINDIFF to be quite helpful.

DFSUTIL.EXE

DFSUTIL.EXE is useful for querying and troubleshooting DFS. It has a number of powerful options, and may require some learning in order to be truly useful.

DSKPROBE.EXE

Disk Probe is a sector editor that allows local Administrators to directly manipulate disks on the system. One important feature of this tool is its capability to save and restore the MBR and partition table to standard files. Beware: This tool is not for the faint of heart, and can quite easily destroy data or render a system unbootable.

FILEVER.EXE

The FILEVER utility displays version information about .exe and .dll files. In verbose mode, it can produce much more information about a file than the Version tab in Windows Explorer.

RSDIAG.EXE

Administrators who take advantage of Remote Storage may find the RSDI-AG tool helpful for troubleshooting RS problems. Used in conjunction with the next tool, RSDIR.EXE, you may be able to recover data believed to be lost.

RSDIR.EXE

The RSDIR utility functions similarly to the familiar DIR command, except that RSDIR is used on Remote Storage reparse points.

WINDIFF.EXE

WINDIFF is an excellent tool for comparing two files or directory structures for differences. Its capability to display the differences between two files in a single view makes it quite easy to determine the differences between the files.

Migration Utilities

The utilities in this section may be useful to you during your migration to Windows 2000. After you are in a pure Windows 2000 environment, you probably will no longer use these tools.

CLONEPR.DLL

CLONEPR is a COM component for use on Windows 2000 domain controllers. Once installed, it can be controlled via WSH scripts. Its purpose is to allow for duplication of user accounts in an NT or 2000 domain. Although similar to the MOVETREE utility, CLONEPR works only between forests.

DOMMIG.DOC

Several utilities in the Resource Kit aren't executables at all. This is one such tool. The focus of this Word document is on planning your NT to 2000 migration.

SIDWalker Suite

The SIDWalker suite is a group of tools devoted to managing or migrating security ACLs. The suite is made up of three separate tools. The first utility, SHOWACCS.EXE, is used to display current ACL settings. Output from this tool can be used to plan a migration to a new domain and is also used as the input for the second tool, the Security Migration Editor. This tool is an MMC snap-in. The purpose of this tool is to map the current SIDs to new SIDs in preparation for migrating the ACLs. Output from this tool is then fed into SIDWALK.EXE, which performs the ACL remapping.

Network Utilities

These powerful tools allow you to configure or test certain network components, such as AD, DNS, Kerberos, and trusts. You'll no doubt find one or more of the tools in this category to be invaluable.

ADSI Edit

ADSI Edit is a powerful tool for editing the AD. It's an MMC snap-in, and uses the ADSI API to perform its work.

DNSCMD.EXE

DNS configuration is the specialty of DNSCMD. Running from the command prompt, it allows you to view and edit the configuration of DNS servers. It also replaces DNSSTAT.EXE, which was included in earlier Resource Kits.

DSACLS.EXE

Typically, AD security is configured via the MMC. However, this tool allows you to view and change ACL entries on AD objects from the command prompt. It allows you to script ACL changes.

DSASTAT.EXE

The DSASTAT tool exists to compare different domain controller's naming contexts. The DCs can been in the same domain or the Global Catalog can be used to cross domains. DSASTAT can also discover whether DCs accurately reflect the current state of their domain.

KSETUP.EXE

If your organization uses Kerberos outside of Windows 2000 for authentication, this will be an important tool for you. KSETUP allows you to configure Windows 2000 machines to join a Kerberos domain rather than a Windows 2000 domain. It then allows users of the Kerberos domain to log on to the machine.

KTPASS.EXE

Although KSETUP allows Windows 2000 machines to participate in Kerberos domains, this tool allows non-Windows 2000 Kerberos computers to utilize Windows 2000 domains for authentication.

LDP.EXE

LDP uses a GUI interface to query LDAP servers, including Active Directory. It allows you to perform all the common LDAP operations, and displays the metadata associated with objects.

MOVETREE.EXE

The MOVETREE utility is used for moving OUs and other AD objects between domains in an AD forest. You would likely use this utility if you consolidate domains after migrating to Windows 2000. There are a number of caveats when using this tool, so be sure to read the documentation prior to using this tool.

NETDOM.EXE

The NETDOM utility has three capabilities. It can manage and create the machine accounts used by all domain member computers. It can also manage the secure channel between machines. Finally, it can manipulate the trust relationship between domains.

NLTEST.EXE

As the name of NLTEST implies, this tool is used for testing. It tests the capability of a machine to properly retrieve information such as the list of DCs and the status of domain trusts. This tool is useful when troubleshooting domain connectivity problems.

REMOTE.EXE

The REMOTE utility allows you to run commands on other machines as if you were at the console. However, this tool has no security mechanisms, which is a significant shortcoming. As a result, it should be used only in fully trusted environments. Other tools are available for allowing the same functionality with better security capabilities.

REPADMIN.EXE

REPADMIN is used to view and manually configure the replication topology used for AD. This is typically unnecessary, but may be required in certain troubleshooting situations.

REPLMON.EXE

The Active Directory Replication Monitor is a COM object that can be used in conjunction with WSH or other COM-aware languages to provide a graphic display of the AD replication topology. It can also monitor DC status and force replication.

SDCHECK.EXE

Although SDCHECK can display the ACLs for any AD object, I think the true usefulness of the utility is that it displays a hierarchy of any objects that provide inheritance to the object being queried.

SEARCH.VBS

This tool is a VBScript that runs under WSH. It allows you to search for objects in LDAP servers.

WSREMOTE.EXE

The WSREMOTE utility is quite similar to REMOTE, except that it allows connections over IP sockets in addition to named pipes. It also requires a username and password prior to allowing access, but better security would still be appreciated.

PC Management Utilities

Although many of the other tool categories are focused on the network, server, or performance, this category is focused squarely on helping you manage workstations. Several of these utilities are very important for workstation administrators.

DUMPCHK.EXE

The DUMPCHK utility verifies the integrity of crash dumps. Although it can be used to provide some information about the crash, most administrators won't find this output useful. The main function of the utility is to verify the dump prior to sending it to a vendor for analysis.

KILL.EXE

If you've worked with Windows 2000 for any length of time, you've encountered situations where you have a runaway process that won't halt. KILL can stop such tasks, either through a normal application shutdown, or by forcing the task to end.

MEMSNAP.EXE

As the name implies, MEMSNAP takes a snapshot of current memory usage by all running tasks. You can compare multiple snapshots to discover usage trends.

MSICUU.EXE

This tool removes Windows Installer-related Registry settings for installed applications. If these settings are corrupt, using this tool will allow you to rerun the install again.

MSIZAP.EXE

MSIZAP is the command-prompt version of MSICUU. Both have the same purpose.

POOLMON.EXE

The POOLMON utility reports memory usage for tasks and can be useful for discovering memory leaks.

REG.EXE

REG is an important tool because it allows access to the Registry from a command prompt. The Registry being used can either be local or on a remote computer. It can perform all the normal query and modification tasks. The only shortcoming is that it can't report or modify Registry ACLs.

TLIST.EXE

The TLIST utility is a command-prompt tool for displaying a list of all running tasks. It can also show the tasks in a parent-child hierarchy, so you can see which process spawned other processes.

W2000MSGS.CHM

This tool is a help file that lists error messages generated by Windows 2000. It explains them and provides guidance on potential actions to resolve the problem.

Performance Utilities

The performance utilities focus on discovering the performance of a specific application, rather than enhancing overall system performance.

PMON.EXE

If you used the TOP command in UNIX, you will be familiar with PMON. It displays output similar to the Processes tab of Task Manager, except it's done at a command prompt rather than via a GUI.

PVIEWER.EXE

The PVIEWER tool shows quite a bit of information about a single process via a GUI. In addition to displaying resource utilization, you can also change the process priority or kill it.

Troubleshooting Utilities

These tools will help you resolve problems with Windows 2000 computers. They range in level from those that your help desk may use daily, to those which you might not use unless told to by Microsoft's support group.

ACLDIAG.EXE

ACLDIAG helps you to troubleshoot AD ACL problems. It can compare existing permissions to the defaults, fix delegation problems, and display effective permissions.

APMSTAT.EXE

The APMSTAT tool assists with troubleshooting power management problems. It works on machines that support APM or ACPI, and will report related Registry, HAL, and BIOS information.

BROWSTAT.EXE

If you've worked with Microsoft's networking protocols, you've likely encountered problems with browsing the network. This tool helps you to fix such problems. It displays the current master browsers, and can display the contents of the browse list. You can also force a browser election.

DEPENDS.EXE

The DEPENDS utility allows you to discover what .dll and similar files are required in order for a utility to run. If any of the utility's dependencies have dependencies of their own, the tool will show this. As a result, you can find all the executables used by a given program.

GFLAGS.EXE

GFLAGS allows administrators to modify the global flags in the kernel. The tool is used mainly by programmers for debugging purposes. Microsoft's support group may direct you to enable certain flags when troubleshooting a problem. Aside from these functions, it's best to not use this utility without a full understanding of its use and implications.

NETDIAG.EXE

The NETDIAG utility is a much-welcomed addition to the Resource Kit. It can be used to troubleshoot IP functionality on machines; not only those running Windows 2000, but on any Microsoft 32-bit OS. It tests an extensive list of functions, including subnet mask, gateway, DHCP, WINS, DNS, and several domain tests. The help desk will no doubt find this tool a welcome addition to their tool chest.

PPTP Ping

The PPTP Ping utility is made up of a server and client executable. It's used to verify that the route between a client and server supports PPTP connections.

SNMPUTILG.EXE

SNMPUTILG is an SNMP tool that can query and set information on SNMP resources. It can also save retrieved data for later use.

Index

Symbols

A

T

Windows 2000 Answers

Selected Windows 2000 Titles from New Riders Publishing

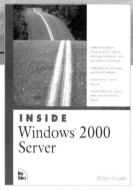

This is the updated edition of New Riders' best-selling *Inside Windows NT Server 4*. New Riders proudly offers something unique for Windows 2000 administrators—an interesting and discriminating book on Windows 2000 Server, written by someone in the trenches who can anticipate your situation and provide answers you can trust.

INSIDE
Windows 2000 Server

ISBN: 1-56205-929-7

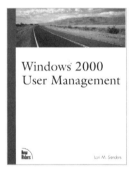

Windows 2000 User Management

ISBN: 0-6205-886-X

Managing the user and the user's desktop environment is a critical component in administering Windows 2000. *Windows 2000 User Management* provides you with the real-world tips and examples you need to get the job done.

Windows 2000 Active Directory is just one of several new Windows 2000 titles from New Riders' acclaimed *Landmark* series. Perfect for network architects and administrators, this book describes the intricacies of Active Directory to help you plan, deploy, and manage Active Directory in an enterprise setting.

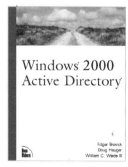

Windows 2000 Active Directory

ISBN: 0-7357-0870-3

Advanced Information on Networking Technologies

New Riders Books Offer Advice and Experience

LANDMARK

Rethinking Computer Books

We know how important it is to have access to detailed, solution-oriented information on core technologies. *Landmark* books contain the essential information you need to solve technical problems. Written by experts and subjected to rigorous peer and technical reviews, our *Landmark* books are hard-core resources for practitioners like you.

ESSENTIAL REFERENCE

Smart, Like You

The *Essential Reference* series from New Riders provides answers when you know what you want to do but need to know how to do it. Each title skips extraneous material and assumes a strong base of knowledge. These are indispensable books for the practitioner who wants to find specific features of a technology quickly. Avoiding fluff and basic material, these books present solutions in an innovative, clean format—and at a great value.

MCSE CERTIFICATION

Engineered for Test Success

New Riders offers a complete line of test preparation materials to help you achieve your certification. With books like the *MCSE Training Guide*, and software like the acclaimed *MCSE Complete* and the revolutionary *ExamGear*, New Riders offers comprehensive products built by experienced professionals who have passed the exams and instructed hundreds of candidates.

Coming Soon from New Riders...

Windows 2000 Professional
By Jerry Honeycutt
1st Edition, April 2000
450 pages, $49.99
ISBN: 0-7357-0950-0

MCSE Training Guide: Windows 2000 Professional (70-210)
By Gordon Barker
1st Edition, June 2000
ISBN: 0-7357-0965-3

Windows 2000 DNS
By Roger Abell, Herman Knief,
Andrew Daniels,
and Jeffrey A. Graham
2nd Edition, April 2000
500 pages, $39.99
ISBN: 0-7357-0973-4

MCSE Training Guide: Windows 2000 Server (70-215)
By Dennis Maione
1st Edition, June 2000
ISBN: 0-7357-0968-8

Windows 2000 Deployment and Desktop Management
By Jeffrey Ferris
1st Edition, April 2000
400 pages, $34.99
ISBN: 0-7357-0975-0

MCSE Training Guide: Windows 2000 Network Security Design (70-220)
By Roberta Bragg
1st Edition, July 2000
ISBN: 0-7257-0984-X

MCSE Training Guide: Windows 2000 Network Infrastructure Design (70-221)
By Dale Holmes and Bill Matsoukas
1st Edition, July 2000
ISBN: 0-7357-0982-3

Windows 2000 Routing and Remote Access Services
By Kackie Charles
1st Edition, May 2000
400 pages, $34.99
ISBN: 0-7357-0951-3

Windows 2000 Thin Client Solutions
By Todd Mathers
2nd Edition, June 2000
600 pages, $45.00
ISBN: 1-57870-239-9

MCSE Training Guide: Installing and Administering a Windows 2000 Directory (70-217)
By Damir Bersinic and Rob Scrimger
1st Edition, July 2000
ISBN: 0-7357-0976-9